Aggravated:

The True Story of

How a Series of Lies

Sent an Innocent Man to Prison

by

Michael Sirois

Cover Design by Michael Sirois, based on an original photograph by Jody Davis, jodylehigh@gmail.com

Aggravated: The True Story of How a Series of Lies Sent an Innocent Man to Prison
Print ISBN 978-1-7327903-0-8
eBook ISBN 978-1-7327903-1-5

Published by Truth Boots Publishing, LLC
Spring, Texas
https://truthbootspublishing.com/
info@truthbootspublishing.com

First Edition

Contents

Disclaimer

This is a true story, filled with lies. The lies are real, but I have changed the names of nearly all of the people, towns, counties, and businesses in and near the area where a 2006 trial took place, as well as the names of a couple of states. For example, Deep Springs, Texas, doesn't exist, and neither does Ashwell County, but those names do represent a real Texas city and county where certain incidents allegedly took place.

The only names which have not been changed, aside from my family's names, are the name of a private investigator and a few other people who don't live in Ashwell County and don't have any connection to the case. All of the pseudonyms in the book were chosen at random by opening several phone books and pointing to a last name on one page and a first name on another page. A few of those names were later modified slightly in order to adapt to misspellings on official documents. All of the pseudonyms were then cross-checked against everyone's real names to ensure there would be no duplication.

If any of the substitute names used in this book happen to match the names of any real individuals or entities, living or dead, it is by sheer coincidence, and you should assume by default that any people, locations, businesses, or other entities which happen to have those same names have no connection to any of the events in this book. I did, however, continue to use the real names of some cities and towns (like Austin, Arlington, and Beaumont) which aren't near the area of the alleged incidents. I have also, for the sake of clarity, kept the real names of some other entities (like CPS, NOAA, and CASA), which are statewide and/or national in scope.

See *People, Places, and Things* at the end of the book for a comprehensive list.

Dedication

To my mother, Joy Shaw Sirois Sen, who died two years after my brother, Steve Sirois, was imprisoned; and to Steve's wife, Robin Henry Sirois, who died during Steve's fifth year of incarceration. He was not allowed to attend either funeral.

Acknowledgments

Some of those who helped with the extensive research and preparation for this book require a special mention. First, my brother Steve, for allowing me, for years now, to question him at length, often on subjects which must have seemed to bear no relation to his unjust incarceration. My niece and nephew, Marri and Beau, also endured numerous odd questions from me on the tiniest details. They helped me gain a fuller understanding of the circumstances their family found itself in; and my other brothers and sisters deserve thanks for filling in gaps in a great deal of biographical information.

As always, my wife, Minay, was amazing. I don't know how she put up with all these years of me trying to find slivers of fact marbled inside piles of false information, and still managed to listen to me ramble on about a great deal of material usually not discussed in polite company.

The information in Tom Swearingen's investigative interviews was instrumental in helping me gain an overall understanding of my brother's accuser. Tom's material also helped me tremendously by providing a central point of comparison to everything else I was able to gather. Many thanks also to Sarah Koenig and her crew for permission to quote briefly from Season One of the podcast, *Serial*; to Zeke Yewdall for his extensive knowledge of Ford Courier trucks; to the many attorneys, judges, clerks, legal librarians, and others who gave me guidance while I researched arcane legal rules and gathered evidence for the book; to Maureen Munsen (a pseudonym), who tracked down payments made to one of the expert witnesses in Steve's trial; to Dan Perez, from the Texas Department of Transportation, who straightened me out on road naming conventions in Texas, and whose best piece of advice was "Go to the source if you're not sure," which applies to a lot of other areas as well: and to Carolyn Levin of Miller Korzenik Sommers Rayman LLP, whose thoughtful advice helped tremendously in the final shaping of this book.

A special shout out to Michael Hall, Executive Editor at Texas Monthly, who helped shepherd the manuscript of this book through the first few years of its existence at the Writers' League of Texas' Summer Writing Retreat Workshops, and provided me with invaluable research, structure, and editing information. He's also a heck of a musician.

In particular, though, to all of the people who refused to talk to me, or were warned not to talk to me, or lied to me, thank you for helping to confirm my suspicion that there was something to hide.

I'm Biased/Foreword

I'm biased. You need to know that from the beginning.

This book is about my brother, Steve Sirois, and about a crime that I believe was committed against him, instead of him committing the crime he was accused of. I'm telling you this in advance so you'll understand that my approach in the book isn't a neutral one. I've done my best to present all sides of the story, but when I did lean it was in the direction of my brother and his family, not toward the person who accused him of a horrific crime. All I ask is that you keep an open mind as you read, and let the facts speak for themselves.

I also realize, given the recent outpouring of sexual abuse accusations against a number of people, that this might not be the best time to release a book of this nature, but I have to. The goal in these pages is to prove that my brother, who was convicted in 2006 of aggravated sexual assault of a child, is, and always was, innocent of that crime.

Any form of child abuse (physical, verbal, sexual, psychological, or neglect) is a terrible thing, one for which the abuser deserves punishment. Having said that, I want to assure you that this is the culmination of a multi-year search for the absolute truth of what happened (or didn't happen) to Hanna Lee Penderfield between the dates of September 1, 2001 and February 14, 2004.

> **Note:** The renaming has begun. Hanna Penderfield is not her real name. You can assume the same about nearly everyone else in the book, especially if they live in or near Deep Springs, Texas. Those who have retained their real names are members of our immediate family and a few other individuals.
>
> See the chapter, *People, Places, and Things*, at the end of the book for a list of all of the major and minor characters, locations, and entities mentioned in the book.

As the subtitle of the book states, I believe that a series of lies resulted in my brother being tried and sentenced to thirty-five years in prison for a crime he didn't commit. We have an epidemic of lying in this country. Politicians, business executives, sports figures, and people from all walks of life often lie with impunity, with no consequences for their prevarication. Lies shouldn't have any place in public life, much less in a courtroom or on official documents. Unfortunately, I believe that the case against my brother was built upon false statements made in affidavits, in court testimony, and in interviews. We usually expect that a guilty person will lie under oath, but once they are convicted of a crime they don't get tried for perjury as well. Being sentenced for the crime is apparently enough; but what if the person who lied throughout Steve's trials wasn't Steve? How could I possibly prove it was them instead? I hope to do exactly that.

A quick word about styles used in the book.

Pronunciation: The 's' on the end of Sirois is silent. My family pronounces it SIR-ROY, like Illinois.

Grammar and Format: Any quotes from the trials, or from official documents, are spelled and punctuated the way they were originally, whether grammatically correct or not. I also compressed the dialogue to save space, which made this book hundreds of pages shorter. I have done my best, though, to make sure that no meanings were altered.

Ellipses: In dialogue from recorded interviews I used ellipses in front of a word to indicate an …interrupted thought, or a …brief pause; but an ellipsis directly connecting two words...like this, still indicates that some text was removed from that place in the sentence.

Emphasis: To emphasize certain words or phrases I usually just underlined them without saying [*the* emphasis *below is mine*] every time.

Alleged and **Allegedly:** I believe that Hanna's descriptions of her molestation are false, but using the words "alleged" or "allegedly" every time I described an incident would have grown old quickly. So, whether I call something an alleged incident or not, just assume that I don't believe it happened unless I say otherwise.

If you're a stickler for grammatical rules and sentence structure, I apologize. It may take a little getting used to, but I hope it won't be bothersome. The content is what's most important. To find out why I pronounce Sirois differently from the rest of my family, and to see a more detailed account of these and other grammatical variations I've used in the book, check out this post on the book's blog:

https://aggravatedbook.com/stylistic-differences-in-aggravated/

What I Need From You as a Reader: This book is about a search for the truth about what happened before and during two trials against my brother, and during my investigation of the accusations against him. I hope to be able to prove to you that the case against Steve, with unwavering specificity, targeted the wrong person. I'm not asking you to instantly accept my position, but I am asking you to not immediately believe Hanna Penderfield's either. I have freely admitted I am biased so you'll know what my position is, but when I first started examining Steve's case I was willing to believe either way.

To keep an open mind I had to accept that it was possible he could have done those things, so the first time I visited him in prison, I said, "Before we get started, I need to ask just one question." He said, "Sure, what?" I asked, "Did you do it?" His face registered shock, of course, and I saw hurt welling up in his eyes, so I quickly added, "It won't change the way I feel about you. I'll still support you, but I have to know one way or the other." He shook his head and said, "No, I didn't. The whole thing is ridiculous. I would never do something like that."

That single statement of innocence from Steve gave me as much "actual evidence" as either of his juries had when they made their decisions, because (aside from two medical exams, one for Hanna and one for Steve, both conducted after the charges were filed) there was no physical evidence, no

DNA, and they weren't able to use Steve's exam in his trials. The prosecution's case mostly consisted of statements from one person, Hanna. If Steve had indicated any guilt at all to me, I would gladly have helped him deal with being in prison, and would have continued to visit him regularly; but having heard him announce his innocence, I could at least start trying to find out the truth about what happened.

Truth is a slippery substance. Our perception of the world around us often influences what we believe, and our biases can get in the way of the actual truth. So, as you read the book, please be aware that I *am* presenting it with a particular bias in favor of my brother; but please don't let any of your own biases prevent you from keeping an open mind. I hope you will be able to see the truth hidden within the many lies that will be detailed in the upcoming pages. One of the main reasons I need you to understand this at the outset is because, although I have honestly searched for the truth in this matter, finding facts in the official record was difficult (for reasons that will soon become clear). This forced me, in a few instances, to speculate about what happened, or why it happened. I pulled my material from public documents, like court records, affidavits, and documents obtained through Freedom of Information requests whenever possible, but when answers weren't available in those, I did occasionally have to make assumptions. When I do that in this book I will let you know if a statement is a carefully reasoned conjecture instead of an established fact. When I did have to speculate about something, however, I supported my thoughts and analysis with a variety of other facts, statements, and data to help prove or disprove a particular claim.

Let me quickly define a lie and how I will use that word in the book. My supposition is that a lie is a false statement, deliberately made, with an intent to deceive others. Sometimes in the book (but rarely) a lie will be a single statement that I can prove to be false on its own, but more often a lie or lies will be enclosed within a series of statements made at different times about a specific act. Each statement, taken on its on, could possibly be true (or false). If they all come from only one individual, though, and some or all of those statements disagree with each other in some substantive way, at least one or more of them must be untrue. That will be my standard operating guideline throughout this document. Some of my conclusions about lies may not have been proven, but in those instances my choices about what I believe were lies were based on my own years-long, thorough investigation of witness testimony and court records.

You should also be aware that there are many passages in the book, usually taken directly from the trial record, which contain graphic depictions of sexual acts. Acts which, in my opinion, were *not* committed against Hanna, but her descriptions are still there. I apologize in advance, but that *is* what the entire case was about. You've been forewarned.

Let's start with a few short scenes. They skip around a bit in time, but the first one takes place in the near-past.

A Few Short Scenes

"The mass of men lead lives of quiet desperation."
Henry David Thoreau

"The incarcerated lead noisy lives of quiet desperation."
Michael Sirois

Late 2019, a Typical Winter Saturday

Pre-Dawn: A few miles south of the Spindletop Oil Field near Beaumont, Texas, two dozen concrete and steel structures gleam harshly white and gray under more than a hundred 277-volt high-pressure sodium parking lot lights. Additional lights, mounted high on the exterior of every building in the complex, cast their beams downward to ensure that very little is in shadow.

Stiles Unit, a prison operated by the Texas Department of Criminal Justice, rests on a flat, featureless section of the Southeast Texas coastal plain. The prison is bounded by a loop road which is shaped a little like home plate in a baseball diamond, but this is no game. Fifty feet inside the loop road, two parallel rows of twelve-foot high chain-link fence surround the prison, but three-foot circular coils of razor wire push it even higher. Between the two fences is a no-man's land, a twenty-foot stretch of packed dirt and gravel, all of it easily visible to the guards with high-powered rifles who man the four towers which are placed at strategic positions along the perimeter fence.

It's 3:30 in the morning inside W-Pod, one of Stiles' dormitories. A nasal voice, bellowing over a loudspeaker, cuts through the thwupping of huge exhaust fans and the dozens of scattered snores of inmates to announce the opening of the Pill Window. Most of the inmates in the pod stir at the sound of the impossible-to-ignore raucous voice.

My brother, Steve, normally picks up a pack of his diabetes medicine once a month, something he didn't need when he got here in 2006; but he doesn't need any medication this morning. Many of the other inmates don't either, but the loudspeaker wakes them all anyway; as do the guards who turn on the lights and work their way through the pod twice each night, kicking beds and waking everyone long enough to verify their presence by having each inmate recite his last name and bunk number.

"Larsen, 48." "Sirois, 49." "Pardillos, 50."

It's impossible for any of them to fall asleep and stay that way, but Steve at least has one advantage over the others. By sleeping on his left side, his glass right eye acts as a built-in sleep mask, and he can ignore the on-again off-again lighting changes, but he still has to ID himself for the guards. This morning he huddles under his thin, scratchy blanket to ward off the chilly air, and tries to grab another minute of relative quiet while it's still possible. Relative quiet because the grinding of the exhaust fans' motors are audible 24/7. One of them even vibrates the wall near his cubicle. As soon as the other sixty-one inhabitants of his pod start to stir, though, his senses will be overwhelmed with incessant chattering, shouting, screaming, blaring TV's. There won't be anything approaching a quiet moment until tonight.

Steve swings his legs over the side of his small bunk. Once everyone is awake, they all line up for the 4:00 am chow call. Their days are ruled by numbers; their ID numbers, their bunk numbers, and the numbers 4:00, 10:00, 2:00 and 10:30 (breakfast, lunch, dinner, and lights out). At first, the timing seemed odd to Steve, but he eventually realized that when he ate or slept was now just another arbitrary decision made by someone else, like everything in his life would be for many years to come.

He also no longer worries about being naked in front of other people. At any moment, a guard could tell him to strip for a search. Showers and going to the bathroom are also done in only marginally private circumstances, but a shower is his first order of business for today. I'm coming to visit him, so he needs to get cleaned up as quickly as possible. He has less than four hours before I will likely make it inside the building and he has a lot to do first. He strips to his boxers, grabs his towel, and heads down the steel stairs to the urinals. After draining his bladder, he crosses to the showers. No one else is using them yet, but he knows there will be a crowd soon, so he works up a quick lather, managing to get a semi-lukewarm stream of water going after a couple of minutes. The other three nozzles are occupied long before he finishes shaving his head and face, and he can hear a grumbling line forming behind him, so he grabs his towel off the low shower wall, steps out of the spray, and dries himself off before making his way back upstairs to his cubicle to dress in his prison whites.

The scent of baby powder rises in the stale, cold morning air. It's the best alternative to more expensive deodorants so most of the inmates use it. Back down the stairs again, Steve joins his freshly-talcumed roommates by the pod's outer door, hoping to be in the first group to be let out for chow, even though breakfast will just be the usual starchy crap. He hasn't had bacon since he arrived here.

He shouts toward the door, "Open the pod bay doors, Hal. We're hungry."

Someone down the line says, "Who's Hal? A new guard?"

It's nearly 5:00 am before Steve finally gets inside the chow hall. Hundreds of inmates are filing along the right-hand wall, moving gradually forward toward the trays and the serving counter. A roughly equal number of inmates are lined up against the opposite wall. They've finished their fifteen-minute meal, and are waiting to be allowed to go back to their pods. It could be as much as another half hour before they're outside again. The Dylan song, "I Shall Be Released," starts playing in Steve's head.

That's what we spend our whole time doing here, he thinks, *waiting to be released. From the pod, from the gatehouse, from the chow hall. From prison.*

He knows it will be a long time before he has a chance to get out on parole, though. His first chance will come at least halfway through his sentence, but the parole board's tendency to release prisoners who won't admit to their crimes is almost nonexistent. In order to win release, he will have to admit to the crime, show remorse, and demonstrate a willingness to reform.

The problem is, I didn't do it. And I would rather die in here with the truth than live out there with a lie.

He makes it back to his pod by around 6:30. Getting to and from breakfast took over two hours, typical for most days.

I arrive at Stiles at 6:45, having left Spring, Texas, before 5:00 am. A little over a hundred miles in less than two hours, thanks to 70 and 75 mph speed limits most of the way, not too bad. I will still have some hoops to jump through before I can get inside (first a car search; then a slow-moving line of visitors at the guardhouse, each of whom has to be searched; a metal detector; a pat-down; and two more checkpoints after that). Steve won't make it to the Visitor's Room until I've been there for a while anyway. They won't let him know I'm here until I'm inside, and then he will have to walk halfway across the prison. I usually wait twenty minutes or more in the Visitor's Room before he gets there. When he does arrive, after submitting to a strip search in an adjoining room (something the inmates call Stupid Human Tricks), a guard writes down the time and allows him to enter the Visitor's Room. After a quick hug, we have just two hours to try to hear each other talk over the din created by a packed room of other inmates and visitors attempting to do the same. Then he returns to his pod and I head for home again.

Note: Parts of the scene above were previously used in a short story I wrote, called "99 Miles for a Snickers and a Dr Pepper." Though it is a piece of fiction, it's an accurate portrait of a small part of a day in Steve's life. The rest of his days are very different, though. I haven't mentioned some of the hardships he does face on a daily basis. Also, there are some things I can't and won't talk about while he is still in prison.

So far he has managed to cope with everything remarkably well. He's taking college classes, and is doing well in them. The prison has found his skills as a construction worker useful. He has worked on their A/C systems, their generators, their boilers, and has done replacement and repairs to their lighting system. His aging body and his diabetes make it hard for him to work at the level he did before he was incarcerated, though. And some days have been difficult for other reasons. He was in Stiles while his wife's health deteriorated, and when she died. He was there when our mother died. He has missed major events in his children's lives. His five brothers and sisters are all older than he is. If he serves his full sentence, he will be 81 when he gets out, and 35 years of his life will have been stolen from him. I'm 74 right now, so if I manage to exceed the current average life expectancy for the United States (78.87 years), and am still around in 2041, I will be 95. It's more likely, though, that I and several of Steve's other siblings will be gone then. That's only a small part of the price he's paying for someone else's lies.

Much of the rest of this chapter is derived from court documents, a few investigative interviews, and hundreds of hours of recorded conversations I have had with Steve.

Let's go back in time now, to an afternoon sixteen years ago (as of the publication date).

Wednesday, April 7, 2004

When Darla Belisle arrived home from work that day, her fifteen-year-old daughter, Hanna Penderfield, told her she had been sexually molested by my brother, Steve, who was at that time a friend of their family. Darla jumped in her pickup and drove the twenty-plus miles from the town of Alderson to Steve's house in Saddleview Cove, a subdivision on the eastern side of Lake Ashwell, intending to confront him or kill him, she wasn't sure which.

According to Steve, he was mowing the lawn after a long day as a Park Ranger at the Lake Ashwell State Park when he spotted Darla's pickup pulling into the driveway. "What's she doing here?" he wondered, "She never comes over during the week." Then he remembered. She had asked him to research battered women's shelters in the area for a friend of hers. "Aw, shit. I forgot." He had meant to make some calls that morning, but got busy and didn't do it. He shut off the mower and headed for the gate to the front yard. As soon as she was in sight he said, "Darla, I'm sorry. I forgot all about it. What's up?"

Darla glanced over at Steve's daughter, who was playing basketball in the driveway. "Marri," she said. "You need to go inside so me and your dad can talk," then she turned her back on Steve and marched toward the driveway. While Marri complied, Steve grabbed a beer from a cooler on the front porch and followed Darla to where she stood rigidly waiting by her truck. He reached for the tailgate, intending to drop it down so he could sit while they talked, but his hand never made it to the latch. Darla squared off against him and said, "Don't touch my fucking truck." Steve froze and backed up a step, wondering what she was so angry about. She said, "You..." She paused. Tension hung in the air. "Did you think she wouldn't tell me?"

Steve was completely confused. Was she upset because he hadn't called her back with the information right away? It had been a tough day. He was tired, and not in a mood for any of her histrionics. He had been her go-to person for almost everything lately, complaints about her brothers, or her ex-husband, or bill collectors, or her boyfriend, or anyone else who had slighted her in some insignificant way. He said, "Darla, don't say it. Just don't say it." Those eight words would come back to haunt him later.

She stared at him a moment longer before saying "Get the hell out of my way!" That was an odd comment, he thought, because she was on the driver's side, close to her door. She turned on her heel, climbed back in her truck, started it up, and slammed it in reverse, flooring it. As she swung the wheel to the right, Steve barely had time to step aside. The front of the truck swerved across a bit of the yard, flinging up chunks of aggregate, and Steve had to jump back to keep from getting hit. She was almost to the corner of the street before Steve, dazed, got his cell phone out and dialed her number. No answer. She wasn't picking up.

Shaking his head, he wandered into the house to tell his wife, Robin, about the crazy encounter he had just had. He tried to reach Darla a few more times, but she didn't answer. Robin said, "Wait until tomorrow. We'll get to the bottom of this." He called Darla the next morning at her workplace, knowing she would have to pick up the phone there, and asked her what she was so mad about. She just said, "You know what's going on. You need help, Sirois," and slammed the phone down. That was the last time Steve ever spoke to her.

A week later, he sat across a desk from Sheriff's Deputy Willard Knox, who told him he was being accused of aggravated sexual assault of a child.

Twenty-eight months later, August 15, 2006:

Cleveland Sanford, Steve's third defense attorney, faced a jury in the county courthouse in Deep Springs, Texas, and said this as part of his opening statement.

> "The evidence will show you that the police did not investigate whether or not Hanna was telling the truth. And that the police did not even consider anything other than Hanna said it, must be the truth, Steven Sirois must be guilty. As a result, we sit here today. The case is about the power of words, it's about the power of the words of Hanna Penderfield...somebody decided she was telling the truth and the Government never turned back."

Two days after that, August 17, 2006:

They say that life can turn on a dime, but sometimes it can turn on a phrase and a word. In my brother's case, the word was "guilty" and the phrase was what he had said to Darla over two years earlier, "Darla, don't say it. Just don't say it." What Steve meant by those eight words was, "Darla, I'm tired, and I'm not in a mood to listen to you gripe about somebody who's done you wrong." Steve's meaning was turned into something entirely different during the trials, though.

Late on the afternoon of August 17th, Sanford's opponent, Ashwell County Assistant District Attorney (ADA), Elmer Ross, ended his closing statement like this, using Steve's own words against him.

> "Counsel told you from the beginning about the power of words. It's an ironic statement given the fact that when Hanna's mother confronts the Defendant and says, 'Did you think she would never tell me?' the Defendant didn't want to hear any words, did he?
>
> "'No, don't say it Darla, don't say it.' It wasn't referencing anything specific, anyone specific, just, 'Did you think she would not ever tell me?' And he knew exactly what she meant.
>
> "'No, don't say it, Darla, don't say it.' Folks, he has been telling you now for four days, 'Don't say it. Don't say it.'"

Ross picked a large book up from the prosecution table before continuing.

> "But there is one powerful word you need to say..."

He slammed the book down, causing everyone in the courtroom to jump.

> "...to this man. You need to say it three times. Count I, guilty. Count II, guilty. And Count III, guilty. Those are the words he needs to hear now."

3:15 pm: The jury began their deliberations. This was the second time Steve's case had been heard in this court. Less than a month before, his first trial had ended in a mistrial, with the jurors unable to reach a unanimous verdict on any of the three counts.

5:00 pm: Judge Preston Hawes received a note from the jury indicating that their "last vote was seven guilty, five not guilty, with no recent progress." He brought the jury back into the courtroom and gave them some further instructions. He told them that if they couldn't agree on a unanimous verdict, he would have to declare a mistrial again and let them go home; but he cautioned them that the case would likely be retried, and that the next jury, the third one for this case, would be chosen in the same way they had been, and they would probably hear nearly identical evidence to theirs. He said that any new jury would wrestle with the same questions they were dealing with, so it wouldn't be any easier for a new group to come to a decision. He asked them to "continue deliberations in an effort to arrive at a verdict that is acceptable to all members of the jury if you can do so without violation to your conscience. Don't do violence to your conscience, but continue deliberating."

6:30 pm: Another hour-and-a-half passed with no further word from the jury, so Judge Hawes sent them a note, asking them to let him know what the current status of their deliberations were. He received notice from the jury that they were split nine to three, with no indication whether they were leaning toward conviction or acquittal. They also said they thought they were making progress, and didn't think they were hopelessly deadlocked, so the judge arranged for supper to be brought to them and instructed them to keep at it.

Just after 8:00 pm: Supper was finished, and they had arrived at a verdict. Steve's attorney noticed as they filed in that one of the female jurors was crying, and didn't think that would bode well for Steve. It didn't. The jury said Steve was guilty of Count I for aggravated sexual assault; but not guilty of Counts II and III for sexual assault, a verdict that, years later, Sanford would tell me made no sense in a case like this. The jury was polled, and all twelve of them agreed that was their verdict. The next day, Steve was sentenced by Judge Hawes to thirty-five years in prison. He began his fourteenth year of incarceration on August 19, 2020.

Why This Book?

Quid est Veritas? (What is Truth?)
John 18:37

"Facts are the bare bones from which truth is made."
Shelby Foote

You may be wondering if I've given away the ending to the story by telling you that Steve was imprisoned and is still there. No, I haven't. I believe he is innocent of this crime, and I plan to prove it to you. Unless he gets a new trial, he is scheduled to be incarcerated until mid-August 2041. He will turn 81 in March of that year. He will technically be eligible for parole in 2024 at the age of 64, but he won't be granted it because he won't admit to something he hasn't done. In Texas, parole without admission of guilt and an expression of remorse rarely happens. Steve has always maintained his innocence, and he refused plea deals before both trials that would have kept him out of prison. He turned them down because, as he said, "I would still be registered as a sex offender, and that would be a lie." Was Steve a saint? No, and I won't paint him as such in the book. He was an ordinary human being who tried to do good things in his life, but also made mistakes. He worked hard to correct those, and had largely succeeded until these false accusations wiped all of that away.

After studying the trial transcripts for years, along with recorded interviews and material from Texas Public Information Act (TPIA) requests, I did an extensive breakdown and analysis of everything. Some new evidence and some previously unused data came out of that analysis. I think I can now prove that this entire case was a perfect example of a justice system run amok. One where I believe that provable lies were told, where my brother's guilt was assumed with little consideration given to other possibilities, and where its prosecutor seemed more intent on getting a win than in finding the truth.

Someone who read an early draft of the book said they could tell I used to be a teacher because it read like a textbook. I hope it does, because I'm not trying to create a great literary work here. I need this document to be accurate, clear, and precise, not a work of art. I don't have receipts, or video, or eyewitnesses to establish anyone's veracity, but I do have court records, and transcripts of testimony from both trials. That testimony and Hanna's affidavit are the only records she made while sworn in. Her other statements (to a counselor and an investigator) weren't under oath, but I will still quote from them to prove that someone was lied to. Wherever possible I used factual data to support my suppositions. If I had included all of the relevant data I gathered and analyzed over the past decade, the book would be well over a thousand pages long; so I have tried to keep it as simple as possible (which was harder than it should have been because Hanna told so many different versions of the same scenarios). If there are some areas of the story that need a more thorough coverage than I can give you here, I'll provide additional details on the book's blog.

The rest of the book is divided into five sections, *Before the Trials*, *The Trials*, *Proof of Innocence*, *After the Trials*, and *Endnotes*.

Before the Trials covers what happened between April 2004 (when Hanna made her accusation) and July 2006 (when the first trial began). It also examines a few additional side issues which don't have anything to do with the trial or the accusations, but could have everything to do with why the jury may have arrived at the verdict they did.

The Trials deals briefly with the few months leading up to July 2006, and explores the facts, or as Shelby Foote said above, "the bare bones" of what was revealed in both trials.

If *The Trials* is the skeleton of the story, the *Proof of Innocence* section should be considered the muscle and fat and organs (hopefully the brains) of it. In that section I break down Hanna's accusations by comparing statements she made at different times, and debunk them with various facts, data, and logic. I don't believe that any of her accusations were true, and will try to prove that by analyzing several crucial incidents (a cross-country track meet; several sleepovers; a drive to see the first Harry Potter movie; a ride home from a rodeo, and a 21st birthday party). If you find yourself wanting to skip ahead to that section of the book, I suggest that you forego the temptation. Read the earlier chapters first. Everything in *Before the Trials* and *The Trials* lays the groundwork for a more complete understanding of the *Proof of Innocence* chapters.

The last two sections, *After the Trials* and *Endnotes*, are there to wrap up a few details and provide some links to additional material.

I also need to make it clear that I have had no direct access to Hanna or her brother, Aaron, although I would welcome the opportunity to interview both of them. I have been warned away from contacting Hanna by her mother, Darla. Anything I tell you from Hanna's point of view will come primarily from trial transcripts, a two-and-a-half hour recorded interview Hanna did with an investigator, a few other sources, and a twenty-minute talk I had in September 2014 with her mother. After that conversation, a number of people in the Deep Springs area refused to talk to me, I presume because someone warned them not to. That is the main reason I have been forced to speculate occasionally. In my opinion, that's their loss. I would have been happy to have given any of them equal time to tell their side of things. There is a lot of detail here, so what I'm asking you to do as a reader is to follow the evidence I will present, and be Spock-like in your judgment. Base it on logic and facts, not emotion. That's what the jury was instructed to do but apparently didn't.

Before the Trials

The Accusation and the Aftermath

"Oh, what a tangled web we weave
When first we practice to deceive."
Sir Walter Scott, *Marmion*

"Nobody who has not been in the interior of a family can say what the difficulties of any individual of that family may be."
Jane Austen, *Pride and Prejudice*

[Subsections in this Chapter: A Brief Family History // April 7, 2004 - An Abuse Presentation // A Slight Pause // Hanna's Affidavit // Creating the Affidavit // The First Analysis]

Some of you might be wondering why I haven't given you any specific details yet about what Hanna accused Steve of. I'll cover that in this chapter, but there were instances where several people disagreed about when Hanna told them she was having sexual experiences with an older (unnamed) man. Hanna said she told some of her friends at sleepovers in 2003. One person said it might have been as early as 2002, and another person said she didn't tell her friends until after she had lodged the accusations in April 2004. Knowing *who* Hanna told, and *when* they were told, will be vital to understanding what really happened. Pinpointing exactly what she said, and when she said it, has sometimes been difficult because she told so many contradictory versions of her story. If she did tell her friends she was being molested before the charges were filed and they told no one, are they culpable in perpetuating a crime? If she didn't tell them until after the charges were filed, though, the rest of her story falls apart. I'll do my best to lay everything out in a way that clarifies those discrepancies, but the timeline of the alleged events is a crucial issue, and I will return to it often. After you've read the book, I'll be happy to address questions about the case on the blog as long as I'm not asked to identify individuals or give out any information which might reveal their identities.

https://aggravatedbook.com

In a minute we'll look at the oral statement Hanna made to a speaker at her school, a comment that led to the accusations against Steve.

But first...

A Brief Family History

I have five brothers and sisters. I'm the oldest and Steve is the youngest. There is a fourteen-year span between us. I was born in Dayton, Ohio, in 1946. My parents met at the Wright-Patterson Air Force Base there. My mother, Joy Shaw, was in the Women's Army Air Corps. My father, Stanley Sirois, was stationed at Wright-Patterson as a member of an entertainment troop for *This is the Army*, a Broadway play and a movie which used a number of U.S. military personnel in the cast. After the war, Joy and Stan married and I showed up the following year. Between then and 1954, we moved from Dayton to Deep Springs, Texas, to Tucson, to New York City, to Boston, and then to Toronto. Two of my sisters, Jamie and Cece were born in New York, and Maritia was born in Toronto. In 1954, we moved from Toronto to El Paso. My brothers Phillip and Steve were both born there (in 1957 and 1960, respectively). We were there for a little over eight years, and moved to Deep Springs again in 1962 to live with Mom's parents on their farm. That was in the middle of my freshman year in high school. Steve was only two years old, so Deep Springs was the only town he thought of as home until he was in high school. You can see pictures of all of us on the blog.

https://aggravatedbook.com/images-of-people/

Although it wasn't talked about, I could tell we had less resources than some of the other kids at school, so I'm sure most of our family's many moves were for financial reasons. I moved to Houston in the summer of 1970. Steve was barely ten then, but I moved out of the house five years before that, and into a series of dorms and apartments, when I started attending the local college, Stockman University. Since I was gone from the house during that time, my memories of Steve are mostly as a little kid. I only saw him as a teenager once. In 1975, when he was fifteen, he visited me for a couple of days in Houston.

Mom took some college courses in Deep Springs before WWII, but left short of a degree when she joined the WAAC's. She divorced our father in 1975, and later married Bill Sen, who lived in Lexington, Massachusetts. After living in Lexington with Mom and Bill for about a year, Steve returned to Deep Springs to stay. Our father was still there, but the rest of us were scattered across Texas by then, except for Cece, who moved to Alaska after several years overseas as an Army MP.

I did go back to Deep Springs a few times after 1970. My wife, Minay, and I stopped and saw Dad and Steve briefly in 1982, on our way back to Houston during our honeymoon. The whole family gathered in Deep Springs in 1993 when Mom graduated from college. She finished her remaining nineteen hours of college in Massachusetts. Stockman accepted her credits and awarded her a bachelor's degree, so she came back there for the graduation ceremony. It only took her fifty years or so, but we were proud of her and all gathered there to see her graduate. Apart from instances like those and a couple of high school reunions, though, I rarely visited Deep Springs. When I first heard about the accusations against Steve it almost felt like something I might hear on a news broadcast, about a person I didn't know. We weren't an especially communicative family before that, so Steve's life from the age of ten on was mostly a blank space for me. That changed radically after the charges were filed, of course.

Let's jump ahead to 2004, just before and just after Steve's confrontation with Darla in his driveway.

April 7, 2004 - An Abuse Presentation

About six weeks after Hanna's 15th birthday, most students in the Alderson Independent School District were probably thinking summer couldn't arrive fast enough, but this afternoon they were getting a break from the classroom through an assembly program. In 2004, the entire town of Alderson was populated by less than 400 people. Just over 200 students attended school in the district, and roughly half of them were in grades seven through twelve. This assembly was for them. Blake Goudy, who had the grand title of Director of Prevention and Awareness for Cradle's Rest, a local domestic violence shelter, gave them a presentation about abuse. In his trial testimony, he said he spent from 12:30 to 3:30 telling the students "about relationship abuse, child abuse, and reporting procedures." As he ended his presentation, Goudy said, "If anyone is abusing you or hurting you in any way, tell someone that you trust, tell your mother, tell your father, tell the school counselor, your teacher, your minister. And if you cannot tell anyone else, Blake Goudy is standing right up here. When we're through, come tell me and I will help you."

If his talk actually was three hours long, I couldn't help but wonder how many of the students managed to stay awake through the whole thing. At the age of fifteen, a month-and-a-half before school let out, I probably wouldn't have been good for more than thirty minutes. During the presentation, Karla Spivey, one year older than Hanna, noticed that she seemed agitated, maybe nervous or upset. She sat down beside Hanna and asked her what was wrong. "Nothing," Hanna said, but Karla pestered her until she gave in and relayed what had allegedly been happening to her. Karla insisted that Hanna had to tell Mr. Goudy, and despite Hanna's protests, said, "I'll walk up there with you. You need to tell him." So, at the end of the presentation, the two girls approached the speaker. Then, Karla left to give Hanna some privacy. After she told Goudy about her abuse, he gave her his card and said to have her mother call him so he could advise her what to do.

That's the story Hanna told in both trials, with slight variations from one trial to the next. Karla (who didn't testify in either trial), later gave an account that sheds an entirely different light on what Hanna might have said that day; but for now we're just going to look at Hanna's version.

A Slight Pause

Moments like this will crop up occasionally in this book, where I feel the need to explain something before continuing. What I've written above is based on recorded data (court documents, interviews, state records, etc.) and is to the best of my knowledge true, with the caveat that I believe Hanna often lied, and much of this information originated with her. At several stages in the book I'll analyze the claims she made and try to separate truth from fiction. For now, though, I'll mostly just try to present an accurate picture of the way these alleged incidents were described to investigators and testified to in court. The one thing I would ask is this: Don't accept everything you read as absolute truth (especially in these early sections) until I give you an analysis of it, because you will be viewing the incidents almost entirely from Hanna's viewpoint. Her versions, while they seemed to me to be constructed out of thin air, were often set within a framework of real events, which might have made them seem truthful to others. The only hint I'll give you now about the above scene is this: What Hanna told the investigators, and what she said in the trials, may not be everything she told Karla. If the differences between her story and Karla's had been known then, I think it could have completely changed the outcome of the trial (or even have determined whether Steve would have been tried at all).

Let's take a look at the document that started it all.

Hanna's Affidavit

Anyone can create an affidavit. They just have to put their statement on paper, sign it in front of a witness, and have it notarized. In a criminal proceeding, an officer of the law usually helps prepare it, though, and that was the case here. I'm not going to dwell on Hanna's statement too much now, except to say that, even though the Ashwell County Sheriff's Office appears to have botched the document badly, it still didn't stop the district attorney from bringing the case to trial.

I have no idea what the day of the affidavit was like for Hanna. I don't know whether she went to school, or whether Darla had her stay home, but the affidavit was signed at 5:00 pm on April 8th, after what Hanna told Tom Swearingen was a discussion of about an hour or so. Regardless of where she spent her day, from the time she told her mother until she appeared at the sheriff's office she had nearly a full day to think about what was going to happen next. Even if you believe she was telling the truth, I think she must have realized the seriousness of what she was about to do. I suspect it's likely that Hanna got very little sleep that night, possibly spending the evening and most of the rest of the next day running through a mental checklist of what she needed to say when questioned by the sheriff's office.

There was some testimony in both trials about what Hanna said to Karla Spivey and Blake Goudy, as well as about what she said to Deputy Knox the next day. Let's compare her affidavit to her other statements, and see how well they match up. The wording, spelling, and punctuation in this transcription is identical to the original, but I've also added a couple of [*redactions*] to replace identifying information. The first paragraph might seem odd at first glance, but I'll explain why below.

I need to remind you that graphic language and descriptions of sexual scenes will occur throughout the book. This is one of those spots. I won't warn you every time. Just expect it.

AFFIDAVIT
STATE OF TEXAS
COUNTY OF ASHWELL

Before me, the undersigned authority in and for said county and state, on this the 18 day of April, 2000 personally appeared Jennilea Hubbard who, after being by me duly sworn, deposes and says:

My name is Hanna Penderfield, I am 15 years of age having been born on [*date redacted*]. I live at [*address redacted*] in Alderson, Texas. I am currently in the 9th grade at Alderson High School. I do read, write, and understand the English Language.

While I am not sure of the exact dates, I do remember several times over the past 3 years that I have been sexually assaulted by a man known to me as Steve Sirois. My family has known Steve Sirois for several years and have visited his home on numerous occasions.

The first time I was sexually assaulted by Steve Sirois was in late August or early September 2001 when I was 12 years old. This happened the first time I had spent the night at Steve Sirois's house. I remember I was sleeping in the same bed with Marri Sirois who was about 9 years old. Sometime during the night I was awaken by Steve, by him shaking my shoulder. When I started to say something to him he put his hand over mouth to keep me quiet. I further remember I was wearing a T-shirt and blue jean shorts. He then removed my shorts and underwear. I remember he then started kissing on me and he then put his mouth on my vagina. I further remember he then stuck his tongue inside my vagina. He did this for several minutes. After he stopped, he told me goodnight and he left the bedroom.

I wish to state that during the past three years this has happened several times while I was visiting his home. I have not been able or willing to talk about this until I met Blake Goudy at school. After listening to him about sexual abuse, I decided to tell him.

The last time I remember anything happening between Steve Sirois and me was February 14th of this year. I remember my mother, brother, and I had gone to Steve's home to have a BarBQ to celebrate his son's birthday. After several hours, his wife Robin got drunk so she went to bed. I further remember my mother had left for awhile and so had Marri. I was in the house along with Steve while my brother, Aaron, was outside at the fire. I was helping Steve put up the food when he started trying to kiss me again. I told him this had to stop but he would not listen to me. He then grabbed my hand and led me into his bedroom where Robin was asleep. He then unzipped his pants and pulled out his dick. He then forced my head down and he stuck his dick in my mouth. He made me suck on his dick until stuff came out. After he let me up he then pulled the draw string on my pants and he stuck his hand inside them. He then stuck his finger inside my vagina. He did this for a few minutes and then he let me go. I then went into the bathroom.

I wish to state I remember him telling me he would not have sexual intercourse with me because I was a minor and that he did not want to hurt my mother or his wife. He further stated he did not want to lose his job and go to jail. He also stated he would deny doing anything, even if he stood in the gates of "hell". I wish to state I did not tell anyone about what was happening except a friend of mine named Josh Chilmark. I remember Josh stated he would go beat the man up but I would not tell him what Steve's name was.

The above affidavit is true and correct to the best of my knowledge and memory and I give it freely and voluntarily.

It was signed by both Hanna and Darla on April 8, 2004 at 5:00 pm. Let's see how it was created, and what it means.

Creating the Affidavit

Late in the afternoon on April 8th, at the Ashwell County Law Enforcement Center (referred to locally as the LEC), Hanna and Darla met with Willard Knox so he could interview Hanna and construct an affidavit detailing her abuse. She was sworn in, and Knox began the interview. His job was to get as much legally valid information from her as possible, to help the district attorney build a case against her perpetrator.

An affidavit, like a newspaper article, should try to answer (as completely as possible) the *Who, What, When, Where, Why, and How* of the accusations. I honestly don't know how this one even passed muster as an acceptable legal document, but it did give me a starting point for examining the changes Hanna made to her claims during the two years leading up to the first trial. Let's examine it.

The ***Who*** in the affidavit is primarily about Steve and Hanna, but she also mentions her mother and brother, and Steve's wife, daughter, and son. A few other names show up in the document too, Josh Chilmark, Blake Goudy, and someone named Jennilea Hubbard.

The ***What***, of course, is Hanna's accusation, and the ***When***, ***Where*** and ***How*** are partially sketched out, but the ***Why*** (the motive) isn't covered at all. Let's break everything down a little, starting with the affidavit's opening declaration:

> "Before me, the undersigned authority in and for said county and state, on this the 18 day of April, 2000, personally appeared Jennilea Hubbard who, after being by me duly sworn, deposes and says:"

What's wrong with that sentence? A lot. The name Jennilea Hubbard is only there because of the way the sheriff's office prepared the affidavit, by using a previous affidavit as a template (one which already had someone else's name and an incorrect date). It's a good example of the apparently careless way they approached the rest of the investigation. Also, the date should have been April 8th, 2004 — not April 18th, 2000. Hanna crossed out the number "1" and initialed it, changing the date from the"18th" to the "8th," but if they caught that mistake, why didn't they also see that the year (2000) was four years too early, and that the person making the affidavit was Hanna, not Jennilea Hubbard? Why didn't they just retype it?

Hanna was fifteen in April 2004. When she was seventeen, during her 2006 interview with Tom Swearingen (his real name), he asked her about that day. She said, "I kept getting on his [*Knox's*] nerves because I would be asked to proofread it, and I would be like, 'Oh, you need to put a comma there, and a period goes there, and you need to pull this out...'" She paused to laugh before saying, "...and I'd get on his nerves because I'm just really good at English." As we look at the trial transcripts and other documents, you will notice that Hanna sometimes attempts to elevate her status above those around her, in this instance by denigrating Knox's language skills, but that leaves us with this question: If Hanna was so "good at English," and she made all those corrections, why does the affidavit still contain so many mistakes? Setting the document's obvious flaws aside, though, the affidavit was the basis for deciding what Steve would eventually be charged with, so let's look at some of the details.

The affidavit stated that Hanna wasn't "sure of the exact dates," but that "several times over the past 3 years" she had "been sexually assaulted" by Steve. She said that the first incident was "in late August or early September 2001" when she was twelve years old, and that was the first time she spent the night at Steve's house. She described the circumstances of that night in some detail, saying that she was sleeping in the same bed as Marri, that Steve shook her shoulder to wake her up, that he put a hand over her mouth to keep her quiet, that she was wearing a t-shirt and blue jean shorts, that he removed them, that he performed oral sex on her, and that he said good night before he left the room.

The accusation of oral sex became Count I against him (for aggravated sexual assault of a child). Each count contained a specific thing the prosecution had to prove. In order to convict him for Count I, they had to prove three things: that he performed oral sex on Hanna that night, that she was under the age of fourteen at the time, and wasn't married to Steve. Here's the count as it was presented in court.

> "Count I, Steven Barker Sirois, hereinafter styled the Defendant, on or about the 1st day of September, 2001, and before the presentment of this indictment, in the County and State aforesaid, did then and there intentionally or knowingly cause the penetration of the sexual organ of Hanna Penderfield, a child who was then and there younger than 14 years of age and not the spouse of the Defendant, by the Defendant's tongue."

The next paragraph was devoted to the final two incidents of abuse, which Hanna claimed happened the night of Beau's 21st birthday party. She gave a specific date, "February 14th of this year" (2004), and said that she and her family went to Steve's to celebrate Beau's birthday. Then she said that Robin was passed out drunk in her bed, that her brother was outside, that Hanna's mother and Steve's daughter were both mysteriously gone, and that she and Steve were inside the house. Also, oddly, although it was Beau's birthday, in this scenario, even Beau wasn't there. She claimed that Steve grabbed her hand and pulled her into the bedroom where Robin was, unzipped his pants and forced her to perform oral sex on him. Then she said he pulled the drawstring on her pants and stuck his finger in her vagina for a few minutes.

Those two actions (oral sex and digital insertion) became Counts II and III against Steve. In other words, Steve was indicted for performing oral sex on her once, for her performing oral sex on him once, and for him placing his finger in her vagina once. To convict Steve on all three counts the prosecution would have to prove those three items.

Here's one other tiny detail to think about. Hanna testified in the trials that she told Blake Goudy that Steve was her abuser, but in the affidavit, which was created the very next day, Hanna didn't say what she told Goudy. I'll revisit that later with an important additional twist.

Once Hanna and her mother left, Knox entered a brief set of notes into the LEC's computer system. Knox's note is recreated below with the same redactions, spelling, and punctuation.

SUPPLEMENT DATE: 04/08/04
INV. GEORGE KNOX

On date I Inv. Willard Knox, made contact with [*full name redacted*] and her mother , Darla Belisle in reference to the above investigation. The purpose of the contact was to obtain a Affidavit from [*first name redacted*] describing the events surrounding the Aggravated Sexual Assault by Steve Sirois. During the interview, [*first name redacted*] estimated she had been sexually abused by Steve Sirois about 50 times over the past 3 years. She then described the first time Steve touched her in a sexual way was when she was 12 years of age. She also described the last time he touched her in a sexual way, which was February 14th, 2004. She stated she remembers this date because it was Steve's sons birthday and they had a cookout at Steve's house. (See Attached Affidavit)
Investigation to Continue...

Here are a few things to consider before we move on.

About the Affidavit: Were the flaws in the document unimportant to the DA's office? Why did they allow it to be used in the trial as it was? Once it was created, did they not have any other choice? Much of it doesn't make sense to me. One example: If the incidents in Counts II and III happened at Beau's birthday party while Hanna's brother was "outside at the fire," why weren't her mother, or Marri, or Beau, or any of his friends, or neighbors, or other relatives also there? When we start comparing it to other documents you should notice a great many more details that appear to be missing from her account.

About Willard Knox's Note: If the purpose of redaction is to disguise the identity of the "victim," why didn't the sheriff's office also redact the name of Hanna's mother in the material they gave me? If Hanna gave Knox the more specific number of "about 50 times" during the interview, as he said in his note, why does the affidavit say "several times" instead of fifty? Did she actually tell Knox it was fifty times? If so, didn't he believe her? Did he think that fifty times would be impossible to prove, so he used the word "several" in the affidavit to help the prosecution? Wouldn't he have a responsibility to be accurate in a legal document? To discover the truth as opposed to bolstering the prosecution's case? Shouldn't the premise of "innocent until proven guilty" apply to law enforcement investigations as well as the courts?

In May 2006, Hanna told Tom Swearingen that she and Willard Knox talked for "a good hour, maybe." Shouldn't there be an hour's worth of Knox's notes somewhere? Or possibly an audio recording? According to the sheriff's office, there isn't. Also, shouldn't they or the district attorney's investigators have interviewed Steve's family and friends and neighbors, and some of Hanna's friends? They didn't at first. They eventually interviewed a few other people, all on Hanna's side, but did almost no investigating beyond that. With their suspect in hand, did they just not bother? I wrestled with some of these questions for over a decade. I can't promise you answers to all of them, but maybe I can clear up the most important ones.

During Hanna's 2006 interview with Tom, she talked about how difficult it had been to edit the affidavit. She said that Knox "asked me to go into detail about what had happened, and ...I ...it was so hard for me ...it was so hard for me, because the last incident had only taken place like maybe two weeks ago." Tom asked her, "Did he try to coach you any?" She asked what he meant by that. He said he wanted to know if Knox had tried to lead her into the answers he wanted. Sounding hesitant, Hanna said, "Yeah," then paused before saying, "There's just ...oh, I don't really remember. It's so long ago, and I was so uncomfortable. I think I kind of snuffed it out." One of the things Tom would naturally try to discover would be whether an interrogation had been handled fairly or not. Hanna isn't unintelligent, and it felt to me (whether this is a valid thought or not) that she was wondering how to answer that question. Maybe she felt it was a trap. As soon as she said, "Yeah" (that Knox *did* lead her into some questions), she backed off, saying she didn't remember.

[*A skilled interrogator can shape an interview through the way they ask questions, but I think Knox completely misread Steve during his interview with him (that's coming up in the next chapter), and missed a number of important details in this interview with Hanna. He also seemed willing to shape the affidavit in a way that would help the prosecution, like using the phrase* "several times," *instead of listing the details she gave him. I believe the poor quality of the affidavit is indicative of the sloppiness with which this was handled.*

Did you also notice that Hanna said the last incident happened "like maybe two weeks ago?" Even assuming that she meant two weeks before the affidavit (not Tom's interview), February 14th was nine weeks before April 8th, not two. In the Proof of Innocence *section you'll see that Hanna's sense of time was very fluid. It seemed to expand when she needed it to be longer, and contract when that suited her needs.*]

One thing that Hanna didn't mention in the affidavit was an incident which she said happened after a cross-country race in September 2001. Without Willard Knox's full notes or a recording, I doubt we'll ever know if they discussed it or not. Hanna inflated her performance in that race when she brought it up in both trials. The race was also mentioned briefly in a summary from Hanna's counselor and in her interview with Tom. In the trials, though, it felt to me like she was using the race as a mechanism for remembering the first alleged incident, which, by that time, was unrecognizable as the incident she described in the affidavit. I'll break the changes about that incident down in the chapter, *A Cross-Country Meet, The First Lie*.

The First Analysis

Words matter.

Steve's attorney for Trial #2, Cleveland Sanford, said in his opening statement, "This case is about the power of words. And in particular, it's about the power of the words of Hanna Penderfield." What he wanted the jury to understand was that no one from CSI was going to sit on the witness stand and explain about semen stains or sex tapes. There weren't any. Hanna's claims about what happened were the only evidence. She also claimed that other people were actually present during many of the incidents and said they should have seen something, but (except for one minor instance, on the night of the rodeo), all of those people said they didn't see anything. All that most of her other witnesses could do was repeat what she had told them, so her words were still the only evidence in the case against Steve.

I believe that Hanna may have accused Steve because of some invented fantasies she had bragged to her friends about. If so, Blake Goudy's abuse talk at her school might have placed her in a position of having to choose to either admit to her friends that she had been deceiving them or to continue to pretend that she had actually been molested. Let's break down what she told Deputy Knox. In the affidavit she said, under oath, that she had been assaulted by Steve at his house "several times" over the previous three years, but the affidavit only lists two incidents. She said the first one occurred the first time she spent the night at the Sirois' home (according to her in August or September 2001), and that the final incident happened on the night of Beau's birthday party (February 14, 2004). That second date might be the only accurate one she gave in the affidavit, because it was the night of a real event, but even it might have been off by a week. Those two dates (one loose and general, and one specific) were used by the prosecutor as markers for the beginning and ending of the abuse, bookend dates for the "several" incidents that Hanna claimed.

Why is the affidavit so vague and inaccurate? Did she not give Knox enough details because she hadn't decided what all the details would be yet? If she did tell Knox that she had been assaulted fifty times, why did he only include those two incidents in the affidavit? As the book progresses, we'll continue to compare the affidavit to other documents and statements. The differences between them are remarkable.

Here's one more thing about the affidavit before we move on. In it, Hanna said, "I have not been able or willing to talk about this until I met Blake Goudy at school. After listening to him about sexual abuse, I decided to tell him." In that same affidavit, though, she also said, "I wish to state I did not tell anyone about what was happening except a friend of mine named Josh Chilmark." According to Hanna, she started talking to Josh about her abuse in April 2003, a year before Goudy gave his presentation at her school. Which of those two statements is the truth? Wait. Before you try to figure that out, in both her 2006 interview and her trial testimony she said that, in addition to Josh, she also told several of her friends about her abuse while they were at sleepovers. The friends aren't mentioned in the affidavit, but if Hanna told both Josh and her friends before Goudy, then Hanna certainly *was* willing to tell someone else, and did. Isn't at least one of the two comments in her affidavit (about who she told) a false statement under oath? Could both of them be false? Wouldn't a good investigator catch a mistake like that and rewrite the affidavit before having it signed and notarized? Couldn't the DA's office, once they noticed the discrepancies, have Hanna create an amendment to the original affidavit or a new affidavit to correct it? They didn't.

Also, in both trials, Josh testified that Hanna told him what was happening to her, but said she didn't tell him who was abusing her. Hanna, in Tom's interview and both trials, said she told her friends about some of the things that were happening to her because it made her more popular. Rhonda Bresnick, though, a friend of Hanna's, testified that Hanna first told her friends about her abuse after the accusations were made, at a sleepover. None of Hanna's other sleepover friends testified.

Pop Quiz: The affidavit and the trials were all held under oath. The interview with Tom Swearingen wasn't. In the affidavit, Hanna said that she told no one about her abuse before Goudy; but she also said that she told no one but her friend Josh. Hanna said numerous times that her conversations with Josh were in 2003; and also said several times that she told her friends about it at more than one sleepover (in 2002 and/or 2003). She also said that, just before she talked to Goudy, she told Karla Spivey what had been happening to her, but she didn't mention Karla in her affidavit at all, and didn't give Karla's name to anyone until she was asked about her by Tom in 2006. The Goudy talk was the day before the affidavit was written, so why weren't Karla or any of Hanna's other friends mentioned in the affidavit?

Looking at the previous paragraph, can you figure out how many times Hanna may have lied under oath? Was it in her affidavit, or to Tom, or in the trials, or in all of them? The answer is unknowable, of course, but that's what most of the research for this book has been like. If you don't have an answer yet, hang in there. For now, just keep this in mind: Logically, at least one statement in a series of statements is false if one or more of those statements materially contradict the other statements. Two of Hanna's conflicting statements under oath were given in the same document, the affidavit. Some of the others were made under oath during the trials. The affidavit is just the first data source for this exploration of truth versus falsehood. A meticulous examination of it and the other documents revealed that they are all flawed in various ways. This document, though, however inaccurate, wasn't questioned by the sheriff's office, the DA's office, or the grand jury that gave the go-ahead to try Steve.

Yes, words do matter, but too often in this story the only words anyone heard were Hanna's, or the words of other people simply parroting what she told them. You'll see, though, that many of her pronouncements disagreed with other statements she made about the same incident.

A Few More Things to Consider: What if the "victim" wasn't a victim at all, but only *said* they were victimized for some other reason? Doesn't that make the accused person the victim instead of the accuser? If Hanna actually *was* a victim of abuse, but lied about who her abuser was; wouldn't the accused person also be a victim? Also, how did Hanna's claim of fifty incidents of abuse (which Willard Knox declined to put in the official affidavit) become ninety incidents between April and September?

We'll get to all of that. Let's look at the time period leading up to the two trials.

The Long Wait Before the Trials

"How much of human life is lost in waiting."
Ralph Waldo Emerson

"He's supposed to send the investigator out.
I don't think he ever did."
Hanna Penderfield

[Subsections in this Chapter: Sheriff's Investigation // A Medical Exam // Five Counseling Sessions // A Question About Innocence // Hiring a Lawyer // April to June, 2004 // Thoughts to Consider // July 2004, an Arrest // Willard Knox's Final Interview // Hiring Tom, and His Early Interviews // A Short Interlude About Drinking // Tom's Other Interviews // Josh Chilmark's Two Interviews // A Missing Rape Kit? // Money Problems // Trip to Florida]

Sheriff's Investigation

We've already touched on the initial investigation in the previous chapter, which was getting that statement from Hanna, however imperfect it might have been. I don't know why they didn't follow up on it immediately, but it took five days for Deputy Knox to call Steve and ask him to come in and make a statement. Steve wanted to know what it was all about, of course, but Knox, after asking Steve if he knew Darla Belisle and Hanna Penderfield, would only say that an accusation had been lodged against him and he would need to come in to find out what it was about.

So, the next morning, April 14th, Steve and Robin drove to the Law Enforcement Center together. The LEC is a multi-purpose building. The sheriff's office, the county jail, the city's municipal Court, and the police department are all housed there. Deputy Knox asked Robin to stay in the waiting room, then ushered Steve though a heavy metal door into the sheriff's area. He led Steve down an institutional beige cinderblock hallway to his office. Once they were inside, Knox told Steve what the allegations were, advised him of his rights, and asked him to sign a Waiver-of-Rights form. Steve did. An affidavit wasn't created from that interview, but the note Deputy Knox later entered into his file hints at the nature of the meeting. Here's part of it, using the same redactions and punctuation as the original.

> "Sirois stated he has never touched [*name redacted*] in a sexual way. He stated she is just a little girl and he would never do anything like that. I then talked with Steve Sirois about specific incidents which he also denied. Steve did admit he and [*name redacted*]'s mother, Darla Belisle did have a few sexual encounters out in his shop. He went on to say that on two separate occasions, Darla Belisle did perform oral sex on him while they were in his shop. Sirois continually denied any sexual contact with [*name redacted*]."

I'm guessing that a comment about Hanna's mother, Darla, caught your attention, but let's deal with Steve's reaction to the interview first. When Knox told him what the allegations were, Steve couldn't believe what he was hearing. He tried to rationalize it, but he just couldn't imagine why Hanna would say such horrible things. He thought back to Beau's birthday party, the last time her family was at the house. He wondered, *Did I hug her too hard when they left? Did I say something wrong? What's going on?*

He told Knox the charges were ludicrous, and he would never do that. While they were talking, Knox received a phone call and took it in front of Steve, saying things like, "Oh, he's going to lawyer up? Oh, well, that just means he's guilty." Steve didn't think about it at the time, but he's now certain the call was staged, trying to scare him into confessing. When he got off the phone, Knox asked Steve if he would be willing to take a lie detector test.

In 1973, Steve's 7th grade science teacher, Merle Pyburn, used a lie detector in class to demonstrate some bodily functions (heart rate, respiration, etc.). Steve participated in the experiment, even though he was massively nervous about it. At the end of Steve's turn, Mr. Pyburn looked at the readout and jokingly told Steve he should never, ever take a lie detector test. He said Steve's nerves were so apparent that he would flunk it for sure (even though polygraph tests are rarely admissible as proof of truth in court). Steve told Knox that story, but said, "I'll take one if my attorney tells me it's okay." Knox said, "Oh, so you need an attorney now? I've been doing this a long time. Do you know what kinetic energies are?" Steve said he didn't. Knox told Steve that he was lying because "You always look up and to the left when you're lying."

Steve lost his right eye when he was younger, after an accident with a seam ripper punctured his eyeball. (Yes, ouch!) When Knox made that comment, Steve took his glasses off and tapped on the surface of his glass right eye with his fingernail, generating a clacking sound, and said, "Which eye were you looking at?" Knox just stared at him for a moment before saying, "Well, I guess we're done." Steve said, "Yes, sir. I guess we are," adding that he would have his attorney contact him. Knox didn't mention the eyeball tapping in his file.

Note: Steve said Knox used the phrase "kinetic energies," but that would refer to the energy of bodies in motion. I've seen the phrase "kinetic communication" used, but in reference to non-verbal languages (like American Sign Language). Whatever phrase Knox used, he was likely referring to micro-expressions, tiny, brief movements which appear on our faces under certain circumstances. Some say these can reveal whether someone is lying, but the accuracy of the technique has been disputed. In a June 2011 article in the FBI Law Enforcement Bulletin, "Evaluating Truthfulness and Detecting Deception," the authors outlined a situation where an interrogator assumes a suspect is lying because they look up to the left (as Knox had claimed), or register one of several facial gestures. The article concluded that the "investigator likely would be wrong," and added that "23 out of 24 peer-reviewed studies published in scientific journals reporting experiments on eye behavior as an indicator of lying have rejected this hypothesis. No scientific evidence exists to suggest that eye behavior or gaze aversion can gauge truthfulness reliably." In Steve's case, with his glass eye, monitoring his eye movements would be especially useless.

When Steve left the room, he saw Lonnie Hartness, one of the investigators who had spoken to Darla the week before, striding toward Knox's office, as if he wanted to get there before Steve left. Hartness glanced at Steve, shook his head, then lowered his gaze and wouldn't look at him. Steve thought that was a cold way to treat him, since Hartness had been friendly to him in the past. I asked Steve if he thought Hartness had been observing the interview, maybe through a two-way glass, but Steve said they were just in an office, "There was no glass, but he had to be listening somehow," maybe through an intercom system which allowed other detectives and deputies to follow interviews while they were in progress. Hartness could even have been the person who called Knox about "lawyering up" during Steve's interview.

In 2014, I spoke to Willard Knox, now retired. He said that the notes from all of his interviews should still be available, and the sheriff's office or the DA should have them. He also said it was now standard practice to record all interrogations, but he couldn't remember if the interview room was set up to do that in 2004. Since the interview was held in Knox's office instead of an official interrogation room, and Steve didn't see any recording equipment out during the interview, probably not. According to the sheriff's office, no tapes or transcripts or even any additional notes exist of Steve's interrogation or of Hanna's deposition. Is that likely? I think there should have been more, and so did Deputy Knox, but several Texas Public Information Act (TPIA) requests, phone calls, and emails only yielded the few pages I received from them, and I saw no signs of extra notes when I examined the DA's files.

Sex with Darla: Here's the part I suspect grabbed your attention in Knox's note, that, "on two separate occasions, Darla Belisle did perform oral sex on him while they were in his shop." Let's clear up a few things. Steve didn't have a shop of his own, but he did say that the oral sex happened. Steve worked for Darla's brother, Leon, at his business, Leon Belisle Builders, and Steve and Darla first met there. Steve worked for Leon for about ten years, and then took a full-time job with the City of Deep Springs in 1999. During that earlier decade, Steve had a standing agreement to work for Leon when he didn't have a better job somewhere else. For example, Steve worked for a year building the city's medical center, which was a steady, well-paying job. When it ended, he went back to work for Leon until something better came along. One of Steve's jobs was constructing cabinets in Leon's shop, which was attached to the office. In 1997, after Darla got divorced, she started working for her brother as a bookkeeper. She and Steve became friends, and sometimes she would bring a couple of beers out to the shop and unload her latest issue on Steve.

In 2017, I asked him to tell me about the incidents in the shop. He was vague at first, saying that Darla was "all stressed out over some dumb thing or another, and pretty much just one thing led to another…but Darla was always very aggressive, which is no excuse." When I asked Steve for a physical description of Darla, he said, "Uh, big. I don't know how else to describe her." Steve said she was slightly shorter than his 5' 11," but she weighed "over 200 pounds…220, 230." He added that her breasts were "very large. She was always doing the bounce-her-boobs-off-you thing," and said that "alcohol was always involved with Darla. There's no doubt she brought beer, and she brought liquor that time out at Magnolia Street [*a third time, when Steve said he and Darla had intercourse, not mentioned in the trial documents*]." He explained. "She's just ...and I hate to use the term aggressive, because it sounds like I was forced to or something, and I wasn't. I did it, and it was wrong, but, I mean, she *is* overly aggressive. She's very intense. So, I don't know what else..." I waited, giving him time to add more. He said, "The boob thing…was her main thing. That was what she liked to do more than anything...she would just come up and ...and put your arm between both of them and rattle you with them, you know. Or she'd just come up and shake them in front of you or something. Shake them with both hands type of thing."

I asked Steve for some details about the third incident. He was working for the City of Deep Springs then, and was checking on one of the major pumping stations for the city. He said almost all of the sewage water for Deep Springs and the neighboring town, Bloom, flowed through the Magnolia Street lift station. Darla called him while he was there, and asked where he was. He told her, then continued running his checks on the station. Steve said, "I had actually backed out, and was pointing toward town when she pulled up and got out with a bottle of liquor." I asked him what kind, and he said, "Oh, it's tequila. It was always tequila with Darla." He said she had been hinting for months that they should have regular intercourse, and when she arrived she said something like "We're going to do this thing now." I asked him to verify if they had intercourse in Darla's pickup. He said, "Yes, in the front seat."

Is any of this important? Steve didn't mention the third incident to any of his lawyers, but he did tell them and Willard Knox about the oral sex in Leon's shop, and Knox's notes were handed over to the DA early on. Could the DA have asked Hanna and Darla about those incidents? That could explain Hanna's later insistent denials to Tom when he asked her (in 2006) if Darla and Steve had any kind of relationship. Hanna said it was just "friendship… and that's it." Tom tried again, asking her if there was anything "other than friendship." Hanna, sounding defensive, immediately said, "No. They had a business relationship if that's what you mean." Tom pressed her some more, asking if she thought they might have gone out together, or "snuck around." She said, "No, my mom is not that kind of person." Tom said he wasn't trying to criticize her, and Hanna said, "Oh, I understand, but no, my mom would never do that because ...he's married, and she was not attracted to him like that, because he …is disgusting. You've seen this guy, right?" Tom said he had, so Hanna added, "He's pretty nasty looking. She has better taste than that." She went on to say that Steve didn't have clean teeth, was "going bald, one eye, fat, nasty." She paused before saying, "but, uh ...no, they never, they never had any kind of relationship like that. Not once." I've often wondered why Hanna would so vehemently deny the possibility that Steve and her Mom might have dallied a bit. Did she know or suspect that her mother might have had liaisons with Steve or with other men? There's no way of knowing the answer to that, but it does raise an interesting question, though. If Hanna thought Steve was too disgusting to date her mother, why would she have allowed him to do those things to her?

Also, when I interviewed Steve's third attorney, Cleveland Sanford, in April 2017, he said something that floored me. He said he didn't find out until later that Steve "was having an affair with Hanna's mother." Sanford said that, if he had proof that Hanna had known about it (and was angry at her mom or Steve), it could have helped Steve's defense. When I mentioned this to Steve, he said he thought Sanford did know about it since it was in Knox's notes, but he also said that one of his big mistakes was assuming that his attorneys knew everything he did. It wasn't until later that he realized that the lawyers only knew what he and others told them. Sanford was hired after the first trial was over, and had less than a week to prepare. I think he did an outstanding job, especially considering the time constraint he was under. Maybe he wasn't told about Steve and Darla, or maybe he missed that bit of information in the midst of everything else. Either way, I agree that it could have been a different trial if he had been able to pursue that line of inquiry (or had known about some of the other evidence I discovered later).

We've done a bit of time-shifting. I'll try not to do that too often, but sometimes I will need to add some extra detail or explain something. Let's get back to the time period just after the accusations.

A Medical Exam

On April 21, 2004, two weeks after the accusation (and more than two months after the last alleged incident), Hanna's mother took her to see their family doctor. The doctor gave Hanna a standard HEENT (Head, Ears, Eyes, Nose and Throat) exam plus a pelvic exam. It took another full year and a court order before the results were given to the attorneys.

In Trial #2, Cleveland Sanford read this sentence from the exam to Hanna,"She has essentially virginal female introitus with the hymen mostly intact, with just a minimal amount of tear noted on the posterior aspect," and asked her to verify if he read that correctly. Hanna said he had. He asked her if she knew what that meant, and she answered, "I think it means that the little pieced [*sic*] of skin that defines a virgin has a minimal tear in it." He asked her if she understood that to mean that she was a virgin at the time of the test. She said, "Yes."

In other words, a medical doctor examined Hanna 74 days after she claimed the last incident occurred, and determined that she was a healthy, normal fifteen-year old girl who probably hadn't had sexual intercourse involving penetration before that exam.

Five Counseling Sessions

Also in late-April 2004, three weeks after creating the affidavit, and a week after seeing the doctor, Hanna had her first session with Ada Dixon, a counselor in Deep Springs who, according to her website, "specializes in helping victims of rape, incest, domestic violence, abuse of all kinds." The website indicated that Dixon was also active in the community as a speaker at local churches, colleges and schools, business organizations, and at various state and national conferences. Dixon's speeches were often of a religious nature (she's a member of the American Association of Christian Counselors); but, between 2000 and 2005, she also gave at least fourteen talks on abuse, most of them about sexual abuse and the abuse of children. A TPIA request also revealed that Dixon conducted three training sessions for Court Appointed Special Advocates (CASA), an organization which assigns volunteers to represent the interests of children involved in court cases. The subject of CASA will surface again in the chapters about the jury voir dire for the second trial.

In September 2004, Roland Mathis filed a motion requesting records from the DA for any medical or psychiatric reports they had, especially copies of Hanna's medical exam and a summary that Ada Dixon had created from her sessions with Hanna. It was April of 2005 before the doctor's reports were submitted to the court. I don't know exactly when Dixon released her summary to the court, but it was mentioned during a December 2004 brainstorming session that Tom Swearingen recorded in Mathis' office. The latest session that Dixon included in the summary was in early-September 2004, so the summary must have been submitted to the court shortly after that. From what Steve has told me, she put up quite a fight to keep from releasing anything, but she eventually agreed to create a summary of her notes for Judge Hawes' approval. It consisted of two typed pages of notes, covering only five of the sessions Hanna had with her. Hawes reviewed it, ruled that it would be acceptable, and gave a copy to the DA, who gave Mathis a copy.

During the trials, Dixon testified that Hanna saw her once a week at first. There were fifteen weeks between the first and last sessions detailed in the summary, which means that Dixon may have only included information from as little as a third of Hanna's earliest sessions; three of them from May 2004, one from mid-August, and one from early-September. I believe Dixon chose the details from those sessions that were most likely to indicate that Hanna's victimization. Try to also keep in mind that everything Dixon was told came strictly from Hanna, not from any other witnesses or forensic proof. Even so, Dixon's first sentence in the summary is instructive. It was an unquoted sentence, just as I've displayed it below.

> At age twelve (12), the abuse started and lasted almost three (3) years.

Aside from everyone on Hanna's team overselling the amount of time available, a topic I'll return to often, Dixon stated that length of time as a fact. She didn't say, "Hanna told me that, at age twelve..." She said it as though it was irrefutable proof. By saying that it lasted almost three years, though, she expanded Hanna's timeline by an extra five months over Hanna's own claim (which was already three months too long). We'll get to all of that soon.

Dixon also approached her testimony in the trials the same way. In Trial #2, Elmer Ross asked her, "Is there anything in your discussions and your experiences with Hanna which lead you to believe that she has not been the victim of child abuse?" Dixon answered, "I <u>know</u> that she has been the victim of child abuse. There is <u>absolutely no doubt</u> in my mind. I <u>know</u> that." Cleveland Sanford asked her if her testimony was based on the assumption that Hanna's allegations were true. She said, "Yes, sir." He said, "So, you agree with me that if the allegations that are relayed to you are not true, then your foundation is faulty, correct?" She said, "The allegations are true." Dixon seemed unwilling to believe that she could have been wrong about Hanna, or even entertain the possibility that Hanna could have been lying to her. In his closing statement, Elmer Ross cited Dixon's belief in Hanna, hammering Dixon's quotes home as if they were proof of truth just because Dixon and others believed Hanna, despite a lack of actual evidence. Expert witnesses aren't legally permitted to testify to someone's truthfulness, but Dixon did exactly that in Steve's trial (see the blog post below for more information about how that happened).

https://aggravatedbook.com/hannas-counselor-part-7/

By the time I read Dixon's summary, I had already read the transcripts of both trials and had listened to Hanna's interview with Tom. In the interview, Hanna said she kissed Steve in a truck on the way to see the first Harry Potter film. The kiss wasn't mentioned at all in Dixon's summary, even though Hanna later claimed that her brother, Aaron, saw the kiss and commented on it aloud. I believe this kissing incident is one of the most ridiculous of Hanna's stories. I'll prove how false it is in the Harry Potter chapter, but here's the strange part. Hanna told Tom that Dixon knew about Aaron seeing the kiss, and said that Dixon had spoken to Aaron, adding, "He don't even want to think about it, and he already told Ada, my counselor, that he does not remember anything. And he does not want to know what happened." In Trial #2, she also tried to squeeze that same information into her testimony, but was unsuccessful. If Aaron had been in town during the trials, would the DA have wanted to put him on the stand? What if he *was* there, but didn't show up at the courthouse until the first trial was over? What would that indicate? Hint: He might have been.

I wanted to ask Dixon if she actually had spoken to Aaron about this, and met her at her office in April 2015. She was cordial at first, but as soon as I identified myself as Steve's brother, she told me she couldn't say anything." I said I understood, and wasn't asking her to violate a patient's rights, that my questions weren't about Hanna. She said she couldn't even tell me that Hanna was her patient. I explained that I had read all the trial transcripts, that it was public information, so I already knew who everyone was, but asked her, "Can you at least tell me if Hanna was your *only* patient in her family." She said, "I can't tell you that either. HIPAA regulations won't allow me to do that." Steve had already told me how strongly she fought to keep from releasing her case notes, so I didn't expect her to reveal anything useful. When she asked me what my interest was in the trial, I told her I was planning to write a book about it. She asked me what the book was for, and I said, "I'm just trying to find the truth." She responded by saying, "Well, the truth was in the courtroom." I felt like saying, "Yes, but it wasn't your patient who was telling it," I didn't, though. Eight months earlier, Darla made a nearly identical comment when she told me, "If you have the transcripts, then you know what happened, then you know the truth." Transcripts only contain truth if the participants in the trial have been truthful, though, and I don't think that happened in this case.

I had hoped Dixon would at least admit to me whether she had or hadn't spoken to Aaron, but she didn't. When I did finally get a copy of her summary from the Ashwell County DA's Office a year later, I found that Aaron wasn't mentioned in the summary at all. Steve is mentioned in it, and Robin and Beau and Marri, and Willard Knox and Josh Chilmark, but Aaron doesn't appear anywhere in it, not by name or even identified by the phrase "my brother," not when Hanna talked about the night they went to see *Harry Potter*, or any other incidents. Hanna did tell Dixon about the ride to see the movie, and who was in the truck, but the incident is described as if Aaron wasn't even there. As if he didn't exist.

Those early sessions with Dixon were held only a few weeks after the accusations were made, but two years later, in Tom's interview and in the trials, Hanna insisted that Aaron had been a witness to a kiss in the truck, and that he had told Dixon he didn't remember it. Again, we only have Hanna's word for it, but the one other person besides Aaron himself (Dixon) who could have confirmed whether Aaron was asked about it, cited HIPAA regulations and avoided answering a question that could either have been beneficial to Hanna's case or could have damaged it further. I believe that HIPAA, which is designed to protect the privacy of patients, but had already been bypassed in the courtroom through Dixon's summary and her testimony, could at least have allowed for a voir dire examination of Dixon (with the jury removed, if necessary) to get to the truth of the matter, but no one asked her during either trial if she spoke to Aaron about witnessing a kiss, or whether Hanna even suggested there had been one.

How likely is it that Dixon talked to Aaron about an alleged kiss? Her first session with Hanna was on April 27th, and Aaron left town to live with his father in Michigan around the first of June. The second and third sessions were on May 6th and 13th. Those are the sessions where Hanna told Dixon about the cross-country meet and going to see *Harry Potter*. The next listed session was May 26th, two weeks later. Hanna said she went every week for a while, so there should have been a session around May 20th. Did Hanna skip a session that week, or did she possibly say something then which Dixon didn't include in the summary?

I Have Multiple Questions: Since the summary does mention the ride to see *Harry Potter* and the other incidents inside truck and the theater, but doesn't say anything about a kiss on the way there, did Hanna decide to add that detail later? Did she even tell Dixon about Aaron witnessing a kiss in the truck? If Hanna told her about a kiss, Dixon would have asked Aaron to corroborate Hanna's claim that he witnessed it, wouldn't she? If Aaron did talk to her, what did he say, and why isn't that in the summary? Or was the conversation with Aaron, the kiss in the truck, and other incidents that night just more of Hanna's inventions? Aaron could have been a crucial witness for Hanna, so why didn't he testify? If Aaron told Dixon there had been no kiss, I believe Dixon would have to have realized how strongly that could have affected the trial? She would have had ethical and legal obligations to report it. If, on the other hand, Dixon didn't talk to Aaron, was Hanna lying to Tom about it, and did she also attempt to lie in court about it? Did Hanna try to mislead the defense, or did her counselor withhold exculpatory evidence?

Vaginal Sex (and some analysis): In the first few sessions with Dixon, Hanna made no mention of vaginal intercourse (and didn't in her affidavit either). Within four months, though, she had added that element to her story. At the end of the summary, Ms. Dixon provided the judge with a bullet list of nine types of things Hanna said Steve had done to her. The last two items were "dry intercourse" and "vaginal intercourse." Did Steve and Hanna have vaginal intercourse? Here's the passage from Dixon's summary for August 18, 2004. It's spelled and punctuated as it was in the summary.

> "He entered me twice. I don't remember when he did it the first time. On February 13th or 14th, the night of his son's birthday party, when everyone went home and went to sleep he said, 'six more years and we can f***, then five years, four years, etc.' (This happened at the first of the abuse.) Once he gave me a margarita at his house. He also offered my wine coolers and a shot of whiskey at other times."

Dixon enclosed that entire paragraph in quotation marks as if they were all Hanna's words, but the parenthetical comment near the end (*This happened at the first of the abuse*) seems to be Dixon saying that Hanna's "six more years" remark happened in 2001. No matter whether it was an insertion from Dixon or whether Hanna actually said that, it makes no sense. If the phrase in parentheses was about giving Hanna alcohol, it should have <u>followed</u> the closing parentheses marks, not preceded them. Hanna did testify, by the way, that none of the kids were allowed to drink, and Steve said he never gave any alcohol to any of the kids. If the parenthetical comment was about Steve telling her they would have to wait x-number of years before having sex, though, it still makes no sense (no matter who was speaking, Hanna or Dixon). Hanna's quote clearly stated that Steve told her this after Beau's birthday party (which was in February 2004), but she was fourteen during the party. Hanna would need to be eighteen to be of legal age, so the "six more years" quote would only make sense if Steve started telling her that on her twelfth birthday (in February 2001), but Hanna and Aaron weren't even visiting the Sirois' until the fall of 2001. If the 6, 5, 4 quote is from Hanna (as it appears to be), she seemed to be lying to Dixon. If the parenthetical remark was from Dixon, then Dixon apparently was clueless about how long Hanna claimed to have been abused. I wondered if Hanna was lying to her as well as everyone else. Dixon might have assumed (without verification) that the countdown started back in 2001, when Hanna was claiming the abuse had begun, but I couldn't understand why she apparently continued to assume that Hanna was telling her the truth, even as the stories grew more and more ridiculous.

If Steve had attempted to have vaginal intercourse with Hanna <u>for the second time</u> on the night of Beau's birthday party in February 2004, why didn't she mention those for several months? In fact, in the affidavit she said, "I remember him telling me that he <u>would not</u> have sexual intercourse with me because I was a minor and that he did not want to hurt my mother or his wife." Why didn't she include the attempts at intercourse in her affidavit? I think she just hadn't decided that intercourse would be a part of her story yet. Some evidence of this is included in a note taken by Officer Duke Chapman at the sheriff's office the night before Hanna met with Willard Knox. Hanna's mother spoke with Officer Chapman and Sgt. Hartness to make arrangements for Hanna's statement to be taken. Darla gave them some basic details about Hanna's accusation. The last line of those details read, "Darla said that [*name redacted*] told her that Steve had molested her stating that they have done everything except intercourse." Looking at both the affidavit and this note from Chapman, it seemed obvious to me that Hanna didn't decide to include attempts at intercourse in her story until she told Dixon about it in August 2004, three-and-a-half months after her counseling began.

Can I prove this was another invention of Hanna's? In her interview with Tom, and in the trials, Hanna also talked about the attempts at vaginal sex, but did she tell anyone else before she accused Steve in April 2004? In 2003, Hanna spoke often with her friend Josh Chilmark. In 2005, Tom Swearingen asked Josh if Hanna had said there were certain things she wouldn't let her abuser do. Josh told him, "Uh, other than they never had intercourse. Other than that, I think they pretty well did everything in the book that I can think of." Lots of different things, in other words, but not vaginal intercourse. In the trials, Josh also testified, saying, "She said it wasn't intercourse," but, when questioned further, he said she told him it was just "oral sex," that she was performing fellatio on her abuser, and that she had said nothing about her abuser performing any sexual acts on her. Josh's testimony, by the way, contradicts many of the rest of Hanna's stories.

One other potential source of information about this could come from the sleepovers Hanna had with her friends. If her revelations at these sleepovers actually happened (although some data suggests otherwise), Hanna started telling her friends about this during their 2002-2003 school year, roughly the same time she was talking to Josh. According to everything I've seen, though, she didn't tell any of them that there was even an attempt at vaginal intercourse. The closest mention of anything similar was when Rhonda Bresnick, a witness in Trial #1, said that Hanna "brought it up at a sleep-over that she had lost her virginity. And she said that it wasn't her decision." Rhonda repeated that in Trial #2, but she also said that sleepover took place in April 2004, after Hanna made her accusation. Rhonda was also the only witness besides Hanna who testified about a revelation at a sleepover. Apparently, Hanna made no mention of attempts at intercourse before the affidavit was written, but soon after creating it she may have started telling her friends "she had lost her virginity," and then, in August, told Dixon that Steve had "entered" her twice. I wondered how many untruths were buried in all of that?

Questions: How does that information square with the doctor's exam, which said that her hymen was mostly intact? The exam took place two weeks after the accusation, or a little over seven weeks after the alleged final molestation. Based on Rhonda's testimony, the exam also took place fairly soon after Hanna may have told her friends she had lost her virginity. For a moment, suppose that someone who hadn't had any sexual contact with anyone, made false accusations like these against another person, but then found out she was about to be examined by a doctor. Also, assume that this person was concerned that their reputation with their friends (and likely their school and family) was in serious danger. If they were truly desperate, how might they get ready for their upcoming doctor's exam? I'll leave it at that.

Dixon's Summary, and Hanna's Expanding Story: Between April and September 2004, Hanna nearly doubled the number of times she claimed to have been abused. By early-September, she was telling Dixon, "We had sexual experiences approximately ninety times," and also told her that it "lasted almost three years." The length of time is close to a year too long, but could it have been her sessions with Dixon that caused the number of incidents to increase from her original claim of 50 (to Deputy Knox) to the "80 to 90" number she used in the trials?

The only other event that became a factor in the trials, but wasn't mentioned in either Dixon's summary or the affidavit, was a ride home from a rodeo that Steve gave Hanna and Rhonda Bresnick in 2003. I think the reason it wasn't included in the summary was because Rhonda waited until August 2005, two years after the rodeo, to give Darla Belisle an undated, all lowercase, peculiarly-worded, typewritten note about the ride home. The prosecution used that note to make the ride seem like a debauched descent into depravity; but, even though neither of them had anything to do with the counts against Steve, I'll still disprove everything connected to both of them in the chapter, *The Night of the Rodeo*. Also, in the chapter, *A Timeline as Final Proof*, I'll refute Hanna's "80 to 90" number, reduce her three-year time period to just over two years, and attempt to prove that Steve didn't have enough time or opportunity to commit the acts that Hanna claimed.

Dixon's Book: Dixon wrote a book called *Overcoming and Dealing With a World of Abuse* (not its real title). In it she listed the symptoms that victims of abuse might typically display. During Trial #2, Cleveland Sanford asked Dixon if she had given Hanna a copy of it. She said, "I give a copy to all my victims." The book was published in April 2004, so it was brand new when Hanna walked through her door for the first time. She might even have been Dixon's first "victim" to have a copy.

Because of its title, I thought the book would fall into the category of psychological self-help, but it isn't that at all. It does contain statistics, real-life examples, and lists of symptoms an abuse victim could be displaying; but nearly every page also includes inducements to heal through prayer and religion, so it can hardly be considered scientific. One egregious flaw in the book is Dixon's stance that homosexuality can be "cured" through gay conversion therapy, something which has been debunked numerous times. As early as 1973, the American Psychological Association (APA) opposed describing homosexuality as a mental disorder, capable of cure through treatment. Over twenty years later, in 1994, they said that "societal ignorance and prejudice about same gender sexual orientation put some gay, lesbian, bisexual and questioning individuals at risk for presenting for 'conversion' treatment due to family or social coercion and/or lack of information." They also said that they opposed descriptions of LGBTQ individuals "as mentally ill due to their sexual orientation," and supported "interventions in order to counteract bias that is based in ignorance or unfounded beliefs," but Dixon still apparently believed in conversion therapy ten years after that, in 2004, when her book was printed.

The APA, as of 2019, was still saying that professional therapists shouldn't tell their clients that they can change their sexual orientation through conversion therapy. After thoroughly analyzing her book, I think I can safely say that it isn't based in science. I've covered it on the blog in six posts, beginning at:

https://aggravatedbook.com/dixons-book-part-1/

I think that Hanna may have found a number of items in the book helpful as a study guide, though, like the symptoms of abuse. Asked about them in Trial #2, Dixon listed, "Depression, anger, nightmares, sleeplessness, a change in grades, a change in friends maybe, very, very angry, feeling very, very betrayed." She admitted under questioning that those didn't all need to be present, and insisted that Hanna's symptoms proved that she had been abused. Just because Hanna said she had some of those symptoms didn't mean that she actually did experience any of them, though. It could simply mean that once she knew what the symptoms might be (having read about them in Dixon's book) she could have openly displayed signs of them, and made sure people were told about them. I have no record of Hanna talking about nightmares before the accusation. She also didn't mention them in her affidavit, but in a session with Dixon about a month after she started seeing her, Hanna said, "I'm having nightmares about the abuse."

She also testified in Trial #1 that she was prescribed Zoloft and Lexapro after telling her doctor, in August 2004, that she was waking up with panic attacks (another symptom from the book). She testified that, because of the anxiety drugs, "more and more of the details and memories would just get blocked." She added, "Of course, it may not have been the medication. It could have just been a natural defense mechanism." Chapter Six in Dixon's book is, coincidentally, about defense mechanisms. In Trial #2, though, the words "PTSD," "traumatic," "stress," "syndrome," "panic," "nightmare," "nervous" "prescribed," "Zoloft," "Lexapro," and "medication" don't appear in any of Hanna's testimony. Why were they prominent in the first trial, but not in the second? I don't know, but her comments about panic attacks and anxiety drugs disappeared between the two trials. Did she, or the DA, adjust her testimony because the first trial was a mistrial?

Another topic covered in Dixon's book is grooming, and Dixon and Blake Goudy both gave lengthy testimony about it during the trials. Grooming is a gradual pattern of intimacy, introduced slowly over a long period of time, to prepare a child for sexual abuse. It's also something I hope to prove didn't exist in this case, and couldn't have.

Why do I believe Dixon's book might have helped Hanna develop her story? Since the numbers and types of acts increased the longer she saw Dixon, attending the therapy sessions and having a copy of the book should both be considered possible catalysts for the widening of her story. The book could have given Hanna a handy primer for how to persuade others that she had been abused; but, if her counselor was one of the most immediate people she had to convince, she would need to keep inventing new scenarios for her, or expand on old ones. Hence an ever-enlarging story.

In the book, Dixon said, "Children are not born with an inherent ability to describe demeaning sexual acts. They can only give detailed reports of such experiences if they have personally lived them." I would argue that, especially in the twenty-first century, by the age of fifteen, children *can* give detailed reports of such experiences, if they: 1) have talked to friends who have had sex; 2) have watched cable TV; 3) have seen videos on the Internet; or, 4) have been given a book which describes them. The amount of knowledge available to children today (even as early as 2004) is astounding. Unless they have been completely isolated, we can no longer assume that the age of an individual indicates the level of knowledge they actually have about any given subject. An anecdote: In 2004, a few months after the charges were filed, Steve and Robin were discussing the accusations. Twelve-year-old Marri was in the room; so, to disguise the adult nature of some of it, they used acronyms. When they referred to "oral sex" as a "BJ," Marri perked up and said, "I know what that is." Steve, surprised, asked her how she knew that. Marri answered, "They do it on the bus."

Dixon's summary also detailed other claims of Hanna's, including incidents in trucks, on beds, in a movie theater, and after a birthday party, with other people present or nearby each time. All of those stories have a couple of things in common. Hanna was the only one telling them; and the people who were there said they didn't see anything. When I spoke to Darla in 2014, I said, "According to Hanna, some people witnessed various things, but nobody's been able to prove that." She said, "They didn't know what they were witnessing." Later, when I cover some of those incidents, keep Darla's phrase in mind, and ask yourself how anyone who allegedly saw acts like those could possibly have been confused about what they were seeing.

Final Comment about Dixon's Summary: The summary only covers five dates, all in 2004 (three in May, one in August, and one in September), but Dixon continued to see Hanna at least until the trials in mid-2006, once a week at first, then roughly once every two weeks. According to Dixon that was nearly eighty sessions. The five excerpts Dixon prepared for the court were therefore taken from roughly twenty of just the earliest sessions, representing (I believe) the ones that were the most negative toward Steve, or that best illustrated the charges against him. Regardless, they were still based solely on the information that Hanna gave to Dixon.

A Question About Innocence

On June 18th, 2004, a week after Steve was indicted, the DA's Victim Assistant Coordinator sent Hanna a letter, telling her that she might be able to get some compensation as a victim. She and her mother did apply, and they did receive some money from the Crime Victims' Compensation fund. I don't know how much it was, but she told Tom in her interview, "I remember we didn't know how we were going to keep paying for the counseling, because... we don't have the money." By the time Hanna said that, Steve's family was on the verge of bankruptcy, while her family had paid nothing for the investigators and the state prosecutors who represented her. I'm not saying Hanna's family wasn't going through any stress, just that there was a tremendous imbalance between the financial cost for the two families.

Pop Quiz: A defendant is considered innocent until proven guilty. In the eyes of the law Steve was technically innocent until he was convicted, but Hanna received money for being a victim before she was legally established to be one (by Steve's conviction). When that happens, does the state, by giving an accuser funds before a trial, ratify his or her innocence, and legally brand the defendant as guilty before they are tried? Also, if an accuser lies to the state, and receives money for it, are they guilty of fraud?

Hiring a Lawyer

Steve didn't officially have a lawyer when he and Robin walked into the LEC on April 14th to see Deputy Knox, but halfway through the interview he knew he needed one. He and Robin drove directly from there to Roland Mathis' law office. It was located in one of the storefronts surrounding the County Courthouse, where the trials would be held a little over two years later. Steve had been worried ever since the confrontation with Darla. It had put him on edge because he didn't know what the problem was, but now he knew how serious it was. He asked Mathis about the possibility of hiring him, saying, "This ain't good. These people are out to get me." He filled his new attorney in on everything he knew so far, including the eyeball-tapping "kinetic energies" episode, and about Knox asking Steve to take a lie detector test. Steve said Mathis' response was, "Hell, no. You're not doing a lie detector test. Not from Ashwell County." I don't know whether that says more about taking lie detector tests or about Ashwell County justice.

Then Mathis made a comment that would have given me pause. According to Steve, he said, "I need to tell you up front that my father is Carl Belisle's tax accountant, and I've done some legal work for Carl; but that won't be a conflict of interest, and I want you to know that I'll do my best for you." Carl Belisle is Darla Belisle' uncle, Hanna's great-uncle, and he owned a prosperous local agricultural business, along with some other concerns, but at the time, Steve accepted Mathis' comment at face value. As the case dragged on, and 2004 turned into 2005 and then 2006, he began to question whether Mathis was the best legal representative for him. For the moment, though, he was happy with his choice.

Ask yourself a couple of questions: Assume that you are a lawyer who has a potential client standing in front of you who isn't rich, but will probably be able to pay for your immediate services; but another client of yours owns an important business in the community, and is related to someone who has just accused your prospective client of multiple counts of sexual abuse. Which of those two individuals would most likely affect your future earnings? Which of the two would you be most tempted to be loyal to? I wasn't there, of course, so I can't judge Steve for decisions he made under a great deal of stress and panic, but after hearing what Mathis said, I wouldn't have hired him. Steve did, though. He paid him a small retainer, thinking that at least would give him enough time to see if he could find another lawyer who didn't have a business connection with his accuser's family. Steve has always been a trusting sort, though, so Mathis became his lawyer for the time being.

April to June, 2004

Following the accusation and the affidavit, several things occurred that will crop up later, so let's take a quick look at them. The case was officially filed on May 11th. Willard Knox notified Roland Mathis that they would be presenting the charges to a grand jury. Based on all the records I've seen, it seems to me that the sheriff's office didn't do any serious investigating following the initial interviews. Knox didn't interview anyone in Steve's family; and the records show that he didn't interview anyone else concerning Hanna's side of the story until September.

Early in June, Hanna's brother, Aaron, moved to Michigan to live with his father, Nate Penderfield. Aaron, who turned thirteen in December 2003, had been lobbying Darla to let him go "since he was probably 12," according to her trial testimony. Of course, Darla didn't want him to, but she eventually gave in. In June of 2004, Aaron left for Michigan, over 1,200 miles away. I find it interesting that Hanna didn't mention Aaron witnessing any incidents in any kind of official record until the trial. She did tell Tom Swearingen (in May 2006) that her brother witnessed a kiss in Beau's truck, but her conversation with Tom wasn't under oath. Also, the name "Aaron" only appears once in her 2-hour, 28-minute interview with Tom, and Tom was the one who spoke Aaron's name, not Hanna. Was it a coincidence that Aaron moved across the country to live with his father shortly after Hanna lodged the accusations? Probably, but if he saw a kiss happen between Steve and Hanna, that would have been a key piece of evidence for the prosecution. He didn't testify in either trial, though. Why wasn't he brought back to be a witness for his sister? What Aaron saw or didn't see will get full coverage in the chapter, *Count I - The Night of Harry Potter*.

On June 10th a grand jury indicted Steve on the three counts you've already seen (cunnilingus, fellatio, and fingering). That decision was undoubtedly based on Hanna's affidavit alone. I can't imagine what other evidence the DA would have presented to them. Grand juries function in secret. The only way a defendant would have a sense of what was happening during a grand jury hearing would be if they were called to answer questions, but Steve wasn't; and no members of Steve's family were, or any of his friends or employers. Since the inquiry is held in secret, and the results are rarely published, only the members of the grand jury, the prosecutor, and witnesses who were called, would know anything about what evidence was presented. It's a commonly held belief that most grand juries just act as effective rubber stamps for prosecutors. Sol Wachtler, former Chief Judge of the New York Court of Appeals, said in 1985 that district attorneys could influence grand juries so easily that they could even get them to "indict a ham sandwich." When Steve's indictment was handed down, though, he knew his situation was officially underway, and he might have to stand trial for something he didn't do.

Thoughts to Consider

The DA's office took more than two months before they indicted Steve. By the end of June, the sheriff's office had only talked to Hanna and Steve. To the best of my knowledge, they only interviewed three other people before the 2006 trials; two in September 2004, and the last one not until April 2005. Those other individuals (Blake Goudy, Tiffany Sperger, and Josh Chilmark) all became witnesses for the prosecution. Shouldn't Willard Knox also have interviewed other people to verify Hanna's claims? Shouldn't a law officer at least make an attempt to discover the truth of a situation? It was five months after he talked to Steve before Knox placed a phone call to Blake Goudy to verify what Hanna told him. The next day he interviewed Tiffany Sperger, but he didn't seek her out, Tiffany's mother arranged the interview.

The sheriff's office also interviewed no one on Steve's side. They zeroed in on him based on Hanna's accusation and apparently didn't try to look for anyone else. I can think of at least two other possibilities they didn't consider, though, and they will be a large part of my argument: 1) Someone else may have molested Hanna; or, 2) Hanna wasn't molested at all, and she invented everything (for reasons I will cover later), but simply found herself in a situation where she had to name someone. She chose Steve.

July 2004, an Arrest

The following conversations have been reconstructed from Steve's recollection of events. He told me that, on April 13th, right after he got the initial phone call from Willard Knox, he called Patrick Houseman, the superintendent at Lake Ashwell State Park, and told him something was up. Steve had been working at the park since the previous September, less than a year, but had recently applied for the lead ranger job. After meeting with Deputy Knox the next day, Steve told Houseman everything. Houseman thanked him for letting him know, and said he would fully support him. On July 1st, the sheriff's office called Houseman at the park and asked him to arrest Steve there at work. Houseman had been in law enforcement for over thirty years, and still held a peace officer's license, but he refused the sheriff, saying he wasn't an officer that day, he was an employer. He found Steve in the maintenance shop and told him an officer was on the way to pick him up. Steve started to change back into his street clothes, but Houseman told him to leave his ranger uniform on. That would force them to take his mug shot in it. Later that day, they did take his picture with his uniform on, but cropped it just under his chin so you couldn't tell what kind of shirt he was wearing.

When Officer Theo Rossiter got to the park he said "My god, Steve, what the hell is this? They've got you on a $50,000 bond." Steve said, "It's a bunch of bullshit that never happened. What do I do now?" Rossiter and Houseman waited while Steve called Robin and a bondsman to arrange for bail. Steve told me that he felt he had an ally in Rossiter that day, but found out later that it wasn't true.

Near the end of August, Houseman gave Steve his annual evaluation. In spite of all the drama surrounding Steve, it was a glowing report, with Houseman summing it up by saying, "I recommend retaining Steve Sirois on permanent status. Steve has proven to be a very reliable, dedicated employee. He is knowledgeable in his duties and works well with all staff and the public." In October, though, the state changed Steve's status to "on leave without pay," essentially cutting the family's income in half. Houseman argued against that, but let Steve know that if the mess cleared up, as far as he was concerned, the lead ranger's job would be his. Steve said he would never forget him for that. It was a vote of confidence that meant a lot to him when so much else was going wrong.

Once Steve was charged and arrested, the court assigned October 11th, just a few months away, as the trial date. Roland Mathis immediately applied for a continuance to give them more time for an investigation. He also made motions for all legally discoverable evidence in the DA's files, asked for Hanna's medical records, and requested an interview with Hanna; but Darla and the DA refused to let Hanna talk to him. Her medical records weren't released by her doctor until April 2005, following a court order. That would have been long after the trial was over if it had been held when originally scheduled. The records I obtained from the DA's office showed that the date for the trial was set and re-set at least sixteen times before the first trial finally took place in July 2006.

Willard Knox's Final Interview

Meanwhile, it seemed to me that Willard Knox was doing whatever he could to avoid investigating. Aside from taking those statements from Hanna and Steve in April, he did nothing else on record until September 15th when he made a quick phone call to Blake Goudy, and interviewed Tiffany Sperger the next day. Here's Knox's note about his phone call with Goudy. Notice that the sheriff's office gave it to me without any redactions.

> "According to Goudy; he had talked with a group of students at Alderson School District about child abuse and what they should do if ever victimized by someone. During his presentation he told the students if anything ever happened to them they should tell their parents or another trusted adult. He even told them they could talk with him after class if they so desired. Goudy went on to say after the presentation was over he had approximately 5 students that approached him wanting to talk. One of these students was Hannah Penderfield which told him she had been touched by a man for several years. She did not go into any details with Goudy. He did tell her she needed to tell her mother about what was happening which she stated she would. Goudy stated that was all he knew about the situation with Hannah Penderfield."

Goudy told Knox that "approximately 5 students" talked to him, but during the trials he said, without hesitation, that five students came up to him afterward. Despite Goudy's certainty, though, Hanna testified in both trials that she was the only one who came forward to talk to him. Why would she insist that she was the only one? Was Goudy exaggerating or was Hanna trying to make her situation unique? Either or both are possible.

Also, Goudy told Knox that Hanna "did not go into any details" with him, and "that was all he knew about" her situation. There's no mention in the note about whether Hanna named anyone to Goudy, but two years later, Goudy testified to a specific name, Steve's. If Hanna had named her molester to Goudy, I can't imagine he wouldn't have told Knox so. And, Knox, if Goudy had given him that information, would have put it in his report, wouldn't he?

By the time of the trials, both Goudy and Hanna said she named Steve that afternoon in 2004. Did she or didn't she? Wouldn't that have been a vital question for a competent investigator to ask? Isn't that an answer Knox would want in his report, especially since Hanna hadn't said in her affidavit whether she told Goudy or anyone else *who* her molester was? I find it odd that neither of them mentioned that crucial detail in their initial interviews, but both were certain of it by the time of the trials. Is it possible that one or both of them lied on the stand, or could there be another explanation?

Here's a possibility. Hanna might have told Goudy the same "sexual experiences" story she had been telling her friends at sleepovers, but didn't give Goudy anyone's name. Then she had the rest of the afternoon, until her mother came home from work, to decide what to tell her. Maybe she told her mother it was Steve because he was someone they had been around a lot, or maybe because she was angry with the Sirois' (for reasons I'll cover later). Even though both Goudy and Hanna testified that she had named Steve as her abuser that afternoon, maybe Goudy actually heard Steve's name from Darla when she called him later that evening, not from Hanna. Maybe he just forgot that detail during the next two years. One reason why Goudy might have told Willard Knox that Hanna "didn't give him any details" was because she might not have.

Why is that important? If it's true, Hanna likely spent the rest of that afternoon knowing she had to give her mother an explanation, but she obviously couldn't say she didn't know who had been "touching" her for "several years." Maybe by the time Darla arrived, Hanna had sketched out a basic plot for her story, and spent the next two years adding to it and embellishing it. What *is* undeniable, though, is that both Hanna's and Goudy's original stories had changed by the time of the trials.

Why did Willard Knox wait until September 15th to call Blake Goudy? Could it simply be that he put the case out of his mind once he had produced the initial affidavit? Maybe when he got a phone call from Glenda Sperger, saying that her daughter Tiffany had some information about the case, he remembered that he hadn't done any real investigating yet, so he called Goudy. Hanna herself said, in her 2006 interview with Tom, that she felt the DA wasn't doing enough. She said, "He's supposed to send the investigator out. I don't think he ever did." I'm not sure Hanna actually wanted them to do any further investigating, but I think she might have been right. I haven't uncovered anything to suggest that either the DA's or the sheriff's offices were actively trying to discredit Steve or to verify Hanna's story. There was little evidence of an actual investigation in the files they showed me in 2016. I also didn't see her brother Aaron's name in the DA's files either, even though he was there for the entire time period that Hanna alleged. Why was he so conspicuously absent in the DA's files and in Hanna's testimony?

On the afternoon of September 16th, Tiffany Sperger's mother, Glenda, brought her to the LEC to talk to Willard Knox. Tiffany's information had to do with something she said Marri told her at school one day. I asked Beau what Tiffany was like. He said, "Spoiled. Pretty well got everything she wanted," and "was real clingy to her parents." Steve, echoing Beau's comment, said,

"Tiffany has always been very superficial and vain." One of the things Steve remembered about her was that she bragged about what he thought was an ordinary oboe, letting everyone know that it "was found on E-Bay by her mother and cost over $6,000." I have no idea whether Tiffany was serious about playing the oboe, or even any good at it, and I do know that oboes can be expensive, but $6,000 is getting into the low-end cost for a professional one. My guess is that either Glenda paid way too much for an average oboe, or Tiffany was wrong about the price. Either way, Steve said she seemed awfully proud that it cost that much. Keep her seeming tendency to exaggerate in mind while you read her affidavit. Here's a transcript of it, exactly as it was entered into the trials as evidence.

> I wish to state I have known a girl named Marri Sirois for about 9 years having attended school with her. Over the past years I have spent the night in Marri's home on several occasions. I wish to further state about 1 1/2 to 2 years ago Marri and I were at school when she approached me and stated she needed to talk to me. I remember she told me I could not tell anyone about what she was fixing to say so I promised her I would not. I remember she seemed very upset that day and I was wondering why. She then told me she had walked into the bathroom at her home and she saw her father, Steve Sirois and another one of her friends named Hannah Prinderfield. She stated Hannah was sitting on the toilet and her father, Steve Sirois was lying on top of Hannah. I remember she stated when she saw them she turned and walked away. She told me she did not know what to do or who to tell.
>
> I wish to further stated it was about a month later when I told my mother about what Marri had told me. I further remember my mother told Marri she needed to talk to someone about this and suggested her mother or their preacher.
>
> I wish to state this is all I can remember about what Marri told me that involved her father and Hannah Prinderfield.

Aside from the misspelling of Hanna's first and last names, when the prosecution saw this they might have thought they finally had something to corroborate part of Hanna's story; and, according to Tiffany, that person was Steve's own daughter, Marri. This doesn't look good for Steve, does it? In light of this new information, Steve's case probably seemed a little less certain to Roland Mathis too. He decided to hire an investigator, Tom Swearingen.

Tom's first interview, the one I refer to as the brainstorming session, was with both Steve and Mathis. The audio began with Tom looking through a batch of papers, asking Mathis if that was all the district attorney had given them. Mathis said that the DA's office "produced some reports, and I went and talked to them, and they basically admitted that their case stunk, that they didn't have anything, and they offered probation...and I ...*we* turned them down. And then they decided they needed to go back and do some more investigation. So that's when Tiffy [*Tiffany*] showed up."

I'll have more to say about Tiffany's affidavit in the chapter, *Pre-Prejudice Against Steve*, but with it providing the first hint of evidence other than Hanna's own statements, it probably did make it more likely that the case would be tried. The first trial was still 22 months away, though.

Hiring Tom, and His Early Interviews

Tom Swearingen was hired in December 2004. For the next four months he made trips from his home in Brady, Texas, to Ashwell County, and talked to a variety of people, at first concentrating on Steve and his family, friends, and neighbors. Those interviews were largely favorable to Steve, most of them expressing disbelief that Steve could have done anything like that. Some people in the neighborhood did hold negative views, though.

In 2013, Tom gave me permission to use the audio files of the interviews he recorded as part of Steve's defense team. The brainstorming session was one of them. It was recorded at Mathis' office, ran for around three hours, and was a sort of audition for Tom, an initial meeting to allow the three of them to get to know one another and discuss strategy. Tom used the session to gather enough background from Steve to know what questions to ask everyone else. This session gave me a sense of how Tom worked, allowed me to see what Mathis' basic legal strategy was, and also let me view Steve's attitude at this crucial juncture. I was relieved to find out that Steve's comments then were essentially the same as they are today (that he didn't do anything to Hanna, and wouldn't have under any circumstances). At that time, his trial was scheduled for February 22, 2005 (about a year after the final incident supposedly occurred). It had already been postponed several times, but he had no way of knowing that the first trial still wouldn't take place for another year-and-a-half.

Let's look at just a few details from that session. It might make it easier to see what the defense knew roughly seven months after the accusation. Early in the audio, Tom asked Steve what Hanna had accused him of. Steve said it was "pretty graphic" stuff, "over ninety times, and just all the time, anytime, anywhere." He added, "It's impossible, basically," because Hanna said it "happened in front of my daughter, in front of my wife, in the bed. Everywhere. In the truck with my son. It just goes on and on."

Since Tom was asking Steve to tell him everything he possibly could about the case, the brainstorming session served as a checklist for me, giving me little bits of information I could follow up on. The recording repeated things Steve had already mentioned to me, but I didn't realize the significance of some of it until I heard him giving the same unwavering details to Tom and Mathis. A few of the things I started paying more attention to after that were: Steve and Darla's sexual encounters; Darla's boyfriend (Eddie Higham, a man who dated Darla from the fall of 2002 until the summer of 2003, and possibly longer); all of the people who claimed that Steve never had any chance to be alone with Hanna; and the relationship that formed in late 2003 between Josh Chilmark and Steve's niece, Liz Brailford (because that may have sparked some of Hanna's apparent animosity toward the Sirois family).

Another bit of information in the brainstorming session that piqued my interest came from a comment by Mathis. Forty-five minutes into the audio he said, "Clyde Sledge is the editor here at the Deep Springs Gazette, and he has called me up once, and he stopped me on the street one day also; and has told me he's getting calls from PI's in Houston, and PI's in Austin—or San Antonio—and several other people, and they're all basically saying, now we're going to find out who really committed …who really killed Jenny Luborsky." He added that there was a "kind of subculture out there" who believed that Steve was the one who killed her.

That's something else that doesn't sound so great for Steve, does it?

I knew very little about this. I didn't realize, until Steve mentioned it during one of our phone calls, that he and my dad had both testified for the prosecution at a rape and murder trial. The defendant, Billy Gasnick, was convicted and eventually executed. Steve said that, before Gasnick's trial began, his family spread rumors about several people, trying to deflect blame away from Billy, a tactic that Steve said they had used previously with great success. Steve said he became one of their targets, and, even though he wasn't involved in Jenny's death, the Gasnicks' rumors about Steve persisted. During a 2014 research trip to Deep Springs, I talked to Mathis and Sledge separately, and asked them about Mathis' comment about the private eyes. They both said they didn't remember having that conversation, or saying anything about hearing rumors about Steve being a suspect in Jenny's murder. The next year I visited them again, and played that portion of the recording for them. Neither denied saying it this time, but they both passed it off as just a casual conversation, something so unimportant that they didn't remember having said it. I wanted Sledge to tell me who the PI's were who called him, but he said he didn't remember; and when I asked him if he would still have any notes about that conversation or about Steve's trials, he said he wouldn't have kept any notes about it. A journalist not keeping notes on everything they wrote, knowing that they might have to back their story up someday, seemed odd to me. Also, if their conversation was so unimportant, why did Mathis make a big deal of it the day of the brainstorming session? I'll dig into Gasnick's case in greater detail in the *Pre-Prejudice Against Steve* chapter.

What struck me the most, though, after listening to the brainstorming recording, was that Steve sounded so hopeful. Even though he must have realized the seriousness of his situation, he almost seemed amused by the charges in the indictment. He said several times that he just couldn't believe them, that they were ridiculous, and there was no way those things could have happened. I agree, the charges were ridiculous, but Steve's biggest mistake might have been believing that the truth would be on his side, and that an Ashwell County jury would be able to (or even want to) see through the falsehoods they would be told about him.

After he was hired and had completed some research, Tom did several interviews. The first one was with Steve's family at their home, on Sunday, March 13, 2005. I found the interview with Steve's son, Beau, especially useful. It allowed me to compare Beau's answers to several of Hanna's statements. I'll cover some of those as we get into the discussion of the trial, but Beau's comment about one post-accusation encounter was especially informative. Beau said that a few days before, on Friday, he and his girlfriend were at the Taco Bell in Deep Springs around midnight. He spotted Cliff Polinger and stopped to talk to him. Polinger graduated from Saddleview High School a couple of years after Beau, so Beau was twenty-two at the time and Polinger was twenty. Polinger was there with another guy and two girls, who were sitting nearby. After talking to him briefly, Beau and his girlfriend sat down in another booth. A few minutes later one of the girls walked up and, pointing back at the other booth, said, "Hanna really wants to talk to you." Beau hadn't noticed that the other girl was Hanna. He told the girl he didn't think it was a good idea because they would be on opposing sides in the upcoming trial. The other girl said, "Well, she just wanted me to tell you that no matter what happens, she'll still think of you as a big brother." Beau and his girlfriend ate their food as quickly as possible and left. Was Hanna trying to "recruit" Beau to her side? Should she even have attempted to talk to him?

At first, Beau's story didn't register with me as anything more than just a curious chance meeting. Deep Springs is a small city, and running into someone you know is a common occurrence. Later, though, I realized that the important point was that Hanna, who had just turned sixteen, was hanging out at midnight with much older guys. I wondered whether her mother had given up on monitoring her activities and with trying to keep her safe. Maybe that was an unfair thought, but several things I discovered over the next few years led me to believe that it was entirely possible that Darla no longer had any control over Hanna. When we get to the chapters on the trials, pay attention to one of the first questions the prosecutor asked Hanna. It was about where she was living then. That's all I'll say for now.

The other important items that were covered in Beau's interview had to do with what happened on key dates in Hanna's statements. It seemed obvious that the prosecution was going to focus on the first and last times Hanna spent the night at the Sirois' home because those were listed in the indictment. After examining everything in the trial transcripts and Tom's interviews, though, I still had a lot of unanswered questions, so I started sending Steve letters, peppering him with questions about the case, asking him for corrections about speculations I had. We also talked on the phone at least once a week, so it was easy to make some of the changes to my notes while I talked to him.

For the first six or seven years, between 2007 and 2014, I was mostly helping Steve prepare his appeals. While doing that, I was also writing and editing my novels, finishing one in 2012, and publishing another one in 2015. A few other partly completed novels have been set aside for the time being. I didn't begin seriously thinking of writing *Aggravated* until late-2015, after Steve had filed what ended up being his next to last appeal. The courts ruled against both of them. Along the way, my mountain of notes had generated a variety of questions, so I interviewed Beau and Marri in 2014, and added their comments to my growing pile of information. I followed those with interviews of other individuals, with some TPIA requests, and with a great deal of online and in-person research. After poring over all of it, I ended up with quite a few ideas about what I thought probably did or didn't happen to Hanna. I'll cover most of that in the section called *Proof of Innocence*.

After Tom interviewed Steve's family, he dropped in on various people in and near Steve's subdivision. His first stop, to see Matt and Vivian Percet, was, coincidentally, on April 7, 2005, exactly one year after Hanna spoke to Blake Goudy. Matt and Vivian were neighbors and good friends of the Sirois family. Vivian had known Robin for decades because their parents had been friends, and they had known Steve since at least 1985 when he and Robin were married. They were regulars at Steve's and Robin's get-togethers, which meant that they had been there nearly every time Hanna and her family had been. Vivian testified in both trials, and the information in Tom's interview closely patterned the testimony she gave in 2006. Both she and Matt were sure that Steve couldn't have done what he was accused of. Matt told Tom almost immediately, "I have no direct evidence whatsoever, but nothing I know about this whole situation would lead me to believe that Steve could have ever done anything like this." Vivian, referring to Steve's confusion when Darla confronted him, said, "I didn't even realize anything blew up until Darla came out and accused Steve of what they were accusing him of, and Steve was dumbfounded. He didn't know what she was talking about. You know, they were close friends."

Before Hanna accused Steve, as far as I can tell from everything I've seen and heard, no one in the neighborhood, or in Hanna's or Steve's families, felt that Steve would ever have done anything like that.

A Short Interlude About Drinking

The subject of drinking came up during Matt and Vivian's interview. Drinking was one of the major weapons Hanna tossed around frequently, claiming multiple times that Robin and Steve "drank 24/7," and that "Robin would wake up with a beer in her hand, go to bed with a beer in her hand." Steve and Robin *did* drink, but not as much as Hanna claimed, at least not at first. Matt, Vivian, and Hanna's mother were also drinkers. Matt said, "Darla would come over there with a bottle of tequila." That wasn't the first or the last time I heard that about Darla. Steve felt that Darla's influence was a big factor in their increased drinking. According to him and others, he and Robin were beer drinkers, and so were most of their friends, but Darla was the one who shifted their habits toward harder stuff. In 2014, I asked Beau how Robin's and Steve's drinking habits changed once Darla started attending the get-togethers. He said, "There was a lot more liquor brought in the house." I pushed him on the subject, and he said, "Darla always wanted Dad and Mom, either one or the other, or both, to take shots of tequila with her," and, he added, "She brought a bottle with her every time she came out there."

Tom asked Hanna, in her 2006 interview, if there was a lot of drinking during the get-togethers. Hanna said, "Every time I was out there Robin was drunk. She passed out most of the time." A minute later, she said that Steve would feed Robin shots "and get her drunk whenever I was there so she'd pass out, because that's one more person who could possibly witness." When Tom asked about Darla, though, Hanna [stressing several words] said, "My mom drank, but never got drunk. I've never once seen my mom drunk. She knows her limit. She knows when to stop." Tom asked her what Darla primarily drank. After a 3-second pause, Hanna said, "She drank beer." Tom waited. After another long pause, Hanna added, "She would have ...a shot of whiskey, maybe like ...one, and that was it. She wouldn't have very much at all." Just about everything Hanna told Tom about her mother's drinking has been contradicted by people who were at the weekend get-togethers for years, people who witnessed how much Steve and Robin drank. They all admitted that Steve and Robin did drink, but they also said they hadn't seen them so drunk they were out of control, and had never seen either of them pass out. Beau, on the other hand, said that he saw Darla drunk "quite often." He said there were times when Robin and Steve "would beg her not to drive home, and she'd do it anyway," sometimes taking the kids with her, sometimes not. Was Hanna trying to mislead the defense before the trial by selling the idea of Steve's and Robin's heavy drinking to divert attention from what might be perceived as her mother's own excesses? She needn't have worried. The words "drink," "drunk," "drinking," "beer," "tequila," and "whiskey" don't appear in Darla's testimony in either trial. Unlike both Steve and Robin, Darla wasn't even asked about it in court. Beau also told me that, as much as his parents' drinking was amplified under Darla's influence, Robin's got even worse after the charges against Steve were filed. Her drinking also increased and her health decreased after Steve was incarcerated. She died in January 2012, at the age of 51, a little over five years after Steve landed at the Stiles Unit.

In Trial #2, Hanna helped steer the course of the trials toward Steve's and Robin's drinking. Ross asked her if the Sirois' spent any time at her house in Alderson, and she said "Very few times." He asked her why, and she replied, "Well, Sirois and his wife drank a lot. They were always drinking beer and whiskey. <u>On rare occasions, tequila</u>. They would come to our house in Alderson very rarely because they would have to leave early or they would be too drunk to make it home safely." That statement gave Ross the perfect opening to bring up the drinking that occurred at the "parties" at Steve's house. Could that interchange between him and Hanna have been planned? What I found intriguing, though, was Hanna's mention of tequila. Everyone I have asked about it said that tequila was Darla's drink, not Steve's or Robin's. When I asked Steve about Hanna's statement about her mom just drinking beer, or maybe just one shot of whiskey occasionally, Steve laughed, and said, "Darla never brought a pint of tequila in her life. It was always a half-gallon." Could Hanna have mentioned tequila because that was what she saw around her own house? Also, if Hanna's idea was that the Sirois' didn't visit them because they would get too drunk to drive home, what does that suggest about the kind of drinking that might have occurred at her house?

Hanna sometimes cited Steve's drinking as a rationale for why he allegedly molested her, but their neighbor, Vivian, had a different take on it. She said, "I've just never seen Steve approach her in any inappropriate way, no matter how much he'd had to drink, you know. He's just ...and there's been too many other young girls spend a lot of time over there that are so appalled at this, you know, that it just makes it unreasonable." From the tone in her voice, Vivian made it clear that the girls she referred to were shocked that Steve had been arrested or charged in the first place.

Vivian also contradicted Hanna's claim that Robin often passed out, or that Steve tried to get Robin drunk. When asked about Robin's drinking, Vivian admitted that Robin did sometimes get drunk, but she said, "When she does, she's up and down all night. She keeps getting up, trying to go to the bathroom, and she can walk, and we watch her close, and help her to the bathroom and everything," and added, "she's a ...a roaming drunk...She'll lay down for a little bit, and then I guess she'll sleep it off a little bit, and then she's always trying to get up and moving." Tom asked her how long "a little bit" was. Vivian said, "Sometimes an hour, two hours. But she's mumbling the whole time, and moving around, and it's just not..." Tom interrupted to ask if Robin was a sound sleeper. Vivian, without hesitation, said, "No." Near the end of the interview, the talk shifted to the treatment of children. Matt said, "You show affection to a child, but...it's not sexual in any way. And that's the way Steve has always impressed me about his approach to young girls. And I just do not believe this shit. Never will. I can't prove it, but I don't believe it," adding, "she is just a child, or she always was to me, and I'm sure she always was to Steve." Vivian said, "He always treated her like a daughter. She was the daughter of his friend, and that's the only way he ever treated her."

Tom's Other Interviews

The next day, following a lead, Tom went back to Saddleview Cove to talk to the owner of The Spinnaker, a local café located on the northern outskirts of Saddleview Cove. She wasn't there, so he talked someone who identified herself as Rebecca Luborsky Benway, one of the café's waitresses. Talking loudly over the clatter of dishes and the clang of silverware being washed in the background, Tom introduced himself, saying he was a private investigator and was "doing some background checking on this deal with Steven Sirois." Rebecca said, in a plaintive voice, "Please let me know if he actually did what he's being accused of." Tom explained that he was out there to try and find out. Rebecca said, "I've known Steve forever. When my mom told me what had happened, I freaked out. He's never touched me." Tom asked how she knew Steve. She said, "His son, Beau. Me and him have known each other since before kindergarten."

Then Rebecca mentioned her sister's murder. In 1993, when Rebecca was ten years old, her sister Jenny was raped and murdered by her stepfather, Billy Gasnick, and Rebecca tried to work that into the conversation, but Tom kept the topic on Steve. He asked Rebecca how Steve had acted around other young ladies, and she said, "Me, when I was younger, it was nothing. He used to hit on my mom, tried to get in her pants a lot. I've seen it." If Tom was surprised at this, it didn't register in his voice. He said, "Mm. Your mom's name is...? Rebecca told him her mom was Karen Suhler, and said that Steve came to their house, knocked on the door, and wanted her mom to let him in, and asked if she was lonely and wanted to sleep with him. Rebecca said her mom told Steve to leave, and added that she didn't tell Beau about that because Beau was her best friend. Steve denied that anything like that happened, saying that Karen actually used to hit on him before he and Robin introduced her to Gasnick. He felt glad about the introduction at the time because he thought that Karen might leave him alone. Once they found out what Gasnick was really like, though, he felt horrible about having gotten them together. We'll get to all of that in the next section, *Pre-Prejudice Against Steve*.

Tom asked Rebecca if she knew of anyone else in the area who might know something about Steve. She said that Steve's neighbors, Amy and Eldon Carragan, didn't like him "because of everything that's going on." He asked if she thought they actually knew something, or were just feeding off the rumors. She said that the Carragans worked at Shaper Unit, a state prison just outside the city limits, "and she has access to files, and she does have a copy of the charges against him," quickly adding, "but I'm not supposed to know that." Then she mentioned other people who didn't like Steve. A woman named Alice, but Rebecca said she didn't get "very much from her." And a man who "doesn't really know him, but he don't like him." They seemed to be people who were just spreading the type of typical gossip that cascades out after an incident.

Rebecca then fumbled a bit before saying, "Here's something I know, no one needs to know about. Marri had walked in on her dad on top of a girl naked." Rebecca's next few words were badly garbled when Tom bumped his recorder, but her sentence ended with "...told me it was a little girl." Tom asked, "Who told you that? Marri did?" Rebecca apparently nodded yes, then she said, "Nobody knows about that." Tom asked her when Marri told her that. Rebecca said, "two months ago," and added, "I told the cops." Did Rebecca really tell the police about Tiffany's story? There's no record of it. Wouldn't there be a note in Steve's file if she had? There isn't. Tom asked her what Marri said "her dad and the girl" were doing. Rebecca replied, "The girl said he was cleaning her ears. And another little girl told me the same thing. Marri told her." Tom seemed confused. "Did Marri tell you that, or did...?" Rebecca said, "Marri told me that, *and* another little girl told me that Marri told her." Tom asked her who the other girl was. Rebecca said, "Glenda ...uh, Glenda's daughter."

Let's unpack that. Glenda's daughter is Tiffany Sperger. You remember that Tiffany's affidavit stated that Marri told her that she had walked in on Steve, lying on top of Hanna, who was on the toilet. Rebecca said that both Marri and Tiffany told her about that incident, the same one that she told Tom "<u>no one needs to know about</u>." In the version Rebecca heard, though, Steve was on top of an unnamed girl, and either the girl was naked or they both were (it isn't clear in her description). Also, in Rebecca's version, the girl used the excuse that Steve was cleaning her ears. The cleaning her ears excuse hasn't been mentioned by anyone but Rebecca. Hanna did testify that Marri caught her and Steve in a compromising position once, and said that she explained it away by telling Marri that Steve was trying to get something out of her eye. Marri has said many times, sometimes under oath, that she never said anything like that to Tiffany, and told me that she didn't tell Rebecca anything either.

I have no proof, of course, but if made me wonder if Hanna or Tiffany spread that story around Steve's neighborhood, and elements of it became warped, like a game of Telephone, where a message is whispered down a row of people. Those in line mishear the message, and the changes get passed down the line. The alteration might be subtle at first, but it soon gets distorted beyond recognition. Gossip works exactly like that. I don't know where Rebecca heard this rumor, but it's clearly based on Tiffany's September 2004 affidavit. After seven months of it being passed around the rumor mill, though, parts of it had changed. Steve has said, unequivocally, that nothing happened at all, and that the incident is stupid on the face of it. "Lying on top of her on a toilet? How is that even possible?" Could Hanna have even developed her excuse about getting something out of her eye from a twisted rumor she heard, which was in turn based on Tiffany's affidavit?

Steve didn't hear any of Tom's interviews before the trials, and has no way to play them in prison, so I usually sent him printed copies after I finished transcribing them, or sometimes just read parts of them to him. When I read him Rebecca's comments, he said he didn't blame her for saying those things, that she was just doing what she had seen others do dozens of times, grab at a bit of fame. A man showed up at her workplace looking for information for a trial which was bound to be a topic of conversation. She gave it to him. Some of it favored Steve and some didn't, and most of what she said was patched together from rumors; but Rebecca did say that Steve never touched her, and that she had been around the family since she was in kindergarten with Beau.

Tom also spoke briefly to Shirley, one of the other waitresses, and asked her if she knew much about Steve. She said, "Naw, I don't know anything about him, except what I've read." He asked her, "What all have you read and heard?" She answered, "Well, the only thing I did read was that book, *A Gruesome End*, but I don't know the man at all." The book, about the Billy Gasnick case, was published in 2002 (which you might notice is just two years before Hanna made her accusation). We'll get to the book and the Billy Gasnick trial very soon. I promise.

Eldon and Amy Carragan lived on Percheron Drive, one street to the east of Steve's street, Mustang Drive. A corner of the Carragan's lot touched the back corner of Steve's. Tom found Carragan's house easily, and introduced himself after getting past a barking dog. As they stood in front of the house and talked, he asked Carragan if he knew anything about his neighbor, Steven Sirois. The audio on this particular interview was horrible. It was sometimes hard to understand because of a combination of street noises, the yappy dog, and several very young children conducting what sounded like a game of demolition derby at the tops of their lungs. In the midst of the cacophony, Tom did learn a few interesting things, though. First, Carragan did confirm that both he and his wife worked for the Texas Department of Criminal Justice. He said his wife was inside sleeping because they worked different shifts at the Shaper Unit, a state prison which was located just south of Deep Springs. Tom didn't let on that he already knew they worked there, or that he had located them through Rebecca. Carragan revealed that they were the source of the printed copies of Steve's indictment that had been posted throughout the neighborhood. He said, "Me and my wife got a copy of the indictment and had it posted out here," adding that his stepdad was the person who posted them. Steve and Beau spent one afternoon driving around the neighborhood, tearing all of them down.

Carragan said, "If we could tell you something, we damn sure would. I don't know anything. I know he don't look in *my* yard. He don't come *to* my yard. If he does come to my yard, he's going to wish he *hadn't* come to my yard." He said that Rebecca Benway had done some babysitting for them, and had told him, "If there's one thing I could do, I'd get his daughter out of that house with him," something she hadn't said to Tom. Continuing, Carragan said he had worked in the prison system long enough that he could "pretty much look at somebody and tell whether or not I want to be around them or not. My instinct with him is no, I don't want to have nothing to do with him." He also said, "From what I understand—and you know this is just a bunch of hearsay—there's more than one little girl that's accused the guy." Tom asked whether Steve and Robin drank a lot. Carragan said, "I don't think they do as much now as they did. They used to throw a lot of parties. I mean a *lot* of parties, but they kind of ...they slowed down a lot on that." Carragan added, "I believe everybody should get a fair trial, but they sure wouldn't want me on his jury."

For someone who told Tom he didn't want to mess in other people's business, Carragan certainly seemed willing to prejudice the neighborhood against Steve without proof, using untrue rumors like "more than one little girl" having accused Steve of molestation. Hanna's accusation was the only one ever brought against Steve. Even after Carragan said that this was "just a bunch of hearsay," he passed it along anyway. Bias, like a cancer, grows when people believe an unfounded rumor and pass malignant messages on. People like Rebecca weren't helping to create a level playing field either. She had known Steve since she was a child, and said she knew that he wasn't like that, but still seemed willing to spread groundless rumors about him.

The majority of interviews Tom did in the subdivision were either favorable to Steve, or at least neutral, but Saddleview Cove was a small community, and most people there knew Steve. Their reaction was usually one of disbelief, and their comments were more along the lines of, "Steve? No, I don't believe it. I've known Steve for years, and he just wouldn't do something like that." There were a few comments, though, like, "Oh, he's that guy who molested that little girl" from people who reacted like Eldon Carragan. Even in his own neighborhood, rumors were spread about "the toilet thing," about other girls accusing Steve, and about Steve's links to Billy Gasnick. Imagine what it must have been like in areas where they didn't know him.

During all of this, Steve was trying to maintain a positive attitude, despite having to scramble to find odd jobs. He still believed that something would happen to clear everything up, or that Hanna would recant and say she was sorry, or say she didn't know why she accused him of such a thing, and everything could go back to normal.

Obviously, that didn't happen.

Josh Chilmark's Two Interviews

Tom Swearingen did one more interview in 2005. It was with Josh Chilmark, and it took place just a few days before Craig Conner, a sergeant with the sheriff's office, also interviewed Josh. Conner had taken over the investigation from Deputy Knox. In her affidavit, Hanna said she had confided in Josh and told him what happened to her. Obviously, Josh was someone who could verify parts of Hanna's story. She swore in her affidavit that she hadn't told anyone about what was happening except Josh (in the Spring of 2003), but she also swore in the same document that she hadn't told anyone until Blake Goudy gave his talk at her school (in the Spring of 2004). Tom wanted to find out if either statement was true. After several attempts to pin Josh down, Tom finally arranged a phone interview with him in April 2005.

Josh told Tom that Hanna wanted to date him, but he said he wouldn't do that because she was too young. Six months after Hanna told Josh she was being abused, Josh started dating Liz Brailford. Liz was three years older than Hanna, and was Steve and Robin's niece. Liz and Josh got married in December of 2004, but Hanna found out they were dating when she ran into them at the county fair in January 2004.

Josh said he had known Hanna since the beginning of his ninth grade year (her fifth grade year). She didn't confide in him until his senior year, though, when she was in the eighth grade and he was a teacher's aide in her gym class. He explained that, in 2003, "These girls were making jokes and stuff, and they brought up about Hanna being a virgin...she started crying and stuff later. I never knew what it was about, and she got real mad, and she ended up telling me that she wasn't sure if she was or not, and ...then she just told me about all this different stuff ...about how he would touch her and stuff, but...I guess it was consensual on her part." Tom asked him what she and her abuser did. Josh said Hanna told him that this man "fingered her, went down on her, she went down on him. Just stuff like that. I'm pretty sure she said they never had intercourse." Tom also asked him when the abuse started, and Josh said, "I think she said she was twelve, because she was fourteen then [*in 2003*]."

Tom also wanted to know why Hanna spoke to Blake Goudy. Josh said that "<u>one of her friends</u> thought she had been acting kind of funny afterward, and asked her what was wrong, and she told her friend." Tom asked him who the friend was. Josh couldn't come up with Karla Spivey's name, but he did say that he thought Hanna *had* also told one other guy, but he couldn't remember his name either. Josh finished by saying that, as far as he knew, he and those other two people were the only ones who knew about Hanna's abuse before she told Blake Goudy. Compare that with what Hanna said in her affidavit, that she hadn't told anyone else before Blake Goudy (except Josh), but Josh thought she had also told another boy and a girl at her school before Goudy. Did she tell no one? Or just Josh? Or Josh and two other people? Or several of her friends at sleepovers? I'll dig into the topic of who knew what (and when they might have heard it) in the chapter *Sleepovers, Confessions, and Lies*.

[*One thing Josh's interview revealed was that Hanna had already formulated a narrative about having sexual experiences with an older guy as early as Spring 2003. The description apparently changed with each retelling, but it was the same pattern she used in both trials. The fact that Josh knew about Hanna telling Karla means that Hanna continued talking to Josh after Goudy's April 2004 speech. Also, Hanna portrayed Karla to Josh as a friend of hers. During the trials, though, Hanna tried to distance herself from Karla by calling her* "a girl that I wasn't very close to."]

Just a few days after speaking to Tom, Josh also gave an interview to Sgt. Conner. The only record of the interview I have is this note in Conner's computer file, sent to me as is, without redactions.

> Victim: Penderfield, Hannah
> Offense: Aggravated Sexual Assault

On Monday, April 25, 2005 I Sgt. Craig Conner followed up on this case. Joshua Chilmark came into the office and gave me an affidavit regarding this case. Chilmark could not remember a lot of details about this matter but documented what he remembered by giving an affidavit.

End of Supplement; Sgt. Craig Conner 04/26/05

I obtained that note as part of a second TPIA request to the Sheriff's Office. I found it remarkable that at least half of the documents they sent me whited out Hanna's name [*which they fairly consistently misspelled as Hannah*], but the rest of the documents didn't redact it. Sometimes it was redacted on one part of a single document, but was in full view somewhere else on the same document. That was also true of several of the files I got from the DA's office.

It's also interesting that Sgt. Conner said Josh couldn't remember much, but Josh spoke to Tom for an hour, and managed to tell him quite a bit. The DA's office sent Roland Mathis a notice three weeks later to let him know Josh's affidavit would be available to him. Oddly, the affidavit wasn't entered into evidence in either trial, the DA didn't have a copy of it in the files they showed me, it wasn't in the documents the sheriff's office gave me, and Mathis told me on two separate occasions that he had no records left from Steve's case. What happened to Josh's affidavit? Shouldn't both the DA and the sheriff's office have copies of it? Shouldn't one of Steve's attorneys have a copy? Why wasn't it entered into evidence in the trials? Was there something in Josh's affidavit that they didn't want anyone else to see?

A Missing Rape Kit?

In addition to Josh's affidavit and Deputy Knox's notes, another piece of information also seemed to be missing. In March 2005, still with no permanent date established for the first trial, Roland Mathis sent a fax to Assistant District Attorney Elmer Ross. Mathis reminded Ross that, several weeks before, Ross had told him that there was "a rumor that a rape kit had been taken from Ms. Hannah Penderfield." He asked Ross to send the results to him. Ross then sent a fax to Sgt. Conner. This is what it said:

"Victim and her mother claim she was seen at Locklin Memorial [*Hospital*] and a Rape exam was completed. Inv. Knox told me he did not think such an exam was done. Please check and confirm whether a report exists of the exam ASAP. Thanks."

Ross didn't word the fax as if this was a rumor. He said "Victim and her mother claim," as in, *I didn't just hear this in the wind, Hanna and her mother told me this as if it was a fact*. Copies of the two faxes were in the DA's files, but there was no response from Conner, and no note about it in Conner's files either. I called him in 2019, and asked him why there was no answer to that question in the DA's files. He said that it sounded like the kind of request he would have checked out with a simple phone call, adding, "if there wasn't nothing to ...nothing found, or nothing to find, then I would have probably just picked up the phone and said, 'Hey, there's nothing here.'" *Did* Hanna have a rape kit done? Knox didn't think so, and neither did Conner. If she did, when was it done? Her doctor should have known about it, but there's no mention of one in the medical files that were entered into evidence in the trials. I wondered why this became an issue almost a year after the accusations. If a rape kit was done in the spring of 2005, how could it possibly be connected to Steve? If no rape kit was done, why would Hanna and Darla tell Elmer Ross it had been? What possible purpose could that have served?

Let's move on.

Money Problems

In the same way that money gives the rich advantages that aren't available to the poor, it also allows the rich to have a better defense in a legal proceeding. The truly poor, those who can't afford to hire a lawyer at all, are usually saddled with overworked and underpaid public defense attorneys who don't have enough time to prepare an adequate defense for their clients. The vast majority of defendants are encouraged to take plea deals, sometimes even coerced into taking them. By accepting the deals, they are given lesser sentences in exchange for pleading guilty (whether they are guilty or not). Plea deals also can give prosecutors a win even if they don't have a viable case. If Elmer Ross had thought the case could stand on its own merits, would he still have offered Steve multiple plea deals that would have allowed him to serve no prison time? Maybe so, but Steve refused them all because, as he said, "I would have to register as a sex offender, and that would be a lie."

Plea deals are an advantage for the courts, the prosecutors, and the public defenders, maybe even for the guilty poor, but not for the innocent defendant. The courts and attorneys get to dispose of cases quickly, without trials. That saves them time, effort, and money, but innocent defendants who are poor can have their rights stolen just because they can't afford an adequate defense. Steve fell between those two extremes when he was accused, but by the end of the first trial the family's finances were completely wiped out. For Steve, the two years between the accusation and the first trial were largely consumed with trying to earn enough money to help keep the family afloat and still afford legal fees, but it was difficult because a lot of people weren't willing to hire him with the cloud of a sexual offense hanging over him.

Steve and Robin were making decent money by 2004. Robin was an engineering tech at a manufacturing firm, and had been with them for twenty-four years by then. Steve seriously pursued a career as a club DJ after high school, and did that for several years, working in clubs between Deep Springs and Fort Worth. After he and Robin got married in 1985, though, he started doing construction work because it allowed him to stay closer to home and help care for their disabled and ailing relatives (Robin's parents, and later, our father). Robin's mother, Iline, died in 1988, and her father, Jeff, passed away in 1994. Our father, Stan, died in 1996. By that time, Steve's DJ'ing days were long behind him. Construction provided a decent income, and he did that for over ten years. In 1999, he got the chance to work for the City of Deep Springs in their water department. The income was steady, and there were prospects for advancement, but he left the city's employ in September 2003 for another opportunity, working for the state as a Park Ranger at Lake Ashwell State Park.

During the first nineteen years of their marriage, between his salary and Robin's, they brought home a solid middle class income, and felt secure.

Everything changed when the charges were filed, though. They soon found out that the cost of his defense could easily wipe them out financially, and they didn't know what to do. After he was arrested, Steve made arrangements with the bail bondsman to pay his $5,000 fee (ten-percent of $50,000) in installments. He obviously couldn't continue to work for Darla's brother, Leon, which would have been his fallback position under other circumstances, so he did some odd jobs for a few people, but many had heard about the charges and were reluctant to hire him. As further expenses arrived, it became clear that their savings wouldn't last long. If Steve couldn't find work, they would have to rely exclusively on Robin's pay (which was then covering some but not all of their bills). In addition, Roland Mathis was primarily an estate planner and tax lawyer, not a criminal defense attorney. Steve kept his eye out for someone to replace him. He looked at two law firms, one local and one from California.

The local attorney, Claude Tisbury, had an aggressive reputation, and was unafraid to take on the county's entrenched good-ole-boy system. Steve worried about using him, though, because he thought Tisbury might antagonize the DA and the judge, and Steve still believed the truth would come out before going to trial. The California firm bragged extensively about their win record, but wanted a lot of money. After seeing the fees most law firms wanted, Steve knew that the family's resources weren't going to be enough. He decided he had to find more money somewhere else. He called me in July 2004, not to ask for a loan, but to explain that he was having a legal problem, and asked about the possibility of borrowing against his inheritance.

If you're wondering why he didn't just ask our mother for a loan, he had a good reason. In 2003, at the age of eighty, our mother was officially diagnosed with Alzheimer's. She had been showing symptoms for a few years before that, but had managed to hide her condition from us by using calendars and a diary as to-do lists, reminding her of each day's commitments. Years before that, she had appointed me and my other brother, Phillip, as executors of her estate, and had given us powers of attorney for legal, financial, and medical matters. By 2002, along with a variety of other health issues, I discovered she was having difficulty paying her bills. She would double-pay some of them, and not pay others. I took over her finances in May of that year, and continued to do that after we moved her (late in 2004) into an assisted living facility just a couple of miles away from Phillip, in a Dallas suburb. I was so focused on Mom's situation at the time that I was barely aware of Steve's problems.

We knew that Alzheimer's is a disease that robs a person of their very essence, and usually works at a brutally slow pace. When Mom was officially diagnosed, we were told that it could be ten years or more before she passed away, and that her regression would strip her of all of her memories while it also wasted away her body. Our primary concern was to visit her as often as possible while she could still recognize us, and to make sure she would have the best possible care for as long as necessary. Fortunately, she was set up financially in a way that would allow that to happen. Steve called me because he knew I was handling Mom's finances. He was reluctant about asking, but a little panicked as well. Unfortunately, I had to tell him it wasn't a decision I could make. I didn't have the authority to withdraw funds for anything other than Mom's care. I had him call her lawyer, Harry Newbold, because I couldn't authorize something like that on my own.

After Mom remarried in 1976, she moved to Massachusetts with her new husband, Bill Sen. All of us kids were out of the house before then except Steve, so he was the only one to go with her. Mom worked for Harry's law firm, Newbold Vanderhoop, when it was in its infancy, and she and everyone there became lifelong friends. When Bill died in 1996, Harry's firm continued to manage her legal and financial affairs. When we brought Mom to Texas, Harry worked with us to consolidate Mom's finances, placing everything in a trust. The law firm deposited money from some annuities into her checking account each month, and I used that to pay her bills, which were mounting because of her condition. The purpose of the trust was to ensure that she would be taken care of for as long as possible, so I was obligated to only use it for that purpose. Acting as a troika, though, Harry, Phillip, and I could make joint decisions beyond that.

None of us "kids" were rich, we were mostly schoolteachers, so the odds of any of us being able to help Steve financially were slim, and I believe he knew that, so he made every attempt possible to try to take care of it on his own, even thinking that the cost to him would be small because he was sure the trial wouldn't happen once everyone realized that the allegations were false. He soon found himself staring into a financial abyss that seemed endless, though. During a conference call with me and Phillip, Harry explained Steve's situation, and wanted our opinion on whether he should tap into some of Steve's inheritance in advance. Harry told us that Steve had found an attorney that he thought could be very good (the one from California), someone who had defended against this kind of charge multiple times. The lawyer was also a female, which Steve felt would make a better impression on the jury because it was a sexual assault case; but she wanted $100,000 to try it. We discussed a lot of the pros and cons of hiring her. Harry thought that bringing a lawyer in from out of state might be overkill, causing the jury to wonder why Steve needed that much firepower.

Neither Phillip nor I had any experience in having to pay lawyers such a huge sum. It seemed like a ridiculous amount of money to us (and still does). We also had to balance it against Mom's needs. Even though we knew there was a possibility that all six of us could eventually receive at least a small inheritance from Mom, we had no way of knowing how much she might need over the next decade or longer. We decided to not advance Steve funds for the California attorney. Harry contacted Steve and let him know, but told him if he could find a local attorney who would work for less, he would revisit the idea of dipping into his inheritance. If that seems like a callous action on our part, we felt cold-hearted having to think that way, but we had no idea how many years Mom had left and our obligation had to be for her first. The main thing we knew about Alzheimer's was that it moved slowly, and that her care would likely get more expensive as her condition worsened, which it did.

After discussing it with Robin, Steve told Harry that he would keep Mathis as his attorney. Harry spoke to Mathis about costs, and they both agreed that it seemed to be a simple "he said versus she said" case, with no physical evidence. Mathis thought the case could be done for $5,000 to $15,000, but "if the matter were dropped immediately" it would be much less. Harry paid him

$2,000 to begin with, but once Tom was hired, more money was needed for him to conduct his investigation. By the end of 2004, Newbold Vanderhoop had paid Mathis $7,500 out of Mom's trust, but within the next four months the total had risen to $27,928. Steve and Robin pulled money from Robin's 401K, and repaid $13,928 of that to Harry's law firm. That squared Steve and Robin for about half of what they had borrowed against his inheritance, but it also nearly depleted everything they had saved for their future. Their financial situation was looking grim.

Trip to Florida

Some people *were* looking out for Steve, though. In October 2005, The state officially let Steve go after a year of being on leave with no pay, but their good friend, Del Weaver, called Steve with an idea. Del had been offered an opportunity to work in Louisiana as an insurance adjuster for Hurricane Katrina losses, but wasn't interested in doing that, so he gave Steve a number to call. Steve, who hadn't been working for a year at that point, jumped at the chance. He talked to someone named Benjy who assured Steve he could get him a temporary license, which would allow him to operate as an adjuster for ninety days, but said it might be a while before he could line up a job. Steve got the job just a couple of weeks later, but it wasn't Benjy who hired him.

A detailed account of what happened is on the blog at:
https://aggravatedbook.com/finding-money-for-defense-part-3/

Here's the short version. After spending $300 the family could ill afford, and taking a three-day class in another Texas city, Steve had a temporary adjuster's license, and an application for a permanent one. Before he left for home, he added his name to an email networking list. A few days later one of the emails read, "Want to go to work? Contact Gabe Gorman." Gabe owned an insurance adjusting company, and he wanted temporary adjusters to handle claims from Hurricane Wilma in Florida. Steve had to be in Ocala, Florida, by 9:00 the next morning to get started. Without thinking it through, Steve told Gabe he'd be there. After clearing everything with the family and Roland Mathis, he asked his brother-in-law, Marvin Foxwell, for help. Marvin loaned Steve $1,500 cash and let him borrow his credit card. Somehow he managed to make it to Ocala with seconds to spare.

Steve worked hard adjusting claims for over three months. After Steve's car broke down, Beau even drove there toward the end and acted as his helper. When they were finished, Steve had earned $39,600, about what he normally made in a year working construction. After expenses, including the cost of a trailer to tow the car back, gas, meals, lodging, and repaying Marvin, there was about $20,000 left. All of it disappeared instantly, paying bills they were behind on, including the bail bondsman, but at least they weren't $20,000 in the hole. The trip had served its purpose by giving them a little breathing room. Even if he were convicted, which he continued to believe he wouldn't be, he wouldn't leave his family with massive debt. Steve returned from Florida thinking the trial would happen right away and he could finally put this whole ordeal behind him. Hanna, by the way, had the gall to tell Tom Swearingen that Steve had "probably found a little girl there" in Florida.

Pre-Prejudice Against Steve

"Prejudices are what fools use for reason."
Voltaire

"What a sad era when it is easier to smash an atom than a prejudice."
Albert Einstein

[Subsections in this Chapter: The Billy Gasnick Trial // Input From Other Media // Flyers at the Lake and a Family Feud // Debunking Tiffany's Story // Analysis]

This chapter isn't about Steve's innocence, it's about why Steve didn't, or couldn't, get a fair trial, and why some of the jurors might have believed he was guilty long before they heard any evidence. I think that a long-standing prejudice against him, coupled with a visceral bias against child molesters (and, by extension, those accused of the crime, guilty or not), ensured that Steve drew partially-biased juries for both trials. In his first appeal, in 2007, Steve argued that some people in the area were determined to convict him, no matter what. Let's look at several items that might help prove that was true.

Before the trials were even held, the deck was partially stacked against him simply because he was charged with sexual assault of a child. During jury selection, several people said they considered Steve guilty simply because he had been charged. Is it impossible to believe that some prospective jurors might have withheld similar biases and ended up on the jury? I think feelings like that were brewing against Steve for the entire two years between the accusation and the trials. That extended period allowed rumors to spread more thoroughly into the potential jury pool. I also believe I can prove that at least one of the jurors in the second trial might have wanted to convict him no matter what the evidence was.

Even the judge and the prosecutors expressed doubts about being able to find an untainted jury. During Trial #2, Judge Hawes and both of the attorneys were wrestling with how many prospective jurors they would need to go through in order to successfully choose twelve jurors and one alternate. Elmer Ross told Hawes, "You know how much I want to try this case, but I can't see going to jury selection without fifty people here, especially on the punishment issue <u>with all the information that's been going around town</u>." He was admitting that people were talking about this case a lot. Judge Hawes said, "I know that last time on the Sirois case [*during the first trial*], we came very close to not having a whole panel." The 95 potential jurors they had started with had decreased to 64 within an hour. We'll cover that process, called voir dire, in the chapter on the second trial. Steve's ability to get a fair trial in Ashwell County, though, began eroding over a decade earlier. After reading this chapter, I hope you will be able to see that there might have been a great deal of bias against Steve, especially in this area, long before his trials got underway. Let's look at one of the reasons.

The Billy Gasnick Trial

I mentioned earlier that Billy Gasnick raped and killed his step-daughter, Jenny Luborsky, and that Steve and our father testified against him. I also told you about Clyde Sledge telling Roland Mathis that private investigators and other people from around the state were telling him that, now that Steve was going to be tried for sexual assault of a child, they would finally find out who killed Jenny. Billy Gasnick was arrested for that crime in 1993, and tried and convicted in 1995. Why would Steve still be a suspect in 2004? Sledge's comment sent me off on a search for evidence of a hidden prejudice against Steve.

We saw that Rebecca Luborsky Benway, in her 2005 interview with Tom Swearingen, was spreading gossip about Steve, and mentioned Gasnick. I think that was because the Gasnick case was connected to *her*, because it was *her* sister who was killed. Regardless of whether Rebecca was hoping that her name would appear in the news or not, her attempt to bring that up during a discussion about Steve suggests that there were rumors of a connection between Gasnick and Steve. What she failed to tell Tom was that Steve was taking care of several kids on the day Jenny went missing, and Rebecca was one of them. He was occupied that entire day, which should have kept armchair jurors from suspecting him of having any involvement in the Gasnick case, but it apparently didn't. Here's a brief rundown about what happened in 1993, but a more detailed, three-part post about it is on the blog, beginning at:

https://aggravatedbook.com/the-billy-gasnick-trial-part-1/

Some of the following information comes from the book, *A Gruesome End*, but is mostly from police reports, interviews, newspaper and magazine articles, and from Steve. As with the rest of *Aggravated*, the following names (as well as *A Gruesome End's* title) are pseudonyms.

In the late 1980's, Steve was doing installations for an outfit called A-Plus Superior Roofing, and he was assigned to work with an installer named Billy Gasnick. During one of our early phone calls Steve asked me if I had read *A Gruesome End.* I have since, but I hadn't at that time. He said he tried to read it once, but he only got partway into it before it pissed him off and he quit. He told me that he and Gasnick were co-workers at one time, but the writer "kept saying I was Billy's best friend, and that's just not true." The author, Marcia Jagger, did refer to Steve several times as "Gasnick's best friend," occasionally adding comments like "Steve would do anything for Billy." Steve said that he thought Jagger got that incorrect idea because she relied too heavily on what the matriarch of the family, Martha Gasnick, told her.

Steve and Robin introduced Billy to Robin's friend, Karen Suhler, in 1989. Karen and Billy were both single and Robin thought they seemed lonely, and they may have been. They were married within six months. Steve has said several times that he regretted introducing them because he was sure that Jenny would be alive today if the two hadn't met, but you can't know in advance what effect a single action might have, can you?

One of the things Gasnick frequently asked Steve to do was to help him move from one place to another. In the brainstorming session, Steve said,

"I got tired of moving him. He'd live in a house until they had to evict him, or had to get him out, and then he'd scrape up the money to do another one, which was probably more money than the rent, but you couldn't explain that to him." Being used that way got old quickly, but when Gasnick asked Steve for help, he usually did. After several moves, though, he managed to find reasons to not be available to help. In some ways, Steve felt his relationship with Darla Belisle was a lot like his with Billy Gasnick. Steve didn't consider either of them to be a best friend, but they both turned to him repeatedly for help. He said that, when Darla bought a new computer, she called Steve to get it hooked up. If she had a problem with a boyfriend, she called Steve to complain. If she was short on money, she called him and whined about how she wasn't making enough. He said her grumbling was never-ending. When Steve started thinking of Gasnick as a user, he pulled back from helping him so much. The two families still saw each other occasionally, though, because of Robin's friendship with Karen.

Early in May 1993, Billy, Karen, Rebecca, and Jenny moved into a house near Dwyer, Texas (without Steve's help that time). Dwyer, barely a town, is located less than ten miles north of Deep Springs, and a little to the east of Lake Ashwell. Their newest house was dilapidated, and the water wasn't connected. Water service could have been set up, but it would have cost a few hundred dollars, and they didn't have it, so they hauled barrels and bottles of water to the house for drinking and bathing. That place was worse than the previous one. The family seemed to be on a downward slide.

Near the end of that first month, Gasnick and Jenny spent the day at the house while Karen, Robin, and Nancy Foxwell (one of Robin's sisters), played in a bowling tournament in Arlington, Texas. Steve and our father, Stan, were at Steve's and Robin's house, caring for Jeff, Robin's paraplegic father, and also babysitting five kids (Beau, Marri, and Rebecca; plus Nancy's kids, Leo and Gail). When I asked Beau what he remembered of that day, he said that he and the kids were at the house during the morning, but that afternoon Steve drove them to Joubert Junction, a small community on the other side of the lake, to spend several hours painting the Bywater Baptist Church along with a dozen or so other church members. Later in the afternoon they went back to the house so Steve could fix supper for the kids. Steve agreed with Beau's memory, adding that the church had taken a video of everyone while they painted. For all those rumor-mongers, Steve was around a lot of people that day, and some of it was captured on videotape. Steve said that still didn't stop the Gasnick family from later trying to divert suspicion from Billy by trying to pin Jenny's rape and murder on him and others.

That night, Gasnick called Steve between 8:30 and 9:00 pm, and said Jenny was missing. Steve told him he would be there as soon as he could. He asked Stan to watch the kids and Jeff for a while, and drove over to Gasnick's, about a dozen miles away. When he got there, Gasnick told Steve he had looked everywhere for Jenny, and just didn't know what to do. When Gasnick said he hadn't called the police yet, Steve waited while he did, and then they called Karen and Robin. The wives wanted to know if they should come home. They had finished bowling for the day, but they had been drinking and stormy weather was predicted. Steve said, no, they shouldn't be driving in the rain if they were tipsy. Not wanting them to worry, he said he was sure Jenny would turn up, and told them to come back in the morning. He said he would call them if there was any news in the meantime.

Sheriff's Deputy Greg Stavens arrived a little after 10:00 and helped them look until nearly midnight. Steve suggested mobilizing a volunteer search team to help. Stavens agreed, and put in a call to set that up. Steve drove back and forth between Gasnick's and his house a few times to make sure the kids were okay, and looked for Jenny on the way. Police and volunteers searched the property most of the night, but a heavy rainstorm caused them to stop for a few hours. Steve said that Gasnick seemed nervous and fidgety during the rain; and Karen's brother, Buddy Suhler, testified that, once the rain stopped, Billy hopped in his Ford Escort and drove off, saying he needed to get away for a bit, but returned ten minutes or so later. The next morning, REACT team volunteers made sweeps across the property, helicopters hovered overhead, and cadaver dogs were deployed, but there was no sign of Jenny. When one of the dogs "hit" on Gasnick's Escort, though, police found blood splatters and small bits of brain matter in the car, so they took Gasnick in for questioning. Late in the afternoon of the next day, May 24th, Jenny's body was found in a culvert, a little over two miles from the Gasnick house. She had been raped and bludgeoned to death.

Steve found out later that Gasnick had previously been tried for other horrible crimes, including rape, kidnapping, and murder, but he said that the Gasnick family closed ranks whenever Billy got into trouble. According to Steve, when Gasnick was tried for an earlier murder, one of his sisters claimed he was with her in a different state, and he was acquitted. No one in Deep Springs was aware of any of this until the sheriff of a nearby county heard about Jenny's disappearance. Steve said that sheriff came to the Gasnick house when Billy was arrested and said, "What do you expect from the most dangerous son-of-a-bitch in Keegan County?"

With the evidence mounting against Gasnick, Steve decided he needed to talk to the investigators; and he and our father submitted to interrogations and gave DNA and pubic hair samples which cleared them of suspicion. They also both agreed to testify for the prosecution. Steve also said that, while they were at the sheriff's office, Deputy Walton told them that, when Gasnick drove off after the rainstorm, they believed he had driven to the culvert to make sure the rain hadn't washed Jenny's body out. The Gasnick family didn't take kindly to Steve and Dad agreeing to testify against Gasnick. According to the book, *A Gruesome End*, during the two years leading up to his trial, Gasnick told his attorney and his family "a number of times" that he believed Steve was "capable of murdering Jenny."

Steve also told me that when the Gasnicks found out that he was planning to testify, they turned on him. He said that Gasnick's sister, Melanie, even threatened to have him killed. Beau, who was only ten years old at the time, said that Melanie approached them while they were sitting in Steve's truck after Gasnick had been arrested, and said she asked Steve, "You don't think he did it, do you?" Steve answered her with what he thought was the truth, "Yeah, I'm pretty sure he did." Acting shocked, she said, "You're his friend. You have to stand behind him." Steve replied, "No, I don't." Beau said that Melanie "got right in Steve's face and told him that she's got people ...that she *knows* people, and they could put him where no one could find him." Beau said that he must have looked visibly upset after Melanie walked away because Steve told him not to worry, that he would be safe. Steve remembered it a little differently, with Melanie saying "I know people in Mississippi. They'll never find your body." He admitted that the encounter was frightening, but he wouldn't have let Beau know that, and testified against Gasnick anyway. Melanie's threat wasn't mentioned at Billy's trial or in *A Gruesome End.*

Steve said that, as the trial approached, Billy's preacher mother and his siblings not only tried to convince everyone that Billy was a good Christian boy who would never do anything evil, but they also offered up alternate suspects, like Steve and Jenny's uncle, Buddy Suhler. That may not seem like a very Christian way to act, but according to Steve, they had done this sort of thing for Billy before. This time they mounted a barrage of what I believe was misinformation to divert suspicion away from him. In the trial, Martha testified that a man approached her at Billy's house and told her that someone with curly red hair had been driving up and down the road in a tan-colored pickup truck, yelling obscene things at neighborhood kids. She said she wrote a note about the man for the detectives, handed it to Steve, saw him hand the note to Deputy Walton and heard him repeat her information to the deputy. She said that the deputy pocketed the note, but did nothing about it. When I asked Steve about it, he said that was "a great lie." He thought Martha might have been at Gasnick's house toward the end, but not during the search, and he didn't remember her writing a note or giving it to him to deliver. It seemed obvious to me that Martha was saying that to discredit Steve, but if there *was* a note, and she actually *was* close enough to hear what Steve said to the deputy, why didn't she just tell the deputy or give him the note herself?

Martha's red-headed stranger made a reappearance later in the trial when Billy's sister, Erica, tried to connect this mysterious man to Steve. She testified that she went to a nearby motorcycle shop to question people, and said that a man in a tan pickup, with red hair and a mustache, was there. She claimed he was acting "kind of off-the-wall," and said she saw a blanket on the floor of his truck that was covering a lump of something. She said she gave the truck's license number to the police, inferring that they did nothing with the information. Gasnick's lawyer, Roy Lane Dunnigan, asked her if she saw this red-headed man after that. Erica said she saw Steve with him at an area convenience store, and said, "Steve Sirois told the man that he had two weeks to get him his money, or else." She added that they stopped talking when they saw her, but the two of them boxed her in on the road when she left, Steve in front of her and the red-headed man behind her, but she said she got away from them when some other traffic appeared. Steve told me that none of that was true, that there was no red-headed man, no confrontation at a store, and that he didn't box Erica in on the road.

The trial lasted over a week, but at the end of it Billy was convicted of raping and murdering his step-daughter and was sentenced to death. A number of news reports indicated that, for the next five years, while Billy was appealing his conviction, the Gasnicks continued their campaign to free him. A last-minute retesting of the DNA evidence established that Gasnick was guilty by such a huge margin that there was no doubt of his guilt. One of the lab technicians testified that the DNA could only have come from Billy or an immediate family member. Interestingly, Steve said that once the lab report showed that a family member was the only other possible candidate for Jenny's murder, the Gasnicks seemed to back away from Billy temporarily; and that, just after the lab technician's testimony, Erica even apologized to Karen outside the courtroom. An article in the Chicago Tribune pointed out that a later test run by the Texas Department of Public Safety, on semen stains that were on Jenny's shorts "matched Billy Gasnick's DNA, with only a 1 in 65 quadrillion chance that someone else would have the same DNA pattern."

The damage to Steve's reputation was probably already done, though. By the time Gasnick was executed in September of 2000, the rumors had apparently spread so widely that they surfaced again when Steve was indicted in 2004. That's when Clyde Sledge contacted Roland Mathis with the news that private investigators were saying they believed that Steve could have been Jenny's killer. The publication in 2002 of the book, *A Gruesome End*, halfway between Gasnick's execution and Steve's indictment, probably added even more fuel to the local gossip fire. I believe that all of the book's references about Steve being Billy's best friend, and about Gasnick telling his family and his lawyer that Steve could have murdered Jenny, only made it more likely that some of the local populace would already have a bias against Steve by the time of the trials. Steve said the book was so popular in the Deep Springs area that it sold out at the local bookstore immediately. He had to order a copy and wait several weeks before he could try to read it.

I suppose I would be remiss if I didn't also mention, for what it's worth, that *A Gruesome End* was also published about the same time that Hanna claimed to have started telling her friends she was having sexual experiences with an older man.

Input From Other Media

As if the seven years' worth of media coverage for Gasnick's trial and appeals weren't enough, along with numerous statewide and national magazine articles and television coverage, followed by the publication of *A Gruesome End* in 2002, and compounded by all of the rumors about Steve, there also were a number of articles and stories about Hanna's 2004 accusations and Steve's arrest and indictment in the local paper, and on area radio and TV stations. Then, on July 19, 2006, the opening day of Steve's first trial, a local blog posted an article with this headline, "Steve Sirois, that name sure sounds familiar. Is this Billy Gasnick's friend?" Even before the first jury had made their decision, some of the people who would likely end up in the jury pool for the second trial were given a reminder of Steve's association with Gasnick. If the blog owner made the connection, so had other Ashwell County residents.

Also, between the two trials, the newspaper flooded its readers with a series of articles that could have raised the bias level against Steve even higher. On July 19th and 20th, the Deep Springs Gazette ran front page stories about the first trial, going into some detail about the charges; and, of course, mentioned Steve, but not Hanna, by name. Three days after that, the paper began running an eight-day series of front-page articles called "Sexual Assault and Abuse: The Most Personal Crime." In eight consecutive issues, the paper ran eight main articles, one of which, titled "Prosecutor says online predators are everywhere," featured Elmer Ross, the prosecutor for Steve's trial. There were also ten other articles about sex crimes and abuse, one editorial about the prevention and survival of sexual assault, and two more articles about local arrests for sex crimes. Twenty-three articles in eleven days either about Steve's trial or about sexual assault. Some of the articles in the series were written by Clyde Sledge, the Gazette editor who claimed, according to Roland Mathis, that private investigators from around the state were sure this trial would expose Steve as Jenny Luborsky's real killer. Obviously, a twenty-three-article salvo about sexual assault in the local newspaper, one of which highlighted Steve's prosecutor, might have further tainted the jury pool for his second trial, but the newspaper still wasn't done.

On August 7th, the originally scheduled start date for Trial #2 (just eighteen days after the first one ended) the paper published an article about Steve's attorney dropping out because Steve couldn't afford to pay him any more money. Then, on the 10th and 11th, there were two more articles (about soliciting sex on the Internet, and registered sex offenders), plus, on August 13th, the first of four more articles about the second trial was published. They covered jury selection, the two days of testimony, and the guilty verdict. Five of those seven articles were written by Clyde Sledge.

In 2018, the Deep Springs Gazette had a print circulation of about 6.000 (out of a little over 7,000 households). The 2009 online version received about 4,000 page views a day. Given the state of newspaper and magazine publication today, the print readership was probably higher than 6,000 in 2006, and the online readership lower. Deep Springs isn't a huge city. In 2006 the population was under 20,000, but the population of the whole county, from which the jury was drawn, was only about 15,000 more than that. In small communities, word spreads quickly and lasts long. Between the two trials, in addition to the 26 articles in 23 days, local radio and regional TV broadcasts, and probably a few sermons, the usual small-town gossip engine kept chugging along. I imagine that all of that sexual assault coverage must have had some influence on the second trial's potential jurors when they gathered at the county courthouse on August 14th.

Roland Mathis, during the 2004 brainstorming session, told Steve that he shouldn't worry about *A Gruesome End* influencing jurors because "people don't remember what they read." I don't think that's true, but please try to remember what you read in *this* book. Mathis may not have been worried, but Cleveland Sanford apparently was. One of the items he listed on the defense's Motion in Limine was that there should be no mention of "Any evidence or reference to Billy Gasnick." A Motion in Limine is an agreement between the judge and the attorneys that certain subjects will be off limits during a trial unless the attorneys first make an argument to the judge, showing why it would be necessary to present that information in open court. The judge would then decide if presenting it to the jury would be prejudicial to the defendant or not. None of the attorneys mentioned Gasnick during either trial, even though

Hanna hinted to Tom that they ought to. I'm firmly convinced that some of the people who ended up as jurors on both trials were well aware of Steve's connection to Gasnick and carried some of that prejudice into the jury room with them. I think others were also predisposed to believe Steve was guilty just because of the nature of the crime. In the chapter, *Jury Stuff*, I hope to convince you that the principle of "innocent until proven guilty" wasn't always in play during jury selection.

Also, the effect that the book, *A Gruesome End*, may have had on Steve's reputation can't be discounted. One reviewer of the book, Warren Hathaway, said in a review, "I worked as a private investigator before the 2006 prosecution of Steven Sirois, a prominent figure in this book...In the course of working this case, questions continually arose about Sirois and his involvement with Gasnick. This book sure didn't help Sirois' case." I spoke with Hathaway in 2020, and discovered he had worked with Tom briefly during the investigation. He also said he met Steve a few times, and could see that Steve found the book's references about him being Gasnick's "best friend" worrisome.

It's highly doubtful that Steve could have been given a fair trial in Ashwell County, maybe not anywhere in the State of Texas, partly because of his association with the Gasnick case, but also because, in addition to the media coverage, a number of other local elements might have corrupted the truth too. They were put into play against him before and during the trials. You've read about some of them already, but let's look at them as a group.

Flyers at the Lake, and a Family Feud

In April 2005, Eldon Carragan admitted to Tom that, he and his wife put flyers up in Steve's neighborhood that outlined the charges against him, spreading the word through the neighborhood that a suspected child molester was living near them, and notified them that it was Steve. Based on something Steve said during the brainstorming session, I believed for years that Tiffany Sperger's mother, Glenda, had probably posted the flyers. During the session, Roland Mathis handed Tom one of the flyers, saying, "This has been kind of posted around the lake." Steve said, "In my personal opinion, I think Glenda did it. The lady that runs security at Galley Shores told somebody else they knew who it was, but was not going to say." Galley Shores is one of three subdivisions that are clustered together on the northeastern edge of Lake Ashwell. The other two are Orchid Beach and Saddleview Cove. Steve and his family lived in Saddleview Cove, and Tiffany lived in Galley Shores. Don't let the names mislead you, these weren't wealthy, gated communities. Most of the houses were mobile homes or pre-fab construction. Tiffany's and Marri's houses were just two miles apart, and the two girls played together often. Steve felt that Tiffany's affidavit, with its claim about Marri seeing Hanna and Steve in a compromising position on a toilet, could have been generated because of a horrible experience Glenda might have had as a child, or even because of a minor feud Glenda had with Steve.

The Horrible Experience: This is something I couldn't verify, but Steve told me that, "When Glenda was a child, she was sexually molested by her father, and when Glenda's mother found out, she shot and killed him. Of course, Glenda has had issues about that ever since." Whether true or not, any person who had been through that kind of ordeal might be even more opposed to the abuse of children than the average person. Just knowing about her childhood might have been enough for Steve to suspect her of posting the flyers, but the Spergers were also upset with him about a disagreement over an auto repair.

The Family Feud: One day, long before the accusations, Steve drove Marri to Tiffany's house in Robin's Jeep so they could play. He said that Glenda's husband, Gilbert, was in the back yard, using a skid steer loader to cover the drainage pipes for his septic system, and the loader had become stuck in one of the trenches, so Steve offered to pull it out with the Jeep. He was successful after several attempts, but they noticed a clattering coming from the Jeep's engine. The skid steer loader was considerably heavier than the Jeep, so Steve thought the strain might have floated the Jeep's valves. The Spergers owned an auto repair shop in Deep Springs, so Gilbert said to bring it by and he would look at it. Steve did, and Glenda said they would give him a discount on the repair since he had hauled Gilbert out of the trench. When he picked the Jeep up, Glenda handed him a bill for over $700, and told him they had knocked some time off the repair just for him. Steve paid the bill, but when he started the Jeep it still made the same noise. He went back inside and complained, but Glenda tried to convince him that the noise wasn't that bad, and that it wasn't the same noise. Heated words were exchanged and Steve stormed out of there. He said the Jeep never ran right after that. Later, he heard that Glenda blamed him, saying the engine was already damaged. When the flyers went up in the neighborhood, Steve's immediate thought was that Glenda had done it. He didn't know that Eldon Carragan had admitted to creating the flyers until I told him a few years ago.

Here's what Steve said about Tiffany's testimony.

> "Tiffany said [*in the trials*] that she had been over at our house approximately eighty to ninety times. Which is a very strange number, considering that it matches the number of incidents Hanna was claiming soon after the charges were filed. Tiffany also claimed that she told her mother about what Marri told her. Here's what's weird. After this bathroom incident supposedly occurred, Tiffany testified that she continued to come over to visit Marri for dozens of weekends. Marri claims that she might have also stayed once at our house overnight. I don't really remember. In fact I only remember her from school and an occasional visit over many years. If any of what Tiffany said was true, why did Tiffany's mother, Glenda, allow Tiffany to continue to come over to our house? And, if the story was true in any way, shape or form, why didn't Glenda freak out a year to a year-and-a-half before the charges were filed, when Tiffany said she first told Glenda, or when Glenda supposedly 'counseled' Marri 'to tell her mother or their preacher' about it? Something Marri says never happened. Why didn't Glenda freak out then? This was clearly invented out of thin air, either caused by Glenda's reaction to the possibility of a child molester in the neighborhood, or as an opportunity to continue the feud against me for the crappy job they did on the Jeep (but wanted to blame

me for somehow). Or maybe both. Also, if Glenda did know about all this, where was she during the trial? Why didn't Ross have her testify? During the trial, Tiffany told a huge lie about Robin somehow chasing them on the highway. If this was so, don't you think they would have had her [*Glenda*] testify to corroborate Tiffany's story, and to verify that she had been told all of this by Tiffany? I believe that there was something in what Glenda was going to say that Ross didn't want the jury to hear."

Something else happened after the flyers were torn down. Child Protective Services received a complaint against Steve, saying he needed to leave the house because he was a sex offender and his daughter was only twelve years old. When CPS investigated and found out that he hadn't even been tried yet, they dropped the complaint. The call likely came from someone in the neighborhood, someone who was aware that Marri was twelve. Steve suspected that the same person who posted the flyers could have been the one who called CPS too. While Glenda could have called CPS, it could just as easily have been the Carragans, or Rebecca, or anyone else in the neighborhood. Whoever it was, CPS took no action against Steve.

There was one curious exchange during the second trial, though. Cleveland Sanford asked Tiffany if she or her mother reported Marri's comment to CPS. Tiffany said, "There was one time, I think it was my mom, who reported their family to CPS, but it wasn't because of that." Sanford, probably assuming she was referring to the CPS call that happened after the flyers were torn down, said, "Okay. But that would have been long after these allegations were made, correct?" Tiffany said, "Actually, no -- well, my mom reported it back in…" Sanford stopped her from finishing the sentence by objecting to her statement as hearsay, and Judge Hawes sustained his objection. Was Tiffany about to admit that it was her mother who made the call to CPS after the flyers came down, but was confused about the date? Her testimony did seem to indicate that her mother did call CPS at some point, but we don't know when or what for.

What is undeniable is that at least a few people in Steve's own neighborhood were bothered by the accusations against him long before he came to trial. These are just a few samples of the vitriol displayed against Steve by Ashwell County residents. Guilty until proven innocent appeared to have been part of the local *modus operandi* long before the trials happened.

Debunking Tiffany's Story

I will occasionally dispense with an accusation when it arises instead of dealing with it later. This is one of those times. I've given you two reasons why the Spergers could have had some animosity toward Steve (Glenda's possible childhood trauma and the feud over the Jeep repair), but here's why I believe Tiffany's story is actually untrue. In her affidavit and in the trials, Tiffany claimed that Marri told her she saw Steve lying on top of Hanna, on the toilet, in the Sirois' bathroom. Tiffany also testified that, a month after Marri told her this, she repeated the story to her mother, and said that her mother told Marri to tell her mother or her preacher about it. According to Marri, none of that happened.

This chronology for the summer of 2004 might help explain what did happen, though. After Steve was indicted in June, Eldon Carragan had derogatory flyers posted in their neighborhood. In July, Steve was arrested, but posted bail that same day and was released on bond. After that, someone called CPS, complaining that 12-year-old Marri shouldn't be living in the same household with a child molester. On September 16th, after the CPS complaint was dismissed, Glenda brought Tiffany into the sheriff's office to give a sworn statement about what Marri supposedly told her. Think about the progression of those events. I'll come back to them in a minute.

Nearly two years later, when Tiffany testified, her story had changed. Every time she was asked about her conversation with Marri, she qualified her answers. In the September 2004 affidavit, she said the conversation with Marri was "about 1 1/2 to 2 years" before that (which would be sometime between September 2002 and March 2003). In Trial #1, she said it took place "sometime in 2002," but later in that trial she said "it was maybe about a year or two" before the affidavit (which expands the time of the talk with Marri to anytime between September 2002 and September 2003). In Trial #2 she said they "might have been in about" the fifth or sixth grade. Marri and Tiffany were in the 5th grade in 2001-2002, and in 6th in 2002-2003.

About, *sometime*, *maybe about*, *might have been*, *fifth* or *sixth grade*. Taking all of that into account, Tiffany's alleged conversation with Marri could have been between September of 2001 and May of 2003. That's quite a spread. Why didn't any of the attorneys try to pin her down to a date? Her vagueness about when it took place was one of the first things in the trial that forced me to use a calendar and create a timeline.

In Trial #1, Elmer Ross asked Tiffany how she was able to remember the exact details of what Marri told her. She said it was because "I told my mom what she told me, and I wrote it down. I don't have it, but I went and told -- I think it was Willard Knox, is the sheriff I talked to." Ross asked her when she talked to Knox. She said "September 16, 2004." Was the jury supposed to believe that more than two years later she could remember the exact date she gave an affidavit, and the name of the man she gave it to, but couldn't remember the year or even the grade she was in when the conversation with Marri allegedly took place? It makes more sense to me that her dates were so fuzzy because the conversation was invented.

If I took Tiffany's testimony literally (that *she* wrote it down, but she didn't have what she wrote, but then she told Willard Knox, so *he* wrote it down, and that's why she remembered it), it makes very little sense to me. Also, according to that testimony, the conversation took place sometime between eighteen months and three years before she spoke to Knox. How did waiting that long help her remember the details?

Despite Tiffany's assertions about what Marri supposedly saw, when Ross asked Tiffany if she had ever seen "any inappropriate touching or anything like that" between Steve and Hanna, she said, "No, sir." When she was asked if Steve had ever made "any type of inappropriate move" toward her, she answered, "No" to that too.

Marri, in Trial #1, was asked whether she told Tiffany about witnessing an incident in the bathroom between Hanna and Steve. She said, "No, sir." When she was asked if she told anyone anything like that, Marri answered, "I just told Tiffany that I thought she [*Hanna*] was following him way too much." In Trial #2, Elmer Ross asked her if she had ever seen Hanna and Steve "doing anything inappropriate," and whether she had ever seen them in a bathroom or on a bed together. She answered, "No, sir" to both of those.

Marri has been consistent, in conversations I've had with her since, in saying that she didn't say anything like that to Tiffany or anyone else, and never saw anything inappropriate happen between Hanna and Steve. I asked her about the "following him way too much" comment, and she said she did tell Tiffany about Hanna following Steve around, but not about anything else. She said she might have mentioned that to Tiffany because she was angry at Hanna over something that happened when they were all preparing an enchilada dinner. She said, "I used to like to help Dad cook, and there was one time I got upset because she didn't want me to help…from my perspective, it's my house, it's my dad. Why can't I help?" I asked her how Hanna reacted to that. She said, "I don't really remember her reaction, but I know she wasn't happy after that. She always wanted to be upset about something." Steve told me that Hanna marched off into one of the other rooms and pouted the rest of that night, saying she didn't want supper, but said that later Robin saw her in the kitchen, eating enchiladas out of the casserole dish. Both Beau and Steve verified that Hanna did follow them around sometimes, and they would give her odd jobs to do to keep her busy, like cleaning the gunk off the pickup when they were working on it. They have both also said that Hanna maintained a fairly constant state of anger, often complaining and having shouting matches with her mother over trivial things.

I don't know if Marri's "following him way too much" comment adequately explains the origins of Tiffany's story about Marri, but there's more from Tiffany's testimony we need to look at. She was asked a variety of questions to establish whether she was ever in a position to witness anything happening between Steve and Hanna. In Trial #1, she was asked if she had ever spent the night at the Sirois' house. She said, "<u>Many times</u>." She was asked if Hanna spent the night the same night she did, and Tiffany answered, "Probably once or twice." She was asked to verify if it was unusual if she and Hanna spent the night at the same time, and Tiffany agreed, saying she "<u>didn't really spend the night over there that much</u>." Did Tiffany spend the night many times, as she testified, or not that much, as she also testified?

Later, when Bevin Jenkins cross-examined her, he asked how many times she was there when Hanna was. Pressed for a number, she said, "Eighty, ninety, maybe. It was up there. I was over there a lot." In Trial #2, Tiffany was asked about it again, and repeated her assertion that she had been to the house "Ninety-ish" times. In Trial #1, Steve was asked if Tiffany was "regularly at your house in the years between 2001 and 2004," the timeframe of the allegations. He said, "No, sir, not actually. She had been at our house, but my daughter spent more time over at Tiffany's house than ours." Steve didn't testify in the second trial, but he has said several things since about Tiffany's statements. Aside from not remembering her being at the house very often, he didn't remember her ever spending the night. He told me that, typically, Glenda usually insisted on Marri playing at their house rather than the other way around. If the story about Glenda's childhood is true, that would be understandable. She would naturally want to keep her daughter close to home. I asked Marri if Tiffany ever spent the night with her, and she said, "No, I don't believe so." I asked, "You don't think she did at all?" She said, "No, I don't think she ever did. I always stayed at her house." I asked Beau the same question, and he said, "Honestly, I don't remember that. I don't remember if she did or not. I don't *think* she did. I think Marri always stayed over there."

So, Tiffany gave what appears to be a highly inflated number for how often she had been to the Sirois' house to play with Marri, but also said that she had maybe spent the night a couple of times (which might also have been inflated). Her numbers, "Eighty, ninety" and "Ninety-ish" are interesting in view of the fact that everyone else says she wasn't there much at all, but also because, by the time of the trials (according to their trial testimony), Tiffany and Hanna considered themselves to be friends, and "80 to 90" also happens to match the number of times Hanna claimed she was molested. When did Tiffany become friends with Hanna? After the charges were filed in April 2004? Or when Steve was indicted that June? Or after the anti-Steve flyers were posted in his neighborhood? Or after Steve was arrested in July? Or after someone called Child Protective Services with no result? Or could it have been after Tiffany's affidavit was created in September? Is there a connection between any of those events and Tiffany's and Hanna's friendship?

I realize that the people who are refuting Tiffany's story are members of Steve's family, but here's some food for thought. If it actually was true that Tiffany told her mother "about a month" after Marri allegedly shared this supposed secret with Tiffany (sometime between September 2001 and mid-2003), why on earth would Glenda—especially if she did experience a childhood trauma herself—allow Tiffany to continue to go over to the Sirois' house for another year or more? If Tiffany's story is true, why didn't Glenda report the incident to CPS in 2002 or 2003? And why didn't Glenda testify in either trial?

For proof of a different sort, let's look at the bathroom itself, and compare it to Tiffany's claim. You might want to take a look at the floor plan of the bathroom on the blog. It will help make it obvious why this incident didn't happen.

https://aggravatedbook.com/other-images/

In the affidavit, Tiffany said that Marri told her she walked into the bathroom, and saw Steve and Hanna inside, and saw that "Hanna was sitting on the toilet" and saw that Steve "was lying on top of her." Here's a two-part question. How likely is that physical act, and how likely is it that Marri could have seen it?

In Trial #1, Tiffany said that Marri "walked through her parents' bedroom and into the bathroom where she saw the light was off and she saw her father and Hanna Penderfield." She added, "I'm almost positive that she mentioned near the toilet. It was a really long time ago." She was asked what Marri said they were doing, and Tiffany said, "She said that he was on top of her. And that right when she saw it she got scared and confused. She turned around, walked away."

In Trial #2, when she was asked what Marri saw in the bathroom, Tiffany said that Marri told her "that the door was kind of open, kind of -- not really cracked open, but, you know, probably about maybe that big, you know, somewhere around there…" [*Tiffany apparently held up her hands to indicate how wide she thought Marri must have meant by* "kind of open." *Would that be called a hearsay by gesture comment?*] She continued, "…and she kind of looked in because she had to go to the bathroom. That bathroom is used a lot, you know, all the time. And so, she kind of looked in there and I think she mentioned something about a night light. And that's when she saw her father, Steve Sirois, on top of Hannah Penderfield." After listening to Tiffany take those five convoluted sentences to get to the point, Elmer Ross asked her if Marri said anything about what Steve and Hanna were doing, and Tiffany said, "No, sir, she did not." He then asked her if Marri had said where in the bathroom Steve and Hanna were. She took another six sentences to explain that the sink was to the left of the door and the tub and toilet were to the right, and that Marri said they were "near the right-hand side, kind of."

[*Let me make it clear that this was an interior bathroom with no windows, and would have been completely dark if the lights were off. We started with Tiffany's affidavit, where she said that Marri just walked in and* saw them, *definitely* on the toilet, *but there was no mention of lights. Then, in Trial #1, Tiffany testified that* the light was off, *but Marri* still saw them, *and they were* maybe somewhere near the toilet. *In Trial #2, though, she said the door was* "kind of open," *and described its state of openness as* "maybe that big," *even though she wasn't there to see it herself. But this time she said that there might also have been* a night light, *and Steve was definitely* on top of *Hanna, but they were* "kind of," *sort of,* "near the right-hand side" *of the bathroom. Somewhere? Maybe? Sort of? Tiffany's story seemed to be shifting like a queasy stomach on the high seas.*]

We've already established that Tiffany was unsure about when Marri allegedly told her this tale. She also gave the sheriff and the courts three different versions of what happened, all under oath, and each successive version seemed more uncertain than the previous one. This would be a good time to look at the floor plan on the blog if you haven't already.

It's 5 feet from the right wall of the bathroom to the edge of the door. In that space are a 3-foot-wide bathtub and an 18-inch-wide toilet (which leaves 3 inches on each side of the toilet). Try to figure out if the following acrobatics are physically possible. For Hanna to have been sitting on the toilet, and Steve to have been lying on top of her, he would have to lie crosswise, either facing the sink or facing the tub. He obviously couldn't face her and lie on top of her while she was on the toilet. Facing the sink, he would have to have been sideways in the 3-foot-wide tub, but Steve is almost 6 feet tall. Also, the rim of the tub is 26 inches off the floor, but the toilet seat is only 16 inches high, 10 inches lower than the tub rim. What kind of balancing magic would that have required, what kind of sex act could they have been doing, and how could Marri have even seen anything at all in a room that dark?

If he had been facing the tub instead, his body would have blocked the door, and no one would have been able to enter at all. Neither of those positions work physically. And, in a house where, as Tiffany testified, the "bathroom is used a lot, you know, all the time," people were constantly in and out. If someone had been stupid enough to try something like that, wouldn't they have closed and locked the door, not left it ajar? Even if they did lock the door, whoever was waiting to use the restroom would see them both when they left. I believe this was just an absurd fifth grade fantasy that was invented five months or so after the charges were filed. It also appears that Tiffany recognized the ridiculousness of her "on the toilet" remark because her story changed in Trial #1 to say that Marri told her that Steve and Hanna were somewhere "near the toilet," not on it. And her description then became even more vague for the second trial, when she said they were "near the right-hand side, kind of."

Obviously, I don't know why Tiffany would invent this tale, but if we couple her family's background and the ongoing feud with Steve with the notoriety of the Gasnick trial and the subsequent rumors in the area, it's easy to believe that Tiffany might have been encouraged by someone to come forward as another way to either get even with Steve or to do her part to rid the area of a child molester. Her story doesn't make any sense for all the reasons listed above, but here's one more bit of testimony to seal its fate.

Hanna did claim, in Trial #2, that Marri had seen her and Steve engaged in some sort of sexual activity on two other occasions. She said that one of the times happened when she and Marri were asleep in the same bed. She said that Marri woke up for a second, and that, later, maybe the next morning, Marri asked Steve if he had been in the room with them. Hanna also claimed that on another occasion she and Steve "snook" into his bedroom, and Marri walked in on them on the bed together (where Robin was supposedly passed out). Marri completely denies ever witnessing anything like either of those incidents; and, of course, Steve denies that anything happened, period.

Here's the statement that I believe destroys Tiffany's testimony about this, though. Cleveland Sanford, in Trial #2, asked Hanna if there were "any occurrences as far as Marri witnessing anything that occurred in a bathroom." Hanna said, "No, sir, I believe that was mistaken." So, Hanna also apparently saw the ridiculousness of Tiffany's claim and disavowed it. Interestingly, Hanna made that statement in Trial #2 before Tiffany testified, undermining Tiffany's affidavit and all of her testimony, but the prosecution had Tiffany testify anyway. Why would they do that? Steve has offered a simple explanation. He's sure that Tiffany's primary purpose was just to discredit Marri's testimony. Marri was on the prosecution's witness list, even though her testimony would almost certainly be in Steve's favor. Why? I believe they had Tiffany testify after Marri in both trials to keep Marri from fighting back against anything Tiffany said. If the jury believed Tiffany, then Marri's testimony against Hanna would have had less value, but even Hanna said that the weird incident in the bathroom didn't happen.

Was Hanna responsible for the spread of rumors about Steve during the two years between the accusation and the trials? I don't know, but she did appear to be sowing seeds of mistrust as late as her May 2006 interview with Tom. He asked her if there were any *women* in the area that Steve might have had affairs with. Apparently ignoring the intent of his question, Hanna said, "I have suspicions about his daughter. I am very concerned for her, and I wish that he would get out of that house. I understand that he moved out for a short time because Vivian Vaughn threatened to call the cops if he was not dealt with, because of the charges that were filed, and his daughter is underage."

Steve said that, as far as he knows, there was no one named Vivian Vaughn in the area. She might have meant Steve's neighbor, Vivian Percet, but she didn't call the CPS about Steve. In fact, she testified in his favor in both trials. Steve never moved out of the house. He was out of state for those few months in Florida, but to earn money, not because he was forced to leave, and Hanna was apparently aware of the Florida trip anyway, because she told Tom, "He went to Florida for a few months for a job or something. He probably found a little girl there. I have no idea, but I wouldn't put it past him." With her Vivian Vaughn comment, though, Hanna appeared to be saying that Steve was gone from the house twice after the accusations, once by court order, and once for work. It isn't true, but I felt that much of what Hanna said clouded her tale with additional layers of confusion.

Contreltophobia: Even if we assume that only a tiny number of people in the United States suffer from a clinically serious fear of sexual abuse, rape or molestation (a condition known as contreltophobia), it is still highly likely that a large percentage of the population does at least worry about the possibility of those acts being committed against them or their loved ones. One likely reason for that level of concern is because of the number of sensationalized stories about a wide variety of crimes that we are bombarded with every day. Robberies, rapes, murders, and other violent crimes are splashed across our nightly news broadcasts and in our news feeds so frequently that it's easy to believe that our entire society is out of control.

The truth is that our perceptions of danger are way out of proportion to the probability of those acts actually happening to us individually, but many people are still worried about the possibility. We warn our children to never talk to strangers, and we have locks and alarms on our cars and our houses, and now many even have cameras in their doorbells. It's almost as if we are in prisons of our own making. Some of these fears are wired into our DNA, but they're reinforced by the continual reporting of terrible things on the nightly news. Things like sexual predation.

Since a large percentage of the population understandably has a natural dislike, or even a hatred of people who commit sexually predatory acts, isn't it also likely that many of those same people feel an inherent bias against anyone who has been *accused* of committing a sex crime, whether that person is guilty or not? Cleveland Sanford told me that, as a defense attorney, when he stood in front of a pool of prospective jurors he would often say, "Okay, how many of you, when you came in here today…said, 'I wonder what he did?' Because it's human nature, you know. It's not, 'I wonder what he's accused of.' It's not 'I wonder why he's here.' It's 'I wonder what he did.'"

I've already mentioned Ada Dixon's book, and how I believe Hanna may have used it to help her learn how to convince a jury that she had been molested. I don't agree with the nature of the book in several respects, but I do agree with one statement Dixon made about jurors. She said, "A juror may enter the courtroom with preconceived ideas about what type of girl gets raped or physically abused." I do agree that some jurors go into trials with specific, built-in biases about victims of abuse, but they may also have equally strong or stronger biases against child molesters, and I think some of the jurors in Steve's trial did as well.

Prospective jurors often assume that the defendant should have to prove they are innocent, even though the burden of proof legally rests with the prosecution, not with the defense. The way jurors approach a trial seems to me to often be the exact opposite of the way they are legally required to. The difficulties innocent defendants must overcome are hard enough without the albatross of "guilty until proven innocent" hanging around their necks too.

Analysis

A Reminder: This chapter hasn't been about Steve's actual innocence. Its purpose has been to display that a frame of mind existed that very likely affected the ability of some of his jurors to decide rationally, based on the evidence presented to them, instead of emotionally, which may have led to an unfair trial for Steve.

In the two years and three months leading up to his first trial, a number of rumors were started or continued, all of which portrayed Steve as the guilty party. Any one of those rumors could have been damaging by itself. When blended with rumors circulated between 1993 and 2000, and then followed by the publication of *A Gruesome End* in 2002, false stories about Steve likely permeated Ashwell County and were recycled multiple times, long before his first trial got underway. Hanna attempted to insert the Gasnick case into her interview with Tom when she brought up the subject of "the Billy Gasnick thing," telling him that Steve "was a suspect in that case" even though the DNA and pubic hair samples he gave had ruled him out. Her comments, and her mother's comment to me, show that they were both familiar with *A Gruesome End*, and likely with whatever else was being ground in the county's rumor mill at the time.

The subject of prejudice also surfaced during jury selection, sometimes against Steve because he was the accused, and sometimes against the fear of sexual assault itself. Consider the responses people had in Steve's neighborhood and around the area; and the coverage online and in newspapers and news programs. Add to that the unjust rumors being spread by locals, and it's easy to see how those fears and prejudices could have infected the minds of some jury members. I hope to be able to show you, in the *Jury Stuff* chapter, how only one or two members of a jury, with a mindset like that, could have swayed the other jurors into trading votes, and (in possible violation of the judge's instructions) may have made decisions that sent Steve to prison for thirty-five years. We'll cover that in the next section, *The Trials*.

The Trials

This section, *The Trials*, is divided into three chapters, *Just Before the Trials*, *The First Trial*, and *The Second Trial*. Aside from covering a few important last-minute interviews and some decisions Steve made as the trial approached, there is also a basic overview of each trial, who the participants were, what the basic arguments were, and what the outcome was. The second trial will be more detailed, since (because it was the trial where Steve was convicted) it's the more important of the two in a legal sense. From there we'll move on to the *Proof of Innocence* section.

Just Before the Trials

"Desperation is sometimes as powerful an inspirer as genius."
Benjamin Disraeli

"Steve's money comes out of Yankee-ville. They give me money, and I spend it for a while, and I go ask for more money."
Roland Mathis

[Subsections in this Chapter: Pre-Trial Desperation // The New Lawyer // Tom's Final Three Interviews]

Pre-Trial Desperation

As the trial got closer, Steve's doubts that Roland Mathis would do a good job for him resurfaced. He called me in early-March 2006, a few weeks after he returned from Florida. All the money he had earned there evaporated almost instantly, and the family finances were back to zero, but at least they weren't in the hole. Worried about Mathis' ability to represent him, he was panicked and wanted to revisit the idea of hiring the expensive lawyers from California. After we spoke, I sent an email to my other siblings, letting them know that Philip and Harry Newbold and I were going to discuss the possibility of Steve borrowing another advance against his inheritance. I asked them for their input, and to let us know how they felt about that. They mostly deferred to whatever Phillip, Harry, and I decided. The first trial was scheduled for March 20th, so we all thought it could happen very soon. I don't think any of us realized that it was still another four months away, or that it had been scheduled and postponed at least a dozen times already. As far as Steve knew, when we talked to Harry the trial was right around the corner, marching rapidly toward a collision with him.

As I explained earlier, none of us knew what kind of an inheritance we might eventually get, or when that would be, so our primary concern was with making sure Mom was taken care of. As it turned out, after she passed away in 2009, we each did get an inheritance, but it was modest. Steve's share wouldn't have even covered the original quote from the California firm, and there still would have been no guarantee they would have won that first trial. Win or lose, Steve and his family would have been saddled with a mountain of debt.

Harry did agree to advance Steve the money to hire Bevin Jenkins, a Texas member of the California firm, who agreed to try the case for a flat fee of $25,000. Steve released Mathis and hired Jenkins.

When Mathis originally hired Tom Swearingen, at the 2004 brainstorming session, he asked Tom for a cost estimate, knowing it could depend on some extrinsic factors like the difficulty of locating individuals. Tom said it might be "as much as $2,000" by the time he had interviewed everyone, explaining that his rate was $75 an hour. Mathis told Tom that "Steve's money comes out of Yankee-ville" [*Massachusetts*], adding, "They give me money, and I spend it for a while, and I go ask for more money." Mathis turned to Steve and asked him if he knew how much more was available, Steve said that he and Harry had spoken, and that Harry "didn't say it was drying up." He thought there was still money available for them to use. Mathis had enough cash in the account to get Tom started, so he gave him a $600 retainer.

A year after Mom died, Harry sent me an accounting of the funds that had been paid out to Mathis for Steve's defense. By the time of the brainstorming session, sometime in late-November 2004, Mathis had already received $7,500. Before he was replaced with Bevin Jenkins in March 2006, though, he had received $30,613.02. Some of that went to Tom, of course.

The New Lawyer

For several months before this, Steve had been feeling that Mathis wasn't doing enough for him. He couldn't pinpoint exactly what it was, but he just thought Mathis' heart wasn't in it. He also wondered if the Belisle family had been exerting some influence on Mathis. Since Carl Belisle was a client of Mathis' father, and also a potential future client for Mathis, Steve thought that he must have been sweating bullets, probably thinking something like, "What if I get Steve off for having molested Carl's grand-niece? He'll never hire me again." Steve wondered how good a job Mathis would do in court with thoughts like that swirling through his head, so, on March 17, 2006, with the trial scheduled for March 20th, Steve filed for permission to switch lawyers. Harry wired a check for $15,015 to Bevin Jenkins. Another $10,000 followed near the end of April. In March and April, Mathis was also sent two final checks for an additional $2,684.20 to settle accounts.

Nearly $60,000 had been paid out to the two lawyers, and the trial was still over two months away. When I told Steve (in 2010) that Mathis had received over $33,000, he was shocked. He had been under the impression that it had been about half that amount.

The trial was rescheduled for May 15th, and Steve and Jenkins got busy, believing they had just under two months to prepare. Tom Swearingen was retained again to help bring Jenkins up to speed. Of course they couldn't know then that the trial would be rescheduled twice more before finally getting in front of jurors in mid-July. When I asked Steve if he ever regretted making the decision to switch lawyers at that point, he said, "Something Roland said has always bothered me. When I went to tell Roland that I had hired Bevin Jenkins, he said, 'Well, there's not much else I can do. It's all in god's hands now anyway.' This bothered me more because of the way he said it. He was very nonchalant about it as if he were expecting it, or was relieved. What I wanted to tell him was, 'I thought I was hiring a lawyer. If I had known I was getting God along with it, I would have felt better.' I bit my tongue and let it pass."

Bevin Jenkins was paid $25,015.00 for defending Steve at his first trial, and he gained a mistrial. Once that verdict was rendered, Jenkins asked for another $20,000 to represent Steve at the second one. When he found out Steve didn't have it (the family was completely broke by that time), Jenkins dropped out. Would Roland Mathis have done a decent job representing Steve in that first trial? We can speculate forever about how much money Steve would have had for his defense in a second trial if he hadn't changed from Mathis to Jenkins; or how much more easily they would have been able to regroup their finances if Mathis had won, but there's no way we'll ever know what the outcome of that would have been.

Tom's Final Three Interviews

As the first trial edged closer, there were still people that Tom wanted to interview. He had been trying to talk to Hanna since early 2005, but her mother and the DA were resolutely opposed to the idea. In May 2006, though, Tom did manage to get an interview with her, and with Angie Womack and Betty Stavens, two friends of Hanna's. Here's how that happened.

Hanna's Interview: Tom's interview with Hanna took place in May 2006, a full thirteen months after Josh Chilmark's interview. Hers lasted for two-and-a-half hours and was wide-ranging. After I got an audio copy of it from Tom in 2013, it became my primary touchstone in trying to determine what was true and what wasn't. By comparing the differences in Hanna's affidavit to comments she made to Ada Dixon and to Tom, and then to what she testified to in each of the trials, I was able to finally realize how many potential lies were spread across the spectrum of her narrative. I'll cover a few things here from the interview, but will rely on it most often in the *Proof of Innocence* section.

Mathis had tried to arrange an interview with her from the very beginning, but his requests had all been refused. Now, with a new attorney, Tom was tasked with digging for information again, and he got a break. He heard a rumor that Hanna had an older boyfriend who worked as a bouncer in a local night club. Tom told me that the club manager found out that the boyfriend had obtained a fake ID for still-underage Hanna, and that he had been letting her into the club. Hanna was banned from the club and the boyfriend was fired. Tom verified this with the manager, tracked the boyfriend down at his job at a local restaurant, and spoke to him briefly, leaving a business card with him. Tom said he thought the guy was just "kind of a boyfriend. I think he wanted to be a boyfriend more than she wanted it." Shortly after that, Hanna called him and said, "You've been talking to my boyfriend. I want to talk to you. I want to tell you my side of it." Was Hanna, not knowing how much her boyfriend had told Tom, trying to do some damage control? I don't know, but that's a possibility.

In the interview, she provided Tom with a massive amount of

information about incidents that would become important to me in my investigation, but she still managed to not give him any details about the three counts against Steve. Either Hanna intentionally avoided talking about those things or Tom wasn't able to steer her toward them. She did veer off track frequently, and Tom had to keep pulling her back to the topic at hand. For example, they did talk about the night they went to see *Harry Potter* (but not about later that evening, when Count I supposedly took place); and about the night of the rodeo (but not what might have happened after they arrived in her home town); and about the night of Beau's 21st birthday party, but she told Tom she didn't think she was there later that night (when the incidents ostensibly occurred). Despite dodging those topics, she did give him a lot of detail about several other things (like the cross-country meet, multiple sleepovers with her friends, and her discussions with Josh Chilmark).

Tom also asked Hanna for the names of people who could verify her story, and for the names of any other girls who had regularly been to Steve's house. Finding someone who could corroborate her story was a theme he returned to again and again. Toward the end of the interview she gave Tom the names of eight people she said could help him, along with a few of their phone numbers. The names she gave him only resulted in interviews with two people, Angie Womack and Betty Stavens, but what those girls said didn't help Hanna's case any. The interviews also weren't important to Hanna in any legal sense because neither of those girls testified in the trials, but they did reveal a few things that were enlightening when considered with other material. Let's look at both of them.

Angie's Interview: Hanna probably thought that Angie Womack would support her story, but her version varied enough from Hanna's that it just made me doubt it more. Angie was a schoolmate and friend of Hanna's. Tom only got to talk to her for about ten minutes before someone interrupted them and said Angie's mother didn't want her to say anything else. Before she was cut off, though, she did disclose a few interesting things.

Hanna's and Angie's estimates of when a particular sleepover took place are at odds with each other. Angie said that Hanna told her and one other girl, at a sleepover, that she was being sexually abused. She said this sleepover happened in April of "2003? 2002? Somewhere around there," and said that a group of girls were talking "about guys" when "Hanna got upset over one of the comments that was made…got really sad about something, and ran into the bathroom." She added that she and a girl named Suzanna Bushnell followed Hanna into the bathroom, where she "just broke down and told us." Angie said that Hanna "wouldn't tell us who it was," but "he forced her to do, you know, sexual activity." Angie also pointed out that the girls at that sleepover weren't talking about sex at all because they were in junior high, and "everybody in that room didn't really know about sex."

In contrast, Hanna told Tom that all the girls were talking about their sexual experiences with guys when Angie (with no mention of Suzanna) took her into the bathroom and asked, "Who is doing all this to you?" In the trials, Hanna said nothing about being sad and rushing into a bathroom, but said that she told all of the girls openly. She told Tom, though, that Angie pulled her away from the others so she could talk to her in private. Unsurprisingly, Hanna didn't mention either Angie or Suzanna in either trial, and neither Angie nor Suzanna testified. Telling her friends about her abuse at sleepovers isn't included in either her affidavit or in Dixon's summary. Looking at just Tom's interview and the two trials, she told three different variations on the same theme. What's common to most of Hanna's versions is that she said she attended sleepovers (plural) in 2003, during which all the girls told the others how far they had gone with guys, and she said that the girls who had gone the farthest without actually having sex gained the most popularity within the group. In Trial #1, though, Hanna placed the focus on herself, saying that they were her sleepovers, and she gained the most popularity because she had the most experience. Hanna putting herself at the center of attention wasn't unusual.

Betty's Interview: Based on what Tom found out, I believe Hanna probably didn't want him to to actually interview Betty Stavens. I think she mentioned Betty's name only to be able to bring up the subject of Billy Gasnick. Here's how that happened.

Tom asked Hanna repeatedly if she knew of any other young girls who might have been involved with Steve, but during most of the interview she couldn't come up with any names. She seemed to struggle, trying to remember one particular girl for several minutes, before saying, "I thought about it, and I still can't remember that girl's name, and it really bugs me because she was a friend of mine. I keep thinking it starts with a "B," but I don't know what it is." She paused, then groaned in frustration. Tom asked her if the girl was still living in the area. Hanna said, "Her mom's name is ...Karen. I think it's her mom. It's..." She had a sudden realization. "Her name is Betty. Her name is Betty." Tom was confused at first, asking if the mother's name was Karen Betty, but Hanna told him no, the girl's and the mother's first names were Betty and Karen, but she couldn't remember what the last name was. She said that Betty's mother was friends with her mother, and that Betty's "real dad's name is Andy," and that they met Andy and Karen and Betty through Steve. Hanna said, "I don't know what his last name is. He works for the police department, I do believe. I think he was a deputy or something."

In the brainstorming session, Steve told Tom about Betty and her parents, Andy and Wendy (not Andy and Karen), so Tom already knew who Betty was, and knew that Andy's father, Greg Stavens, had been the chief investigator on the Gasnick case. When Hanna said that Betty Stavens' dad was a deputy, Tom fed her the rest of it, "There was an Andy Stavens that was a deputy." Hanna's voice brightened up. She said, "That's what it is. It's an Andy Stavens, because it's Betty Stavens."

Tom asked her whether Steve was involved with Betty. When Hanna said she didn't think so, Tom asked her why. She paused before answering, then said, "I never saw him act the way he does with me around anybody else, but then again he was very good at hiding things. [*Here it comes.*] Did you know he was also indirectly involved with the ...Jenny ...something ...gee, I don't remember ...Jenny..." [*She paused again, wait for it.*] "...Jenn-- ...the Billy Gasnick thing? Jenny Luborsky, I think? He was a suspect in that case. And I ha-- …I …my instinct tells me that he probably either messed with her while Billy was doing it, or before ...but no, he didn't kill her. He doesn't have the balls." Tom said, "So you think ...you think he messed with her?" Hanna said, "I think so." Tom informed Hanna that Rebecca, Jenny's sister, denied that Steve had ever touched her (which was the common comment from all of the other girls Tom interviewed). Hanna quickly changed the subject, suggesting that Tom might try to talk to "any of Marri's little friends" instead. It felt to me that Hanna spent all of that time and effort faux-fumbling for Betty's name so she could bring Billy Gasnick into the conversation, and then accuse Steve of possibly murdering or at least molesting Jenny Luborsky. There were also a number of other places in the interview where Hanna seemed to be trying to send Tom off onto wild goose chases or to make him believe that some unfounded rumor was true.

Tom did talk to Betty with her mother, Wendy, present. They lived in a town about sixty miles away from Deep Springs, but Tom interviewed them there at their home. Betty's voice was that of a quiet, shy teen girl, possibly embarrassed at having to have this conversation with an adult male, but she did seem sincere in her answers. To begin with, she said she had known Steve since she was a baby, and she came to the house to visit Marri "about once every six months, not very often." Betty was only connected to Jenny Luborsky because, after Billy Gasnick had been sent to prison, Betty's father, Andy, married Jenny's mother, Karen. Was that tenuous connection to Gasnick enough for Hanna to have brought the subject up? Maybe, if she was desperate enough to discredit Steve. Betty did say she knew Hanna, having met her at the Sirois' house. She said it was typical for the adults to sit outside while she and Marri were inside watching TV. She said that she and Hanna weren't really friends (as Hanna claimed), more like acquaintances, and she mostly hung out with Marri while she was there.

Tom asked her the usual series of questions: Did she ever see Steve touch Hanna in any way that would be inappropriate? Or see him hug Hanna or hold her? Or ever pat her on the rear end, or anything like that? She answered "No" to all of that. Just to be sure, he asked, "So, nothing that you know of happened to either you or to Hanna while you were there?" She said, "No, nothing ever happened to me. Nothing ever happened to Hanna that I know of." And he asked, "Have you ever seen Steve act inappropriately with any young lady?" She said, "No." In response to other questions, she indicated that she didn't know why Hanna would have made the accusation, and that she didn't know whether Steve was ever alone with Hanna. She did say, though, when Tom asked her, that Steve and Robin did drink a lot. Tom also asked her if she could tell him who else might have been there when she was. She mentioned several people: her dad and her stepmother and stepsister (Karen and Rebecca), also Jessica and Judy Higham, and usually several neighbors. She said that Tom might want to talk to the Highams [*he already had, and Judy testified for Steve*]. Tom asked if Steve made a habit of going into the house a lot while the kids were inside. Betty said, "He went in there just to get a Coke, or get another beer or something, and he'd come in there and check on us for a bit, and then he'd go back outside."

Betty didn't remember being there when Hanna threw the fit over cooking enchiladas, but when Tom asked if Hanna ever got mad about anything else, she said, "Well, she would. She had a short temper. She'd get mad. I don't know what she'd get mad about, but she was mad pretty much all the time she was over there." Tom asked her for some specifics, and Betty said, "Well, she always had, like, an attitude. I didn't really understand why." Tom asked her what that looked like, and Betty said, "She would always say, 'I'm so mad,' and just, like, walk off, or just go sit by herself the rest of the night." When Tom asked her if she could think of any reason why Hanna accused Steve, she said that she had been shocked when her mother asked her about it.

Wendy entered the conversation at that moment to explain that Andy had wanted her to ask Betty if Steve "had ever tried anything with her, touched her or anything." Wendy said they had a long talk where she made sure Betty understood that she would not be at fault or to blame if Steve had, but they needed to know the truth. Tom asked Betty once again if, in her opinion, anything had happened between Steve and Hanna, but Betty said, "No, I don't think it happened." Tom asked her why not, and she said, "I don't think Steve is that kind of guy."

Betty's statements don't support any of Hanna's story, and they don't support Hanna's contention that Steve might have been involved in Jenny Luborsky's murder. Just to remind you, though, Steve gave DNA and pubic hair samples which cleared him of suspicion in the Gasnick case, and he was babysitting and caregiving when Jenny was murdered. While everyone might have been a suspect early in the investigation, which is typical, Steve was removed from suspicion after he provided his DNA for testing. That didn't keep the rumors from spreading, though.

The 2002 publication of *A Gruesome End*, undoubtedly refueled the rumor machine about the Gasnick case, and it had apparently been a topic of conversation in Hanna's family too, which might be why it was on her mind during her interview with Tom. When I spoke to Hanna's mother in 2014, she also raised the specter of Gasnick. I believed I had proof that she had lied on the stand about whether Eddie Higham had lived with her during their relationship. I asked her why she had done that, but instead of answering my question, she countered by saying that Eddie was "somebody that Sirois could blame stuff on, just like he did with Gasnick." It sounded to me like she felt the verdict in the Gasnick case should have been reversed, so I asked her what she meant. She again didn't answer, but asked if I had looked into the Gasnick story. I said I had, and added that it had no bearing on Hanna's case against Steve. She said, "Well, it's the same sort of deal, you know. He molested her too." Not believing what I was hearing, I said, "Steve did?" She said, "Yeah," so I asked her what proof she had. Sounding offended, she said, "I didn't say I have proof." Our conversation went downhill from there, with her accusing me of being in some sort of scheme with Steve, saying "...he's trying to pull shit." She added that she had already talked to the DA's office, and that she works for three attorneys, and that "if something needs to get done, I'll get it done." I think those comments were just threats to try to scare me away from investigating any further. I tried to reason with her. She didn't bend to my way of thinking, but I didn't expect her to. We ended the conversation on a reasonably neutral note, but it's just another indication that prejudice against Steve was probably alive and well in Ashwell County even as late as 2014, and likely still is today.

A Couple of Questions: If Hanna, as late as the Spring of 2006, just a couple of months before the first trial, was actively trying to spread rumors, and was falsely accusing Steve of being a suspect in the Gasnick case, could it have been because she was worried that her own story wouldn't be well-received in court? Could she also have been the source for some of the rumors against Steve that were spread across the area earlier than that? Yes, I do believe that's a possibility.

Betty Stavens was the last person Tom interviewed before the trials began. He wasn't able to reach any of the others. There is at least one person I wish he had been able to find, Karla Spivey. She plays a small but important role in our story. We'll see what her revelation was in the chapter, *Sleepovers, Confessions, and Lies*.

Let's take a look at both trials before moving on to the *Proof of Innocence* section.

The First Trial

"Prosecutors have a higher duty than other lawyers;
they must seek justice, not a conviction."
Comment, American Bar Association Rule 3.8

"My lawyer and my mama are going to be mad about this."
Hanna Penderfield

[Subsections in this Chapter: The First Trial in Brief // A Previous Conviction Rears Its Ugly Head // A Last Minute Surprise // A Questionable Tactic // Analysis]

The First Trial in Brief

The first trial began on July 17th, 2006, and ended on July 19th with a hung jury and a mistrial. Hanna and Steve were the two primary witnesses for their respective sides. Hanna's side also had a few witnesses who were there to verify her version of events, but could generally only parrot what Hanna had told them. Steve's witnesses could largely only testify to his good character and say that they had never seen anything untoward happening between him and Hanna or any other young girls. It looked like the trial would be a classic case of *he said vs. she said*, but things are never that simple, are they? I've already referred to testimony from this trial several times, but just a reminder: The inconsistencies and untruths I might point out in this chapter will still just mostly show how unfair the trials were. The chapters that detail how and why Steve wasn't guilty will mainly be in the *Proof of Innocence* section.

A Previous Conviction Rears Its Ugly Head

I'm not going to try to convince you that Steve was perfect. He was a regular human being who made some good decisions in his life and some bad ones; and a few times he was in the wrong place at the wrong time. You've seen an example of being in the wrong place at the wrong time in the story about Billy Gasnick. Right now, though, I want to tell you about something Steve did decades earlier, but shouldn't have, and show how the prosecution used that against him in both trials. Steve used to smoke marijuana, and was convicted of possession in 1982. He started using it in the mid-1970's when he was a teenager. Shawn Mansbach, a friend of his, was fairly wealthy, had a fancy car, and ran wild often enough to convince our mother that he was a bad influence. He introduced Steve to cannabis, and they smoked it regularly.

Steve was sixteen when he met Robin for the first time, but they had barely started dating when he had to move to Massachusetts with Mom in 1976. When Steve came back to Deep Springs a year later, he and Robin dated on and off. He liked Robin about as intensely as she hated drugs, and she had a good effect on him, settling him down. They got married in 1985, but long before that he was winding down his use of marijuana. He quit completely after his possession arrest. In 1982, three years before he married Robin, nine years before Marri was born, Steve was 22, and was having some success as a club DJ. He told me he was rooming in Fort Worth with a guy named Vince Amaral, who owned the club Steve worked at, and described him as a "muscleman, an enforcer-type." Steve DJ'd on the weekends, but had several days off during the week, so he would often go back to Deep Springs to see friends. All he wanted to do was DJ, but he said that Amaral had an extra chore for him. According to Steve, occasionally, when he left for home, Amaral would put a package in his trunk and tell him to stop in Brewer and give it to Edgar Madeiros, the club's previous owner. Steve described Madeiros as "intimidating," and said that, although he never saw what was in the packages, he was aware that delivering them was probably wrong; but said he felt like he couldn't say no to Madeiros because it would be like crossing the Godfather.

One day in 1982, during a trip home, he was stopped by police in Brewer, and was arrested for possession of the marijuana in the package. Madeiros hired Roy Lane Dunnigan to be Steve's lawyer. Dunnigan advised Steve to plead guilty in exchange for a probated sentence. Steve told me he "was scared to death…to not take the probation." He felt like he had to accept the plea deal, so he did. He was convicted of possession of marijuana, and was given a four-year probated sentence. Steve said that, to pay for the lawyer's fee, Madeiros gave Dunnigan some buildings to use for a skeet range and moved them to Dunnigan's property. They had Steve operate the machinery to dig the ditches to lay the water and electric lines for the range.

Did the name Roy Lane Dunnigan sound familiar? He was Billy Gasnick's lawyer thirteen years later, in 1995. In Gasnick's trial, Dunnigan tried to use Steve's marijuana conviction to discredit his testimony against Gasnick. I don't think that's exactly ethical, since he had been Steve's lawyer during the earlier trial. Fortunately, the judge, Arthur Seabury, didn't let Dunnigan introduce it. Would Judge Hawes act the same way in 2006, twenty-four years later? We'll see.

After that arrest, Steve stopped using marijuana, and said that he hasn't had any illegal drugs since then. The important thing here is that, at the time of his 2006 trials, he hadn't used any for twenty-four years, more than half his life at the time. He met all the requirements of his probation (paying a $1,000 fine and completing 250 hours of community service). In 1986 the conviction was discharged. Here's how that document reads:

"...it is accordingly considered, Ordered and Adjudged by the Court that the judgment of Conviction heretofore entered against the same [*Steven Sirois*] is hereby <u>set aside</u>, the <u>indictment dismissed</u>, and the <u>Defendant discharged</u> from said probation, and the Defendant is hereby <u>released from all penalties and disabilities</u> resulting from the Judgement of Conviction in this cause."

Steve wondered how an indictment could "be 'set aside' and still remain a conviction." If there was no indictment, how could there have been a conviction?

Back to the 2006 trials. Texas' Rule of Evidence 609 says that a prosecutor can only attack the credibility of a witness with evidence of a previous crime if three circumstances are present: 1) If the crime "was a felony or involved moral turpitude;" <u>and</u> 2) If the "probative value of the evidence outweighs its prejudicial effect;" <u>and</u> 3) if "it is elicited from the witness or established by public record." In plain terms, a prosecutor can't bring up a defendant's previous conviction for a crime unless it was a felony or something immoral; <u>and</u> the judge has to decide that revealing it will produce more valuable information than the harm it might cause the defendant; <u>and</u> the prosecutor can't just spring this information on the defendant. Even if the first two conditions exist, the defendant also usually has to make some statement that "opens the door" [*by saying something that gives the prosecutor the opportunity to ask questions about it*].

Rule 609 also sets conditions on whether that evidence can be used if it's more than a decade old. If it's an older conviction, the judge is supposed to give careful consideration as to whether the quality of the information (its "probative value") is worth more than any harm it could cause the defendant ("its prejudicial effect"). This is supposed to keep defendants from being attacked with an earlier crime, especially if a sizable amount of time has passed with no criminal activity on the part of the defendant (as was the case with Steve). In my opinion, a fair judge wouldn't have allowed that information in, especially considering how far in the past it was. Judge Seabury didn't allow it in 1995, but Judge Hawes did in 2006. Even though Steve's conviction happened twenty-four years before the trials, Hawes allowed it, so it was introduced anyway. Here's how they brought it up in the first trial.

About thirty minutes into Steve's testimony, his attorney, Bevin Jenkins, was wrapping up his questioning. He asked Steve if he had been shocked by Hanna's allegations. Steve said, "Yes, sir, very much." Jenkins asked him if he would "ever have done anything to hurt Hanna Penderfield," and Steve said, "No, sir, not any child, sir." Jenkins asked if he would do anything to hurt or injure his daughter, or his wife, or risk doing anything like that. Steve said, "No, sir. Never." He asked if he would have done anything right in front of his family, as Hanna said he did. Steve again said, "No, sir."

Jenkins passed the witness to Elmer Ross, who asked Steve a number of questions about the three counts against him. Ross had very little success with that because all he could do was to ask Steve if certain things happened, and Steve told him they didn't. In a discussion that became contentious, Ross also spent a great deal of time asking Steve about the ride home from the rodeo. Steve argued that Ross misquoted one of his earlier answers to make it seem like he was changing his testimony about whether he had touched Hanna improperly on her back. Just for the record, Steve was right. No one had even asked him a question about that. They went back and forth on that, but Steve wouldn't budge.

Ross, in my opinion, tried to slip a bombshell in at that point. He said, "You do realize what I'm doing now is called cross-examination?" Steve said, "Yes, sir." Ross said, "And you're not unfamiliar with testifying in court, you've done it before, correct, Mr. Sirois?" Steve answered, "Yes, sir, once." Ross was referring to Steve testifying for the prosecution in the Gasnick trial. Jenkins objected before he could continue, and called a sidebar conference between the judge and the attorneys to find out why Ross was bringing up that question. The sidebar wasn't included in the testimony, so we don't know what was said, but once the jury returned Ross shifted to a different topic. If Ross' intent had been to let the jury believe that Steve had been accused of crimes before, he accomplished that, but he also made a move to introduce Steve's marijuana conviction soon after that anyway. He asked for another sidebar conference, as he was supposed to, and the jury was sent from the room again.

A discussion ensued about whether to let any of Steve's criminal record be heard by the jury. Ross produced certified copies of the 1982 conviction, and the 1986 discharge from probation, and said, "I believe it is permissible to impeach his testimony of a prior felony conviction." At that point in the trial, no one had even mentioned the marijuana conviction, so I don't believe there wasn't any "testimony of a prior felony conviction" to impeach. Bevin Jenkins objected to it because of the age of the felony, and because it had nothing to do with Steve's character at the time of Hanna's accusation two decades later. Judge Hawes asked if Steve had "any intervening offenses" since the 1982 conviction, "misdemeanor or otherwise." Ross couldn't come up with any, but he said that there had been a previous marijuana conviction in 1978, and a misdemeanor DWI in May of 1982. Both of those were before the September 1982 marijuana charge, not after, so they weren't "intervening" charges. Hawes clearly wanted to know if Steve had committed any crimes in the period between September 1982 and 2004, so why did Ross even mention the other two? Hawes asked Ross why he thought he should be allowed to bring the conviction up, especially since it had been "more than ten years since he was convicted." Ross said it would be relevant because Steve testified "that he would not participate in illegal activities," and revealing the conviction would be proof that he wasn't credible. Hawes asked him if he was referring to Steve's statement about never doing anything to hurt a child. Ross said, "Yes, it's a felony conviction which directly goes to his character." Jenkins countered by saying that Ross' view (that Steve would commit a crime now because he had committed one in the past) "is absolutely irrelevant and improper evidence."

Judge Hawes took a recess to look up some case law on the matter. When he returned, he said he had decided that allowing the jury to hear about Steve's conviction *would be* prejudicial to his case; but, because Steve had said "that he wouldn't do anything that would risk harming his family and others... the probative value does outweigh the prejudicial nature because there has been a false impression that he would never do anything that would harm his wife or child or even risk doing anything like that when, in fact, he has been previously convicted of a felony," so he decided to let Ross ask Steve about it. Before he did, though, Hawes told the jury they could only use the information they were about to hear to determine "the truthfulness of the Defendant as a witness in this case and for no other purpose."

What followed was almost anti-climactic. Ross asked Steve if he had "a previous felony conviction." Steve said, "Yes, sir." Ross asked, "From September 8th of 1982?" When Steve answered yes to that, Ross moved on to another subject without even eliciting what the conviction was for. That was it. After all that wrangling to get the information into the trial, the prosecutor got what he wanted. The jury heard that Steve was a convicted felon, and Ross just let it hang there. When Bevin Jenkins cross-examined Steve, he tried to clarify the matter. He asked Steve if the earlier conviction was for anything like the current charges against him. Steve said, "No, sir," and said it was for possession of marijuana, and that it "was in '82, and I was a kid."

Steve's first appeal argued against the unfairness of bringing that conviction up just for the purpose of casting doubt on his honesty, especially considering the age of it, that he wasn't even married to Robin when it occurred, and that it happened nearly a decade before Marri was born. The appeals courts all sided with the district court, though, saying that revealing that information didn't matter because the jury didn't convict him on all three counts. I believe that was a misguided assessment on the part of the appeals court, because Steve's jury may have voted based on a deal they made to swap votes, not on the evidence. I cover the appeal thoroughly on the blog, beginning at:

https://aggravatedbook.com/steves-appeal-part-1/

Judges often view cases with different lenses than the general public, and they do have the legal power to interpret the harm or the benefit of a piece of evidence as they see fit. Even though Judge Seabury, in 1995, wouldn't allow an 13-year-old conviction to be used in his court, Judge Hawes chose to allow the same conviction 24 years later, in spite of the 10-year limit imposed by Rule of Evidence 609, which also says "Evidence of the conviction is admissible only if its probative value, supported by specific facts and circumstances, substantially outweighs its prejudicial effect," I can't see what "specific facts and circumstances" the 2006 jury could have heard. Ross didn't attempt to connect the earlier conviction to any "facts" or "circumstances." He simply had Steve admit that he had been previously convicted of a felony, and let the scent of "*Eau d'Criminel*" linger in the courtroom. I don't think the information should have been allowed in front of the jury the way it was, but I wasn't the judge. Jenkins did step in at the first opportunity to establish that the conviction was for a totally unrelated type of crime, one which happened when Steve was much younger, but the damage had already been done.

Why does any of that matter? It matters in this context because the prosecution brought up a conviction that was supposed to have been expunged after Steve completed his probation. Even though it was for a completely unrelated crime, I believe it was done for one reason only, to telegraph to the jury that Steve was scum, undeserving of their sympathy. Steve had reformed, though, no longer did drugs, and quit being a DJ to do construction work so he could be nearby to help Robin care for her ailing parents. I think his previous convictions shouldn't have been used to ascertain his truthfulness or his character because they didn't reflect the man he was during the 2006 trial, or the man he had been since 1982. Was he perfect? No. Did he still make mistakes? Yes, of course. Did he do the things Hanna accused him of? No. Evidence of that is coming up soon, in the *Proof of Innocence* section.

Here's one more (very important) moment from Trial #1.

A Last Minute Surprise

Judy Higham was one of the final witnesses called in Steve's defense. Eugene Guthrie, Bevin Jenkins' second chair, asked Judy the usual questions, establishing that she was sixteen years old, that she had known Steve for many years, and was good friends with both Marri and Hanna. She said she had been to the Sirois' home "a lot. I really can't give you a number." Guthrie asked her if she had been at the house when Hanna was there. When she said yes, he asked her how often. Judy said, "Almost every time she was there, I came over because me and Hanna, we're really good friends." He asked if she had seen anything inappropriate happening between Hanna and Steve, or had seen them go off by themselves, or had seen anything happen with any other young girls, or any kids, or whether Steve had ever been inappropriate with her. Judy answered, "No, sir" to all of that, saying she had never seen Steve do anything wrong with anyone. Continuing, Guthrie established that Judy thought Steve was a loving father, and that his kids were close to him. She admitted that she wasn't there every single time that Hanna was, but said that she was there "a large majority of the time," and added, that when she was there, Hanna was rarely out of her sight. Finally, he closed by asking her once again, "Did you ever see anything inappropriate going on between Mr. Sirois and her?" Judy said, "No." Guthrie passed the witness, and Elmer Ross took over.

Under cross examination by Ross, Judy was asked if she spent the night when Hanna did. She said, "Majority of the time." Ross, of course, would probably have preferred a different answer, one that would have reduced number times when Judy and Hanna spent the night at the same time, minimizing the number of witnesses during Hanna's claimed eighty to ninety instances of molestation, but Judy also established that it wasn't just her. She said there were a lot of people there, adults and kids both. If you will remember, Tiffany Sperger said the same thing, although she didn't claim to have spent the night as often as Judy did. I don't see how the questions Ross asked Judy helped Hanna. The more people there were, the more likely someone would be caught *in flagrante delicto*, but I believe the reason no one ever caught was simple. There never was any *delicto*. If we believe that Judy was at the Sirois' house nearly every time Hanna was, and spent the night there most of those times, then Judy has to be figured into the potential witnesses who should have seen something. Like all the other witnesses, though, Judy said she didn't see anything inappropriate happen between Steve and Hanna.

Ross used those questions, about friends and family and lots of kids being around, to lead into questions about drinking, and he did get Judy to say that, yes, the adults drank. Ross passed the witness back to Guthrie, who had Judy emphasize that there was only one bathroom in the house, and agree that, yes, people were "in and out of that bathroom all the time." She had done a good job for the defense, and had probably helped Steve's case.

Judge Hawes excused Judy and asked Guthrie to call his next witness. He had just called Meredith Winstead, the granddaughter of one of Steve's neighbors, when he suddenly realized he had forgotten to ask Judy an extremely important question. Doing what was probably a textbook case of groveling, he said to Judge Hawes, "Your Honor, I'm sorry, I need to call back Judy Higham. I have a couple more questions. I apologize." Judy had already been excused. Hawes could have said "Too late, you had your chance," but if he had he could have opened up an avenue of appeal for Steve. Prosecutors and judges hate having their trials overturned, of course, so Judy was called back to the courtroom. Guthrie thanked the judge and they got Judy back on the stand. As soon as she was back, Guthrie asked for a side bar conference. Guthrie wanted to be sure the judge would allow him to ask a certain sensitive question. Hawes excused the jury so they wouldn't hear what was about to be discussed. The side bar wasn't made part of the transcription, so we don't know what they said, but it did include an objection from Ross. Hawes wanted to see what questions Guthrie was planning to ask before he made a ruling on Ross' objection, so with the jury gone they asked Judy some questions on the record.

Guthrie asked Judy who Eddie Higham was, and how he was "connected with Hanna." Judy said that Eddie was her uncle, and added "I believe he used to date her mom." Then Guthrie asked, "Okay. And what is the problem with Eddie Higham?" Judy said, "I can't remember if it was a friend of the family or part of our family had accused him of sexually molesting her or something like that." She added, "And like he had gotten five years or something." To clear up any ambiguity, Guthrie asked her if it was true that Eddie was a registered sex offender. She answered, "Yes."

He passed the witness to Ross who asked her only two things, whether she knew if Eddie "was even in the home when Hanna was there," and whether she had heard any allegations that "anything was improper between Eddie Higham and Hanna Penderfield." She answered "No, sir" to both questions. Hawes ruled that the current information was too vague, but gave the attorneys an opportunity to ask more questions. That was followed by close to ten minutes worth of arguments and objections about the relevance of the information. Hawes finally decided that Judy's comments would be hearsay, so without a certified copy of evidence that Eddie was a sex offender at the time he dated Darla, he couldn't allow the jury to hear that evidence.

They brought the jury back in, and, after testimony from Meredith Winstead and Nancy Foxwell, both of whom said they had never seen any inappropriate behavior from Steve, another sidebar conference was called, and the jury was excused once more. During Meredith's and Nancy's testimony, Charlotte Felton, a therapist who was assisting the defense, went to the District Clerk's office and got a certified copy of Eddie's conviction; which made me wonder, if they were aware they were going to ask Judy that question, why didn't they have that document in hand already?

After some further argument and objection back and forth, Judge Hawes agreed to allow the document into evidence, and they had Judy return to the witness stand. In front of the jury this time, Guthrie asked Judy who her uncle was. Elmer Ross immediately objected. Judge Hawes overruled him. Judy said, "Eddie Higham." Guthrie asked if Eddie had ever dated Hanna's mother. Judy said, "Yes, sir." He asked if she remembered when they dated. She said "2002, 2003." Guthrie asked if Hanna was also there whenever she saw Eddie and Darla together. Judy said, "Yes, sir." Guthrie then tossed her the big question, "Now, what's the problem with your Uncle Eddie?" Ross again objected, saying it was hearsay. Hawes overruled him. "Judy said, "He was accused of sexually molesting a friend of the family." Guthrie asked her if Eddie was convicted of that crime. She said, "Yes, sir."

The document detailing Eddie's conviction was entered into evidence and the jury was allowed to see it. On cross examination, Elmer Ross had Judy clarify that Eddie had been convicted of molesting someone else, not Hanna, and he established that Judy didn't know how often Hanna was around Eddie. When Guthrie got his turn again, he had Judy verify that every time she saw Eddie and Darla together, Hanna was with them. Then she was excused, for good this time. Judy was Steve's last witness.

Did the prosecution already know about Eddie, or was he someone Darla and Hanna hid from the DA's office? No one else on either side, Hanna's mother in particular, got a chance to say anything about what they knew about Eddie because the previous witnesses had all been excused. Steve had already testified as well, so he wasn't able to tell the jury about going to the CPS in defense of Darla when she was summoned there because of her relationship with Eddie. Judy's testimony was a bonus for Steve's side. Even though there was no proof that Eddie molested Hanna, the jury got to hear that Hanna's mother dated a registered sex offender during the time period Hanna claimed she was molested. As you might suspect, the subject of Eddie came up again in Trial #2, but much earlier that time.

There's one final thing to be aware of. Despite their connection as friends, and having spent time together at the Sirois' house, Hanna—who usually seemed eager to claim that someone was her friend—didn't mention Judy at all. Not in her affidavit, not in Dixon's summary, not in the interview with Tom, and not in her testimony in either trial. Was Hanna trying to hide Eddie's relationship with her mom from the jury? By ignoring Judy's existence, was Hanna hoping they wouldn't ask her questions about Eddie?

A Questionable Tactic

I don't know if the subject of Darla dating Eddie Higham caught Elmer Ross by surprise at the end of the first trial or not, but Hanna's answer to one of the first questions he asked her in that same trial might have. A surprise statement is something all lawyers hope never happens, especially when it's something their own clients say in a trial. After establishing Hanna's name and her ages during the timeframe in question (twelve years old in early September 2001, and just shy of fifteen at Beau's birthday party in 2004), Ross asked an innocuous question, "Where do you live, Hanna?" She said, "Deep Springs, Texas." [*Hanna had lived her whole life in Alderson. Was Ross caught off guard by that?*] He followed that with, "Who do you live with?" Hanna said, "My cousin." [*Did he know she was going to say that?*] Ross asked who the cousin was, and she said, "Eva Kern." He asked if her mother lived in the area too. When Hanna said, "Yes," he asked her who her mother was. She said, "Darla Belisle." Then [*maybe hoping they had both moved in with the Kerns*] he asked where her mother was living. Hanna said, "Alderson, Texas." I'm not sure if Ross even knew how to word his next question, but he plunged ahead. "How long has it been since you weren't living -- or you stopped living with your mom?" Hanna answered, "Three days." He moved on to other topics at that point, but I suspect that he wouldn't have asked those specific questions if he had known that Hanna wasn't living at home. Once it was out in the open, though, he couldn't change Hanna's testimony. Was it true? I do think she was living with someone other than her mother during both trials. Whether it actually was with her cousin, and whether she had only been there for three days, I don't know, but I'll try to settle that in just a minute.

She was apparently still not back home a little less than a month later,when Trial #2 began. Once the DA's office knew they were going to retry Steve, it seems logical that they would have regrouped and discussed how to approach everything the second time around. The reason I believe Ross may have been surprised in the first trial by Hanna saying she had moved out of her mom's house was partly because of his seeming hesitation before asking where Darla was living, but also because of the way he reworded his questions during Trial #2. That time he started by asking, "Who is your mom, Hanna?" She said, "Darla Belisle." He asked, "And where does your mom live?" Hanna said, "At Alderson, Texas." Ross asked, "And is that where you have lived most of your life as well?" She said, "Yes, sir." Then he asked, "And so, right now, it's just you and your mom in terms of family that is living here in Ashwell County; is that right?" Hanna said, "Yes, sir."

Deep Springs and Alderson are both in Ashwell County, so Hanna's answers were technically correct. Did Ross, by rewording his questions, and by not asking Hanna where she was living then, intentionally alter the substance of Hanna's Trial #1 testimony (giving the second jury a false impression that she was still living in Alderson with her mother)? That was the end result, but was that information so significant that he felt he had to hide it? Regardless, it's clear from the careful way he fed those questions to Hanna in the second trial that he didn't want her to again say that she, at seventeen, wasn't living at home. Cleveland Sanford, being new to the case, didn't pick up on that detail, and Steve (who admitted he was largely numb through large chunks of the second trial) didn't catch it either, so the second jury spent their entire time believing that Hanna was still at home with her mother. Did Ross think his case was that fragile, or that the thought of a young girl not living at home might have been a contributing factor in his failure to get a conviction the first time? Was he cheating by keeping the new jury from having that information? It depends on your viewpoint. It seemed to me that he was hiding information which looked bad, but that information wasn't part of the charges against Steve. Also, the defense could have questioned Hanna about it during cross-examination (and I'm sure they would have if they had known about it).

I wondered, though, whether Hanna really did leave her mother's house only three days before the first trial, and whether she actually was living with her cousin, Eva Kern. Having seen so much information from her and her family that I believed to be lies, I had an inherent distrust of anything she said, including this. A few excerpts from her interview with Tom Swearingen might help you decide what's true, though. Tom recorded the interview (and this is important) on a Thursday night, May 25, 2006. The audio recording is 2 hours, 28 minutes, and 30 seconds, but it was interrupted a few times when Tom's and Hanna's cell signals dropped out and they had to reconnect. Since it began at roughly 8:00 pm, Hanna was up quite late that night (possibly after 11:00 before they were done). She was also talking to an adult male about a variety of things, many of them sexual in nature. That may seem like a trivial thing at first, but bear with me, and I'll show you why it wasn't.

Tom said that Hanna first attempted to call him around 7:00 pm, while he was on the road, driving back to Brady from Deep Springs. He asked her if he could call her back once he got home because he had an issue with his phone battery. They both complained several times about the poor quality of cell service in the area, indicating that they were both on cell phones when the actual interview occurred. When he first tried to call her back, there was a lot of electronic noise on that part of the audio, but I could hear the voices of other people in the background. When Tom asked her if she had a few minutes to talk to him, she hesitated, sounding exasperated. He said, "I hope it's not a bad time, ma'am." She said, "Uh, kind of a bad time. Why don't you try back in about a half an hour? I'm kind of dealing with something right now." Tom said he would do that. She thanked him and hung up. When Tom reached her later, the noises of people in the background were still there. After exchanging hellos, Hanna said, "Uh, are you going to be busy later? I'm kind of in the middle of the same thing…" Tom said "Okay," but sounded doubtful. She said, "Promise I'll call you back." Tom suggested instead that he call her about eight o'clock. Hanna said, "Yes. Thank you. I appreciate it."

[*Even though Hanna said she wanted this interview, Tom didn't want to wait by the phone for a call that might not come. Around 8:00 pm he called her back.*]

Here's the important bit. After exchanging hellos again, Hanna said, "Yes. I'm sorry about that. I had some domestic trouble." Tom laughed, and said, "Sounds like you had some little ones you were sitting with in the background." Hanna said, "Well, <u>they might as well be</u>."

[*Like Tom, I thought Hanna was babysitting too until she said* "they might as well be." *The clear indication is that she wasn't with young kids. Who was she with? Would Darla let her have friends over on a Thursday night, even if it was near the end of the school year?*]

Twelve minutes into the audio, an unintelligible <u>male voice</u> interrupted Hanna. She said, "I don't know where your phone is. I'm kind of in the middle of something." The voice said, "Sorry." Hanna told him, "It's very important, thank you."

[*If Hanna was in her own home, after 8:00 at night, why would a male be asking her if she had seen his phone?*]

Then, thirty minutes into the discussion, Hanna suddenly said, "Excuse me for one second. [*she called out*] Hey, do <u>y'all</u> have a Nokia phone charger?" A male voice in the background said something unintelligible. Hanna said, "Where?" The male voice responded [*I still couldn't understand him*]. Hanna said, "Okay, thank you." To Tom again, she said, "My phone's going dead. ...going to get <u>his</u> charger."

[*Even though I can't tell what the male in the background was saying, it's clear that this is no juvenile voice. There is a bass quality to his tone. Also, while the word, "y'all"* can *be used in Texas to indicate one person, it almost always refers to two or more people, a group.*]

So, let me pose a modified version of my earlier question. Would Hanna's mother let her have <u>male friends</u> over <u>on a Thursday night</u>, while Hanna was <u>a junior in high school</u>, and while she was talking to an investigator for the defense, about sexual matters, just before a trial in which their family had a huge stake? No, of course she wouldn't.

Here's one other tiny quote from the interview. Tom, From the very beginning, went to great lengths to verify that Hanna was speaking to him of her own free will, and knew that she could terminate the interview at any time. He said, "That's why I want to identify myself so there's no doubt. Because you don't have to talk to me in any way, shape or form. You don't have to say a single word to me." Hanna said, "Right. My lawyer and my mama are going to be mad about this."

[*If Hanna knew this was something that both the DA and her mother didn't want her to do, she was clearly not in her own home. She was either in someone else's house on a school night, or her mother wasn't there; which also doesn't make any sense, because the interview finished late at night, and the next day, a Friday, was a work day for Hanna's mother.*]

Obviously, this is speculation on my part, but the interview was in May and the first trial didn't begin until July. Could Hanna have moved out of her mother's house a month or more before the date she swore to in court? If that's the case, why wouldn't she just say so? Obviously, of course, moving out of her mom's house, at her age, three days before the trial, wouldn't look nearly as bad as moving out months before; but was it so bad that Ross would want to keep that information out of the second trial?

Analysis

The first trial ended up being a practice run for the second one. Whether it was the last minute revelation from Judy that Darla had been dating a sex offender, or for some other reason, the jury members couldn't unanimously reach the same conclusion, and that forced Judge Hawes to declare a mistrial. Since all twelve jurors need to vote guilty to convict a defendant, one or more of the jurors in that first trial didn't vote to convict Steve on any of the three counts. Whatever the final vote was, the prosecution must have believed they were on the right track, though, because the questions they asked in the second trial, with just a few exceptions, were very close to the ones they had asked in this one.

Let's take a look at that second trial now. Like the first one, I'll be quoting from it extensively in the *Proof of Innocence* section, so this next chapter won't follow it step-by-step through the whole thing, but there are several things I'd like to show you.

The Second Trial

In effect, the DA was saying: Even if they got the date wrong, as long as Hanna said it happened before they gave the details to the grand jury, it would still be a valid indictment.

Michael Sirois

"...the truth doesn't change. If the truth doesn't change, and you have two different versions of it, then you're lying."

Cleveland Sanford

[Subsections in this Chapter: A Third Lawyer // The Trial Begins // Voir Dire // Ronelle Wilcox and the Voir Dire // Analysis of the Voir Dire // Believability and Witnesses (Expert or Otherwise) // Overview of the Trial Itself]

A Third Lawyer

The first trial ended in a mistrial, but the prosecution immediately announced their intention to retry Steve. The new trial was set for August 7th, just three weeks after the first one ended. It was postponed once, but did begin on August 14th. That trial was patterned closely after the first one. The prosecution fielded the same roster of witnesses, in a slightly different order. The big changes for Steve this time were that he didn't testify, and he had a new lawyer.

At the end of Trial #1, Bevin Jenkins told Steve that he would represent him again for another $20,000, but two years of legal fees had wiped the family out. Steve released Jenkins, and started looking for someone else. On August 7th, Clyde Sledge published an article in the Deep Springs Gazette, "Attorney for Sirois asks to withdraw from case." Sledge wrote, "Attorney Bevin Jenkins of Keller, said in the motion filed in 555th District Court that he wants to withdraw because Sirois has been unable to pay attorney's feels." Sledge, of course, meant "fees" instead of "feels," but he gave the impression in the article (by saying "has been unable") that Steve cheated Jenkins by not paying him what he owed him. Steve had, however, already paid Jenkins the agreed upon $25,000 to represent him in the first trial ($15,015 on March 14th, and another $10,000 on April 28th). Steve and Robin just couldn't afford to give Jenkins an additional $20,000 to do a repeat performance. They were broke, a not uncommon situation for people of modest means after being kept on the string for over two years awaiting trial. Beau, only 23 at the time, put up a number of items for collateral, and took out a loan in order to hire Cleveland Sanford. After the trial, he sold the Jeep, his Kawasaki Mule, his 16-foot bass boat, and two flatbed trailers to repay the loan.

Once Sanford was hired, he did his best to prepare for the second trial despite the limited amount of time he had. I interviewed him in 2017, and we talked at length about a number of things, but I especially wanted to know how he got ready for the trial. He had less than a week, but I assumed he had at least received copies of all the court documents and the materials from the previous lawyers, everything that two years of work and $58,312 had paid for. Unfortunately, Sanford told me he got none of it. The first time I talked to Roland Mathis in person, in 2013, I asked him if he still had any materials from Steve's trial. He said he didn't, so I asked if he had given them to Bevin Jenkins. He said, "I guess so." That seemed oddly non-committal, so a year later I asked him once more if he was sure he didn't have any materials left from Steve's trial. He again told me he didn't. That was also the same day I asked both him and Clyde Sledge about Mathis' comment about the PI's being interested in Steve's connection to Billy Gasnick. Both of them said they had no materials left, and neither remembered having the conversation about the PI's. I know that Steve's case might have been a non-issue for them eight years later, but I still found it unbelievable that all physical traces of it had been wiped as clean as the Sahara Desert after a scirocco. It seemed odd to me that attorneys and reporters wouldn't keep records?

Cleveland Sanford did.

When I stopped to see him on my way back to Houston after that 2013 research trip, he had a banker's box full of documents from the trial, which he graciously let me have access to, even copying some of the trial transcript for me. I don't know what records Jenkins may have received from Mathis, but he didn't pass anything on to Sanford. When Sanford was hired, he started from scratch. He said, "I went and met with the court reporter, and it was one of those things where she was like, 'Can you tell me what it is you need, not what you want, because…to get all of it is going to be really...'" He didn't finish the sentence, but the implication was that it would be costly and time consuming. Earlier that same trip I had asked the same court reporter, Mindy Camillo, to transcribe Darla's testimony from the first trial so I could compare it with the second one. A month later I had a twenty-page document that cost me $100, five dollars a page. To transcribe the whole trial would have been over $6,000, which I believe was only a little less than Sanford was paid to represent Steve. Sanford had Camillo do just the essentials: the testimony for Hanna and Steve, and a few key witnesses on Hanna's side, but not the two expert witnesses, Dixon and Goudy. He was also, of course, given copies of all the evidence from the first trial: the doctor's reports, affidavits, etc., but after that he was on his own.

He was officially hired on Wednesday, August 9th, 2006, and only had until the next Monday to prepare for the trial, but the transcripts he ordered weren't finished until Friday the 11th. In three days, he read the transcripts, took notes, and formed a strategy. He re-hired Tom Swearingen to help with a quick investigation, which gave him access to all of Tom's interviews. He also had Tom sit at the defense table with him during the trial to fill him in on important details when necessary, but he said that, in the few days leading up to the trial, "I shut everything else down, and didn't do anything but this case." He rented a motel room in Brady, where Tom lives, and worked on the trial during the day while Tom was interviewing people. Then at night they listened to the interviews, took more notes, and discussed trial strategy. He said they did that for a couple of days, but on Sunday he came to Deep Springs to interview

Steve and his family, take pictures to use as evidence, and finish getting ready. In other words, Sanford tried the case without the benefit of Jenkins' or Mathis' materials, but still did a credible job of defending Steve without the years of preparation that Mathis had, or the several months that Jenkins had.

While reading the transcripts for the first trial, Sanford probably noticed that Steve seemed to have a difficult time on the stand. Remember Steve's science teacher telling him to never take a lie detector test because he was so nervous? Steve also has a tendency to be a step ahead in conversations. I do that too to some degree, so our phone conversations often consist of the two of us stepping on each other's sentences. It happened in the brainstorming session, and Sanford could probably see it happening on the printed page in the first trial's transcript. Here's a quick excerpt from Trial #1. I've kept it in transcript format for clarity. Judge Hawes had already cautioned Steve several times before that to let the attorney finish his question before responding, but Steve had just stepped on the end of a question again when Hawes interrupted.

HAWES: Again, wait until he...
STEVE: I thought he did.
HAWES: ...finishes the question.
STEVE: I thought he did.
HAWES: You may anticipate he is through, but wait until he finishes...
STEVE: I'll give him time.
HAWES: ...before you begin your response. Okay?
STEVE: Yes, sir.
HAWES: See, you're not even letting me finish. Now go ahead.

Sanford convinced Steve it would be in his best interest to not testify in the second trial. Was that a good decision? I don't know. The prosecution couldn't try to trap him like they had in the first trial, but they still managed to use his marijuana conviction against him by having the court reporter read parts of his Trial #1 testimony aloud to the jury. Steve said that, once the trial was underway, he felt powerless. He had to just sit there and listen to people lying about him and try to not react badly.

Sanford told me that Hanna's testimony was the most important thing he needed to be familiar with, because, "When she gets up there and she says something that doesn't coincide with what she said previously, that's when you're pointing out that there's discrepancies. And the truth doesn't change. If the truth doesn't change, and you have two different versions of it, then you're lying." During the trial, Sanford did catch her in a number of inconsistencies, changes from one piece of testimony to the next. For example, when Sanford read in court from her affidavit, "During the past three years this has happened several times while I was visiting his home," she agreed that she had said that. He then reminded her that she had testified that there had been "between 80 and 90" incidents, and asked her if she "would agree that several is not 80 or 90." She said, "Yes, sir." He asked her if she would also agree that her story had expanded since the affidavit. She agreed with that too. In another exchange, Sanford pointed out that Hanna had said earlier in this trial that "kissing and touching and fondling occurred between 10 and 12 times" between the cross-country race and the movie, but in the first trial she had said that it was "maybe six to eight times." She said she didn't remember saying that, but agreed that her numbers had grown, which was an all too common occurrence in her narratives. Sanford challenged her on a number of statements like that during the trial, along with other examples of shifts in her testimony, some of them fairly outlandish.

Even if a defense attorney points out a multitude of falsehoods, though, the final choice of whether a defendant is guilty or innocent rests with decisions made by twelve ordinary citizens. As you saw in the *Pre-Prejudice* chapter, though, some of them might have already decided to convict Steve because of untrue things they had heard about him.

The Trial Begins

August 14, 2006, arrived. Steve had survived the ordeal from less than a month before, but was having to endure it all over again. Put yourself in his place. Someone has accused you of a horrific crime, one you didn't commit. There is no forensic evidence, no semen stains or pubic hairs or blood splatters to provide DNA evidence, no weapons, no sex tape. You believe that the truth is on your side, and you know you didn't do this, but it's now going to be your word against your accuser's. Steve said he had been in the same courtroom twice before the first trial, once during Gasnick's trial, and once when he officially adopted Beau, but this was entirely different. Sitting in front of the jury panel, he felt them looking at him as if he were "a poisonous spider under a glass dome, with someone holding a hammer over it." He said that, during the trial, he and the attorneys faced the judge, the jury, and the witnesses; but during the jury selection, they were on the opposite side of the defense table, facing everyone in the gallery, looking at the jury panel for the whole day, unable to say anything. "All you could do," he said, was "stare at them with your most honest look" while they talked about you and what you were accused of. "You can go take a break every few hours," he said, "but it's with the same people, and you can't even say 'hi,' or 'excuse me.' You've been told that this could make you have to start the process over. Yep, just the old honest face. I always thought I had an honest face, because I was honest. I never realized how hard it was to think about looking honest until they told me to try. The whole process is the most nerve-racking thing I've ever done. I don't think many people could keep it up for long."

Steve sat there facing the jury pool until mid-afternoon, trying to look honest and not like a poisonous spider, while the judge and the attorneys listened to excuses and questioned the prospective jurors.

They were conducting a process called voir dire.

Voir Dire

There's a great deal I could say about the voir dire that day, but I've pared it back to the key details here and posted a more extensive version on the blog, beginning at:

https://aggravatedbook.com/the-voir-dire-part-1/

Voir dire is French for "to speak the truth," something all potential jurors are sworn to do. Unfortunately, some of them lie in order to get on a jury (and others lie to avoid being on one). The phrase is pronounced several different ways in the United States, largely depending on where you are. The French pronunciation is something close to *vwa deer*, but in Texas and much of the Deep South you're more likely to hear *vor dīre* (like *four tire* with soft consonants). During voir dire, attorneys question potential jurors (also known as venirepersons) in order to choose the best possible jury. When this is well-conducted, with a cooperative group of venirepersons, the attorneys can gain some sense of who they might want (or not want) on the jury. The prosecution attempts to eliminate people who could be sympathetic to the defendant, and the defense tries to remove those who would favor the victim. They do this by striking (excusing from duty) those they don't want on the jury. The end result should be a neutral jury because the most extreme outliers will have been excluded from serving, resulting in jurors who will hopefully make their decisions based on evidence, not on personal biases. Unfortunately, venirepersons sometimes have agendas that they either hide to get on a jury or expose openly to be excused from serving. Let's find out why one specific person might have wanted to be on this particular jury.

Judge Hawes swore everyone in, explaining that the oath they took was a promise "to answer <u>truthfully the questions that I ask</u> concerning your qualifications or <u>any of the questions asked later by the attorneys</u> during the process of jury selection and that <u>those answers will be truthful</u>." He also explained that "<u>an incomplete answer</u> could result in a juror being seated that was not qualified to be there," which could cause a mistrial. "So, it's very <u>important that you are truthful</u> in your responses, and I'm sure you will be."

Was everyone truthful in their responses? No. I believe that at least one person lied about personal connections that would have prevented her from being on the jury. If that had been discovered during the trial and a second mistrial had been called, the prosecution would have been forced to either give up or have a third trial at great expense. This person flew under the radar, though, and did end up on the jury. I also think she may have helped convince other jurors to convict Steve. How much influence could one person have on the decisions of eleven other people? A lot. Let's look at a little of the voir dire process first, then at how it applied to that one venireperson and why she was seemed to be trying to get on this jury.

A Reminder: Everyone's names, aside from those previously identified as real, are pseudonyms.

After cautioning them to be truthful, Judge Hawes allowed anyone who felt they needed to be excused to come forward and talk to him. Some of the prejudices against Steve, including general biases against child sex offenders, were on full display during this early stage of the voir dire. Elias Levy, one of the first to come forward, said, "I read in the newspaper that there would be a child molester trial, and I don't feel that I would be adequate to judge upon a person, a child molester." Hawes explained that even though someone has been accused, "it doesn't mean they are guilty of anything." Levy said "it just sickens me for -- even the allegation that someone would touch a child." Hawes asked him if he could set that thought aside and base his verdict on the evidence alone, but Levy insisted, "To me, if they have been accused of it, they've done it." Hawes did the right thing, and put Levy on a civil jury panel that would meet that afternoon, rather than allowing someone to remain who might have been an adverse presence on the jury. Consider this, though. If Levy had wanted to be on the jury, and had kept those feelings to himself and calmly sat in the jury pool making benign, neutral comments when he was spoken to, could he have ended up on the jury? Of course he could have.

There were several others, like a man who announced that they had already tried the case in his office, and a woman who said, "I think he is guilty, so I would be whatever you call it." Hawes put both of them on the civil panel; but, if either of them hadn't expressed a clear bias, or hadn't said they had already made up their minds, could they have ended up on the jury? Again, yes, they could have. Hawes also put a few others, who said they knew Steve or knew his kids from school, on the civil panel. After listening to a variety of reasons from 37 excuse-requestors, Hawes kept 6 of them, let 23 of them go home, and sent 8 of them to the civil panel. He then gave everyone a half-hour break while the court clerks shuffled the 64 remaining juror information cards and assigned numbers to each of them. After the break, with everyone seated according to their assigned numbers, Hawes explained that the chances of being chosen were greater for those who had been seated closer to the front and on the left side of the room. It's the same principle that causes students on the front row of a classroom to get more attention, and why some students deliberately sit in the back of the room. If they're not noticed, they might not have to answer. If someone wanted to get on a jury, though, their best bet would be to hope for the lowest number possible, and become noticed enough that they seem reasonably intelligent, but avoid revealing anything that one of the attorneys would decide could be negative toward their side.

A Stray Thought: The "shuffling" of the information cards (to assign numbers to the jurors) was done while the venirepersons were outside the courtroom. If those who are seated with the lowest numbers are far more likely to be put on a jury, as Hawes explained, how hard would it be for the cards to be "shuffled" so certain people end up with their cards near the top of the stack?

This would be a good time to take a look at the floor plans of the courtroom.

https://aggravatedbook.com/images-for-the-second-trials-voir-dire/

The venirepersons were seated on the gallery benches according to the number they were assigned by the random shuffling of their information cards. Facing the gallery, the first person on the left was labeled Juror #1, the next person to their right was Juror #2, and so on, ten people to a row on the left-hand side. Number 30 completed the third row on the left side of the room. Everyone else was seated on the right-hand side, eight to a row for the first three rows, beginning with #31 on the left side of the right-front row, and the fourth row on the right ending with #64. They held numbered cards in front of them so the court reporter, Ms. Camillo, could type their number in her stenotype machine when they spoke. There were too many people for her to be able to capture their dialogue and look up each of their names at the same time. Later, when she transcribed the trial, she could turn #2 into Ms. Wilcox, #5 into Ms. Benson, or #20 into Mr. Timmons, etc. By the way, #2, Ronelle Wilcox, is the person this chapter segment is about.

Judge Hawes turned the proceedings over to Elmer Ross, who said he would be asking them about their backgrounds to find out who "would be an effective and impartial juror on this kind of case." He added, "there are no wrong answers, except for the answer that you don't give us because you're too shy to speak up," and said he would be asking about "your background so we can make a decision as to whether we feel you would be able to be a fair and impartial juror on this case." In effect, he was putting them on notice, even though they had already been warned by Judge Hawes that they were sworn to be completely truthful.

After giving them some biographical information about himself, Ross asked if any of them would be uncomfortable deciding whether or not someone had committed a crime. Several hands went up. They came up to the judge's bench and spoke privately to Hawes and the attorneys. Two jurors from the first row, Jurors 3 and 7, had issues related to sexual assault. Juror #7 said a relative of hers "went through something like this. I have him guilty till he is proven innocent. I'm backwards." From the second row, Jurors 18 and 19 also had difficulty being impartial. Juror 19 said. "I just wouldn't feel comfortable sending somebody to prison." Hawes put the four of them on that afternoon's civil panel. Notice that #19 seemed to believe that Steve would be convicted no matter what. With Jurors 3, 7, 18 and 19 gone, the first two rows were down to eight possible jurors each.

As voir dire continued, several people had strong feelings about the sexual assault of children. One said, "I'm a first-impression person. And the impression I get is that this guy is …I don't know…but he just gives me that impression." Cleveland Sanford stepped in to ask if his "first impression" was that Steve was guilty. The juror said, "Well, yeah." Sanford asked for him to be removed from the panel because the juror had indicated he couldn't be impartial. Judge Hawes agreed and put him on the civil panel. Then Ross asked Steve to stand up, and asked if anyone recognized him. Juror #1, Andrea Brailford, raised her hand. She said, "I'm his sister-in-law." Andrea was Liz Brailford's mother and Robin's sister. Being related to Steve, and also being the mother-in-law of one of the trial's witnesses (Josh Chilmark) who had been married to Liz for almost two years by then, was probably an automatic disqualifier, but Judge Hawes asked her anyway if she thought she could be impartial. She said, "Probably not." He put her on the civil panel. Another juror was gone from the front row.

Wesley L. Sawyer, #12, a juror on the second row, said he went to school with a Sirois, and that he graduated in 1967. Ross said Steve was in his mid-40's, which made Juror #12 a dozen years older than him. I graduated from Deep Springs High School in 1965, and my sister, Jamie, graduated in 1967, so #12 was probably thinking of either her or me. As a good indication that the city is small, others said they lived near Steve, knew him from high school, or met him when he worked for the city. One said that Marri and her daughter played together sometimes. All said they would have no problem being fair. None of them made it onto the jury, but #12 did. The others were put on the civil panel. After another question about whether the venirepersons already had any information about the trial (a few said they did), Judge Hawes announced a lunch break. Five potential jurors were gone, all but one of them from the first and second rows on the left.

Ronelle Wilcox and the Voir Dire

After lunch, Elmer Ross still had the floor. His first question was answered by Juror #2, Ronelle Wilcox. My focus will be on her for the rest of the voir dire, but I should remind you that Wilcox's role in the voir dire proceedings has nothing to do with Steve's actual innocence. I do believe it may have been a factor in why he was convicted, though.

I believe that Ronelle Wilcox may have been intentionally trying to get on the jury. I'm not saying that she had help getting placed in the #2 slot (as interesting as it is to think about that possibility), but her position right in front made it that much more likely that she would get picked as long as she didn't say or do anything that would make one of the attorneys question her qualifications. She spoke up twice during the voir dire, but it was what she didn't say that convinced me she was angling to become a jury member.

The first time she spoke was when Ross read a list of potential witnesses for the trial, "Hanna Penderfield, Darla Belisle, Blake Goudy, Marri Sirois, Ada Dixon, Joshua Chilmark, Rhonda Bresnick, Tiffany Sperger, Craig Conner, and Willard Knox," and asked, "Anyone on the left side of the room recognize any of those names? We will start with the first row." Jurors 1 and 3 had been excused earlier, and Wilcox, #2, who was on the front row in a roomy space all her own, raised her hand. I'm going to leave this next little bit in transcript format for clarity.

ROSS: Juror No. 2, who do you recognize?
MS. BENSON: Craig Conner.
ROSS: How do you know Mr. Conner?
MS. BENSON: He dated my daughter when they were in high school.
ROSS: Boy, I'm treading into dangerous territory, but let me ask, as a result of that experience, do you have any biases or anything…
MS. BENSON: No.
ROSS: …which would make it uncomfortable for you to be a participant as a juror?
MS. BENSON: No.
ROSS: Thank you ma'am.

First, I need to clear up one thing about the trial transcript. As you can see, it identified Juror #2 as Ms. Benson. Crystal Sue Benson was also a venireperson, but she was #5. Ronelle Wilcox was #2. I know steno machines are designed very differently from QWERTY keyboards, but I think the court reporter just hit the wrong key (5 instead of 2 when identifying the speaker).

I spoke to Ronelle Wilcox in May 2016. To verify her identity, I asked her if she was the juror who said her daughter dated Craig Conner. She said, "That was me, yes."

Also, did you notice, when Ross asked if she had "any biases or anything," how quickly Wilcox jumped in with her "No" before he could finish his sentence? Was she a little too eager to establish that she was bias-free? Maybe, but here's the larger issue. Blake Goudy and Ada Dixon were also on Elmer Ross' list, and Ross read their names before Conner's. Wilcox had a connection to both Dixon and Goudy (one much stronger than the other), but when she admitted to knowing Craig Conner, she said nothing about either Goudy or Dixon. Ross was trying to establish if a connection to <u>anyone</u> on the list could jeopardize his case, and cause a second mistrial. Cleveland Sanford was also watching for such connections because he might need to use strikes against anyone who could be biased against Steve.

As Ross moved around the room, several other people said they knew some of the people on Ross' list. Goudy was recognized by one person, and <u>Dixon was recognized by seven</u>. Sheriff's Deputy Willard Knox came out on top, though, with eight people who knew him or knew of him. Ross had to be standing near Wilcox while he talked to some of the people behind her on the second and third rows. She would have heard Dixon's and Goudy's names when Ross first read them aloud, and then heard them repeated over and over again when people around her spoke about them, but Wilcox only mentioned knowing Craig Conner, no one else.

I repeated Ross' question to Ms. Wilcox, and asked her, "Did you recognize either of the names Ada Dixon or Blake Goudy? Those were the two I was interested in. Do you remember how you answered to those?" She said, "No, not ...I knew who Ada Dixon was. I knew what she did in town, but other than that, no, that's all I knew," adding unnecessarily, as if clarifying her point, "I just knew what her profession was." It felt to me like she was fumbling a bit, over-explaining it. Even if she didn't know Ada Dixon personally, and only knew *of* her, why didn't she include her name along with Craig Conner's when she spoke up? Several others around her mentioned knowing or just recognizing more than one person on Ross' list. If Wilcox *had* known Dixon personally, though, she definitely should have mentioned her, shouldn't she? Hang on to that thought. We're just getting started.

To see where the venirepersons were all sitting at this point, take a look at the courtroom floor plans for the voir dire on the blog, at:

https://aggravatedbook.com/images-for-the-second-trials-voir-dire/

As Ross wrapped up his portion of the voir dire, Ms. Wilcox got another reminder about withholding information. Ross said to the group, "If you were representing either of the parties in this case…would you have something in your background that you would want, as that person, to know about prior to selecting you as a juror in this case. In other words, something that maybe I've danced around or I haven't asked the specific question, or <u>anything in your background</u> that you think, after you've listened to our discussion so far this morning, that the participants in the trial would like to know. Anyone on the left side of the room?" No response from Wilcox.

After Ross was through, it was Cleveland Sanford's turn. He began by giving them some personal information, as Ross had. He talked about his educational background and his family. Then, he told them about some things that would have prevented him from serving on that jury. He said, "I don't qualify under the question about CASA and Cradle's Rest and Victims Compensation Fund." That statement should have kicked Wilcox's consciousness into gear because she was more than familiar with at least one of those items, if not all three. Cradle's Rest was on his list because Blake Goudy worked for them, and the Victims Compensation Fund and CASA were there because they both provide aid for victims, and because people who had utilized them might be predisposed to look unfavorably toward anyone charged in a case like this.

If Wilcox wanted to be on this jury, and heard the defense attorney say that he wouldn't be to get on it if he had an association with a group like CASA, she would realize that CASA or anything dealing with abused children were subjects she had better not mention. But, Sanford then asked a question she *could* respond to, one that might make her look good to both sides. He asked, "Is there anybody here that has never broken the law? I mean never had a speeding ticket, never had any problems with the law? Surely there is somebody." Wilcox (who was identified as herself in the trial transcript from this point forward, not as Ms. Benson) raised her hand, and Sanford asked, "You've never had a speeding ticket?" Ross objected, on the grounds that Sanford was asking about the personal histories of jurors, but Judge Hawes overruled him. Sanford turned to Wilcox. "No. 2, if I understand you correctly, you've never been convicted of a crime?" Wilcox said, "Yes." Sanford asked her if it was safe to assume that she wouldn't "commit a felony in the next five years." She said, "No. I may be charged with one, whether I commit it or not." Sanford was trying to point out that anyone could end up in Steve's position simply by someone accusing them of a crime. Wilcox's response showed that she was intelligent, was paying attention, and said exactly the right thing.

Sanford then asked the group questions about whether they knew or had associations with people in the legal profession or people who worked for the courts, or in law enforcement, police, probation, and parole. Several people answered, and Sanford discussed with each of them whether they could be fair and impartial. Wilcox was silent through all of that.

Then [*and this is the most important bit*] he said: "Does anyone here work for or have a family member or close friend that works in any sort of position dealing with abused victims? By that, I mean, basically working in a shelter of some form, anything that would have special training dealing with abused, possibly work as a CASA rep or a psychologist, anything along those lines? Let's start on the first row on the left side. Anybody?" There was no response from the first row, where Wilcox was sitting silently. "Second row?" Some venirepersons said that they or family members had worked as social workers or respite providers in the past, and some said they currently were engaged in those professions, or that they had foster kids, or were counselors, among other things. Wilcox was silent through all of that.

Ronelle Wilcox didn't raise her hand or speak up in response to that question (or to the earlier ones about Dixon and Goudy), and she got on Steve's jury. When Sanford asked his question about CASA there were seven out of ten potential jurors remaining on the front row. Juror #1 was gone, and so were

#3 and #7. Wilcox had one empty space on her right and another on her left. She was alone in her own space. Sanford was standing in front of the row, separated only by a short railing, and must have looked right at Wilcox when he said "Let's start on the first row on the left side. Anybody?" He had already, in his opening statements, mentioned the likelihood of his disqualification from jury service in this trial if he had personally had an association with CASA, and he had just mentioned CASA again. Wilcox had been so responsive during the voir dire so far. I find it difficult to believe that she didn't hear him ask about CASA.

Let me pause to say that there is nothing wrong with CASA (Court Appointed Special Advocates) as an organization. There are thousands of CASA chapters across the country, and they provide a wonderful service for children who are caught up in the legal system. Barbara Osler, the executive director of the Deep Springs chapter of CASA, told me that "each child in the custody of Child Protective Services has a guardian ad litem and an attorney ad litem. Our program, CASA, serves as the guardian ad litem…so the kids have an attorney who represents their legal rights and interests, and CASA represents the child's best interests." She said they typically "get involved in cases where Child Protective Services, or CPS, removes children from the home." When a child has to appear in court, a CASA volunteer is assigned to help that child get through that experience as effectively as possible. Volunteers are required to have thirty hours of specialized training before they are allowed to be an advocate for CASA, and they are required to complete an additional twelve hours of training every year to maintain that status. Their sole focus is supposed to be on the needs of that child.

In September 2015, I was trying to locate all of the jurors who served on Steve's second trial so I could interview them. When I Googled Ronelle Wilcox's name, I found a March 2001 article in the Deep Springs Gazette about a new chapter of CASA being formed there. Ronelle Wilcox was one of only ten volunteers who were sworn in by Judge Preston Hawes as the first CASA representatives for that chapter. Yes, the same Judge Hawes. The founding of that CASA chapter was his special project. At the end of the article, there was also a list of the members of that CASA's governing boards. Ada Dixon was on their Board of Directors, and Blake Goudy was on their Advisory Board. The article also indicated that the representatives had completed their required thirty hours of training to become CASA volunteers. At their swearing-in ceremony, and afterward, the volunteers obviously met Judge Hawes and could have met some of the board members then as well. When Steve's jury panel was asked if they recognized any of those names, did Wilcox intentionally refrain from mentioning Dixon and Goudy because she did know one or both of them as early as 2001? Even if she didn't know who they were before her March 2001 induction into that chapter of CASA, I find it ridiculous to believe that she didn't know them by August 2006.

We're not done.

I told Wilcox that one of the attorneys had asked a question about working with abused victims, and about working as CASA reps. I asked her if she remembered how she answered that question. She said, "Well, I had been a CASA representative, so I guess I answered that I had been a CASA representative." I just said, "Oh, okay," not letting on that I knew she hadn't revealed that in court. She added, "An advocate. I had been an advocate for CASA." I said, "You were a volunteer for CASA, right?" She said, "Yes."

Earlier in our conversation Wilcox said, "I knew who Ada Dixon was" and "what she did in town," but "no, that's all I knew," just "what her profession was." TPIA requests to the Deep Springs chapter of CASA revealed that Ada Dixon, on two dates in February 2001, taught Wilcox and the other original CASA volunteers two of their required pre-service training classes. The first was called "Understanding Children," and the second one was titled "Dynamics of Child Abuse and Bonding and Separation." So, Wilcox, in a class of only ten people, in two separate sessions, received two-and-a-half hours of training from Ada Dixon, some of it related to child abuse.

Ms. Osler told me that Dixon also gave talks to their CASA group in May of 2001, and February and May of 2004 (those talks were all during Wilcox's tenure at CASA). And Dixon had other associations with the group. She spoke at an annual CASA conference in Dallas in 2003; and gave speeches in 1999, 2000, and 2003, at the Governor's Prevent Child Abuse Texas Conference in Austin. Also, in February 2000, the year before she taught the training classes to Wilcox's group of CASA volunteers, Dixon was the featured speaker at the Ashwell County chapter of a statewide educational organization [*which I won't name here*]. Guess who has held high-ranking positions in both their Ashwell County chapter and in their statewide organization. Yes, Ronelle Wilcox. Could she have even met Dixon as early as 2000 at that speech in Ashwell County? Since Wilcox was in the first cadre of volunteers for the Deep Springs CASA chapter, it seems impossible that she could have been a member of such a small group and not known someone who was as heavily involved with the group as Dixon was, especially since she received personal training from her on two separate occasions.

Osler also sent me documentation showing that Wilcox served as a CASA volunteer from March 2001 to January 2005, and worked on two abuse and neglect cases during that time. As to how much time was typically spent on those cases, Osler said, "The number of [*court*] hearings held for a case varies between four and six during the Temporary Managing Conservatorship status (first 12-18 months), and then twice per year during Permanent Managing Conservatorship status." Osler added, "While I do not have a record of specifically how many times Ms. Wilcox appeared in court for CASA, she appeared in the 555th Judicial District before District Judge Preston Hawes and Associate Judge Jordan Decker." Wilcox was inducted into service in CASA by Judge Hawes. CASA of Deep Springs was his baby. He got it started. Wilcox volunteered for CASA for just shy of four years. Using the low end of the estimate above, Wilcox would have appeared in court in front of Judge Hawes and/or Judge Decker at least a dozen times.

To sum that up: Cleveland Sanford, in five separate questions, asked all of the venirepersons to respond if (by the time of the trial) they knew, or were themselves, people who worked for the courts [*Wilcox knew and appeared before Judges Hawes and Decker*]; or people who work in any sort of position dealing with abused victims [*Wilcox knew Dixon, possibly knew Goudy, and almost certainly dealt with abused victims herself*]; or people who worked in some sort of shelter [*Goudy*]; or people who had special training dealing with the abused [*Wilcox knew Dixon, possibly knew Goudy, and had special training herself — from Dixon*]; or people who worked as a CASA rep [*Wilcox did, and should have known some or all of the other nine CASA representatives, as well as some new volunteers during her four years there*]. By not revealing any of this, I believe that Wilcox may have lied by omission during voir dire; and by doing so, may have committed an intentional, blatant act of disregard for the law, possibly in order to influence a trial.

My Thoughts: In 2006, Wilcox wasn't with CASA any longer, so she wasn't helping children directly. Maybe her jury summons seemed like an opportunity to defend a child once again. It was well known in the area that the first trial had ended in a mistrial. Remember Elmer Ross telling Judge Hawes he was worried about being able to form a jury "with all the information that's been going around town?" This is just supposition, of course, but Wilcox, having heard some of the gossip "going around town," could have seen an opportunity to help a victimized child by preventing the second trial from ending the way the first one had. Did she keep silent because she didn't want the defense attorney to know about her connections? If she had doubts about what he meant, she could easily have said, "I used to volunteer for CASA, does that count?" She didn't, though, and that didn't afford Sanford the opportunity to question her further, which may have deprived Steve of a fair and impartial trial. When I interviewed Sanford, he put it this way. "If the lady who was Number Two in the jury pool had been a CASA volunteer for four years, and I asked the question, she's obligated to answer." I asked him what he would have done if he had known about Wilcox's service with CASA. He said, "I wouldn't leave somebody that was a CASA volunteer on a child case. I mean, I just wouldn't do it...unless I didn't have *any* other options. If I have the first potential juror who says that 'I've been a CASA volunteer for four years prior to this, and I quit being a CASA volunteer within the last two years,' I absolutely would have used a strike on that person." Sanford sent me an affidavit, which Steve submitted as part of an appeal in June of 2017. Here's what Sanford swore to.

> "I was recently informed that one of the Jurors selected in the case was a CASA volunteer and that she remained silent when I asked questions directly on point to identify any potential jurors that had prior experience working with or for CASA or any other victim services type of organization. I was also recently informed that this Juror knew Ada Dixon, one of the State's main witnesses, and may have known her quite well, despite the fact that she did not disclose this information during jury selection. Irrespective of this Juror's knowledge of, or relationship with Ada Dixon, I would have further inquired into her CASA involvement in an attempt to raise a challenge to this Juror for cause, and if unsuccessful, I would have used one of my peremptory strikes to prevent this potential juror from ultimately being seated on that Jury. Due to the nature of the case, I am 100% certain that I would not have left this potential juror on the Jury had I known that she was a CASA volunteer."

Based on Sanford's affidavit, I believe that Wilcox wouldn't have been on Steve's jury if she had done what Judge Hawes had instructed her and the others to do, tell the truth and don't withhold anything. This also made me wonder whether judges, when they spot irregularities, have a responsibility to inform the attorneys, or to strike a juror *sua sponte* (on their own). Hawes founded the Deep Springs chapter of CASA. He swore those volunteers in, and Wilcox was in his very first group. She likely appeared in his court numerous times between 2001 and 2005. During the voir dire, if he realized that she had been one of his CASA representatives, I wondered whether he should have said or done something? Sanford has been a district judge in Texas, on the same level as Judge Hawes, since 2015, so I asked him what he would have done, as a judge, if a CASA question was asked during voir dire, and he saw someone that he knew had been a CASA volunteer remaining silent. Was there any legal requirement to inform the attorneys or to strike the venireperson on his own? He said, "My gut is that, legally, you do not have any obligation," but "...I think morally ...well, let me tell you this."

He told me a story about a woman who had been on a jury panel the week before we spoke. He knew she had worked for one of the lawyers trying the case, but she had a different last name. He didn't know if she was possibly divorced and had regained her maiden name, so he didn't want to mention it in front of everybody unless he had to. He said, though, that the attorney who had been her employer immediately mentioned that she used to work for him. Sanford said, if that hadn't happened "I would have called the attorneys up, because I would have felt a moral obligation to make sure that the other attorney knew, particularly when she used her maiden name on her card, because that made me think she's trying to deceive to get on the jury." She apparently wasn't trying to do that, but Sanford felt that warning the opposing attorney would have been the right thing to do. He added, "That's a scary thing because we do have people sometimes who are trying to get on juries."

My potential score: Sanford 1, Hawes 0.

Analysis of the Voir Dire

I hope you believe by now, as I do, that the combination of Wilcox's tenure with CASA, her personal association with at least one if not both of the expert witnesses, and her connection to Judge Hawes and the Ashwell County court system, should have been disqualifying factors for being a jury member on Steve's trial. Not revealing any of that information during voir dire felt to me like a willful act, an attempt to get on the jury so she could manipulate it against the defense. Thanks to post-trial testimony from another juror, Emma Barrens, we do know that someone on that jury came up with the idea of swapping votes in order to convict Steve. It wasn't hard for me to also believe that it could have been Wilcox's idea, or that she helped someone else convince the others to go along with that scheme. Once the verdict was rendered, though, Judge Hawes, even if he had wanted to, was restricted from using Ms. Barrens' testimony to reverse Steve's conviction. Because of Texas' Rule of Evidence 606(b), what happens in the jury room can't be used as evidence to overturn a verdict except under a few specific circumstances. My personal opinion is that Rule 606(b) and its counterpart, Appellate Rule 21.3, exist for primarily one reason, to keep courts from having to retry cases. The two rules will likely never be eliminated, although I think they should be modified to cover certain situations. I won't say anything more about them here, other than I don't agree with them. I've covered both rules on the book's blog.

https://aggravatedbook.com/606b-and-21-3-legal-rules-in-conflict/

Steve's last writ was primarily about what Wilcox did and didn't say during the voir dire, with backup from Sanford's affidavit, but the courts wouldn't look at it. They declared the writ invalid without considering the evidence, saying that too much time had passed before he filed it. Unfortunately, as I understand it, all of the evidence in the writ about Wilcox's connections is now technically dead and buried, and can't be used to Steve's benefit.

Believability and Witnesses (Expert or Otherwise)

The prosecution's case depended on believability, but their witnesses were all operating on information generated by only one person, Hanna. Should the juries have believed it? Elmer Ross asked them to accept Hanna's honesty as the definitive "evidence" against Steve. He even suggested that they should believe her because a young girl wouldn't put herself through the ordeal of a trial if this hadn't actually happened to her. Which reminds me of a comment Hanna made near the end of her interview with Tom. She may not have wanted to undergo the trial after all. He had asked her for phone numbers of anyone who could help prove that her story was true, and she did finally, after some struggle, give him names of several people, and numbers for a few of them. Tom warned her, though, "The thing that would be most damaging to you, is if I went to these people, and they said, 'Well, we never heard anything about it.'" Oddly, Hanna said, "I was hoping, all of a sudden we would come to a plea ...if we have to." Was she admitting to Tom (by wishing that Steve would take a plea deal) that her accusations were false, and her friends might tell a different story than hers? I think the last thing Hanna wanted was for her story to be examined in a trial. Had she been hoping all along that Steve would accept a plea deal so she wouldn't have to go to court? He was offered several deals, all of them involving no prison sentence, but he refused them.

Tom told her that his job was just to find the truth and turn that over to the lawyers. Everything after that would be up to them. Her response to that was, "The problem is it's going to be a little bit vague, because like I said, it's been a long time. It has been at least three years." [*April 2004 to May 2006 was barely over two years*] She paused and then added, "But, no, everybody says that they would stand up for me, and support me, no matter what."

Was that just bravado? The only "friends" of Hanna's who testified on her behalf were Tiffany Sperger, Josh Chilmark, and Rhonda Bresnick, but they might not have been her friends at all. Tiffany was actually an ex-friend of Marri's, not Hanna's, and the prosecution primarily used her testimony to attack Marri's credibility as a witness, not to corroborate Hanna's story. Even Hanna said that Tiffany's strange tale about Marri witnessing something in the bathroom wasn't true.

Marri's testimony contradicted all of Hanna's except those things that were undeniable elements (like riding in a truck to see *Harry Potter*). Above all, Marri denied witnessing any of the incidents that Hanna claimed happened in her presence.

Josh was friendly toward Hanna, but not really a friend. She had a crush on him, but he graduated shortly after she began confiding in him. Hanna's ever-changing timeline is questionable, but Josh did confirm that their talks began sometime in April of 2003, and he graduated at the end of May. He started dating Steve's niece in December of that year, soon after he returned from Marine training. That effectively ended any friendship he and Hanna might have had. All Josh said in his testimony was that Hanna told him about some sexual experiences she claimed to be having with an older, unnamed man. He didn't know who her alleged abuser was until the charges were filed in April 2004.

Consider this possibility: Hanna, who might not have been abused at all, found out in January 2004 that Josh was dating Steve's niece. Could that have made her angry enough at Steve to do what she did?

The other "friend," Rhonda Bresnick, testified at both trials that she was no longer friends with Hanna, and all she could say was that Steve gave them a ride home from a rodeo, during which she didn't witness any sexual activity between Steve and Hanna. She tried to support Hanna's case, but her statements mostly contradicted Hanna's.

In the interview with Tom, and during the trials, Hanna mentioned friend after friend after friend, but only Tiffany, Rhonda, and Josh testified for her. One of her friends, Suzanna Bushnell, had been to Steve's house. Why didn't she testify? Why didn't Angie Womack? Why didn't any of Hanna's other friends testify for her? Judy Higham testified, but for the defense, and said she never saw any hint of impropriety from Steve, and didn't believe that he could have done any of those things. Two other people who should have been witnesses if Hanna's accusations had any credibility were Hanna's brother, Aaron, and Karla Spivey. I have no idea what Aaron would have said, but he could at least have cleared up the matter of the kiss in the truck and whether Ada Dixon had talked to him about it. Karla could have testified about the day she convinced Hanna to talk to Blake Goudy, and could also have testified about what Hanna told her that day. The prosecution could have subpoenaed both of them, but didn't. Did the prosecution fail to ask Ada Dixon about her discussion with Aaron for the same reason they didn't subpoena Aaron? Wouldn't the DA have subpoenaed Hanna's other friends if they had any substantive information that would have backed Hanna's story up?

Before their testimony was over, though, both Dixon and Goudy were asked if Hanna was telling the truth. Both of them said, yes, they were sure of it. Both of them cited their years of working with children, and dealing with cases of child abuse as evidence of their abilities in determining truth. Is it likely that Hanna could have convinced both of these "experts" (Goudy for about fifteen minutes, and Dixon for a little over two years) of something that wasn't true? Let's look at both of them.

Blake Goudy's Believability: Goudy only spoke briefly to Hanna, so all he could say was that she told him she had been molested and he counseled her about what to do next. He also testified that she named Steve as her molester, but, as we've already covered, she might not have named anyone to him that day. Even though Willard Knox's note said Goudy told him that Hanna "did not go into any details" with him, and that all he did was talk to her for a few minutes, the prosecution still managed to fill up 32 pages of the trial's transcript with a discussion of Goudy's credentials and a repeat of nearly everything Hanna had told the jury. The prosecution's questions to Goudy were largely couched in hypothetical terms, but they patterned what Hanna had testified to. In essence, the jury heard her assertions repeated by an authority figure, even though she hadn't given him "any details."

What were Goudy's qualifications? Ross began by having him recite a list of his credentials. Goudy said he was currently "an independent social services contractor providing services to a number of entities in Texas," and before that had been "a licensed chemical dependency counselor intern," had worked for "eight years with Child Protective Services as lead investigator," was "a certified parenting specialist," was "a specialized investigator who worked all over the State of Texas," who had worked "over 1,200 investigations of child abuse and neglect," who also did a "three month training through CPS," and had done "800 hours of continuing education" from "the University of Texas and also the Dallas Police Department's Crimes Against Children's Unit." Ross asked him if he had testified in "courts in the State of Texas in the area of child abuse expert before." Goudy said, "Numerous times."

Ross asked him "Have you personally treated many children who have been sexually abused?" The question of "treatment" should probably have been asked of a doctor or psychologist, but Goudy answered, without correcting him, by saying, "I have investigated over 300 allegations of sexual abuse against children involving anywhere from one to six children per investigation." Ross asked if certain things "occur in the course of a sexually abused child." Goudy said, "You see certain traits, you see certain reactions. You just gain a variety of experience in interviewing over 3,000 children during the course of my career." Sounds pretty impressive, doesn't it? Let's take a closer look.

In 2004, when he gave the talk at Hanna's school, he worked for a domestic violence and sexual assault shelter in Deep Springs called Cradle's Rest. In the two years between then and the trials, he apparently worked as an intern for a company that did drug counseling, and then (by the time of the trials) was an "independent contractor." Not as impressive sounding as "lead investigator" for CPS. It seemed to me like he was trying to make his background look as strong as possible. Results from a TPIA request showed that Goudy worked for CPS from September 1, 1992 to September 30, 1999. That's seven years and one month, almost a year short of the eight years he claimed in the trial. His CPS records included a termination code of "Dislike/Unsuit Assigned Duties." There's a fairly large chasm between "disliking" something and being "unsuited" for it, so that's not particularly helpful in determining if he was a good investigator.

He was 52 at the time of the trials, and had graduated in 1978, at the age of 26, with a BS in Sociology from Stockman University, the local college. The trials were 28 years later, so our potential timeline for Goudy's career activities is from 1978 to 2006. If he started at Cradle's Rest as soon as he left CPS, he would have been there about three-and-a-half years when he gave the talk at Hanna's school in 2004. According to his testimony, his job at the shelter carried the title of "Director of Prevention and Awareness," and he described his duties as "doing a variety of public relation services, speaking to groups, doing radio ads, newspaper articles, talking to civic organizations, religious organizations, and schools throughout the area about abuse and neglect, primarily spousal abuse, elder abuse, and child abuse." In other words, he was a media representative for them, not an investigator.

I have no idea if he worked in any fields related to child abuse in the fourteen years between graduating from college and starting to work at CPS; but, even if we assume he hit the ground running when he started there in 1992, and was investigating cases as soon as he finished the three months of required training, he would have to have been Energizer Bunny busy to do over 1,200 cases in "eight years." Or, actually, 6 years and 10 months (7 years and a month minus 3 months for his training). Let's give him the benefit of the doubt, though, and round the cases down to a flat 1,200. For him to handle that many in 6 years and 10 months, he would have to take on 184 new cases every year. That would mean investigating an average of .504 new cases every day (including Saturdays and Sundays), or 3.53 new cases every week. Let's round those down too, to just 3.5 cases, even though that would give him a freebie of 11 cases over the 85 months. Since those cases can sometimes stretch into weeks and months, he obviously didn't investigate and dispose of them as soon as they landed on his desk. If we use that average of 3.5 cases a week, he had 3.5 cases by the end of the first week, 7.0 by the end of the second, and 10.5 by the end of the third, etc. Eventually, some of those would be resolved, but new cases would still continue to appear at roughly 3.5 a week, or 182 a year.

How long does it take before a case is resolved? Barbara Osler, from CASA, speaking of CPS cases of abuse and neglect (the exact type of case Goudy said his were), said that her CASA volunteers had four to six court hearings in the first year-and-a-half of each case, then twice per year after that, indicating that some cases might last for quite a long time, years perhaps. Even under the best of circumstances, using Goudy's numbers, he could have had hundreds of cases open at once that would need periodic handling. Is a single CPS investigator's case load really that heavy? At the end of his first year, how many cases would he still have open out of the 182 that were begun that year? How many of those would also carry over into Year Two? Year Three? How many would he be juggling at once? Is what he claimed even possible?

We could assume he meant that he had handled 1,200 cases in his entire career, instead of just seven years, but that would still be a lot. From his graduation until he started at Cradle's Rest was 21 years. Even if we give him that extra 15 years, his case load would still average 57 cases per year. How would he have the time to do all of that plus the "800 hours of continuing education" training, and the "numerous times" he testified in court as a child abuse expert? And, in which of his professions other than CPS would he have been working on cases like those anyway? Does it sound to you like his credentials were being oversold? It does to me.

Let's look at the other expert witness.

Ada Dixon's Believability: In Ross' closing argument, he said, "Is it reasonable for a child to go through these kinds of experiences and then if they didn't happen, be willing to go to counseling for three or four years?" Aside from his odd phrasing (of going through experiences that didn't happen), Ross was vastly overstating the length of time; in this instance regarding how long Hanna was Dixon's patient. By the time of the trials, Hanna had been seeing Dixon for two years and four months, not "three or four years." Dixon testified that she had seen Hanna 78-80 times, which is an average of once every week and a half, and we only have Dixon's word for that rough number. She looked up other dates during the trials, like the exact date Hanna first saw her. Why couldn't she have looked up an exact number? Could it have been less than that, or maybe more? Dixon gave other rough numbers too. When Ross asked her how many times she had testified in court "as an expert in child abuse cases," she said, "Oh, 30, 40, guessing." The 25% difference between 30 and 40 isn't an insignificant amount for her to "guess" at. Did Dixon really testify that many times, or did she say that to bolster her status, as Goudy may have done? According to her website, she opened her counseling office in 1994, twelve years before Steve's trial. Even if she was instantly overflowing with patients, for her to testify in 30 cases by 2006, she would have to have testified in (an average of) 2.5 child abuse cases per year, and 3.3 cases per year to achieve 40. Did she handle that many child abuse cases every year that also ended up in court? With all of her public speaking, and training she was doing for CASA, when did she find the time? I'm not saying it was impossible, it just seems highly unlikely to me. How can we know what's true if she won't open her records?

We could try looking it up elsewhere.

If Dixon did testify in 30 to 40 trials in just twelve years, her name might appear in legal databases. Nine years after Steve's trial, a 2015 search of the Lexis-Nexis legal database showed zero instances of her name appearing in appeals documents before Steve's 2006 trial. Her name did appear twice, but one was for Steve's 2007 appeal, and another was for a 2011 appeal of a trial we'll call *Gonzo v. Texas*. In that appeal, the defendant alleged that "Dixon could not testify to the truthfulness of the victim" because she hadn't met the criteria for Texas' Rule of Evidence 702. That rule, essentially says that testimony from an expert witness about the truth of the matter at hand can't be opinion-based, it must be backed by facts or data, and must be generated from reliable principles and methods. An expert witness simply saying, "She told the truth" without concrete proof is not allowed in a court of law, but she did exactly that in *Gonzo*, and she did it in Steve's case too. Dixon also testified in another post-2006 trial, *Texas v. Munsen* (2013). In that one she was asked how many times she had testified before. She said, "I couldn't give you a definite number, but over 21 years a lot." Also, in that trial, she claimed she couldn't produce the documents the court had subpoenaed because she lost them when her computer "crashed, as well as my whole 21 years of practice." As I said to Toby Billings, the person who gave me copies of the *Munsen* transcripts, "If she really only kept her records on her computer, she's an utter fool. Computers crash. Every computer in existence will fail someday," but did her computer really conveniently crash just before she was required to produce records for a trial?

A Small Side-note: How many computers have you had in the past 21 years? When you got a new one, did you move all the records for your home or business that were on that first computer to your new one each time you upgraded, or did you keep paper records, or backups on discs or CDs or DVDs or some other method of storage? Wouldn't it be inherently foolish to keep your "whole 21 years of practice" on just one computer?

Another Small Side-note: According to Dixon, she opened her business in 1994, which appears to be 19 years before the Munsen trial, not 21. Was that another attempt to pad her resume? In Steve's trial she said, "I have been in private practice about 13 years." From the beginning of 1994 to the end of 2006 is 13 years, but did she open her office on January 1st, 1994, and was Steve's trial being held in late December of 2006? No, it was mid-summer 2006. I know. I'm being picky, and it's a very minor point, but I believe Dixon, like Goudy, might have been expanding her credentials.

In the Munsen trial, Dixon was also asked to produce documents that listed the cases where she "testified as an expert on sexual assault of a child at trial or by deposition in the past ten years." She said, "I wouldn't have a list because I wouldn't want to break HIPAA laws reporting who I'd seen and stuff like that." That court ultimately didn't force the issue and require her to produce the list, but it would have answered some of my questions, and HIPAA shouldn't have prevented her from providing a list with generic dates (like "three trials in 1998, two in 1999," etc.). In Steve's trial, she admitted that she had brought Hanna's mother into some of the sessions, but no one asked her if she had also spoken to Aaron as Hanna had claimed. Would Dixon have refused to answer that in court because of HIPAA, as she did with me, or did she even know that Hanna had claimed that she had asked Aaron about whether he saw a kiss in the truck? Did her "computer crash" prevent her from producing the records the *Munsen* court asked her for, and let her bring in only the materials she could "find," documents that happened to be unfavorable to Mr. Munsen? I believe she obtained a similar result in Steve's trial by convincing Judge Hawes to let her summarize just five out of the earliest twenty sessions for him to review. Those twenty, by the way, based on her estimate at trial, represented less than a quarter of Hanna's eventual sessions with her. Did the summary alone provide a complete picture of Hanna's sessions with Dixon, or was it one that was primarily biased against a sexual offender? Without full disclosure, it's doubtful that we'll ever know.

Regarding Dixon's court appearances, a TPIA request by Maureen Munsen, Alan Munsen's mother, asking for information about payments made to Dixon revealed that Dixon had been paid a total of $1,775 for "professional services" by Ashwell County, on three separate dates, which could have been for testifying, but could also have been for other things (like teaching training classes to CASA volunteers, for example). Two of the dates were in February and May of 1996, and one was in June of 2001. The county had no records of payments to her after 2001. Requests by Ms. Munsen to other nearby counties yielded no results at all. Brewer County and Dutton County found no records of Dixon testifying. Seward County's records only went as far back as 2007, but they also had no listing for her, and no one at the Seward County courthouse recognized her name. Cutter County's records only went back to 2002, but Dixon wasn't in any of theirs either. There is very little record of Dixon testifying on behalf of any of her clients between the time she opened her offices and the 2006 trial. Without examining every single trial held in Ashwell County and the surrounding counties from 1996 to 2006, I can't prove that she testified far less than she swore to in court, but I also haven't found any evidence that she did testify that many times. To see an accounting of the lengths Dixon went to during the Munsen trial to circumvent court procedures, check out the blog posts, *Hanna's Counselor – Parts 3, 4, 5,* and *6*; beginning with this post:

https://aggravatedbook.com/hannas-counselor-part-3/

To get back to Ross' question about whether a child would be willing to go to counseling for that long if they hadn't been molested, my answer would be, yes. I do believe Hanna was willing to continue seeing Dixon, at least until the trials were over, because attending those therapy sessions would add credibility to the idea that she was suffering because of this. I've often wondered if she stopped seeing Dixon fairly soon after the end of the second trial, but Dixon wouldn't answer any of my questions, citing HIPAA.

In Trial #2, Dixon listed a series of sexual abuse indicators. "Depression, anger, nightmares, sleeplessness, a change in grades, a change in friends maybe, very, very, angry, feeling very, very betrayed." They were also listed in her book (absent the multiple "very"s). According to Dixon, Hanna's anger was a symptom that she had been abused. Hanna told Tom, though, "I wasn't mad, and that's the problem. Ada was actually mad at *me* for not being mad at him. I was ...just wasn't mad at him. I ...I'm mad at him now, but at the time the charges were filed, I wasn't mad ...I felt ...I was mad at myself because I felt like I was betraying a good friend, and, after I had been to counseling for a while ...um ...it got to where I had no feeling for him at all. He just didn't exist." After a few moments of silence she added, "Now I'm mad at him and he's very real. He's like a living nightmare." Notice how Hanna managed to work both anger and nightmares into the comment?

[*If true, would Dixon becoming angry with Hanna, when Hanna was ostensibly vulnerable and experiencing trauma, be a recommended therapy by most psychological associations? According to Hanna, if that really did happen in her therapy sessions, Dixon succeeded. Of course, there is always the possibility that Hanna was just using Tom to refine her story, changing the outward expression of her feelings to match what Dixon's book said a victim of abuse should feel. It's also possible that Hanna's anger discussion with Dixon never happened at all. With Hanna, there's no way to tell. Her claims of having nightmares, by the way, according to all the documents I have, didn't begin until after she started her sessions with Dixon.*]

Another Side-note: For the record, "a change in grades" was also one of Dixon's symptoms. Hanna's grades did fall a little, but very little. This is just speculation on my part, but the drop in Hanna's grades may have been about the same time she got caught cheating on her school's self-paced computer learning program by logging on with other students' ID numbers to see their answers on tests before entering her own. Hanna brought the subject up to Tom, telling him that she had done that. When I visited her school, I asked two Alderson School District officials about it, and they verified that it was true.

Overview of the Trial Itself

"On or about" is a phrase the prosecution used to great effect in both trials, but it limits the ability of innocent individuals to defend themselves because it allows for the accuser to use distorted timelines. During the jury voir dire, Elmer Ross said that the prosecution was able to do that because "the law requires that a date be alleged, but the law will allow the testimony to prove that date in a different way other than saying specifically that date." He added that, in sexual assault of a child cases, "it is sufficient, the date that is alleged, to place the Defendant on notice as to a timeframe. And that the offense occurred either on that date alleged, before that date alleged, or after that date alleged, but as long as it occurred before the case was presented to the Grand Jury for the handing down of the indictments" because "a child is not aware of specific days, like an adult would be."

[*In effect, the DA was saying: Even if they got the date wrong, as long as Hanna said it happened before he gave the details to the grand jury, it would still be a valid indictment. Presumably, that also means that she could even claim there were incidents that happened before the first incident she swore to in her affidavit, and after the one she also swore was the last one, and that would have been okay with the law too.*]

One basic argument the prosecution gave to justify using imprecise dates was that children view time differently than adults. Presumably because adults have fixed work schedules and routines which make them more aware of dates and times, and children generally don't, Ross implied that children have imprecise memories of days and dates and hours of the day. I could largely accept that notion as it applies to very small children, but Hanna was in junior high and high school during this time period. She did have specific things to do at specific times on specific days; a schedule, in other words. A simple glance at her school activities, in fact, suggests a fairly regimented, active schedule. She was faced with remembering details on a daily basis, and she did come up with presumably exact dates when she needed to (the cross-country race on September 8, 2001; a sleepover on April 18, 2003; and Beau's birthday on February 14, 2004, for example). She was also able to cite exact times of the day (like a 9:00 pm movie, as well as other specific times when certain incidents allegedly occurred), and usually stated those dates and times clearly, as if she remembered exactly what they were. Her times and dates were often wrong, though. You'll see several examples of that as we continue. Regarding the alleged incidents, Hanna was the source for all of the numbers and dates and times that were used in the trials, like the "80 to 90" times she claimed to have been molested. In her 2004 affidavit, though, she said she couldn't remember exact dates for any of them except the last one.

The date she gave in her affidavit for the first alleged incident was only semi-specific, "in late August or early September 2001...the first time I had spent the night at Steve Sirois's house." Since the indictment was based on the affidavit, they took her fuzzy date, split the difference, and came up with "on or about September 1, 2001." The prosecution's job was to then prove that the information in the indictment was true. If both elements had been true (the first incident happening close to September 1st, and happening the first time she and Aaron spent the night, which was in November), the prosecution, under ordinary circumstances, would have been faced with a dilemma. How could they prove that early September and late November were the same thing? They didn't even try. They just ignored the disparity because the phrase "on or about" let them get away with listing September in the indictment but still claim almost any date in the trials.

If a bank was robbed, and the witnesses all said the robbery happened just after 10:00 am on September 1st, a person who was accused of that crime might be able to prove whether they were there or not. Witnesses could verify the defendant's presence elsewhere, or receipts from businesses could show they were buying something in a different part of town. But if the indictment just said that the robbery might have happened sometime in August or September, or earlier, or maybe later, and (oh, by the way), none of the security cameras were working and the robber was wearing a mask and gloves (i.e., no DNA and no eyewitness ID), then you come closer to the situation Steve was in. All he could say was, "I didn't do it. It never happened." If a prosecutor can interpret time as loosely as that, what chance does a defendant have in a case like Steve's? He could attempt to prove that his accuser is lying, but there are also restrictions on what the defense can do to discredit a "victim." It's supposed to be the prosecutor's job to prove that the accuser is telling the truth (or that the defendant isn't). I don't believe they did that in either of Steve's trials, but, unfortunately, this tactic also made it nearly impossible for Steve to counter Hanna's claims.

Something else to consider: Hanna told Tom during her interview that she became sexually active after April 2004. If that was true, I believe that activity could have provided her with specific details that she fed to Tom, Dixon, and the DA, and testified to in both trials. When reading Hanna's testimony, it's clear that she had some knowledge of sexual acts; but keep in mind that she had over two years between the accusations and the trials to continue to invent and refine her story, and also to experiment. Especially in light of the many changes she made to her narrative after the accusation, everything she said should be treated suspiciously. Think of her changes as script pages undergoing revision and polishing, getting all the dialogue just right before the show opened.

The Part Eddie Higham Played: In Trial #1, Attorney Guthrie didn't attempt to establish too much when he questioned Judy Higham. He just introduced the idea of Eddie Higham being in Hanna's life, brought up his background, and let the thought of him hover there. That might have been a good trial strategy, but why didn't they probe other elements of his relationship with the Belisle/Penderfield family? Eddie was a known quantity to the defense since the very beginning. Why wasn't he interviewed, and possibly called as a witness? I should also point out that Hanna didn't mention Eddie in her affidavit, and he also isn't mentioned in Ada Dixon's summary. I'm not saying that Hanna should have volunteered that information, just that she was silent on the subject of Eddie until Tom asked her about him in 2006.

What lengths would someone go to in order to protect their reputation? Would they lie in a court of law? I believe that Hanna often did lie, but proving it has sometimes been difficult; and proving that she and her mother both lied on the stand in the second trial might require a higher level of difficulty. I think it's fair to say, though, that when a witness drastically changes their testimony about a factual matter from one trial to the next they may have committed perjury in at least one of those trials. I think it's also accurate to say that a prosecutor who knows that his client has changed their testimony but doesn't attempt to correct it could possibly be suborning perjury.

I believe that Hanna's accusations were formed through some sort of bizarre fantasy involving males she knew (Josh in particular, maybe Beau, Steve, or Eddie; and possibly others). Unfortunately, I don't have a way to establish which of her statements are invented, or whether any of them could be true. I'm positive that, using the criteria mentioned above, I can prove that some of them are false, but I often can't prove which statements might be lies; or, conversely, whether any of them might be true. If, for example, I said that I bought only one kind of fruit yesterday, and told one person that I bought bananas, told someone else that I bought apples, and told a third person that I bought oranges, at least two of those statements would be lies, but it's also possible that all three were. I could have bought grapes, or no fruit at all. Some of Hanna's statements veer into that kind of territory. Right now, though, we're only going to look at what I think might be one major lie (and possibly a couple of supplemental ones). In the *Proof of Innocence* section, though, I'll tackle several sets of whoppers.

Eddie Higham was a convicted sex offender who served five years in prison for aggravated sexual assault of a 13-year-old girl. Here's the question: Did Eddie live with Darla Belisle and her children for any length of time during the timeframe of the accusations (September 1, 2001 to February 14, 2004), and did Darla and Hanna lie about it? I believe he did and they did, but can I prove it? Let's begin with what Steve and others have told me and then we'll look at the testimony. The following information comes largely from Steve, but Eddie's criminal record and other information has been confirmed by members of his family, and by court and trial records.

Some Background: In October 2002, Robin and Darla and the kids were at Saddleview Cove's swimming pool. Before everyone got back, Fred Smith, Peggy Higham's husband, showed up at Steve's house and told him that Peggy was at the pool with her brother, Eddie. He said that Eddie had recently been in prison for having sex with a minor, and that Darla seemed to be attracted to him. According to Steve, Darla and Eddie started dating that same day. Steve said that, after that, every time he talked to Darla she would rave about Eddie (he's so thoughtful, he's such a gentleman, etc.). Concerned for Darla and the kids because of what Fred had told him, Steve went to the county clerk, obtained information about Eddie's incarceration, and told Darla about Eddie's past, but Darla said she already knew about it. According to Peggy, Eddie told Darla about it when he met her, and Darla took him home with her the same day they met, even though she had two young kids in the house and knew he was a registered sex offender.

Steve said that, a few months later, he got a call from Darla. She was panicked, saying someone had turned her into Child Protective Services because of Eddie, and they wanted to take her kids away. Steve agreed to go there with her to support her, but was shocked when he heard Darla tell the CPS worker that she was no longer seeing Eddie (which he was sure wasn't true). He didn't say anything, though, thinking Darla would now tell Eddie she couldn't date him anymore. He vouched for her, saying that she was a good mother who loved her kids. CPS dropped the case, thinking the relationship was over. It wasn't. How would the rest of this story have played out if Steve hadn't gone to CPS with Darla?

He also said that Darla went to a local lawyer, Patricia Lindeen, and asked her if there was any way she could keep dating Eddie under the circumstances. Lindeen advised her to disassociate herself from him right away. According to Steve, Darla said, "That bitch. Fuck her," and kept dating Eddie. CPS wouldn't reveal who filed the report against Darla, but I assume it must have been a neighbor, or someone who knew her well enough for her to have mentioned Eddie's past, or to have seen him hanging around her house.

Steve discussed Eddie with Roland Mathis soon after he hired him, and the subject also came up in the brainstorming session, but the next mention of Eddie didn't come until Tom's interview with Hanna. She must have been thinking about what to say for a couple of years by that time. Two hours into the audio, Tom asked her if Eddie "was your mother's boyfriend, or lived with y'all for a while?" Hanna said, "He never lived with us. He stayed over a couple of nights, but that was it…and there was only one time when him and I were alone, and nothing happened." Tom told her that would probably come up in the trial, "because Eddie was a convicted, uh..." He paused, and Hanna said, "Exegist, yes."

[*I've listened to that section multiple times, and it really does sound like she said* "exegist" *on the audio, but an exegist is someone who's an expert in explaining Bible texts. Maybe she was trying to say* "sexist."]

Whatever she did say, Tom just agreed with her and asked if Eddie ever tried to approach her. Hanna said, "Not once." Hanna must have known it would look bad in court if a sex offender had been living with them. Was she trying to lighten the impact of that by reducing the amount of time he might have been around them? Let's see what she and Darla said in the trials.

They weren't asked any questions about Eddie during the first trial. That fell to Eddie's niece, Judy at the end of Trial #1. During Trial #2, though, the subject of Eddie surfaced soon after Cleveland Sanford got a chance to cross-examine Hanna. He asked if she knew "anybody named Eddie Higham." She said, "Yes, sir, I do…He is my mom's ex-boyfriend." He asked her when Darla dated him. Hanna said, "Between the years of 2002-2003." He asked if her mom dated him for a period of time, and she answered "Yes." To make sure, he asked, "It wasn't like two dates?" She said, "No," and added, "He is not the most reliable person. To me, he seemed like a pretty nice guy. I didn't have a problem with him." When Hanna was released from questioning, she went to wait outside with her family. The court took a lunch break at noon, then six other witnesses had their turn before Darla was called to the stand around 3:00 pm.

Elmer Ross asked Darla if she had any information to indicate that anyone other than Steve molested Hanna. Darla said, "None at all." Then he asked her if she knew who Eddie was, and she answered, "Yes, I do." He asked her how she knew him. She said, "I met him out at the lake." He asked her if, beginning sometime in 2002, she had "a dating relationship with Mr. Higham." Darla said, "Yes." He asked her if she had any information that Eddie had "done anything inappropriate to Hanna." She answered, "Oh, none at all. He never had the opportunity." When he asked her what she meant by that, she said, "I mean, I never left him alone with her. There was never an opportunity. No."

[*None at all - never - never - no. Darla wasn't asked any questions that should have caused her to lie about Eddie, but she may have lied just then anyway, when she said she* <u>*never*</u> *left him alone with Hanna.*]

Ross passed the witness to Sanford. I've <u>underlined</u> the most relevant phrases in their exchange. He asked Darla how long she had dated Eddie. She said, "Eight or ten months, <u>maybe</u>." He asked her if "those eight or ten months were all between September of 2001 and April of 2004." She said, "Yes." He asked her to verify that she had just told Ross that in those "eight or ten months of dating this man, he never had an opportunity to be alone with your daughter at all?" Darla agreed that, yes, she had said that. Just to be sure, Sanford asked, "Not even for a minute?" She said, "Not to my knowledge." Then he asked her, "He never gave her rides?" Darla said, "One time, one ride. <u>I just figured that was coming</u>." Sanford said, "Where did he take her?" Darla said, "He went to pick her up at Sirois'." Sanford asked her if that meant she was changing her earlier testimony. She said, "I'm saying one time he went to pick her up. I couldn't get a way to go get her. And Sirois called me the minute they left." Sanford objected, saying her answer was unresponsive [*i.e., she wasn't answering the question he had asked*], and Judge Hawes agreed. Sanford asked, "if he went and picked her up and brought her back to your house, then he was alone with her, wasn't he?" She said, "Just long enough to do it, yes." Sanford asked her if it was 23 miles between the two houses. Darla wasn't sure, but agreed that was close. [*It's actually a little over 21.*] Then Sanford asked the next big question. "Aside from that ride, <u>did Mr. Higham spend the night at your house</u>?" Darla said, "<u>No</u>." He asked her, "<u>Never once</u>?" Again, she said, "<u>No</u>."

[*I wasn't there, so I can't pretend to know what Darla's attitude was when Sanford was questioning her, but her answers feel argumentative when I read them, so I've usually pictured her as being a bit belligerent at that moment. I'm assuming that Darla's line, "Just long enough* <u>*to do it*</u>*" meant "long enough to drive Hanna home," not to "*<u>*do*</u>*" anything else.*

Darla said she dated Eddie for "eight or ten months, <u>*maybe*</u>*." Could* *their relationship have lasted longer than eight to ten months? Even if it only was eight to ten months, that would mean she continued to date a registered sex offender for four to six months after her visit to CPS, continuing to risk the possibility that her kids could be taken away from her. In comparison, the prosecution used Steve's 1982 marijuana conviction as proof that he was dishonest and was willing to harm his wife and kids even though he had stopped that behavior over two decades earlier, before he was married to Robin, and before Marri or Beau were even born. Darla, on the other hand, continued to expose her children to a registered sex offender long after she had been warned (by CPS, and by Steve, and by an attorney) to not see him anymore. Are those two sets of circumstances even remotely equivalent?*]

If Darla dated Eddie for "eight or ten months, maybe," and she started dating him in October 2002, is that length of time true? The word "maybe" connotes vagueness. In this case it could either mean less than eight or ten months or it could mean longer. Let's look at both possibilities. If you had been doing something for a year or so, and you didn't want people to think you had been at it for that long, you might low-ball the amount of time, and say something like "eight or ten months, maybe" to give the impression that it was in that general neighborhood but probably not quite that long. If, however, you wanted people to think you had been at it longer, you would likely say something along the lines of, "Oh, at least ten months, maybe more." The wording of Darla's statement indicates she might have been trying to play down the actual length, possibly so the jury would believe it was briefer than it really was. The Ashwell County Rodeo was held at the end of July 2003, which was about ten months after Darla met Eddie. In the chapter on the rodeo, I will argue that Darla might have still been dating him then, but could it have been even longer than that? I have no proof of it, but Darla's relationship with Eddie possibly ending as late as when the charges were filed, in April 2004, does fit into one of the theories I have about why Hanna accused Steve instead of someone else.

Back to the trial: When Sanford asked Darla, "Never once?" he gave her an opportunity to correct her statement, but she didn't. Did you notice the lie she may have given just before that? When she said, "I just figured that was coming," it seemed to me that she was admitting that she not only lied when she said that Eddie was never alone with Hanna, but also that she suspected that the defense might ask her about the ride, but she lied anyway, knowing how it could look if she admitted to have knowingly placed her kids in proximity to a registered sex offender. The next potential lie may have been only a few lines later, when she said "No" to the two questions about whether Eddie ever spent the night at her house. We'll take them one at a time.

The Lie About the Ride: Steve and Robin and the kids, including Hanna, were at home one Saturday morning in 2003, waiting for Darla to pick Hanna up, when Eddie drove up in Darla's pickup. Steve said, "For some reason, Aaron was not with her that time. She was by herself, because that was what upset us so bad." Shocked to see Eddie instead of Darla, Steve asked him what he was doing. Hanna came out of the house before he could answer, climbed in the pickup, and they drove off. When Steve told Robin, she said to call Darla right away. He did, and told her that Eddie shouldn't be alone with Hanna. He made her promise to call him when they arrived.

In the second trial, when Sanford asked Darla, "Never once?" her response was, "I'm saying one time he went to pick her up. I couldn't get a way to go get her. And Sirois called me the minute they left."

I'm going to pick those three sentences apart a little.

First sentence: "I'm saying one time he went to pick her up." I believe that Darla and Hanna knew this ride was going to be a problem for them once they realized that Darla's relationship with Eddie might be brought up in the trial. That's could be why Hanna was so forceful when she told Tom "...there was only <u>one</u> time when him and I were alone," and why Darla testified that there was only "<u>One</u> time, <u>one</u> ride," followed by "I'm saying <u>one</u> time he went to pick her up." <u>One</u>, <u>one</u>, <u>one</u>, <u>one</u>. Did Darla and Hanna really expect the jury to believe, with Darla working until late afternoon every day, that in the space of eight to ten months (or longer), Eddie never had <u>any</u> access to Hanna, and was only alone with her <u>that one time</u>, for that <u>one brief ride home</u>?

Darla's next sentence: "I couldn't get a way to go get her" could be a mis-transcription by the court reporter. Saying "<u>a way</u>" suggests that she didn't have the means to get to Steve's (i.e., no car, or no ride). A better transcription might be "I couldn't get <u>away</u> to go get her," meaning she was involved with something and couldn't leave right then. Steve doesn't remember how it happened that morning, but typically Hanna or Aaron would call Darla when they were ready to leave, and she would drive the 21.3 miles from Alderson to the lake to bring them home. And she did have "a way" to pick up Hanna. She had her pickup, but instead of driving it herself, she apparently sent her boyfriend in it instead.

Third sentence: "And Sirois called me the minute they left." Was Darla suggesting that she asked Steve to call her when Hanna left? Steve called her to let her know that he didn't think it was a good idea for Hanna to be alone with Eddie given his background. This may actually be a better expression of Steve's character than it is of Darla's concern for her own daughter. I believe he was worried about Hanna's welfare when Darla apparently wasn't.

The Lie About Eddie Living With Them: Cleveland Sanford closed his questions to Darla by asking her if Eddie ever spent the night at her house. She said, "No." He asked her, "Never once?" She again replied, "No." A couple of months before that, Hanna told Tom Swearingen that Eddie "never lived with us," "he <u>stayed over a couple of nights</u>, but that was it."

[*Hanna's and Darla's dogged insistence that Eddie had been alone with Hanna "only one time," just "one time, one ride," feels to me like they were trying to hide the exact opposite of that. Darla knew that Steve was aware of Hanna's ride home with Eddie, and how it would look to a jury. Was that why she lied about it? I also believe that Hanna was lying to Tom about whether Eddie lived with them or not, but can I prove it?*]

Tom didn't get to interview Darla, and she wasn't asked about Eddie in Trial #1, but when Sanford, in Trial #2, asked her if Eddie had ever spent the night, she emphatically denied it, and she attempted to lie about the ride moments before that, even though she seemed to believe that Steve's lawyer knew about it [*he did*]. Isn't it conceivable then, or even likely, that she also lied about Eddie living with them? Someone reported Darla to CPS because of Eddie, so other people had to have known he was there.

Eddie's sister, Peggy, was in the courtroom when Darla said Eddie had "never once" spent the night at her house. As soon as she could (later that same day), Peggy told Steve that she knew Darla had lied in court because she had brought Eddie's things to him at Darla's house. Steve called Tom and Sanford immediately, but Sanford said he couldn't put Peggy on the stand because she had been in the courtroom when Darla testified, and procedural rules wouldn't allow her to be a witness if she heard any of the testimony. Peggy could have been called as a witness if there had been a third trial, and her testimony could have been introduced then. In 2014, Peggy gave me an affidavit, which states, among other things, that "Darla Belisle knew Eddie Higham was a registered sex offender from the beginning of their relationship, and Eddie lived with Darla, Hanna, and Aaron, in Darla's house. I know this because I brought him his clothes and some personal items when he moved in with her in October, 2002."

All of that could be introduced in a later trial, along with Peggy's accusation of Darla's perjury. The statute of limitations on perjury for the 2006 trial expired a number of years ago, but, I believe, if there ever were a new trial, and Darla and Hanna were asked the same questions under oath, they would be forced to lie again or come clean.

Questions About Eddie: Did the Assistant District Attorney, Elmer Ross, know about Eddie, or did Darla and Hanna hide that relationship from him? Why did it take so long before anyone investigated whether Eddie lived with Hanna, Aaron and Darla, and how long he lived there? The defense knew about the relationship soon after Steve hired Mathis. Shouldn't they have had documentation and affidavits, and possibly even an interview with Eddie underway as early as 2005? Wouldn't that information have been something a defense attorney could use? I asked Tom Swearingen (late in 2017) if any of Steve's attorneys had given any consideration to the idea of talking to Eddie about whether he had lived with Darla, or how long they dated, or had thought about calling him as a witness. Tom simply said, "Not that I can remember." I can understand the rationale behind an attorney not wanting to interview people associated with their opponent, just in case they might reveal something that would harm their case, but I think anything Eddie might have said would have been more useful than harmful.

I have a list of people I would very much like to interview eventually. Eddie is one of them, and Aaron is another. I would also like to talk to several of the jury members I wasn't able to reach (I've spoken to five so far, but they were all very non-committal), and I have already attempted to speak to several other people, like Ada Dixon (who refused to say anything, citing HIPAA regulations), and attorney Patricia Lindeen, who also refused to talk to me.

Jury Stuff

"The jury, passing on the prisoner's life,
May in the sworn twelve have a thief or two
Guiltier than him they try."
William Shakespeare

"If the system worked the way the system was supposed
to work, you wouldn't be writing a book."
Cleveland Sanford

[Subsections in this Chapter: Distortions of Fact // Jury Deliberations and Verdict // Things the Juries Didn't Hear About // Analysis]

Distortions of Fact

Before the jury could begin their deliberations, the two attorneys had to give their closing statements. Throughout the trial, but especially in its final moments, the prosecution made a number of comments which I think bent the facts in various ways. Here are a few of them to give you the basic idea. Don't forget, though, that this chapter is only about proving that the trial was unfair. I will still poke holes in the comments below, but the *Proof of Innocence* section is where I'll prove to you that Steve didn't do the things Hanna claimed.

Here's what ADA Elmer Ross said in his closing statement.

> "So, let me remind you what Hanna told you began to happen in September of 2001. After several years of her family socializing with the Defendant, after several months of the Defendant cultivating a relationship with her, where he would talk to her about things, attempting, she thought, to encourage her, to make her feel better about herself, how she was going to do great things in the future. Folks, this is a perpetrator cultivating a child for what they are about to do to that child. Both Blake Goudy and Ada Dixon told you that. And this Defendant did that with great specificity. As he spent time and time and time with Hanna."

That statement is full of misrepresentations. Let's look at them.

1) *"After several years of her family socializing with the Defendant..."*

The prosecution tried to paint a picture of Steve and Hanna in isolation together for years. According to Steve, that didn't happen. Not before September 2001, and not after. The families socialized when they got together. Steve cooked, usually barbecuing or grilling outside, except in the winter when they had fewer get-togethers anyway. The kids played outside or watched TV inside. The adults usually sat under the carport and talked, and yes, drank; but Ross' time period was way off base. According to Hanna's own testimony, she and Aaron first met Steve at her uncle's business in 1998, when Steve worked there, and Darla brought them to Steve's house once (probably in 1999). Darla visited the Sirois' a few times by herself between 1999 and 2001, but not often, and the kids didn't visit again until September 8, 2001, the day of Hanna's cross-country meet.

2) *"...after several months of the Defendant cultivating a relationship with her..."*

Hanna and Aaron weren't regular visitors until the cross-country meet. After that, they didn't come every weekend, and, when they did come, it was almost always just Fridays. There were ten Fridays between the cross-country meet and when they went to see *Harry Potter*, but they only visited roughly every other weekend. How did a few hours, on four or five Fridays, become months of time alone with Sara when Steve was also cooking meals and socializing with the adults? He might have said "hi" to the kids when they got there and probably talked to them occasionally during the evening, but he had no time alone with Hanna.

3) *"...he would talk to her about things, attempting, she thought, to encourage her, to make her feel better about herself, how she was going to do great things in the future."*

Steve said, sure, he talked to her. He talked to everyone. Did he say encouraging things to her? I hope so. Any decent person would treat children with respect. And that would be true for any of the kids who were around from time to time: his own, Darla's, Marri's friends, whoever was there. And there *always* were other people there. In the first trial, Darla herself testified about the get-togethers, saying *"There was usually quite a crowd there. There was other kids and parents and, it was like a, the home base, you know, everybody would come."* Steve had no time alone with Hanna.

4) *"And this Defendant did that with great specificity..."*

Ross was saying that Steve targeted Hanna deliberately, and paid her concentrated, detailed attention, trying to win her trust, but how could he have accomplished that? Ross used Hanna's statements in the trial to build up a scenario that placed her in the center of Steve's attention as if he had no desire to interact with anyone else, but it wasn't true. They were never in a vacuum, and he had no time alone with Hanna.

5) *"...he spent time and time and time with Hanna."*

Darla was asked in the first trial if Hanna ever spent time with Steve other than the cook-outs, and even she said. *"No. I mean, there was, I guess, times that he, not just her alone to my knowledge. There were times that he would take a few of them to the movies or, you know, here and there. But just one on one, no...he was usually one to have his daughter with him or his son or somebody. I mean he was rarely alone."* Taking both his kids and Darla's to the movies didn't happen until November 2001, when they went to see *Harry Potter*, and even Hanna's mother said Steve wasn't alone. Do I need to say it again? I will anyway. Steve had no time alone with Hanna.

[*Ross painted a picture that fit the pattern of grooming a child for molestation, something which was also hammered home by both of the expert witnesses, Goudy and Dixon. Ross' presumption was that, after* "years of her family socializing," *and "several months" of grooming, Steve was able to take advantage of Hanna the first time she spent the night, but those several months didn't happen, and neither did the years. There were no more than four to six evenings (if that many) before the first time they spent the night, and other people were usually around. There was no time for grooming. The* "time and time and time" *that Ross claimed Steve spent with Hanna just didn't exist.*]

There were a number of other ways that Ross' closing statement altered the facts in subtle ways which made things seem worse than they were. Hanna claimed that there were eighty to ninety separate instances of molestation. Was stretching the time period a way to make that number seem possible? In his closing statements Ross said, *"And the testimony is uncontroverted that she was over there in the period from 2001 to 2004, at least every other weekend, if not more than that."* Uncontroverted testimony? Who proved the truth of her claims? No one did, and even Hanna and Darla said it wasn't that often. Ross made it seem like there was a full three years' worth of weekends (156 of them) for Steve to carry out his evil manipulations, but that amount of time didn't exist, which is something I will thoroughly debunk in the chapter, *A Timeline as Final Proof*. For now let me just say that the time period of Hanna's claims should instead begin near the end of November 2001 and extend to February 14, 2004, which automatically eliminates 40 of Ross' 156 weekends.

Here's another example where I believe Ross stretched the truth. He told the jury that Hanna had been *"in counseling now for over three years."* At the moment he was saying that, Hanna had actually only been seeing Ada Dixon for two years and three months. He even extended that ridiculous time period a few minutes later when he said, *"Is it reasonable for a child to go through these kinds of experiences and then if they didn't happen, be willing to still go to counseling for three or four years?"* He slipped an extra year into an already-too-long-to-be-true supposition. He even tried to get the jury to forget some of Hanna's testimony when he said, *"And what the Defendant's own daughter saw in the bathroom was the Defendant on top of Hanna during the timeframe these events were occurring."* I've already discredited Tiffany's statement, as well as the reason she was testifying, but Ross ignored his own client when Hanna herself said, in response to whether Marri witnessed anything happening in a bathroom, *"No, sir, I believe that was mistaken."* Did Ross think the jury would have forgotten she said that? Maybe they did.

Had Hanna just revised her stories so often that even her own lawyer couldn't keep up with the changes? It seems to me that, between the two of them, they not only altered basic details for most of the claimed incidents, they also tried to change space and time in a variety of ways. I'll cover more of them in the *Proof of Innocence* section.

Jury Deliberations and Verdict

Just to remind you, Steve was charged with one count of aggravated sexual assault of a child, and two counts of sexual assault of a child. Count I was an aggravated charge because Hanna was under fourteen at the time of the alleged first incident. She was fourteen, though, almost fifteen, when the final two counts were alleged to have happened, so those two counts weren't aggravated charges (a legal distinction). To convict on all three counts, all twelve jury members had to unanimously vote guilty on each count. That second jury deliberated for nearly five hours, from 3:15 pm until 8:04 pm. During that time, there were a few notes back and forth between them and Judge Hawes. At 5:00 pm they were stuck. Hawes sent a reply, reminding them that if they couldn't reach a decision, he would have to call a second mistrial, and the case would probably be tried again. He told them that the next jury would be in exactly the same predicament they were in, and said they should keep trying to reach a verdict that would be acceptable to all of them. He closed his note, "Don't do violence to your conscience, but continue deliberating."

In answer to a 6:30 pm status request from Hawes, they said they were split "nine-three," with no indication how many of their votes were guilty and how many were innocent. None of the jurors indicated that some of them felt Steve was partly innocent and partly guilty. All their notes were worded as if some thought he was completely guilty and some thought he was completely innocent. They finally did reach a verdict just after 8:00 pm, though.

What happened in the ninety minutes after their 6:30 note? Food happened. After reading the note, Judge Hawes said, "I'm going to leave the jury alone and let them continue to deliberate," and arranged for supper to be brought to them. They must have made their decision while they ate. Assuming the food arrived around 7:00, they didn't have much time to eat, and had less time to argue. I can imagine one of the jurors making a comment between bites of a hamburger or a slice of pizza: "If they're feeding us, they probably expect us to be here all night. Let's settle this thing and go home." During the discussion and the eating, some of them convinced those who had been voting not guilty to trade votes with them. This resulted in the guilty verdict on Count I and the acquittals on Counts II and III, and was documented in the affidavit that juror Emma Barrens submitted to the court a month after the trial. As I mentioned before, though, Judge Hawes couldn't allow the affidavit to be used to grant a new trial because of procedural rules.

A few years ago, Cleveland Sanford told me, "I've tried a lot of cases…and this one stands out, you know, and not for a good reason. I don't think the system worked." I asked him why. He said, "The way the system is supposed to work, you have to prove it beyond a reasonable doubt, and they didn't." He added that "there's perfectly good evidence of that in the jury's verdict, because you couldn't delineate out the one count from the other two and say..." He paused and tapped on the table to illustrate a juror saying, "I'm convinced beyond a reasonable doubt that he did <u>this</u> [*first tap*], but I'm not convinced that he did <u>this</u> or <u>this</u>." [*second and third taps*] "You either believe it or you don't, because at the end of the day it comes down to the credibility of Hanna. And if Hanna's not credible as to Count Two and Count Three, then Hanna wasn't credible as to Count One either. Just no way. It shouldn't have been a guilty verdict. Just shouldn't have been."

Emotion crept into his voice as he added, "I was really upset afterwards." I told him that Steve had noticed that, and had asked me "to thank you for all you did, because he understands you were doing the best you could, and sometimes it's a crap shoot." Sanford said, "Looking back on it, there's probably some things I would've done differently…and I still feel like I pointed out enough discrepancies and lies that ...I just didn't think she was credible at all." I asked him if he'd had many juries that had rendered split decisions like Steve's. He said, "No. Not as a lawyer *or* as a judge. That's the only case I ever had that happen where the case was sexual in nature. And I had quite a few. I tried quite a few sex cases...and as a judge I haven't had any either where they split it. I mean, they have to be really distinct, separate events, for a jury to separate it out. And in this instance, it was all just this hodgepodge of ...well, because Ada Dixon created a hundred events. That was the real issue."

Things the Juries Didn't Hear About

The Trucks: There were two incidents that supposedly happened inside two different trucks, one on the ride to see *Harry Potter* (in a large 1998 Chevy Silverado, extended cab pickup), and another during a ride home from a rodeo (in a small, early-1980's model Ford Courier, single bench seat pickup). I'll cover those incidents (and those trucks) in detail in their respective chapters, but I want to say something about the jury's impression of these two trucks. They heard descriptions of the trucks; how old they were, what make and model, the type of seating and transmission, etc. They saw photographs of the smaller of the two trucks. They saw one photograph of the back seat of the larger truck, but they didn't see either of the trucks in person. Tom borrowed a Chevy Silverado from a nearby car lot (exactly like the truck they went to the movies in), and parked it outside the courthouse during the second trial. He had hoped to show that Hanna's claims about what happened in the truck couldn't have happened at all, but the demonstration didn't take place. If it had, I think that jury members who weren't already prejudiced against Steve would have had a far greater incentive to push back against the deal-making that happened in the jury room.

In 2015 and 2019, Beau and his girlfriend and I took some video inside two similar model Chevy Silverados to demonstrate that Hanna's story was impossible. I'm not happy with a lot of the footage (very shaky). I might eventually edit it into a YouTube video that will help prove the ridiculousness of part of Hanna's story about that night. In the meantime, you'll find a still frame from the footage in the chapter, *The Night of Harry Potter, Part 1.*

Steve's PPG Test: Something else neither of the juries heard about was Steve's PPG test. In May 2005, Steve was given a complete sexual evaluation by Bernard Stein, PhD, a forensic and clinical psychologist. Dr. Stein administers these regularly for the State of Texas to quantify the likelihood of convicted sex offenders reoffending after they are released from prison. Steve wanted to be tested to prove that he wasn't capable of what Hanna accused him of. He was taking quite a risk by doing this. If the tests had shown anything negative, like a propensity toward underage females, for example, he could have been jeopardizing his entire defense, but he wanted to do this to prove that he wasn't capable of committing the crime he was accused of. Unfortunately, while the state believes these same tests are accurate enough to assess sex offenders after they are released, they, like lie detector tests, aren't admissible in court to prove innocence. Because of that, the results were never shown to the jury. Dr. Stein administered a battery of tests: personal history, checklists for psychopathic personality traits, aggression questionnaires, sexual history and inventory tests, a sex offender risk appraisal, reviews of all available trial records, and a PPG test. PPG stands for Penile PlethysmoGraph. Here are Dr. Stein's results, broken down into several categories. I've underlined some important phrases.

Psychopathic Personality: "Individuals who have psychopathic personality disorders are described as having a callous and remorseless disregard for the rights and feelings of others, and an irresponsible, impulsive, thrill-seeking and anti-social lifestyle," Stein said. To measure it he used the Hare Psychopathy Checklist, "a 20 item structured interview with scores that range from 0-40." His report read, "non-criminal men receive an average score of 9. Male pretrial jail detainees receive an average score of 22-23, and relentless reoffending male felons labeled psychopaths receive scores of 30 or higher. Steve Sirois received a low score of 11. Mr. Sirois is not a psychopath. He was also administered the Personality Assessment Inventory (PAI) and the Structured Clinical Interview (SCID), both of which ruled out any personality or social disorder."

Sexual Reoffending: Steve was administered two tests, the SORAG and the STATIC-99, to determine whether he might commit additional sex crimes [*even though he hadn't committed this one*]. Stein described the SORAG (the Sex Offender Risk Appraisal Guide) as "a well-established, reliable, and valid method for predicting sexual re-offending 7 and 10 years in the future." The test evaluates "indicators of negative childhood adjustment, demographics and criminal history. Mr. Sirois received a low score, which out of nine categories of all convicted sex offenders, places him in the third category. This represents a low risk of sexual or violent re-offending." He was also tested with the STATIC-99, which tries to determine the offender's risk to his community. Of the results of that test, Stein said, "Mr. Sirois is in the lowest risk category for sexual re-offending over the next 24 years in the community."

Ability to Successfully Complete Community Supervision: To test this, Stein used what he called "a reliable and valid 54-item checklist used by State and Federal Prisons and Probation and Parole departments to predict an individual's response to community supervision, and to suggest an appropriate level of supervision based on a 'risk and needs' approach. Mr. Sirois' results on this instrument show that only a minimum level of supervision/service is needed for him. His results also show that his probation guidelines suggest medium surveillance. He has a 23% chance of recidivism for general or technical re-offending." According to the National Institute of Justice, 68% of prisoners released in 30 states in 2005 were re-arrested within three years of their release, and 77% were re-arrested within five years. The possibility, though, of Steve getting arrested again, according to Dr. Stein, was very small.

Aggression and Sexuality: According to Dr. Stein's analysis, "Scores from the Aggression Checklist show that Steve does not have an aggression management or anger management problem. Results from the self-report sexuality questionnaires do not show any evidence of deviant sexuality."

The PPG: Penile plethysmograph testing (AKA phallometric testing) measures the level of sexual arousal in males when shown sexual content like photos or movies. A strain gauge is placed around the shaft of the male's penis. Even small changes in its circumference are noted while the man is shown erotic images. Reactions to pictures of adult women and men versus the reaction to children, young men, and young women are measured and quantified. The test does have lots of critics, but some reports (such as "Sensitivity and specificity of the phallometric test for pedophilia in non-admitting sex offenders," March

2002, Blanchard, Klassen, Dickey, Kuban, and Blak) indicated that there is a distinct difference in males who were sexually interested in adult women to those interested in children. Dr. Stein's assessment of Steve after testing with the PPG was, "Results from using penile plethysmograph showed he has an interest in adult females. No sexual interest was shown for underage females." The results of this test could possibly have swayed some of the jurors in favor of acquittal, but it wasn't allowed as direct evidence, so the jury didn't see it.

Stein's final comment was, "Mr. Sirois' history shows a positive work ethic and a strong commitment to his family. Psychological testing shows that he is not a psychopath and does not lead a criminal lifestyle, has no evidence of deviant sexuality, and has a low probability of re-offending sexually or violently as measured by two risk assessments."

Steve has always contended that he never dated under his age by more than a few years. In high school he was interested in high school girls. In his twenties, he was interested in young women in their twenties. He was generally faithful to Robin once they were married (Darla was the lone exception), although he did flirt with other women roughly his age, usually his and Robin's friends, and usually with Robin present.

Darla and Steve and Sex: Steve said he had sex with Hanna's mother three times. I've already told you about that, but it's worth noting (considering the PPG results above) that Darla is four years older than Steve. If you'll recall, Steve said that Darla presented Steve with a beer and herself, and "one thing led to another." He wasn't proud of it, and he knew he shouldn't have done it, but he said that Darla performed oral sex on him on two separate occasions. He thought that was the end of it until a couple of years later, when she arrived at one of his work locations with some tequila and they had intercourse in her truck. Would the trial have turned out differently if the jury had known about that? I don't know. During my interview with Sanford, he said, "One thing that bothered me…I heard at a later date that he was having an affair with Hanna's mother, of some form or fashion, and I didn't know that, and he didn't tell me, and, obviously, she wasn't going to tell me." Steve had told his other attorneys, and it was mentioned in the brainstorming session, so I said, "I thought that was known to everybody." Sanford said, "No, I didn't know that." I was surprised, because Steve had been so up front during his initial interview with Deputy Knox, and to Mathis and Tom. He also told Robin the same day as the brainstorming session, placing himself in hot water with her for quite a while afterward. Deservedly so. Sanford explained that he could have used that information. He said, "Because, what you really need in this type of case, from a defense standpoint, is you need a logical explanation as to why someone would make the allegations, and they're not true." A minute later he clarified that a little further. "In order for you to be not guilty, there has to be an explanation for why she's saying you did it ...and, in my mind, it seems like...there wasn't a good explanation, but if he was sleeping with her mom, that's a pretty good explanation...and I'm like, Why would you not tell me that Steve?" When I asked Steve, he said he thought Sanford did know about it, but admitted that he was in such a state of numbness by that time, that he really didn't remember if he had told him or not.

Hanna's Credibility: I've spoken with several people who sat in the gallery during one or both of the trials; and, yes, they were friends or acquaintances of Steve's, but all of them said, in one way or another, that they didn't believe Hanna. So, why did the jury believe her? The answer is that some of them didn't. Emma Barrens' affidavit clearly said they were at a stalemate before they made a deal to swap votes. I do believe it's possible that some jurors may have ignored discrepancies in the evidence because they knew how they planned to vote before they walked into the courtroom. Some readers of this book also had their minds made up early on (yes, you know who you are). Those readers haven't paid any serious attention to the arguments I've made so far (or, even more likely, they aren't reading this sentence at all because they stopped reading the book ages ago). "Why should I read a book about a danged sex molester?" This was probably the attitude of some of the jury members too.

Steve's choosing to not testify in the second trial could have been another reason why some of those jurors might have believed Hanna instead. Juries usually want to hear a couple of things from a defendant. They want to hear an alibi, and they want clarification of critical details in the accuser's claims. Steve couldn't do either of those things in either trial whether he took the stand or not. All he could say about most of her accusations was "I didn't do it. That never happened," but some of the jurors may have at least wanted to hear it directly from him.

Hanna's knowledge of sex may also have influenced some of the jurors' decisions. It was probably obvious to them that she seemed to know things that no one should know at twelve to fourteen years old, but Hanna wasn't a preteen during the trials. She was seventeen then, and fifteen when she made the accusations. In the two years before the trials she had multiple opportunities to test scenarios during her counseling sessions with Ada Dixon, and by retelling her story to her friends; plus she admitted to Tom in her interview that she became sexually active after the charges were filed. Many of her descriptions of sexuality could just as easily be behaviors she experienced or learned about after April 2004.

Analysis

There was an extremely high likelihood that, if the jury hadn't made a deal to trade votes, the second trial would have either ended in an acquittal or another mistrial, with a mistrial being the more likely of the two. There were holdouts on both sides, people who weren't budging from their respective innocent or guilty positions. If the prosecution had decided to try Steve one more time, though, it might not have made much difference. The family was completely broke by then. There was nothing left to borrow against except their house. The poor and the broken have very little chance against overzealous prosecutors with deep pockets.

Are you ready to move on to the chapters about Steve's innocence?

Proof of Innocence

How This Section Works

"There are two ways to be fooled.
One is to believe what isn't true;
the other is to refuse to believe what is true."
Søren Kierkegaard

"They didn't know what they were witnessing,"
Darla Belisle

Everything you've read so far has been setting the stage for what follows. The previous chapters were concerned with Steve as a person and his circumstances leading up to and during the trials. Most of what you've read so far has been about why Steve didn't get a fair trial, not about his innocence, but the topic of his innocence will inform the rest of the book. What you read from this point forward will be entirely about proving that he didn't do what Hanna said he did. The next six chapters examine Hanna's accusations against Steve, detail why they aren't true, and why they didn't and couldn't have happened. I'll also break down the three counts against Steve to prove why I believe they were all based on lies.

This is the point where the book becomes even more like a textbook. In some sections it will resemble a combination, history, legal, and math textbook, which means that most of the chapters from now on are dense with details (facts, figures, quotes, etc.). Several of the chapters are also structured around a series of questions about various aspects of that particular accusation. Wherever possible I will answer them with thorough details drawn from the trial record and other sources, and at the end of most of them I will analyze that question before offering a conclusion. Many of the details will include a wide range of often contradictory information from Hanna and others. Rest assured, I will bring all of the details together by the end of each chapter.

The first item we'll examine is what I believe was a lie about a cross-country track meet. I realize that it might not seem important at first. Hanna didn't say anything about it in her affidavit, but she did mention it to Ada Dixon and to Tom, and she did bring it up in both trials. Even though it isn't one of the counts against Steve, examining it is crucial to establishing how and why Hanna might be lying.

In the other chapters we will look at sleepovers where Hanna may have lied to her friends about being abused. We'll also examine Count I, the count Steve was convicted of, which allegedly happened on the night they went to see the first Harry Potter movie. We will also explore an incident which supposedly happened during a ride home from a rodeo. And then we'll examine Counts II and III, both of which were initially alleged to have happened within moments of each other on the night of Beau's 21st birthday party.

Before arriving at any of my conclusions, I meticulously sorted through a variety of texts and data, cataloging them by topic and date. Hanna's claims were then analyzed for comments which I decided might be provable one way or another. Where that wasn't possible, I compared her comments to other statements about the same topic to see how widely or narrowly the comments diverged from each other. Hanna didn't cooperate by being consistent, though. By the time of the trials, her original versions of what happened (the three counts in the indictment) had been discarded in favor of completely different accusations. Now, having analyzed everything thoroughly, I firmly believe there is more than enough information to establish that Steve shouldn't have been convicted.

But, just to make sure I leave no doubt in anyone's mind, I will provide a timeline, using dates and details which prove that it wasn't possible for Steve to do what Hanna said he did.

On to the cross-country race.

A Cross-Country Meet, The First Lie

"I do believe her, though I know she lies."
William Shakespeare

"Anyone who doesn't take truth seriously in small matters cannot be trusted in large ones either."
Albert Einstein

This chapter is about a day when Hanna claimed she was first abused, and then she said it wasn't then, and then she ...well, you'll see. I believe that her testimony about this event also happens to be a perfect illustration of the way she may have been telling untruths from the very beginning. I call this The First Lie because it was the first statement of hers that I thought I could prove to be false, but I don't believe it was the first one she told. Ultimately, I spent as much time researching this part of the story as any other element of the case.

Here it is. Hanna claimed that, at the age of twelve, when she was in the seventh grade, she ran in a one-mile cross-country race for her school, against 300 or so other girls, and placed 16th. Was that a lie? Or maybe a half-lie? As was true of most of Hanna's other fabrications, this one is partly grounded in reality. At the age of twelve, Hanna did run in a mile-long cross-country race for her school, and the race did happen during her seventh-grade year. I think the rest of that is false, though. The reason this event even appeared in the trials was because Hanna used it to introduce the first alleged molestation. We'll look at both the race and the abuse (which she said happened after the race), but we'll do the race first.

Her basic story of that day was that her mother invited the Sirois' to watch her run in a foot race in Langford, Texas, about 80 miles away. Afterward, they all ate a large lunch at a restaurant there, then drove home, stopping at the Sirois' to relax for a few hours. Hanna said that, while they were at Steve's house, he forced himself on her, then she and her family went home. She altered that story several times before she testified about it, but I believe I can prove that parts of those versions were true, and other parts weren't. One thing is certain, though, each new version was clearly different from the previous one in some way.

[Subsections in this Chapter: The Cross-Country Race // The Ultimate Score // The Alleged Post-Race Molestation // Some Extras]

The Cross-Country Race

Hanna, who was twelve in September 2001, and fifteen when she created the affidavit in April 2004, didn't mention the cross-country meet in her affidavit at all. In it she said, under oath, that the first time she was molested was in "late August or early September 2001," but she also said that was the first time she spent the night at the Sirois' house. Her specific details of that claimed molestation (oral sex performed on her) became Count I against Steve.

A month after creating the affidavit, Hanna told Ada Dixon that an incident involving kissing and groping "happened after the first cross-country meet in August 2001," but she said nothing about oral sex occurring.

Two years later, In her interview with Tom Swearingen (May 2006), Hanna said, "On September 8th of 2001, I had a cross-country meet in Langford. It was my first meet." She said that her mom encouraged the Sirois' to come see her run, and said, "I did really good in the meet. I was very proud of myself."

Two months later, in Trial #1, she was asked how she remembered she was twelve when the molestation started. She said, "Because it was around my first cross-country meet. I was in the seventh grade." She also said, "I remember that day particularly, because I had ran against 300-some-odd girls and I had gotten 16th place. And I was very proud of myself because I was one of the youngest girls there." She said that the race was in the "late morning, around 10:00, 11:00 or so," and added that it finished "whenever you got done running. It was normally over about maybe 20 minutes after it started. It was very short. It was only a mile." That's more detail than before, but have any runners already spotted something that's wrong with her story?

In Trial #2, Ross again asked her how she knew she was "12 when it started." She said, "I remember I was in the seventh grade, and I ran cross-country. And my first meet was in Langford, and I ran a mile. I got 16th place out of 300 and something girls. And I was really proud of myself and I will never forget it." Ross asked when the meet was. She said "It was September. On the 8th actually." Ross asked her how she remembered that specific date. She said "It's also a very good friend of mine's birthday." Later in the trial, she identified Rhonda Bresnick as the friend.

In Tom's interview and in both trials she also followed that testimony with details about some alleged sexual encounters that night. We'll get to them.

[*Notice how practiced Hanna's spiel became by Trial #2, and how much her story changed? Instead of waiting to be asked, she squeezed all her answers in at once: still remembering the race because she was proud, but also because it was her* "good friend" *Rhonda's birthday. Oddly, no one asked her about her race time, something a good runner might remember, although she did hint at a 20-minute time to Tom. Note: Rhonda, who features prominently in the chapter,* The Night of the Rodeo, *was, indeed, born on September 8th, but when we get to that chapter, remember that Hanna testified that Rhonda* <u>*is*</u> *(as in* <u>*currently, now, right that moment*</u>*)* "a <u>very good</u> friend" *of hers.*]

Let's see whether this is a provable lie by exploring her statement that she came in 16th out of 300 other girls. That result seemed highly unlikely to me, so I decided to find out what actually happened. Her comment about being proud of her place in the race because she was one of the youngest girls there also struck me as false immediately because it was a seventh-grade race, which meant that all of her competitors were the same age she was, but the number of runners and her ranking especially didn't make sense. How I researched the lie is a story in itself. I'll give an abbreviated version here, but there's a fully detailed four-part account on the blog if you're interested.

https://aggravatedbook.com/the-first-lie-part-1/

I also talked about this race during a research talk I gave in 2015. You can see the YouTube videos of the talk at the URL below. The part about the race starts at the beginning of Video #2.

https://aggravatedbook.com/researching-aggravated-a-talk/

In 2013, after reading the trial transcripts, I started trying to find data on that particular cross-country meet, a seventh-grade race held in Langford, Texas, in late August or early September of 2001. I made calls and sent emails to runner's organizations and schools in Langford. Those led nowhere. I asked Steve and Beau what they remembered about the race. Robin's health started going downhill once Steve was incarcerated, and she died in 2012, so I never got to talk to her about it, and Marri was too young in 2001 to remember much. Steve and Beau didn't remember the name of the school that sponsored it, but both were certain that 300 was way too many runners. Beau remembered a field of "around 20 or 30," and neither of them recalled Hanna placing higher than the middle of the pack. I wondered if it was possible that Hanna had actually finished in 16th place, but had only run against 30 girls. That would have been a middle of the pack finish. Had she increased the number of her competitors tenfold just to make herself look better?

In 2014 and 2015, I met with officials at Alderson ISD, Hanna's school district, and told them I was writing a book about the trial. We talked about Hanna, and they were very helpful about a number of other things, but they assured me they didn't have records of track meets that far back, and didn't know of any meets the school attended in Langford. Most of the rest of my search happened on the Internet, by phone, and through email. In 2015, I stumbled across a race results sheet for a cross-country meet in a town I'll call Miler, Texas, and Alderson was listed as one of the teams. Miler is a small town only ten miles or so away from Langford. I had found the right school. Further Internet searches led me to more race results for Miler's annual cross-country meets for 2011, 2013, and 2014, but not as far back as 2001. I added those other stats to 2015's, and gathered new ones each year, adding 2016 through 2019 (eight sets of records so far). The stat sheets listed the last names of the runners, the schools they represented, and their ranks and times. Comparing the statistics from year to year gave me enough information to make a good guess, but I wanted more.

When I contacted the school at Miler, they said they didn't have records for their own meet as far back as 2001, but they did give me the name of their 2001 cross-country coach, Charlie Correll. Alderson ISD also gave me the name of Hanna's 2001 coach, Hope Dawson. Neither of them were still teaching at those schools, so I had some difficulty finding them at first, but I finally did, and asked them if they remembered whether a 7th grade female runner from Alderson had placed 16th out of 300 runners in 2001. Mr. Correll said he didn't know how well any individual runner did in the 2001 race, but said, "We never had 300 girls running in any division. Probably closer to 150 at most." Ms. Dawson didn't respond to my voicemails or emails at first, but I kept trying. In June 2016, she replied briefly, saying it was too long ago for her to remember anything. I asked her if she remembered anything at all about the number of runners or how well her girls did. She didn't respond. A year later I tried again, several times. She eventually did answer, maybe just to shut me up, saying that "any races we attended were small," and confirmed that the 7th grade races Alderson competed in were "between 20 and 50 runners." That narrowed it down a lot.

Also, in 2016, I emailed one of Miler's current coaches, Curtis Hamner. He remembered the 2001 meet, but couldn't give me any details. He did say, though, "I do know that we did not have 300 kids in a 7th grade race, ever," and added, "We had our biggest meet ever this year and there wasn't but 800 kids running from 7th grade thru 12, boys and girls, total."

Here are the basic conclusions I arrived at, but (if you're interested) a thorough rundown of Miler's race stats are in the blog's posts about the race. In 2011, 45 girls ran in Miler's 7th grade girl's race, 62 ran in 2013, 90 in 2014, 105 in 2015, 123 in 2016, 145 in 2017, 115 in 2018, and a big jump of entrants in 2019 — 192 girls ran in the 7th grade race. That's a pattern of a meet that was growing nearly every year. It doesn't make sense that it would have been three times as popular in 2001. None of those 7th grade races came remotely close to the 300 runners than Hanna claimed she ran against. Her story seems to be hyperbole at its most extreme.

I also compared actual race times. Since Hanna claimed she was 16th out of 300, I looked at the times for 1st, 16th, and last places in the 7th grade girls' races from 2011 on. The best 1st place finisher out of all eight years had a time of 8.32 (8 minutes, 32 seconds), the worst 1st place finish was 9.41. The average of those times is 9.02. The 16th place finishers ranged from 9.44 to 11.27, for an average time of 10.46. And the last place times ranged from 16.08 to 19.02, for an average time of 17.55. In Trial #1, though, Hanna testified that the race was over "whenever you got done running," "maybe twenty minutes." Even the worst times beat that. In the records I have, Alderson's runners didn't fare well at any of the Miler meets. They didn't compete there in 2011, 2013, 2014, or 2019, but they did participate from 2015 through 2018.

In 2015, out of 105 runners, Alderson's best 7th grade girl placed 62nd at just over 12 minutes. Other Alderson 7th grade girls finished 70th, 91st, 96th, 97th, and 102nd.

In 2016, 123 girls ran in the 7th grade race. Alderson only fielded three 7th grade girls. Their best 7th grade runner placed 55th, with a time of 11.51, slightly better than the middle of the pack time. The other two Alderson runners finished 69th and 83rd.

In 2017, Alderson's 7th grade girls still ranked low. They only had two 7th grade runners that year (out of 145). They finished 90th and 118th. The girl who finished in 118th place had a time of 13.22.

In 2018, with 115 girls running, Alderson entered only one girl in the 7th grade race. She finished 110th, with a time of 14.30. Alderson's runners, both boys and girls of various grades, didn't fare very well in any of the stats I have. Almost all of Alderson's runners, year after year, 7th through 12th grades, were middle of the pack or worse at this meet, often at the tail end.

I don't say this to belittle the team, but to point out that Hanna's performance, if it had been anything close to what she claimed, would probably have been considered a remarkable achievement at her school. I realize that the performance of other 7th grade girls from Alderson in different years isn't proof of Hanna's actual time, but given the low performances I've seen so far, I would think that any Alderson 7th grade girl who placed 16th out of 300 girls, or even out of 50 (the high number Hope Dawson quoted), would be a sort of school hero, at least for a while. Somebody would have remembered her doing that. No one does, though, not even her former coach.

Also, Hanna said in Trial #1 that the race finished "whenever you got done running. It was normally over about maybe twenty minutes after it started. It was very short. It was only a mile." The worst 7th grade 16th place finisher in those eight years of stats had a time of 11.27. The worst last place finish out of all the years was 19.02, which means that every runner finished in less than twenty minutes. In 2018, the Alderson girl who finished 110th out of 115 runners had a time of 14.30. Did Hanna actually take "about maybe twenty minutes" to run a mile? My wife, who is 65, regularly walks two miles in about forty minutes. How could Hanna have placed 16th with a roughly twenty-minute time if the other 16th place runners were at least nine minutes faster than that, and even the last place finishers consistently beat twenty minutes? Here's one more question. If Hanna was as good as she claimed in her very first race, why was she only on the cross-country team in junior high? She participated in a lot of athletics and other school activities, but according to the school's yearbooks didn't do cross-country in high school at all.

Why did she portray the race and her performance as so much better than reality would dictate? Was it to make herself seem more accomplished than she was? Her need to boost her popularity and be the center of attention was a topic I ran across over and over again. Even if other people hadn't told me she was that way, it's evident in her own words and actions. Keep your eyes peeled for signs of that as we continue, and see if you agree. Why wasn't she satisfied with just saying "I did well," instead of her astounding "16th out of 300" claim? If she thought the people who saw the race couldn't contradict her, she would have been right. During trials, witnesses have to wait outside the courtroom. When Hanna said something that didn't match what she told Deputy Knox, he couldn't hear it. If she changed some element of her therapy sessions, Ada Dixon didn't hear what she said. The people who were at the race (Darla, Marri, Robin and Beau) didn't hear her testimony about it, and Steve was never asked about it. Did she think no one would check? No one did, not for years.

Finally, in the records I have found so far, Miler's largest 7th grade girl's race had 192 runners (over a hundred runners less than Hanna's claimed 300). Everyone I talked to agreed that Hanna's numbers were off. Beau said that, in the 2001 race, he could only remember "around 20 or 30" runners. Hanna's 2001 coach, Hope Dawson, said that the races they competed in only had "between 20 and 50 runners." Charlie Correll, the 2001 Miler coach, said that they "never had 300 girls running in any division." Curtis Hamner, current Miler coach, said that Miler "did not have 300 kids in a 7th grade race, ever." Is that enough proof that Hanna probably lied about her ranking and the size of the race?

The Ultimate Score

Over time, Hanna *was* consistent about a few things: She said that there was a cross-country race in Langford, in 2001, that she ran against "300 and something girls," and that she finished in 16th place. The race wasn't in Langford, but it was nearby, and it did happen. Hanna told Ada Dixon that it was in August, though, and told everyone else it was in September. It likely *was* on Saturday, September 8, 2001, as she eventually said, but the number of runners and her placement in the race are demonstrably false. I would love to be able to find a record for that specific year, but nobody seems to have one, not even the schools involved. I always thought that keeping records (as in, "this is going to go on your permanent record, young man") was one of the major things that schools do, but apparently it isn't important to keep everything.

I believe that Hanna's multiple versions of this event are indicative of someone who is telling a story that is probably false. Generally, a convincing liar will try to tell it the same way each time, but of course they can't. They add details that they think will make it seem more realistic, or will make them look better, but when one version is compared to another, the changes often make it obvious that something in the story isn't right. The trick, of course, is finding out which of the versions contain lies, or whether they all do; but if there are lies in at least one version of a story, it reinforces the possibility that all the versions could contain lies. Hanna's account of this race triggered my first suspicion that she might be a pathological liar. Based on the numerous changes in all of her other stories, and some of the ridiculous claims she made, it still seems a likely possibility to me. I can't prove that she is one, though, and it's not a diagnosis I'm qualified to make anyway.

Is the race legally important? It isn't mentioned in any of the counts against Steve, but Hanna used it to introduce the idea that an incident occurred after the race. If her seemingly false story about the race itself did anything, it forced me to pay closer attention to everything else she said. I hope you will too, especially from here on out. Let's look at her story about this first supposed molestation, the one that she said happened after the race.

The Alleged Post-Race Molestation

A month after signing her affidavit, Hanna told Ada Dixon, "One time he hugged me for no reason and tried to kiss me on the mouth, but I thought it was just because he was drunk. He kept turning my head. This happened after the first cross-country meet in August 2001. He had me against the wall and started kissing me on my neck and groping me." None of that incident, or anything even resembling it, was mentioned in the affidavit. She said in her affidavit that the first time she was sexually assaulted by Steve was the first time she spent the night there, and said that was in late August or early September, but she and Aaron didn't spend the night until ten weeks or so after the September cross-country meet.

Two years later, she said something similar to Tom about the day of the cross-country race, but added a twist. She said her family stopped at the Sirois' home after they all ate lunch in Langford. There's some confusing phrasing ahead, but I'll try to clean it up after we get through it. Here's what she told Tom.

> "It was kind of a cool night, mid-September you know, and everybody was sitting outside, and I was inside, in the kitchen, doing something. I was probably like picking at the food. I was just sitting there, just snacking or whatever...He came in there and said, 'Here, give me a hug.' 'No, it's hot.' This isn't the second incident, where something actually did happen. The first time he just told me to give him a hug and he tried to kiss me, and I just turned my head away, and then I backed off after a second after he didn't stop, but I don't ...I think that was like a week before ...and then, this event I'm talking about now is something that actually did happen. He told me to give him a hug, so I did. He kept trying to kiss me. I turned my head away, just like the last time, and then ...he ...there's a little bitty walkway, not even really a hallway, just a little walkway that leads back to his bedroom. You cannot see the walkway from the kitchen because there's a little wall there. He took me behind that wall, not into his bedroom, but just in the little walkway and stood me up against the wall. Not hard, but just enough where I couldn't move. And he started kissing me. I did not kiss him back. And he started massaging my breast, and kissing me and licking me and I don't even know what, all over my neck."

Despite all her extra embellishments (like snacking after eating, Steve asking for a hug, the strange description of the hallway [*it* is *an actual hallway, by the way*], and the kissing and the weird licking on the neck, and the "too hot" reference on a night that she said was "cool"), she still talked about this as if it had been one single incident, but she also told Tom that there had been a previous similar incident. When did that happen?

[*How can* "kind of a cool night" *and* "it's hot" *sensibly be in the same description? This wasn't the only time she made a strange statement about the temperature, though. You'll see more incorrect hot and cold comments from her as we continue.*

Her statement about the attempted kiss being "just like the last time," *which she thought* "was like a week before," *is also interesting. She was alleging an earlier encounter, a week before this one. How is that possible if this was the first time they visited as a family since she was ten? She also seemed unsure about why she was inside the house,* "probably picking at the food," *just* "snacking or whatever." *What food? They ate a big meal at a restaurant. Steve didn't cook while they were there that day. Also, it wasn't nighttime. It doesn't take the rest of the day to drive from Langford to Deep Springs (about 80 miles). They arrived at the Sirois' in early-to-mid-afternoon, if that late.*]

Did she change any of that when she testified? In Trial #1 (July 2006), Hanna upped her game by adding two more incidents.

First Incident: She said "he was cooking supper," "we were just talking," then "he said, Come here give me a hug, give me a hug." "And I knew he had been drinking. He drank a lot. And he leaned in to kiss me and I kept turning my head away." "I backed up because he had his arms around me and I backed up and he finally let go and he just kind of smirked." Ross asked her how that made her feel. She said, "I was confused." Then he asked her if Steve had ever tried anything like that before. She explained that there had been another incident "that took place a week before that. And it -- He just tried to kiss me the same as before."

Second Incident: Ross asked her what happened next. She said, "And then a few minutes later, he came back in and he cornered me in the hallway right outside the kitchen." Ross asked her where everyone else was. She said "They were still outside." "He began kissing me, and I wouldn't kiss him back. I just stayed still. I didn't move. I didn't -- I didn't do anything. I just stood there." "He started on my mouth and he worked his way down my neck. And he started licking me." Ross asked her where he was licking her. She said, "On the side of my neck, on the right side. And then his hands were rubbing my breasts over my clothes. And he just kept on. He wouldn't stop." She said it lasted "two to five minutes."

Third Incident: Ross then asked if anything else happened that night. She said, "Yes. A little later that night...he came back in and he was doing something in the sink. He was rinsing off a dish or something. And I was kind of standing to his right a few feet. And he reached over with his right hand and rubbed my breast and asked me if it felt good." Ross asked her how she reacted. She said "I just turned my head." Ross again asked where everyone was. She said, "Still outside." He asked if anyone was inside the house, and she said, "Just their dog. That's it."

[*Suddenly, two months after she talked to Tom, her story about that evening expanded from one incident to three incidents, accompanied by all kinds of additional detail that wasn't in any previous version. This time she had Steve attempt one kiss and smirk when it failed, take a ten minute break, then come back, find her in the hallway (and kiss her but she didn't kiss back, and lick her on the neck and rub her breasts for two to five minutes), then take another break, but come back to rinse dishes and rub her breast again, just one breast this time (with wet hands?). She again said that Steve tried to kiss her a week before that.*

Hanna described these things happening after supper. According to Steve, her family was only there for a few hours in the afternoon, and they didn't eat there. Compared to earlier versions, this was a full blown performance.]

Did the story change again for the second trial?

Yes, in Trial #2 (August 2006), she reverted to saying there were two incidents, not three.

First Incident: She said, "I was in the dining room. I don't remember what I was doing. I just know that he came in there and washed his hands and then he started kind of talking to me like he always did. And then, he said, 'Come here, give me a hug.' 'Give me a hug.'" "And he leaned in and tried to kiss me. I kept turning my head away because I didn't know what was going on. I just knew it was weird." She added, "He kind of puckered up his mouth a little and was kind of leaning towards me." "I tried to back up, but he had his hands around me and I couldn't move." Ross asked if she got away from him. She said, "Yes I did." He asked how that happened, and she said, "He let go." "He just kind of snickered." "I just kind of backed up slowly and then I just -- I guess I gave him a funny look, because he kind of looked at me funny. Then he said, Well, I better get back out there, and he turned around and walked back out." Ross asked her if anyone else was "inside the house." She said, "Not that I know of. I mean there wasn't anybody there. I don't know about in the house." He asked, "But no one in the room that could have seen what was going on?" She said, "No."

Second Incident: She said, "15 or 20 minutes later," "He came back in, and I don't remember, I was in the kitchen doing something, getting a drink or something like that. I don't remember, but he came in and he started like -- just kind of took me, led me over to this little hallway that was really close to his bedroom and just kind of pinned me up against the wall, like just held me there. It wasn't forced or anything. He just held me there where I couldn't move. He started kissing me on my mouth and I wouldn't kiss him back, but then he started moving his head down to my neck. And it just felt really warm and wet. He had one hand on my hip and his other hand was on my chest." Ross asked her what she meant when she said something was "warm and wet," She said, "He was licking me." Ross asked if there was anyone else in the house. She said, "I don't really recall. My best guess is that my little brother and Marri were in the front room watching TV, which is out of sight from the kitchen and the dining room and the hallway." He asked if anything else happened. She said, "He was just kind of slowly thrusting his hips into mine." Ross asked what happened next. She said, "He just kept going. After a couple of minutes, he just stopped and just kind of gave me this look that implied I wasn't supposed to say anything, and he just left."

Hanna added several more actions this time, Steve puckering his lips and leaning toward her, snickering instead of smirking, and dragging her into the hallway instead of "cornering" her there. This was closer to what she told Dixon in May 2004 (an attempted kiss, followed by kissing and groping in the hallway), but she split it into two incidents instead of one, and completely dropped the third incident she had used in the first trial. She also added some new details this time, like Steve "thrusting his hips" against hers, and the other kids being in the living room. Being able to see someone in their kitchen, by the way, is just a matter of a few steps from the living room, or just a lean to the right if they were sitting on the couch.

[In Trial #1, there was a slight difference in the order of events. In Trial #1's first alleged incident, she said she backed up so he let her go. In this trial she said he let go and she then backed up.

In two of the incidents, across all of the versions, Hanna portrayed Steve as intensely and continuously drunk (to Dixon and in Trial #1), but in describing this incident in Trial #2 (and in her interview with Tom) there was no mention of Steve drinking that night. I'll push back on the drinking comments in various ways later, but for now let me just say that, according to Steve, he and Robin didn't drink at the level that Hanna claimed, and they didn't begin drinking hard alcohol to any degree until Darla started bringing tequila to the house. This would have been long before their drinking accelerated.

Also, they had just returned from a morning track meet and a big lunch. It was mid-afternoon, not nighttime. Since they didn't eat another meal before Hanna's family went home, why did she say Steve was cooking? And why, in Trial #2, did she insert Marri and Aaron into the scene for the first time but disappear the dog?]

There are five different versions of this: The affidavit, Dixon's summary, Tom's interview, and the two trials. Each new one is different from the previous one in some way. Looking at them as a group, there were huge changes. The race wasn't mentioned in the affidavit, and the kids didn't spend the night after the race, so that's a major time discrepancy in the affidavit. The third incident in Trial #1, and the rubbing of her breast at the sink weren't mentioned anywhere else. Hanna flip-flopped back and forth. In one scenario she was snacking, in another she was just in the dining room doing "something." In another Steve was cooking, in another he was rinsing dishes, and in another he came inside to wash his hands (all on an afternoon when he didn't cook). Everyone else is outside in four of the versions, except the dog is inside for tone of them, and in the last one the other kids are in the living room and the dog is gone. Why didn't Elmer Ross correct all of these drastic changes in her testimony?

Hanna indicated several times that these alleged incidents weren't visible to any of the other people who were there, whether they were inside or outside the house, so you might want to take a look at the floor plan on the blog. It includes sightlines that show how much someone might be able to see from the front door or the utility room door.

https://aggravatedbook.com/other-images/

The house had three doors, but the one in the living room was rarely used. The other two allowed entrance to the house from the front and from the utility room. Both of those doors were easily accessible from the carport where the adults were sitting. Anyone standing in either of those doorways could see a great deal as soon as they opened the door. Anyone watching TV in the living room would have been just a couple of steps away from a full view of the kitchen and dining room, and possibly only a few more steps away from seeing into the hallway Hanna talked about. Anyone who was sitting on the right side of the living room couch could see the dining room and the kitchen from there. The only way to get to the bathroom was through the kitchen and the hallway. If, as Hanna said, the adults were all drinking beer, and the kids were drinking sodas, there would have been a steady stream of people (no pun intended) from the carport to the bathroom and back again.

Steve would have to have been a complete and utter idiot to have attempted any of the actions Hanna claimed. Even if he, as she claimed in one of her scenarios, pulled her into the hallway leading to the bedroom, that hallway is narrow, with no room to break apart, and no place to hide. Anyone poking their head around the corner would see whatever was happening.

Some Extras

A Minor Point: After the race, the two families ate what Steve described as a really large lunch in Langford before driving back to Deep Springs. He said that he and Robin and Darla sat under the carport, while the kids played around the house. What struck him as weird were the comments from Trial #1 about him cooking and rinsing the dishes. They had just eaten a big meal in a restaurant. Why would he be cooking or washing dishes? I don't think any of Hanna's claims about this are valid. I think the two families arrived at the house full from lunch. The adults sat under the carport and talked, and yes, possibly had a few beers. The kids played in and around the house until late in the afternoon when Darla and her kids went home. Also, September 8th was a Saturday, another reason why they wouldn't have stayed into the evening. Hanna and Aaron rarely ever spent the night on Saturdays because the two families attended different churches.

Other than a few important exceptions (which I'll detail in the chapter, *A Timeline as Final Proof*), from that point on, Hanna's family only came to visit occasionally for an evening cookout (almost always on a Friday). It wasn't every weekend, but (according to Darla) it averaged about every other weekend for a while. Some of Steve's neighbors and friends were usually at the cookouts too, and they have also verified (sometimes under oath) that Hanna's family didn't visit every weekend. Also, late in 2003, according to Hanna, it even slowed to very few visits and no sleepovers for around six months. This visit in September 2001 was just Hanna's family stopping for a few hours on their way home. It was the very first in a string of semi-regular get-togethers between the two families, but Steve had been doing this with other friends and neighbors for years. He doesn't remember this particular one stretching into the night, and he doesn't remember cooking a meal, as Hanna claimed in Trial #1 (something she changed her mind about in Trial #2).

[*Again, it's less than a 90-minute drive from Langford to Deep Springs, about 80 miles, and they had just eaten a big lunch. Why was Hanna in the kitchen eating, and what was she eating? Steve didn't cook, and no food would be out if they had just been to a restaurant.*]

Hanna and the Weather: Hanna made one other claim about something I could verify, the weather. It cropped up in nearly every one of her descriptions of the alleged incidents. Was she told in one of her English classes that the addition of detail makes scenes seem more real to the reader? She loaded her descriptions with all kinds of things, but the clothes people were wearing and the weather seemed to be her two favorites.

Hanna told Tom, "It was kind of a cool night, mid-September you know, and everybody was sitting outside, and I was inside, in the kitchen, doing something." She didn't testify in the trials about any weather-related hints about this day. She only mentioned this to Tom. Let's see what the weather actually was like.

Based on datasets from the National Oceanic & Atmospheric Administration (NOAA), the country's department for everything weather-related, the temperature in Deep Springs on September 8, 2001, ranged from a low before dawn of 74° Fahrenheit, to a high of 96° in late-afternoon. The day before and the day after (the 7th and the 9th) were also hot, 91° and 93° respectively. Hanna's comments to Tom were odd, though. She first said it was "kind of a cool night," but moments after that she said she told Steve she didn't want to hug him because "it's hot." Which was it? Was she trying to cover all the possible bases? Any suggestion of it being a cool mid-September night, though, is ridiculous. Before we're done, we'll see weather information from NOAA several more times (especially in the chapters on Counts I, II, and III, and the ride home from the rodeo).

What Supposedly Happened First? Hanna's testimony also had some problems with chronological order. She said in the affidavit that the first incident of a sexual nature happened the first time they spent the night. Then she told Ada Dixon that this post-race kissing and groping *was* the first incident, but she didn't say anything about spending the night. After that, she clouded her story with additional information. In several of the documents, she alleged that incidents occurred in a different order, and that they included earlier incidents that weren't in any of the other versions. In 2006, she told Tom about the incident after the race, but said, "This isn't the second incident, where something actually did happen. The first time he just told me to give him a hug and he tried to kiss me, and I just turned my head away, and then I backed off after a second after he didn't stop, but I don't …I think that was <u>like a week before</u>, and then, <u>this event I'm talking about now is something that actually did happen</u>."

[*Was the other* "event" *not an event, but this one was, and the earlier one that* "happened" *also* didn't *happen? I know, try to make sense of that. Her dialogue is often incomprehensible. This makes no sense anyway because this was the first time they visited. There was no* "before." *Here's more, though.*]

Hanna also mentioned earlier pre-race incidents in the first trial, and talked about all of the quality time that she and Steve spent together, all by themselves. This next excerpt is a good example of that. Elmer Ross asked her what happened after the race. Hanna said, "We were just talking. He used to talk to me like I was an adult. We would talk for an hour-and-a-half, two hours, and just talk about everything. And <u>we did this for several months</u>. Then, finally, he said, 'Come here, give me a hug.'" She also said that Steve "would start conversations and we would talk about school and how I was going to grow up and be really beautiful and successful and have to beat all the guys off with a stick. And he wouldn't talk to me in little kid voice you sometimes see parents talk to their children. He spoke to me like I was an equal." Ross asked her how that made her feel, and she said, "Important."

During the second trial, Hanna's story started the same way, but then an odd twist occurred. When Ross asked her if this was "the first time that anything like this had happened," Hanna said, "Yes, sir." Probably surprised, because he had expected her to talk about the <u>earlier incident</u> and the "several months" of talking together that she had testified to in Trial #1, he tried again. "Had anything <u>close to this</u> happened between you and the Defendant <u>prior</u> to this time?" Hanna said, "<u>No, sir</u>." He gave it one more shot, asking, "Did <u>anything else</u> happen that day?" Hanna said, "<u>No, sir</u>."

[*In Trial #2, she downgraded her story about this day from Trial #1's three incidents to two, and then (unlike everything she had said earlier) denied that anything had happened before that day, even after Ross gave her three opportunities to reverse her statement. Ross was trying to establish a time period long enough for grooming to occur, but Hanna killed that effort by testifying that nothing happened before September 8, 2001. As you know, I believe she lied in both trials, and that nothing happened, period; but her testimony makes it clear that she lied about these alleged incidents in at least one of the trials, if not both. The Trial #2 jury, of course, didn't hear her Trial #1 testimony, but, if they had been paying attention, they would have noticed that Hanna had just testified that there were zero incidents of a sexual nature before the day of the cross-country race. After that, how did Ross continue to justify pushing the idea that Steve had conducted months and months of dedicated grooming of Hanna? Maybe by just ignoring her testimony?*]

Non-Existent Get-Togethers, Invisible Kids, and Drinking Adults: About an hour into Hanna's second trial testimony, she changed her story again. Elmer Ross asked her why they stopped at the Sirois' after the cross-country meet. Hanna said, "So many times before -- and I'm thinking this happened the same way -- Sirois would just say, Why don't y'all come back to the house and hang out for awhile, just relax. That's what we would do. Nine times out of ten, that's what he would say." Ross then asked her what the adults did when they got there. She said, "I remember they went outside after awhile, they were sitting out there having a beer or two. And I was in the house because I wasn't allowed to be out there most of the time." He asked her why she wasn't "allowed to be out there." She said, "Because I was a kid and I wasn't supposed to hear what the adults were talking about. I wasn't supposed to be around the drinking." Ross asked her a minute later if there was anyone else in the house, and she said, "I don't really recall. My best guess is that my little brother and Marri were in the front room watching TV, which is out of sight from the kitchen and the dining room and the hallway."

[*Here's the problem with that reasonable-sounding dialogue. Using the phrases, "So many times before" and "Nine times out of ten," sent a message to the jury that there had been previous get-togethers, many of them. Statements like that also reinforced Ross' opening comments about Hanna's family visiting often before that day, but everyone in Steve's family has told me that (after the one visit in 1999, when Hanna was ten and Aaron was nine) this was just the second time that all three of them had visited. Darla had dropped by occasionally before the day of the cross-country race, but without the kids.*

Hanna's other comment, about being in the house alone and not being allowed to be outside because the adults were drinking, is missing a very important detail. The other kids. If she wasn't allowed outside at twelve years old, then Aaron and Marri had to have been in the house too. In reality, the kids were usually all over the place, outside and inside, playing in the yard or watching TV. If the other kids were in the house, watching TV, the incidents Hanna described would have been nearly impossible. A few steps from anywhere in the living room, and they could have seen into the dining room and kitchen, which was also just a few steps away from the carport if any of the adults decided to come inside to use the bathroom or get something else to drink. And Beau went to the cross-country race with them too. Where was he in this scenario? You'll see other examples of Hanna's tendency, as we continue, to disappear people from a story when their presence was inconvenient for her. Also, by stating that she was alone in the house, she made it plausible that Steve would encounter her there when he came inside.]

A Theory: Why did Hanna's story change so much after she created her affidavit, and then change even more each time she relayed part of it? Let's speculate a little about how she might have constructed it. In the affidavit, Hanna said the first incident of molestation happened the first time she spent the night. Then, once she started having sessions with Ada Dixon, and remembered that she and Aaron didn't spend the night until November, she could have realized that the original version of her story didn't work anymore. Also, in April 2004, Dixon, according to her trial testimony, gave Hanna a copy of her brand new book, which included information about grooming. Once Hanna read about that, she might have also realized that, in order to convince Dixon she had actually been molested, Steve would have needed extra time to implement this slow grooming process. Since there clearly wasn't enough time between the race and the movie (just ten weeks), she created a hazy set of earlier incidents that stretched over a longer, but non-existent, series of visits. Because of the restraints she already placed on her narrative in the affidavit, the starting point of the alleged first instance of abuse had to be moved three months into the future, but then she had to fill those three months with something else. What did she do? I believe she lied about something as simple as her ranking in a footrace, and invented a new set of incidents [*which weren't included in the affidavit*] so she could change her story about when the alleged molestation started. Before long another version of her deeply flawed story was gestating.

Speaking of lies, here's a chapter about a period of time when Hanna might have lied to her friends and confidants about being abused.

Sleepovers, Confessions, and Lies

"Truth becomes fiction when the fiction's true;
Real becomes not-real where the unreal's real."
Cao Xueqin, *Dream of the Red Chamber*

"It is not that hard to fool people around here."
Hanna Penderfield

While this chapter is about disclosures that Hanna may or may not have made to friends at sleepovers between mid-2001 and April 2004, I'll explore a few other related "confessions" as well. Personally, my mind is split about what might have happened to Hanna during the timeframe of the accusations. I would like to believe that she wasn't abused at all; but after poring over thousands of pages of testimony and transcripts, the only thing I'm positive of is that very few of the elements which comprise her stories are true. How, you ask, could I possibly make an argument about whether she was or wasn't abused? It depends a great deal on which parts of her stories are true and which parts aren't.

I don't think Hanna ever intended to end up in court. I think she had a far simpler motive for fabricating these tales, but as soon as they were out in the open she may not have seen a way to back away from them and save face. Once she was on that path, she may have become aware that her story had to be based on some basic truths for it to have any credibility. A number of people (teachers, school officials, Hanna's friends, etc.) have said that she was smart, but was she smart enough to have convinced an entire community and a court system that a series of incidents happened if they actually hadn't? The prosecution did get a conviction on one of the three counts against Steve, but does that say more about the possible ability of Hanna to deceive or more about the average juror's willingness to be deceived, especially about a story with high emotional content?

Let's look at a ruse that Hanna may have perpetrated on some of her friends. She claimed to have told them, at sleepovers, that she was having sexual experiences with someone. She also said that she never named the person, and that she did it to become more popular with her friends. Exactly who she told these stories to, when she told them, and what she said, is hard to verify because only a few of her friends were ever interviewed, and only one of them testified. I believe that most of what Hanna told her friends was false. There is even a possibility that she only mentioned it to one person before she accused Steve. It depends on which version of her stories you examine, and whose testimony you believe.

Why did Hanna construct these stories to begin with, though? I think there might be a few potential reasons.

During her early teens:

1. She desperately wanted to date a boy named Josh Chilmark;
2. She had a strong need to be the center of attention; and
3. She hated it when any of that attention was diverted toward someone else.

How could those elements lead to her accusing Steve of molesting her? Please understand, I'm not saying that Hanna deliberately accused Steve in order to destroy his life. I would personally like to believe that her testimony and statements about lying to gain attention from her friends is true, but it's only one of several possibilities. Her versions also tend to be very fluid, sometimes shifting and changing within a single statement, which makes the truth incredibly hard to pin down. Fortunately, along with everything generated by Hanna, I also had a great deal of fact-based information.

In 2003, Hanna began trying to get Josh's attention, possibly hoping that he would become her boyfriend. In her 2004 affidavit, she said that Josh was <u>the only person</u> she told about her abuse; but, in that same affidavit she also said that she didn't speak <u>to anyone</u> until Blake Goudy came to speak at her school. Both aren't possible, of course, and both statements were made in the same document. She didn't mention telling her friends about her abuse in the affidavit, but she did tell Tom about some confessions to her friends when she spoke to him two years later. Some of her friends' statements don't concur with hers, though. Since Hanna's sleepovers weren't mentioned in the affidavit or Dixon's summary, let's start with Josh's interview with Tom. Josh wasn't at any of the girls' sleepovers, of course, but he acted as Hanna's confidant in mid-2003, and he testified in both trials. Much of what he said is relevant to this chapter. The other sources we'll look at are: Tom's interviews with Hanna and Angie Womack, and trial testimony from Hanna and Rhonda Bresnick. We'll look at everything separately, and in roughly that order, but I'll also blend in some quotes from other sources along the way. Call it freeform chronological.

[Subsections in this Chapter: Josh's Interview With Tom // Hanna's Interview // Angie's Interview // The Trials and the Sleepovers // An Investigation of a Confession // Chapter Analysis]

Josh's Interview with Tom

We're starting with this, but we'll flip back and forth between Josh's and Hanna's interviews a bit. Tom spoke to Josh on the phone for nearly an hour on April 25, 2005. Josh was almost twenty then, but was a 17-year-old senior in high school when he and Hanna (a 13-year-old eighth grader) started communicating in 2003.

Tom began by asking Josh how he and Hanna became friendly. He said that he was "a teacher's aide" for an eighth grade PE class, a sort of mentor for the younger kids, and Hanna was one of them. When Tom asked him how she began confiding in him, Josh said, "These girls were making jokes and stuff, and they brought up about Hanna being a virgin...and she started crying and stuff later…and she got real mad, and she ended up telling me that she wasn't sure if she was or not, and then she just told me about all this different stuff about how he would touch her and stuff." Josh said that, as far as he knew,

Hanna had "never had a boyfriend in school, and explained the teasing during Trial #1 by saying that he had walked in on some girls who were "talking during that class about virginity and Hanna seemed to be upset. Later, she told me the reason she was upset is because she wasn't sure if she was a virgin or not." In Trial #2, he made no mention of the teasing, but simply said he thought Hanna had told him about her abuse on the school bus.

[*Did Josh actually overhear the girls teasing Hanna, or did she just later convince him they had been teasing her? Given the quality of investigation I've seen by law enforcement and the DA's office, I'm fairly certain that no one other than Tom talked to any of Hanna's friends to see if anything like the teasing or the sleepovers took place. Aside from Steve, Hanna, and Josh, very few potential witnesses spoke to investigators or the DA. Tiffany Sperger did, but her mother approached the sheriff's office, they didn't seek her out. I also saw no record of an interview with Rhonda Bresnick in the DA's files. A note from Rhonda to Hanna was submitted to the DA by Hanna's mother, not by Rhonda (I'll cover the note in* The Night of the Rodeo*). Was the prosecution afraid to find out whether any of Hanna's assertions had holes in them? Whether some girls teased Hanna or not is unimportant, but she told Tom that, on the bus, she intentionally* "manipulated the conversation" *so Josh would ask her if she was a virgin. Could Hanna have just made the teasing up? What if she simply told Josh that the girls had been teasing her about being a virgin, but he didn't actually overhear them?*]

Tom asked Josh how he and Hanna communicated, "on the phone, or just face to face, or...?" Josh said that "a lot of it was face to face. She called me quite a bit, though." Tom also asked if their communication was at school or elsewhere. Josh told him it was "just at school" because he worked after school at a nursing home.

[*So, according to Josh, they didn't see each other much outside of school, if at all, but he did say that Hanna talked to him on the phone a lot. How late did Josh work at night? Was Hanna calling him* "quite a bit" *later at night without her mom noticing? Angie Womack, when Tom interviewed her, had a different take on where and how Hanna and Josh talked. We'll look at that after Hanna's interview. I'll put everything together at the end of the chapter.*]

One thing that bothered me while I was reading through the interviews and the testimony was the realization that (if Hanna's stories were true) people who supposedly knew about Hanna's abuse for years didn't report it. Josh was one of them. He told Tom that he had urged *her* to report her problem to the police. Tom asked him how Hanna responded to that. Josh said, "She told me, 'No,' because they thought she would think that she was like a little slut or whore." Tom asked him, "So she was afraid of her friends thinking it was her fault?" Josh waited a moment before answering. He said, "Yeah, and …I didn't tell anybody because she told me that she would make an assault charge, and she was afraid of him, and she told me she wasn't. I don't know if it started out with her being afraid of him. Like I said, it's been going on two ...two-and-a-half years, something like that, she told me."

[*Did the phrase* "they thought she would think that she" *feel as strange to you as it did to me the first time I heard it? One inconsistency was Josh saying (in April 2003) that it had been going on for* "two ...two-and-a-half years, something like that." *That would put the start of the abuse between October 2000 and April 2001. Either date was way before her family started attending get-togethers at the Sirois' house, and not at all what she claimed in her affidavit. That would really mess up her timeline (although Elmer Ross would have probably been tickled to death with the extra grooming time). If that* is *what she told Josh, she was claiming that she had been abused since she was eleven years old, which also contradicts huge swaths of her testimony. It felt to me at times like her story had no outside boundaries, as if it began and ended wherever she wanted it to at any given time.*

Also, Josh, by making the "little slut or whore" *comment, seemed to believe that her friends didn't know about her predicament. That, of course, contradicts Hanna's testimony about the brag sessions with her friends. Was she telling Josh he was the only one who knew about her situation?*

And I don't understand the bit about Hanna telling Josh she was afraid of the man but also wasn't afraid of him. Did Josh misunderstand Tom's question, or did Hanna try to make her situation appear more drastic to Josh? Did she think she needed to be in some sort of danger for Josh to want her? If so, it backfired. He was concerned for her, but wasn't interested in dating her.]

Here's one quick quote from Ada Dixon's summary about Josh's and Hanna's discussions. Sorry, it's going to add another contradiction to her story. In August 2004, Hanna told Dixon, "Josh knew since the beginning of my eighth grade year, but he couldn't get me to tell my mom. The abuse had been going on one year when I told him."

[*Hanna's 8th grade year started in September 2002. A year before that would match the affidavit's beginning date of* "late August or early September 2001," *but (to Tom and in the trials) Josh and Hanna both said they started talking in April 2003. September 2002 would be eight months too early. Did Hanna tell Dixon that so it would agree with the affidavit, but changed her mind later? From one version to the next, her narrative seemed to shift to match her whim of the moment.*]

Tom asked Josh what information Hanna gave him about the man who was abusing her. Josh said, "I didn't know the guy's name, nothing like that." Tom asked him what she did tell him, though. Josh said, "Just his age. That he was a friend of the family. And he lived somewhere out by the lake. She didn't tell me which lake, but I assumed Lake Ashwell." Tom asked if she gave Josh any other description of him. Josh said, "No," then paused before adding, "Oh, yeah. His family... wife, son, daughter ...about her age." Tom asked, "No names of any of them, huh?" Josh said, "Naw, she wouldn't give me a name."

[*According to Josh, Hanna gave him no names, but did tell him the age of the man, that he was married, lived near Lake Ashwell, had a daughter about Hanna's age, and a son, and that he was a friend of her family's. Even without the names, that's a lot of information. When Tom interviewed her, Hanna said she had told Josh far less than that. Did Josh possibly get less detail from her, but remembered it differently in hindsight?*]

Tom asked Josh if he thought Hanna might have said those things to make her friends think she had more experience than they did. Josh said, "Nah, I don't think so. Because I think she would have told family, not me. She knew I wouldn't tell anyone."

[*This is another question that Josh answered oddly. Tom didn't know about the sleepovers when he interviewed Josh; and I presume Josh didn't know about them either. I don't know if he just didn't hear Tom correctly (he does have an ear problem that kept him from joining the Marines), but his answer about Hanna telling him instead of her family might make sense if he thought Tom was asking if Hanna* wanted *other people to know that she was being abused.*]

When Tom interviewed Hanna (May 2006), he asked her when she first told Josh. She paused for seven seconds, and then groaned before saying, "Let's see. The school year was '02 and '03." [*another pause*] "And I didn't really get to know him until... [*another pause*] ...Let's see, I did not tell him [*a hesitation*] until about [*3-second pause*], let's see, the sleepover was in April. [*another pause*] I probably didn't tell him until about May ...April ...no, uh, end of April. Yeah, about the end of April, because..." Tom interrupted, "Of '03?" Hanna said, "Yes."

[*That was a lot of pausing from Hanna, but she eventually gave Tom an end-of-April date for the bus ride where she said she told Josh, and for the sleepover she was going to. The date might have been contradicted by Angie Womack, though, and was also disputed by Rhonda Bresnick's testimony.*]

Possibly curious because of Hanna's hesitation, Tom asked her to verify that she told Josh in April 2003 and made her accusation in February 2004. She agreed those were the right dates. He asked her if that meant that Josh knew about the abuse for almost ten months. She said, "Right."

[*Actually, Tom was two months short. The alleged last incident was in February 2004, but Hanna didn't come forward until April 2004. Josh held on to the information for about a year.*]

Tom asked Hanna why she didn't just go ahead and file charges in 2003. She said, "Because I was scared. I didn't want anything to happen to my mom, or him ...or Sirois, or me." He asked her if she told Josh to impress him, but she said, "No, I was telling him because I needed a friend, and I trusted him." Tom asked her what Josh did to get her to stop the abuse. She paused again [*4 seconds this time*], then said, "He tried to convince me verbally, he tried to convince me over the Messenger [*MSN's chat program*], he just kept talking to me, saying 'You have to tell him, this is serious stuff, you have to tell, you have to tell.' And first ...before ...before he kept saying that, he just kept on saying, 'Where does he live? Me and...' his friend at the time, Cliff Polinger...he and Cliff were going to go beat him up." She said she told Josh no, she didn't want him hurt, and that she also didn't reveal Steve's name or where he lived. Tom asked her how much she told Josh about Steve. She said, "I just said he was a friend, was in his forties, had two kids, and it all is in motion."

[*According to Hanna, even though Josh urged her to report it, she wouldn't. She also said in her affidavit, and to Tom, and in the second trial, that Josh offered to go beat the evil villain up but she wouldn't let him. Interestingly, the affidavit mentioned Josh offering to go beat the man up, but didn't mention Cliff Polinger. Josh also didn't tell Tom anything about wanting to go pummel Steve. You might recall that Polinger was the older guy who was with Hanna at midnight at the Taco Bell in 2005. Did Josh and Cliff even know each other?*

I tried to get an interview with Josh for years, using Beau and Marri as my intermediaries, but he kept avoiding it, so I've had no personal contact with him. I tried one final time, in September 2019. I asked Marri if she would ask him two simple questions. 1) Was he friends with Cliff Polinger in 2003? and 2) Did he tell Hanna that he and Cliff would go beat the bad guy up for her? Responding to Marri, Josh said, "Me and Cliff were friends. But that was at least 15 years ago and I don't recall saying that." That contradicts all of Hanna's statements (in the affidavit, to Tom, and in the trials). Was Polinger's name just handy in Hanna's memory when she spoke to Tom (because she began hanging out with him after the accusations), so she lumped him and Josh together in her "beat Steve up" story? Maybe, but Josh didn't remember even offering to do that. Was Josh's willingness to do that something Hanna invented to make his defense of her seem more noble, or was it something designed to send Tom off on a snipe hunt?

There's also one more disparity between Josh's and Hanna's versions about what she told him. The end of her last sentence above, "and it all is in motion," *seems to say that she told Josh (in April 2003) that she had already arranged to go to the authorities. That contradicts her affidavit, where she said that Blake Goudy (in April 2004) was the impetus for her speaking up (even though it could also have been Karla Spivey's prodding that forced her to talk to Goudy). I believe the reason Hanna didn't give Josh the name of her abuser was because her story wasn't true, but she may have faced a different set of circumstances when she talked to Goudy.*]

Tom asked Hanna if she ever dated Josh, or ever played around, or "ever got into any kind of heavy petting?" She just said, "Nope" to all of those. Then he asked her, "Did y'all ever get alone? Were y'all ever alone anyplace where someone could *say* you got into any heavy petting?" After a two-second pause, Hanna said, "One time." Tom waited. A moment later she said, "And that's because I needed a ride home and he gave me a ride home, and that was it. He told me he could *not* give me a hug, and I walked in my front door."

[*Does that sound familiar, a little like the* "one time" *she got a ride home with Eddie? Why did Hanna mention the hug that Josh* "could not" *give her? Did she ask for one, or try to hug him?*]

Tom asked Josh if Hanna tried to stop the abuse, and Josh delivered another strange sentence. "She told me she wasn't afraid of him, and she told him it couldn't happen anymore, and she did that, and it did happen the same time she told him, but after that, she told me it didn't happen anymore." [*I know. Translation, please?*] Tom also asked him when Hanna last had sex with her abuser. Josh said, "I guess it was the day exactly, sometime after she told me, and I told her I was not going to tell anybody, and she told me it would never happen again." Tom, still trying to understand what Josh meant, asked if he was saying that Hanna *did* stop the abuse. Josh said, "She said they did it one more time, I think. She said she couldn't help herself is what she told me," and added that Hanna wrote him a letter about what she told the man. Josh said, "Like she wrote out the entire conversation."

[*Why would Hanna tell Josh that she couldn't resist so she had sex again? Was that an attempt to seduce him, or keep him interested in her and maybe date her? Possibly. Did it work? No. Josh graduated at the end of May, and was in the Marines shortly after that, but by December he was back in town and dating Steve's niece. Unfortunately, Josh burned Hanna's letter because he didn't want his girlfriend (now wife) to find it. Understandable, but a shame. There could have been a lot more information in it.*

What if Hanna, just to titillate Josh, invented this older abuser, using Steve or someone else as a model? Then, when she was faced with naming someone to Blake Goudy, she told him it was Steve because his name surfaced easily. What if her model was someone other than Steve, though, and she gave that name to someone else just before she talked to Blake Goudy? That story is at the end of this chapter.]

During the brainstorming session there was some discussion about Josh's and Hanna's relationship. Roland Mathis said, "I feel she's been sexually active with Josh." Tom, following up on Mathis' comment, asked Josh if he had ever dated Hanna. Josh said, "No, I didn't." Tom tried again, asking if they any sort of intimate relationship. Josh said, "Nope." Tom waited, and after a little silence, Josh said, "Uh, just hugging is about all, but all my friends do ...and stuff like that. So, nothing..." Tom, continuing, asked if Hanna ever expressed a desire to have a relationship with him. Josh said, "Yes." Tom asked if she tried to get him to date her. Josh said, "No. Well, not really, just suggestions to go out with her and stuff." Tom asked him what kind of suggestions. Josh said, "Just that she ...well, she liked me, thought I was attractive. I told her maybe when she was older, but it never happened." Tom asked if he thought that Hanna might have told him that to impress him, but Josh said, "I don't know if that would have been the case or not."

[*When Tom asked Hanna if she and Josh had ever been alone, she said that Josh would* "not" *give her a hug in the car, but Josh told Tom that the kids hugged all the time. It made me wonder if something else happened in the car (or* didn't *happen) that Hanna told Tom was just an unfulfilled hug.*

Hanna tried to convince Josh that she was worldly and desirable. She told him she thought he was attractive, said she liked him, and wanted to go out with him. He wouldn't date her then, just offering a "maybe" for when she was older, but shortly after that he was in the Marines.]

There is some evidence that they did continue to communicate after Josh left school. Marri told me, "Hanna and Josh used to write each other. I remember her coming to me and showing me the letters. He sent her a picture of him in his army wear with it. I cannot tell you specifically what the letters said, but I do remember her telling me that he would write in the letters that when he got out and she was old enough that they would be together. If this was true, because she wouldn't ever let me read them...I do remember the letters and I remember the picture."

[*Since Hanna wouldn't let Marri read the letters, should we believe that Josh told her they would be together when she was older? Josh said he gave her a* "maybe" *on the possibility of dating when she was older, not an* "of course, yes." *Would Hanna be thoroughly pissed off if she found out that Josh didn't intend to ever be her boyfriend? What if he* did *write her and say they would be together someday, only to appear a few months later, hand in hand with Steve's niece, Liz. Could that have been a potential recipe for jealousy on Hanna's part? Or for anger? Or revenge? Or all three? Would she be tempted to take that out on Josh, or Liz, or maybe even on Liz's relative, Steve?*]

What did Hanna tell Tom about all of this?

Hanna's Interview

There are no mentions of sleepovers in Hanna's affidavit or in Dixon's summary (both in 2004). The first recorded comment I have about them was to Tom (in 2006). When he asked Hanna why she finally decided to make the abuse allegations, she said, "Well, the more often I was around him [*Steve*] the less likely I was to say anything, but towards the end there we started going out there less and less, because my mom kept getting mad at Robin or something, for drinking so much, or something like that, and we'd just go out there less and less. And since I didn't see him for like two or three weeks at a time ...it was just ...it became easier and easier for me to say something ...but I never did. I hinted to my friends, because at sleepovers, or whatever, that I went to, they'd be like, 'Okay, who has the most experience with boys?' Just silly girl stuff. And I would always have the most experience, but <u>I would never tell them with who</u>." Tom asked her for the names of any of those girlfriends who "would have been aware that something was going on." Hanna paused, then said, "Um," then paused for five more seconds before saying, "Hmmm," and paused again. He shifted the subject to the sheriff's investigation for a minute, but later brought it back to requests for friends' names.

[*Why would Hanna be so hesitant to give Tom any of the girls' names? Was she afraid they wouldn't corroborate her story? Here's something to think about until we get to the* Timeline as Final Proof *chapter: Hanna told Tom that* "towards the end" *she found it easier to* "say something." *Is that a clue that there were no revelations to her friends until after the charges were filed in April 2004? To Tom and in the trials, though, she portrayed the sleepovers as a regular ongoing thing where she and her friends vied for bragging rights about their sexual experiences. Why did she wait that long to say anything about them?*

Here's one other discrepancy. Hanna said that she and her friends bragged at their sleepovers about how far they had gone with sex, and Hanna claimed that she always won, which made her more popular with her friends. If the dozen girls in her grade (it's a very small town) thought she was a virgin and had no boyfriend, who was she bragging to about sex? The girls at her sleepovers couldn't have been the same girls who were teasing her if she was bragging about sexual experiences to them. It doesn't make sense.

Also, Hanna maintained that these girls who were told about her experiences knew about it for years, or at least one full year under the most liberal interpretation of her statements. Think back to your junior high days, especially if you were from a very small town. How long could members of your group of friends have kept a secret like that? A few days? A month?]

Tom asked Hanna why she told Josh about her molestation. She said, "When I was around Sirois, I kind of learned a little manipulation on my own, and I had a huge, *enormous* crush on him [*Josh*] for the *longest* time, and I had to ride the bus to my friend's house for a sleepover <u>or something</u>…<u>and he rode the same bus</u>. He was a senior in high school at the time, and we got to talking about something, and I kind of manipulated the conversation so I knew he would ask. I don't know, we were just being silly, just talking about girls, and I manipulated the conversation, and he asked …well, I don't remember what I said, but he goes, 'Well, *are* you a virgin?' I said, 'I don't know,' because I didn't know ...but if I had to tell somebody, and I trusted him, I just didn't know how to go about it, so that's what I did, but I had to tell somebody, and I was like 'Oh, I'll talk about it later,' and you know I just kind of blew it off, and then we were chatting on the Internet, on MSN Messenger one night, and he was like, [*She began acting out all the parts*] 'So, what did you mean?' I said 'About what?' 'You're just playing dumb.' 'Um, you mean about being a virgin? I don't know.' 'What do you mean, I don't know? It's a yes or no question.' 'No, it's not.'"

[*Hanna said she told Josh because she wanted him to notice her, and said she tricked him into asking about intimate things because she had a crush on him. What better way to appeal to his better nature than to* "manipulate" *him into thinking she was a damsel in distress. She told Tom she deliberately broached the subject of her virginity on the bus, and gave Josh the details later, but she told a different story during the trials.*

Their discussions took place near the end of Josh's senior year. Were they her last-ditch attempt to spark some interest from him before he joined the Marines, maybe disappearing from her life altogether? She was vague about why she was riding the school bus to her friend's house (for "a sleepover <u>or something</u>"), *but in the trials she was positive it was a sleepover.*

Also, why was Josh riding the bus if he had a car and went to work every day after school? The main thing to remember for now is that Hanna said she intentionally got Josh to talk to her about sex. More on that and other inconsistencies as we continue.]

Tom also wanted some detail about the "one ride" home that Josh gave her. She said they drove "from school. Which is like less than two miles from my house." Tom asked if they had gone straight to her house. She said, "Yes. There were <u>no</u> detours." He asked if they hung around together after school. Hanna seemed to take offense at that idea. "No," she said, "We never hung out outside school. <u>**Never**</u>!" Tom asked her if she and Josh mostly talked on the Internet and the phone, instead of in person. She agreed. "We didn't spend a lot of time together at school or anything, there was just..." He interrupted, "So you were not together in personal contact." She said, "Not really. He would give me a hug, just throughout the day he'd see me. 'Hey, hi,' and he would give me a hug. He knew I had a crush on him, and he said, 'No, we cannot date until you're older.' Which he's married with a kid now anyway, so it really doesn't matter, and I'm with somebody else."

[*Hanna said Josh drove her home, emphasizing that* "there were no detours." *Alderson's town boundaries are just under a mile from north to south, and only 3,400 feet wide at its widest point. The school complex is in the southwest corner of town, and Hanna's house was in the middle of town, roughly 2,400 feet away from the edge of the school grounds. So, yes, Hanna's house was definitely* "less than two miles" *away from the school. Did she actually need a ride home, or just want Josh to give her one? And if he freely gave her hugs at school, why wouldn't he give her one in his car? Have you been keeping track of everything? I know, it's hard. Don't worry, I'll tie everything together soon.*]

Tom again asked Hanna for the names of any of her girlfriends who might be able to verify her side of the story. She mentioned Angie Womack, and Tom asked who she was. Hanna said, "She's a very good friend of mine. We've been friends since about the fifth grade. She was at the sleepover, and one time ...we were at my friend's house ...had a sleepover, we kind of got into a det- ...we got into a detail with all those girls about experiences with guys ...and ...and she took me into the bathroom ...and she's like 'Who is doing all this to you?' and all sorts of stuff, because I don't really remember what was said. She would remember better than I would."

[*Hanna said that Angie,* "was at the sleepover, and one time ...we were at my friend's house ...had a sleepover." *Did she slip up by saying* "the?" *In Trial #1, she said,* "I had sleepovers" *(plural), as if to say they were* her *sleepovers, but no one else has said she hosted any of them. To Tom, though, she only talked about the sleepover, and it was at a friend's house. Was there actually only one? She also said* "...we got into a detail with all those girls about experiences with guys..." *Who is* "we?" *Her and Angie? Her and someone else? How many girls were there for it to be* "all those girls?" *Also, in the trials, Hanna testified that she talked about her experiences because the other girls were all talking about theirs. If that was so, why would Angie pull her into the bathroom to question just her? Wouldn't Angie be worried about some of the other girls too? Did Hanna* "manipulate" *her friends like she did with Josh, maybe to gain sympathy? Were the other girls even talking about sex? When Tom interviewed Angie, she painted a very different picture of that sleepover. That's coming up.*]

Tom also asked Hanna how much she told Angie. Laughing, she said, "Ohhh ...a lot. At first I told Josh more than I told her, but now she knows everything. I keep a lot of people updated on the court thing, because they want to know." Tom asked her what Angie could testify to. She said, "Well, I told her what had happened to me at a sleepover before I came out to my mom about it. I don't know if that would do any good to me or not." [*Warning: Lots of conflicting information ahead*] Tom asked her how much time passed, after she told Angie, before she told her mom. Hanna said, not exactly answering the question, "Oh, good grief [*long drawn out "uhhhhh"*] ...about two years ago. I think I told her ...I think I told her. The day I told you I manipulated that conversation with Josh, I think I told her that night." Tom, to be sure of the date, said, "Okay, so that was about April of '03?" Hanna answered, "Yes. It was the middle of April. Um, the friend's birthday that had the sleepover? Her birthday's on the 18th, or somewhere very close. It was on that Satur... No. That was Friday night, because I remember riding the school bus. It was that Friday close to the 18th. I don't know what date it was exactly."

Tom asked her if Angie knew Steve. Hanna said, "No. Never met him." Tom asked if Angie had "any exposure at all to Steve." Hanna said, "No." Tom asked Hanna if she had told Angie who Steve was. After a four-second pause, Hanna said, "Yes." Tom asked if there was anyone else that Hanna had made outcries to. After another long pause, followed by another "uhhhh," followed by a three-second sigh, she said, "Let me think." Seven seconds later, she said "I know that Suzanna Bushnell had been around Sirois. I don't know if I told her before I told Blake [*Goudy*] or after."

[*Let's start with the date. Tom's interview was in May 2006. She said the sleepover was around the 18th, on a Friday in April,* "two years ago." *April 18, 2004 was on a Sunday (after Hanna signed her affidavit). April 18, 2003, was on a Friday, though. Hanna's* "two years ago" *comment would have put the sleepover in 2004, but Josh's testimony that their talks were during his Senior year would more likely place the sleepover in 2003.*

Hanna also told Tom that Angie Womack was one of the people she told about her abuse, "at a sleepover before I came out to my mom about it." *Days before telling her mother? Hours before? Years before? We know that Hanna did tell her mother on the same day she told Blake Goudy (which was April 7, 2004). The only two days that the sleepover could have been on in April 2004 (and also be before the 7th, and not on a school night, were Friday or Saturday, April 2nd or 3rd, 2004. Could a revelation to some of her friends a few days before Goudy's talk have helped Hanna decide to come forward to him? Hanna ruined that possibility, though, by telling Tom that she let Angie know about the abuse the same night she manipulated Josh (April 18, 2003), but she also told Tom that the sleepover with Angie was "about two years ago," which would have been after she accused Steve. Was Hanna talking about two different sleepovers? Hanna also told Tom that she did tell Angie who Steve was. According to her affidavit, though, she told no one who her abuser was before Blake Goudy (and, as I've mentioned, she may not have named anyone to him either). If your mind isn't already completely jumbled, Angie's interview is coming up soon. Get ready for another 180° twist.*]

Tom continued to ask for the names of any of Hanna's friends who could corroborate her story, and added, to explain why that was important, "I've talked to a lot of young ladies out there [*in Steve's neighborhood*], and he either has a lot of people fooled..." Hanna interrupted. "I believe that he does, because of my parents' divorce. My dad had a lot of people fooled, and it is not that hard to fool people around here." Tom asked her how she believed her dad fooled people. She said, "Just lies. So many lies." He asked her what type of lies she thought her father told. She said, "I don't really know. I was very young at the time. Um, I just know that he ...I believe to this day he's a compulsive liar. He lies even though the truth would help him out more, because he's lied to me several times by just saying, 'I did not say that,' and he just kept his look on his face like you had no choice but to believe him. And after he skipped town, after my parents' divorce, my mom had people coming up and apologizing to her saying 'I'm so sorry I ever believed him. I apologize for treating you the way I did. You didn't deserve it. You're a good mom.' Blah, blah, blah, blah."

[*I'll preface this by saying that I don't know the exact circumstances of her parents' divorce, but Steve said it was a bitter one. Hanna said she was aware that her father lied, but also said that she didn't know what his lies were. How could she know one and not the other? The logical assumption is that her belief that her father was a* "compulsive liar" *came from her mother. One thing she seemed to have learned after the divorce, though, was that people will have sympathy for you and give you attention if they believe something awful happened to you, or that you have been wronged. She didn't react to the apologies to Darla as anything important. She referred to them as,* "Blah, blah, blah, blah," *but the attention itself appeared to stir something in her. She said that Steve taught her how to manipulate people, but I believe there could be a different source, her father. She seemed to have learned from him that, if she kept a straight look on her face and looked right at people when she spoke, they would believe her whether she was telling the truth or not. In my opinion, though, her most important phrase came after she had taken the measure of her small town and said* "...it is not that hard to fool people around here."]

Hanna, who had occasional pauses during the interview (as anyone normally would), seemed to have exceptionally long ones when she was trying to think of names for Tom. After the revelation about her father, Tom asked her again for names. This time there was a twelve-second pause before she said, "Mm," followed by a four-second pause before she said, "I don't know if he would be of any help, because I did tell him what had been going on before the charges became filed, but just never said with who." Tom asked who she was referring to. She said, "His name was Sean Luedeman…He's an extremely good friend of mine. Him and I still talk. He promised to be there to support me whenever we go to court." She said that Sean lived nearby, was sixteen (a year younger than her), and knew her from school. She didn't remember how they became friends, possibly "walking home together after school." She said, "…we just kind of started talking and getting to know each other and now ...we're really close." Tom asked her what she had told him. She said she told him "everything that had happened, but there were no names involved." He asked her when she told him. She said, "Oh, it was about a year or so ago I started talking to him. It was before charges were filed [*more pauses, first a two-second one*] ...um [*another two-second pause*] ...it was about ...let's see [*another two-second pause*] ...oh, gosh [*a four-second pause*] ...yeah, about ...yeah, about the year '03."

[*When Tom interviewed Hanna (May 2006), she had already had over two years to think about everything. The DA had also undoubtedly spent time encouraging her and Darla to find people to testify on her behalf, but so far they only had Rhonda Bresnick and Josh Chilmark. Josh didn't give an affidavit until April 2005, and Rhonda didn't come forward until August 2005, when Darla asked her for her note. Tiffany Sperger testified for the prosecution too, but I consider her an outlier. Even if we count her, that's only three witnesses beyond her mother and Dixon and Goudy. How could Hanna, after all that time, be unable to think of people who could verify her story? Could it be because (despite what she had been claiming) Hanna's friends might tell stories that wouldn't support any of her versions?*

And, as far as the time is concerned, Hanna said she started talking to Sean "a year or so ago," "before charges were filed," "about the year '03," *but a year before May 2006 would be in 2005, not 2003. Despite her claim that Sean* "promised to be there to support me whenever we go to court," *he was never on any witness list, and didn't testify in either trial. Hanna's dates are vaguely all over the place. When in 2003 did she tell Sean about* "everything?" *Her conversations with Josh were during the spring and maybe the summer of 2003. Could Sean have been Josh's replacement (maybe in the fall of 2003)? She would have been shifting her focus from an 18-year-old boy to a 12 or 13-year-old one. Did she tell Sean after she told Josh and the others, but before the charges were filed, or did she actually tell him* "...a year or so ago" *(in 2005, when he would have been around 15)? Or did she tell Sean anything at all? I don't know. There's a layer of ambiguity on top of a layer of obscurity.*

A Reminder: She swore in her affidavit that she hadn't been able to tell <u>anyone</u> until Blake Goudy gave his talk at her school, the same document where said she didn't tell anyone except Josh. Are her comments about telling her sleepover friends, and now Sean, all lies? Aside from Josh, did any single one of these individuals know about Hanna's supposed molestation before Blake Goudy? What's real? What's the truth? It's impossible to know, but one thing is certain, multiple stories appear to have been told to multiple people.]

Before we shift to Angie's interview, here's one more of Hanna's comments about what she told her friends. Tom was still asking for the names of anyone she told about the abuse <u>before Goudy</u>. She followed a three second pause with an "Uhhhh" that sounded like a long drawn out sigh, and said, "Let me think." Then, after an eight-second pause, said, "I know that Suzanna Bushnell had been around Sirois. I don't know if I told her before I told Blake or after." Tom asked for Suzanna's phone number, and Hanna promised to get it for him [*she didn't*]. Tom asked her what she told Suzanna before telling Goudy. After a brief pause, Hanna said, "Ummhhh" [*then a 6-second pause*] "I don't really know. It's kind of hard for me to remember how much I talked to her about it because her and I have talked *a lot*, and some people I've tried to tell what had happened, <u>when they asked who, I lied to them and said it was someone else</u>." Tom asked who she told them it was. Hanna said, "I wanted to be cool. Like I said, I cared about what other people think. Now I really don't care, but at the time I did, and it's not cool to say, yeah, this forty-something-year-old man did mess with me. That's not cool. So <u>I said that it was Beau</u>, because he was nineteen at the time. And that's cool. I mean, a nineteen-year-old, that's cool to junior high kids." Tom said, "Did Beau ever mess around with you?" Hanna said, "No! He never even gave me a hug ...he gave me a hug like once in a while, but that was about it." Tom asked her if Beau ever attempted anything. "No," she said, "Nothing whatsoever." They talked a bit about Beau, with Hanna insisting that there was nothing physical between them. She finished by saying, "No, he never did any of that. He is a good man."

Tom asked Hanna when she told Suzanna. She said, "I don't ...really ...remember what I told her. I don't know if I told her *after* I filed charges, or not." Tom asked her again if she told Suzanna before or after Goudy. She said, "I remember [*a pause, then a sigh*] I remember exactly where I was when I told her. I remember what we were talking about *before* I brought it up…but I don't remember when it was. It was right before school started, when I was a [*3-second pause*] ...freshman, I want to say, or just going into my freshman year. Yeah, I was just going into my freshman year I told her. It was a week or two before school started." Tom said, "September or August of 2003?" She said, "It was about the end of July, beginning of August. '03, yeah."

[*There's a lot to unpack in this one. This doesn't just contain statements that I believe are lies, but also an admission from Hanna that she* did *lie under certain circumstances. She said,* "...when they [*her friends*] asked who, I lied to them and said it's someone else," *admitting to Tom that she deliberately chose to lie about certain things, and also that she told them it was* "someone else," *or that it was Beau because* "...a nineteen-year-old, that's cool to junior high kids." *Does that mean that she told some of her friends it was Beau and told other friends it was someone else? Or did she tell the same friends that it was both Beau and someone else who had abused her? Which of those statements about lying to her friends is the truth? Is either one true? Beau, by the way, was shocked when I read Sara's statement to to him. He couldn't believe she would have said such a thing about him.*

No matter how cool Hanna's friends might have found it, Beau was six years older than her, and Romeo and Juliet laws wouldn't have applied. She was still describing what would have been a crime. And, if the sleepover was in April 2003, as she claimed, Beau was twenty then, not nineteen. Did Hanna not know Beau's age even though her own birthday was within spitting distance of his, or did she make this up to throw the defense off track? If the sleepover, as others have said, was in 2004, Beau was twenty-one then, and Hanna and her friends weren't in junior high. Would it actually have been "cool" to them, though? Angie didn't think so. She's up next.

Hanna said that she and Beau were just friends, that there was nothing physical between them. When Tom pressed her, she said, "No. He never even gave me a hug ...he gave me a hug like once in a while." *Did Beau (like Josh) give her hugs, or didn't he? This was a recurring pattern in her interview and the trials. She would start to say something, then would stop reverse course, saying something else; as if she thought it wouldn't sound good, or wouldn't help her side of the story.*

Hanna also told Tom that she couldn't remember how much she told Suzanna before she talked to Goudy and how much she told her after. About the sleepovers, though, she said she told her friends everything except for the guy's name; but she also told Tom that she lied to them and gave them Beau's name and/or someone else's name.

Hanna told Tom that she told to her friends about having sexual experiences because her friends were bragging about similar things and it would make her more popular if she had some experience with sex too. According to Angie, though, they weren't *talking about sex. I know, that's* another *contradiction. It's time to see Angie's take on these sleepover revelations.*]

Angie's Interview

We briefly looked at Angie Womack's interview in the chapter, *Just Before the Trials*. She also had a lot to say about one particular sleepover and about Hanna's and Josh's relationship. After establishing that the girls were in the eighth grade when this sleepover took place, Tom asked Angie if she could give him an approximate date for it. She said, "Uh, yes," gave a single laugh, then sighed and said, "It was in April, uh ...of two-thousand ...um ...2003? ...2002? Somewhere around there, and, um ...it was at my friend's, Gloria Moore's."

[*Hanna and Angie were in the eighth grade from September 2002 to May 2003. Could Angie's fumbling statement have been because she was genuinely trying to recall when it happened, or could she have been trying to produce a date she had been asked to remember? She did come up with a month right away, but not the year.*

If the sleepover had been in April 2002, would those girls have allowed Hanna's situation (whether true or not) to continue for two full years before she made her outcry to Blake Goudy? Even if it was in 2003, a more likely date, it would still mean that none of them said anything for at least a year after they heard about her supposed abuse. I find it hard to believe that teenagers, especially in a tiny town, could keep a secret like that for any period of time, much less a year or two. Assume instead, though, that none of Hanna's girlfriends heard about the abuse until <u>*after*</u> *her outcry to Goudy. Their testimony would be meaningless as evidence in the trial. Could that be why almost no one appeared in court on her behalf? If the sleepover was in April 2004, everything else Hanna said about the sleepovers was a lie. Which date was the correct one, 2002, 2003, or 2004? Angie and Suzanna didn't testify. Wouldn't the DA have wanted them to verify that Hanna told them about the abuse as early as 2002 or 2003, while it was still happening? One more little detail. Rhonda Bresnick, who testified that Hanna told them at a 2004 sleepover,* <u>*after*</u> *Hanna accused Steve, wasn't mentioned by anyone as having been at any of the sleepovers.*]

Early in the interview, Angie told Tom that "Hanna got upset over one of the comments that was made" at the slumber party. He asked her what the comment was, and Angie said, "I, uh ...it was about guys, because, I mean, it was a girl's slumber party. Tom laughed, and Angie said, "Yeah, we were talking about guys..." [*some words were lost while Tom continued to laugh*] "...got really sad about something, and so we thought that she was sick or something. We had just been playing, dancing, jump-roping, and hula-hooping, and stuff like that, and then we ate cake, so I figured she was ralphing in my friend's toilet. Suzanna went in there to go talk to her, and I went in there afterwards ...and she just broke down and told us." She said Hanna told them that "something was going on and it was bad and she didn't like it. And that she wouldn't tell us who it was, but ...like, I'd never been around them ...because I was like the new kid in the..." Tom, laughing again, said, "You were the newbie, so you had to..." Angie jumped in with, "Yeah. I hadn't really like been around much of ...their family ...or their friends ...or anything like that, and they had grown up together since kindergarten ...so, you know, I didn't know how these people think, and, like I was asking my friend, Suzanna, I was like 'Who would it be?' and she was like '...Sirois?' She was like 'because he's the only one with the ...you know ...that's friends with her mom, and they go over there,' and ...you know ...stuff like that." Tom asked her if Suzanna thought it might have been Steve. Angie said, "Yeah. She's the one that should've ...but she just told me, and ...you know, in..." [*she paused*] Tom suggested, "In confidence?" Angie said, "...in confidentiality, because ...I didn't know. I was like 'What's she talking about?'"

[*Yes, that's a lot of strange phrasing. I think Valleyspeak had made its way to Central Texas by then. Basic Translation: They had been doing all sorts of physical things and eating cake, so when Hanna went into the bathroom, Angie thought she was about to throw up, so she and Suzanna went to see if she was okay. Notice that Angie said Suzanna went first and she followed her. In Hanna's version, <u>all the girls</u> were talking* "about <u>experiences</u> with guys ...and she [*Angie*] <u>took me</u> into the bathroom." *Hanna didn't mention Suzanna, but said that Angie* pulled her *from the room because of what she had just revealed to the group, not because she left the room suddenly. Where was Suzanna in Hanna's version? Not there. Where was she during the trials? Not there.*

Also, Hanna said she told Suzanna about her situation near "the end of July, beginning of August, '03." *If the sleepover was in April of either 2002 or 2003, Suzanna would already have known about the abuse, so Hanna wouldn't have told her again in August 2003. Was Angie wrong about when the sleepover was, or could she and Hanna have just poorly coordinated a story for Tom? Is any of it true? In Angie's version, Hanna told both her and Suzanna what was happening to her, but gave them no names. Angie said they figured it out <u>after</u> Hanna had left the bathroom. If there was anything even remotely true about this version, and Suzanna had spent the night at the Sirois' house, wouldn't she have testified on Hanna's behalf? She could have provided all sorts of details about the sleeping conditions and how Steve treated Hanna, and what happened at that sleepover. Why wasn't Suzanna called as a witness?*

Angie also told Tom she was new to the group, and hadn't been around them very much, but Hanna called Angie "a very good friend," *and said they had* "been friends since about the fifth grade." *If we take Angie's comment at face value about the sleepover taking place in April of 2002 or 2003, when she and Hanna were in the 7th or 8th grades, they would have known each other for two to three years by then. How was she a newcomer to the group if their school class was only about two-dozen kids, half of them girls?*]

Angie also said, "And I told my mom, and my mom was like 'Well, does her mom know?' And I was like, 'I'm sure her mom knows.' So we didn't push the issue." Tom asked her why she thought Darla knew about it. Angie said, "I think that her mom knew because her mom was friends with the man, but, like ...I guess she didn't know." Angie said she had believed that Hanna would have told Darla because, "the way I was raised, I communicate," and she said, "My mom was like 'Well, we don't really know any of the facts, or anything like that. We don't know if she's lying, you know. We're not going to start anything between mother and daughter, you know,' and..."

Before Tom could ask his next question, Angie suddenly added, "I didn't tell my mom until a year later." Tom, surprised, said, "Oh, so, you waited until …you waited a year?" Angie said, "Yeah, because Hanna said that everything had stopped, when it in reality hadn't, because she ...I guess she realized that she made a mistake by telling us ...because she knew that she would go back, and like now that I knew she had lied to us, and told us it had stopped ...and it really hadn't, it made me mad, and I felt ...because I should have done something, you know ...but, like ...I mean ...we're in junior high, and that's just not right." Tom asked her, "Do you think she would have lied about any of this?" Angie answered, "No. I really don't. Like she ...she's a really smart girl ...and she has a good head on her shoulders." Tom asked if Hanna might have said all of this to impress her friends. Angie said, "No, because we weren't talking about anything [*she paused for a nervous laugh*] ...like sexual. Once again, we're in junior high ...and, like sex wasn't ...like something ...like that, and ...like, you know ...everybody in that room didn't really know about sex ...so [*she gave another nervous laugh before adding*] ...except for her."

[*Let's break that down a little. First, how could Angie not see the irony of saying that she was raised to communicate with her mother, but waited a year before she told her about Hanna's problem? Seriously? I also found it interesting that Angie's mother assumed that Hanna might lie about being abused. Did she know something about Hanna's ability to lie? Or about her own daughter's veracity? If there was even a remote possibility that Hanna* was *being molested, though, why would any mother hesitate to say something? Just to avoid being in the middle of a mother-daughter squabble? One more thing, did Angie actually tell her mother, or could that have been part of another diversion concocted by Hanna? I know, I have more questions than answers about parts of this. As far as the date of the sleepover, if we believe Angie, it took place in either 2002 or 2003. If it happened in 2002, and Angie waited a year before telling her mother, it meant that she and her mother held onto that information for another year before the charges were filed, and would also mean that Angie and Suzanna kept it from the authorities for at least two years. If the sleepover was in mid-April 2003, and Angie's mom didn't find out until a year later, then Hanna would already have accused Steve by then. Even if I was willing to believe Angie, there are huge flaws in both scenarios.*

Something else disturbed me about the rest of this excerpt. Angie said that later (after Hanna told them that she hadn't stopped having sex with the man) she realized that Hanna had lied to her, but when Tom asked her if she thought Hanna would have lied, Angie said that she didn't think Hanna had because "...she's a really smart girl." *That would have been a perfect moment for Tom to tell Angie that smart people often make the best liars, but being a good investigator, he wanted to keep her talking, so he didn't.*

Hanna said several times that the girls bragged about who had gone the farthest with boys, but Angie said it wasn't like that at all; that they were just junior high kids, and none of them except Hanna were experienced sexually. Was Angie at the same sleepover as everyone else, or was the bragging about sexual exploits another figment of Hanna's imagination? Angie painted a very different picture than Hanna's idea of what was "...cool to junior high kids."

Neither Angie nor her mother testified.]

These next few quotes might be the most important in this chapter, but they also add one more layer of inconsistency to everything. When Angie tried to explain why Hanna left the room at the sleepover, she said, "It was just like ...she just got really upset about one of the comments someone made." When Tom asked her what the comment was, she said, "It was something about ...like a rodeo? Or something ...and like ...she was just like ...she was sitting there, and she was just ...just got up and left a little bit after that. And it wasn't like a dramatic scene, because hardly anybody realized she..." Tom finished her sentence, "Realized she had left. Yeah."

[*Angie said* <u>*someone mentioned a rodeo*</u>*, and that was what sent Hanna out of the room, but Hanna said she had told her friends about her sexual experiences multiple times. Angie talked about this as if it was a one-time incident. The rodeo Hanna and Rhonda went to was in July 2003. To believe that Hanna's reaction had something to do with the rodeo, it would have to have taken place* <u>*before*</u> *the sleepover. Was Angie making up that bit of information to help bolster Hanna's and Rhonda's stories? One other obvious possibility is that none of Hanna's comments about telling her friends at sleepovers were true. Was Rhonda's testimony about that final sleepover (where she said Hanna told everyone that she had lost her virginity), the only true statement in the bunch? True that Hanna told them at that April 2004 sleepover, not at any earlier time.*

Witnesses aren't supposed to meet with each other and discuss strategy before a trial. Did Angie and Hanna try to get their stories straight in advance; or was Angie, on her own, trying to help her friend by coming up with a reason for Hanna telling them she had been molested? Wasn't Angie's earlier statement about them all talking about boys good enough? Couldn't that have triggered something that bothered Hanna? If the sleepover actually was in 2002 or 2003, it's a better explanation than saying that a rodeo that hadn't happened yet was the catalyst for Hanna's freakout. None of the three girls seemed to have a firm grasp on when anything took place, but the ride home from the rodeo was obviously before April 2004. Darla would never have asked Steve to give the girls a ride after the charges had been filed.

There is yet another possibility. If the sleepover did take place in April 2004 (not 2002 or 2003), Hanna could have told her friends about her supposed abuse for the very first time (yes, <u>*after*</u> *she had accused Steve), and then convinced them to come to her rescue to keep this evil monster from having a chance to molest other girls. I can imagine her looking them right in the eyes and saying something like,* "I'm sorry I never told any of you before. I was ashamed and didn't know what to do. If you don't help me he'll just get away with it. Could you tell everyone I've been telling you about this since we were in junior high, but I didn't tell you who it was?" *That could provide an explanation for why Tiffany Sperger didn't give an affidavit until September 2004, and why Rhonda Bresnick didn't come forward until August 2005. That scenario only works, though, if Josh Chilmark was the only person Hanna told about her supposed abuse. If any one of those versions are true, though, all of her other versions fall apart, which would be another good reason to remember what she said to Tom.* "It is not that hard to fool people around here."]

One last thing from Tom's interview with Angie. He asked her if she knew Josh Chilmark. She tentatively answered, "Yes." Tom asked her if Josh was older than them, and Angie said, "He's like ...a couple of years ahead of us." Tom asked her if Josh and Hanna used to hang out together. Angie hesitated, but said, "Uh, they were ...they were friends. Like he had a car, so, like [*she paused for a couple of seconds*] ...they'd drive around." Tom asked her if Josh took Hanna places very often. Angie said, "No." Tom just said, "Okay," and waited. After another pause, Angie said, "Like mostly, if they did get into his car ...it was just to sit there." Tom asked if they just sat in his car and talked. Angie said, "Yeah. <u>I think</u>." Tom asked if that happened at the school. Angie said, "I think she spoke to him a lot about stuff, because he was like a brother figure."

[*This exchange made me wonder why the defense team didn't try to get Angie on the stand. They knew about her because Tom interviewed her shortly after he interviewed Hanna. Angie seemed reluctant to talk about Josh. Her voice was barely audible when she answered* "Yes." *Why would the mention of Josh's name worry her? Did she suspect that Josh and Hanna did have a relationship, or could Hanna possibly have hinted to her that there had been one? Hanna told Marri that Josh had said they would be together when they were older. Could she have said the same thing to some of her friends? In the brainstorming session, Roland Mathis, possibly because of that type of comment, said he believed that Josh and Hanna might have had some sort of sexual relationship.*

Why did Angie say that Josh was only a couple of years older than them? She can count. He was a senior when they were eighth graders, four years older than them, and he was gone after the 2002-2003 school year. By the time of her interview, Josh hadn't been there for three years, and she and Hanna still had one more year of school left.

Angie also said a couple of things that contradict each other. She said "...he had a car, so ...they'd drive around," *but she followed that with,* "...if they did get into his car ...it was just to sit there." *Did Josh and Hanna sit in his car a lot, or drive around, or was Angie making up what she thought might have happened? And if Josh worked after school, how much time did he have to pal around with anybody, or sit in his car and ...talk? Tom asked Hanna if she had been alone with Josh long enough that* "someone could say you got into heavy petting?" *Hanna answered,* "One time," *and she said it was so he could drive her home. Josh, on the other hand, said their interaction was mostly face-to-face at school, and on the phone and the Internet, plus she wrote him <u>one letter</u>. Three people, three different stories.*]

Let's take a look at what Hanna said about all of this during the two trials.

The Trials and Sleepovers

Just a quick reminder that everything said during the trials is done under oath. We'll start with Trial #1. There's a brief repeat here. Hanna told Elmer Ross, "<u>I</u> had sleepovers, and <u>I</u> gained popularity because <u>I</u> had the most experience with boys. <u>I</u> would never tell them with who, <u>I</u> would never tell them anything about what had happened, but I would tell them what I had done. Because after I got a little bit older, the further you went, it was cool as long as you didn't have sex and you weren't a 'hoe,' basically." Ross said, "At this point, you had not had sex..." Hanna interrupted him with a quick, "No," before he was able to add "...with the Defendant, correct?" She then said, "No. Yes, correct."

[*Barely eight weeks after Tom's interview, Hanna testified that she told her friends at her sleepovers, and that it made her popular. It's also interesting that Hanna was so quick to interrupt Ross and say she hadn't had sex before Ross got out the words* "...with the Defendant." *Did she think her own lawyer was about to ask if she had become sexually active after she made the accusations, as she had admitted to Tom? Why would her lawyer do that? And there's this strange sentence,* "I would never tell them anything about what had happened, but I would tell them what I had done." *Don't the phrases* "what had happened" *and* "what I had done" *mean the same thing in that situation?*]

Ross asked Hanna if she told Josh that someone was molesting her. I don't know if she wasn't paying attention, or possibly expected a different question at that point, but instead of just answering "Yes," she said, "By this time I was going out to the Sirois' less frequently. I couldn't take it. I had to tell somebody. And at that point in time, he was the only one I trusted fully." Ross kept pace with her and asked, "Why did you trust Josh?" She said, "The same reason I trusted Sirois. He never did anything to ever break my trust. He never harmed me in any way, harmed anyone that I knew. He was always very sweet to me. He was just -- He was a good friend." Then, to set a time period, Ross asked if their talks happened during her eighth-grade year. She agreed.

[*Hanna could have just answered "Yes," and let Ross ask for specifics. Instead, she rambled about not being able to visit the Sirois' as much, and how much she trusted this older boy, but never actually answered the question about what she told Josh. Then, oddly, she said she trusted Josh because he treated her like Steve did, using words and phrases like* "very sweet," "never harmed me," *and* "a good friend." *Does that make any sense in light of what she was accusing Steve of?*

How did Hanna and Josh get to be such good friends? Josh told Tom that he knew Hanna since his freshman year (when he was 14 and she was 10). I seriously doubt that Josh was hanging out with her when she was ten. They probably didn't have any personal interaction until he became an aide in her 8th grade PE class. Hanna said she had a "huge crush" on him, but I doubt they were more than just school acquaintances until Hanna told him about her alleged dilemma. I also don't think she talked to Josh because she "trusted" him. I believe she just wanted to get him to notice her, but since he was probably treating her like all the other kids her age she took things into her own hands.

One other point needs to be made here. Hanna testified that the frequency of their visits to the Sirois' were already decreasing when she and Josh started communicating. That was in April 2003, a full year before she made the accusations. She will talk about the number of visits shrinking even more before we're through. How often Hanna's family visited the Sirois' may be one of the more important reasons not to believe her accusations. Hopefully that will become clear soon. If it doesn't, the chapter, A Timeline as Final Proof, *should settle the matter.*]

Here's more from Trial #1. Ross asked Hanna what she said to Josh. She answered, "I don't remember how I had started the conversation. I just know that I would give him a little bit of information that something wasn't right, and he would keep pressing me and pressing me until I just gave in and I poured out the whole story. It was through MSN Messenger over the Internet. It was an Internet conversation." Ross asked her if she ever gave Josh her abuser's name. She said, "No. I never mentioned where he lived, who he was. All that he was -- All that Josh was told was how old he was and that he was married with kids." Ross asked her, "How old did you tell Josh this person was that you were doing things with?" She said, "He was about 42, 43 at the time." Ross also asked her if she remembered exactly what she told Josh. She said, "I told him everything that I remembered in detail. Or not so much detail as I have today, but enough to where he got the idea." Ross asked her how Josh responded to that. Hanna said [*acting out the parts again*], "He kept -- He just said, 'I want to ask you one question.' I said, 'Okay.' He said, 'Who is he?' I said, 'I can't tell you.'" Ross asked her why she didn't name anyone. Hanna said, "Sirois, while he wasn't messing with me, was like a father figure to me. My father had never been there for me, and he was."

[*I believe Hanna spent much of her time before the trials trying out parts of the story on people like Ada Dixon and her friends. Two months before the trial, she told Tom in great detail about the massive crush she had on Josh, and how she* <u>*deliberately manipulated*</u> *the conversation, but when she testified she said she couldn't remember how it started. The idea of her "manipulation" of Josh had completely disappeared from her story, and she said nothing about her and Josh being on the bus together. She only mentioned having an Internet conversation, something that (unlike sitting side-by-side on the bus) involved no face-to-face communication, or touching, or a possible shoulder to cry on, so the jury only heard about conversations with Josh that were safely removed from any physical contact. And, I know this is picky, but when Ross asked her what she told Josh about her abuser's age, she responded by saying that* "He was about 42, 43 at the time." *Steve* did *turn 43 in March 2003, but her testimony only stated how old Steve was,* <u>*not that she told Josh*</u> *how old her alleged abuser was.*]

Ross then asked her if she told anyone else what was happening to her. She testified, "I had told some friends of mine what had happened, but not with who. I always made up some lie about how he went to a different high school and he was on the football team and things like that that would be more appealing." Ross asked if she ever told anyone "that it was an older man that was married or anything like that." She said, "No." He asked her if it would be "safe to say that you told Josh more than you told anyone even though you didn't tell him the name of the person responsible." She said, "Right, yes, sir."

[*As you can see, her story changed again during the trials. There she shifted from saying that she didn't tell her friends who the person was, to saying that she lied to them, and told them it was a boy—a football player—from another school. This is one more admission from her that she was capable of lying to protect her reputation. She also testified that she didn't give her friends any information about this person being older or married. Who were these friends? She didn't name them during the trials. What did she say she told Josh and Angie and Suzanna? Josh's and Angie's stories don't match hers. How many potential lies does that add to the total?*]

Here's one other important bit from Trial #1. This is about Hanna telling her mother about the abuse. She said, "I just wasn't sure how to break it to her. Because I had only told one other person before this, and that was hard enough, and it wasn't even face-to-face. It was over the Internet."

[*Hanna said,* "I had only told one other person before this." *Before her mother? Before Goudy? What about all of her girlfriends? The* "other person" *she refers to is obviously Josh. He said, though, that most of their discussion <u>was face-to-face</u>; and Hanna said her manipulated discussion with him <u>was face-to-face</u> on the school bus; Angie said that Hanna <u>told her and Suzanna face-to-face</u> in the bathroom, and Angie said Hanna <u>talked to Josh face-to-face</u> at school and in his car; Hanna said she <u>told multiple friends about it face-to-face</u> at the sleepovers; and she said she <u>told Suzanna about it face-to-face</u> near the end of summer in 2003; and that she also <u>told one other girl face-to-face</u> during Goudy's speech (that's next); and what about Sean, her buddy from school? She said she told him all about it on their walks home? What happened to him? She didn't mention him in either trial, but she told Tom <u>they talked in person</u> about her situation. Why did Hanna tell this seeming lie in court, under oath? Or was that the truth and no one except Josh knew anything until after Goudy's speech? Are the possible lies piling up?*]

Despite what she said in her affidavit, and everything you read above, Hanna also told one more person about her abuse just before she told Blake Goudy. In Trial #1, Hanna testified that Goudy said, "At the end of this if you need to come talk to me, you're more than welcome." Ross asked her how old she was then. She said, "I was -- It was either right before -- maybe a day or two before my 15th birthday, or a day or two after. It was very soon after that." Ross, possibly aware that wasn't correct, guided her by asking if the speech took place in April 2004. She said, "Yes it did. It was at the beginning of April, if I remember correctly." He asked her if that meant she was already fifteen. She said "Yes, sir." He then asked her what her reaction was to the abuse presentation. She said, "I became extremely upset. It was written, I guess, all over my face, because a girl that I wasn't very close to, I hadn't talked with much, had kind of looked behind her, and she saw that I was upset, and she came and sat beside me. And for the rest of the presentation, she kept kind of just messing with me to get me to tell her what was wrong. And finally after about 15 minutes, I told her. And she said, 'You really need to go tell the guy. You need to go tell him.' I said, 'I can't do that.' She said, 'Yes, you can. Yes, you can. It's okay, I'll walk up there with you.'" Ross asked Hanna how she felt about talking to this girl. She said, "I wasn't crying or tearing up or anything. I was more in shock than anything because I found out I had a way out."

He asked her if she told Goudy what had happened. She said, "Yes," although she may not have told him much. Goudy, according to Deputy Knox's note, said that Hanna "did not go into any details" with him.

[*There are numerous examples of Hanna's inaccuracy with dates, like Dixon saying, after Hanna talked about the cross-country race, that she* "lost concept of time." *This is one reason why establishing accurate details about Hanna's story has been difficult. I found it odd that she could be so fluid with time, but still be so specific about other things (like clothing and weather). It was one reason I came to believe she was making her stories up as she went along. This testimony about her birthday is an example. It seemed like she was about to say, "I was fifteen," but stopped herself. She had to have known when her own birthday was. She turned fifteen about six weeks before Goudy's talk. Was she pausing to calculate whether she could get away with saying she was only fourteen when he gave the talk at her school?*

The girl who sat beside Hanna and encouraged her to talk to Goudy was Karla Spivey. It seemed to me that they let Hanna get away with delivering a lot of hearsay testimony by replicating Karla's comments when Karla wasn't there to corroborate them. Also, notice how Hanna tried to distance herself from Karla. "A girl that I wasn't very close to, I hadn't talked with much." *Why would Hanna say that unless she was trying to hide who the girl was? Karla will reappear with a startling revelation near the end of this chapter.*]

When Steve's attorney, Bevin Jenkins, got a chance to cross-examine Hanna, he asked her if it was true that she told her friends that she had sexual relationships with guys from other schools when she really hadn't. She said, "The sexual relationship happened, yes, but it was not with guys from other schools or anybody like that." He said he understood, but wanted to know if she had told her friends that. She answered, "Yes." He asked her if she had mentioned any guys' names. She said, "No, I did not." Knowing what she said in her interview with Tom, Jenkins asked her if she had ever claimed that Beau was her abuser, but Elmer Ross lodged an objection, saying the question wasn't relevant, and that Jenkins might have violated one of the Motions in Limine [*an agreement that they would clear certain subjects with the judge before mentioning them*]. Jenkins countered by saying that he wasn't asking her about having sex, he was asking her if she had lied about who she said she had sex with. Judge Hawes pointed out that Hanna had already said that she hadn't mentioned "<u>any guys' names</u>" (and Beau would be included in that category, of course). Hawes ruled in favor of the prosecution. Hanna didn't have to answer the question.

[*Aside from Hanna's testimony that she lied to her friends about some things, the judge ruled that she didn't have to answer about saying that Beau was her abuser because she had already said she didn't name anyone, and Beau would be included in the category of "anyone." I believe, though, that based on her testimony that she <u>hadn't mentioned any guys' names</u>, she either lied to Tom or to the court (which includes the possibility that she could have lied to both). She wasn't under oath when she talked to Tom (or to her friends), but she was under oath during both trials. Jenkins didn't press it any further. Maybe he thought it would be unwise to cross the judge at this point, but I wonder how different the trial would have been if the defense had introduced Hanna's interview with Tom into evidence. In it, she clearly told Tom that she* *told her friends she was having sexual experiences with Beau, and/or some unnamed football players, or just guys from other schools (no one who could be identified except Beau). Couldn't Jenkins have used that interview to help establish Hanna's pattern of lies? If the recording or a transcript of it had been introduced as a defense exhibit, he could have quoted from it, or played some excerpts, and that would have forced more of her constantly changing statements out in the open. The important thing to remember for now, though, is that Hanna potentially added at least one more lie to the scoreboard, and got away with it. How many is that?*]

Hanna made another comment during Trial #1 that I think is significant. Jenkins asked her if she had ever lied to get attention, and she said, "Exaggeration, yeah. A bold-faced lie, no."

[*I believe that Hanna telling her friends or investigators or a jury, at sleepovers or in a courtroom or elsewhere, that she was having sexual experiences with an older man, or a football player from another school, or Beau, in order to get attention and gain popularity (or for any other reason) is about as close to a* "bold-faced lie" *(or even a bald-faced one) as we're going to get. At least it will be until we get to the night they went to see Harry Potter, and the ride home from the rodeo, and the night of Beau's birthday party. There are some big whoppers ahead.*]

Let's look at Rhonda Bresnick's Trial #1 testimony. In August 2005, long after the charges were filed, she gave a typewritten, undated note to Hanna's mother, claiming that she wrote it in 2003, shortly after Steve gave her and Hanna a ride home from the Ashwell County Rodeo. In Trial #1, Ross asked Rhonda about this sentence from it. "I figured that it was nothing to be concerned about." He asked her if something later changed her mind about that. When Rhonda said, "Yes, sir," he asked what that was. She said, "She had brought it up at a sleep-over that she had lost her virginity. And we questioned it. And she said that it wasn't her decision." Ross asked if that was when she realized that the ride home was not so innocent. Rhonda answered, "Yes."

[*We'll cover Rhonda's note in great detail in the chapter about the rodeo, but when she said* "...we questioned it," *she was indicating that her friends didn't believe Hanna when she told them she had lost her virginity. In April 2004, two months after the last incident supposedly occurred, a medical exam found that there was a slight tear in her hymen, but it was still "essentially virginal." Unfortunately, Hanna didn't mention Rhonda having been at any sleepovers, and Rhonda didn't say who was at the one she attended; but Hanna's sleepover references usually didn't mention any names anyway, mostly just saying something along the lines of* "my friends" *or* "the other girls." *Convenient, right?*]

In Trial #2 (August 2006), Elmer Ross again asked Rhonda about the sleepover. That time she revealed some new information. He asked her why she wrote the note, and she repeated what she had said in the first trial, "Because she had told us, me and several of my friends from school, at a sleepover that she had <u>lost her virginity</u> and it was not her decision." He asked her when Hanna told them that. Rhonda said, "It was a couple of years ago in

April." I don't know what Ross' facial features revealed to the courtroom at that moment, but he did ask Rhonda, "So, it would have been after April of 2004; is that right?" Rhonda said, "Yes, sir."

[*Did Ross slip up, not knowing what Rhonda was going to say, or did he introduce that date on purpose, thinking the defense had information that the sleepover occurred after the accusation? They didn't know that, but Rhonda's new information generated even more questions for me. Was Rhonda not at any of the other sleepovers where Hanna supposedly told her friends about her abuse, or was there only one sleepover where Hanna did a big reveal? Did that sleepover take place after the accusations, making all of Hanna's other testimony about telling her friends at sleepovers a lie?*

Rhonda and Hanna were the only ones who testified about sleepovers at all, and Angie was the only other friend we have on record who said that Hanna revealed anything at a sleepover. Angie's "2003? 2002? Somewhere around there" date was so fuzzy, though, she could have been talking about Rhonda's 2004 sleepover for all we know (especially in light of Angie's statement about the word "rodeo" sending Hanna toward the bathroom). Hanna said there were multiple sleepovers where she and her friends talked about sexual experiences, but Rhonda said that Hanna told several girls, at one sleepover, after the accusations, that "she had lost her virginity" (*which is obviously different than Hanna's entire premise of being abused for two-and-a-half years without completed penile-vaginal intercourse).*

Finally, Rhonda testified that she wrote her note a few weeks after the 2003 rodeo, but she also testified that she wrote the note because of Hanna's big reveal at the 2004 sleepover (which was eight or nine months after the rodeo). What truths (or lies) are we supposed to glean from that?]

In Trial #2, the sleepovers didn't appear in Hanna's testimony until Cleveland Sanford cross-examined her by reading bits of her first trial testimony, and asking her if she had said certain things at the sleepovers. Hanna did agree that she had said she "gained popularity" with her friends because she "had the most experience with boys," and that, once the girls were "a little bit older, the further you went, it was cool as long as you didn't have sex." Ross then asked her if she had given her girlfriends any specific details. She said, "Not really, sir." He asked her if she ever said who the man was, or how old he was. She answered, "No, sir, I didn't."

[*By saying that they went further as they got* "a little bit older," *isn't she indicating that this was something that they were all doing, and that it happened over a long period of time? Would Angie, who said that most of them didn't know anything about sex, agree with that description of their activities?*

Hanna testified that she never told any of her friends who was molesting her, had never given them a name, and had never said anything about the age of the person, but she told Tom that she told her friends she was having sexual experiences with Beau. Then, in the first trial, she said she never told anyone the name of the person, but said he was a football player from another school. Angie and Josh both told Tom that Hanna didn't name Beau or anyone else to them. At least one of those statements must be a lie. Why weren't Suzanna and Angie called to testify about Hanna's freakout at the sleepover? A number of other people who could potentially have helped Hanna's story (Gloria Moore, Angie Womack, Karla Spivey, Sean Luedeman and Suzanna Bushnell) could also have been called as witnesses. Why weren't they? Did any of them hear about any of this before the accusations were made, or were they were told something completely different, and at a different time, than what Hanna told the juries?]

What about the parents? Hanna said she told her friends she was being molested, but none of her friends' parents came forward to say that their daughters told them anything. As far as I know, the report to CPS against Darla about Eddie Higham living with her was the only report made to CPS or a law enforcement agency about Darla and her kids, and that happened in early 2003. I have to believe that no one called Darla to forward a rumor they heard about Hanna. If Hanna actually told her friends a year or two before April 2004, isn't it odd that almost none of them told their parents? Angie said she did, but can we believe her? I know of at least one other person who did, but not until April 2004. Karla Spivey went home the very day of Blake Goudy's speech, and told her mother what Hanna had said to her earlier that day.

This raised a whole host of questions for me. According to Tiffany Sperger, she told her mother about Marri's "secret" sometime between September 2002 and March 2003, but her mother didn't bring Tiffany to talk to the authorities until September 2004. If Tiffany did tell her mother a year to a year-and-a-half earlier, why did her mother still allow Tiffany to play with Marri until April 2004? Angie Womack, who thought the sleepover was in either 2002 or 2003 (or "somewhere around there"), said she told her mother, but waited a year to do it. So, did she tell her mother in 2003 or 2004, and in what month? Was it before or after Hanna accused Steve? Did Angie actually tell her mother anything, or did she just tell Tom that she had? Did any of these girls tell their parents about Hanna's plight before the charges were filed? Did they even know about her situation before April 2004, or was Josh the only one Hanna "confessed" to in 2003? Josh said he didn't report it to CPS or to law enforcement because Hanna asked him not to. I believe she asked him to be quiet because it was all a lie. I do think it's even possible that there was no abuser; or, if there was, the abuser might be someone Hanna couldn't accuse because of who that accusation might hurt.

If Hanna did tell her friends about it, I find it difficult to believe that a secret like that would stay that way in a town of only 400 people for any length of time, much less for over two years. Having spent high school and part of college in Deep Springs, I know how fast local news traveled there, and Deep Springs is nearly fifty times the size of Alderson. If Hanna actually told her friends she was being abused, I find it inconceivable that no one did anything about it. If she did tell her friends, why didn't CPS see a flurry of reports from the girls' parents, instead of the one report, early in 2003, that complained about a different issue, Darla's boyfriend, Eddie?

Why didn't more of Hanna's friends, or any of the friend's parents, appear as witnesses? Were the girls actually telling similar stories about themselves, and that's why they didn't tell their parents? If their parents knew about Hanna's abuse and didn't report it, they would have been in violation of Chapter 261 of the Texas Family Code, punishable by imprisonment of up to 180 days and/or a fine of up to $2,000. Shouldn't at least one of them have been civic-minded or law-abiding enough to have said or done something?

Could there have been other reasons? Sure. Maybe what Hanna told her friends before she made the accusations was more innocent than what she later claimed. Or maybe she didn't tell any of her friends except Josh until after she had accused Steve (but that would make her testimony about previous confessions at sleepovers a lie). Maybe she only told a few people after April 2004, and steered Tom toward them because they had already agreed to cover for her. Even so, isn't it reasonable to assume, if any of these parents had been told that an adult was molesting one of their daughters' friends, that at least one of them would have notified Hanna's mother, or the authorities, or would at least have gossiped about it with their friends? Why, then, were there no reports of any kind against Steve during the two years and eight months between September 1st, 2001 and when the charges were filed in April 2004? Isn't the most likely possibility that Hanna didn't tell her friends about her alleged molestation until after she had accused Steve?

The final thing to notice about these interviews (Hanna's, Angie's and Josh's) is that every bit of information in them originated with Hanna. Neither Josh nor Angie actually witnessed anything. The only information they had was what Hanna had told them, and much of that, as you have seen, was contradictory.

There is just one more item to cover before I summarize everything and wrap this chapter up, and it's a big one. Karla Spivey was the girl who spoke with Hanna during Blake Goudy's speech. Let's find out what Hanna may have said to Karla.

An Investigation of a Confession

Early in my research for this book I made several trips to Deep Springs to search for information and interview as many people as possible. I was especially curious about some discrepancies between various documents about Blake Goudy's presentation at Hanna's school. Everyone agreed that he gave his talk on April 7, 2004, in the Alderson School auditorium, that it was about abuse and its prevention, and that one or more students asked him for advice. There was some disagreement about the number of students who talked to him, though. In her affidavit, Hanna simply said "I decided to tell him," and mentioned no other students. Willard Knox's records had Goudy claiming that five students, including Hanna, approached him afterward.

I also wanted to know about Hanna's interaction with Karla Spivey. Here's what she told Tom about how Karla got involved that day. "One of my friends that knew nothing about what was going on, she just saw the look on my face. She said, 'What's wrong?' I said, 'Nothing.' She said, 'No. That's bull. Tell me what's wrong.'" Tom asked her who the friend was, and Hanna said, "Her name is Karla Spivey." Hanna said that Karla convinced her to talk to Goudy, even though she was reluctant to, and added that Karla walked to the front with her, and left her there to talk privately with him. Hanna said she "told Blake Goudy what was going on. Blake gave me his card and said to tell my mom as soon as possible."

In Trial #1, Hanna told the same story, with a few additional flourishes, but distanced herself from Karla, calling her "a girl I wasn't very close to, I hadn't talked with much, had kind of looked behind her, and she saw I was upset, and she came and sat beside me. And for the rest of the presentation, she kept kind of just messing with me to get me to tell her what was wrong." Hanna also played Karla's part, saying, "You really need to go tell this guy," and "It's okay, I'll walk up there with you." Ross didn't ask Hanna who the girl was, and Hanna didn't volunteer her name. In Trial #2, she repeated the same information, but again didn't mention the name of the girl who pushed her to talk to Goudy. Fortunately, Cleveland Sanford asked her, and Hanna said (as the court reporter entered it), "Carla Spivey." He also asked Hanna where Carla was now, and Hanna said, "I honestly don't know." Then Elmer Ross asked her if she gave the girl any specific information. Hanna said, "I don't really remember, sir."

[*Tom asked for her name as soon as Hanna mentioned the incident. She told him it was "Karla Spivey." No one asked for her name in either trial until Sanford did in Trial #2. Unfortunately, the court reporter spelled it Carla with a "C" instead of a "K," and that hindered my initial search for her. Despite having revealed several things in Trial #1 about her and Karla, when Ross asked her in Trial #2 if she gave Karla any specific information, Hanna said she didn't remember. How could she have been so forthcoming with both Tom and Ross, but completely forget those details between trials? I also wondered why Karla wasn't contacted by sheriff's investigators or the DA. Hanna told Tom she would get Karla's number for him, but Tom said she didn't. Why wouldn't she want Tom or the DA to talk to Karla? All Karla could possibly say was that she encouraged Hanna to talk to Goudy, right?*]

I also wanted more information about the other four students who supposedly talked to Goudy. Did any of them say they had been abused? Did they recant, or just not tell their parents? I tried several times to locate Goudy with no success; and I tried to find Karla Spivey, thinking she could tell me more about Goudy's talk, but the misspelling of her name in the trial record kept me from locating her for a while. In August 2014, though, I did a search on just "Spivey" and "Deep Springs," and found a Facebook page for a Spivey, first name Karla (not Carla), who worked at a fitness center and a rest home there. A month later I drove to Deep Springs to do some interviews and investigating. What follows is an abbreviated version of that information and the search for it, but full details of that trip are covered in four posts on the blog if you're interested. The first post is at this URL.

https://aggravatedbook.com/searching-for-karla-spivey-part-1/

I first tried to find Karla at the fitness center, but they told me she quit her job when she went back to college. Later in the day, I got the same story at the rest home, but a friend of hers who worked there said she would contact her. I left her my card, not expecting to hear from her (I have found that people rarely return calls). After talking to several other people, I had managed to gather at least a little useful information, so I went back to my hotel room. While I was writing up my notes and planning the next day's to-do list, I was surprised by a phone call from Karla. She told me she had a vague memory of Goudy's speech, but said that her mom, Margie, would remember everything. That seemed a little strange to me, but she gave me her mother's phone number. I called, and got her voicemail. I left a message, explaining that I had spoken to Karla, and asked her to call me back.

I wrote a few more notes and crashed on the bed, figuring that was all I would get done that day. While I was resting, Margie called me. I told her I was writing a book about a 2006 trial, and said that Karla had been mentioned in the trial's transcript. Margie gave me a word for word recitation of what Karla told her that day. When she finished, I thanked her, and hung up. I had been half asleep when she called, and I wasn't used to using my new digital recorder yet, so I didn't think to record the conversation, but I took notes the whole time. The last sentence in my notes read, "Hanna said that her mom's boyfriend was abusing her."

It was a short call. Here's a basic replay of our conversation. I started by telling Margie how much faith Karla had in her memory. She said, "Well, she came home from school and said, 'Mom, you'll never guess what happened at school today. We had this speaker, talking about sexual abuse and that kind of thing. Hanna Penderfield was sitting there, kind of shaking and crying.' And she went over to her and asked her what was wrong, and Hanna at first didn't want to tell her, but she said that Hanna finally told her that she was being abused, so she questioned her some more, and Hanna said that her mother's boyfriend, or maybe her dad, was abusing her." I asked, stunned, "Her mom's boyfriend?" Margie said, "Or maybe her dad. I don't remember exactly. I think she said it was the boyfriend."

As soon as we hung up, I transcribed the call while it was still fresh in my mind, and I believe it's close to perfect. I'm positive that the important part of it (that Karla told Margie that Hanna had said she had been abused by her mother's boyfriend) is completely accurate. I realize, of course, that Margie's statement to me was second-hand hearsay (and is third-hand when I repeat it to you), so it's completely invalid in a legal sense. I have sworn to it in an affidavit, though, and I am willing to testify to our conversation, under oath, in court, should the opportunity arise.

[*That was quite a revelation. Hanna's parents, by the way, divorced when she was seven. Her father had been living in Michigan for nearly eight years when Goudy gave his talk, which makes it a fair certainty that her father wasn't who Hanna told Karla was her abuser, but, according to Karla's mother, Steve wasn't either. Let me make it clear that I am not accusing Eddie Higham of that, and that he has never, to my knowledge, been investigated as a possible suspect. Also, in revealing my conversation with Margie, I am repeating an unsubstantiated statement about what Hanna allegedly said to another individual. That's a recollection twice removed. Definitely not eyewitness testimony on my part. How would the trial have changed, though, if Karla had been called to testify?*]

The next day, Darla Belisle called me while I was on my way back to Houston. She told me that Karla had been upset and had called Hanna to tell her what I was doing, and Hanna in turn had called Darla to complain.

[*Pause for a moment to consider something. Why would Karla have been upset? She suggested I talk to her mother because she trusted her mother's memory, and I told Karla that Hanna had mentioned her in the trial, and that I was writing a book about it. She had all of that information when she gave me her mother's number. The trial was held in open court, and was heavily publicized. It's hard to believe that Karla didn't know that I wanted information about what she and Hanna talked about, so she must also have known what her mother would tell me. Did Karla get upset after she called Hanna to tell her about it? Was Karla even upset at all, or did Hanna just tell her mother that Karla was? I don't know, and (naturally) I may never find out.*]

I tried to assure Darla that I was looking for the actual truth of what happened, but she kept pointing me toward the trial transcripts, insisting that the answers were all there. I told her that the transcripts were filled with fabrications, and I was trying to sort the truth from the lies, but that didn't seem to matter to her. We did end on a somewhat conciliatory note after I explained that I would be using pseudonyms for everyone.

I still believe that Hanna might not have been abused, but she said that Karla pressured her into talking to Goudy, so she might have felt forced into telling him something. If she actually had been telling her friends stories about being abused, that could have doubled the stress on her to speak out. Maybe Hanna hadn't meant to mention anyone's name. Telling Karla that it was her mother's boyfriend could have just slipped out. Maybe Hanna was mad at her mother and said it on purpose. Who knows? At any rate, by the time Karla had nudged her up to the front, Hanna had a serious decision to make. If she told her mother that Eddie had been abusing her, how would Darla take that? According to Steve, "Darla thought Eddie hung the moon and the stars." Did Hanna dare accuse her mother's boyfriend?

We know that Hanna did talk to Goudy, but I'm not even sure that she named anyone to him. Willard Knox's September 2004 note indicated that Goudy said that Hanna told him "she had been touched by <u>a man</u> for several years," that "she <u>did not go into any details</u>" with him, and "that was <u>all he knew</u> about the situation with Hannah Penderfield." None of that indicates that Hanna gave him anything beyond the barest details, and it doesn't say that she named anybody. Goudy testified in both trials that Hanna had named Steve to him, but his statements to Deputy Knox make it sound more likely that he got Steve's name from Darla, not Hanna, when Darla called him later that day.

Chapter Analysis

Sleepovers and Confessions: Hanna said that, at the sleepovers, the girls bragged about who had the most sexual experience, and that her advanced knowledge in that area helped make her more popular. She said she never told them who she was having these experiences with, but she also said that she lied and told them it was a football player from another school, or it was Beau (who was only nineteen [*when he was actually probably twenty*], so that was "cool to junior high kids"), or she could have lied about lying to them. Which of those is the truth? Is any of it the truth?

If there were sleepovers where Hanna revealed her sexual experiences to her friends, they would have to have been between September 2001 and February 2004, wouldn't they? That was the time period of her supposed abuse, unless, of course, the alleged abuse began back when she was ten or eleven, in 2000-2001, as Josh seemed to indicate at one point. But that would be ridiculous. The earliest sleepover mentioned by date was the only sleepover that Angie mentioned, and she said it was in either 2002 <u>or</u> 2003, "somewhere around there." Angie's sleepover had the girls having fun, playing games, eating, talking about boys, being innocent little lambs, until someone mentioned the word "rodeo," which set Hanna in motion toward the bathroom. Angie said that, in the bathroom, Hanna broke down and told her and Suzanna what had been happening to her, and that she revealed these experiences as if they were traumatic events (not something she was saying to gain popularity). Angie also said that Hanna gave them enough information for Suzanna to believe she was talking about Steve. Soon after that, according to Angie, Hanna told them the abuse had stopped; but, a year later (2003? or 2004?), Hanna told them it hadn't stopped after all. After realizing that Hanna had been lying to them, Angie said she told her mom, but said that her mom didn't want to tell Hanna's mom because Hanna might be lying and she didn't want to get in the middle of a mother-daughter squabble. Was Hanna's entire story about revealing her abuse at sleepovers just a story that Angie was repeating for Hanna's benefit?

A lie, repeated often enough, though, from enough different sources, can become truth in the minds of those who hear it.

Josh was, at first, an object of desire for Hanna, but I believe he also unwittingly became an information conduit for her (to Tom and in the trials). He said he heard a bunch of eighth grade girls, 13-year-olds like Hanna, teasing her that she would be a virgin for a long time because she didn't have a boyfriend.

[*Was Josh implying that, in 2003, most of the 13-year-old girls in the Alderson School District were already having sex?*]

He said that later (maybe that same day), Hanna confided in him, saying she was upset and she didn't know if she was a virgin or not. Hanna told Tom that same story, but said she used the girls' teasing to "manipulate" Josh into talking to her on the school bus. Then, over days or weeks, as they continued to talk, Hanna filled Josh in on all the sordid details, except for who she was having these experiences with. By the time of the trials, though, Hanna's story was that their discussions were mostly on the Internet. Josh, however, said it was face-to-face at school, through letters Hanna wrote, on the phone, and over the Internet. Angie, in opposition to both of them, said it was while sitting in Josh's car. Josh later testified that Hanna told him quite a few personal details about her abuser, but not his name; and said he thought that the abuse consisted entirely of "blow jobs." He said he encouraged her to stop, and that she told him she had, but later told him she hadn't.

Rhonda wasn't included in any of Angie's or Hanna's sleepover stories. She testified that she *was* at a sleepover (in 2004), but neither Hanna nor Angie mentioned her being at any of them. Rhonda, in her version, only mentioned Hanna by name. Rhonda also testified that she wrote her note about the ride home shortly after the 2003 rodeo. Angie, however, said that Hanna got upset at the mention of the word "rodeo" in April of either 2002 or 2003, both of which were before the 2003 rodeo. Rhonda also testified that Hanna told them in April 2004 that she had lost her virginity, and that Hanna's 2004 revelation was the reason she decided to write the note in 2003. Is there a lot of contradiction there? Yes. Regardless of when Rhonda actually wrote it, though, she still didn't give it to Hanna's mother until August 2005 (seventeen months after the 2004 sleepover, and more than two years after the 2003 rodeo). It seems that Rhonda either felt it was unimportant, or she didn't actually write it until August of 2005 (after Darla asked for her help). One way or the other, Rhonda may have lied in court.

Clearly, comparing everyone's statements also exposes some serious time and logic conflicts. Which brings us to the subject of...

Time Sequence Discrepancies: Hanna, in her interview, said that she didn't confide in Josh until a month or so before he graduated at the end of the spring 2003 semester, but Josh told Tom that he had known Hanna since he was a freshman (when he was fourteen and she was ten). In the second trial, he referred to their discussions as having happened over "a series of weeks," which Elmer Ross then characterized as a "two-week period." Hanna and Ross might have wanted to minimize the length of her relationship with Josh, but Josh had no reason to lie about how long he knew her. As I said earlier in this chapter, I made repeated attempts to interview Josh, but aside from the question he answered (through Marri) which contradicted Hanna's claim that he offered to beat Steve up, he has so far avoided giving me an actual interview. Tom and Deputy Conner also had difficulty pinning him down for their interviews.

In her interview with Tom, Hanna said that she told Suzanna Bushnell what was happening to her, but at first said she didn't remember if that conversation was before or after she told Blake Goudy. Then, a moment later, she "remembered" telling Suzanna in late-summer 2003 (seven months before Goudy's speech). According to Angie, though, Suzanna was the other girl who followed Hanna into the bathroom at a sleepover (in April of either 2002 or 2003) when Hanna reacted to hearing the word "rodeo." Did Hanna tell both Suzanna and Angie in April of 2002 or 2003 (before the rodeo)? Or did she tell Suzanna in late-summer 2003 (after the sleepover *and* the rodeo)? Was Angie told in April 2002 or 2003, or did she hear about it with everyone else in April 2004? Was Suzanna at the 2004 sleepover? Was Angie? Several elements in Angie's story conflict with some of Hanna's multiple versions, but Suzanna was never interviewed and neither Angie nor Suzanna testified. Rhonda testified, but her date for the sleepover was after the affidavit. All of Hanna's multiple versions of her story conflict with each other, but they also conflict with the stories of her friends. Logically, some of those versions must contain lies.

April is the only month that was associated with any sleepovers. Hanna testified that the sleepover she went to on the same day she "manipulated" Josh on the bus, was on April 18, 2003. Angie said the sleepover where Hanna broke down in front of her and Suzanna was in April 2002 or maybe 2003. Rhonda testified that the sleepover where Hanna revealed the loss of her virginity to everyone was in April 2004, but all of those statements were made after the accusations had been lodged, and long after the events they described. The only thing we can say for certain is that Hanna and some of her classmates might have had one or more sleepovers between 2001 and 2004, and that during at least one of them Hanna could have claimed to have been abused, or to have lost her virginity, or to have had sexual experiences (with either a man, or a boy, or another boy, or Beau). Is that as clear as mud?

Final Thoughts: We can only be sure of one thing. Lies were told. Nothing in this chapter provides absolute proof that Hanna lied about this during Steve's second trial (the crucial one, legally), but the comparisons show that almost none of her testimony in that trial accurately matches what she said before that. There is no consistency to her narrative. Who should we believe? Everyone disagrees with everyone else. Josh's testimony, and his and Angie's interviews, contain definite contradictions to the testimony Hanna gave in both trials. Rhonda's trial testimony also contradicts Hanna's. Looking at the second trial alone, Hanna's story seemed to me to be just a confused, rambling tale with moments of startling specificity popping out of the jumble. I don't think those specific moments were truer than any of the haphazard ones, just more direct and detailed.

Our brains have a wonderful (but also disturbing) quality of being able to rearrange memories to suit our particular worldviews, adapting and shifting those recollections to benefit the survival of our personal psyches. Over time we can convince ourselves that stories we have invented about something are what actually occurred. I think that could have been what happened to Hanna. She may have told herself a particular story (i.e., imagined a particular scenario) long enough for parts of it to become real for her.

Here's one of my theories: I think that Hanna may have felt abandoned after her father left, and became convinced—possibly by her mother's stories of how bad he was—that they were well rid of him, but she kept an eye out for a replacement, even a surrogate one. I think that she probably enjoyed the trips to the Sirois' home, aside from having to play with kids younger than her. She did sometimes compensate for that by inviting friends (like Suzanna Bushnell and Judy Higham) to visit her while she was there.

During her eighth-grade year (2002-2003), according to her own statements, she developed a crush on Josh Chilmark, and being a bright girl, constructed a game plan for getting him to notice her. It wouldn't be the first time a teenager has concocted a plot to obtain the affections of another student. The girls at her school may have been innocent, but (as kids will do) might have talked a bigger game. Even if they weren't innocent, the theory still works. Either way, Josh could have had the misfortune of interrupting a conversation where some of the girls were teasing Hanna because she wasn't dating anyone (at the age of thirteen), and Hanna saw her chance. It's possible they weren't even talking about virginity. It would be a fairly easy matter for someone who believed that it wasn't "that hard to fool people" to convince Josh that he really stumbled into a different discussion and "manipulate" him into asking about her virginity. It's also entirely possible that Josh didn't hear the girls teasing Hanna at all. Convincing him that she had been teased could just have been part of her plan.

Emboldened after getting Josh to talk to her, she might have started telling her friends some falsehoods about sex to gain popularity; or maybe she had already been inventing these fantasies for them. The order in which that happened is also unimportant. It's easy to see how things could snowball from there, forcing Hanna deeper into the lie than she wanted to be. Then, when a speaker at their school said that anyone who had been abused should come talk to him afterward, how could she not go forward, especially after being pushed to by Karla Spivey? She either had to walk up front or admit to her friends that she had been lying to them all along. For the next two years, feeling trapped even further, she honed her stories, getting ready for the trial, possibly hoping that Steve would accept a plea deal, as she told Tom, so she wouldn't have to testify. This is just one possibility. We'll see some other variations on this theme before we're done.

Next up: The crucial chapters in proving that Steve was wrongly convicted for Count I, and that he didn't commit the acts that Hanna accused him of doing (during a ride to a movie, inside the theater, and later that night), *The Night of Harry Potter, Parts 1 and 2.*

The Night of Harry Potter, Part 1

"When you have eliminated the impossible,
whatever remains, however improbable, must be the truth."
Sir Arthur Conan Doyle

"I don't know what time it was whenever we finally got to go in there,
but I know it was really, really late when we got out."
Hanna Penderfield

In this chapter I intend to disprove Hanna's claims about what happened before and during a showing of the first Harry Potter movie. The next chapter, *Part 2*, deals with what supposedly happened after the movie. Both chapters began as a decade's worth of legal pads filled with notes from affidavits, interviews, trial transcripts, maps, social media, weather data, and personal observations. All of that eventually coalesced into 141 single-spaced typewritten pages of analysis. It was trimmed down considerably for this book, of course, but I believe you will still be able to see Hanna's duplicity clearly.

I will also mention several images during this chapter. You'll find them on the blog at:
https://aggravatedbook.com/images-for-the-night-of-harry-potter-chapters/

In her affidavit, Hanna claimed that she was first sexually assaulted by Steve when she spent the night <u>for the first time</u> at the Sirois' house "in late August or early September 2001," but she didn't spend the night in August, or in September, or in October. It was near the end of November before she and Aaron spent the night, after they saw the first Harry Potter movie with Steve, Marri, and Beau.

The Basic Story: One night in November 2001, they went to see the movie, *Harry Potter and the Sorcerer's Stone,* at the Bloom Junction Mall in Bloom, Texas. Hanna was 12, Beau was 18, Marri was 9, Aaron was 10, and Steve was 41. They drove there in Beau's pickup, and went to the Sirois' home after the movie was over. What happened after they got back to the house will be covered in *Part 2.*

Hanna's Version: She said they left after dark. Beau drove, Steve was in the passenger seat and she sat behind him in the back seat. She masturbated him during the ride to the theater, gave him a kiss (or maybe two) while they were both buckled in, and then more molestation happened inside the theater. Her version is radically different from everyone else's. To sort between them we're going to look at some questions about that night.

[Subsections in this Chapter: Before the Movie // During the Movie // Final Thoughts About Part 1]

Here are the questions: **(Before the Movie)** "What was the date and time of the movie?" "What was everybody wearing?" "What was the weather like?" "Where was everyone sitting in the truck?" "What happened on the way to the movie?" "Did anyone in the truck see this happen?" **(During the Movie)** "Where was everyone sitting inside the movie theater?" "What happened inside the theater?" "What happened when they left the theater?"

If some of these seem odd, please bear with me. There's a reason for all of them.

Before the Movie

What Was the Date and Time of the Movie?

Why is This Important? The prosecution's case was based on a range of dates between September 2001 and February 2004, but Hanna, possibly because of something she said in her affidavit, changed the starting date of her supposed molestation from late-August to the night they saw this movie. We can't assess her claims about what happened that night without having a reasonably accurate date for the movie, and knowing when it began and ended. Let's briefly see what everyone said.

Tom asked both Beau (in 2005) and Hanna (in 2006) when they saw the movie. Beau said, "It was around Thanksgiving...I was out on Thanksgiving Break, and we went. I think it started at 7:45, something like that."

Hanna said, "And we went to go see *Harry Potter*, the first one." He asked her if she remembered the date, but she said, "No. Whenever it was in theaters. I don't know. The first couple of days it was in theaters." She added, "I remember it was cold, so it must have been a couple of months after September. It must have been like the beginning of 2002, or the end of 2001. It had to have been."

[*The first Harry Potter movie opened nationwide on November 16, 2001, but Beau's return from college for Thanksgiving Break makes it more likely they saw it the second weekend, not the first. The movie was gone from the Deep Springs area by January 2002.*]

In 2014, I talked to Marri and Beau. They were sure the movie was on a weekend because Beau was home from college. I asked them how dark it was when they left the house. Marri said the sun wasn't down, but was going down. Beau agreed, saying, "It was getting dark. It was dusk." In 2015, I asked Steve what night of the week it was. He said, "It would have to be Friday or the weekend." "I would not be going out on a work night to go to a movie."

[*Steve felt it had to have been on Friday or Saturday because of his work schedule with the city.*]

Everyone agreed that it was an evening showing, near Thanksgiving, 2001, and the only place it was playing in the area was at a multiplex in Bloom, Texas, just east of Deep Springs. Why don't we know the exact time and date? That's easy. Steve bought the tickets with cash and no one kept a stub. We can narrow the day and time down, though. None of the parents would have allowed their nine-, ten-, and twelve-year-old kids to be up very late on a school night. The only logical days when they would have gone to a nighttime showing of the movie would have been a Friday or Saturday. This was also true of all the other visits to the Sirois' home as well. Hanna's family typically didn't visit on more than one day during any single week; and, since the adults worked during the week, visits were almost always on a Friday instead of a Saturday because of church and other activities on Sundays.

What about the movie's start time? On the first weekend (November 16 and 17), the evening showings were at 6:30 and 9:45 in one screening room, and 7:00 and 10:15 in the other. By the third weekend (November 30 and December 1) the showings had been reduced to 6:30, 7:00, and 9:45 (still on two screens). They saw either the 7:00 or the 9:45 show on one of those three weekends, but most likely on Friday, November 23rd, the day after Thanksgiving. My bet is on the 7:00 show. Here's why.

At the trials, four-and-a-half years later, Hanna had a vested interest in the jury believing they went to a later show. For her story to make sense, they had to drive to the theater in the dark, and had to leave late at night. According to her reasoning, if they finished watching the movie earlier in the evening, they wouldn't have spent the night, because Steve would have driven them straight to her home afterward. It also had to be dark inside the truck for most of the actions in her story to be plausible to a jury. If they had gone to a 6:30 or 7:00 pm show they would arrive at the theater while it was still light out, but no one other than Hanna suggested that they saw a late showing.

Let's analyze Beau's and Marri's statements that the sun wasn't quite down. In November 2001 (from the 16th through the 30th), sunsets in Ashwell County began between 5:38 and 5:33 pm, getting earlier as it got closer to December. Astronomical twilight, though, the time when the vague light above the horizon is difficult to tell from night, ended between 7:03 and 7:00 pm those nights. If they left in time to get to the 7:00 show it would still have been partially light during the drive, as Beau and Marri said.

Beau also thought "it started at 7:45, something like that," but Hanna said they saw "the 9:00 show." Oddly, with actual show times of 7:00 and 9:45, they were both off by 45 minutes, and the actual times would have supported their individual arguments better than the times they remembered, but there is another, simpler reason to believe they went to the earlier show. *Harry Potter and the Sorcerer's Stone* is a very long movie, 152 minutes if you don't count the previews. We do need to count them, though. Previews add roughly fifteen minutes to a show's runtime, so three hours and fifteen minutes were scheduled for each showing. If they had gone to the 9:45 show, it would have started at 10:00 (after previews), and would have finished at 12:32 am, but the 7:00 show would have started at 7:15, and ended at 9:47. We can, however, take eight minutes of that back, because the end credits for the first *Harry Potter* ran eight minutes and five seconds, and very few people stay for the credits.

Hanna even tried to build extra time into their evening, giving three ever-expanding versions of how that happened. She told Tom, "We went to like the 9:00 show, or something like that, but we ended up having to wait because the movie got messed up or something, so we stood outside for an hour, and didn't get back to his house until <u>one in the morning</u>." In Trial #1, though, she said, "It was a late show. We were going to go see the 9:00 show, or somewhere around that timeframe. And something had happened to the movie we were supposed to watch. It didn't play like it was supposed to or something. So, we had to wait even longer before the movie actually began playing. They had to switch it to a different theater." She added, "By the time we got back to Sirois' home, it was <u>about 1:00, 1:30</u>." In Trial #2, she said, "It was already a late show. I believe it was about 9:00 or so. And something had happened with the movie, either -- I don't remember if it was the one that was playing previously or not, but, something went wrong with it and it messed up somehow and they had to move the movie to a different theater. And that took a while. And so, we had to stand out there in the hallway where all the theaters are for a long time. And then, I don't know what time it was whenever we finally got to go in there, but I know it was really, really late when we got out." Ross asked her what the plan was for after the movie, but, instead of answering him, she said, "By the time we got out, it was maybe <u>1:30, 2:00 o'clock</u> by the time we finally got to the house."

[*Her stories jumped from* "one in the morning" *to* "about 1:00, 1:30." *to* "maybe 1:30, 2:00 o'clock," *pushing it a little later each time. Did you notice that in Trial #1 she said <u>they waited outside,</u> but in Trial #2 she said <u>they waited in a hallway</u>? Convincing the jury they got to the house extremely late was crucial to Hanna's story. If the jury believed that Steve had taken advantage of an ultra-late movie to keep them at his house that night, Hanna could claim a point in her favor. The real reason they drove straight to the Sirois' house after the movie, though, instead of taking Hanna and Aaron home first, is explained in Part 2 (After the Movie). It had nothing to do with a delay.*]

In 2015, Steve and I talked about Hanna's claim that they got to the house after midnight. He said, "I don't remember ever being home that late with the kids." I asked him what time he thought it had been. He said, "Just as soon as it was over, but more than likely it would have been earlier or we wouldn't even have gone to the movie. I'm just not going to stay up that late with the kids. Never did." I asked about his schedule with the city, he said, "Always on call. 24/7."

[*By 2015 Steve didn't remember when the movie ended, but he was sure they wouldn't have gone to any show that would have let them out after midnight, partly because he wouldn't have kept the kids up that late, but also because he often had to make the rounds of the city's water towers on the weekends, checking them for overflow problems, etc.*]

Analysis: Was the movie really delayed and moved to another screening room? The theater chain now has new owners, and they told me that all the previous records were gone. I posted a request on some Deep Springs social media groups, asking if anyone had seen the first *Harry Potter* at the Filmland Theater in 2001. Burl Conley, who worked at the theater then, said, "I don't believe we had any delays." That would tend to negate Hanna's version about the show starting late; but another area resident, Maggie Mae Joyner, said that the movie did break when they went to a late showing, and they "waited in the roped line they had inside forever." That supports Hanna's version about the film being delayed, but why didn't any of the others remember that happening when they saw it? Maggie Mae also said that she didn't see it on opening night, but "there were church people outside" protesting the movie because it was about witches, and the protesters "scared my youngest son because they were hollering." Burl agreed. "There were some local church groups protesting the film, passing out tracts and holding signs." If our group of five went the night the film was delayed, why didn't Hanna or any of the others also remember seeing the protesters?

Based on the local comments, and what Steve, Marri, and Beau said, I don't think anything unusual happened at the movie theater that night. Maybe a friend of Hanna's told her there was a delay when they saw it, so she just folded that detail into her story, but it's just one more excuse layered onto the others to help create the idea that they left the theater very late that night. Was she worried that the rest of her story wouldn't be believable if she couldn't give a reason for them going straight to the Sirois' home after the movie?

As with all of her stories, Hanna started with small details, but over time the minutiae expanded. That does happen. I can vouch that stories often do take on a life of their own. Maybe Hanna should have been a little more Hemingway with her creations and a little less Proust.

Conclusion: I can say with certainty that the movie played at the Filmland Theater in Bloom, Texas (the only place it played in the area), and that all five members of the group said they saw it sometime in late-November 2001 (except for Hanna, who told Tom that it must have been "the beginning of 2002, or the end of 2001."). Was that another example of her trying to throw Tom off the scent? She certainly remembered Thanksgiving as the date eight weeks later at the first trial.

Does it matter whether they saw an early or a late show, or whether it was delayed? Based on the multiple variables Hanna and others have suggested, the movie could have ended as early as 9:39 pm, or as late as 1:24 am (minus the film's credits). The time matters if you're on Team Hanna, because an after-midnight ending could lend some credibility to her claim that Steve was using this fortuitous delay of a late movie to convince Darla to let them spend the night. But what if Darla didn't want the kids to come home that night anyway? I'll cover that in *Part 2 – After the Movie*.

Considering the kids' ages (9, 10, and 12), and Steve likely having to work the next day, it's obvious that they went to the 7:00 pm show. Hanna might have wanted the jury to think otherwise, but didn't she lie at least twice by pushing the end time later and later? A film break that caused a long enough delay for them to end up returning to Steve's house after midnight would also have been a fine excuse, but did it happen that night? None of the others remembers having to wait that night before they went in, or getting home that late. Aaron could have had a say in the matter, but he didn't testify.

An Important Side Note: Hanna was the only one who was asked any questions in either trial about when the movie began and ended, or about delays, or what time they left the theater or when they arrived back at the Sirois' house that night.

I can't prove which showing of the movie they saw, but (bias aside) I would be tempted to vote for the 7:00 pm show through simple logic. The three youngest members of the group were 9, 10, and 12 years old. Marri and Aaron in particular were too young to be kept up very late, and Hanna was barely older than they were. It makes far more sense that they went to an earlier show. Also, if you thought you might have to get up and go to work the next morning, you wouldn't choose a show that was going to let out after midnight when you could go to a 7:00 pm show and be home by around 10:00.

Just common sense.

Let's look at the clothing Hanna said they had on.

What Was Everybody Wearing?

Why is This Important? The only reason this question is here is because Hanna ladled constantly fluctuating description onto her narrative. It's vital to address this because so much of her story included details about what she and others were wearing when the alleged incidents occurred. Sometimes those descriptions were inconsequential, but a comparison of her differing accounts of clothing, along with other things she inaccurately described, like the weather, should help prove that Hanna's testimony was false. So, what did she say they were wearing that night in November 2001?

In her affidavit, she said she was wearing blue jean shorts and a t-shirt the night she was first assaulted (which she also said happened in late summer, and that it was the first time they spent the night). Within a month, she had changed that story, telling Ada Dixon that it happened the night they went to see *Harry Potter* (which *was* the first time they spent the night). She told Dixon that she had on pants and a jacket (instead of shorts and a t-shirt).

She began her 2006 interview with Tom by talking about the difficulty she might have at the trial because she couldn't remember dates or what Steve wore "because I haven't thought about it for so long." Ten minutes later, though, when Tom asked her how Steve was dressed that night, she said, "he was wearing those black denim shorts. I don't remember what kind of shoes he had on." She laughed and just said "they were ugly." Tom asked about the shorts, and she said, "They came down to about ...mmh, inch or two above his kneecap." He asked about Steve's other clothes, and she said he wore a "polo shirt," with a "collar like with two or three buttons." After a lot of hesitation, she said the shirt had "horizontal stripes that were either dark blue or black," with stripes that were "either gray or white," adding, "I don't remember. I just know that they were contrast colors."

[*That's quite a description from someone who said she* "cannot remember what he wore," *but she still weirdly insisted that Steve was wearing shorts and a polo shirt in late-November. Brrrr.*]

I think it became obvious to Hanna that her own shorts and t-shirt were a ridiculous outfit for November, so she changed it. She told Tom she was wearing jeans, but still insisted that her jacket was just "a blue and black windbreaker." After she claimed that Steve was rubbing her leg under her jeans, Tom asked her how he managed to do that. She said, "Well, they were those flare leg type." She called them "flare-legged jeans" from then on.

In the first trial, Elmer Ross asked her what she wore that night. She said, "I was wearing a pair of jeans. They were flare-legged and they rode up on my waist, not on my hips. They were old-fashioned from Goodwill. And I had on a red shirt that was fitted. It wasn't skin tight, but it was a little bit tight. And it was kind of short." Her only description she gave of Steve's clothes was that he wore "pants" [*not shorts?*] inside the movie theater.

In Trial #2, she again said that Steve wore "a t-shirt and denim shorts." "He wore close to the same outfits a lot…but it was always a t-shirt." About her outfit, she said she was in "a t-shirt," and "flare-legged" jeans that came up to her waist, but "they weren't the hip-huggers." She added that her "shirt was red and kind of a strawberry pattern. It had two layers. It had little bitty holes, so it looked like where the seeds on the strawberries would go. It was a fitted shirt. Not skin tight, but just fitted. And it was kind of short, so it came down to meet the top of the jeans."

[*Hanna's descriptions shifted slightly each time, her jeans becoming flare-legged jeans and a t-shirt, which became a "shirt" then a "fitted shirt" with two layers and little holes all over it to represent strawberry seeds. Later in Trial #2, she oddly insisted that this layered, fitted shirt was actually a t-shirt. Did her original* "T-shirt and blue jean shorts" *become Steve's* "t-shirt and denim shorts" *after she abandoned the idea of wearing them herself? Also, why did she replace Steve's polo shirt with a t-shirt? Too preppy?*]

Beau, when asked about it in 2005, told Tom that he wore "kind of about what I've got on now. Just a jacket, pair of blue jeans, and a nice shirt." He also said that Steve probably wore about the same, plus "his cowboy boots," and maybe a jacket "like this one," [*the Carharrt he had on*].

[*This wasn't a memory from Beau, just what he thought he and Steve were likely wearing that night, typical Central Texas male gear.*]

In 2015, I asked Steve, Beau, and Marri what they wore that night, but none of them could remember specifics. I asked Steve what he would normally wear toward the end of November. He said, "Blue jeans. It would have been blue jeans of some type. But it would have been a long-sleeved shirt, and either my lace-up boots or cowboy boots, one of the two." I asked him if he remembered how Hanna was dressed that night. He said, "No." I also asked him if he would have had his own jacket with him, and he said, "Absolutely."

Marri said, "Probably clothes for warmth. Jacket. Pants." I asked her if she could "remember how Steve or Hanna was dressed," but she said, "No, I couldn't tell you."

After telling Beau about the shorts that Hanna said Steve had on, he said, "I very seldom remember Dad going to town in shorts." I asked him why, and he said, "Because most of the shorts he had, Mom wouldn't let him wear out of the house."

[*Regardless of the weather, Beau said that Robin wouldn't have let Steve go to town in beat up shorts. And, again, why would he have been wearing shorts and a t-shirt, or a polo shirt, and no jacket in cold weather?*]

Conclusion: Hanna's detailed descriptions of clothing only prove that she had enough opportunity in the two-and-a-half years between the Fall of 2001 and the Spring of 2004 to see the kinds of clothes Steve wore, and was capable of describing her own wardrobe (even though her descriptions of both shifted and changed regularly). Ordinarily, small inaccuracies wouldn't bother me, especially after a great deal of time has passed, but look at the phrases some of the others used in describing clothes they might have been wearing. Beau said, "kind of about what I have on now," and "probably about the same, "and "I think he had a jacket." Marri said, "probably clothes for warmth." They were guessing because, after that many years, they obviously didn't remember. It was just an ordinary night at the movies to them. My suspicion is that Hanna didn't remember what she or Steve were wearing either. I believe all of her clothing "memories" were created during the two years leading up to the trial. Some proof of that is the definitive statement she made in her original affidavit on April 8, 2004: "I further remember I was wearing a T-shirt and blue jean shorts." Once she changed her scenario from late summer to November, she changed the shorts and t-shirt to flare-legged jeans and a red, fitted, collared shirt, with strawberry-seed holes in it, but even that description happened in stages. Her clothing descriptions in all of the documents weren't memories. They were inventions. The real mystery, though, is, with all those changes, why didn't she give Steve winter clothes too?

Here's my theory. After the charges were filed, Hanna probably realized she couldn't just say this happened without something to back it up. Especially after she started sessions with Ada Dixon, and had read her book, it should have been obvious to her that she would need to construct a more complete narrative than the one in her affidavit. She probably also noticed that she had made a big mistake. The first night she spent at the Sirois' home was near the end of cold, cold November. Based on what she was reading about grooming in Dixon's book, she also couldn't continue to say that the first incident happened in a few stolen moments on one of the very first days they visited the Sirois family. Unless her story included a number of times alone with Steve, during which he "groomed" her for these sexual experiences, the thinness of her original story would collapse under the weight of any thorough questioning. I believe that, at that point, she started making adjustments and beefing her narrative up.

After changing the date from late-summer to near-winter, she also had to change the clothes she was wearing; but why did she continue to keep Steve in shorts and a polo shirt (or t-shirt) without a jacket? Those would have made perfect sense in a late-summer scenario, but not in November. There aren't any details about Steve's clothes in the affidavit, but maybe Hanna said something to Willard Knox about Steve being in summer-like clothes too, and thought it would be in Knox's notes? She may have also thought that Steve's attorney would have a copy of those notes (he didn't), so maybe she just tried to match what she told Knox. That's complete conjecture on my part, just a possibility. In most cases, though, Hanna's stories changed with each retelling anyway, almost as if she treated each time as a rehearsal, refining it before "opening night" (the trial).

Do you remember what you were wearing on any given day last month, much less years ago? No one but Hanna remembered what they were wearing. I think she used that level of detail primarily to appear confident in front of the jury. No matter how poised she might have seemed, though, the details still shifted and changed each time. Unfortunately, neither of the juries could compare what Hanna told them to any of her earlier versions.

My final thought on the matter: Hanna's testimony may have given the jury the impression that she knew what she was talking about, and that she could be trusted to remember details, but most of her descriptions of clothing are unimportant to her story, just window dressing.

Actually, let me rephrase that: I believe that Hanna's descriptions aren't just window dressing; I think they're bullshit dressing, poured thickly to cover a side order of lies.

Let's check out the weather.

What Was the Weather Like?

Why is This Important? I don't know why Hanna insisted that Steve wore summer clothes in late-November, but I'm glad she did. Here's the problem she generated for herself. In order to believe that Steve was dressed that way, we would also have to accept that the weather was warm enough for him to have been reasonably comfortable in just shorts and a t-shirt. All of her descriptions had him dressed that way, but she also claimed that he borrowed Marri's jacket during the movie because he didn't have one with him (we'll get to that once we're inside the theater).

Hanna tried to pinpoint when they saw the movie by how cold it was. She told Tom it was so cold that it "must have been like the beginning of 2002, or the end of 2001. It had to have been." In Trial #2, Sanford asked her if the movie was in late November. When she answered, "Yes," he said, "Generally pretty cold in late November?" She again answered, "Yes."

[*If Hanna agreed it was cold, why was she happy to dress herself in a jacket and jeans, but still keep Steve in shorts and a t-shirt with goosepimply arms and legs?*]

Burl Conley, an employee at the Filmland Theater in 2001, said he remembered that *Harry Potter's* opening night "was a chilled fall evening." The low was 61 degrees that day (cool, but not terrible), but the next two weekends were colder. See the chart on the next page. Temps ranged from just cool to very cold. The opening weekend never got out of the 60's, even during the day, and it was rainy both days (nearly 2 inches on opening day). Rain is another thing no one mentioned, so that helps us eliminate the first weekend. The 23rd and the 24th (just after Thanksgiving) were a little warmer during the day (in the 70's), but dropped to 45 and 46 in the evenings, definitely cold. Twenty to thirty degree swings in temperature are not unusual in Texas, especially when a front moves through the area. The third weekend (November 30th - December 1st) was just below freezing the first night, and just above it the second night. While everyone said the weather that night was cold, no one said it was freezing, which also helps establish the date of Friday the 23rd as the most likely night.

In the trials, Hanna was the only one who was asked about the weather and what clothes they wore, but the details she gave often made no sense. She also said it was cold at night on a July 2003 evening, claiming it was so cool she had to wear double layers. See the chapter, *The Night of the Rodeo*, for details about the record-breaking heat that July.

Here's some weather data from NOAA for Deep Springs. These are the six Fridays and Saturdays when they most likely saw the movie.

NOAA Weather Data, Deep Springs, Texas (November 2001)			
Date	**High**	**Low**	**Rain**
11-16-2001	63	61	1.82 in.
11-17-2001	68	58	0.24 in.
11-23-2001	74	45	0.00 in.
11-24-2001	79	46	0.00 in.
11-30-2001	45	30	0.00 in.
12-01-2001	66	33	0.00 in.

Conclusion: It was clearly getting colder from mid-November on. Ask yourself, would you go out in mid-40's weather in shorts and a polo shirt, and not even bring a jacket?

Exactly, neither would I.

Where Was Everyone Sitting in the Truck?

Why is This Important? For reasons which will soon become obvious, Hanna had to sit behind Steve during the drive to the theater for any of her story to be remotely believable. No one entirely agreed with anyone else about this question, but I'm going to keep this simple. Since I need to prove that Hanna's statements about that night were lies, I need to use her seating arrangement as if it was the correct one, and still show, using her own circumstances, that the rest of what she claimed wasn't possible.

There was no mention of the movie in Hanna's affidavit, but she did tell Ada Dixon about the ride there, "His son was driving, I was behind him [*Steve*], and his daughter was in the back in the middle."

[*This was Hanna's first description of this on record. Although Hanna rarely mentioned Aaron by name, by process of elimination he was sitting to Marri's left, behind Beau. She made nearly identical statements to Tom and in both trials, so that's the seating arrangement I'm going to work with.*]

There were some differences of opinion about who sat where in the truck, but everyone did agree that Beau was driving and Steve rode shotgun. If Hanna couldn't convince the jury that she was sitting behind Steve, none of the rest of her story about what happened in the truck works. Marri, in Trial #1, said that Hanna was sitting behind Beau, and Steve had an opportunity to agree with that, but he didn't. He simply testified that he didn't remember who sat where in the back seat. I asked him why, and he said, "Because that was the truth. I really didn't remember," which I think speaks volumes about his character.

Conclusion: Even if Hanna's version of everyone's location in the truck was correct, she still wouldn't have been able to do the things she claimed. That's next. Here's what she said happened during the ride.

What Happened on the Way to the Movie?

Why is This Important? Count I alleged that an incident happened later that night. The movie and the ride to the theater aren't mentioned in the affidavit at all. The prosecution's case rested on what happened at the Sirois' home the first time Hanna spent the night (even though the night in question happened three months later than the September 1st date specified in the affidavit and the indictment). To gain a conviction on Count I, they had to prove that the one act of oral sex occurred at the Sirois' house later that night, so why should we care what Hanna said happened earlier that evening? Because, if I can prove to you that she lied about what happened during the ride and in the theater, it makes her assertions about everything else suspect as well.

Warning: Graphic descriptions ahead. We'll start with a series of quotes about what happened during the ride to the movie. The first batch is all from Hanna.

In the Affidavit (April 2004): Not one single word was said about any incidents happening on the way to a movie, but a month later she said...

To Ada Dixon (May 2004): "He reached behind the seat and started rubbing my leg and he got my hands. I was leaning up against the seat. He put my hand on his dick. I thought how gross!"

To Tom (May 2006): "I leaned up. We used to like hold hands once in a while, which I thought was kind of cool because I never had a boyfriend or anything, and I thought that's what couples did, and in my state of mind, so I could deal with it, he was like a boyfriend, but ...not." "That's what it was like to me. I was only twelve, you know. What am I supposed to know? But, uh... I went to hold his hand, and I felt something, and I thought it was his finger, so I just kept playing with it, just being silly, and it wasn't his finger. It was ...you know. I don't really feel comfortable saying it. And the first thing that went through my mind was like, Oh, god. As soon as I ...it hit me what it was." "He, uh ...he'd unzipped his pants, and I didn't know it but I was playing ...with his penis, and [*2-second pause*] ...uh, for a minute I didn't know what to do, I just kept going. I didn't ...I've always been the type to kind of worry about what people think, and I didn't want him to think I was a chicken. And so I just kept going because I didn't know what else to do. I didn't want ...I wanted to prove to him that I was an adult, so I just didn't stop. And [*2-second pause*] ...um ...he leaned back and cocked his head to one side, towards the door one time, and I up and kissed him." "He reached back with his right hand and he pulled my leg up in between the seat and the door...and would just stroke my shins, my calf, or just that area of my leg, not real high up." She paused for a few seconds, then said, "So [*pause*] ...um [*pause*] ...he kind of stopped there when we got close to the theater because the lights got real bright, because of all the lights they got there in the parking lot."

[*I found it interesting that Hanna could use the word* "dick" *three times in her affidavit (about other incidents), then a few weeks later use it to Ada Dixon, but to Tom (and in the trials) was suddenly embarrassed to say the word? I believe that her alleged kiss, by the way, will prove that all of her comments about inappropriate behavior that night were a lie. We'll get to that. Patience, grasshopper. I do think she may have made one true statement in the middle of everything else, though. She said,* "I've always been the type to kind of worry about what people think," *which I believe could have been at the root of all the actions she took and the statements she made.*]

To Elmer Ross, Trial #1 (July 2006): Ross asked her if masturbation occurred that night. She said, "Yes. In the truck on the way to the movies." "I was sitting behind him in the truck on the passenger side. And he reached back with his right hand under the seat in between the seat and the door and he started rubbing my calf." "He kind of tugged on my jeans a little bit. I knew he wanted me to lean forward, so I did. I was just like a robot." "He fished around for my hand. And grabbed it and then he took it up and put my hand on his stomach. I thought, 'Well, that is kind of weird.' Then he lifted up his shirt and he put my hand on something. I didn't know what it was. It was just hard and smooth. And then I was just kind of touching it. I didn't know what it was." "There was one time, he had leaned back -- he had leaned back his head and kind of like that, and he made a little kissy face at me. So, I leaned up to give him a kiss and my little brother was like, 'Hanna, did you just kiss Sirois?' And I was like 'No.' And I tried to come up with an excuse, and I couldn't think of anything. I just said, 'No, you're just tired.'"

[*She told Tom that Steve pulled her leg between the seat and the door and stroked her leg, then the other actions followed. In Trial #1, though, her leg stayed where it was. In that version, Steve didn't pull it* "up in between the seat and the door," *but if her leg wasn't hidden by the seat, wouldn't the others have been more likely to see Steve's hand and wrist stroking her leg? And, when did she have time to become* "like a robot?" *She also repeated the kissy face story for the trial, but that was the first time she said anything about his shirt covering his penis, and the way her hand ended up in his lap was different. I'll put that all together in a minute.*]

To Bevin Jenkins, Trial #1: Jenkins asked her (probably using his best skeptical attorney voice), "And not only was there masturbation, but was there also a kissing incident?" Hanna answered, "Yes." Jenkins asked her when Aaron commented on the kiss. Hanna said, "It was after the second -- it was the second time that we kissed on that particular incident."

[*Yes, that's what she said – a second kiss.*]

Steve to Bevin Jenkins, Trial #1: Jenkins asked him if it was possible for someone to reach from the back seat and fondle someone's genitals in the front seat. Steve said, "No, sir," and added, "Nobody rides in our vehicles without their seat belts on. Jenkins also asked him, "Did Hanna ever put her hand on you in any way?" "Did she kiss you in the truck?" and "Did you put your hand on her?" He answered, "No, sir" to all of those.

[*No kissing. No touching. Yes, seat belts. It's the law. Why do you suppose Elmer Ross didn't ask Hanna whether everyone was buckled in?*]

That trial was a mistrial. They held Trial #2 less than a month later. Most of the Trial #2 questions and answers were repeats, but not all of them.

Hanna to Elmer Ross, Trial #2 (August 2006): "He kept putting his right hand down the side, like behind the seat, and he kept rubbing my calf under my pants leg. He kind of tugged on it a little bit and I just kind of leaned forward." Ross asked her if that sort of thing was happening a lot by then. She said, "By this point, I kind of figured it was going to happen. It was just like a routine. I just kind of started behaving like a robot. Every time something would happen, I would do my best to shut my mind off to what was going on." Then she said, "I leaned forward and put my right hand -- I reached around like out to the front of the seat, and I was just kind of playing with his hand, just real affectionately. And he took my hand and drug it farther toward the middle of the seat. And I felt his shirt and then I felt something else and I didn't know what it was." "It was hard and soft, and it was kind of like a finger, but not." Ross asked if she had ever touched his penis before that. She said, "No." Ross also asked about the amount of light in the truck, and she said that there were "just the dashboard lights, just to show speed, things like that, just gauges." Then she said, "He looked back at me at some point towards the outside of the truck and just kind of made a kissy face, I guess you would call it, at me. So, I leaned up and I gave him a real quick kiss." Ross asked her where she kissed him. She answered, "On the mouth," and repeated her story about Aaron witnessing the kiss. This time, though, instead of saying that Aaron was "<u>just tired</u>," she said "No, you're <u>just weird</u>."

[*Again, Robotic behavior? How long did Steve have to program her, a few visits? Does that make any sense? Her leg was also still out in the open where everyone in the back could have seen it getting stroked. If it was dark enough to hide what they were doing, how was it light enough for her to see Steve make a kissy face <u>on the other side of the front seat's headrest</u>? Also, why was Aaron weird that time instead of tired?*]

Cleveland Sanford, Trial #2, asked Hanna if she was wearing her seat belt in the truck that night. She said, "Yes, sir, I was. I didn't have the front strap over my shoulder, however...The strap that goes across the actual body, it was behind me." Sanford asked her to verify that she had testified that she managed to massage Steve's penis while she was in the back seat. She said, "Yes," and continued to respond in mostly monosyllables after that. — Sanford: Did you go over the seat? "No." — Sanford: You went around the seat? "Yes." — Sanford: Was that under his arm or over his arm? "Under." — Sanford: Did my client ejaculate at that point? "No." — Sanford: And it's your testimony that my client turned around and gave you one kiss or two? "One."

[*The ejaculation question will come up again, so I'll wait until we've reached that point before saying more about it. Hanna seemed ready with a seat belt answer that time, though. Did she think that eliminating the shoulder strap would give her more movement? It doesn't work that way. See the illustration in the analysis. She also dropped from a claim of two kisses to just one, and then denied that she had said it was two kisses in the first trial. Did she lie about the kiss/kisses in the first trial or in this one? Or in both?*]

Steve to me (2015): I asked if everyone wore their seat belts. He said, "Sure, had to be. We didn't go anywhere without everyone buckling up." I asked him if he saw Hanna unbuckle her seat belt, or slip the chest strap behind her. He said, "No. I don't remember ever looking at any of the kids." I then asked him a series of questions: "Did she at any point reach around the front seat and grab your hand?" "Did you and she touch each other in any way on the drive there?" "Did you hear Aaron ask Hanna if she had just kissed you?" He said "No" to them all, laughing at the ridiculousness of the last one.

[*Steve, wasn't hazy on these, he flatly said that none of what Hanna claimed was true.*]

Analysis of What Happened in the Truck: Let's first look at some inconsistencies. Hanna **told Dixon** that Steve rubbed her leg, and he pulled her hands along the side of the seat and onto his penis, but she **told Tom** that she "went to hold his hand," and thought she was holding his finger but it was his penis. She said she also leaned up and gave him a kiss (without losing hold of his penis, and with her seat belt still on). She said Steve pulled her leg between the seat and the door and stroked it, and that she continued to stroke Steve even after Aaron caught them kissing. **In Trial #1**, she said Steve rubbed her calf, but didn't say he pulled her leg between the seat and the door. She said he tugged on her pants to make her lean forward, and grabbed her hand and pulled it onto his lap. She said that, while she was stroking his penis, he made a kissy face, so she "leaned up to give him a kiss" (still strapped in) and claimed that was the second kiss in the truck. **In Trial #2**, she again said that he stroked her leg and tugged on her pants leg, so she reached around the seat to play with his hand, but he grabbed her hand and pulled it onto his lap. While she stroked his penis, he covered her hand with his shirt. Then he gave her a kissy face, so she leaned up and "gave him a real quick kiss" (yes, still buckled in).

Her story changed from one version to the next. In some he grabbed her hand, in one she was reaching to find his. In all the others, Steve "pulled" her hand onto his penis. In two of the versions there was a single kiss, in one of them there were two kisses, and in Dixon's there were no kisses at all. In some there was calf-rubbing and pants-tugging followed by masturbation, but in others the masturbation came first. In some the activity was covered by Steve's shirt. In others it wasn't. There was no consistent order to the sequence of events, but that was true of many of her other descriptions too.

In order for Hanna's claims about that night to be viable, several different conditions had to be in alignment. We need to look at the time available, the amount of light, and the restrictions of seat belts.

The Time Available: Not the twenty minutes in the truck, the ten weeks between the cross-country race and the ride to the movies. Hanna told Tom that Steve "was like a boyfriend" by this time, and they would "hold hands," and she thought that "was kind of cool," because "that's what couples did." So, when Steve played with her leg in the truck, and pulled her hand onto his lap, she said she just accepted it. Her premise was that there had been enough time for Steve to groom her for that sort of activity. In Trial #2, she said, "...by this point, I kind of figured it was going to happen. It was just like a routine. I just kind of started behaving like a robot." Elmer Ross also pushed the idea of months and years of visits between the families before this night, but you could probably count the number of visits on one hand, and only one of them was before the cross-country race.

Grooming Hanna for molestation was a primary theme in the case against Steve, and the prosecution's two expert witnesses, Goudy and Dixon, were questioned extensively about the process. After spending a great deal of time cultivating a friendship with their victims, child molesters gradually, over many months, introduce children to perverted things (like a little bawdy talk, or some mild pornography); and patiently, slowly, win them over to the idea of having sex. Hanna said several times, in her interview and in the trials, that Steve's grooming was "step by step, just getting deeper and deeper into it very gradually. It was extremely gradual." She enhanced that premise sometimes with her phrasing, saying things like he "<u>would</u> stroke my leg," implying that it was a commonly recurring action, something he had done with her for so long it had become habit, but there's a flaw in those statements. The time required for grooming didn't exist.

Hanna said (to Tom and in both trials) that one of the first incidents happened in early September 2001, after her cross-country meet in Langford, when her family stopped by the Sirois' home. She said that Steve groped her and kissed her inside the house, slobbering gooey spittle down her neck. Romantic, right? Steve said, if he had been her, he would have screamed bloody murder and run for the hills. Her boyfriend/girlfriend statements in the trial, insinuated that—even before the drooly September incident—she and Steve had found multiple occasions to talk for hours and get acquainted with each other. So many opportunities that, by the time they went to the movie in November, Steve had her completely trained. Trained so thoroughly, in fact, that the behavior in the truck was not only acceptable to her, but she reacted to it automatically, like Pavlov's dogs. Elmer Ross also bolstered that idea with many inaccurate comments about the months and months and years and years they had known each other. Stopping after the cross-country meet, though, was their first visit as a family other than one brief visit a couple of years before, when the kids were much younger. After the race they only came one day each time, almost always on a Friday, and they didn't visit every week. It was closer to every other weekend on the average. Darla, Steve and Robin all got off work late in the afternoon, so the visits usually didn't last more than a few hours from late afternoon into the evening. During the get-togethers, Steve was the cook. After everyone ate, the kids went inside or into the yard and played while the adults sat under the carport, talking and drinking.

During those initial, brief, roughly five visits between the race and the movie, where was the opportunity? Between Steve's cooking, and talking with the other adults, and the kids off playing somewhere, when did he find any time to spend alone with Hanna? There would have to have been a lot of continuous "alone" time if he had been able to talk to her for "hours and hours," and even more time to prepare her for this intimate act she said they committed in the truck. So, when Hanna said, "by this point," what did she mean? Are we supposed to believe that he could do all of that in a scattered moment here and there, over the space of just a few visits, with people moving around, in and out of the house?

Remember Hanna's descriptions of the incidents after the cross-country race? One incident to Tom, three in Trial #1, and two in Trial #2. She testified that each of them only lasted a few minutes before Steve dashed back outside so he wouldn't be missed? She had to describe brief, quick incidents because everyone there has said that, when Steve did go in the house, he wasn't gone for long stretches of time. When would he have groomed her before the night they saw the movie? How did he create those magic chunks of extended free time? In Trial #2, she claimed "we would talk for an hour-and-a-half, two hours, and just talk about everything? And we did this <u>for several months</u>." Even Hanna's mother testified in the first trial that Steve was rarely alone, that there was usually someone else around. The number of months didn't exist. That multiple hours of time didn't exist. The grooming didn't happen. And, Steve is not a foolish man. Why on earth would he do those things in front of his daughter, in front of his son, and in front of Hanna's brother?

The Amount of Light: Hanna needed darkness to explain why no one saw her masturbating Steve and kissing him, but it wasn't that dark. In my opinion, of course, darkness wasn't the reason no one saw them. It was because she didn't do those things. Even if it *had* been dark when they drove there, a fair bit of light emanates from the dashboard of the Silverado, plus there were street lamps on the way, and light from cars on the road. In late-November 2001, there was also a three-quarter to nearly-full moon. It would have provided some light too. Also, even if the inside of the truck was as dark as Hanna might have wanted us to believe, the eye's iris widens in the dark to allow us to take advantage of whatever light is available. Beau, who ostensibly would have had the best view of Steve's lap, has vision that works better in darkness than in bright light. He didn't see anything, and neither did anyone else. We'll cover Beau's eyesight in the next question.

The Restrictions of Seat Belts: Hanna said that Steve made a "kissy face" at her, so she leaned forward and gave him one or two kisses (Tom – one kiss, Trial #1 – two kisses, and Trial #2 – back to one kiss). When Cleveland Sanford questioned her about that, she denied under oath that she had said there were two kisses in Trial #1 even though it was in the trial record. How many potential lies happened there, and why wasn't she held accountable?

Hanna admitted she was wearing her seat belt. Steve said, "Nobody rides in our vehicles without their seat belts on." Everyone agreed that, in addition to being the law, it was also a family rule. Hanna tried to counter that by saying she slipped the chest strap behind her. Unless she had unusually long gorilla arms, she still couldn't reach as far as she claimed she did. According to trial exhibits, Hanna was only 5'2" in February 2001. The ride to the movie was ten months later, so maybe she grew some, but she was only 5'4" in October 2002. Let's split the difference and say she could have been 5'3" in November 2001. She said that sliding the strap behind her allowed her to lean forward, but that isn't the issue. Even when it's fastened properly, your chest strap will move forward with you if you move slowly enough. What you *can't* do easily is move your waist forward. Even if she had been able to reach around the side of the seat and place her hand in Steve's lap, the belt would still have held her in place at the waist. See the illustration below? When someone is buckled in, their head follows a trajectory like the arrow in the picture unless some other object impedes its motion, like the back of a seat. The kiss was impossible.

Hanna also told Tom that Steve reached back, tugged on her jeans, and pulled her "leg up between the seat and the door." We decided to test that (along with the rest of the scenario), so I videotaped Beau and his girlfriend, Laura, reenacting the sequence in the truck. Beau (at 5'11") and Laura (at 5'4") are roughly the same heights that Steve and Hanna were in 2001, although Laura is probably a little taller than Hanna was. We borrowed an extended-cab Chevy Silverado pickup with the same dimensions as Beau's former truck, and tried Hanna's story out. The video clearly shows that the incident couldn't have happened. Take a look at this screenshot.

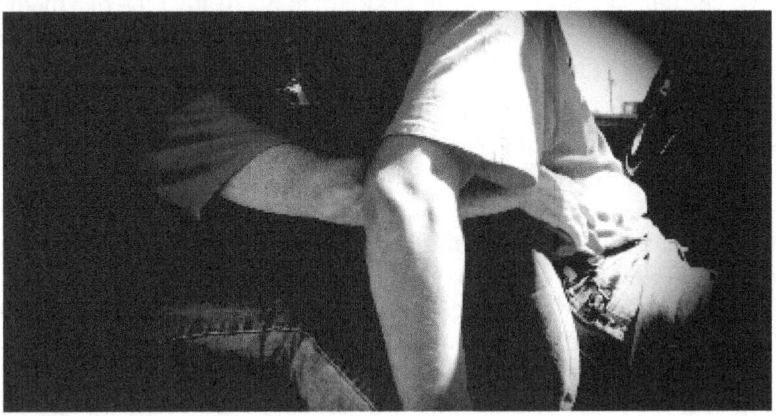

The side doors opened from the middle on that Silverado, so we were able to get a full view of both the front and rear seats. Beau's seat was as far back as it could go, but Laura couldn't reach past Beau's waist. Even if Hanna could have reached Steve's crotch from the back seat (which you can see that she couldn't), her story still has other problems. Buckled in, Laura couldn't flatten her body against her legs like I originally thought Hanna might be able to. She was so close to the front seat that she couldn't bend that far forward. Her face was smashed against the back of the front seat so tightly that she couldn't even see Beau when he made a "kissy face" at her. The only way a kiss could have happened would be if both of them had completely unbuckled their seat belts and Beau turned around to face his head toward the back seat (or pulled off a 180-degree *Exorcist* neck twist). Even then it would have been quite a stretch for Hanna. Also, when Beau tried it with his seat pulled forward, his knees were up against the dashboard, and Steve wouldn't have been sitting that way. Laura could bend a little flatter with the front seat all the way forward, but then Beau was even farther away.

We're not done yet, though. That test was done with the doors open. With the doors shut, conditions were even worse. After we closed the doors, Laura tried to fit her hand between the seat and the door, but couldn't get it past her wrist. See the photograph on the blog which shows her trying to do that. Beau couldn't get his arm along the side of the seat at all. With the door shut, he could barely reach the cuff of Laura's jeans with his fingertips, and her foot and leg wouldn't fit between the seat and the door, period. Hanna not only said that her foot and leg fit into that space, she also said that her arm was under Steve's arm when she reached his crotch. Two arms won't fit into that space at the same time. None of what Hanna claimed was physically possible. If anyone would like to try to recreate this scene, feel free to. You'll find the same thing I did. Be sure to use a Chevy Silverado or GMC Sierra 3/4 ton extended cab pickup, late 1990's model, and people of appropriate sizes.

One other small point. Hanna testified that, during the twenty-minute ride, Steve didn't ejaculate. Even if she had pulled off the miracle stretch that allowed her hand to reach Steve's lap, how long would she have been masturbating him before they arrived at the theater and had to stop? Half the time? Maybe ten minutes? I'm not going to try to make any kind of a medical or physiological diagnosis here, but I'll just say that ten minutes of masturbation can be a *really* long time.

Conclusion: Hanna claimed that Steve stroked her calf inside her pants leg and made a kissy face, which caused her to lean forward and kiss him on the mouth (for the second time?) while her hand was still on his penis. That isn't physically possible. Look at the seat-belted figures on the previous page, and at the photograph of Laura and Beau inside the truck. One thing is clear. When the hips are fixed in place, and someone bends at the waist, their head has to follow a downward curve. It can't do anything else, and it definitely can't move higher than the line the circle inscribes. The mouth has to follow that curve too. It would have been impossible for Hanna to reach anyone in the front seat with her mouth, which was probably six inches down from the top of her head. She would have to stretch even farther, buckled in, for that kiss. During the trial, a demonstration with a stick figure on a pad of paper, and a curve drawn with a piece of string would have shown that she couldn't possibly kiss someone in the front seat no matter what her height was. Better yet, having the jury watch a live demo in a pickup would have put all doubts to rest about whether Hanna was telling the truth about that. Tom had arranged for one, but it didn't happen. Opportunity wasted.

I believe this entire part of Hanna's story is a fantasy. Even if everyone in the back seat had blinders on and didn't see her bent over at the waist, with her face smashed up against the front seat, and her right arm stretched between the passenger seat and the door, she still couldn't have reached his lap with her hand. And she clearly couldn't have reached his mouth with hers. It just can't be done.

Did Anyone in the Truck See This Happen?

Why is This Important? There were three other people in the truck. They had fifteen to twenty minutes to witness Hanna push her seat belt's chest strap behind her, reach around the edge of the front seat and fondle Steve's penis; and see Steve tug on her flare-legged jeans, fondle her calf, pull her leg into the tiny space between the seat and the door frame, pull her hand into his lap, unbuckle his seat belt, unzip his jeans and pull his genitals out; to see her lift her seat-belted body off the seat to kiss Steve once or maybe twice (while they were both buckled up); plus to hear Aaron ask about the kiss. Maybe this question should actually be "Why on Earth Didn't Anyone See This Happening?"

Going to the movie wasn't in Hanna's affidavit. She told Ada Dixon about it, but Dixon didn't list anything in her summary about a kiss in the truck, or about anyone witnessing it. If Hanna had told Dixon there had been a witness to a kiss (which would have been very damning evidence against Steve), Dixon would have included that in her summary, wouldn't she? When Tom interviewed Hanna, she said, about Aaron seeing the kiss, "He don't even want to think about it, and he already told Ada, my counselor, that he does not remember anything. And he does not want to know what happened." Tom asked if she thought Aaron was hiding from remembering it. Hanna agreed, saying, "Basically he's in a lot of denial…He's a very strange person." Then she giggled.

[*Dixon wasn't asked about Aaron during the trials. She would have been required to report an exculpatory statement if Aaron had made one. Do you find it peculiar that Aaron moved to Michigan shortly after Hanna accused Steve, and was the one person who could corroborate this detail, but Hanna claimed that he didn't remember anything and didn't want to talk about it? Would Aaron actually be "in a lot of denial" about something if he didn't see it in the first place? We only have Hanna's word that Aaron saw, or did, or said anything in the truck that night. He wasn't called as a witness in either trial, but I've been told that he* was *seen in Deep Springs (at the courthouse), in the summer of 2006. We'll come back to that.*]

Hanna told Tom that the others in the truck didn't react to Aaron's comment "because we were all kind of laughing and joking around." She said she convinced them instead that she had "just made a funny joke about Beau," because she "was always teasing Beau about something. He was like my best friend. And we all kind of laughed it off or whatever, and I got kind of nervous after that -- didn't do it again. I kept my hand under [*Steve's shirt*], because I didn't know what else to do."

[*Were they quiet or raucous? Hanna, who had been portraying this incident as if it was happening in its own silent little bubble, now had to explain why only her brother saw the kiss, so she said everyone was laughing and joking (*"or whatever"*), and said that she somehow convinced them that Aaron's comment about the kiss was a joke she made about Beau, but no one else remembers Aaron saying that, or Hanna making any kind of joking comment about a kiss or anything else.*]

In both trials, Ross asked Hanna about Aaron seeing the kiss. In Trial #1, she said, "I leaned up to give him a kiss and my little brother was like, 'Hanna, did you just kiss Sirois?' And I was like, 'No.' And I tried to come up with an excuse, and I couldn't think of anything. I just said, 'No, you're just tired.'" In the second trial, she gave the same answer, but that time said, "No, you're just weird." Ross asked if that satisfied Aaron, and Hanna said, "Well, he's the kind of person that comes up with a lot of random things that normally a person can't follow, so I just kind of blew him off."

[*Weird? Tired? What happened to the "funny" joke about Beau? Also, why was Hanna allowed to quote Aaron when he wasn't there to verify it? Wouldn't that be a violation of the hearsay rule?*]

Beau's Eyesight: Hanna told Tom, "Beau has a problem. He cannot see at all. His vision is like 200/400, something like that. He has to wear special glasses to drive. So his focus is completely on the road. So he would not have noticed anything because of his eyesight." She also said that his vision was "really, really bad," and "he has to wear special glasses," and "he could get arrested, and have those glasses taken away if he should not have those glasses on him behind the wheel. They have to be on his face." She finished with, "He could not see anything out of his peripheral, considering the lighting was really bad. Like I said, it was only dashboard lights."

[*Did that diatribe shut Beau down completely, and make him useless as a witness? Hang on to that thought for a few minutes.*]

In Trial #1, after talking about Aaron's comment, Bevin Jenkins asked whether Beau or Marri said anything. Hanna said, "No, they stayed quiet." She again mentioned Beau's "very poor eyesight" and his need for "a lot of concentration for the road." Jenkins asked whether Beau and Marri were aware of what was happening, but Hanna brushed it off, saying, "At the time, they probably thought it was just one of Aaron's random things. He does not have a lot of common sense. So, it was dismissed as nothing. And I would have done the same if I had been one of them."

["They stayed quiet?" *What happened to all the raucous playing around and joking? Hanna shifted gears again and blamed their non-response on Aaron's lack of common sense, as opposed to the other choice, that nothing happened for them to respond to.*]

In the same trial, Jenkins asked Hanna, "When was the first time that you had touched his sexual organ?" She answered, "It was that night in the truck." To verify, he asked again, "In the truck?" And she confirmed. "Yes."

[*After two years of learning about grooming, Hanna peppered her testimony with mentions of the months of time alone with Steve in which he supposedly built up her self-esteem and made her feel special; but, after taking those vast stretches of time (which didn't exist) to so meticulously prepare Hanna for this, why on earth would he choose to have her touch his penis for the very first time in full view of his son, his daughter, and her own brother?*]

Jenkins asked Marri if she saw Hanna kiss Steve, if she and Aaron were asleep during the drive, and if she saw Hanna reach around the seat and do anything inappropriate. Marri answered "No" to all of that. When he asked her if she was sitting right next to Hanna, she said, "Yes," but when he asked if Hanna had any opportunity to reach around the seat without anyone seeing, she said, "No." Then, finally, he asked her if it was possible or impossible. She said, "Impossible."

[*Marri was sitting right next to Hanna in the truck, and didn't think Hanna could have done what she claimed without being seen. If Hanna wanted everyone to believe that Aaron, sitting on the other side of Marri, saw what was happening, she can't also expect everyone to believe that Marri wouldn't have seen it too. And, just for the record, how dark was it supposed to have been in the truck? Apparently, according to Hanna, everyone could see a lot.*]

In Trial #2, Sanford asked Hanna, "Did my client ejaculate at that point?" Hanna said, "No." He asked if she gave Steve "one kiss or two." She replied, "One." Sanford asked if it "was a kiss on the lips." She answered, "Yes." Sounding incredulous, Sanford said, "And nobody saw it?" She said, "I believe my little brother did." Sanford said, "But he is in Michigan, correct?" Hanna said, "Yes," but added, "And he was asked about it. He claims he doesn't remember." Sanford objected to her extra comment. Judge Hawes instructed the jury to disregard everything Hanna said after "Yes."

[*During Trial #1, Hanna didn't get the information in about Aaron not remembering the kiss. She did here, but did she also lie? She told Tom there was one kiss, but in Trial #1 said there were two kisses. When Sanford asked in Trial #2, she said there was only one kiss, and denied that there had been two kisses. Statements 2 and 3 were under oath. The third statement agreed with the first one, but Hanna denied saying the second one.. At least one of the statements under oath had to be untrue. And, of course, they all could have been. Sanford's objection to the rest of Hanna's comment was because she tried to squeeze something in that Sanford didn't ask for. It also would have been hearsay because she can't legally speak for Aaron if he isn't there to corroborate her comment. Which again makes me wonder why he didn't testify.*]

When Beau took the stand in Trial #2, Elmer Ross followed up on Hanna's comments about his poor vision, asking him if he needed to pay extra attention when he drove at night. Beau said, "Not any more attention than anybody else would." Ross tried again, asking him if he was looking at the road or looking back and forth from Steve to the kids in the back seat. Beau said, "I was looking at the road and I would look over and talk to them."

[*In other words, the way most people drive. Did Beau gain back any points there?*]

Cleveland Sanford asked Beau whether he saw or heard anything inappropriate on the way to the movie, and whether he thought anything had happened. Beau said, "No, sir" to both of those. Sanford also wanted to clear up the matter of Beau's eyesight, so he asked Beau if he had a driver's license. Beau said, "Yes, sir." Sanford asked if it was a valid one. Beau said, "Yes, sir." He asked if it had any night driving restrictions. Beau said, "No, sir." Sanford asked him if the State of Texas thought he could see well enough to drive at night. Beau said, "Yes, sir."

[*Beau didn't see or hear anything inappropriate, and you can't get a driver's license without passing a vision test. Let's talk a bit about Beau's vision.*]

I didn't think Beau got enough of an opportunity to explain his eyesight, so I asked both Marri and Beau about his vision when I interviewed them in 2014. Marri said "We drive to Beaumont at nighttime all the time [*to visit Steve*]. I don't think it affects him at all, in any kind of way." I asked her if his vision would prevent him from seeing things to his left or right. She said, "No, because I can be sitting there, and he's like, 'Are you texting?' I mean like he can see what I'm doing, while driving." I said, "So his peripheral vision is okay." Marri said, "Yes, sir." I'm her uncle, and I keep telling her she doesn't have to call me, "sir," but she does anyway. She's so polite.

[*Marri said that Beau's night vision is good. Beaumont, where Steve is incarcerated, is over 300 miles from Deep Springs. They drive there the night before so they can arrive at the prison when it opens for visitation at 7:00 am.*]

I asked Beau to describe what his vision is like, and how it affects his ability to drive, especially at night. Beau said, "My vision ...it's hard to explain because I've always had it all my life." I asked if there was a medical term for his condition. He said, "Yes. Iris Colaboma. It's where I'm missing part of my retina. And it's also caused my pupil to be tear-shaped, so they don't dilate like they're supposed to. If anything, I've always been able to see better at night, because glare during the day sometimes bothers me, but at night my eyes don't have to dilate, and I can see better when it's dark. As far as driving, I drive just fine. I wear a set of driving glasses, and they help me read the road signs. I can see good enough to drive. I can see the lanes, I can see cars, I can see people. All they do is help me see far ahead and read road signs." He explained that the glasses have "a telescope in the very top part of the lens." I asked if that's to increase the size of objects overhead like road signs. Beau said, "Yes. Ninety-percent of the time I'm looking through the bottom that has no prescription in it whatsoever." I asked if there was anything abnormal about his peripheral vision. He said, "No, I've got real good peripheral vision. The only vision that's altered as far as my peripheral is up." I asked him if his vision would prevent him from seeing what somebody was doing in the passenger seat while he was driving. Beau said, "No." I also asked him if it was true that he could be arrested, as Hanna had claimed, if he wasn't wearing the glasses. Beau said, "No. I can get a ticket, just like anybody else can that doesn't drive without their glasses on if they've got prescription lenses."

[*Hanna's mention of Beau's* "special glasses" *and how* "he would not have noticed anything because of his eyesight" *seemed deliberate to me; and while Beau did a good job in his testimony of explaining that he has no restrictions on his driver's license other than having to wear corrective lenses, he didn't get to fully explain to the jury that his side-to-side peripheral vision is fully functional, and that he actually sees better at night than he does in the daytime. His glasses, in other words, are just like the graduated lenses or bifocals that millions of people wear so they can see clearly from eighteen inches away while working on a computer, and still see signs clearly on the road when they're driving. His are just designed to increase the size of overhead signs in the distance. How does Hanna's testimony about Beau's terrible eyesight stack up now?*]

Analysis: Did anyone in the truck see anything? Hanna said that Aaron witnessed a kiss, but she didn't say that Beau saw a kiss, or that Marri did. They were both there, and they both testified. The only person she claimed saw a kiss was her brother, but he didn't testify even though he could have been a key witness for Hanna.

Beau, who had a full view of Steve's seat, and Marri, who was sitting right next to Hanna, said they saw nothing at all. In addition to the fact that some of Hanna's claims are physically impossible, no one said they saw Hanna pull the seat belt's chest strap over her head, and slip it behind her. Or saw Steve reach his right hand back and stroke her leg. Or saw her lean forward, or saw Steve pull her hand onto his lap. Or saw him turn his head and make a "kissy face." Or saw her kiss him (once, or twice, or once) on the lips. Or saw Steve pull out his penis. Or put it back for that matter. When I mentioned that there were lies in the trial transcript to Hanna's mother she said, "They didn't know what they were witnessing." I find it hard to believe that if Beau or Marri saw their father being masturbated, or saw a kiss between him and a young girl, that they wouldn't recognize those acts for what they were.

According to Hanna's testimony, Aaron was her only witness to the alleged incidents in the truck; but she claimed that, when he saw the kiss, he was so traumatized that he blocked it out and then refused to talk about it. She said that Aaron "already told Ada, my counselor, that he does not remember anything. And he does not want to know what happened." Isn't it more likely that Hanna made it all up, and Aaron (if he actually *was* asked about it) doesn't remember it because it didn't happen? Aaron began living with his father in Michigan in June 2004, placing him safely far away, but more than two years passed between the charges and the first trial, so the DA had plenty of time to put him on the witness list. He could have testified, but he didn't. I didn't see anything in the DA's files about Aaron, which makes me believe that he wasn't asked to give an affidavit or a deposition. It felt like they didn't want to hear what he might say. Ada Dixon wasn't asked during the trials if she had talked to him. I tried to ask Dixon about it, but she wouldn't even admit that Hanna was her patient, even though she had testified that she was in open court. If Dixon did talk to Aaron, and he told her he didn't witness a kiss, his comment would have been exculpatory evidence, useful for the defense. If Aaron did tell her anything that contradicted Hanna, Dixon would have been legally required to give that information to the court and the DA, and that information would also have to have been given to Steve's attorney, but there's no mention of it in any documents I have. According to Steve, Dixon fought to avoid turning any of her materials over to the court. Judge Hawes accepted a summary from Dixon of just five of Hanna's sessions instead, which in effect allowed Dixon to choose what to give to the court as evidence.

I said earlier, that Dixon, in the *Texas v. Munsen* trial, instead of producing her files, claimed that her laptop had crashed and that she had lost her "whole 21 years of practice." In that case, when she was asked her opinion about providing the files, she stated, under oath, that she would "fight to protect those records because I don't want to make anything where it's easier for a defense attorney to try to come up with stuff to say that, you know, this didn't happen. <u>I know</u> what happened."

By saying that, it seems to me that Dixon placed herself above the law, essentially saying that she would decide matters of law for herself. Toby Billings, who worked on the *Munsen* case, filed a complaint against her with the Texas Board of Examiners of Professional Counselors, saying that she "contrived a fraud by playing a shell game with the records." The board dismissed the complaint, but having said, under oath, that she would "fight to protect" her records from defense attorneys, is it beyond belief that she could, potentially, have withheld information in Steve's case? On the other hand, isn't it also just as likely that Aaron never talked to Dixon in the first place, and that Hanna's comment was just one more lie? I've often wondered, as a legal question, if Aaron did dispute Hanna's account to Dixon, couldn't anyone who knew about that, but didn't reveal that information to the courts, be considered complicit?

Here's more. According to Peggy Higham, Aaron *was* in town during one of the trials, and could have testified. She gave me an affidavit which said that Aaron sat with Hanna and her mother while the jury was deliberating. The affidavit partly states, "during the deliberations, Hanna and her family (her brother, Aaron; and her mother, Darla), along with Hanna's boyfriend, sat near the jury room and laughed and joked, but whenever the jury went into or out of the deliberation room, they switched to sad faces and cried." Peggy, in case you forgot, is Eddie Higham's sister, but was also good friends with Steve and Robin, so she sat with them during deliberations. Were there people on Hanna's side who didn't want Aaron to testify? The only person whose word we have for what Aaron knew or didn't know, or what he saw or didn't see, is Hanna. He could have cleared up the matter of the kiss, and also could have provided a second eyewitness account of the nights they spent at the Sirois' house, but no one put him on the stand. The main reason I can think of for why Hanna's family might have wanted to hide him until the trial was over would have been because they were afraid of what he might say. Hanna also didn't seem to have a very high opinion of Aaron, telling Tom that he was "a very strange person," and in the trials saying, "It was just one of Aaron's random things. He does not have a lot of common sense," and he "comes up with a lot of random things that normally a person can't follow." Was she saying, about own brother, that even though he might have seen that kiss (or kisses), everyone ignored him because he usually made stupid comments?

Did anyone in the truck see Hanna bending at the waist, right arm stretched around the side of the passenger seat? Did anyone see her lift up off the rear seat after magically converting her seat belt into a bungee cord so it could stretch that far? No, they didn't. The reason Hanna gave for why no one paid any attention to Aaron's comment was that "we were all kind of laughing and joking around," even though she said that after initially describing everything as if she and Steve were in a quiet isolation bubble, separate and apart from everyone else. To justify no one responding to a comment (that I don't believe Aaron made), Hanna created a sort of mini-chaos, that may or may not have existed, with everyone laughing and joking. If they were actively looking around and joking, wouldn't it be that much more likely that someone would have noticed something? Which was it, a chaos or a bubble of calmness?

Also, think about the mechanics of her claim. She said she kept her hand under Steve's t-shirt while she was kissing him (a new comment she didn't add to her narrative until Trial #2). Did she have magic arms that could stretch farther than anyone else her size (to make it to Steve's lap), and then also manage to keep her hand in his lap while, buckled in, she lifted two feet off the seat to kiss him? Was her left arm strong enough at the age of twelve to counter the tightness of the seat belt and pull her body away from the rear seat that far? How could she see him make a kissy face if her head was pressed up against the back of the front seat? It's just mind-boggling.

Also, if Aaron's comment made Hanna nervous, why didn't she just pull her hand out of Steve's lap, and sit back and laugh and joke with the others? Why would she stay bent over at the waist, with her face pressed against the front seat, and her arm shoved along the right side of the seat, under Steve's arm, with her hand still in his lap? Wouldn't that have been a strange and obvious body position for someone to remain in who was trying to not get noticed?

Let's try one quick test. Sit in the passenger seat of a car or truck. Fasten your seat belt, then unbuckle your pants belt, unbutton your jeans, and unzip them. Wait, you say you can't do that while your seat belt is still buckled? All of that would have to happen for Steve to expose his penis. Wouldn't Beau and Aaron and Marri have noticed if Steve unbuckled his seat belt, then his own belt, then unbuttoned his jeans and unzipped his fly? Wouldn't an alarm go off in the truck when he unbuckled the seat belt? Did anybody see any of that happen on the way there? No, they didn't. And wouldn't he need to lift up off the car seat to slip his jeans/shorts partway down? Just unzipping them wouldn't be enough to free his penis. To accept Hanna's version, we would have to either believe that Steve managed all of that without unbuckling his seat belt, or that he was so sure of himself that he unzipped and slid his pants partway down before Beau started the truck. Wouldn't it have been obvious to anyone climbing in the back seat from the passenger side, that the guy in the passenger seat had his pants unzipped and pulled down? My vote? He never unzipped them in the first place.

There's one more detail that relates to what might or might not have happened in the truck and inside the theater. There's a side effect that occurs after masturbation even if a man hasn't ejaculated. Can you guess what that might be? We have one more masturbation incident to go, so I'll cover that in the analysis of *What Happened Inside the Movie Theater?*

Conclusion: It's obvious that the reason no one saw Hanna do anything to Steve, like fondle him or kiss him, was because she didn't do either of those things. If Aaron didn't remember seeing a kiss, or remember saying something about it, it was because he didn't witness what didn't happen; and it didn't happen because Hanna couldn't have physically done any of what she claimed. That entire part of her story isn't possible. I believe it's just a lie, concocted to make the already egregious accusation against Steve seem even more heinous.

During the Movie

Just to remind you, the questions I'm going to cover in this section of the chapter are: "Where was everyone sitting inside the movie theater?" "What happened inside the theater?" "What happened when they left the theater?"

Where Was Everyone Sitting Inside the Movie Theater?

Why is This Important? Where they sat inside the theater was integral to Hanna's claims of what happened there. Just like in the truck, everyone had a slightly different opinion about where they sat and who was sitting next to them; so, like the question about where they sat in the truck, I'm going to use Hanna's seating arrangement because hers is the one I have to disprove.

Here's what everyone did agree on, though. The screening room had typical multiplex stadium-type seating. It was tiered, with one single area of seating near the screen that extended the full width of the room. The upper tier was comprised of a wide middle section and two smaller side sections. The upper tier extended from the center of the room up to the back wall. Our group of five sat somewhere in the middle section of that upper area, and the first person entering their row sat five seats in from the aisle.

Hanna told Tom, "We were sitting on the edge of the aisle -- whatever you want to call it -- I was sitting on the edge, and then it was him [*Steve*], his daughter, um ...and then either Beau or my little brother. I don't know." Tom asked her if she was in the aisle seat. Hanna said, "Right." Tom asked if she was on Steve's right side or his left side. She said, "Left."

In Trial #1, in response to a question from Bevin Jenkins, Hanna said, "...we were sitting in the very back row." [*Why do you suppose she would want to claim that location?*]

In 2015, I asked Steve where they sat that night. He said, "Somewhere around the middle. As best as I remember, it was somewhere around the middle. It wasn't too far to see, and, of course, Beau always picks that." I asked if he sat in an inside seat or one on the aisle. He said "I would have been on the outside." I asked him how full it was, and he said, "Over half full."

There's not much else to say about this. I believe that Hanna created a scenario that best fit the needs of her story (that she and Steve sat side-by-side to the left of everyone else). Whether it's true or not, Hanna's scenario has her (when facing the screen) on the left side, then Steve, then Marri, and then Aaron and/or Beau. Steve being on the aisle makes more sense, though, if he thought he might have to go to the restroom or smoke a cigarette, as he said he sometimes did a couple of times during a long movie; but, to give Hanna the best possible opportunity to make her case, I used her seating arrangement and her own words when analyzing her claims.

Conclusion: Even if Hanna was on the outside of the row, with Steve between her and Marri, Marri would still be able to see whatever was happening right next to her. No matter whether we put Steve on the outside of Hanna or not, Marri was still sitting next to one or the other of them. She would have seen anything they were doing. Also, keep in mind that Marri thought she might have been sitting between Steve and Hanna. We're just using Hanna's seating arrangement to show that it wouldn't work anyway.

What Happened Inside the Theater?

Why is This Important? As with the question about what happened in the truck, Hanna gave very specific, but mercurial details about what happened or didn't happen in the theater that night. I think those details will help prove her wrong here too. Pay attention to how she refined her story with each new retelling. I've underlined some comments about the jackets for reasons that will soon become clear.

During her May 2004 session with Ada Dixon, Hanna said, "We got to the movies and got popcorn and butter and shared it. He got his daughter's jacket, put it over his lap, and told me to put my jacket on backwards. Then he felt my boobs. He would constantly touch my boobs. He tried to get into my pants, but I wouldn't let him. We hadn't gotten that far yet."

[*Was Hanna's mention of sharing the popcorn meant as some sort of "proof" that Steve was treating her as his girlfriend? Did they actually share it? We only have Hanna's word that they did. Also, here's another use of phrases indicating that extensive grooming* had *occurred before that night. She said,* "We hadn't gotten that far yet" *and* "he would constantly." *Her family had only visited the Sirois' five or six times by then, if that many.*]

Two years later, Hanna told Tom, "...he reached over and got his daughter's jacket. No wait. Hang on ...yeah, he got his daughter's jacket ...jacket, and put it across his lap, and said, 'I'm cold, I need to borrow...' and she's like, 'Okay, Daddy,' and didn't even think about it, and she got back into the movie, and she was like ...er, he leaned over and was like 'Put your jacket across your shirt.' I was like, 'Okay. What if I'm not cold?' [*pause*] Um, but, uh, I put it across me, and it was really, really hot in there. I was 'I'm not cold, I'm not cold.' He's like, 'Yes you are. Just put the jacket across you.' I was 'All right!' And I did and then ...the jacket ...was kind of long so it fit across my entire torso, and then some of my legs. Not quite to my knee, though. And, um ...he ...reached over with his ...hand, and put his hand up my shirt, and felt my breasts. And, then his hand slid down and he went and undid the button and zipper of my jeans, and started to put his hand down there. I would not let him go under my underwear, because we hadn't gone that far yet. I didn't know what would happen. I was scared. So I just put ...I just put my hand there to stop him."

[*Does most of that feel like she was trying to decide what to say instead of remembering what happened?* He got her jacket, no he didn't, no wait, hang on, yes he did, etc. *And did you notice that she managed to suggest that her windbreaker was gigantic? More on that later.*]

She also told Tom, "And then he kept like watching around and being real careful, and then he, uh, [*3-second pause*] ...he kept looking over at ...we're ...he kept looking across the aisle at these people that were sitting there, because they kept kind of glancing over, and he said, 'We better stop because they're kind of getting suspicious.'" After waiting seven seconds for her to continue, Tom asked her what else happened. After three more seconds, she said, "That was it. He tried to mess with me once or twice after that, not real long, and then quit..."

[*Doesn't that also seem like she was inventing this bit for the first time?*]

For some reason, in Trial #1, Elmer Ross didn't ask Hanna anything about what happened inside the movie theater. As soon as she said they arrived at the theater, he asked her what went on at Steve's house later that night. When Bevin Jenkins, who had heard Tom's interview with Hanna, asked if there had been any incidents at the movie, she said, "Yes, there were several."

[*The DA's office had a copy of Ada Dixon's summary in their possession since the fall of 2004. Ross must have known about Hanna's claims about what happened inside the theater. Why didn't he ask Hanna about them? Was he just anxious to get to Count One?*]

Jenkins continued, and asked Hanna to describe the incidents, even though the prosecutor had failed to. I'm glad he did, because her answers, when compared to her other testimony, made no sense. After explaining that Steve left "every ten minutes for a smoke break," Hanna said that he told her to "Take off your jacket and put it across your chest." She ran through the same "it's-hot, no-it's-not" disagreement she had told Tom about, but said that she eventually complied. Jenkins asked if anyone noticed them. She said, "Across the aisle in the very corner of the theater -- we were sitting in the very back row. To the very corner to my left, there were about three or four teenagers, and they were being kind of loud, making smart remarks. And Sirois said, 'Well, better calm down, I don't want them to notice.' He had also borrowed Marri's jacket and set it across his lap. He unzipped his pants, drug my hand over to his penis and made me massage it while he reached over with his right hand and fondled my chest. He unzipped my pants and got as far down to the underwear line before I grabbed his hand. And he kept trying to push, and I was trying to pull his hand back because I hadn't done anything like that before."

[*Was it actually hot in the theater? Wouldn't a hot/cold disagreement like that just attract further attention to what they were doing? Also, if he was fondling her with his right hand when he* "drug" *her hand to his penis, he had to drag with his left hand, correct? Did she stick with that story in Trial #2?*]

Ross missed his opportunity in the first trial to ask Hanna about what happened inside the theater, but in Trial #2, as soon as he finished asking her about the incident in the truck, he said, "What happened when you got to the movies, Hanna?" She repeated her story about Steve leaving, only this time she said it was every "5, 10 minutes," but said that he asked her questions about what was going on in the movie each time he got back because she "had read all the books." Then she said Steve asked "Marri to borrow her jacket, saying he was cold, and put it across his lap. He told me to take my jacket off and to kind of cover up with it like a blanket. Not really put it on, just lay it over my front." Then, acting it out, she said, "He took my right hand and drug it over and put it on his penis." Ross asked if Steve's penis was under or over his clothes. She said, "Over. He had already had his pants unzipped and everything." Then she said that Steve's penis was "Hard, swollen," and that he "just kind of -- moved my hand up and down really slowly so it wouldn't draw attention," and then said that "He took his left hand -- he put his right hand on my hand, took his left hand and kind of reached across as best he could and somehow managed to get up my shirt and under my bra and started fondling my breasts." She said that continued "for a couple of minutes," then "he tried to unbutton my pants, and I wouldn't let him…I took my left hand and I put a really firm grip on his hand. He kept trying to mess with the button. I just grabbed his hand the best I could to stop it from moving." She then acted out the rest of their dialogue. "Why not?" "Because." "Why?" "I just don't want to," and then she said, "it just gradually stopped. He kept having to leave for a smoke break, I guess. And that was the end of it. Nothing else happened."

[*Hanna said she covered her torso with her jacket, and Steve did the same with Marri's jacket, then he dragged her right hand over to his already-out-of-his-pants, "hard, swollen" penis. When did he unzip his "pants" (not shorts) and pull his penis out? Which hand did he do that with? According to her, while he fondled her breast with his left hand, she masturbated him with her right, but, when he tried to do the same to her, she wouldn't let him. She then described a somewhat argumentative conversation, followed by Steve leaving to have a smoke. And Marri didn't hear any of that? Or notice what was going on under her teeny, tiny jacket? Or wonder why her father was leaving the screening room every 5 to 10 minutes? Marri would have to have been the most oblivious person in existence to have missed all of that.*]

When Sanford questioned Hanna, he asked her to verify that she had said, "you took your right hand and you placed it on his penis," and that Steve took "his left hand and massaged your breast." Hanna agreed, adding that massaging with his left hand "was very difficult for him, but yes." When he asked her why nobody saw that, her response was just, "There were jackets."

He asked where they were sitting. She said, "Toward the top." He asked if she meant at the back of the theater. She said, "The back, yes." After she agreed that she had been to many movies, Sanford asked "If you are sitting closer to the screen and someone else is behind you, if you turn around, they are in the light, correct?" Hanna said, "Yes." He asked if she would also agree that everyone in the theater could have seen what they were doing if they had turned around. Hanna said, "Yes," but quickly added that "the theater was nearly empty because of the lateness of the show." Sanford objected to her statement about the emptiness of the theater, and Judge Hawes told the jury to ignore it, but can a jury actually ignore a statement once it's out in the open?

[*Contortions on top of contortions, but nobody saw anything? I'll have a lot more to say in the analysis about why seeing the movie was all that happened inside the theater, and we'll also look at the process of fumbling around under the jackets; but, yes, Hanna flip-flopped on which hands Steve used (unspecified to Tom, right hand on breast in Trial #1, and left hand in Trial #2). Also, the light from the screen would definitely shine on them. Many of the scenes in the first* Harry Potter *movie were brightly lit. Those scenes would bounce a lot of light onto the audience, and, if they were at the back, anyone turning around could have seen what they were doing.*]

Sanford asked Beau if he would believe that improper things could happen while he was in the same room. Beau said, "No, sir." Sanford asked if he sat on the same row as Steve in the theater. Beau said he had, so Sanford asked if he saw or heard anything. Beau said, "No, sir."

[*Beau was on the same row as Steve but he didn't see or hear anything improper.*]

In 2014, I asked Marri if she remembered Steve leaving several times during the show. She said "No." I asked if he usually left a lot. She said, "No, not that I can recall." I also asked if she remembered Steve borrowing any of her clothing that night. Marri said, "No." She wasn't asked any of those questions in either trial.

[*Steve said, in October 2015, that he might leave a show once to smoke a cigarette, or twice if it was a really long show, but that was all.*]

I also asked Steve some questions he wasn't asked during the trial. — During the show, did you borrow Marri's jacket and cover yourself with it? Steve said, "No." — Would you have had your own jacket with you? "Absolutely." — So there wouldn't have been any reason to borrow Marri's? "No, and if it was November and I'd have walked from the truck to the theater, I would not have left my jacket in the truck. I would always have had it with me." — Did you tell Hanna to cover herself with her own jacket? "No." — Did you touch Hanna in any inappropriate way, under jackets or otherwise, during the movie? "No." — Did she touch you? "No." — If Marri was sitting next to you, would she have noticed if you were doing any of the things that Hanna claimed was happening under the jackets? "Sure. I don't see why not. Anybody would notice."

[*Flat denials. He said he didn't do it, and anybody would have noticed. There's also the issue of Marri's jacket to consider. Steve is 5'11." Marri, even today, nineteen years later, is just over five feet. In 2001, at the age of nine, she was truly tiny. Check out the picture of ten-year-old Marri on the blog.*]

https://aggravatedbook.com/images-for-the-night-of-harry-potter-chapters/

Let's break those questions and answers down a little.

Analysis: Hanna told Ada Dixon that Steve fondled her breasts inside the theater and attempted to put his hand down her jeans, but didn't say a word about masturbating him. I can't imagine that Dixon would have left that piece of information out of her summary if Hanna had said anything at all about it.

As an indication that parts of Hanna's scenario were possibly still being written two years later, in her interview with Tom she seemed unsure about what happened inside the theater. Her sentences were broken into fragments like "...and then we got ...he didn't do anything..." "...got his daughter's jacket. No wait. Hang on ...yeah, he got his daughter's jacket ...jacket." It seemed as if she was still working out the details. Also, as with Dixon, she said nothing to Tom about masturbating Steve in the theater. Was Elmer Ross surprised when Bevin Jenkins brought up the fondling and masturbation in the theater? Wouldn't he have questioned Hanna about that himself if he had known about them? Could Hanna have decided to add the masturbation in the theater after she talked to Tom, just two months before the first trial?

Hanna also told Tom about the teenagers who supposedly noticed what they were doing, saying that the fondling and the attempts to slip a hand inside her underwear <u>were already underway</u>, and that prompted Steve to say, "We better stop because they're getting kind of suspicious." When Tom asked her what happened next she first said "That was it," but then added, "He tried to mess with me once or twice after that, not real long, then quit." That's another example of her changing her mind in mid-thought, then adding more, as if she had suddenly realized that he wouldn't likely have stopped that quickly. Also, why would she make a point of saying that Steve put Marri's jacket over his lap if she wasn't going to claim that she masturbated him? Was she hiding information from Tom that she intended to use in court?

In the first trial, she was more specific than she was with Tom, as if she had ironed out the kinks in this part of the story, but had she? In that trial, she painted a picture of them reclining in the movie theater chairs, with jackets covering their torsos, but <u>before</u> they could get started, the loud teenagers were "making smart remarks." She said that Steve told her to calm down so they wouldn't notice. Within two months, "stop" (<u>because</u> they see us) had become "calm down" (<u>so they won't</u> see us). Her scenes were also chronologically out of order. She told Tom they were already fooling around, and stopped because they were attracting attention, but in Trial #1, she said the rowdy "teenagers" noticed them covering themselves up and made their lewd remarks before they did anything. Two different versions.

Hanna said she was hot when Steve wanted her to pretend she was cold. One of the questions I asked on some local social media groups was about the temperature inside the theater. Maggie Mae Joyner simply said that the inside temperature "wasn't too bad." I also interviewed the theater's manager, who said the company's policy was to adjust the temperature to maintain a constant temperature between 65 and 75 degrees. That's a cold-to-moderate range, but certainly not hot. The only way it might have been warmer would be if the theater was jam packed with bodies, but Hanna said it "was nearly empty." Appearing to bend the temperature to suit her whims happened a lot in the documents I have, but I believe it was just another sign that she might not have actually remembered any of those things, and was just making up whatever she thought would sound good, irrespective of actual conditions.

In Trial # 2, Hanna took a different tack, making little mention of people noticing them, but generally treated the scene (like those in the truck) as if she and Steve were isolated, with no one around to bother them. Unfortunately, just as the jury in Trial #1 couldn't compare Tom's interview with what they heard, the jury in Trial #2 also didn't get to hear what Hanna told Tom or what she testified to in Trial #1. And let's not forget the hand switch. In Trial #1 she said Steve was fondling her with his right hand. In Trial #2, it was with his left.

A Windbreaker Experiment: Before we get to the experiment itself, I need to mention one of Hanna's comments about windbreakers and the available light. Tom asked her what kind of jacket she was wearing that night, and she said "a blue and black windbreaker," which does sound like the wrong gear for cold weather, but he also asked Hanna what kind of jacket Marri had on, because she had just told Tom that Steve borrowed it during the movie. Hanna said, "I don't know what color the jacket she had was or not. I know it was a dark color, but I couldn't see it," giving the impression that it was too dark in the theater to see colors. Didn't she see Marri in her jacket at the Sirois' house both before and after the movie, and in the truck, and waiting in line before the show, and in the light from the screen during the movie? How could someone so unobservant be so sure about her descriptions of everything else?

The movie wasn't mentioned in the affidavit, but fondling under Hanna's windbreaker and attempts to get into her jeans were in both Dixon's summary and Tom's interview. What wasn't in either of those, though, was any hint of Hanna masturbating Steve inside the theater. All three were included in both trials, though.

My wife, Minay, and I did a brief test to see how likely it might be for Hanna's claims to succeed. Just for the record, we are both consenting adults, born mid-twentieth century. We sat beside each other on our couch with our feet up on the coffee table to simulate leaning back in movie theater seats. We draped <u>full-sized</u> windbreakers over ourselves, and Minay reached over into my lap with her right hand while I reached over with my left hand and tried to carry out some of what Hanna said Steve was doing in Trial #2. There were serious problems with the experiment, though, and we didn't have a cup-rest arm-barrier between us, which should have made it easier for us than for them. We were probably in an even more prone position than they likely would have been able to achieve in the theater, but whenever one of us would move, our jackets would slide around. Also, I couldn't slip my hand under her windbreaker without exposing my arm. I also tried rotating my body to the left to better reach her with my right arm (as Hanna said Steve did in one of her versions), but that exposed Minay's right arm even more.

Despite the difficulties we experienced, Hanna testified that Steve reached over and unbuttoned and unzipped her pants after he had already done that for himself (*with one hand? without being noticed? while covered with one very tiny windbreaker?*). Try it. It's impossible to do discreetly. We also tested one other thing while we were at it. Hanna said that her windbreaker was "kind of long," and fit across her whole torso, plus some of her legs, but not quite to her knee. I wondered if windbreakers were long enough to cover someone's entire torso and still go nearly down to their knees. Draping our windbreakers across both of our chests, the bottom hems fell a little below our waists, and Minay is only 5' 1" tall. When we pulled them just halfway down to mid-thigh, our chests were completely exposed. How did Hanna manage to get her windbreaker to cover her entire chest and still come down almost to her knees? What about the arm switch between the two trials? Hanna described Steve trying to fondle her and get into her jeans in two entirely different ways (left hand, right hand) from one trial to the next. In our experiment, neither way worked without exposing arms and other essential body parts.

There's one more crucial element to consider. Steve is 5' 11" tall, but Marri, even today, is barely over five feet. In 2001, at the age of nine, she was tiny. Take a look at the picture of her on the Harry Potter image page on the blog. It was taken in May 2002, six months after they saw *Harry Potter*. Her head is lower than the bed of the Dodge pickup and the hood of the Jeep she's standing in front of. Her jacket would only have fit over a small part of Steve's torso. Why would he borrow a jacket that wouldn't come even remotely close to covering him? Even if it did cover his groin area, Hanna's entire right arm would have been exposed as it slid under the edge of the jacket. Both of Steve's arms would have been completely exposed in any case.

One more thing about the jackets. In her earliest mention of them, Hanna told Ada Dixon that Steve "told me to put my jacket <u>on backwards</u>." To Tom, and in the trials, she switched to saying that Steve told her to "Just put the jacket <u>across you</u>," "put it <u>across your chest</u>." The 2006 comments are distinctly different from what she said to Ada Dixon in 2004. Putting it on backwards means to put your arms through the sleeves with the zipper toward your back. It may have sounded good when she said it, but my guess it that she tried it later and realized how problematic that would have been. She certainly could have done it, but there would have been some distinct disadvantages. First, because of the way her shoulders would fit inside it, the reversed jacket would have pulled higher on her waist, actually reducing the area that was covered. Second, with her arms actually inside the sleeves, everything Hanna described doing would have been hampered, her hands would have been exposed, and the sleeves of the jacket would be visible sliding under the edge of Marri's jacket. Most importantly, the collar of the jacket would press directly into her windpipe. In *Part 2*, Hanna will talk about a phobia of things touching her neck. I don't know if she really had that condition, or if it was just something she said to elicit sympathy, but if she really did have a strong reaction to things touching her neck, she wouldn't have been able to wear her jacket backwards at all. I nearly choked when I tried it, and I'm not sensitive to things touching my neck. After telling Dixon that, it isn't mentioned that way again in any of the documents I have. Her story changed again.

In Trial #2, Hanna said they were under the jackets, and Steve used his right hand to place her right hand on his penis, and held her right hand down with his. Then he "somehow managed" to use his left hand to get under her tight, fitted, strawberry-red shirt with the little holes in it, plus push her sports bra up out of the way so he could start fondling her breasts. With his left hand? He couldn't possibly do that without exposing his entire left arm, which seems to me would have to be done with the arm held high and rotated backwards at the shoulder. Try it.

While he was doing that, he was also supposedly keeping her right hand moving with his right hand, while also making sure the jackets didn't slide around, fall off, or bounce up and down. It would have been easier to just roll in her direction and use his right hand (not his left) to fondle her with (which is what she said he did in Trial #1). Notice that she also said in Trial #1 that Steve placed Marri's jacket in his lap (not across his torso). As small as the jacket was, that would have left both of his arms and Hanna's right arm visible. Anything happening under Marri's little bitty jacket would be extremely obvious. And wouldn't lying on his left side watching a movie have also been particularly noticeable? Besides, if Steve *had* rolled in her direction and used his right hand, the logistics of everything else she claimed wouldn't work, and his arm would have been even more exposed. No matter which version she claimed at any given moment, I don't think it could possibly happen without them being seen.

Changes: Hanna told Dixon that Steve felt her breasts with an unspecified hand; To Tom, she said he put his (also unspecified) hand up her shirt; In Trial #1, she said that he reached over with his right hand and fondled her chest; In Trial #2, she said he held her right hand on his penis with his right hand, and used his left hand to fondle her breasts. [*A hand, a hand, right hand, left hand*]. She told Ada Dixon that he tried to get in her pants, but she wouldn't let him. To Tom, she said that he did unbutton her jeans and slipped his hand inside, but she wouldn't let him go any further. In Trial #2, she said he <u>tried</u> to unbutton her pants, but she stopped him. [*Didn't unbutton, Did unbutton, Didn't unbutton.*] How many sets of lies do you think could be buried inside those conflicting groups of actions?

Unaddressed Topics: Hanna talked about unruly teenagers, and about how Steve was worried about them noticing. Wouldn't he have been just as worried about whether Marri, mere inches away, would notice? Hanna said that Marri was sitting right next to Steve. No one asked Marri if she witnessed any of these incidents in the theater, or if Steve had borrowed her jacket. Even more amazing, in Trial #2, she wasn't asked a single specific question about what happened before, during, or after the show. They could even have had Steve stand up and hold one of Marri's 2001-era windbreakers in front of him to show how small it was, but they didn't.

Also, erections don't instantly dissipate. Hanna said that Steve, because he had no success getting below her panty line, just stopped and left for a smoke break, but she didn't mention that he would first have to sit there in his seat, and wait for his penis to soften and shrink down enough to get it tucked safely inside his jeans/pants/shorts, and he would have to arrange those shorts/pants/jeans before he zipped them up and rebuckled his belt.

Another big omission was about the other side effect of erections — seminal fluid. Men leak. They leak a lot, whether they climax or not. Hanna didn't mention anything of a liquid nature coming out of Steve's penis until later that night (that's in *Part* 2), and yet she claimed she had massaged his penis twice, once in the truck, and once in the theater. There's not a word about stickiness or drippiness in her interview or in any of her testimony until they asked her about Steve ejaculating later that night, and even then the only moisture she mentioned was the ejaculate itself.

Here's the thing I find hardest to believe, though. How stupid would Steve have to be to take a chance on getting seminal fluid or ejaculate all over the inside of his daughter's jacket before he handed it back to her to wear home?

Hanna's story makes no sense.

Conclusion: Seriously, someone convince me that two people, with another person sitting right next to them, could do any of this without being noticed. What about the curious teenagers who were supposedly sitting over their left shoulder, and the audience sitting all around them? Anyone sitting in front of them, just by turning around, could have seen what Hanna said they were doing because of the light from the screen. Also, Marri, sitting right next to them, would have noticed Steve turning on his left side, or would have heard them bickering ("Why not?" "Because." "Why?" "I just don't want to." "I'm hot."), or would have seen Hanna's and Steve's crossed arms, not to mention the shifting jackets while he slid Hanna's shirt and bra up, unbuttoned and unzipped her jeans, unbuttoned and unzipped his own jeans (all with one hand), dragged her arm over onto his lap, and wrestled with her left hand while he tried to slip his hand underneath her underwear. According to Hanna, all of their hands were occupied under the jackets, but what about the arms that would have been out in the open, crossing the space between the jackets? Wouldn't they have been more than obvious? Also, Hanna consistently described these jackets as windbreakers, which are slick and have practically no weight to hold them down. They wouldn't have been able to keep them from, inevitably, sliding around. If Hanna wanted the jury to believe that the people across the aisle would have noticed something, how could she possibly expect them to believe that Marri (or Aaron, or Beau) wouldn't have seen it too? Not credible at all. And, yes, let's not forget the lack of moisty stickiness.

Here's the last question.

What Happened When They Left the Theater?

Why is This Important? It isn't. Everyone agreed about this, but just for the record, let's hear it from Hanna. She told Tom, "...on the way home, on the way to his house, actually, nothing happened." In Trial #2, Ross asked her what happened after the movie. She said, "We all piled back in the truck and went back to Sirois' home and nothing out of the ordinary happened."

[*The movie finished, they went back to Steve's house.*]

They left the theater, drove straight to the Sirois' home, and nothing happened on the way. Why they drove straight there is covered in *Part 02 – After the Movie.*

Conclusion: Given what I believe was Hanna's intent to convince everyone that Steve was a raving sex maniac, I would have expected her to say that he gave it another try on the way home. Considering everything else she had already presented to the jury, did she think another fondling session would be a bit over the top? She had already jumped the shark once with the gymnastics in the truck, followed by the juggling act inside the theater, and she still had to describe the incidents that allegedly happened later that night, with Marri in the same bed. Maybe she decided that there had already been enough sexual accusations to take place during the early part of the evening, so she said, "nothing out of the ordinary happened." And everyone agreed.

Ready to wrap this chapter up?

Final Thoughts About Part 1

First, a quick summary of the opposing viewpoints.

Hanna's final claim (after she ditched the date in her affidavit) was that, sometime near Thanksgiving 2001, five people (herself, Aaron, Beau, Marri, and Steve) drove from the Sirois' home to a movie theater, a distance of twenty-one miles. She said it was after dark when they left; and, in the dim interior of Beau's truck, Steve took her hand, pulled it onto his lap, and had her stroke his penis. Hanna also said that Steve made a "kissy face" at her, so she leaned forward, even though she had her seat belt on—something she didn't mention until she was asked about it—and gave him a kiss (which, in Trial #1, she said was the second one of the evening, and then, in Trial #2, changed it back to one kiss even though her two-kiss testimony was in the trial record). By default, one or both of those statements have to be lies. Hanna also said that Aaron saw the kiss, but forgot that he saw it, and a couple of years later (when Ada Dixon supposedly asked him about it) didn't want to talk about it. When they got to the theater that night, she said Steve made her stop stroking him because of all the lights at the mall.

Then she said that the movie, a late show, was delayed somehow, and they had to wait for about an hour outside (which she said was a hallway in the second trial), but they were finally let in. She said they sat on the left aisle, in the very back row of the theater, and that Steve sat just to her right, Marri was to the right of Steve, and Aaron and Beau were to the right of Marri. Hanna said Steve got up and left every five or ten minutes or so, and asked her questions about the movie each time he returned because she had read all the Harry Potter books. Then she said he told her to take off her jacket and cover her torso with it. She complained because she was hot, but complied after much discussion and disagreement, including raucous comments from nearby teenagers who seemed to be noticing what they were doing. She said that Steve didn't have a jacket, so he borrowed Marri's; and that, underneath their jackets, she played with Steve's penis again, while he fondled her chest and tried to put his hand inside her jeans, but she wouldn't let him. Then, when the movie was over, they drove back to Steve's house, but nothing happened on the way back.

The defense's version of that night is simpler. The same five people drove to the theater in Beau's truck. Beau drove, Steve rode shotgun, and the kids were in the back, with Marri in the middle. They bought tickets, went inside, watched the show, and then drove back to Steve's house. No waiting, no groping, no kissing, no fondling. Just a movie.

Everyone was in agreement that they saw the movie around Thanksgiving 2001, at the Filmland Theatre in Bloom, Texas. Hanna made some contradictory claims about the ride in the truck, first describing the events in a way that made it seem like no one else was paying any attention to what was happening. Then she added the element of the kiss (or kisses), but— to explain how she could get away with that—said that the other occupants of the truck were laughing and joking and didn't notice. If everyone was so active, though, laughing and kidding around, it would have been even less likely that she and Steve could get away with what she claimed. Plus, even if the drive had been under the exact conditions Hanna claimed (in terms of distance, time of evening, darkness, etc.), she still couldn't have physically done what she claimed she did.

Hanna also wanted the jury to believe that it was a late movie, but everyone else thinks they left the house around dusk. Hanna's claim of darkness on the way to the theater was the best way to convince a jury that it was difficult for the others to see what was happening. At that time of year, though, it would have still been partially light out during the drive. Also, since three of the people in the truck were young (9, 10, and 12) none of the adults would have wanted them up after midnight when an early show was available. Steve also wouldn't want to be up late because he might have to work the next day. They almost certainly went to the 7:00 pm showing.

It was a cold November night, by Hanna's own admission (which is logical for that time of year), but she told Tom that, even though Steve didn't have a jacket with him, he was wearing denim shorts and a two or three-button striped polo shirt, which she changed to a t-shirt during her trial testimony. Everyone else, including Hanna, had on jeans and jackets. It doesn't make sense that Steve wouldn't be dressed that way too. Did Hanna dress him as coatless and in summer clothes to create a reason for borrowing Marri's jacket inside the theater? As absurd as Hanna's claims are about using Marri's small jacket, without it none of the claims would have been even remotely possible. Did she come up with the idea of Steve using Marri's jacket after she realized she hadn't given him one in any of her earlier descriptions? And why would he borrow his daughter's extremely tiny jacket to cover up with, knowing that his semen could get all over it. Is it even conceivable that he would take a chance that he might have to hand a sticky unexplainable mess back to his daughter to wear home when, according to Hanna, his purpose for borrowing the jacket in the first place was ostensibly to keep her from discovering what he was doing? Absolutely ridiculous.

Hanna also said the screening room was nearly empty because of the late hour, Beau and Steve have both said it was fairly full, and they weren't the only ones. My request to local social media groups about the movie, returned comments from Nathan Brooks and Maggie Mae Joyner. Nathan said he remembered the theater "being packed." Maggie Mae said the *Harry Potter* showings were running at "full capacity," and even the late showing she saw "was 3/4 full." A near-empty theater also doesn't support Hanna's claim that the theater was overly warm. A packed theater would more logically translate to the possibility of a warmer room. She can't have it both ways.

The details in Hanna's multiple versions shifted and changed with each retelling. She may have worked on this narrative for at least two years, but the trial transcripts, along with interviews and the other sources, show that there is very little in this story that is credible. In addition to Steve's clothing being all wrong for the season, no one else remembers a delay that night, or waiting, or moving to another screening room, or a near-empty theater. Combine all of that with Hanna's ridiculous accusations about incidents in the truck and the theater, and it's obvious that much of it is downright impossible. Add everything together and I believe there might be enough untruths to call this part of the evening a fairly sizable pack of lies.

Finally, during Trial #1, Elmer Ross made an interesting comment when he tried to suggest that Bevin Jenkins might have coached Marri into giving false testimony. His premise seemed to be that, because Marri's testimony was contrary to Hanna's, it had to be false. Ross tried to get Marri to say that Jenkins had talked to her <u>after</u> Hanna testified and had told her what to say. Marri said, no, Jenkins had discussed the case with her and her family days <u>before</u> the trial, and he had talked to them about the <u>kinds of questions</u> they might be asked, as any attorney would have done (as Ross had also undoubtedly done with Hanna). Ross closed his questioning of Marri by asking her, "Nothing out of the ordinary happened to you that night for you to have such a vivid recollection as to where everyone was seated at the time, did it?"

I would have thought that seeing a girl, who was sitting beside her in a truck, masturbate her father, or seeing that girl kiss her father twice on the lips, or seeing additional masturbation and fondling in a movie theater happening under the tiny jacket her father had just borrowed from her, would qualify as more than a little bit "out of the ordinary." How could Marri not have seen all of that? The answer, I think, is obvious. Marri and the others didn't have a "vivid recollection" of the evening because "nothing out of the ordinary" happened that night.

It was just a ride in a truck to see a movie.

The Night of Harry Potter, Part 2

"It were better that ten suspected witches should escape
than one innocent person be condemned."
Increase Mather (Salem Witch Trials, 1692)

"You'll never get mixed up if you simply tell the truth.
Then you don't have to remember what you said,
and you never forget what you have said."
Sam Rayburn

This chapter is about Count I of the indictment against Steve, which alleged that he performed oral sex on Hanna. He was only convicted of that one count. Yes, in case you're wondering, that means that everything I just covered in *Harry Potter, Part 01* has nothing to do with the charges in the first count. Was it a waste to spend so much space covering the ride in the truck and the movie theater? No. The over-selling of Hanna's story that you saw in that chapter and in *A Cross-Country Meet* follows the pattern of other statements she made in the trials and elsewhere. I think it became obvious to her that many of her stories wouldn't stand on their own merit, which could be why she enhanced her testimony with lots of lurid details. She may have thought it was the only way the jury would believe her. It just made me more suspicious.

Elmer Ross went to great lengths during the voir dire to explain to the jury pool how the phrase "on or about" gave them a great deal of leeway as to when Hanna said things happened. That might have been a necessity for their case because, by the time of the trials, Hanna had changed everything she had sworn to in the affidavit. Probably less than twenty percent of the testimony in the trial was directly related to the incidents described in the three counts, and that testimony was distinctly different from what Hanna alleged in the affidavit. The rest of the trial testimony was filled with descriptions of other alleged incidents, the bolstering of those incidents, and with expert witnesses describing hypothetical situations which happened to closely match Hanna's story. The trial, of course, eventually came down to Hanna's word against Steve's. Her additional details were there to create a picture that her audience (the jury) would accept as true; but, as we saw in *Part 1*, a number of Hanna's claims can be disproved. Let's see if we can also do that in *Part 2* as well.

The questions I'm going to explore in this chapter involve what may or may not have happened at the Sirois' home after the movie: "What does Hanna's affidavit actually accuse Steve of?" "What was the plan for after the movie?" "What were the sleeping arrangements?" "What did Hanna and Steve wear to bed?" "What happened at the Sirois' house that night?" "Why didn't Marri notice this?" "What happened the next morning?" And a bonus question, "Why are everyone's memories so different?"

What I'm asking you to do is to look at the things I can prove to be true, and those which I can prove to be untrue, and decide whether Hanna, who seemed to be capable of telling so many lies, was also lying about the few things I can't definitively prove.

I will again reference some images during this chapter. You'll find them on the blog at:

https://aggravatedbook.com/images-for-the-night-of-harry-potter-chapters/

[Subsections in this Chapter: After the Movie // Final Thoughts About Part 2]

After the Movie

What Does Hanna's Affidavit Actually Accuse Steve Of?

Why is This Important? Did Hanna's affidavit say anything about going to a movie? No. Did that matter to the prosecution? No. Thanks to the phrase "on or about," all they had to do to convict Steve of Count I was get the jury to agree that he performed oral sex on Hanna in the general vicinity of September 1, 2001 (apparently that could include a date within a few months or so in either direction). To have a baseline to compare everything to, though, we have to start with the affidavit. It was created from notes that Willard Knox took during Hanna's deposition on April 8, 2004. We already covered the affidavit earlier, so we'll just look at the two excerpts that pertain to Count I.

Here's the part that was used to establish the date and time of the first incident.

> "The first time I was sexually assaulted by Steve Sirois was in late August or early September 2001 when I was 12 years old. This happened the first time I spent the night at Steve Sirois's house."

I believe it's possible that Hanna hadn't been abused by anyone by the time of Blake Goudy's April 7th talk, but after telling Karla Spivey she had been, she said that Karla pressured her to tell Goudy about it. Goudy later told Deputy Knox that Hanna "did not go into any details" with him, but said that he told her to have her mother call him. If she actually hadn't been abused, she could have halted her predicament by simply not telling her mother, but she didn't do that. After seeing the fury in Darla's eyes when she said that Steve was her abuser, Hanna must have known she would have to give the sheriff's office more than the vague version she gave Goudy. She likely spent that evening thinking about what she had already told other people, and started forming a narrative that she thought would satisfy Knox.

Here's the other excerpt from the affidavit, which described the action that became the specific incident spelled out in Count I.

> "I remember I was sleeping in the same bed with Marri Sirois, who was about 9 years old. Sometime during the night I was awaken by Steve, by him shaking my shoulder. When I started to say something to him he put

> his hand over mouth to keep me quiet. I further remember I was wearing a T-shirt and blue jean shorts. He then removed my shorts and underwear. I remember he started kissing me and then he put his mouth on my vagina. I further remember he then stuck his tongue inside my vagina. He did this for several minutes. After he stopped, he told me goodnight and he left the bedroom."

Count I was developed from those two excerpts. Before I try to disprove it, here is the exact wording of the grand jury's indictment for that count.

> "Count I, Steven Barker Sirois, hereinafter styled the Defendant, on or about the 1st day of September, 2001, and before the presentement of this indictment, in the County and State aforesaid, did then and there intentionally and knowingly cause the penetration of the sexual organ of Hanna Penderfield, a child who was then and there younger than 14 years of age and not the spouse of the Defendant, by the Defendant's tongue."

To garner a unanimous vote of guilty from the jury on Count I, the prosecution had to prove that Steve committed this one act of oral sex on Hanna while she was under the age of 14. His conviction and entire 35-year sentence was based on this single act, but her affidavit only bears a superficial resemblance to her testimony. The inaccuracies in the affidavit are striking. The count probably should have begun "On or about November 23, 2001," but when Hanna met with Knox I don't think she even had an inkling that the night of the movie would become part of her story. Later, though, if she realized how flawed that original document was, she may have started inventing additional incidents to make Steve's alleged actions sound more horrendous. It felt to me like her *modus operandi* eventually became: *Don't say he did one thing when I can say he did four or five.* So, at some point the incidents in the truck and at the movie were included, plus additional details and actions were added for what supposedly happened after they had returned to the house. I'll cover all of that in the other questions below.

Analysis: The charge in Count I was that, "on or about the 1st day of September, 2001," Steve penetrated Hanna's vagina with his tongue. In the affidavit, Hanna said that "the first time" it happened "was in late August or early September 2001," but she also said that it happened the first time she "spent the night." Soon after creating the affidavit she started changing her story. There were no physically impossible gymnastic acts included in Count I (like those in the truck), but let's see what I can do with the affidavit's date, its phrasing, and the clothing.

The Date: The prosecution went to great lengths to tell the jury that the phrase "on or about" a certain date allowed them to not be pinned down to an exact day and time. Even if that's true legally, there still should be a reasonable assumption that the date on which the crime occurred was fairly close to the alleged date, shouldn't there? If the prosecution doesn't have to establish a date within a narrow range, how can the defendant possibly be expected to provide an accurate alibi? I think they used "on or about" as a crutch. It allowed Hanna to say whatever she wanted to, because she could easily fall back to a position of, *Well, I don't remember the exact date, I just know it happened.*

Hanna and Aaron didn't spend the night at Steve's until the night they saw *Harry Potter*, but the trip to the movie wasn't in the affidavit at all, and the brief mention of the movie in Dixon's summary didn't say anything about it being the first time they spent the night. Maybe that incorrect statement in the affidavit bothered Hanna as much as it did me, so she spent the next two years trying to adjust it to make it work.

The Phrasing: The last four lines of this section of the affidavit always felt odd to me. Imagine them being read in a Stephen Hawking-style computer voice. Here they are. "I remember he started kissing me and then he put his mouth on my vagina. I further remember he then stuck his tongue inside my vagina. He did this for several minutes. After he stopped, he told me goodnight and he left the bedroom." The wording is so clinical, not at all like the Hanna I heard on the audio recording of her interview with Tom. Those four sentences contain most of the details that became Count I, but none of the other ridiculous things she later claimed happened that night were even hinted at in the affidavit. This is also true for Counts II and III. They also don't remotely resemble the claims she made in the trials either. Why not?

The Clothing: In the affidavit Hanna didn't say what Steve was wearing that night, but she did say that she had on "a T-shirt and blue jean shorts." After she adjusted her own clothing to be more suitable for late-November, why didn't she do the same for Steve? She hadn't mentioned his clothes in the affidavit anyway. Could she have told Willard Knox that Steve was in shorts and a t-shirt too, and assumed the defense had that information?

A Little Side-Note: I don't want to go all crazy conspiracy theory on you, but could Hanna's changes to her story be one of the reasons that Willard Knox's additional notes, documentation, and possible audio tapes on the case have mysteriously disappeared from the sheriff's office? In fairness, they have never given me a definitive answer as to whether interviews were taped in 2004 or not, but they still couldn't find Knox's notes anywhere.

The Additional Details: Of the other things that Hanna mentioned in the affidavit, Marri sleeping in the bed with her and Steve giving her oral sex were the only two items that made it into her trial testimony. Her blue jean shorts were replaced with clothing for colder weather, she said she was both awake <u>and</u> asleep (we'll get to that), and she never again claimed that Steve woke her up by shaking her shoulder or that he put his hand over her mouth to keep her quiet. That was all gone.

Conclusion: When you consider the radical changes that happened to Hanna's story after the affidavit was created, along with the fact that it took over two years to bring the case to trial, it feels like the prosecution was never sure they had a winnable case. I don't know what the impetus was for the changes she made. Maybe Elmer Ross was an influence. Perhaps he expressed dissatisfaction with the skimpy amount of information he had to work with. Or, maybe Hanna's fear of her deception being uncovered caused her to pile detail upon detail. The one thing I can say for certain is that I find it hard to believe those details. Even though the specifics in the affidavit were accepted by the grand jury, and were established in the indictment as the legal parameters for the trial, Hanna changed the date established for the first count, changed her description of the clothes she was wearing, put clothes on Steve that were completely wrong for the season, and added a mass of other details that I don't think were even in her mental incubator when she talked to Willard Knox. If the prosecution had been required to prove Count I exactly as Hanna described it in her affidavit, they might not have even brought the case to trial, especially since Counts II and III also bore no resemblance to the affidavit.

Her versions are full of holes that have been stuffed with nonsense.

Let's find out how Hanna and Aaron ended up spending the night.

What Was the Plan for After the Movie?

Why is This Important? There are (again) two opposing viewpoints here. Hanna said that Steve brought her and Aaron to his home first instead of just taking them home, and waited until they were there before asking Darla to let them spend the night. Hanna said that was a calculated decision on Steve's part, claiming that he took advantage of the lateness of the movie to gain access to her. Let's explore her statements and testimony and see where they lead us.

Hanna didn't mention going to see the movie in her affidavit, and in Dixon's summary she simply said (almost as if that was where they were supposed to be), "We got to his house at 1:00 am." She also told Tom that they "didn't get there until one in the morning," but added, "…um, he called my mom when we got back to his house, and said 'Well, it's really late. Just let the kids stay here, and I'll take them home in the morning.' And Mom, she was like half-asleep, she was like 'Okay,' you know. I mean she just wanted to go back to sleep. I mean she cared, but she was like 'Are you sure they're not a problem? And he was like, 'No, no. It'll be fine, it'll be fine.' She was like, 'Okay.' Because, you know, she trusted him. He was her …best friend."

[*Hanna, after a slight hesitation, told Tom that Steve didn't take them home* <u>*because*</u> *it was so late. Was that an attempt to convince Tom that spending the night wasn't accidental? In Dixon's summary, though, arriving at Steve's house was simply presented as a fact (although, as I've said, I believe they arrived much earlier). There was also no mention of a phone call or a request for the kids to stay overnight in Dixon's summary, and none of the Sirois family members remember Steve calling Darla when they got to the house.*]

During the trials, Hanna advanced the time even later into the night. In Trial #1, Elmer Ross asked her if she had planned to spend the night. She said, "No, I was supposed to go see the movie and I believe he was to take me and my little brother home." He asked her why Steve didn't do that. She said, "Because it was 1:00, 1:30 in the morning. My mom was already asleep. And everybody was just tired. The movie was so long." Ross asked if anyone let Darla know what was going on. Hanna said, "Sirois called my mom as soon as he walked into the door," and, she added, "I was standing about ten or twelve feet away from him, so I heard everything."

[*Hanna waited until the trials to say that they expected to be taken home, and, since she was standing only* "ten or twelve feet away," *she* "heard everything" *Darla said to Steve, so the call must have happened, right?*]

In Trial #2, Ross again asked what the plan was. Hanna said, "Honestly, I didn't know what the plan was, I just knew we were supposed to go watch the movie and then, to my knowledge, he was supposed to take me and my little brother home, but because of the conflict with the movie and how late it was by the time we got out, it was maybe 1:30, 2:00 o'clock by the time we finally got back to his house. So, as soon as we walked in the door, he called my mom and just asked her if it was all right if the kids, me and my brother, could just stay the night."

[*In Trial #1, Hanna said she thought the plan was to take them home, but in Trial #2 she* "didn't know what the plan was." *And she pushed the time again (from 1:00 to 1:30 to 2:00). My guess is they were back at the house shortly after 10:00 pm, so there would have been plenty of time for Steve to take them home to Alderson if that* had *been the plan.*]

In 2014, I asked Beau and Marri where they went after the movie. They both said they went straight home. I asked Beau if that was the first time Hanna and Aaron spent the night at the house. He said, "Yeah. To be honest, I can't remember her staying before that. I can't say it didn't happen, but I can't say it did either." Marri said she didn't remember any discussion about whether to take Hanna and Aaron home, and didn't remember her dad calling Darla when they got there.

[*They went straight home. Beau didn't think Hanna had spent the night before then, but he wasn't positive. Marri, who was only nine at the time, didn't remember a discussion or a phone call to Darla. They just came home.*]

In 2015, I asked Steve why they didn't just take Hanna and Aaron home from the movie. He said, "I don't actually remember, but I'm pretty sure they were supposed to stay at our house already. I'm sure it was already prearranged." I asked him if he had discussed it with Darla, and he said, "Absolutely. I wouldn't have just done it without asking, without discussing it with Darla, and it was more than likely Darla's initiation." I asked him why she would want him and Robin to keep her kids overnight. Steve said, "So she could go out. That's what she always did. Usually to the VFW." I asked if this was the first time she had done that. He said, "I can't say if it was the first or not." I said, "Don't remember?" He answered, "Yeah. You know me and dates anyway, but that specifically I don't remember. It was a common occurrence." I asked him if he remembered calling Darla from the movie, either on his cell phone or once they got home. Steve said, "No."

[*Steve said he didn't call Darla because spending the night was probably her idea. Did she just want some "me" time? Steve said that she would often go out and leave the kids with them.*]

Here's one other point that wasn't brought up in either trial. The prosecution's focus was on why Steve waited until they got back to his house before he called Darla (maybe as late as 2:00 am according to Hanna's fourth version). Think about this, though. If someone (even a person you knew and trusted) took your kids somewhere like to a movie, and was supposed to bring them to your house afterward, wouldn't you be on the phone by around 11:00, trying to make sure he and the kids weren't splattered all over a road somewhere? In the trials, Hanna was the only one who was asked what was supposed to happen after the show. Why wasn't Darla asked if she got a call from Steve? And (if Hanna's story about the lateness of the show was true), why didn't Darla call either Steve or Robin, or both of them, long before midnight? Steve had a cell phone with him. If the expectation was that he was going to drive Hanna and Aaron to Alderson after the show, he would have called Darla from the theater if it looked like the show was going to run late.

Analysis: Was there a plan, or no plan at all? Hanna's claim was that a confluence of events gave Steve the opportunity he had been waiting for, a chance to get her alone so he could molest her. She said in the trials that she thought "he was supposed to take me and my little brother home," and it was only because the show "messed up" that they got out so late. Her arrival times at the house became progressively later with each retelling of the story. She stuck with 1:00 am for both Dixon and Tom, but in the trials she jumped from 1:00 am to 1:30 (Trial #1) to 1:30 am to 2:00 (Trial #2).

Steve said that, if Hanna and Aaron were going to stay there that night, "it would have been cleared one way or the other." He and Beau both agreed that Darla often dumped the kids on them so she could go partying. Steve said, "It was not uncommon for her to go bar-hopping and leave the kids with us." This might have been the first time she did that.

Hanna said that Steve called her mother as soon as they got to his house. The first record we have of her saying that was during Tom's 2006 interview, which suggests that she might not have immediately generated the idea of having the indictment's first incident of molestation be on the night they went to see *Harry Potter*. Why would she tell Deputy Knox that it happened in late summer and then change it to late-November? She may have also confused Ada Dixon about the sequence of events. One of Dixon's comments in the summary read, "At this point all of this was happening every two weeks," which inaccurately made it sound like that night's molestation was just one in an already ongoing series of incidents. Dixon also said "this probably happened at age thirteen (13)." That would only be true if they saw the movie after Hanna's February 2002 birthday, but the first Harry Potter movie was gone from Deep Springs by January 2002. Dixon could have been confused about the sequence because of Hanna's habit of free-form time jumping, and thought they saw the movie much later than they did. That may also have helped Dixon believe there had been enough time for grooming, but in my opinion it doesn't say much for her ability to accurately judge what her patients tell her.

Did Hanna tell the DA that Steve had called her mother? If she had, wouldn't he have asked Darla to corroborate that at the trials? Was the phone call an invention to allow Hanna to blame spending the night on a much-too-late movie? Was her full-blown recitation to Tom of Steve's conversation with her mother a practice run for Trial #1? I'd like to know how she managed to hear her mother's side of the conversation from "ten or twelve feet away." Was she suggesting that Steve had switched on the speakerphone that he didn't have? Does she have bat ears as well as gorilla arms? She did streamline the story for Trial #2, simply saying that Steve called right away "and just asked if it was all right" for them to spend the night. Steve told me, "We would have made sure that Darla didn't want us to bring them home, or whether they were going to stay at the house, or whatever." He also said he didn't make a call to Darla because he believed she had already said she wanted the kids to spend the night. It was a pre-arranged decision, but he wasn't asked about it in the trials, and neither were Darla, Marri, Robin, or Beau (or Aaron, of course). If it hadn't already been arranged, and the movie was running late, Steve would have called Darla from the theater to ask what she wanted him to do.

You can see a map of the potential routes and distances on the blog, but if they had driven Hanna and Aaron home from the theater, the round trip from Steve's to the theater, to Hanna's, and then back to Steve's would have been 54.8 miles (20.6 miles from Steve's to the mall, then 12.9 from there to Darla's, and 21.3 to Steve's from Darla's). If they drove to the Sirois' house first, called Darla from there, and she had insisted on having the kids home that night, the round trip would have been 83.8 miles (20.6 from Steve's to the mall, plus 20.6 home, then 21.3 to Darla's, and 21.3 home again). Why would he take a chance on driving an extra 29 miles when he could have simply called Darla from the theater to ask her? If, however, Steve already knew that Darla was going to come pick the kids up the next morning, his total mileage would only be 41.8 miles round trip from the house to the theater and back again. Maybe the more important question is, if Hanna's version of the events was true, and Steve was supposed to bring her and Aaron home right after the movie was over, why didn't Darla call Steve or Robin long before midnight, asking why the kids weren't home yet?

Conclusion: Whether there was a plan or not depends partly on what Darla did that night. She had been raising two kids by herself for over four years by then. Did she need a night away from them, either just as a break or to seek some adult companionship? I don't know. Hanna made an interesting comment in Trial #2, though. Ross wanted to know how often they went to get-togethers at the Sirois' house. He asked how often her family visited on "weekdays, weekends, or what?" She told him that it was weekends, but added that, "as time went on, my mom went by herself on Wednesdays." Steve and the others have said that they never had get-togethers during the week, and that Darla only visited on Fridays or Saturdays. I've often wondered what Darla was doing on Wednesday evenings that she didn't tell her kids about?

Hanna claimed that Steve was leaving the movie every "five or ten minutes." He might have left once or twice, as he said he did sometimes in long movies, but if he had gone out to the lobby as often as Hanna said he did, he would have had plenty of opportunities to call Darla and say something like, "It looks like this movie is going to run late. Do you want me to bring the kids home as soon as we get out?" The fact that he didn't call her from there could simply mean that he didn't think it was necessary (as opposed to Hanna's idea that he waited until they got to his house so he could have access to her). Neither Steve nor Beau seemed concerned about notifying Darla. Maybe because she had already asked Steve and Robin to keep her kids that night?

In the trials, though, no one asked Darla if Steve had called her, or if she had wanted Steve and Robin to keep the kids that night. Hanna was the only one who said Steve made the call. Did Elmer Ross know Hanna was going to say that in court? If she had told him in advance, it could have been verified with phone records. A prosecutor would have loved having concrete evidence that part of his client's story was true. Hanna was also the only person who said that she and Aaron didn't know there was a plan. Could she have known all along that they were going to spend the night, but decided to selectively forget that to make Steve look a bit more despicable?

Ultimately, if there had been a plan, whether Hanna and Aaron knew about it or not, the plan had to have originated with Darla. Did she ask Steve and Robin to keep the kids that night so she could go do something else? If there was no plan for the kids to spend the night, and Steve hadn't called by late in the evening, Darla would have wondered why her kids weren't home yet, and she would have called Steve to make sure everything was okay. In the summer of 2003, according to Hanna, Darla called her when she was just a few minutes late getting home from the rodeo. If that was true in 2003, wouldn't she have been just as worried about Hanna and Aaron when they were two years younger?

Hanna's story is full of inconsistencies, and can't be trusted.

Regardless, the whole crew made it to the house. What happened next?

What Were the Sleeping Arrangements?

Why is This Important? Hanna claimed that Steve (for his own nefarious purposes) made specific decisions about where everyone slept. This idea, like the ever-changing show times, and the delays to start the movie, and the phone call to Darla, was also a late addition to Hanna's story. She didn't say anything about it in the affidavit, or to Ada Dixon during their early sessions, or to Tom, and no one else was asked about it during either trial. Since Hanna was the only person to have anything to say about it, these excerpts will mostly be hers.

In her affidavit, after giving a vague date of "late September or early August 2001" for the first time she spent the night, Hanna said, "I was sleeping in the same bed with Marri Sirois who was about 9 years old." She didn't mention where Aaron or Beau were, or that they were even there.

[*Just in* "the same bed with Marri," *but no indication of which bed that was.*]

In May 2004, Hanna told Dixon, "We got to his house at 1:00 am. I was asleep beside his daughter in the bed closest to the door."

[*She didn't mean there were two beds, and she slept in the bed that was closest to the door. There was just one bed in the room, and she and Marri were both in it.*]

In Trial #1, Hanna said, "In Beau's room, there was a full-sized bed. And I was to sleep in it with his daughter, Marri." Ross asked if she had been told "how or where to sleep on the bed." [*Was that leading the witness?*] She said, "Yes. Sirois told me to sleep on the side closest to the door." Ross asked her why. She said, "It took me a couple of minutes. I thought, 'Why would it matter to him?' Then it just clicked." Ross asked her what clicked. She said, "He wanted to mess with me. He wanted to touch me."

[*Hanna said that Steve told her which room to sleep in, but did he really tell her which side of the bed to be on? Whose word do we have about that? Right, just Hanna's.*]

In Trial #2, Hanna expanded her story again. She said that Steve told them it was time for bed, and "I asked where I was supposed to sleep. He told me and Marri to go into Beau's room, which is…an incredibly small room. The bed takes up about half the room. It's a full-sized bed. He somehow -- I think after everybody was getting dressed, he took me inside and said, 'Sleep on the side closest to the door.'" Ross asked her why he told her that. She said, "At first, I didn't know. I just thought, Well, okay, maybe it's if I have to get up in the middle of the night and go use the restroom, I won't trip over something or somebody. And then, after a couple of minutes, I knew that wasn't it." Ross asked her why Steve told her she needed "to sleep on a specific spot on the bed." Hanna said, "He wanted to mess with me." Ross asked her if she did go to sleep. She said, "Yes." He asked if Marri was in the same bed, and where Marri was. Hanna said, "…you have to climb over in order to get to the side Marri was sleeping on. When I was laying on my back, she was sleeping to my left."

[*This time she said Steve pulled her aside secretly to tell her where to sleep. The phrase,* "after everybody was getting dressed," *will take on further importance when we get to the night of Beau's birthday party, but I'll briefly mention it once more in just a bit.*]

In 2014, I asked Beau what he remembered about the sleeping arrangements. He said, "I believe Marri and Hanna slept in my room." I asked, "Who decided who slept where?" Beau said, "I believe Dad told them to go in the bedroom. He goes, 'Y'all need to go to bed in there,' because I had a problem with sleeping in the living room on the couch with Hanna being over there. Just because she was a girl." I said, "So the guys went in the living room, the girls went somewhere else?" Beau said, "Right."

[*Beau, because he was shy, asked Steve to separate the boys from the girls.*]

Analysis: I don't often trust Hanna to tell the truth, but I do believe part of what she said above because I have verification. Steve did tell them where to sleep (the girls in Beau's room and the boys in the living room), but not so he could have access to Hanna. Beau said it was because he was embarrassed about sleeping in the same room with Hanna; which is another bit of data indicating that this *was* the first time Hanna and Aaron spent the night. A floor plan of the house is on the blog. It should help you see why it would have been intensely stupid for Steve to do what Hanna claimed he did that night. Of course, for him to do any of the things she claimed would have been way beyond the bounds of common sense.

Nobody except Hanna was asked, in either trial, about the sleeping arrangements. She didn't mention them to Tom or the sheriff's office, and they weren't in Ada Dixon's summary. No one else was asked how the sleeping locations were decided until I spoke to Beau eight years after the trials were over. In Trial #1, Hanna simply said that she and Marri slept in Beau's room, but said that Steve told her to "sleep on the side closest to the door." Following her usual pattern, she didn't even mention that her brother was there or where he slept. In Trial #2, she added that Steve pulled her inside the room and then told her to sleep on the side closest to the door, which painted him as sneaky and controlling.

Conclusion: This was really a non-issue, except Hanna used it to foster the idea that Steve isolated her intentionally (so she would be more accessible to him). Beau deflated that premise when he said it was really his idea to separate the two groups that first night, not Steve's, but no one heard that in either trial. As far as the relative positioning of the two girls in the bed, Marri could have crawled into bed first, scooting over to make room for Hanna. Or Hanna, in an unfamiliar situation, might have hesitated before getting into bed, which naturally placed her on the outside. That's assuming that Hanna's story about which side she slept on was even true. It could just as easily have been the other way around.

Do I need to say it? No one asked Marri which side she slept on.

There's one other factor to consider. If Steve had walked between his bedroom and Beau's room late at night could he have been seen or heard? Yes, he could have. You might want to look at the image of the floor plan on the blog while you read the next bit.

https://aggravatedbook.com/images-for-the-night-of-harry-potter-chapters/

A glance at it exposes a few other flaws in Hanna's story. She said the room was dark, but there are windows in the den, the living room, and Beau's room. Marri and others have said there were usually lights on in the house. Also, the window in Beau's room had a sheer curtain on it, so the near-full moon that night, and the light in the carport, could have sent a fair bit of light into that room. The sightlines on the floor plan also show that Beau and Aaron (on the couch and the recliner in the living room) could see the edge of Beau's bedroom door, but probably not much of the bed. What they both could have seen, though, would be anyone coming or going through the dining room and the den to get to Beau's room. They would also have likely seen any movement in Beau's room, and maybe even have seen anyone who was standing next to the bed.

Why would Steve have taken a chance of being spotted by them or Marri? And there's also a good likelihood that Steve could have been heard by Aaron and Beau as well as seen. I'll cover the noise from the dogs and the house's squeaky floors in the question, *Why Didn't Marri Notice This?*

What Did Hanna and Steve Wear to Bed?

Why is This Important? If Hanna had simply said "I don't remember what we wore," this question wouldn't even be here. She rarely qualified her remarks, though, by saying something like "I might have been wearing," followed by the name of a garment. She usually just named the item as if it was fact, and then described it in great detail. Specificity can make juries believe that a witness really does "remember" something, but what if those specifics aren't consistent with other details in the same story? We already covered this in *Harry Potter, Chapter 1*, so I'll quote less here, and just list the clothes.

In her April 2004 affidavit, about the first time she spent the night, she said she was wearing "a T-shirt and blue jean shorts."

[*How long did she continue to claim that? Not long.*]

By May she was telling Ada Dixon that they went to see *Harry Potter*, but didn't stipulate the month or year. Here are the five phrases from Dixon's summary about what Hanna said they were wearing at the theater: "...my jacket" "...my pants" and "...my underwear." She said Steve's clothes were: "...his pants" and "...his underwear."

[*All generic terms, but notice she did use the word "pants" for Steve, not shorts.*]

Hanna didn't tell Tom about what happened at the house that night, but she did give a description of what Steve wore to the movies: "black denim shorts," "ugly" shoes, and a "polo shirt" with a two or three button collar, blue or black horizontal stripes with "either gray or white" contrasting ones.

[*That's very precise. Did she stick with that description during the trials? Of course she didn't.*]

In Trial #1, Elmer Ross asked her what she wore later that night. She said: "jeans and a t-shirt." She said that Steve was in the "t-shirt and denim shorts" he had on at the movie. She launched into a description of her jeans: "hand-me-down or Goodwill," "they weren't the hip huggers," but were "flare-legged and denim," and her "shirt was red and kind of a strawberry pattern," with "two layers" and "little bitty holes...like where the seeds on the strawberries would go." It was "a fitted shirt. Not skin tight, but just fitted," and "kind of short...so it came down to meet the top of the jeans." Ross asked if she had anything on underneath. She said, "A sports bra." She mentioned Steve's "jeans and underwear..." but, before the jury caught that slip, Ross asked. "Jeans?" and she quickly corrected it to "shorts, denim shorts."

[*Hanna said Steve was wearing a* "t-shirt and denim shorts" *(not a polo shirt), and she wore flare-leg, waist-high jeans and a t-shirt, which she later described as a red, strawberry-patterned, not skin tight but fitted shirt. I can see why she would have worn her clothes to bed (that's what she had on), but why would Steve? Would Robin let him to go to bed fully clothed? Hanna also later said the room was so dark that she couldn't see. If it was that dark, how did she know what he was wearing? We'll get to that.*]

When Hanna said "everybody was getting dressed," what did she mean by that? In nearly every description about spending the night (except the final incident), Hanna said she was wearing what she wore earlier in the day; but when Hanna and Aaron stayed over, the kids all slept in their clothes. No one "was getting dressed" in pajamas or nightclothes of any kind.

[*Did Hanna want the jury to believe she was alone with Steve long enough for him to tell her what side of the bed to sleep on? No one went off to another room in the house to change into nightclothes.*]

I asked Steve what he usually wore to bed. He said, "When Marri was born, I got scrubs, and I slept in either my underwear or my scrubs."

[*Steve said it was usually surgery scrubs or underwear. Not denim shorts or polo shirts.*]

Analysis: Hanna rarely said the same exact thing twice. In her affidavit, she said she "was wearing a T-shirt and blue jean shorts." In her interview with Tom, she said she was in "flare leg type" jeans, not shorts, but didn't mention her shirt. In Trial #1, she described her jeans as flare legged, not hip huggers, old-fashioned, and from Goodwill, and said that her "t-shirt" was red, fitted, but not skin-tight, and short. In Trial #2, she used a similar description, but added the extra detail about her red "shirt" having a two-layer strawberry pattern with tiny strawberry seed holes, not skin tight, but fitted, and that time described its length as being short enough to just touch the top of her jeans. She was also asked what Steve was wearing when he came in after everyone was asleep. She said he was in "the same clothes he was wearing when we went to the movies, a t-shirt and denim shorts," but Steve described his typical bedtime clothes as either his underwear or his surgical scrubs, not ratty denim shorts.

Conclusion: Sometime after her sworn statement in the affidavit became a legal document, Hanna shifted the date of the first incident forward by nearly three months into cold weather. She then changed the description of her clothing to something more suitable for the chilly November climate, and ignored the affidavit's claim of warm weather clothing and an end-of-summer date. Steve, Beau, and Marri all agreed that, by the end of November, Steve would definitely be wearing a jacket and jeans, not shorts. That would make it even less likely that he would wear shorts to bed, much less to the movie, as Hanna claimed. Beau also pointed out that Steve's shorts were ratty, and Robin wouldn't have let him out of the house in them anyway.

If he had planned to walk through the house in November, on the squeaky floor, in the middle of the night, wouldn't he be more likely to wear something that made more sense for a cold November night. I don't know what that would be, maybe a robe over his surgical scrubs. Also notice that Hanna never said anything about Steve's shoes that night. Would he still have on his "ugly" boots, or would he have been barefoot on the cold, cold squeaky floor? Hanna's insistence that he was wearing something that would have been better suited for summertime than winter is just preposterous. And she even added a brand new story in Trial #2 — about a trucker cap. We'll get to that in the question, *What Happened the Next Morning?*

Let's take a look at the alleged incidents.

What Happened at the Sirois' House That Night?

Why is This Important? The first count against Steve was based solely on one physical act, Steve performing oral sex on Hanna, something she swore happened the first time she spent the night. It's especially important to look at this thoroughly because it's the only count Steve was convicted for.

Let's begin with the affidavit. The underlined phrases are the physical actions Hanna said Steve did to her that night. "I was awaken by Steve, by him <u>shaking my shoulder</u>. When I started to say something to him he <u>put his hand over mouth</u> to keep me quiet. I further remember I was wearing a T-shirt and blue jean shorts. He then <u>removed my shorts and underwear</u>. I remember he then <u>started kissing on me</u> and he then <u>put his mouth on my vagina</u>. I further remember he then <u>stuck his tongue inside my vagina</u>. He <u>did this for several minutes</u>. After he stopped, he told me goodnight and he left the bedroom."

[*Can I prove these things didn't happen? I'll try. Just keep in mind that the affidavit refers to an incident which she claimed happened* "in late August or early September 2001," *and she didn't spend the night until late-November.*]

A month after the affidavit, she told Ada Dixon about the night they saw *Harry Potter*. She said, "I was asleep by his daughter in the bed closest to the door. He came in and took off my underwear. I still had on my clothes from the movies. He started french kissing me and then moved down to my boobs and sucked on them. From my boobs he moved down to do oral sex on me. Then he unzipped his pants and pulled down his underwear in the front and then he took my hand and made me masturbate him while he was fingering me. He was trying to get me to do oral sex on him but I refused. He kept trying and said, 'Maybe next time.'" Dixon added: "At this point all of this was happening every two weeks."

[*Within a month, Hanna had considerably expanded the scope of her accusation beyond what she said in the affidavit. She added French kissing, suckling, masturbation, fingering, and a request for fellatio to the list, and changed the date. She also admitted to Dixon that her family didn't visit every week, but the quote,* "this was happening every two weeks," *makes it seem like this wasn't the first time they spent the night. Maybe Hanna hadn't made up her mind about that yet?*]

I need to pause here to say something about how badly Dixon's summary is worded. It's often misleading, but maybe some of her confusion came from Hanna's tendency to jump from event to event with little or no context. Here's an excerpt from the summary about the time period between the cross-country race and seeing *Harry Potter*. It's punctuated exactly like the original, and I've underlined what I believe are Dixon's inserted comments.

> "Then he started looking at me like a boyfriend would. He would say flattering things like, 'you're so sexy and beautiful (<u>age 12</u>).'" <u>This puts Hanna into an adult world to do adult things</u>. "He

> started more touching and grabbing me inside my clothes." This probably happened at age thirteen. "We were on our way to the movies to see Harry Potter in his son's truck…"

It's difficult to understand what Dixon was referring to. Are we supposed to assume that the "touching and grabbing" inside Hanna's clothes happened at the age of thirteen, or that the ride to see *Harry Potter* did? Or both? According to Hanna's own chronology, neither one makes sense. She was still twelve when, following an impossibly brief alleged grooming period, they went to see *Harry Potter*. She described plenty of touching and grabbing inside her clothes in the movie theater (when she still barely knew Steve), and even described some touching on top of the clothes ten weeks earlier, after the cross-country race (when she knew him even less). The statement "This probably happened at age thirteen" can't possibly refer to any of that. Also, if she saw *Harry Potter* when she was thirteen it would have to have been the second film, which didn't open until November 2002. If she didn't spend the night for the first time until then, she would have needed to toss out an entire year's worth of alleged incidents.

Interestingly, Hanna did testify in Trial #2 that the movie they saw was "*Harry Potter and the Chamber of Secrets*," which is the second in the series, not the one they saw in 2001. Did Hanna mix the titles up, or had she been telling Dixon they saw a different movie, which could have confused Dixon about which movie they went to? Or was there another reason, one that didn't originate with Hanna? Dixon prepared the summary knowing it might be used in a court trial against Hanna's perpetrator. I believe it's possible that the information from Hanna's sessions could have been shaped to fit that gradual grooming process: flattery first, then suggestion, then touching on top of clothes, and then inside clothes before any overt sexual acts.

The summary feels to me like an attempt to force Hanna's story to fit specific patterns. Dixon's assertion in the trials was that Steve prepared Hanna over a long period of time, but Hanna's own statements, and the dates of events, contradict that idea over and over again. Hanna and Aaron had previously only visited the Sirois' house one time (in 1998 or 1999). The next time they visited was after the race in September 2001. They went to see the movie only ten weeks after that. There was no opportunity or time for gradual preparation. Also, Dixon should have known that Hanna was twelve when she saw the movie, not thirteen. Shouldn't a clinician (someone scientifically inclined, who actually wanted to record the truth about a patient) ask specific questions about times and dates, and then prepare an accurate record that would reflect that truth? I don't believe that happened with Dixon's summary, which feels to me like it's been shaped to fit the methodologies she espoused in her book.

Okay, back to the first time Hanna and Aaron spent the night.

Here are excerpts from Tom's interview with Hanna about Steve removing her clothing on two other occasions (not after the movie, because she didn't reveal any of that to Tom). These are pertinent because of what Hanna said in the trials about a problem with clothes and her neck.

Excerpt 1: She said, "He never ...he hardly ever took my shirt off, actually. He always just pushed it up." Tom asked her how far it was pushed up, and she said, "Up to my neck."

Excerpt 2: Tom asked about a special shirt she had mentioned. She said, "I wanted to wear it because it was brand new and I thought it was really neat, and he just treated it like any other shirt, just pushed it up to my neck."

[*Hanna didn't express any thought of discomfort to Tom about her shirt being pushed up that high. In the second excerpt she said that he "treated it like any other shirt, just pushed it up to my neck," as if that happened nearly every time. Here's more about Hanna's neck.*]

Trial #1: Ross asked her what happened that night. She said that Steve came in "and pushed my shirt up to my neck. And I can't have anything in this area of my neck or I gag, so I had to have one hand up here to keep from choking myself." Trial #2: Ross asked how high he pushed her shirt. She said, "To my neck. And I put my left hand -- hooked it under the collar of my shirt, because I have a real phobia of anything touching this -- like the lower area of my throat." Ross asked her if she pulled the shirt away from her neck. She said, "Yes, sir. Or else I would gag. I can't breathe."

[*If her gag reflex really was that strong, and he "always" pushed her shirts up to her neck, wouldn't that have been problematic for her each and every one of the 80 to 90 times she said he molested her? If it truly bothered her, why didn't she tell Willard Knox about it, or Ada Dixon, or Tom? If she actually had this condition, why did she wait until the trials to reveal it? Do you remember Hanna telling Dixon that Steve had her put her* "jacket on backwards," *and how I said that would have been impossible with her gag reflex? Did she wait until the trials to invent that condition? It didn't seem to be an issue for her when she told Dixon about wearing the jacket backwards, or when she talked to Tom.*]

I'm going to collapse the next few excerpts more than usual, but Hanna's answers will always be in quotes. Remember that Marri was also in the same bed with Hanna when all of the following was supposedly happening.

In Trial #1, Ross asked, What did Steve do next? "He started kissing me and he was rubbing my stomach, and he lifted my bra and started fondling my breasts." — Ross: Where else did he kiss you? "On my mouth and then he went down my neck and then it ...he went on down my chest and then he stopped to pull my pants down and my underwear." — Ross: Had he ever before removed your underwear? "No." — Ross: Did you say anything? "I was breathing really hard. I was nervous. I didn't know what was going on." — Ross: What happened next? "He kissed the inner part of my thighs, and then he started …started kissing my vagina." — Ross: Had he ever done that before? "No." — Ross: Did he do anything else? "He put his tongue in my vagina." — Judge Hawes interrupted to tell Hanna there were tissues next to her if she needed one. She took one and they continued. — Ross: How did that make you feel? "It was so -- I thought, 'This is so disgusting.'" — Ross: Did you tell him to stop? "I didn't know I could. I asked him what he was doing. He just asked me if it felt good." — Ross: Where was Marri? "She was asleep." — Ross: Did Marri wake up? "No. She rolled over once and he paused and then waited a couple of seconds to make sure she was still asleep, and then he kept on." — Ross: How long did that last? "It was probably about an hour. He also made me masturbate him." — Ross: What do you mean by masturbate? "He took my hand and put it on his penis after he pulled his underwear down. And he would grab me by the wrist and made me move my hand up and down."

[*Hanna alleged that Marri slept so soundly that she and Steve could have conversations while he pushed her fitted shirt and bra up to her neck, pulled her jeans and underwear off, kissed her all over while she struggled against a gag reflex, and also perform cunnilingus on her, plus finger her while she masturbated him; all without waking Marri up? Marri would have been less than a foot away. How could she not wake up with all of that going on?*]

A Side-Comment About the Tissues: Steve told me that, when Judge Hawes showed Hanna the tissues, she took one, and kept taking them as the day wore on. Steve said he never saw her wipe her eyes or blow her nose. She just held them in her hands, then dropped one occasionally before taking another. He started counting after a while, and said he thought there were fifteen to twenty tissues littering the floor when she was excused.

[*Hawes may have shown Hanna the tissues because she was crying; or maybe it was something he did normally during emotional testimony. Yolanda Maldonado, Steve's co-worker at the State Park, said that Hanna's weepy moments felt fake to her, "crocodile tears." Real or not, it does seem like Hanna might have turned the judge's offer into a good prop.*]

Another Comment: This one's about whether Hanna was aware that she could tell Steve to stop. In Trial #1, she testified that she didn't know she could tell him that. Later in the same trial, Steve's attorney, Bevin Jenkins, asked Darla if she and Hanna had a close relationship, and Darla said they did. Jenkins asked, "Did you ever talk to her about appropriate and inappropriate touching?" Darla said, "Many times. For many years. Yes." He asked her what she had told Hanna. Darla answered, "That if anyone other than myself or a doctor touched her anywhere that her bathing suit would touch her, she needed to tell me, or to tell somebody." He asked her if Hanna told her "about other things in her life that were intimate and important to her." Darla said, "Yes, sir, she would talk to me about everything."

[*If Darla's statements about that were true, and she did have those multiple talks with Hanna (and possibly Aaron too), how could Hanna not have known that the things she claimed happened would have been wrong, and that she* could *have said, "No," and* should *have told someone? So, I see a couple of probable choices: Either Darla didn't have any talks with her kids about protecting themselves; or she did talk to them and Hanna denied that she knew what to do.*]

We're still in Trial #1: Hanna said, "Everybody had gone to bed. I stayed awake. I didn't know what was going to happen. I had never stayed at his house before and..." — Ross interrupted: Where was Marri? Hanna said, "She was laying on my left side. She fell asleep. And she is a deep sleeper. She didn't wake up." — Ross: How long before something happened? "To me, it seemed like forever because I was just laying there, looking around." —

Ross: Why did you do that? "I couldn't sleep. I knew something was going to happen. I just didn't know what and I didn't know when."

[*This was another admission that this was the first time she and Aaron spent the night there, but because Marri was in the same bed Hanna had to convince the jury that Marri was a deep sleeper. For now, though, just remember that Hanna said she* "stayed awake," "couldn't sleep," *and* "was just laying there, looking around." *We'll come back to all of that.*]

Still Trial #1: Ross asked Hanna: Was it light in the room or dark? "No, it was dark." — Ross: Had you ever seen an adult man's penis before? "No." — Ross: Describe what it was doing? "It was hard and swollen." — Ross: Did he make you masturbate him? "Yes." — Ross: Did anything happen to his penis after you did that? "Something warm and wet came out of it. A little bit of it caught my hand. I didn't know what it was. It was kind of like water, but thicker. Not quite like syrup." — Ross: During the masturbation, did he say anything to you? "He just kind of moaned and was saying, 'That feels good.'" — Ross: Did you say anything to him? "No." — Ross: What happened next? "He put his finger in my vagina." — Ross: Did that happen before or after the oral sex? "After. And he moved it around, in and out. I don't know what all. And then after awhile, he said, 'I'm tired, I'm going to bed.' He just got up, got dressed and left." — Ross: What did you do then? "I just laid there on my back. I was just frozen." — Ross: Were your clothes still off? "Yes." — Ross: What did you do with them? "As soon as he left, I put them back on. I just laid there and I tried to go to sleep and I couldn't. There was a window that had a kind of a thick curtain. You couldn't really see out of it, you could barely see the outline of any light. I just watched the light turn till it was daylight."

[*Count I only alleged oral sex, not masturbation and fingering (as she also told Ada Dixon but not Tom). Keep in mind that Marri was right next to her that night, and Hanna said there were conversations and noises (*"That feels good," "I'm tired, I'm going to bed," *moaning, etc.), but Marri stayed asleep. One other thing: Hanna's knowledge of a hard, swollen member and semen, while accurate, could easily have been discovered during the two-year wait before the trials (through personal experimentation, in talks with her friends, or from cable TV or the Internet.*]

In Trial #2, the questions were the same, but some of her answers were different. Ross asked what happened after she went to bed, and Hanna said, "Sirois came in later on. I don't know how much later it was, but he came in there and he woke me up and he started kissing me on my mouth."

[*Hanna said that when Steve came in, he woke her up and started kissing her. That isn't what she said in Trial #1, or to Dixon. She said two different things under oath, awake in one, asleep in the other. Which one is true? Are either of them true?*]

Also from Trial #2, this is Hanna's extremely long, very graphic description of the incident. I've underlined some important phrases. We'll review them afterward. — Ross: What happened after he pushed up your shirt? "He started to unbutton and unzip my jeans. I tried to get him to stop. He said, it's all right, you'll like it." — Ross: Did he get them unzipped? "He pulled them and my underwear down and off my right leg and kept them hooked around my left leg." — Ross: Was he doing anything with his mouth? "He was already kissing on my neck, he started moving down, started kissing me on my breast." — Ross: What was next? "His other hand rubbed my stomach and started moving down and he finally put his finger inside my vagina." — Ross: Was that the first time he did that? "Yes, sir." — Ross: How did that feel? "It was really tight and it kind of hurt." — Ross: Did he say anything during that? "No, sir." — Ross: How far inside your vagina was his finger? "I don't really know. I'm almost certain it was the whole finger. I don't even know which finger it was." — Ross: Were you conscious of how far inside you he was? "No, sir. I wasn't really aware, but you could tell or anything that was my first experience and I had my eyes closed half the time and I was still half asleep." — Ross: Did he say anything to you during that? "No, he would just give me little hints here and there. Like whenever he was pulling down my pants, he would say, lift up a little bit so I can pull them down your hips. And I was like, okay. And he was like, keep them hooked around one leg, and just things like that. So, I would do what he wanted." — Ross: Did you tell him to stop? "I grabbed his hand again whenever he first started to pull down my panties. Then after that, I just -- I couldn't get the words out. They were just stuck. They were just stuck. Wouldn't come out. It was going through my head over and over, stop, no, this isn't right, just stop it, go away, none of it would come out." — Ross: What was Marri doing during all of this? "She was asleep." — Ross: Did Marri ever wake up? "No, sir. She never moved."

She still hadn't talked about the action listed in Count I, so Ross asked her if anything else happened that night, and Hanna said, "Yes, sir." — Ross: What was that? "After he was kissing my breasts, he started moving down my stomach, kissing my stomach and licking it. And then he started kissing my inner thighs and then he put his mouth on my vagina." — Ross: Had he ever done that before? "No, sir." — Ross: What happened next? "I don't really know. It was just a really weird sensation." — Ross: What did it feel like? "Like he was kissing it and then I think he stuck his tongue in it. I don't know. I just know it felt really weird and slimy." — Ross: What made you think his tongue was inside you? "Because something was wiggling around. I could barely make out his hand. It was really, really dark in there." — Ross: Did he say anything while that was happening? "No, sir." — Ross: Did you say anything to him? "I asked him what he was doing." — Ross: How did he respond to that? "Just asked me if I liked it." — Ross: How did you respond to his comment? "I said, 'No.'" — Ross: Did he stop? "No." — Ross: How long did he have his tongue inside you? "It was probably about 20, 30 minutes. I don't really know. To me, I thought maybe it was like an hour, hour-and-a-half, but I don't think it could have been that long now that I look back on it."

Then Ross asked, Did anything else happen? "Yes." — Ross: What was that? "He stood up beside the bed at some point, and he had pulled down his jeans and underwear and he took my right hand and put it around his penis." — Ross had her correct her jeans comment to shorts, then asked her: Was there any light in the room at all? "There was a window with kind of a thick curtain, but you could still kind of see through, just barely make out shapes. You had to know what it was to be able to see it." — Ross: Could you see his penis? "I could see it, but I couldn't make out the shape. I had never seen one before." — Ross: After he asked you to put your hand on it, what happened? "He took my wrist and started moving it up and down." — Ross: Did he say anything to you then? "He said, 'Just keep doing that.'" — Ross: Did you reply to him? "No." — Ross: How long did that go on? "It would be about five minutes, and then...I let go because something started coming out of the end of it. I didn't know what it was. It was warm and wet and it was kind of thick. It wasn't like water, but it was kind of close." — Ross: Did he say anything to you during that? "No, sir, not that I recall." — Ross: Had you ever seen a grown man's penis before that night? "No, sir, I had not." — Ross: Had you ever seen anything come out of a man's penis before that night? "No, sir." — Ross: What happened after that? "He just said, 'Um, that felt good.' Then he said something along the lines of, 'I'm tired and I have to go to bed,' or something like that." — Ross: What happened next? "He pulled up his shorts and underwear and he turned around and walked out of the room." — Ross: What did you do then? "I laid there for a second, made sure he was gone, and then I got dressed." — Ross: Did you get dressed while still on the bed? "Yes, I was still laying on the bed." — Ross: What did you do after you got dressed? "I just laid there and watched the light coming out of the window until it was daylight." — Ross: Were you able to go back to sleep after that? "No, sir."

[*In Trial #1, when she was asked if she told him to stop, she said,* "I didn't know I could." *In this trial, when asked the same thing, she said she* "tried to get him to stop," *and said that she grabbed his hand, and tried to say,* "stop, no, this isn't right, just stop it, go away," *but* "none of it would come out." *Saying that she didn't know she could, and saying she did know, and tried to speak but wasn't able to, are two entirely different things. Even though I believe that neither of those statements are true, at least one of them, by default, must be a lie, and both were said under oath.*

Then she described everything happening in a room so dark she could barely see anything, but she somehow still could see that Steve had on jeans (or shorts) and underwear? One of Ross' first questions was, "Was he doing anything with his mouth?" *I think Ross was trying to get her to talk about the oral sex right away. It was the one element he had to prove. Instead she talked about him kissing her on the neck. When he finally got her to describe the subject of Count I, did anyone else notice that Hanna (technically at least) didn't actually say that he gave her oral sex that night? She said,* "I think he stuck his tongue in it. I don't know." *Also, the sequence of events was different from her Trial #1 testimony.*

Her description of the roughly continuous dialogue she had with Steve during the incident is another reason why it's hard to believe that Marri wouldn't wake up with all of that chatty, motion-filled activity happening, on the same bed, less than a foot away. Hanna also contradicted her previous testimony when she was asked if Marri woke up. This time she said, "No sir, she never moved." *In Trial #1, she said that Marri rolled over and Steve waited to make sure she was asleep.*

And, after her account of twenty minutes of something happening that might or might not have been cunnilingus, Hanna said, "He stood up beside the bed at some point, and he had pulled down his jeans and underwear." *Was she saying he was actually* <u>*on the bed*</u> *during all of the physical action she described? He could have done almost none of it if he had been kneeling beside it, as she implied, but if he had been on the bed, how did Marri stay asleep?*]

Marri was asked multiple times during the trials if she was a light sleeper, and she and everyone else except Hanna agreed that she was. In 2014 I asked her about darkness vs. light. "When everybody's in bed at night, were there lights that were left on, typically?" Marri said, "Yes, because I didn't like the dark. I was really terrified. I asked her if they were like night-lights or like table lamps. She said, "They were like table lamps, but sometimes mom and dad…they would leave a light on, so I could find my way, so I could go back there to go to the restroom."

[*If there were lights on in the house, why did Hanna claim it was so dark in Beau's room, maybe because darkness allows for stealthy secrets.*]

In 2015, I asked Beau about some of the same things. I asked him if the blue curtain I had seen in his room when he took me to the house was the same one that would have been there in 2001. Beau said, "I believe so. I can't see why we would have changed it." I showed him a picture I took of sunlight streaming through the curtain, and asked him if there was any light outside on a typical night. He said, "Usually you'd be able to see a little bit in there. I always kept it pretty dark, but I don't remember it being pitch dark."

[*No one has lived in the house since Robin died in 2012. Beau said he thought that was the same curtain that was there in 2001. Hanna described the room as being so dark she couldn't make shapes out, but also said that she looked around while she waited. If there was near-zero light how could she look around? If there* was *some light, though, she should have been able to see those things she said she couldn't see. Which was it?*]

Look at the picture of Beau's room on the blog.

https://aggravatedbook.com/images-for-the-night-of-harry-potter-chapters/

The bed is a standard double size (54" × 75"), and the curtain's sheer material was clearly not meant to block out light. There aren't any street lamps nearby, but the moon from November 23rd to December 1, 2001 was in its 3rd quarter to full phases. Also, Beau said that the light in the carport was usually left on at night, so there should have been some light coming through that window. Hanna said that Marri never woke up during any of the incidents, but they were sleeping side by side in a 54-inch wide bed, which means that the girls would each only have a space 27-inches wide to sleep on. Marri was mere inches away from Hanna. How could she have stayed asleep?

In 2015, I asked Steve, just for the record, if he went into Beau's room and woke Hanna up. Steve said, "No." I asked if he touched her in any inappropriate way. He said, "No." I asked if he had Hanna commit any inappropriate acts on him. He said, "No."

[*His comment was the same as it always has been,* "I didn't do it. It never happened." *It's what he has said all along, despite several opportunities for plea deals that included no prison time.*]

Analysis: I think I have already proved that what Hanna said happened during the ride and the movie is ridiculous, and also that much of it was physically impossible. Just invented nonsense. Maybe the rest of the evening was too. I'll keep this analysis as brief as I can. Let's compare Hanna's claims about three different topics: Their clothing, the darkness, and what happened.

What They Were Wearing: **Affidavit** — She wore a t-shirt and blue jean shorts. No mention of Steve's clothes. // **Dixon** — She wore pants and underwear, and mentioned Steve's pants and underwear. // **Tom** — She wore jeans, a t-shirt and a jacket, and said Steve wore black denim shorts and a polo shirt. // **Trial #1** — She wore old-fashioned flare legged jeans from Goodwill, non-hip huggers, and a fitted, kind of short, slightly tight, red shirt which just met the top of the jeans. Steve wore underwear. // **Trial #2** — She wore her "hand-me-down" "flare-legged jeans and t-shirt," which she said was a red, two-layered fitted shirt with strawberry seed holes in it. Steve wore "a t-shirt and denim shorts."

[*Hanna was all over the place with these descriptions, but I still find it peculiar, given the cold weather, that she would Steve in shorts without a jacket, and that she would wear a t-shirt in November that was too short to tuck inside her jeans (which she later claimed was a fitted, layered shirt). I also wonder if her mention in both trials that the jeans were from Goodwill was done to indicate that her family wasn't well-off, maybe to elicit sympathy from the jury.*]

The Darkness in Beau's Room: **Affidavit**, **Dixon**, and **Tom** — (no mention) // **Trial #1** — It was dark. She lay there, looking around until Steve came in. There was a thick curtain, and she couldn't really see out of it, so she just watched the light turn until it was daylight. // **Trial #2** — It was so dark that she couldn't see through the thick curtain, and could barely see Steve's hand or other objects. She could see Steve's penis, but couldn't make out its shape because she had never seen one before. She just watched the light through the window until daylight.

[*Hanna said it was so dark she could barely see or make out shapes, but she could still look around the room and through the sheer curtain. And there were other lights on in the house, and potentially light from outside. It probably wasn't nearly as dark as Hanna said it was, which means it would have been even more likely that Steve would have been caught in the act. If it had been as dark as she indicated (so dark that she could avoid describing Steve's penis), she wouldn't have been able to tell what clothes he had on. She either could see or she couldn't, but she claimed to be able to do both.*]

The Alleged Actions: The affidavit specified six actions that supposedly happened that night, but Hanna altered them from one statement to the next (often adding other actions, and/or changing the original ones). **Affidavit** — Awakened by shaking her shoulder; Hand over her mouth to keep her quiet; Removed her shorts and underwear; started kissing on her; Mouth on her vagina; Stuck tongue inside her vagina. Six separate actions. // **Dixon** — Took off her underwear; French kissed her; Suckled her boobs; Performed oral sex on her; Unzipped his pants and pulled down his underwear; Took her hand, Had her masturbate him while he fingered her; Tried to get her to perform oral sex on him. Seven separate actions. // **Tom** — (no mention). // **Trial #1** — Awake when he came in; Pushed her shirt up to her neck; She grabbed her collar to keep from choking; Started kissing on her and rubbing her stomach; Lifted her bra, started fondling her breasts; Pulled her pants and underwear down; Kissed her on the mouth and neck again, then her breasts and stomach; Kissed the inner part of her thighs; Started kissing her vagina; Put his tongue in her vagina; Talked about what they were doing; Paused when Marri rolled over; Kept going for another hour; Then made her masturbate him to ejaculation; Moaned and said it felt good; Put his finger in her vagina, and moved it around, in and out; Then said he was tired and was going to bed; Got dressed and left. At least eighteen separate actions. // **Trial #2** — Asleep when he woke her up; Started kissing her on her mouth; Moved down to her neck, kissed her there; Raised up her shirt and bra, fondled her breasts; Pushed her shirt up to her neck; She hooked her hand under her shirt collar; Unbuttoned and unzipped her jeans; She tried to get him to stop; He said she would like it; Pulled her jeans and underwear off her right leg, but kept both hooked around her left; Gave her little hints; After kissing her neck, he moved down; Kissed her breasts one at a time; Rubbed her stomach while one hand was fondling her breast; Put his finger in her vagina; Started kissing her inner thighs; Put his mouth on her vagina; She thought he stuck his tongue inside, but wasn't sure; Put her right hand around his penis, started moving her hand up and down; Ejaculated, said it felt good; Said he was tired and had to go to bed; Pulled up his shorts and underwear, left the room. At least twenty-two separate actions.

[*Hanna said nothing about hooking her jeans and underwear around her left ankle in the affidavit, or in Dixon's summary (where she said she was just in her underwear), but in later versions she was still in her jeans. She did say something similar about hooking the underwear in Tom's interview and in both trials, but to Tom she wasn't referring to this night but to an incident that she said happened toward the end, but she couldn't remember when it was. Did she get the counts mixed up? Or had she told these tales so often that she blended parts of one with another? Did she even try to keep her stories straight from one moment to the next?*]

One final comment about masturbation. Hanna said she masturbated Steve three times that evening (in the truck, in the movie theater, and at the house). She was asked if Steve ejaculated in the truck or in the movie theater, and she said, "No." The first mention of any kind of liquid or moistness discharging from Steve's penis that night was at the house. I think it's safe to say, though, that men, once their penis is engorged and it has been stroked (even if they don't climax and ejaculate), leak a fair amount of seminal fluid. Yet, in all of her descriptions of what happened earlier that evening, there wasn't a single statement that would lead us to believe that Steve's penis was anything other than (pardon the pun) bone dry during both of the earlier stroking sessions. Hanna also didn't say anything about Steve having to wait for his erection to soften in the truck, or when he left for a smoke break after she masturbated him in the theater. None of that is realistic. Is Steve steeped in Indian Tantric practices, or a Kama Sutra master? No, he's not. He's just an ordinary guy, capable of leakage like everyone else. So, why on earth would he borrow his daughter's jacket to cover his torso at the theater and take a chance of getting ejaculate on it?

Hanna was either asleep or awake. Steve either woke her up or he didn't. He either talked to her or he didn't. He either took her clothes all the way off or he had her leave some of them hooked around one leg. Marri either rolled over or she never moved. Steve was either wearing a t-shirt and shorts or he was wearing a t-shirt and jeans or he was wearing a polo shirt and denim shorts. It was either so pitch dark that Hanna couldn't see her hand in front of her face or what clothes Steve had on, or she could see well enough to look around her while she was waiting. Steve either gave her oral sex before she masturbated him and then he put his finger in her vagina, or he put his finger in her vagina before he gave her oral sex and then she masturbated him. He either leaked or he didn't.

Or, more plausibly, none of this happened. Hanna, however, claimed to different audiences at different times that all of these things did happen. Impossible. I think the reason there is so much contradictory minutiae is because Hanna made it all up, but also did a poor job of remembering her previous versions. The sequence of events was so scrambled (from affidavit to therapy session to interview to trial to trial) that I just can't believe any of it.

Conclusion: Was it technically possible for Steve to have committed the physical acts that Hanna claimed he did with her that night? Physically, yes, but I don't think he was psychologically capable of doing any of it. Unfortunately, when the case was presented to both juries, Hanna was the one driving the narrative. There are still a few issues I haven't brought up yet, and we'll get to them in due time, but we have to return to the one major truism we've encountered so far. During all of this, Hanna never told a reliable story. The primary difference between you and the juries is that each of them only heard her version of the moment, and had no opportunity to compare and contrast it with any of her others.

Hanna either told the truth or she didn't, but since she felt compelled to tell so many different versions of her story on so many different occasions, I would have a difficult time (even if I weren't Steve's brother) to find more than the merest kernel of truth in her tales. Those truths I have found in her story have usually been just provable specifics that could fit within the framework of any of her stories (they *did* go to the movies, he *did* give Hanna and a friend a ride home from a rodeo, Beau *did* have a 21st birthday party).

While I can't personally put a *Liar, Liar, Pants on Fire* label to the actions described in this section (only because I wasn't there to witness them not happening), simple logic, coupled with a comparison of all of her different claims, strongly suggests to me that she did lie under oath a number of times.

Why would someone lie if they have the truth on their side? Exactly.

Next is a question that I've raised several times already. Even if Steve could have physically done the things Hanna claimed he did that night, could he have done them without Marri noticing?

Why Didn't Marri Notice This?

Why is This Important? Marri is the only person who could have corroborated this part of Hanna's story, but she didn't. If you're on Team Hanna you might have been hoping for Marri to wake up and say, "What are you doing, Daddy?" But Hanna said that Marri (and Beau and Aaron on many other occasions) *always* slept through everything. Everyone who was asked about Marri's sleep habits (people who are, admittedly, friends or relatives of Marri) disagreed with Hanna, and said that Marri sleeps lightly. Since Marri *was* in the room, it's understandable that Hanna would try to say that Marri didn't wake up when Steve came in, put his hand over her mouth, pulled her jeans and underwear off, shoved her fitted shirt and sports bra up around her neck, molested her for twenty to thirty minutes (or an hour, according to one of her versions), talking to her the whole time, or when he dropped his drawers and had her masturbate him while he was fingering her. Saying it doesn't make it true, though. Knowing that almost anyone in existence would wake up under those conditions, I believe Hanna invented a different Marri: The Girl Who Could Sleep Through Hurricanes. Pay attention to Hanna's comments about her own state of wakefulness as you read these next excerpts.

In her affidavit, Hanna said, "I remember <u>I was sleeping</u> in the same bed with Marri who was about 9 years old. Sometime during the night I was awaken by Steve, by him shaking my shoulder." Reminder: She claimed this was in August or September, not November, but all of the other quotes below refer to the night they saw *Harry Potter*.

[*Hanna said, under oath, that <u>she was sleeping</u> in the same bed with Marri when Steve came in and shook her shoulder to wake her up.*]

Hanna told Ada Dixon, "<u>I was asleep</u> beside his daughter in the bed closest to the door. He came in and took off my underwear."

[*Hanna said <u>she was asleep</u> beside Marri when Steve came in.*]

By the time Trial #1 got underway, Hanna had reversed course. She said, "Everybody had gone to bed. <u>I stayed awake</u>. I didn't know what was going to happen. I had never stayed at his house before and..." Ross interrupted, asking where Marri was. Hanna said, "She was laying on my left side. She fell asleep. And she is a deep sleeper. She didn't wake up."

[*This time Hanna, admitting that this was the first time they spent the night, said <u>she was wide awake</u>, wondering what was going to happen, but Marri was in the bed next to her, sound asleep, deeply asleep, completely asleep (except, of course for that single time when Hanna said that Marri* "rolled over once," *and caused them to pause for a minute).*]

In Trial #2, though, when Ross asked her if she did go to sleep while waiting for Steve, she said, "Yes," and confirmed that Marri was in the bed with her. Then he asked if something happened later that night. Hanna said, "Yes. Sirois came in later on. I don't know how much later it was, but he came in there and he <u>woke me up</u> and he started kissing me on my mouth." Ross asked her what Marri was doing. Hanna said, "She was asleep." He asked if Marri ever woke up. Hanna answered, "No, sir. She never moved."

[*In Trial #2, Hanna mostly reverted back to what she said in the affidavit and to Dixon, saying she was asleep, with Marri in the bed with her, but Marri slept the sleep of the dead this time, no rolling over. Neither jury heard all of those different versions, of course, and the prosecutor didn't correct Hanna's changes from the previous trial.*]

Steve's defense attorney for the first trial, Bevin Jenkins, asked Marri if she was a heavy or a light sleeper. Marri said, "Light sleeper." He asked what she meant by that. She said, "If someone comes into the room where I'm sleeping or something, I'd wake up." He asked if she would hear them walk in. She said, "Yes, sir." Jenkins asked what would happen if somebody came to the front door. She said, "If I was close to the living room, I would be able to hear it." Then he asked a series of questions: "Would you wake up?" "If there is movement in your bed, do you wake up easily?" "You and Hanna actually slept in the same bed on several occasions; is that correct?" "And would it wake you up if she was to get up?" Marri answered, "Yes" to all of those. He asked her if she ever saw Steve and Hanna together in the bed with her. Marri said, "No." He asked if she would wake up if Steve got in bed with them. She said, "Yes." Jenkins asked Marri if she thought there would have been any way he could have gotten on the bed without her knowing about it. She said, "No." And finally, he asked her if she thought what Hanna claimed was possible or impossible. She said, "Impossible."

[*Obviously, Jenkins asked those questions to give Marri an opportunity to push back against Hanna's idea that multiple acts of molestation could have happened in the same bed without her waking up. Just for the record, Beau and Robin also both testified that Marri was a light sleeper, as you would expect.*]

A Quick Bias Test: If you read the testimony above and thought, *Of course Marri would defend her father no matter what the truth was*, then you might have a bias-based belief that any child would lie to protect their father.

A Second Bias Test: If you have so far been thinking that Hanna would have no reason to put herself through these court proceedings, so she was probably telling the truth, then you may also have a bias. If that's the case, hang in there. I don't know how I can prove to you that a daughter wouldn't lie for her father, but before we're done I will show you a number of reasons why Hanna might go through with the trials. I don't think those reasons had anything to do with her being abused, though.

In Trial #2, Cleveland Sanford asked Marri what kind of sleeper she is. She answered so quietly that he had to ask her again before he heard her say, "A light sleeper." Sanford asked if she understood that her father had been accused of committing some inappropriate behavior with Hanna while she was in the same bed with them. She said, "Yes, sir." He asked her if she thought she would have woken up. Marri said, "Yes, sir." He asked how sure she was about that. She said, "Pretty sure." He asked if she ever saw anything inappropriate happen between her father and Hanna. Marri said, "No."

[*Marri said she was a light sleeper. Unfortunately, most of the prosecution's questions to her were about Tiffany Sperger's bizarre story, not about what she might have actually witnessed or not witnessed that night.*]

Robin also wasn't asked specific questions about that night even though she was there too. Sanford asked her several generic questions about how solidly people slept. Of herself, Robin said, "A light sleeper." She said that Beau "is a lot like me. Well, I take it back. He's a little harder to wake up." About Marri, Robin said, "Marri is a pretty light sleeper." Sanford had visited them just a few days earlier, and had seen the house, so his next question to her was to ask if the house had a concrete slab foundation. She said, "No, sir." Sanford asked her if the floor moved at all. Robin said, "Yes, sir." He asked if the floor made any noise. She also answered "Yes." Then he asked if she thought it would be possible to walk around the house without making any noise. She said, "No, sir."

[*Robin said that not only is Marri a light sleeper, but the floor in their home creaks. It does, it's noisy. I'll explain why in the analysis.*]

In 2014, I asked Marri if she would wake up if somebody came in and touched the bed or made any kind of movement in the room. Marri said, "Oh, sure." I asked her if she really was a light sleeper. She said, "Yes, sir." I told her that, while she and Hanna were both on the bed in Beau's room, Hanna had said that Steve undressed her, did several things to her, and then she got herself dressed again while still on the bed. I asked Marri if she would wake up if any of that happened. She said, "Yes, sir." I asked her if she wakes up during thunderstorms. She said, "For sure. I hate thunderstorms." I asked, "Dogs barking?" She said, "Oh, yeah."

[*She's a light sleeper, and would wake up if anything like that had occurred.*]

In 2015, I asked Steve how likely he thought it would be that Marri would wake up if he had been in Beau's room and had engaged in any kind of physical act with Hanna. Steve said, "I have no doubt she would have woken up." I asked him if Marri was a light sleeper. Steve said, "Sure."

[*Steve also had* "no doubt."]

Analysis: There isn't much I can say about this issue to convince you if you already believe otherwise. People who know Marri believe she is a light sleeper, and Marri says she is too. Look at this from a different perspective. Even if Marri normally slept soundly, with everything that Hanna said went on (sustained movement, pushing and pulling of clothes, conversations), how could she not have awakened at least a few times? And, according to Hanna, that night wasn't the only time Marri didn't wake up. She said there were many other incidents when Marri or someone else was there or nearby, sometimes in the same bed, but she said that everyone *always* slept through it.

What Marri supposedly witnessed is completely dependent on Hanna's statements, because Hanna, and Hanna alone, spooled out this narrative. Let's look at this snippet of dialogue from Trial #2. Ross asked Hanna what she was aware of during her encounter that night. She said, "I wasn't really aware, but you could tell or anything that was my first experience and I had my eyes closed half the time and I was still half asleep." Then he asked her what Marri was doing while all this was going on. Hanna said, "She was asleep." Ross asked if Marri ever woke up. Hanna said, "No, sir. She never moved."

If Hanna "wasn't really aware," had her "eyes closed half the time," and "was still half asleep," how could she know whether Marri was asleep or not? This is another example of what I believe is an example of Hanna saying whatever would suit her point at any given moment. And what does that odd phrase, "but you could tell or anything that was my first experience," mean? Was she trying to suggest that everyone should believe it was her first time just because she said it was? And if she did mean that *was* her first experience, wasn't she also saying (under oath) that all the other groping and fondling and kissing that she testified happened earlier that night (and in the "months and months" before that), didn't happen?

Hanna maintained that Marri was asleep during everything, but ask yourself this: If you were sleeping next to Person A on a double bed, and Person A was on their back when Person X came in, woke them up, and started kissing on them, and then Person X talked to Person A while they shoved Person A's shirt and bra up around their neck and pulled their jeans and underwear off, then kissed Person A from their head to below their waist, and fondled them, then spent twenty minutes performing oral sex on them before Person X stood by the side of the bed and had Person A masturbate them while he fingered her, would you stay asleep, or would you wake up?

Also, Person X in that scenario can't be suspended over the bed, hovering in mid-air. He would have to, at the minimum, lean on it no matter how careful he was. In fact, most of what Hanna described wouldn't work from the side. She described some acts in which Person X would have to be parallel to her, above her, almost certainly on top of her. Person X would have to actually be on the bed part of the time (for the twenty minutes of oral sex at the very least). Also, Person A would have to lift their hips, move their arms, and move in a variety of ways during every bit of this. If all of that was happening, including the talking, would you stay asleep or would you wake up? If you had been Marri, could you have slept through all of that?

A Side-Comment From My Wife: Hanna testified that Steve pushed her sports bra up to her neck nearly every time. When Minay read that paragraph, she pointed out that, for most women, taking off their bra is the high point of their day. She didn't know anyone who willingly slept in one. She said it would be like a man gladly wearing his fully-tied necktie to bed. Even if Hanna hadn't brought sleep clothes with her, wouldn't she at least have taken off her bra before she went to sleep?

Let's look at some other facets of Hanna's story about that night.

Shifting Sleep States and Actions: Affidavit — Steve woke her up by shaking her shoulder, hand over her mouth to quiet her, then started kissing on her. // **Dixon** — She was asleep. He came in and took off her underwear, then started French kissing her. // **Tom** — (no mention). // **Trial #1** — She couldn't sleep, just lay there looking around, he came in, pushed her shirt and bra up, started kissing her on the mouth. // **Trial #2** — He came in, woke her up, started kissing her on the mouth, then raised her shirt and bra up while he was kissing her on the neck.

[*That's Asleep – Asleep – no mention – Awake – Asleep. The chronological sequence is also off. From waking her first then kissing her; to waking her when he took her underwear off and then French kissing her; to her already being awake, pushing up her shirt then kissing her; to being asleep, waking her up, kissing her, and then shoving her shirt up). Three of her comments were made under oath. Dixon's summary wasn't. How many potential lies are in that testimony? Could everything have been lies?*

Incidentally, in Trial #2, when Ross asked about the slow progression of incidents (referring to the grooming), Hanna said, "For a long time it was just pecks on the mouth. I wouldn't open my jaws or anything. He tried to get me to French kiss him, and I wouldn't do it for a long, long time," but she told Dixon that Steve began French kissing her that first night as soon as he woke her up. Another change from one version to the next.]

Noise, Bedcovers, and Dogs: Robin testified that the floors creaked and were noisy. During testimony about Counts II and III, Hanna talked about how adept she was at avoiding the creaky parts. When I mentioned that to Steve, he said there were no creaky *parts*, it was *all* creaky. The house, a Magnolia brand triple-wide mobile home, originally belonged to Robin's parents. In 1985, when Robin and Steve got married, her parents gave Robin the house, but continued to live there with them for the rest of their lives. Robin's mom, Ilene, passed away in 1988, and her father, Jeff, died in 1994.

The Magnolia came in a collapsed form, about a third of its final width when it arrived. Once it was fixed in place, installers unfolded the walls and floors out to their finished size. The house, not mounted on a concrete slab, sat on the axles that supported it during transport and on some additional struts for the sections that unfolded. The hinged floors creaked with nearly every step, something I can verify, having been inside it several times now.

Something else not mentioned in any of the documents was bedcovers. Hanna didn't say whether she was lying on top of the covers or under them (in late-November), and nobody else was asked. Based on data from NOAA, the low temperature for those late-November weekends could have been anywhere between 30° and 46° Fahrenheit. I asked Steve how cold the house was in the winter. He said, "As hell." Yes, that's a misnomer since we're talking about temperature, but he meant it was really cold. Steve said it was always cold in winter because they had left a lot of cracks and leaks when they did a poor job adding the living room to the original house. He also said that certain spots, especially along the southern exterior walls (where Beau's bedroom was) weren't insulated. Those walls were essentially trailer sheet metal with minimal insulation. In weather as cold as it was that night, they would have been using sheets and blankets. Lifting them or pushing them aside is something else that should have caused Marri to wake up. And where would the covers have been pushed onto? On top of Marri?

And then there were Podner and Bob, the family's Labrador Retrievers. They were both house dogs. Podner was a black lab they got in the mid-1990's. He passed away in 2003. Bob was a chocolate lab they got as a puppy early in 2003. Marri named him after their neighbor, Bob Laine, who died in late-

November 2002. Podner was inside the house that 2001 November night. In Trial #1, when Hanna described the alleged incidents after the cross-country race, Elmer Ross asked her if anyone else was inside with her and Steve. She said, "Just their dog." In the second trial, she said that the kids typically "watched TV or were outside in the yard, playing with the dog or something." Steve said that Podner and Bob were usually underfoot, and Marri described Podner as "a follower." If anyone stirred, the dogs were right at their heels, usually hoping they were going to get fed. If people were moving around at night, it's a sure bet the dogs would have been wandering too.

So, in addition to all the other possible things that could have caused Marri to wake up, we also need to consider shifting sheets and bedcovers, creaky floors, and wandering dogs, following anyone who might have been meandering late at night, clacking their toenails on the linoleum.

Conclusion: Whether Marri was a light sleeper or a deep sleeper, she *was* physically there. In almost all of Hanna's scenarios, someone else was there with them. That's because someone else always *was* in the same room, or vehicle, or house, or nearby. In Trial #1, even Hanna's mom, Darla, said of Steve, "He was usually one to have his daughter with him or his son or somebody. I mean, he was rarely alone." Unsurprisingly, after a mistrial in that first trial, Darla didn't repeat the comment in Trial #2.

Hanna couldn't deny that Marri was in the same bed with her, so I believe she tried to convince the jury that there was no chance of Marri waking up in the night by planting the idea that Marri couldn't have witnessed anything happening because she slept so soundly that she "never budged" and "didn't wake up at all." According to Hanna, the whole Sirois family, despite their denials to the contrary, were all sound sleepers (when they weren't drunks, another accusation Hanna tried to propagate a number of times). In most of her stories, she kept the focus on her and Steve, as if what they were doing was unaffected by outside forces or noises, or dogs, or cold, or lightly sleeping children. Just the two of them. Alone together.

A technique that's often used in the political arena and by con artists is: Tell a lie often enough, and people will eventually accept the most ridiculous falsehoods as truth. Let's apply Occam's razor here instead: *The simplest explanation is usually the right one.* Here are three possibilities: Out of 80 or 90 claimed incidents, Steve and Hanna never got caught, even though there were lots of potential witnesses around, because:

1) Dozens of people were so clueless that none of them ever noticed anything over the space of two-and-a-half years, even though some of them were frequently present when the acts allegedly occurred; or

2) Steve was such a skilled manipulator that he convinced everyone (especially those who were physically present) that something wasn't happening, even when it was happening right in front of their eyes; or

3) Steve and Hanna never got caught doing anything because they never did anything.

You know which one I choose, of course.

What Happened the Next Morning?

Why is This Important? Part of this is another clothes-related question, which I believe is just more of Hanna's window dressing. It was something brand new that she sprung on everyone during the second trial. She also did another 180° flip flop.

In Trial #1, Elmer Ross asked Hanna if she spent the rest of the evening at the Sirois' house. She said, "I stayed the whole night. And <u>then he took me home in the morning</u>." Ross, to clarify, asked who "he" was. She said, "<u>Sirois. He took me and my little brother home</u>." He asked her if there was anyone else in the car with them. She said, "No." He asked if Steve said anything to her during the ride home. She said, "No. I asked him that morning before we had left his house what happened. I didn't know if it was just a nightmare or what. He just said, 'S-h-h, keep your voice down. I don't want to talk about it now.'" Ross asked her what Steve meant by that. She said, "It meant, shut up, fly right, and don't breathe a word." Ross asked her if she told anyone about what had happened. Hanna said, "I didn't say a word."

[*Hanna said Steve quieted her, letting her know they couldn't talk about it until later, and then <u>he drove her and Aaron home</u>, which meant they couldn't talk about it because Aaron was in the truck with them.*]

Here's the Trial #2 excerpt. Check out how different it is. Ross asked Hanna what happened the next morning. She said, "He was wearing a hat -- I believe this was the same incident. It was like a trucker hat. And he had taken it off and set it somewhere close to the bedside table that was on the side of the bed that I was sleeping on. And <u>I remember that he had had it</u>. And when I got up in the morning, I <u>looked for it and I found it</u>. And then I took it to him and he was like, 'Oh, ___.' and I can't say the other word." Ross asked her what the word was. She said, "It starts with an "s," so..." Ross asked if it was a curse word. She said, "Yes." He asked her if Steve had left the hat in the room the night before. She said, "I know it was the hat he left in the room because he was the only one in there, and that was originally Beau's room and he didn't wear things like that." She added, "I asked him what had happened last night," and "He told me to keep my voice low, not to talk about it." Ross asked her what that meant. She said it meant, "Don't breathe a word. Just shut up, basically." Then Ross asked her if they went home. Hanna said, "Yes. I believe <u>my mom came and got me later that morning</u> after we had all had breakfast." He asked Hanna if she told her mother anything. Hanna said, "Not anything about what happened." Ross asked her why not. She said, "By this time, it had become a habit. And the first time that incident had occurred, it was just kind of implied to keep quiet."

[*This was the first and only mention of Steve wearing a trucker hat (or cap, or head covering of any kind) during one of their encounters, a brand new addition to her story. She said Steve left a trucker hat behind, and she <u>looked for it</u> in the morning. How did she know the hat had been left there if the room was so dark she couldn't see anything? She also said her <u>mom</u> came* *and brought <u>her</u> home (this time not mentioning Aaron). Her claim that Steve wore trucker caps, denim shorts and t-shirts or polo shirts to bed is peculiar as well as incorrect, but her final comment,* "By this time, it had become a habit. And <u>the first time that incident had occurred</u>, it was just kind of implied to keep quiet," *was also odd. There are two strange bits in the comment.* 1) *This was the first time she and Aaron spent the night. The hadn't visited often enough for it to have* "become a habit." *And,* 2) *By saying that Steve had, on an earlier occasion, hinted that she should* "keep it quiet," *she was saying that this <u>wasn't</u> the first time, which contradicts the affidavit, and the rest of her testimony as well.*]

I already knew Beau's likely answer to this, never having seen him without one, but I had to get it on the record, so I called him in 2015 and asked him if he wore trucker caps as early as 2001. He said, "Yes," as I had assumed he would. I told him about Hanna's claim that she found a trucker cap on the floor, next to the nightstand in his room. He said, unsurprised, "Right." I said that she testified that "she knew it had to be Steve's because you didn't wear those kinds of things." Beau said, "Oh, yeah? I always have." I also asked Beau if Steve would ever fall asleep with a trucker cap on. He said, "Only if he fell asleep in the recliner in the living room. Otherwise, no."

[*Beau today has a cap rack by his front door that has a dozen caps on it, and another in his guest room with several more. Look at the picture of Beau's old bedroom on the blog (yes, the room Hanna and Marri slept in). Are there trucker caps in the room? Of course there are. Also, check out the picture of Steve and Beau in trucker caps in 2001.*

I believe that Hanna probably came up with the idea of finding a trucker cap between the two trials to add a little more drama to her story and to use it to introduce a lie about Steve warning her to not tell anyone. The more detail added to a lie, the more believable it will be to some people. How could Steve possibly counter this? All he could do is say what he has said from the beginning, "I didn't do this. It never happened." In this case he could have added, "She didn't give me a cap. We never had that talk," but he wasn't asked about it.

Analysis: How Hanna and Aaron got home the next morning would ordinarily be an insignificant detail, but Hanna once again gave two different statements about it, both under oath. Trial #1 - Steve took her home; Trial #2 - Darla came and brought her home. Why did Hanna change that detail in between trials? It's even possible that she didn't know she had changed her story. During Trial #2, she had difficulty remembering what she had said three weeks before, even though she was given a copy of her testimony after the first trial was over. She admitted in Trial #2, that she had studied it before the first day's session, and again before the second day. If she had been telling the truth, though, she wouldn't have needed to "study" it. As Cleveland Sanford told me, "The truth doesn't change." Studying it would only be helpful if she was worried she wouldn't tell the same story the same way the next time. During the second trial, after she experienced continued difficulty remembering what she had said in the first trial, Judge Hawes loaned her his copy of that trial's transcript to read from. I don't think it was fair for him to give her a cheat sheet, but he's the judge so he can do that if he wants to.

Does it matter who took them home? Yes, because one statement was true and the other one wasn't, and both were given under oath. Darla was the most likely person to chauffeur the kids back to their house anyway, so why did Hanna tell two different stories about this? Maybe because, when she was asked the question in Trial #1, she couldn't remember, so she just made it up. Later, after realizing she was wrong, she changed it. She not only claimed two different rides home, though, she also decorated the new story with those additional details. In Trial #1, she kept it brief, saying that Steve told her to keep her voice down, he couldn't talk about it then, and that he took her and Aaron home. In Trial #2, though, she added the trucker hat. She also had Steve saying "Oh, shit" when she handed it to him. I think she was just pretending that she couldn't finish that phrase because it had a curse word in it.

She also added the false statement about it being Steve's cap because he wore those things and Beau didn't. Why did she add the element of the cap? Did she think the story needed to be punched up for the second jury? I don't know. The one thing I can say for certain is that Beau has worn trucker caps since he was very young (something Hanna had to be aware of, despite her comment). Incidentally, Darla wasn't asked in either trial if she gave Hanna and Aaron the ride home, and Steve wasn't asked about it in Trial #1.

As far as who took Hanna home, Steve was sure it had been Darla. He said, "I wouldn't have done it without clearing it that Darla was going to pick them up, because I promise I wasn't going to take them to the house and turn around the next day and take them home." Taking the kids home the next morning would have cost Steve an additional 41.8 miles, plus the mileage the night before, just to give Darla a night out. Also, Steve said several times that he could have been called in to work the next morning, in which case he wouldn't have been available to take them home anyway.

Cursing, French Kissing, and Innocence: Hanna may or may not have been prone to cursing, but I thought it odd that she said she couldn't repeat the word "shit" aloud, even though she was supposedly quoting Steve. To Tom, she readily quoted Steve as saying, "Damn that hurt," after she claimed that she bit his tongue the first time he tried to French kiss her. She also managed to use the word "dick" three times in her affidavit, and also said it to Ada Dixon. It was only in the trials that she seemed to clean up her language.

About the French kissing, Hanna told Ada Dixon that, after the movie, as soon as Steve removed her underwear he began French kissing her. In both trials, though, she said "It was a long, long time before I would even French kiss him." Which of those is true, that he began French kissing her the night of the first molestation, or after a long, long time? Or never.

How innocent was Hanna by the time of the trials? Her descriptions of sexuality may have led some jury members to believe that Steve did molest her, because how would a twelve-year-old know about those things? One thing to consider is that she wasn't twelve during the trials, she was seventeen. Also, in March 2005, less than a year after the accusation, Beau said he saw Hanna with another girl and two guys at midnight at Taco Bell. One of the guys, Cliff

Polinger, was twenty then and Hanna was sixteen. Just over a year later (April 2006), Polinger was arrested for burglary, a second-degree felony. He pled guilty, and was given ten years deferred adjudication and community service. In January 2008, he was arrested for lying to a police officer about the identity of an individual who was in the car he was driving (the charge was "hindering apprehension of a known felon"). He pled guilty to that, and served 30 days in jail. The following year (in March 2009), he was arrested again, that time for "delivery of a controlled substance" to a police officer (methamphetamine), and for possession of marijuana. He was indicted, pled guilty, and was sentenced to one year in state jail for that. At the same time, though, his earlier adjudication for burglary was revoked, so he ended up serving a seven-year sentence in state prison instead (the remainder of his time on the burglary charge). This was the same guy that Hanna said was going to help Josh beat up her abuser, something Josh claimed he didn't offer and didn't do. Was Darla aware that Hanna was hanging out with older guys like Cliff that late at night? Did she know that Hanna told Tom she became sexually active after the charges were filed? And yet, eight weeks after her interview with Tom, Hanna was on the stand, under oath, portraying herself as someone who was still so innocent that it embarrassed her to say a curse word.

Conclusion: Someone took Hanna and Aaron home the morning after the group went to see *Harry Potter*, most likely Darla. Who did it doesn't matter. What's important is that Hanna (under oath) changed her story from *Steve took me home* to *Mom took me home*. She also added the extra little scene about giving Steve back his trucker hat, and about his cursing, and about her being unable to say bad words aloud. Hanna was trying to convince the jury that she was still a sweet innocent lamb by telling them she couldn't curse. The problem is still the same, though. We only have Hanna's word that she talked to Steve that morning, and her word that she gave him back a cap, and her word that Steve told her to keep quiet, and her word that Beau didn't wear those kinds of hats. I refer you again to the 2001 picture of Beau and Steve wearing trucker caps.

Given all the lies I believe Hanna has told so far, her word on this matter isn't worth much with me, but there are still a lot more of her false statements ahead.

To quote Steve, "It's crazy."

To quote Hanna, "It is not that hard to fool people around here."

The Bonus Question:
Why Are Everybody's Memories So Different?

A person who speaks confidently is usually perceived as being more truthful and more accurate than someone who seems unsure about what they are saying. Steve, Marri, and Beau have said they remember very little about the night they went to see *Harry Potter*. Some people might interpret that as being evasive, but there is a more likely possibility. They may only have a minimal memory of that night because it was just an ordinary night. Driving to town in the truck along a familiar route was a regular occurrence for them. The memory of the ride faded quickly because they didn't try to remember it while the memory was still fresh. It was just a night at the movies. None of them spent hours in front of a mirror deciding what to wear to make the best impression on everyone around them, so they don't remember what clothes they or the others wore. If something unusual *had* happened, like protesters outside the theater the night they saw it, or rain, or bitter cold (things that did occur on some of those weekends), they likely would have remembered that, but none of them did. Since no unusual incidents occurred to spark a memory, they forgot specific details. I think that actually makes their recollection of the night more believable than Hanna's, which might have had more validity if any one of the other four passengers had an equally vivid memory that matched any of her differing claims, but no one remembered it as anything other than an average night. Based on her affidavit, even Hanna didn't attach any extra significance to it when she made the accusations. She mentioned the first time she spent the night in the affidavit, but placed it incorrectly in late summer, and said nothing about going to see a movie the night of her alleged first molestation.

Conclusion: Most people's ordinary memories shift and fade and change, or disappear altogether, if they aren't reinforced through repetition. I believe that Hanna constructed her memories (possibly by telling her friends variations on them long before the charges were filed). Then (in April 2004) she added a new element, a name for her alleged perpetrator. After the charges were filed, I think she continued repeating those scenarios (to herself and to friends). The repetition, along with the therapy sessions with Ada Dixon, and discussions with the DA's office, gave Hanna the perfect practice medium for trial preparation; especially with the addition of Dixon's book as a study guide. She may even have had a dress rehearsal with Tom Swearingen, as evidenced by adjustments she made to her script before the big show. Ultimately, though, I think she had created so many different versions that she couldn't keep them separate from each other, so portions of one sometimes bled over into another.

I also think Hanna was the only one who played with and rearranged these narratives before the trial. Steve and his family had no concrete memory of that night, so what did they have to practice? Having invented her whole story allowed Hanna to say whatever she wanted in the courtroom, which was safe for her to do because none of the other witnesses (except Steve, of course) could hear what she said during the trial. They were all outside of the courtroom, waiting in the hallway for their turn to testify.

Final Thoughts About Part 2

The movie isn't even mentioned in the affidavit. There is also very little in Hanna's interview with Tom about what happened after the movie, and almost no trial testimony from anyone but Hanna about it either. Beau and Marri weren't asked about it. Darla wasn't asked if she got a phone call from Steve. Steve wasn't asked if he made the call. Unbelievably, Steve wasn't asked a single question about what happened after they returned home from the movie. If Count I was so important to the prosecution's case, why was

Hanna the only one who was asked specific questions about what happened after they got back to the Sirois' home?

Hanna's affidavit was created from statements she made to Deputy Willard Knox. The affidavit's date for the Count I incident was late August or early September, about three months earlier than what Hanna claimed in the trials. The affidavit also had her wearing a completely different outfit than she testified to in her trial testimony, one better suited to a summer afternoon than a cold November night (but on that particular summer afternoon, according to her testimony, she remained in her track suit after the cross-country meet, not a t-shirt and blue-jean shorts). In the affidavit, she said she was asleep, but was awakened by Steve when he shook her shoulder and put his hand over her mouth (actions she never claimed after that), and said that he performed cunnilingus on her "for several minutes" before he stopped, said good night, and then left. Even though the indictment was based on that affidavit, Hanna tossed most of those elements aside within a month, changing the date of the first assault, the circumstances, the clothing, the weather, and adding an additional layer of incidents (but keeping the oral sex in the picture, although she said it was for twenty minutes to an hour, not just "several minutes"). After a minimal version of her new scenarios passed muster with Ada Dixon, I believe she began inventing more, and continued to refine them over the next two years, not knowing when the trial might happen.

I think she may have considered her interview with Tom to be a further test. Sounding oddly cheerful and confidant during large parts of the interview, she told Tom several things that were different from her previous statements. Maybe to see what he might challenge her on? Tom, being a good investigator, mostly just kept her talking.

In the trials, her story changed again. In Trial #1, she said she was awake, and, in Trial #2, asleep. Unlike her affidavit, she said nothing in either trial about Steve shaking her shoulder or putting a hand over her mouth. She dressed Steve in clothes he would never have been wearing in November, but also changed their color and style from what she told Tom. She added two entirely new sets of accusations about the early part of the evening, and added fingering and masturbation to the incident later that night, more items not mentioned in the affidavit. Almost everything she said in the trials was different from what she had sworn to earlier. Sanford questioned her about several of the changes she made from Trial #1 to Trial #2, and she backed away from a few of them, but denied even having said others (despite them being in the trial record).

If the prosecution had been required to prove Count I exactly as Hanna described it in her affidavit (happening in late August or early September, etc.), I don't think they would have brought the case to trial, especially since Counts II and III also bore no resemblance to the affidavit. I would also have thought, though, that any jury that was interested in reaching a just conclusion based on evidence rather than emotion, would have found Steve not guilty on all three counts. This jury didn't, and by now you hopefully know why.

Are you ready for a ride home from a rodeo?

The Night of the Rodeo

"…that place was awesome, the echoes are fricking loud ...but anyway, nothing happened there. It was kind of cool.
Hanna Penderfield

"He pulled over into the ditch. It was a really deep ditch. The truck was at a really big angle."
Hanna Penderfield

[Subsections in this Chapter: Questions and Other Stuff // Summary and Analysis: The Night of the Rodeo]

Questions and Other Stuff

In 2003, Hanna was given tickets to see a rodeo, so she asked Rhonda Bresnick to go with her. Steve gave them a ride home, stopping briefly at a water tower on the way. Hanna said that a sexual act occurred during the drive (while Rhonda was also in the truck), and that even more happened after they dropped her off. This wasn't on the DA's radar until mid-2005, and it wasn't referenced in the affidavit at all, but Hanna's story about that night still figured heavily in both trials, filling almost as much of Trial #2's testimony (58 pages) as all three counts combined (66 pages). Why did the prosecution think this night was so important? Why did they spend so much of the trial on it when it wasn't even one of the counts against Steve? And maybe a more important question is: given the nature of the claims Hanna made about this night, why did the prosecution wait more than a year to add this to their game plan?

I've broken this chapter into thirteen related questions and segments. I'll briefly handle five of them right now, and cover the lengthier ones after that. If you want more detail about the first five, complete coverage of them has been posted on the blog, beginning at this URL.

https://aggravatedbook.com/five-questions-part-1/

I'll also reference some images during the chapter. You'll find them at:

https://aggravatedbook.com/images-for-the-night-of-the-rodeo-chapter/

The first five questions/segments are: "When Was the Rodeo?" "Why Did Steve Give Rhonda and Hanna a Ride?" "Did Rhonda Already Know Who Steve Was?" "About the Water Tower" and "About the Truck." Here's the first one.

When Was the Rodeo? Much of the testimony about this was an incoherent mess. Neither Hanna nor Rhonda seemed to know what month or year or even what season it took place, and they weren't in sync with each other about what they did know. Hanna also tried to again stretch the timeline beyond reason. Bevin Jenkins asked her how soon after seeing *Harry Potter* they went to the rodeo. Hanna said, "For me, the years '03 and '04 are extremely mixed up. Because those were nearly two full years of this happening. And I don't remember what year the rodeo was. It must have been '03. That is my best guess." By suggesting that the rodeo could have been in either 2003 or 2004, and by using the phrase "those were nearly two full years of this happening," did she think she could add an extra ten months or so (from February 2004 to the end of December 2004) to her molestation claim? At least eight months of that time would have been after the accusations were lodged.

Both Hanna and Rhonda said the rodeo finished around 10:30 to 11:00 at night, but in the second trial, when Rhonda was asked when they got to the water tower, she said, "It was night around 12:00 or 12:30." They could have driven over a hundred miles between 10:30 and 12:30, but the tower is just 3.3 miles from the rodeo. Rhonda also testified that the drive to the water tower took "about 10 to 15 minutes," which doesn't square with reality or with the time she claimed they arrived there. I don't know why they couldn't get the correct answer to this in the trials. With a few phone calls and a social media post I found out that the rodeo usually ended between 10:30 and 11:00 each night, and the one they went to was likely on Friday, July 25, 2003.

Why Did Steve Give Rhonda and Hanna a Ride? Because Darla called him and asked him to. Darla presumably knew that Steve and Robin had driven (in separate vehicles) to see Robin's sister, Nancy, after they finished work that day, and knew that Nancy didn't live very far from the rodeo. There's more to it than that, of course. Steve told me, in 2014, "I was picking them up only because Darla had called and said she was drunk and didn't need to drive, and asked me to go and get them." Hanna told Tom, though, that Darla asked Steve because she "didn't feel like getting out." She testified, though, that "Mom said she would be too tired to pick us up." When Darla was asked, in Trial #2, if she had asked Steve to do that for her, she just said, "It's possible, yes," as if she didn't remember if she had asked him, but she also admitted that Steve and Robin did help her out with rides, and sometimes watched her kids, as favors for her.

Did Rhonda Already Know Who Steve Was? Rhonda either knew Steve or she didn't, but she and Hanna managed to muddy the waters about this too. The simple answer, is yes, Rhonda did know who Steve was when he picked them up that night. In her 2005 note, though (which we'll get to soon), she only referred to Steve as "the man who picked us up." In Trial #1, she said that Hanna and Aaron "came to our house every day after school, and they mentioned him [*Steve*] on several occasions," but in Trial #2 Rhonda said he "came to pick Hanna up from my house several times." Why didn't she say that in Trial #1? Did she and Hanna discuss their testimony between trials? There's a big difference between hearing someone's name and seeing them arrive at your house.

Hanna added to the confusion when she was asked if Rhonda had ever met Steve before the night of the rodeo. She said, "She met him very few times. He had come over to her house, where I was spending most of my time, and picked us up to take us out to his house." Aaron was at Rhonda's too, but by not mentioning him, Hanna gave the jury the impression that Steve had taken her and Rhonda to his house, not her and Aaron. I asked Steve if he had ever picked Hanna up at Rhonda's. He said that he had only been to Rhonda's house once before the night of the rodeo, and Robin had been with him. He said he couldn't remember for sure, but Darla had either asked them "to go pick her up, or we dropped her off to get rid of her, one of the two." If that seems a little callous, it was just Steve expressing himself honestly. From everything I've been told, Hanna was a handful, usually wanting to be the center of attention, sometimes whiny and petulant, having constant arguments with her mother, and not very pleasant to be around. Maybe they dropped her off at Rhonda's because Darla wasn't home yet. So, yes, Rhonda did know who Steve was the night of the rodeo, but not extremely well.

About the Water Tower. When Steve and the two girls left the rodeo, they passed a water tower and stopped to look inside. Three years later, Hanna and Rhonda appeared to be trying to turn that stop into something it wasn't, something disturbing. Steve was responsible for several towers as part of his job for the City of Deep Springs. Hanna told Tom that they left the rodeo "And he …um …let's see [*6-second pause*] ...uh ...he showed us this big water tower. I don't know where it is. It's ...I don't know. It's kind of in a secluded place. I don't know. It's a big, cylinder-shaped water tower." Was she hesitating so much because she was working out what to say in the trial? She added that Steve <u>let them</u> go inside, and told Tom, "...man that place was awesome, the echoes are fricking loud ...but anyway, nothing happened there. It was kind of cool." You can see a picture of it on the blog.

Hanna said that Steve was working for the state park, but he was actually still working for the city. He didn't start at the state park until a couple of months after the rodeo. To get inside the tower he had to unlock a gate and the door to the tower itself. How could he do that if he wasn't working for the city then? When I asked Steve about it, he said, "I stopped by a water tower which was my responsibility to monitor. The tower was on the way. Records that I acquired for Sanford showed that I had been called out to that tower constantly during the summer months. I just thought it would be nice to show them, and would also be nice for me to check on it to make sure it wasn't about to overflow, and that way I could sleep when I got home without worrying about it."

Both girls insisted that Steve took a number of different turns, and led them way out into the wilderness somewhere. Look at the map on the blog. The route from the rodeo to the water tower consists of only one turn onto a paved, streetlamp-lit road. He didn't take multiple turns down deserted roads heading out into the boondocks. There is a subdivision and a school just north of the tower. No one would build a water tower in the middle of nowhere to service a distant urban population. In Trial #2, Rhonda grudgingly agreed that Steve didn't force them to go there, that he did nothing to them while there, and made no advances toward either of them. The tower was even portrayed by the prosecution as being a romantic place. It's a very old, large, round concrete structure that holds a million gallons of water and is very dusty inside. Interesting mechanically, perhaps, but hardly a place to take someone for flirting and innuendo.

I also think that one of the issues Rhonda raised in the trials was a manufactured one. She said, "When we were walking in the water tower, he would put the hand on, like the bottom part of her [*Hanna's*] back." The prosecution tried to make that seem depraved, but it made me wonder. I had originally pictured the tower having a door that was flush to the ground, but I realized that wouldn't be practical. If the tower was flooded during heavy rains, or in case of one of the many overflows this old tower experienced regularly, the electrical equipment inside could be damaged. I asked Steve if there was any kind of a lip on the tower's door. He said there was. "It's about twelve inches. You have to step over the lip," and said there was also a second lip at an inner door inside the tower. So, touching Hanna's back might have just been to warn her to watch her step and not trip over some obstacle. It was fairly well settled during the trials, and agreed to by both girls, that nothing happened there. I think that (maybe after some urging from others on Team Hanna) Rhonda searched for anything she could think of to help strengthen Hanna's case, and the only thing she could remember was that Steve might have touched Hanna's knee (shifting gears), and that he had placed his hand on her back at the tower. That allowed them to turn what was probably a simple warning into something creepy. As Hanna said, "nothing happened there."

About the Truck. According to Hanna, a sexual incident happened in Steve's truck after they left the water tower. The truck's design itself makes some of her assertions highly unlikely, so (to give you some context for the incident) we need to learn a little about the truck. It was a Ford Courier, which Hanna described as "a small S-10 size, an older model." A collector of Couriers, Zeke Yewdall (his real name), gave me some details about them. Based on a picture I sent him, he said it looked like "a 1978 through 1982 Courier. A standard model, not the fancier XLT. It is a very small truck -- just getting three people in there at all is fairly squished." Small is right. The Courier only had a 61.4-inch-wide truck bed, so the seat width was smaller than that. Even assuming extremely thin doors, the seat was likely only 54 inches wide. Each of them would have had no more than 18 inches on which to place their posteriors. Add shoulder width and elbow room, and it would be nearly impossible to not knock elbows. The average coach seat on most airlines is between 17" and 18" wide, so that should give you an idea of how cramped it must have been for the three of them. I don't know any way to put this delicately; but, in 2003, Steve was 5' 11" and weighed 180 pounds, and Hanna was about 5' 4" and weighed around 140 pounds. I don't know what Rhonda's height or weight was, but she has been described to me as being about Hanna's size. We aren't talking about three exceptionally thin passengers. When Hanna and Rhonda were questioned about the size of the truck they used words like "tiny," and "itty bitty." It had a single bench seat and a standard transmission with a stick shift on the floor. This "itty bitty" truck was providing conveyance for three people, none of whom could be described as wafer thin, so they likely bumped into each other a little during the drive.

Hanna also tried to use the truck to demean Steve by accusing him of theft. When she was asked about the truck in the first trial, she said, "It belonged to a neighbor of his that had passed away." In Trial #2, she doubled down on that by saying "it <u>actually</u> belonged to his neighbor…but he had passed away, died from cancer." Ross didn't follow up either time, but just let the pseudo-accusation hang there for the jury to absorb. In my opinion, suggesting in open court that Steve might have stolen a truck from a dead man was an especially low act. The truck *had* originally belonged to his friend Bob Laine, but after Bob died Steve bought it from Bob's wife, Linsey. By saying it "actually" belonged to a neighbor, Hanna may not have committed perjury, but I think she was being petty and vindictive. The truck was not stolen, or even borrowed from a dead man. Steve owned it. Beau later sold the truck to help pay off the loan he took out to hire Cleveland Sanford to defend Steve in the second trial.

That should get us started. The rest of the questions and segments are: "Rhonda's Note, and When It Was Written" "What Was the Weather Like?" "How Did They Get to the Rodeo?" "How Dark Was It Inside the Truck?" "What Happened in the Truck on the Way to Alderson?" "What Happened After They Got to Alderson?" "Were Rhonda and Hanna Friends? and "Was Steve Physically Capable of Doing What Hanna Claimed?"

Let's begin with Rhonda's note, which was the primary reason the ride home from the rodeo became part of the trials.

Rhonda's Note, and When it Was Written

Why is This Segment Important? In August 2005, Hanna's mother faxed a copy of this note to the DA's office. Even though none of the three counts against Steve had anything to do with this night, I think that Rhonda's note, and that night's events, may have been included in the trials because the DA's office didn't think they had a viable case before its arrival. Steve told me that Seymour Cooper (the DA) was "more of a politician than a prosecutor, and didn't try the case himself because he didn't think he could win it," and that was how Elmer Ross (the ADA) ended up with the case.

By mid-2005, after several postponements, Ross may have been wondering if the trial was ever going to happen. He was likely pushing for more evidence, more details. Anything that could help flesh out what I could imagine (based on the inconsistent, frequently shifting story he had been given up to then) might have seemed like an unwinnable case. Maybe he asked Hanna and Darla if they could think of anyone else who might have witnessed something; because, despite all of Hanna's claims that so many people were present or nearby during incidents, the prosecution still had no substantive witnesses. Maybe, after Hanna remembered the ride home and the brief stop at the water tower, Darla talked to Rhonda about that night. After Darla faxed Rhonda's note to the DA, the trial might have suddenly seemed possible again. I have no idea if that's what actually happened, but several things point to that as a possible chain of events. Does Rhonda's note prove anything? I think I can convince you that it doesn't. Also, while Rhonda said she wrote the note shortly after the rodeo, it could have been created long after Hanna made the accusations. Let's find out if that's true.

Here is the text of Rhonda's undated note, as it was entered into the trial record, typed entirely in lower case, and punctuated exactly like the original. Her signature was the only thing handwritten. I've represented it with large italics.

> hey hanna. i know that we really dont get along but i know that you really need me to do this for you. the night of the deep springs rodeo when you and i went together.....i really dont remember that much from that night or any specific incidents. what i do remeber though is thinking that you and the man who picked us up seemed really involved in each other, or he seemed really envolved in you. i really didnt think anything of it at the time, but now that i sit here and think about it i realize how serious it could have been. all i really remember about that night was that we were in a small truck and you sat in the middle. he took us to a water tower and let us go inside. i also remember that in the truck, everytime i would look over at you he would have his hands on you. i never wanted to say anything because i figured that it was nothing to be concerned about, until you asked me about it. im so sorry that i can not be on more help to you but this is all i remember from that night. i do remember that things did not seem right and i really didnt want him to drop me off and you stay with him. i sensed that something was out of place, and im sorry that i cannot remember more from that night. i really hope that this can, in some way help you.
> all my love,
>
> *Rhonda Bresnick*
>
> Rhonda Bresnick

[*It has kind of an* archy and mehitabel *quality to it, doesn't it? I don't know if that was intentional, but ask yourself this: Does it read like a note written by a 14-year-old girl shortly after an incident, or does it read more like someone trying to imitate a young girl? Also, I find it curious that Rhonda's full name, in a note to a friend, was both typed* <u>*and*</u> *signed, as if she anticipated, back in 2003, that the note might be needed for a future legal proceeding.*]

When I saw the absence of capitalization and punctuation (in words like "dont" and "didnt"), the former English teacher in me rose grumbling to the surface. After a bit of study, I realized that there were only three misspellings ("envolved," "remeber," and "everytime," plus one weird phrase ("sorry that i can not be on more help to you"). Aside from those few things, though, the rest of the note was punctuated nearly perfectly, and was written (for the most part) with clear, logical phrasing. That was my first clue that it might not have been written by a fourteen-year-old. The note's content also contains information that could help prove it wasn't written in the summer of 2003. I did a geeky examination of all of that, and a line by line breakdown of the whole note on the blog, beginning at:

https://aggravatedbook.com/a-grammar-geeks-examination-of-a-note-part-1/

Did someone other than Rhonda type or dictate it? In Trial #2, when Sanford showed her a copy of it, she said, "I <u>typed</u> it." Could she have been truthful about typing it while hiding who composed it? I'm not a forensic linguist, but I believe this note was constructed long after the rodeo. The occasional misspellings and the lower-case lettering seem deliberate to me, as if they are mimicking a fourteen-year-old's style, with the lower-case characters trying to represent the affectations of a young girl. I think it could easily have been written by Darla, or by Rhonda or Hanna when they were sixteen. I have no proof, of course, and this is only speculation, but the note being typed, undated, and all in lowercase just felt deliberate to me. Some of the misspellings are strange too, like "involved" and "envolved" in the same sentence. The "i" and the "e" aren't remotely close to each other on the QWERTY keyboard. Mistakes like that feel intentional, and further reduce the note's credibility.

The most important phrase in the note, though, is "you really need me to do this." It didn't say "might" need me, or "will" need me, it said, "you really need me" (present tense, as in "you <u>do</u> need me <u>now</u>.") Why would Rhonda, right after a ride home (which she said in the note "was nothing to be concerned about"), say it was something Hanna needed right then? And if it was so urgent, in July or August 2003, why did she wait more than two years before giving it to Darla? Also, she said she "really didn't think anything of it <u>at the time</u>, but <u>now</u> that I sit here <u>and think about it</u>, I realize how serious it <u>could have been</u>." Not how serious it <u>is</u> (now, in the present), but how serious it <u>could have been</u> (reflecting back on the past). All of those phrases seem to me as if they were written some time <u>after</u> an event, looking back on it from a distance, <u>after</u> they've had time to think about it.

She also apologized multiple times for not being able to "remember more from that night." If she wrote the note right after the rodeo, why couldn't she remember it? Finally, she closed the note with, "I really hope that this can, in some way, help you." That's a lot of regret for a recent, possibly awkward ride home from a rodeo. It's more akin to what someone might say years later, after they have been convinced that a tragedy had occurred; one they, for example, could possibly have prevented but didn't. Rhonda seemed to have forgotten a lot of detail about that night, information she would have probably remembered if she had written the note soon afterward.

The phrase "…I figured it was nothing to be concerned about, <u>until you asked me about it</u>," is another clue. When did Hanna ask her about it? In Trial #2, Sanford asked Hanna how soon after the rodeo she saw Rhonda again. Hanna said, "The rodeo that I had gone to, I don't remember what night it was, but I know that I saw her that next Monday at school." When Rhonda testified, though, she said, "About two weeks later, she -- me and her talked about it, me and Hanna." The next Monday would have been July 28th. Unless there was school that day, and unless school was in session on August 11th (two weeks after the rodeo), Rhonda and Hanna may have both lied under oath. The first day of school in the Alderson School District that year would have been on August 25th (not July 28th or August 11th) Also, an Alderson school official verified for me that Hanna didn't have summer school in 2003, and wasn't on the campus using any of the school's computer equipment, something she did later when she was trying to graduate early. How could she have seen Rhonda the "next Monday at school" if she wasn't on campus, or if (as Rhonda said) they didn't speak for a couple of weeks? Their testimony was under oath. Were they both truthful?

Rhonda lived with her grandmother. In Trial #2, Cleveland Sanford asked her if she told her grandmother that she was worried, or if she called Hanna to make sure she made it home safely. Rhonda said, no, she didn't do either of those things; but, if she had actually been worried, she would have done something, wouldn't she? She could have tried to convince Hanna to get away from Steve, or asked Hanna to spend the night with her. She could have offered to walk the three blocks to Hanna's house with her, and let Steve go home. She could have gone to the police herself. She could have told a school counselor. But she didn't do any of those things. Did that night only seem serious to her in retrospect, years later?

The best evidence, though, that the note wasn't written in 2003 came when Elmer Ross asked about it in Trial #2, and Rhonda said she wrote it after Hanna told her and some friends "at a sleepover that she had lost her virginity and it was not her decision." She also agreed, when Ross asked her, that the sleepover took place "after April of 2004." Her answers became fuzzier under Sanford's questioning, though. When he asked her if she typed the note shortly after the rodeo, she said, "<u>I'm not sure</u>." Even when he asked her what year the rodeo was, she said, "2004, <u>I think</u>." But when Sanford asked her if she wrote the note after the allegations were made, she said "No," even though she had just testified that her reason for writing the note was <u>because</u> of Hanna's comments at the April 2004 sleepover.

[*She told Ross that she wrote the note after the April 2004 sleepover <u>because</u> of what Hanna had told them, and then told Sanford she wrote it <u>before</u> Hanna made the allegations. Doesn't one of those statements have to be false by default? I'll cover that in detail in the analysis, but didn't Rhonda also seem to be trying to avoid giving a date for generating the note? And how would Rhonda <u>know</u> in 2003 that Hanna <u>needed</u> her help? Was she prescient? How would the note, which claimed that the ride was* "nothing to be concerned about," *have helped Hanna shortly afterward?*]

Just to repeat, when Ross (in August 2006) asked Rhonda why she wrote the note, she said, "Because she had told us, me and several of my friends from school, <u>at a sleepover</u> that she had lost her virginity and it was not her decision." Ross asked when that conversation was. Rhonda said, "It was <u>a couple of years ago</u> in April." Ross said, "So, it would have been <u>after April of 2004</u>; is that right?" She said, "Yes, sir."

[*I can't overstate the importance of that statement. Rhonda admitted that she wrote the note <u>after</u> an April 2004 sleepover where she learned about Hanna's molestation, which Hanna apparently characterized as having* "lost her virginity." *Who were Rhonda's "several" friends?*]

Sorry, there are more discrepancies ahead, but we can't look at any of these comments in isolation. Everything is interconnected. Was Rhonda's sleepover the same one that Angie Womack attended (the one that Angie said took place in April 2002 or 2003, the one where the word "rodeo" freaked Hanna out, the one where Hanna told Angie and Suzanna she was being abused)? Was Angie giving Tom a correct date? How could the mention of the rodeo upset Hanna if Hanna and Rhonda hadn't been to to the rodeo yet? The only way this dichotomy would make sense to me would be if Angie's sleepover was an invention of Hanna & Company. In addition to Angie's recollection, we also need to remember that Hanna testified that she told her friends about her "experiences" at several sleepovers because her friends were boasting about various degrees of sex they had participated in. If the April 2004 sleepover (Rhonda's version) was the first time Hanna's friends heard about her troubles, though, and her school class only had a dozen girls in it, who were the friends she had been talking to for a couple of years? One more point. If these sleepovers did all take place in 2002 and 2003, all of these boastful girls were just 13 and 14 years old at the time. Does that make the brag sessions about sex seem more likely or less likely?

[*Was Angie telling Tom the truth? Could Hanna have told her to say that the sleepover was before 2004? Were Hanna's bragging-rights sleepovers just ordinary slumber parties with no revelations about sexual activity? Did they even happen? When I compare all of their statements, it makes me wonder if any of the versions are true. Anything is possible.*]

In May 2006, Tom asked Hanna when she and Rhonda next talked about the ride home from the rodeo. Hanna said, "I'd have to ask her. It was a while after that, though. It's that ...well, like I said, her letter's vague. It's kind of hard to tell." Tom asked if Rhonda had been interviewed. Hanna paused before answering, but sounding cross, said, "My -- lawyer -- got -- an investigator that was supposed to go talk to her and never did."

[*Hanna was awfully evasive. Tom asked her what she remembered, not what she and Rhonda could agree on. Yes, the note* is *vague, but the content of the note has nothing to do with when they next spoke.*]

In Trial #1, Ross asked Rhonda if someone had asked her "to give a statement about this, later on, several years later." Rhonda said, "Yes, sir." He asked her why she hadn't told anyone before then. She said, "Well, I had brought it up to Hanna later on, but she -- but she wouldn't talk about it." He asked if it was true that she and Hanna "don't really get along now, but you wanted to tell the truth and give her that statement; is that correct?" Rhonda said, "Yes, sir."

[*Ross said* "...you and her don't really get along now," *implying that they did get along at the time of the rodeo. If they* were *friends then, and Rhonda* did *write the note right after the rodeo, she wouldn't have opened the note with* "I know that we don't really get along," *would she?*]

Here's one more bit of Rhonda's testimony. Pointing to the fax copy of the note, Sanford asked Rhonda who sent it. She said, "Belisle Builders, I guess." He asked her to read the date on the header. She said, "August 23rd, 2005." He asked her if she gave the note to law enforcement herself, but she said, "No," and added, "I gave it to Darla Belisle, Hanna's mom." Sanford asked her if that was after Darla contacted her. Rhonda said, "Yes, sir."

[*When was the note written? It could have been anytime between the rodeo and when it was faxed. I do find it strange, though, that enough space was left between the bottom line and her typed name for Rhonda's signature. Isn't that too formal for a note? There is no way to prove when it was typed, or if Rhonda typed it herself, but wouldn't a fourteen-year-old handwrite a note to a friend instead of typing it? I do have serious doubts that the note was written shortly after the rodeo, but more on that in the analysis.*]

When Darla testified, Sanford asked her if she contacted Rhonda about being involved in the case. Darla said, "When Hanna remembered the incident, yes, I did." He asked her if that was after the allegations were made. Darla said, "Yes." Sanford said, "So, Rhonda Bresnick didn't come forward on her own, you contacted her?" Darla said, "Yes, I did."

[*No one asked Darla, though, when the note was written, or asked about her conversation with Rhonda when she asked her for the note.*]

Analysis: Darla faxed a copy of Rhonda's note to the DA's office from her workplace. According to Steve, Darla badgered Rhonda until she wrote it. If Rhonda had something to say, why didn't she give the note to the authorities herself? Why wait over two years, and then give it to someone else? Rhonda was fourteen during the rodeo and sixteen when Darla faxed the note. Obviously, it wasn't written before the rodeo or after it was faxed, which gives us just over a two-year window during which it could have been created. Here's what the header at the top of the fax looked like:

LEON BELISLE BUILDERS; [*phone #*] AUG-23-05 8:22AM; PAGE 4/5

The far right of the header indicates that this note was on the 4th page of 5. The first page would have been a cover page, but I'm curious as to what pages 2, 3, and 5 contained. An explanation from Darla about the ride and the note, maybe? I saw no other pages from the fax in the DA's files in 2016. I only have a copy of the note because it was entered into evidence for both trials. What happened to the other pages? In the 2004 brainstorming session, Roland Mathis said he thought Steve would be tried early in 2005, maybe in January. The fax was sent to the DA about seven months after that. Why hadn't Steve been tried by then? Why did this document appear so late in the game? Was the note what tipped the balance toward finally trying Steve? Possibly, but the first trial still didn't take place until eleven months after the fax was sent.

Conspiracy-Theory-Type Question: I already told you about the missing rape kit. Elmer Ross sent a request to find it in March 2005, five months before Rhonda's note surfaced. Deputy Conner told me that there should have been more information in the DA's file if a rape kit had been done. March 2005 was one month after the original trial date. Could Hanna and Darla have told the DA about a non-existent rape kit when the February trial date got rescheduled, maybe thinking that might create some momentum; then a few months later, after that didn't work, used Rhonda's note in another attempt to make something happen? True or not, it's only one of the many bizarre thoughts I've had about this case.

Back in Non-Conspiracy Land: Here are some logical questions I have about Rhonda's note. If the note was for Hanna, why didn't Rhonda give it to her in 2003? Why did she wait two years until Darla asked for it? Also, if she wrote it shortly after the rodeo because she felt odd about that night, it should read more like a diary entry, shouldn't it? It seems more like a prepared statement that's trying to feel spontaneous. Some of the note's details make it seem less like a letter to a friend, and more like a catalogue of events; almost as if someone was standing over Rhonda's shoulder while she worked on it, saying, "Just type up all of your feelings about that night and what happened. Don't leave anything out. We need you to do this."

Conclusion: I know that the details I've given you about the note are extensive, so I'll keep this short and sweet. You have seen throughout this book that several people have probably lied about a variety of things. I believe that the contention that the note was written soon after the rodeo is likely one more lie. It could have been constructed by Rhonda on her own in 2005 (possibly to get Darla to stop bugging her), or by Rhonda and Hanna working together, or (it *is* all typed) even written by Darla herself. Why? Maybe because she thought Hanna stood a good chance of losing the case. Rhonda testified under oath that she wrote the note "after April 2004." If that's true, the rest of her testimony about the note isn't. Or, if she did write it earlier, her testimony about the April 2004 sleepover giving her the impetus she needed to write the note isn't true. I do think that the proof that Rhonda didn't write the note in 2003 is in the document itself, though. The language is clearly about a distant-past event, not about something that happened just a few days or weeks earlier. I also believe that the information on the previous pages strongly suggests that multiple lies were told about the note and other events related to that night. Each lie adds up, of course, and each new one casts more doubt on the rest of Hanna's claims.

What's next? The weather, of course.

What Was the Weather Like?

Why is This Question Important? Hanna (as she did in her Harry Potter testimony) made a number of statements about the temperature and the clothes she was wearing the night of the rodeo. The truth about the weather that summer could help verify or discredit her descriptions.

In the first trial. Elmer Ross asked Hanna, "What time of year was it, spring, summer, winter, fall? Hot, cold outside?" Hanna said, "I don't remember. We were there in the evening, so I don't really remember. It got kind of chilly a little bit later on. It might have been in the fall, but I don't know. That was the first time I had ever been to the Deep Springs Rodeo. I don't know what time of year it is or anything. Even now, I don't pay any attention."

[*She didn't remember the season because it was chilly? And because it was in the evening?*]

In the same trial, Hanna said that Steve was making small talk after he picked them up, asking them about school, etc. Then she said, "After he got done talking, it got kind of quiet in the truck. And I had my arms crossed because it was kind of cold and the windows were down."

[*Steve told me that the reason the windows might have been down, or at least cracked, was because it was a very old truck, and it had no air conditioning, so he often drove with the windows down in* <u>*warmer weather*</u>*. So, if the windows were down, it must have been warm outside. If it had been cold, the windows would have been rolled up. If it actually was cold, I could understand Hanna crossing her arms for warmth, but would it have been quiet with the windows down?*]

Hanna had one more comment about her wardrobe. She said, "I had been wearing warmer clothes than usual." Ross asked her what she meant by that, and she said, "Well, I had on two shirts instead of one."

[*Of course. In cold weather, you wear warmer clothes and multiple layers, right?*]

She repeated that description in Trial #2. Ross asked her, "What happened when you got back in the truck?" Hanna said, "It was kind of chilly. Because it was <u>still</u> the time of year when it got cool at night. I had already had like two shirts on, I believe. I didn't have a jacket with me or anything, but it was kind of chilly that night." Later she said, about Steve, "He pulled his shirt over his shorts."

[*She said it was chilly, but she's got Steve in shorts again. Would he be allowed to wear shorts to work?*]

In Trial #2, Hanna made one other clothing/weather comment about that night. She said, "I had on like a spaghetti-strapped shirt with the built-in bra and I had a bra underneath that, but, on top of the spaghetti-strap, I had a denim button-up shirt. And he asked me why I had to wear so many clothes and make things so difficult. I said <u>it was cold out</u>."

[*She was still insisting it was cold. Let's check out the weather.*]

Here's some data from NOAA's Climatological Record, using hourly readings for Deep Springs, Texas, sourced from WTXD Radio, the area's official weather reporting agency. The summer of 2003 was a hot one. As early as April there were two days in the 90's. In May there were sixteen days in the 90's and three in the 100's. June had a single 101 degree day and sixteen days in the 90's. July, the month the rodeo was held, had twenty days in the 90's and nine days in the 100's; August had twenty-seven days in the 90's or 100's, and seventeen of them were 100 or above (the hottest was 111). The night they went to the rodeo, Friday, July 25th, the temperature at 11:00 pm, about the time they left the rodeo, was 87.8 degrees (with a heat index of 89.4). If it's still nearly 90 degrees four hours after the sun sets, it was hot that day.

[*How could Hanna make the claim that it was* "<u>still</u> the time of year when it got cool at night" *when, in the three-and-a-half months before the rodeo, there had been nearly fifty days in the 90's and the 100's? No matter how cold she said it was, the thermometer doesn't lie, and 87.8 in the dark is hot by any measure. Also, around 6:00 pm, when they probably left home for the rodeo, the heat index was 99 degrees. Why did she insist it was cold?*]

Analysis: Hanna was so wrong about the weather, almost as if she was making it up. She said it "got kind of chilly," and "it was kind of cold," and that she was "wearing warmer clothes than usual," and "it was kind of chilly that night," and "it was cold out."

In Deep Springs on July 25, 2003, the low temperature (75.2° F.) occurred at 4:30 am. After that it did nothing but climb. The high was 98.6, with a heat index of 104.9. Late at night, between 10:30 and 11:00 pm (about when they left the rodeo to go home), the heat index was 89.4. The whole spring and summer that year was overly warm. Between April and September there were 94 days in the 90's or the 100's, but Hanna said she was wearing two layers of shirts, and had her "arms crossed" because "it got cool at night." When they arrived at the rodeo (maybe 7:00 pm), the heat index was still in the 90's. She would have been sweating buckets through those double layers. Cold weather was logical when they saw *Harry Potter* in November, when it gets down to freezing and below some nights. In mid-summer in Central Texas, though?

Hanna also tried to put Steve in shorts again. Normally, shorts *would* make sense in mid-summer, but Hanna got this one wrong too. Steve said that his work clothes, when he worked for the city, were jeans (even in the summer) and a white uniform shirt. No, he wouldn't have been in shorts.

Conclusion: I have no idea why Hanna said it was cold, or that she was wearing multiple layers, or why she placed Steve in shorts, but it wasn't true. I believe she might have said that because so little happened that night that Hanna may have felt that she had to dress it up with other details, whether true or not; and her go-to items for details seemed to be weather and clothing, even though she clearly didn't remember that evening (or apparently even the season) all that well.

Hot is not cold. Jeans are not shorts. Lies are not truth.

The next question is easily answered, but one aspect of it might not be easily understood without some explanation.

How Did They Get to the Rodeo?

Why is This Question Important? It shouldn't be, but one of Rhonda's answers could be.

Ross asked Hanna in Trial #1, "How did you get to the rodeo?" She said, "My mom had taken us and dropped us off."

[*Hanna's mother, Darla, drove them there and dropped them off. That's simple enough.*]

When it was Rhonda's turn, Ross asked her the same question. She said, "Darla dropped us off, <u>I believe</u>." To verify, Ross asked if Darla was Hanna's mother. Rhonda said, "Yes, sir."

[*Rhonda said she <u>believed</u> Hanna's mom dropped them off? Hold on to that thought.*]

In Trial #2, Ross asked the same questions again. Hanna answered the same way, saying her mom dropped them off, but when he asked Rhonda this time, she just said, "We were dropped off," without identifying a driver.

[*In Trial #1, Rhonda didn't seem positive about who drove them there, but a month later she kept it simple and unambiguous. Why? I have a theory. Here's the analysis.*]

Analysis: According to all the testimony, Hanna's mother did drive them to the rodeo, so why even explore it? Because Rhonda qualified her answer in Trial #1 when she said, "Darla dropped us off, I believe." Admittedly, she also seemed unsure about the month, "…early summer. May, I think" (it was July), unsure of her age then, "13 or 14" (she was about two months shy of turning 15), but I found it difficult to believe that she wouldn't remember if it was her friend's mother who dropped them off. Could there have been another reason for her answer? Remember Eddie Higham, the sex offender that Darla said she dated for "eight or ten months, maybe?" Even if Eddie did leave Darla's house after four months (something Eddie's sister, Peggy, confirmed for me), if Darla continued to see him for four to six more months she could have been dating him in July 2003, the month of the rodeo. Could she also have still been seeing him as late as April 2004, when the charges were filed? That's all just speculation on my part, of course, but it is an interesting idea, especially since (in April 2004, during Blake Goudy's speech) Hanna allegedly told Karla Spivey that she had been molested by her mother's boyfriend (not her mother's ex-boyfriend). Yes, I know, that's hearsay.

I realize I sometimes wring every last scrap of detail out of a document (or a paragraph, or a sentence), but what if Rhonda's "I believe" meant something other than just "I think so?" What if someone else (like Eddie) was with Darla when the girls were dropped off, or was even the one driving Darla's truck? Could Rhonda initially have said "I believe" because she wasn't sure what to say, but just bypassed the issue in Trial #2 by generically saying "We were dropped off?"

Conclusion: I have no reason to believe that Darla didn't drop Hanna and Rhonda off at the rodeo. Whether someone else was with her at the time, though, I don't know.

In all of Hanna's testimony about the alleged incidents of abuse, she tried to offer explanations for why no one else noticed them happening. Under the cover of darkness was one of them.

How Dark Was It Inside the Truck?

Why is This Question Important? Hanna created another outlandish situation inside a truck, including some difficult-to-believe actions, but also said that it was probably too dark for Rhonda to see very much. Let's see if the inside of the truck was more well lit than she claimed.

In Hanna's interview with Tom, he asked her if she thought Rhonda had a hard time seeing because of the dark. Hanna said, "Um, there was just enough light from the dash to probably tell that …she probably saw that something wasn't right."

[*Hanna suggested that there might have been just enough light for Rhonda to tell that something strange was going on, but just barely.*]

In the trials both girls were asked about the time of night, and how dark it was. In Trial #1, Hanna just answered Ross' dark or light question with, "Dark." Rhonda agreed that "it was dark outside." In Trial #2, Hanna again said that it was dark.

[*I agree. It probably* was *as dark as it normally is at night, in a truck, driving on a combination of rural and urban roads. But how dark is that?*]

The maps on the blog will help the following data make more sense. View them on a large monitor if you can. Beau and I took several drives from the rodeo grounds to the town of Alderson. Our aim was to find out just how much light there was along the route. Steve and the two girls drove a total of 22.8 miles that night. Between the rodeo and the turnoff to FM 29 (also known locally as the Ritter Highway access road) the area was well-lit with street lamps and other lights from the rodeo and businesses. From that intersection to the water tower there were 10 more street lamps (a total of 3.3 miles so far), plus there were a number of other lights surrounding Shaper Unit, the prison that was across the road from the tower. In the next 6.6 miles, from the tower to US 179 (the turnoff to Bloom) there were 15 more lamps. In the 1.7 miles from there to the intersection of 179 and US 373 (the turnoff to Alderson) there were another 19 lamps, and a whopping 27 more in the 2.7 miles after that. That only brought them to the eastern city limits of Bloom (population 2,500). The next two lamps were 4.4 miles away; and a mile later there were two more at the entrance to Alderson. Between there and Rhonda's house (less than a mile farther) there were at least 16 more street lamps and assorted lights from homes and businesses.

I'm not saying that the interior of the truck was flooded with light the whole way from the rodeo grounds (and we will only be concerned with how dark it was from the water tower to Rhonda's house anyway), but there were many spots on the drive where the interior of the truck would have been momentarily bathed in light from the outside as they approached and passed under street lamps. Also, as Hanna said, there would have been some glow from the dashboard lights. The longest stretch with no external lighting would have been in the final 4.4 mile stretch near Alderson, but that takes less than four minutes at 65 miles per hour. Near the end of July 2003, a waning crescent moon would also have provided a little light, but it would have been minimal.

Obviously, Steve's truck wasn't in total darkness the whole way. There would have been frequent moments when light would have illuminated the interior very well.

[*The main thing to remember when reading any of Hanna's descriptions is that, no matter how much she may pretend otherwise, nothing was happening in a vacuum. Her narrative always felt to me like she was spinning out the details she wanted everyone to hear, but ignoring things that might give a fuller picture of the surroundings and circumstances.*]

Analysis: For Hanna's story to be believable, she had to convince the jury that it was light enough inside the truck for Rhonda to see something. Actually, there probably was plenty of light for Rhonda to have witnessed everything that Hanna said she did to Steve, but Rhonda testified that she didn't see Hanna do anything (that's coming up soon). Let's start by seeing how well the interior of the truck might have been lit. I have driven this route several times now, cataloging each of the street lamps and other potential sources of light. Drive it with me now, using the maps on the blog, paying attention to the lighting along the route from the rodeo grounds to Alderson. Whenever I indicate that there were two or more street lamps at any individual location there were always lamps on both sides of the road. Here we go.

From the rodeo grounds we head south on US 373. I'm driving, you're in my passenger seat, and someone is sitting between us. We're in a small pickup, on a bench seat. As we leave the rodeo, there are 12 street lamps and lights from businesses in the 1.4 miles from there to the corner of US 373 and FM 29. We pass between two more street lamps at that intersection and three more lamps soon after we turn left onto FM 29, heading east. This is the one and only turn we make on the way to the water tower. Halfway there, three more lamps light up another road heading north, then we pull to a stop across the road from the water tower (on our left) just 3.3 miles from the rodeo. To our right, three street lamps mark the entrance to the Shaper Unit, a state prison. The prison is also surrounded by dozens of vapor lamps, all as tall as the street lamps. It positively glows in the dark, casting some of its light across the road onto the water tower. We took less than four minutes to get here, driving well under the speed limit of 65 mph, and passed a hospital complex, some manufacturing plants, and a few houses along the way. It's far from deserted.

We're on the road again, still heading east on FM 29. Two-tenths of a mile farther, we come to two street lamps at another road that heads north into the city. A half-mile after that FM 29 veers sharply south. There are three more lamps here, plus a well-lit National Guard building off to our right. Every time we pass any of these lamps light floods the interior for a moment. We don't take 29 to the south, though, we just stay straight. Even though we're now on a different road, FM 1517, it doesn't feel like it. We enter a zone of relative darkness. The road curves gently toward the northeast, and for 3.1 miles there aren't any lights from street lamps. This is the second-longest unlit stretch on the entire drive. At the end of this dark zone we reach Rock Squirrel Road, another entrance to Deep Springs. The four lamps here light up this intersection very well. We were in that first dark area for less than three minutes, and left the water tower barely five minutes ago. The next intersection is 1.4 miles farther, where 1517 ends at US 179, known locally as the Ritter Highway. There are four street lamps there too, one on each corner.

We turn left onto 179, slow to 30 mph, and head slightly northwest for 1.7 miles to an intersection known as The Split.** It's obvious why it's called that, three major roads converge here.

**The Split is an invention to help disguise the city represented by Deep Springs. There *is* an intersection at that location, but the actual configuration of the roads there is slightly different. The mileages depicted here are completely accurate, though.

The Bloom Junction Mall, where they saw *Harry Potter*, is on the north side of this intersection. Before we get there, though, we pass 19 street lamps, and then encounter five more at The Split. Any of them we pass at this slow speed flood the interior for twice as long as they did on the roads we were on earlier. We have been in Bloom, Texas, now for a couple of minutes, and it's very brightly lit. We reach here less than ten minutes after leaving the water tower. Sitting at The Split, we are surrounded by overhead lights and lights from businesses and homes. If you looked at me now from the passenger seat, you would be able to clearly see anything I was doing. From here we could go in several directions, but we turn right onto US 373 and head northeast toward Alderson. There are still a lot of street lamps to pass before we leave Bloom, though. Twenty (20) more of them in the next 5.5 miles.

Then, on US 373, we reach our second dark zone. It's another 4.4 miles before we reach the two lamps that announce the end of it, the longest section of unlit road on the whole route. We breeze through it in four minutes flat, though. A mile later we are greeted by two more lamps at the entrance to Alderson. We pass another 16 slightly dimmer street lamps, plus lights from a few businesses, on our way through Alderson. Even after slowing down to 30 while we were in Bloom, though, we still get here roughly twenty minutes after we left the water tower. There were over 120 street lamps, plus light from a scattering of businesses and homes on the road between the rodeo grounds and Rhonda's house. Incidentally, except for the time inside Bloom and Alderson, the street lamps were the only thing tall enough to overhang the road. Most trees were scrub oak, not very tall, and back from the road a bit.

Hanna mentioned one more light source when Sanford asked her how far it was from Deep Springs to Alderson, she said "the way traffic was that night" it would have taken them "between 25 and 30 minutes" to get home. She was then asked if she knew the distance between Alderson and Deep Springs. She said, "13 miles." In other words, there were enough cars and trucks on the road after the rodeo that she believed they would only be able to drive about 30 mph going home. That suggests that there were a lot of cars leaving the rodeo. Heavy nighttime traffic would have generated more light. Add the street lights and the headlamps together, and the interior light in the truck could have periodically been substantial.

It could be argued, since the dark zones filled 7.5 miles of the distance (3.1 and 4.4 miles combined), that a lot of time was spent in them, but they were going 60 to 65 mph while they were in them. In Trial #1, Hanna said that, after Steve "showed us the water tower, he was kind of talking to us a little bit whenever we left," asking Rhonda questions. The first unlit area was only two miles from the water tower. They would have easily reached the dark zone before he stopped talking, so, even if Hanna started in on Steve as soon as they reached the first dark zone, four street lamps would likely have announced the end of it with a blast of light before she could even get his jeans unzipped. After driving slowly through very brightly lit Bloom, the final dark zone would also have come and gone quickly. In those two unlit areas, provided there weren't other vehicles nearby to cast extra light on them, they would only have been in steady darkness for a few minutes each.

Here's one final thing to think about while you're reading the next section. Neither of the girls testified that it was too dark to see. Actually, they said things like "she kept kind of glancing over there," and "he made movements with his hands," and "Rhonda kept looking over." If they could see that, and the dozens of other things they described, wouldn't there also have been plenty of light in the truck to see everything else that Hanna claimed was happening?

Conclusion: Hanna said she wasn't sure if Rhonda could see what she was doing to Steve, and Rhonda said she kept looking over at them, but didn't see anything. And Hanna said there might have been "enough light from the dash" for Rhonda to see "that something wasn't right," but Rhonda had a lot more than just dashboard lights. Most of the route is either littered with street lamps or had at least a few lamps every hundred yards or so. There are only two sections that have no lighting, and they would have passed through those areas quickly. There also might have been a fair bit of traffic to cast headlights their way. If Rhonda looked over even occasionally, she should have seen anything that was happening. She did, in fact, say that she saw Steve touching Hanna's knee (possibly when he shifted gears), and gave a vague comment about his hand being "around her." Remember, they were on a bench seat in a tiny truck. The distance between Steve and Rhonda was eighteen inches at best, and Hanna was between them. There wasn't even a console to hide Steve's lap. Rhonda didn't say it was so dark she couldn't see anything. She said she kept glancing over, *trying* to see something, but didn't.

There was nothing to see.

Now that you have an idea how much light there might have been during the ride, let's see what Hanna said happened in the truck, on the little tiny bench seat, with Cindy sitting right beside her.

What Happened in the Truck on the Way to Alderson?

Why is This Question Important? Hanna made specific claims about what happened during the ride to Rhonda's house. Think about how dark it wasn't while you read what she said. Also, I shouldn't need to warn you by now, but there are graphic descriptions ahead.

Tom asked Hanna what happened after they left the water tower. She said, "He unzipped his pants and drug my hand over to his crotch." Tom asked if Rhonda saw that. Hanna said, "She kept kind of glancing over there, and I thought she might've seen something, and she never actually said anything, and the letter that she wrote is very vague." Tom asked if Rhonda was afraid to talk about it, or if she just didn't see anything. Hanna said, "I honestly don't know, because her and I used to be best friends, and the past couple of years we haven't been that close. It's just typical girl stuff." He asked if Steve put his arm around her or his hands on her while Rhonda was in the truck. She said, "No." He asked her what she thought Rhonda saw. Hanna said "She probably saw that something wasn't right, because my arm was not in a normal position."

He asked what she meant by that. Hanna, sounding frustrated, said, "No, see I …grrr …my arm …my arms were crossed. I was sitting on his right side, but I reached over with my right arm, so it *looked* like my arms were crossed. It looked …it looked kind of funny, because you could tell my arm was straining a little bit." After six seconds of silence she added, "I don't know exactly what she saw. I don't …uh ...I don't know. I was hoping it wasn't obvious at the time, but now I hope to god it was."

[*Hanna told Tom that Steve didn't put his arm around her or his hands on her, but said that he unzipped his pants and dragged her hand over to his crotch, that her arms* "looked like" *they were crossed, and that Rhonda kept* "glancing over." *Compare that to her testimony from the first trial.*]

In Trial #1, Ross asked Hanna what happened after the water tower. She said, "He was kind of talking to us a little bit whenever we left. He would ask a question about Rhonda and I would answer for her because we had been very close at one time, and I knew that she was real shy around people she didn't know very well. She was real quiet. She wouldn't answer a question that was spoken directly toward her." Ross asked her what kinds of questions Steve asked Rhonda. Hanna rattled a few of them off. "Where do you go to school?" "How old are you?" "How long have you known Hanna?" "And I answered for her every time. And then finally he just said, 'I'm not trying to be mean, but I'm talking to Rhonda here.'" Ross asked why Steve wanted to know so much about Rhonda. Hanna said, "No. He -- The way he asked the questions, it wasn't, to me, out of the ordinary that someone would ask, if you just met somebody that is a friend, I thought it only natural for an adult to ask a kid questions just to make them feel like they were getting attention... After he got done talking, it got kind of quiet in the truck. And I had my arms crossed because it was kind of cold and the windows were down. I had my left arm over my right arm. And he reached over and grabbed my right arm and pulled it to the furtherest extent without me actually turning, and put my hand on to his zipper on his jeans. And he kind of -- he kind of made movements with his hands to show that I was to help him unzip his pants...so I did. And he pulled his penis out and put my hand around it and started moving my wrist up and down." Ross asked if Rhonda was still there, and Hanna said, "Yes. He kept glancing sideways at her. I kept doing the same to make sure she wasn't looking or anything."

[*Hanna said that Steve asked Rhonda questions someone might ask if they* "just met somebody," *but Rhonda said she knew Steve because* "He came to pick Hanna up from my house several times." *Hanna said her arms were crossed (left over right) because it was* "kind of cold," *but she told Tom that her arms just looked like they were crossed (right over left, the opposite of what she testified to). She also told Tom they were crossed because of what she was doing, not because she was cold (another difference).*

Question: If Steve could manage to steer, shift gears, grab her hand, make "movements with his hands" *(plural), pull out his penis, put her hand around it, and move her wrist up and down, why did he need her to unzip his pants?*

Side Note: He can't "glance" *sideways to his right (his glass eye).*]

Let's see what Rhonda said. This is still Trial #1. Ross asked her if she saw anything that night that made her feel uncomfortable. Rhonda said, "He put his hand on Hanna's knee. She was sitting in the middle of the truck. He would put his hand on her knee and around her." Ross asked her why that made her feel uncomfortable, and she said, "I just didn't see it as a friend-of-the-family type thing. It seemed more than that." He asked her what it did seem like. She said, "It appeared more like a boyfriend-girlfriend sort of thing." He asked her if anything else made her feel that way. She said, "Just when we were walking in the water tower, he would put the hand on, like the bottom part of her back, and just things like that." Then he asked if she tried to observe them in the truck. She said, "Part of the time, I would turn away toward the window and just look out the window, and I would look over there every once in a while to see what was going on."

[*Hanna sat in the middle, in an* "itty bitty" *truck, next to the gearshift. Rhonda said she saw Steve put his hand on Hanna's knee and touch her back while they were at the tower, and felt that was* "more like a boyfriend-girlfriend sort of thing." *Plus, Hanna said the windows were down. Was Rhonda saying they were up? She also testified that she looked* "over there every once in a while to see what was going on," *but still didn't see* <u>*Hanna*</u> *doing anything, only Steve. Hang on to that thought for a while.*]

When Bevin Jenkins cross-examined Rhonda, he asked her if she ever saw Hanna's hand on Steve's sexual organ. Cindy said, "No." He asked her if she knew what a sexual organ was. She said, "Yes, sir." He asked her if she knew what masturbation was. She said, "Yes, sir." He asked her if she ever saw Hanna do that to Steve. Rhonda said, "No."

[*Rhonda didn't see Hanna masturbate Steve, but how could she not have seen Steve's penis if it was out in the open, and erect, with Hanna's hand wrapped around it, just a couple of feet away from her?*]

When Steve took the stand, Jenkins started by asking him what kind of transmission the truck had. Steve said, "It's a standard." Jenkins then asked him if he had touched Hanna's leg. Steve said, "I could have bumped her shifting gears, but that would have been all it was." Jenkins continued, asking Steve a series of other questions in rapid succession. "Did you put your hand on her and squeeze her leg or anything like that?" "Did you put your hand in her private area?" "Did you put your hand on her breasts?" "Did she put her hand on you?" "In your private area?" Steve answered, "No, sir" to all of those. Jenkins asked, "Does it seem pretty incredible that somebody would do that with a kid sitting next to them?" Steve said, "It's just, I can't believe it. I can't believe any of it."

[*Firm denials. He said he* "can't believe any of it." *Neither can I.*]

In Trial #2, many of the questions were repeats, but some of the answers weren't. Elmer Ross asked Hanna what happened after they left the water tower. After again talking about how cold it was, she said, "I was sitting with my arms crossed, my left arm over my right. And the truck was a standard. Most of the time, he kept his right hand on the gearshift. He reached across with his left hand and took my right hand where I actually had to stretch to move my hand all the way over, he drug his hand over -- drug my hand -- I'm sorry -- over to his crotch and I helped him unzip his zipper." Ross asked her why she did that. Hanna said, "Just a habit. It was something I learned to tolerate." He asked her what Rhonda was doing during this. She said, "I kept watching her, just to keep a close eye on her. She kept kind of looking and then she would turn away and kind of stare out the window for a while. Then she would just kind of glance over and do the same thing again every couple of minutes or so." He asked her what happened next. Hanna said, "She kept doing that over and over again. I was wondering if she noticed anything, because she never said a word. And he had already taken my hand and had put it on his penis, and I just began automatically to move my hand up and down." Ross asked if Steve said anything to her. Hanna said, "No." He asked her how long the masturbation lasted. She said, "We were -- I'm not sure where the water tower was. I still don't know where it is, but I'm guessing we were about 10 or 15 minutes away from Alderson. And it was all the way until we got almost to Alderson city limits. And then he kind of pushed my hand away and covered himself up. There wasn't a dome light or anything whenever Rhonda opened the door to go into her house, but there were porch lights, things like that, streetlights around. So, he pulled his shirt over his shorts."

[*This has so many things I want to talk about, but I'll just mention them now, and cover them in the analysis (hands and arms, unzipping, automatically masturbating him, steering the truck, jeans and shorts, and lighting).*]

When it was the Defense's turn, Cleveland Sanford showed Hanna a photograph of the Ford Courier, and she identified it as the truck Steve drove that night. She agreed that the truck was pretty small, then answered the next ten questions simply with the phrase "Yes, sir." He asked if it was just the three of them in the truck; if Rhonda sat on the passenger side; if she sat in the middle; if Steve was driving; if Rhonda kept looking over; if she "performed manipulation, for lack of a better word" on Steve's penis from the water tower to Alderson; if that lasted for 10 to 15 minutes; if it was true that Rhonda said nothing during the drive; if Hanna used her right hand to masturbate Steve; and, finally, if she had her left hand crossed on top of her right arm during this.

[*Hanna said yes to all of that. Yes, some of it does contradict her Trial #1 testimony, but the important question is: During the drive from the water tower to Alderson, did Rhonda see anything?*]

Then Rhonda took the stand. Ross asked her why she felt uncomfortable that night. She said, "Mr. Sirois would put his hand around Hanna or his hand on her leg and things like that." He asked her if this was inside or outside the truck. She said, "It was inside." Ross asked her why that made her feel uncomfortable. She said, "It just didn't seem like something a family friend would be doing." He asked her if she thought that was appropriate. She said, "No." He asked her why not, and she said, "As a family friend, I don't see that he would need to be doing that."

[*I think Rhonda saw Steve's hand, as Hanna said, "on the gearshift," not her leg. Also, what does* "around her" *mean? Around her waist, her shoulders, in her general vicinity? Hanna told Tom that Steve <u>didn't</u> put his arm around her, or his hands on her, <u>in any way</u> while she was in the truck. Was*

Rhonda (whose testimony was entirely about what Steve did, not what Hanna did) imagining something in 2006 that she didn't see in 2003?]

When Sanford questioned Rhonda, he asked, "When you left the water tower, you went straight back to your house, correct?" Rhonda said, "Yes, sir." He asked if that took about 20 minutes. Rhonda said, "Yes." He asked if it was correct that she didn't see Hanna do anything to Steve. Rhonda answered, "Correct." He asked if it was true that she looked their way multiple times. She said, "Yes, sir." He said, "This truck isn't very big, is it?" Rhonda said, "No."

[*No matter how long it took to drive from the water tower to Rhonda's house, she agreed that she* "looked their way multiple times" *and didn't see Hanna doing anything to Steve.*]

Sanford handed Rhonda some pictures of the truck, and asked her if the first one looked like the truck they were in that night. She said, "Yes, sir." After she had looked through the pictures he asked her a series of questions about them: Was the stick shift very close to the seat; was a quarter in one of the pictures being held in place by the stick shift and the edge of the seat; was the seat only a little bigger than the yardstick that was on it; were all three of them sitting in an area that was only a little bigger than the yardstick; was it true that she didn't see Hanna doing anything inappropriate to Steve; was it true that she had been around Steve and Hanna a few times; and was it true that she hadn't seen anything else inappropriate beyond what she had already testified to. Rhonda answered, "Yes," or "Correct" to all of them.

[*Rhonda agreed to all of Sanford's questions, and again verified that she never saw Hanna doing anything inappropriate to Steve. See the blog for some of the pictures of the truck that Sanford showed Rhonda.*]

If you're looking at the pictures now, the shiny oval thing touching the seat and the gearshift is a quarter, balanced on its end, held there by the gearshift. The gearshift is extremely close to the seat. In fact, it extends up and over the edge of it a bit. The gearshift is mounted on that bulge in the floor, which is called a transmission hump. Hanna told Tom that she straddled the gearshift (in which case she would have had one leg on the left side of the hump, and one on the right), but in Trial #2, she told Sanford that she didn't remember if she did or not. With her seat belt holding her waist in the center of the seat, she could have twisted her body to the right and put her legs on that side of the hump, invading Rhonda's space a little, but can you imagine her doing any of what she claimed if her body was twisted toward Rhonda? Alternately, if both of her legs were on Steve's side he wouldn't have been able to drive. The gearshift is too close to the seat, and he couldn't have operated it or the floor pedals with her legs in the way. Even with her legs on the right side of the hump, her knee would still have been next to the gearshift knob. I can't see Hanna straddling the gearshift either. It would have looked distinctly phallic jutting up between her legs, would have been eminently noticeable, and almost impossible to operate. I think the only likely possibility was that Hanna sat with her legs just to the right of the transmission hump, which would have considerably hampered any movements she made toward Steve.

I had a thought about what Rhonda might have meant when she said

Steve had his hands "around" Hanna, so I ran it by Steve as a hypothetical situation. "Assume that you have to back up your car or truck to get to the road or make a three-point turn." Steve said, "Okay." I asked him, "What do you do with your arms and hands as part of that process?" He said, "It would probably depend on what car or truck I was in." [*I think he had already figured out why I was asking him this*]. I said, "Well, assume it's a small truck, standard shift, a bench seat." He said, "The little truck, in other words." I said, "The little truck, yeah." Confirming my theory, he said, "In most any truck, I'd hook my right arm over the back of the seat when I turn to look back. In those trucks I didn't like to use the side mirrors anyway. They were really small."

[*When I back my own car up, even though I have a rear-view camera, I also reach behind me with my right arm, and hold onto the back of the passenger seat to help me turn toward the rear to look behind me. When Rhonda said she saw Steve's arm* "around" *Hanna, that could have just been Steve grabbing the back of the seat as he backed up. The rest of the time he would have had his right hand on the gearshift knob when he shifted, or on the wheel. Just a thought.*]

Analysis: Let's look at Hanna's feats of arm stretching in the truck while Steve was shifting gears. Somebody sign these two up for the Cirque du Soleil. Hanna told Tom that it only <u>looked like</u> her arms were crossed because she reached <u>over</u> with her right hand, and her "arm was not in a normal position." In the trials, though, she testified that her arms <u>were</u> crossed, but she was still able to reach into Steve's lap with her right arm, which was under her left arm because the left arm was wrapped across her right arm to ward off the "cold" July temperature. Why did she change her story for the trials? Also, she said this arm-crossing maneuver was happening while Steve was operating the gearshift with his right hand. He would have been reaching past her right arm with his right arm to shift, while he was also steering with his left hand, while she masturbated him with her right hand. That may not reach the level of flexibility she claimed in Beau's truck on the way to see *Harry Potter*, but Rhonda still said she didn't see Hanna do anything. I defy anyone to do that and not be noticed by someone less than two feet away.

All Rhonda saw, according to her testimony, was Steve with <u>his hand</u> on Hanna's "knee or around her," which would be hard to avoid whether she was straddling the gearshift or not. Rhonda should have easily noticed Hanna's contortions if they were actually happening. Even though Rhonda said that Steve "would sit his hand on her knee or around her," Hanna told Tom that, while Rhonda was in the truck, Steve <u>didn't</u> put his arm around her or his hands on her "<u>in any way</u>." Rhonda also said that she didn't see any of the sexual act that Hanna claimed she performed on Steve. Rhonda testified that, even though she looked over at Hanna and Steve often, she didn't see anything inappropriate; and her note read, "every time I would look over at you <u>he</u> would have <u>his</u> hands on you," but said nothing in her note or her trial testimony about <u>Hanna</u> doing anything <u>to Steve</u>. No hand movements. No odd body positions. Hanna's claims weren't about Steve touching her knee or putting his hands on her. Her story was largely about what <u>she</u> did, unzipping his pants and masturbating him (none of which Rhonda saw). Why was their testimony so out of sync? Could Hanna have been lying for herself while Rhonda was lying for Hanna, but they didn't coordinate their stories?

And, finally, Hanna couldn't have done what she said. Sitting up straight, with her left arm over her right, her right arm would be at least slightly impeded. Try this. Keep your shoulders flat against the back of a seat; then, without turning to your left, reach for an object that's a foot to your left, at lap height, with your right hand. That's hard enough, but now try it while you're hugging your body with your left arm over your right. The left arm hinders the right, making it harder to stretch to the left. Then try it with your legs placed several inches to the right while your torso is facing straight forward. In order to even reach Steve's lap, torso straight or not, Hanna would have to twist her upper body away from Rhonda and lean to her left, which would make her actions even more obvious, but Rhonda consistently described Hanna as if she was just sitting there.

Some Stray Thoughts and Inconsistencies: In Trial #2, Hanna said, "Most of the time he kept his right hand on the gearshift. He reached across with his left hand and took my right hand" and dragged it "over to his crotch, and I helped him unzip his zipper." If Steve's right hand was on the gearshift, but he grabbed her right hand with his left hand to drag it over, which hand was he steering the truck with? Hanna told Tom that Steve unzipped his own pants and dragged her hand over to his crotch, but in Trial #1, she said Steve grabbed her right arm and dragged it over to his zipper and "made movements with his hands" (plural) to let her know to unzip his pants. Again, who's steering the truck if he's making movements with both of his hands? In Trial #2, though, she said he dragged her hand over and she just automatically started to unzip him. Also, in Trial #1, she said that "he pulled his penis out and put my hand around it and started moving my wrist up and down," but in Trial #2, she said, "he had already taken my hand and had put it on his penis, and I just began automatically to move my hand up and down." That's four changes to her story about just this one part of that night's alleged incidents. This is a good example of how she tested her story and refined it each time she told it, but it still doesn't make it true. Or even probable. Also, if Hanna could see Steve "motioning" for her to unzip his pants, why didn't Rhonda see it too?

To Recap: Hanna told three disparate versions of her actions that night:

1) Steve unzipping his own pants and dragging her hand onto his throbbing member;

2) him motioning for her to unzip him, him pulling his penis out, him dragging her hand onto it and getting her started masturbating him, and;

3) her helping him unzip his pants, him pulling his penis out, and her automatically starting to masturbate him.

As far as I can tell from the audio and the trial transcripts Hanna didn't hesitate when she told any of these versions. With Tom she charged right ahead as if she remembered it vividly, but then said something completely different in the first trial, and a month later told a third variation to a different jury. My belief is that she just forgot which lie she told before. After telling so many different versions to so many different people over such a long period of time, how could anyone keep them straight? I think that each time she repeated part of her story, she probably just did what she said she learned from her father, kept a "look on [*her*] face like you had no choice but to believe [*her*]," and spoke as if it were the absolute truth, each time reinventing her story as well as she could remember it.

In the Harry Potter chapters, I suggested a test, unbuckling your pants belt, then unbuttoning and unzipping your pants without first unbuckling your seat belt. Impossible, of course. Here's a semi-related thought. How many movies have you seen with this plot? A guy is driving down the road, and his date bends forward, places her head in his lap, and gives him oral sex, usually in a highly unrealistic way. The problem with those scenes is that the "action" usually begins immediately. His date's head drops below camera range and his eyes immediately go all googly. Completely unbelievable, just like Hanna's story, and that's why those scenes are often played for comic effect.

In Hanna's post-rodeo story, just unzipping Steve's pants wouldn't have been enough. She would first have to undo Steve's seat belt, then his pants belt, then unbutton and unzip his pants (all with just one stretched-to-its-limits right hand), while she continued to sit up straight and hug herself with her left hand. Have you ever tried to unbutton your jeans with just one hand while sitting down? Or someone else's? It's not easy. And then she would have to deal with getting past his underwear, which also is more difficult than it sounds. More than likely his pants and his underwear would both have to be pushed down some just to get to his penis.

Was Hanna the one getting Steve's pants pulled down, or was he helping? If he was helping, how was he steering the truck? Of all the things Rhonda said she didn't see, wouldn't this one have been too obvious to miss? She was only inches away from Hanna, and less than two feet from Steve. How could she not see Steve unbuckling his seat belt while he was driving down the road, or Hanna doing it for him with one hand before pulling his pants and underwear down and masturbating him for the last fifteen minutes of the drive to Alderson? They would be highly visible during the five to seven minutes they were driving slowly through brightly lit up Bloom, and especially noticeable during the stops at the intersections there. What would be the odds that Rhonda wouldn't see something then? A hundred to one? A thousand to one? More? And Hanna claimed to have done it from an upright position, belted in, with her arms crossed (right over left she told Tom, but said it was left over right in both trials), and all with just her constrained right hand. Would that amount of flexibility be the equivalent of a circus contortionist's, or maybe Elastigirl's?

Conclusion: I think what Rhonda saw was entirely innocent. Her memory of it was probably enhanced by reimagining it years later. Her note partially proved that with the statement, "I really didn't think anything of it at the time." It's likely that, once she had been persuaded to produce the note, and, after several discussions as the trial date approached, Rhonda became convinced that more must have happened than she originally thought.

Hanna said that Rhonda probably couldn't see much because it was dark in the truck, but both girls testified to a great many things they could see with no difficulty, which proves there was plenty of light. Rhonda testified that, during that drive, despite the fact that she "looked back in their direction multiple times," she didn't see Hanna doing anything to Steve, even though she had enough light to see, and plenty of opportunity to witness something as obvious as Hanna unzipping Steve's jeans/shorts and masturbating him two feet away from her.

We also have to consider the disparity between their testimonies. Hanna's comments were about things she said she did to Steve, and Rhonda's were about things she said Steve did to Hanna. They weren't even describing the same situations.

And, once again, despite Hanna's claim that she masturbated Steve for roughly twenty minutes, there was no mention of ejaculation, stickiness, or moistness, just like the night they went to see *Harry Potter*. Her descriptions of both nights were almost clinical, with no resulting climax or other leaky side effects. Very strange (and unrealistic).

I think I can safely say that this was just another bit of invented ridiculousness from Hanna (and this time, maybe from Rhonda too). Nothing happened in the truck on the way to Alderson.

Okay, they arrived in Alderson. What happened next?

What Happened After They Got to Alderson?

Why is This Question Important? This is about what Hanna claimed happened when they left Rhonda at her house and afterward. There's a lot wrong with what she said, but she made one statement that spoils it all for her as far as I'm concerned. See if you can spot it.

In Trial #1, Hanna said, "We stopped by Rhonda's to drop her off, and my house was maybe three blocks from hers." Ross asked her if she said anything to Rhonda. Hanna said, "'Bye, see you later on, hope you had fun.' Just your normal goodbyes. Didn't say anything out of the ordinary." She added, "It was like a big relief came because I didn't have to worry about someone seeing. Because for me, it wasn't so much that I felt it was wrong as much as embarrassing."

[*Hanna said they just said* "normal goodbyes," *and that she was glad Rhonda was no longer with them.*]

Ross asked Hanna what happened after they dropped Rhonda off. She said, "He asked me where was the quickest spot to go to that was secluded. And I directed him to a county road. It was still paved, still within the city limits. He pulled off into the ditch. And then he began to kiss me on the mouth and the neck, and..." Ross interrupted to ask if she tried to resist Steve. Oddly, she replied, "No. I had been wearing warmer clothes than usual." Probably used to her non sequiturs by then, Ross just asked her what that meant. She said, "Well, I had on two shirts instead of one." Playing along with her fashion tangent he asked her why. She said, "Well, it was just the style to wear layers.

Like, you know, for instance an undershirt then there was a shirt pulled over that one that was buttoned all the way down." She added that Steve asked why she wore "so many clothes, it just makes it more difficult." Ross asked how she reacted to that, and she said, "I was just kind of like, 'I don't know, I thought it looked good.'" He asked if Steve did get underneath her clothes. She said, "Yes, sir, he did…He began fondling my breasts and sucking on them. And then he pushed my hand down to his penis and made me massage it and then he pushed my head down to where I put my mouth on his penis again."

Hanna said this continued for about five minutes, but said that her mother called, and asked her, "Where are you, it's been a while since -- shouldn't you be home by now? I said, I'm sorry, we've had vehicle trouble. We will be there in just a second." Ross asked her if that was a lie, and Hanna said, "Yes." He asked her why she lied to her mother. Hanna said, "She [*sic*] already told me that that was the excuse I was to use if my mom called and asked." Speaking her mother's lines, Hanna continued, "She said, 'Well, I hope y'all are okay.' I said 'Oh, we're fine, we're fine.' I was trying to hurry, get her off the phone. I felt uncomfortable. So, she was like, 'Well, be careful.' Then she hung up and we showed up at the house just seconds later. And she asked Sirois what was wrong with the truck, and I don't know what he said." Hanna said that she noticed her clothes "looked messed up," but said she ran up to her room and changed into her pajamas before her mom noticed. Ross asked if her mother realized what was going on. Hanna said, "Not at all." Ross said, "And...?" Hanna replied, "And most of it happened right under her nose."

[*It seemed like she was almost proud that she fooled her mother. I have too much to say about the rest of that passage. I'll debunk it all in the analysis.*]

When Ross questioned Rhonda, he asked her what happened after they arrived at her house. She said, "He dropped me off and I had asked Hanna if she was okay with him by herself." Ross said, "Why did you ask her that?" Rhonda said, "Because I felt that she was uncomfortable with him." He asked her how Hanna responded, and Rhonda said, "She shook her head. Reluctantly, she shook her head." Ross asked her why "reluctantly." Rhonda said, "She just -- I don't think she was sure about the fact that she was okay with him, but she went ahead and went with him."

[*Hanna said they just said* "normal goodbyes," *but Rhonda said she asked Hanna if she was going to be okay and Hanna gave her a reluctant shake of her head. Who's telling the truth?*]

In Trial #2, Ross asked Hanna if they took Rhonda home. Hanna said, "Yes, she was dropped off at her house. We were supposed to go straight to my house, which is straight down that road." Ross asked if that's what happened. Hanna said, "No." He asked her what they did instead. Hanna said, "He had asked -- I'm so sorry [*apparently beginning to cry*]. He had asked me where was a quiet place we could go. I told him, okay, go up to the end, take a right, go down this far. And I wanted to keep going until we were on the back road. He said, well, here is fine. He pulled over into the ditch. It was a really deep ditch. The truck was at a really big angle."

[*By the second trial, Hanna dropped her comment about it being a still-inside-the-town, paved-county-road. Beau and I have driven on all the roads in and around Alderson several times, and I have no idea what road she could be referring to. I'll cover all of that in the analysis too.*]

Ross asked Hanna what happened after they were in the ditch. She said, "He turned off the truck and he started kissing me and just -- it was just the usual pattern." She went on to describe her various layers of clothes, and said that Steve asked her why she wore so many. She said, "Well, it was cold out," adding, "He made me masturbate him with my mouth, so to speak." Ross had her explain that she meant oral sex, and she said, "And I did that for maybe 5 or 10 minutes and then my mom's cell phone started ringing and my mom was calling me wondering where we were. I said, well, we had vehicle trouble, we will be there in just a second…And by the time we got there, we had already gotten up to the door and him and my mom were talking. I looked down and noticed my clothes were still disheveled and twisted around every which way. They didn't look right, so I hurried up to my room to change into my PJ's. As far as I know, he left after that."

[*In Trial #1, she said she was wearing all those layers because she thought they looked good, but in Trial #2 she said it was because she was cold. Then, after rushing home, Hanna discovered that her clothes were all disheveled, but an inattentive mom was the only reason they weren't caught? I don't believe any of that happened, and I'll explain why in the last segment of this chapter, "Was Steve Physically Capable of Doing What Hanna Claimed?"*]

Ross asked Hanna if she saw Rhonda the next day. Hanna said, "No, sir, I didn't." He asked her when she did. She said, "The rodeo I had gone to, I don't remember which night it was, but <u>I know</u> I saw her the next Monday at school." He asked her if they talked about the night of the rodeo. Hanna said, "No." He asked her why not. She said, "Well, I didn't know for sure if she had seen anything or not. And I wasn't going to bring it up and start her asking questions. And if she did see anything, I didn't want to know. I was too embarrassed."

[*We covered this falsehood by Hanna already during the question about Rhonda's note. The school district said that Hanna wasn't on campus that summer. How could she have been so specific about the details of what happened that night (irrespective of how changeable those details were from one version to the next), but still be so unaware of even the basic time of year the rodeo took place? How many other potential lies are buried in all of that testimony?*]

Ross, when questioning Rhonda, read her this line from her note, "I figured it was nothing to be concerned about till you asked me about it," and wanted to know when Hanna did ask her about it. Rhonda said, "About two weeks later, she …me and her talked about it, me and Hanna." He followed that by asking her when she wrote the note, and she stumbled her way through vague comments that never really established when she wrote it.

[*We covered all of that already too, but I wanted to remind you that she said they talked about the night of the rodeo two weeks later, not a couple of days. Hanna and Rhonda were telling two different stories.*]

Ross asked Rhonda what happened when they got to her house. She said, "I got out of the truck, and Hanna also got out of the truck. I asked her if she was going to be okay." Ross asked her why she said that. She said, "Because I just didn't think she should leave with him by herself." He asked her why not. She said, "Because I could tell that she was uncomfortable and I knew I was also uncomfortable with him." Ross asked if she had thought it was unsafe for Hanna. She said, "Yes, sir." He asked her how Hanna responded to that. Rhonda said, "She shook her head and <u>said</u> it was okay." Ross asked her if that made her feel better about leaving Hanna alone with Steve. Rhonda said, "It did. I was a little unsure, but she <u>said</u> that she was okay." He asked her what happened then. Rhonda said, "She got back in the truck and they both left." When it was Cleveland Sanford's turn, he asked her if she went inside her house. She said, "Yes, sir." He asked, "You didn't tell your grandmother, did you?" "No." "You didn't call Hanna to make sure she made it home okay, did you?" "No." "You didn't call Hanna's mom to make sure she made it home okay, did you?" "No."

[*Do Rhonda's and Hanna's statements about arriving at Rhonda's match? No, they don't. Let's compare them.*]

Analysis: Before we talk about specifics, you might want to take a quick look at the rough map of Alderson on the blog. It's a very small town, and apparently a shrinking one. It had 472 residents in 1929, but was down to just over 400 at the beginning of this century, roughly when our story takes place. It was reduced even more according to the 2010 census. The population was 390 then, and was down to 370 in a 2018 estimate.

Hanna said she directed Steve to a paved county road that was still inside the town limits, and he pulled off into a ditch. In Trial #2, she changed that by saying it wasn't inside the town limits, but "It was a really deep ditch. The truck was at a really big angle." Without revealing exactly where Rhonda's or Hanna's houses are, I'll just say they are on the north side of town. Only two paved roads enter Alderson north of Rhonda's house. County Road (CO) 982 runs east and west, along the northern boundary of town. Farm-to-Market Road (FM) 3500 runs north and south, and is labeled Main Street inside the town. The other county roads are on the southern side of town, and they begin at the town boundaries. Beau and I searched, but couldn't find a deep ditch beside any of them.

Hanna's directions also make no sense. She said they were pointed toward "my house, which is straight down that road" (i.e., facing south from Rhonda's). If they drove "to the end" of that street, though, they would pass Hanna's house, running the risk of Darla spotting them. Also, I don't know what she meant by "<u>the</u> back road." All the roads leaving Alderson are "back roads" of a sort, heading out into the countryside past farms and ranches, some dead-ending, and others connecting with roads that eventually intersect with highways. I've driven along every road that enters and exits the town, checking them for ditches, and haven't found anything deeper than slight dips off the side of the road. CO 982 and FM 3500 are the only ones close enough to support her claim that they got to her "house just seconds later" (but it more than likely would have been minutes instead, and they would have needed to break some speed records to accomplish that). Hanna's comment about Steve pulling the truck into "a really deep ditch," causing it to lean "at a really big angle" is wrong on several levels. See a picture on the blog of Beau's truck, parked by the side of the road on FM 3500, just north of Alderson. It's in the deepest depression we could find that was even remotely close to town. Beau's truck is leaning at about a 10° angle because the left tires are almost on the roadway, and the right tires are down in the depression. If we had pulled a couple of feet to the right, though, the truck would have leveled out perfectly flat again, so why would Steve have left it tilted at an angle? There might be some deeper spots somewhere on the two roads, but that was the deepest we could find that was even reasonably close to Hanna's house. I don't think the ditch she talked about exists.

One other thing doesn't ring true. Why would Steve ask her to direct him to a place to park? He spent many hours every week when he worked for the city, driving from one location to another. When he worked for Hanna's uncle, Leon, for a decade, and for other contractors, he had jobs all across the area. He knew the roads in Ashwell County extremely well, and certainly knew the roads in and around Alderson after having worked for Leon for all those years. Steve asking her for directions makes no sense at all.

Hanna, in addition to those specific (but odd) directions to find the road to park beside, also made a number of other changes to her testimony in Trial #2. She offered up more precise changes to her clothing, like the "spaghetti-strapped shirt with the built-in bra," which in Trial #1 was just "an undershirt." Also, Trial #1's "ditch" became "a really deep ditch" in Trial #2; one that caused the truck to slope "at a really big angle," but the comment about her proudly sneaking past her mom disappeared in the second trial. Did she think she didn't give enough specific detail in Trial #1, or was she worried that the comment about fooling her mother didn't play well? Or both? I don't know, but she did make changes.

Rhonda also made a big change to her story about what happened when they arrived at her house. Ross, in Trial #1, asked, "Did you receive any response from Hanna?" and Rhonda said, "She shook her head. Reluctantly, she shook her head," indicating a non-verbal response from Hanna. In Trial #2, though, when Ross asked the same exact question, Rhonda replied, "She shook her head and said it was okay," adding that Hanna seemed "a little unsure, but she said that she was okay." In Trial #1, Hanna was silent, in Trial #2, Hanna spoke. Which of those statements is the true one?

Neither of Rhonda's versions, both of which tell different stories, match Hanna's version where they just said normal goodbyes. It would have been to Hanna's advantage to use either of Rhonda's stories, which portray her as someone who is "reluctant" and worried about being alone with Steve, but she didn't. Ross, in the second trial, maybe not wanting to confuse the jurors with two competing versions, just didn't ask Hanna anything about how she and Rhonda said goodbye. My guess is that Hanna's version of normal goodbyes from Trial #1 was likely the real one. Maybe she didn't change it because she thought Rhonda would have the same (actual) memory she did. As a result, what they ended up with was normal goodbyes from Hanna, and a worried exchange from Rhonda. Which of those statements is the true one?

Rhonda said she didn't see Hanna for a couple of weeks, but Hanna said she saw Rhonda the next Monday at school. Her school district, however, said there was no school in July, and Hanna wasn't on campus then. Which of those statements is the true one? Are any of them true? How do we know?

Cleveland Sanford's final argument in Trial #2 contains a brief passage which explains why we might want to look at Rhonda's testimony with a critical eye. He said, "And if she thought everything was so odd, then why didn't she call Hanna to make sure she made it home okay? Why didn't she call Hanna's mom to make sure she made it home okay? Why didn't she call the police? Why didn't she tell her grandmother? She didn't do anything. What she did was she waited and she came forward long after the fact, long after she talked to Hanna, long after Hanna made these allegations and charges had been filed." And, I would add, <u>not until Hanna's mother asked her to</u>.

[*Sanford's speech makes it clear that Rhonda probably didn't think anything was wrong that night. If she had actually been worried about Hanna, she would have said or done something back in the summer of 2003, but she didn't do anything until she was approached by Darla in the summer of 2005.*]

By the time Darla talked her into providing her note, Rhonda must have known she would also have to testify. If all she remembered was a ride home from a rodeo and a stop at a water tower, she must have spent the next year thinking about the allegations Hanna made, wracking her brain to see things from a different perspective. Despite that effort, she still couldn't remember anything bad happening in the truck or at the water tower. Her note, in fact, said she "really didn't think anything of it at the time," so the rest of her story may have developed from imagining what could have happened, as opposed to what she really saw. Mixing real memories with imagination creates an iffy mental salad, but let's see what we can logically deduce about what did happen after they arrived back in Alderson.

Conclusion: I believe the truth is that they arrived sometime between 35 and 45 minutes after they left the rodeo (which includes 10 to 15 minutes at the water tower). When they got to Alderson, Steve drove north through the middle of town on Main Street, turned onto one of the side streets, and then south onto Rhonda's and Hanna's street. He dropped Rhonda off at her house. Rhonda went inside, then Steve drove three more blocks south and dropped Hanna off before driving home.

Originally, the prosecution didn't even consider this night as something that could be used against Steve. It isn't mentioned in Hanna's complaint, or in Dixon's summary, and wasn't one of the counts against Steve. It wasn't until the summer of 2005, nearly a year-and-a-half after the accusations were first made, that the story about the water tower, the masturbation in the truck, and the oral sex in a ditch on a county road surfaced in anyone's consciousness. Did Hanna add the elements of masturbation and oral sex after August 2005? Rhonda's note only hinted at what she thought might have been some flirtatious behavior. The fact that the prosecution devoted 58 pages of Trial #2's transcript to this night (more than any other single incident, almost as much as all three counts combined) indicates how important this ride home was to their case, but it still doesn't mean the claims were true.

Hanna claimed that Steve made her start masturbating him soon after they left the water tower; but she said that he made her stop when they got close to Alderson, pulling his shirt down over his exposed penis so Rhonda wouldn't see it (because, she said, there were street lamps and porch lights in Alderson). There are four large, bright, street lamps on US 373, near Alderson, but the street lamps inside the town are much older and less brilliant than the modern ones. There were, however, 47 modern lamps that lit their way through the town of Bloom and its outskirts, and dozens more along the rest of the route. There is no way that anyone, after slowing down to 30 mph in Bloom, would have allowed themselves to be masturbated over the several miles of brightly lit city roadway there, unconcerned about being seen, but cover up for less than a mile of marginally lit roads five minutes later in Alderson.

Hanna said they just said normal goodbyes, but Rhonda said that Hanna either reluctantly shook her head <u>without speaking</u>, or reluctantly <u>said</u> she was okay (depending on which trial she testified at). If one of the girls was telling the truth, the other one wasn't, and Rhonda contradicted herself from one trial to the next. It's also possible, of course, that they were both lying, but didn't know the other one was, but it isn't possible that both of them were telling the truth.

It *is* possible to park a truck beside county roads near Alderson, but Beau and I couldn't find anything resembling a deep ditch on any of the roads in or around it, just some shallow depressions.

Importantly, Darla wasn't asked a single question in either trial about what happened that night, and neither was Steve. He told me he didn't remember what Darla said to him, but thought it was probably just a simple "thanks for bringing her home." I asked him if the truck broke down, or if Darla called Hanna on her cell phone. He answered "No" to both questions.

To Sum Up: Steve couldn't have done what Hanna claimed he did in the truck and still managed to drive it. Hanna couldn't have done the things she claimed she did and still maintained a straight upright body position. And none of those things could have happened without Rhonda seeing most or all of it. Also, Steve wouldn't have pulled his shirt over his penis because of the street lamps in Alderson if he hadn't done the same thing in brightly lit Bloom. Either Hanna or Rhonda isn't telling the truth about their goodbyes at Rhonda's house (or both of them aren't), and no county roads in or near Alderson fit Hanna's deep ditch description.

There are too many discrepancies for me to accept that any of the sexual activity in Hanna's versions actually happened. I believe that she embroidered her stories the way she did because she was afraid of losing her reputation. I don't mean the reputation she gained of being the defenseless victim. I think she was okay with that. I'm referring to the one she may have thought she would lose with her friends and her family if they discovered she had lied to them for so many years. I can more easily accept Rhonda's general memory of the drive home, because (even though she was ostensibly testifying to bolster Hanna's story) she still didn't see any of the blatant sexual acts that Hanna swore happened on the way to Alderson. If Rhonda had changed her own story to better fit Hanna's, she would have said she remembered seeing something sexual happen between Hanna and Steve, but she didn't. Based on Hanna's descriptions, though, how could Rhonda not have seen something? I think the only way she wouldn't have seen Hanna's claimed activity in the truck would be if it hadn't happened in the first place.

Were Rhonda and Hanna Friends?

In the trials, both girls were asked if they were friends. Both said they weren't, and the note's first line does read, "I know that we really don't get along, but I know that you really need me to do this for you." Was that sentence the reason the prosecution asked them about their friendship? Possibly. Did Hanna and Rhonda ever have a friendship? Maybe. Maybe not. Elmer Ross still went to great lengths to make sure the juries heard that they were definitely not friends by the time of the trials. Because of that comment in the note, Tom asked Hanna how she and Rhonda felt about each other. Hanna said, "I honestly don't know, because her and I used to be best friends, and <u>the past couple of years</u> we haven't been that close. It's just typical girl stuff."

["...just typical girl stuff." *I'm not sure what that means.*]

In Trial #1, Ross asked Hanna how she knew Rhonda. She said, "We used to go to Sunday school together when we were about two or three years old. We have been going to the same school our entire lives. We went to Alderson since kindergarten." He asked her if they were friends. She said, "To an extent, yes. We used to be best friends, and we've just <u>grown apart with time</u>." He asked if that meant they weren't as close as they had been. Hanna said, "No, sir. I'm afraid not."

[*If they knew each other since they were* "two or three," *that would mean that by the time of the 2003 rodeo they had been friends for at least eleven years, but within the next few years they had* "grown apart with time?"]

Was it since the age of two or three? In the same trial, Ross asked Rhonda how she knew Hanna. Rhonda said, "She goes to school with me." Ross asked her if they had been in the same class for a while. She said, "Yes, sir; since elementary." He asked if she and Hanna were friends now. She said, "No." He asked, "Just acquaintances?" She said "Yes, sir." He asked her if there was a reason why they weren't close anymore, and she said, "No, we just <u>grew apart as time went on</u>."

[*Those are terse answers even though it was the prosecutor questioning her, not the defense attorney. I don't know what Rhonda's tone of voice was, but on the written page she seems to be upset about having to do this. If so, did Hanna do something to anger her?* "Since elementary" *would be from the age of about five or six, not Hanna's* "two or three." *Oddly, though, the phrases* "grown apart with time," *and* "grew apart as time went on," *are almost identical. Friends? Or not friends? That is the question.*]

In Trial #2, Hanna continued the "we went to Sunday school" "since the age of two or three" story, adding, "We grew up together. We went to the same school our entire lives. We were best friends there for a while. And then the past six, seven years, we've just been growing apart. We don't talk near as much as we used to. Now we're just acquaintances." Ross asked her why she took Rhonda to the rodeo. Hanna said that her aunt, " who works at the municipal court, had come by some tickets in one of the boxes there at the arena. And she -- I think they had some other plans or something, but anything, they didn't end up using the tickets…And Mom said, Well, you can go if you have a friend to go with you, you're not going by yourself. So, I said, okay. And it turns out Rhonda wanted to go, too. So, I asked her to go with me. She said, Yeah, sure. So, we went."

Here's Rhonda in Trial #2. Ross asked her how she knew Hanna. She answered, "She goes to school with me." Ross asked her how long they had known each other, and Rhonda said, "We met when we were around four or five." He asked her if they were still friends. She said, "No, sir," adding "We just grew apart as we got older." He asked her if something had happened to cause that. She said, "No. We just grew apart."

[*I found it interesting that Hanna mentioned that her aunt works for the courts (an instant character reference?). Are Hanna and Rhonda telling the same story? There are some differences. Hanna said they knew each other since two or three in Sunday school, but Rhonda said since four or five. Was Hanna's repeat mention of Sunday School not only untrue, but just for the purpose of making her seem more religious? Both girls said they weren't friends, but they* "just grew apart" *(using similar phrases each time). I have some issues with the* "growing apart" *thing, but I'll go over that in the analysis.*]

Here's one final comment from Hanna about their friendship. Early in her Trial #2 testimony, Hanna was asked how she remembered that the cross-country race was on September 8th. She said, "It's also a very good friend of mine's birthday." When asked who that friend was, she said it was Rhonda Bresnick. Hanna didn't say that Rhonda used to be a good friend of hers, she said she is "a very good friend." Then, later in the trial, contradicting herself she said, "…we're just acquaintances."

[*She can't have it both ways. Were they friends at the time of the trials or not?*]

Analysis: Was Rhonda's and Hanna's non-friendship real, or was it just a show for the trial? In her interview with Tom, Hanna seemed worried about what Rhonda would say, because they "used to be best friends, and the past couple of years we haven't been that close. It's just typical girl stuff."

It could have been just typical "Hanna stuff" instead. During the rest of the interview, Hanna named a bunch of other people as friends (Beau, Josh Chilmark, Karla Spivey, Suzanna Bushnell, Cliff Polinger, Angie Womack, Sean Luedeman, and Betty Stavens). She labeled several of them as "best friends" even though she couldn't remember Betty's name until Tom helped her figure it out. When Tom interviewed Betty, she said, "Me and Hanna are friends, but not like close friends." Tom asked, "More like acquaintances?" Betty said, "Yeah." As I pointed out earlier, though, it's possible that Hanna only mentioned Betty as a way to bring up the subject of Billy Gasnick.

In another example, in Trial #1, Hanna described Karla Spivey as "a girl that went to my school, she's graduated now, but her and I were never good friends, never really got along." Did Hanna try to demote Karla in importance during the trials because she was afraid of what Karla might say if she testified? Also, was Hanna really friends with any of those people, or were they just classmates and acquaintances? Hanna told Tom that she and Rhonda hadn't been as close as usual for "the past couple of years," but she testified that "the past six, seven years, we've just been growing apart." Two years isn't six or seven years by any stretch of the imagination, but if we accept that larger figure from Hanna, it would mean they had been working on becoming un-friends since 1999 or 2000. If they weren't friends in 2003, why were Hanna and Aaron at Rhonda's house every day after school? If they weren't friends in 2003, why did they go to the rodeo together?

There was also a post-trial event that, for a few years, I thought could be connected to Rhonda's and Hanna's non-friendship. Here's the part where I say I was wrong about something. In the trials, when Rhonda was asked if she and Hanna were friends, she answered with a flat "No." For several years I wondered why she would say that but would still testify for her. In Hanna's interview with Tom, the subject of Hanna's various boyfriends came up, and Tom asked her if she was dating someone named Dan Dunbar who lived in Truesdale. Hanna said, "No, Dan is my best friend's boyfriend." That particular "best friend" was Suzanna Bushnell, who later married Dan. Pressing on, Tom asked Hanna who she *was* dating. She said, "Uh, his cousin, Rich..." [*and she swallowed a mumbled last name that I have tried dozens of times to understand on the audio, but still can't*].

I wanted to know who this "Rich" was, and if he was the same fake-ID/bouncer boyfriend who might have been the catalyst for Hanna asking Tom to interview her. A search of Texas marriage records showed that Hanna married someone named Richard (Rich?) G. Wheeler in 2007, less than a year after the second trial ended. A social media search also found a 2013 picture of Hanna with another husband, Shane Lancaster. Obviously Rich and Hanna had divorced between 2007 and 2013. Actually, it was fairly soon after 2007. A further search of marriage records and more social media searches found that Rhonda Bresnick's last name is now Wheeler, and she has been married to a Richard G. Wheeler since 2009. I wondered if Rhonda's non-friendship with Hanna in 2006 could have had something to do with a guy that Rhonda felt Hanna stole from her. I realized that was massive speculation, but I still thought it was worth checking out. I discovered that Richard worked at a restaurant in Deep Springs, so on my last research trip there, in July 2019, I stopped in during the restaurant's afternoon lull, and asked if he was available. He met me at the front desk. It was a short interview.

I introduced myself, and asked if he was related to Dan Dunbar of Truesdale. He seemed surprised at the question, and said, "No, I'm from Idaho." I asked him if he had been married to Hanna Penderfield. He said, "Yes," so I followed that by asking if he was currently married to Rhonda Bresnick. He seemed really wary by then, but said that, yes, he was. I told him that I was asking because Hanna had once told an investigator that her boyfriend's name was Rich, and that he was Dan Dunbar's cousin.

Just to verify, I asked if he was the bouncer at a club near downtown Deep Springs who got Hanna a fake ID, and was fired over it. He said, "No, I was seventeen when I met Hanna, so I couldn't have been a bouncer." I explained that I was writing a book about a trial that Hanna and Rhonda were both involved in. He said he knew about the trial, so I asked him if he was saying that he had moved down here after the trial was over and met Hanna then. He nodded, yes, so I thought I'd give it a shot, and asked him if he thought Rhonda might agree to talk to me. He said, "No, I don't think she would." I asked him if she still had some loyalty to Hanna. He agreed she did with a nod of the head. He was clearly a different Rich, so I thanked him and left. I didn't ask him why he and Hanna got divorced because I didn't think his answer would have had any bearing on the book, or would have given me any new insights into Hanna's motivation for naming Steve. Maybe I should have asked anyway.

Were Rhonda and Hanna ever friends? Steve had some thoughts about that. During one of our frequent phone calls I asked him what he knew about their friendship. He said, "How do I prove this? Kids are just kids to me…but we knew all along that Hanna was a snooty, rotten little bitch." I asked if, by that, he meant that nobody liked her. He said, "No. Nobody. She says she has all these friends, but she was arrogant and overbearing, you know, and she always was, but we didn't think that much of it. It was just the way she was." I asked him why he thought Hanna didn't invite someone other than Rhonda to the rodeo if their relationship was on the wane. He said he might have an answer, and told me that Rhonda's grandmother and Darla were friends, and that he thought the two girls' relationship "was probably more forced than anything else. I don't know if that had any effect on anything, but I know that Darla and her were extremely close, but, of course, it's Alderson." I said, "Right. Tiny town, everybody knows everybody else." Steve said, "Everybody, sure." I asked him, "So, you think that maybe when Darla got the tickets, she said something like, 'There's two tickets here. Why don't you take Rhonda?'" Steve said, "Possibly."

I had been wondering for a while whether Hanna really had as many friends as she said she did, or whether she just had them long enough to suit her purposes, or until she got bored with them or they got tired of her? If she had a choice about who she could take, though, and she really did have all those other friends, why didn't she take one of them instead? Did Rhonda and Hanna ever actually like each other to begin with, or was it a forced relationship? It doesn't change what did or didn't happen that night, but knowing the truth could provide a plausible reason why Hanna and Darla may have had difficulty getting Rhonda to help them with the note, and why Rhonda sometimes (on paper at least) seemed to act like a hostile witness.

Was Steve Physically Capable of Doing What Hanna Claimed?

I've been holding something back from you, but it's time to reveal it now. This could prove that most of the accusations Hanna made about Steve committing sexual offenses against her were lies. I waited to bring this up because I wanted you to first see that her accusations had little or no merit on their own before I added this to the mix. Hanna said that the time period of her abuse stretched from the beginning of September 2001 to the middle of February 2004. I'll push back strongly on that range of dates in the chapter, *A Timeline as Final Proof*, but Hanna claimed that, during that time period, Steve was constantly after her to have sex. She told Ada Dixon, "He told me he always wanted me," and "He acted like I was a buffet and he could take all he wanted," and "99.99% of the time we were together he would do sexual things to me." She painted a picture (in her affidavit, to Dixon, to Tom, and in both trials) of Steve trying to find every possible excuse to be alone with her so he could molest her. She claimed he wanted to do it everywhere (in a jeep at his sister-in-law's house, on a four-wheeler while other kids were waiting to ride next, behind a convenience store while Beau was inside buying something, etc.). On February 24, 2003, though (right in the middle of Hanna's time period), while lifting a heavy metal flange at work, Steve suffered an indirect inguinal hernia, which allowed part of his intestines to drop down into his scrotum. Men everywhere are grimacing as they read that. I don't think I need to emphasize why that information, placed alongside Hanna's claims about this time period, is important.

In Trial #2, Cleveland Sanford asked Robin if Steve had any surgeries between September 1, 2001 and February 14, 2004. Robin said, "Yes, sir." He asked her what kind. She just said, "Hernia." He asked if that was something he recovered from overnight. She said, "No, sir." He asked her how long it took. She said, "Well, he went back to work in a week, but he had more complications, so it was probably eight months before he could really say it was over with, and he still has problems." Sanford asked her if she would agree that a hernia was a hole in one of the body's internal walls. She did, so he asked her where on Steve's body the hernia was. Robin said, "The groin area."

[*It was actually much longer than a week before he returned to work, and he was on light duty even then, not supposed to lift anything. Robin simply said there were* "complications," without giving any additional details, but added that, *even as late as 2006, three-and-a-half years after the injury,* "he still has problems."]

Here's what Steve told me about the operation. "I had a hernia surgery, and for at least six months, any attempt at sex, mainly ejaculation, became extremely painful. I have known various types of pain in my life (from a nearly-severed thumb to many surgeries) but I have never experienced the pain that even a cough gave after that hernia."

[*Robin was wrong about the time Steve was off work. His medical records confirm that he wasn't cleared to return to work until April 10th. That's 45 days after the hernia (6 weekends), but he had severe pain from it for many months. The rodeo took place only four months after the surgery. According to Robin's testimony, it was still bothering him to some degree over three years later. Why did I mention the number of weekends specifically? We'll get to all of that in the chapter,* A Timeline as Final Proof. *I promise.*]

Analysis: Steve was injured on February 24, 2003, while working for the City of Deep Springs, and suffered an indirect inguinal hernia. He later told me, "The one time I tried to lift something the right way, it just happened."

Some Medical Stuff: The spermatic cord and the ilioinguinal nerve pass through the inguinal canal, which is a passage along the back wall of the abdominal cavity. There are two canals, one on the right and one on the left. In males, both of the passages descend into the scrotum. The ilioinguinal nerve runs along the outside of the spermatic cord, and is what makes a male's gonads the source of such a wide range of physical sensations, from extreme pleasure, or (when kicked or punched) possibly the most severe pain on the planet. Those who have given birth or passed kidney stones also have good arguments on their side for the worst pain ever. This type of hernia happens when, through weakness or a strain in the canal's wall, a tear occurs in the canal's entrance, which allows some of the abdomen's contents to slip into the canal and descend into the scrotum.

Steve was examined the next day, and had a second exam nine days later. He was operated on a week after that, seventeen days after the injury. He had a follow-up exam a month later, and was cleared to return to work for light duty with a warning to avoid any heavy physical activity. Robin, in Trial #2, said "it was probably eight months before he could really say it was over with." Steve said "for at least six months, any attempt at sex, mainly ejaculation, was extremely painful."

An article in *Anesthesiology 2007*, titled "Ejaculatory Pain: A Specific Postherniotomy Pain Syndrome," stated that "Sexual dysfunction due to ejaculatory and genital pain after groin hernia surgery may occur in approximately 2.5% of patients," and added, "All patients with ejaculatory pain had experienced major negative life changes and deterioration in their overall quality of life and sexual function as a result of the hernia operation."
https://anesthesiology.pubs.asahq.org/article.aspx?articleid=1931147

Steve was one of the people who was affected sexually by his hernia. He experienced ejaculatory pain for many months afterward.

Conclusion: Accusations of Steve committing sexual acts from the end of February 2003 through at least the fall should be considered false because he wasn't physically capable of sex without causing serious pain to himself. The rodeo was near the end of July. Steve injured himself near the end of February and had surgery in mid-March. He wasn't cleared to return for even light duty at work until April 10th, and still had pain for most of the rest of the year. It makes no sense that he would have tried to have sex with someone a few months after an operation like that, especially under the conditions Hanna described. They didn't stress the importance and the seriousness of that injury during the trials, but they should have. I believe that Hanna's claims that Steve would have even wanted, much less tried to have sex with her after the rodeo (or at any other time after February 2003) are not only false, they are ridiculous.

Let's put the pieces of the rodeo puzzle together, but this time keep the hernia in mind while you review each person's versions of that night's events.

Summary and Analysis: The Night of the Rodeo

One night, in late July 2003, Steve gave a ride home to Hanna and Rhonda, who may or may not have been good friends at the time. They attended the Ashwell County Rodeo that night, after being dropped off by someone, probably Hanna's mother. That much isn't in dispute by anyone. The rest of the evening has been told in several different variations that don't mesh well with the others. Let's take a quick look at basic versions of what Steve, Hanna, and Rhonda all claimed.

Steve's version is that Darla called him and asked him to bring the girls home because she said she was too drunk to drive. He came to the rodeo when Hanna called him, and drove the girls to their homes in Alderson, Texas. On the way he spotted a water tower that he had responsibility for as part of his work for the City of Deep Springs, and asked them if they wanted to see the inside of it. They said yes. The tower was just over three miles from the rodeo grounds and was on their route. He showed it to them, then they drove to Alderson. He dropped Rhonda off first, then Hanna, then drove home.

Rhonda's version was that it probably was Darla who dropped them off at the rodeo, and that Steve did give them a ride afterward. She didn't know him well, but he was a friend of Darla's, so she thought it was okay. She said they left the rodeo between 10:30 and 11:00 pm, and Steve drove them (in a direction she wasn't familiar with), to a water tower, but they arrived there after midnight. She felt uncomfortable because she thought Steve was "into" Hanna, and she saw him place his hand on her back at the water tower, and his hand on her knee in the truck. Rhonda kept looking over at them during the drive home, but didn't see anything sexual happening. Steve dropped her off at her house. She said that she and Hanna both got out of the truck, and she asked Hanna if she was okay. Rhonda, at different times, said that Hanna either "reluctantly" <u>nodded</u> yes, or <u>said</u> she was okay. Then Steve and Hanna left.

Hanna's version is that she called Steve because her mom either didn't want to come get them or was too tired to, so Steve came to pick them up. She said "he kept taking different turns," and drove them to a "secluded place" where there was a water tower, let them go inside, explained how it worked, and then they got back in the truck and started toward Alderson. During the drive, she said he had her unzip his pants/shorts, and she masturbated him until they got to Alderson, where he made her stop. In Alderson, he pulled his shirt over his pants so Rhonda wouldn't see (because of the street lamps and porch lights). They dropped Rhonda off and said "normal goodbyes." Then, she said Steve asked her to show him a place to park. She led him to the outskirts of town, and he pulled off the road into a "really deep ditch," where "the truck was at a really big angle." She said Steve struggled his way past the two shirts and bra she was wearing (because it was cold, or because they looked good), massaged and kissed her breasts, and then had her give him oral sex. While they were doing that, Hanna's mom called, wondering where they were. Hanna told her they had car trouble, lying to her because Steve had told her in advance what to say (just in case her mother might call). They got dressed, and were at Hanna's house "seconds later." She said her clothes were "disheveled," but she got in the house and into her pajamas before her mom noticed.

If there's a Rashômon quality to those three versions, it's for a good reason. All three of them contain basic kernels of truth, but there are lies in one or more of them. In telling the three versions above I chose the elements for each that I thought would best represent what their general story was; but, as you saw earlier, two of those stories were altered each time they were retold. I'll address the various changes below, but, if you feel I described any part of an account inaccurately, please point that out to me. More than anything I want this to be a factual representation of what the participants said, which is hard to do when the details keep zig-zagging. I don't believe that anything sexual happened between Steve and Hanna (not on the night of the rodeo, or at any other time). Yes, I'm biased, but look at the total inability of Hanna to tell a truthful story about that night.

Let's look at several facts about that night (along with a little speculation). I started with two dozen of these but I'll just do a Top Ten here. The full list is on the blog at this URL.

https://aggravatedbook.com/the-night-of-the-rodeo-expanded-fact-list/

Fact: The temperature reached 98.6 on the day of the rodeo (with a heat index of 104.9). The late-night heat index was 89.4 at 10:30 pm, and only dropped to 85.6 by 11:30. The heat index at 7:00 pm (when they likely arrived at the rodeo) was still 100 degrees. Despite this, Hanna said she was wearing double-layers of shirts because it was chilly at night.

Fact: Steve did favors for Darla all the time. No one disputes this.

Fact: Darla contacted Steve and asked him to give Hanna and Rhonda a ride home. According to Steve, Darla told him she was too drunk to go get them, and Hanna said it was because Darla told her she was too tired and/or just didn't want to. Maybe they were both right.

Fact: Hanna claimed that Robin and Steve "drank 24/7," and said that Robin "was drunk all the time." Steve worked in different types of jobs for over two decades, but his work was well-respected. Robin was an engineering technician for a cable manufacturing plant for 26 years, and had an exemplary work record. How did either of them do that if they were drunk all the time? The Sirois' are the ones who admitted they drank. Hanna was the one who denied that her mother got drunk. Methinks Hanna doth exaggerate too much.

Fact: They did stop by a water tower. The girls both gave sworn testimony that made it seem like the tower was far off in the wilderness somewhere, but the tower isn't out in the backwoods. It's within 2,000 feet of subdivisions on a heavily-traveled road. They didn't take a bunch of different turns to get to the tower. They took <u>one</u> turn, from US 373 onto FM 29. I think Hanna's and Rhonda's claims of wandering around were designed to deliberately distort the simple truth that all they were doing was getting a ride home. Nothing inappropriate happened at the water tower. They went inside, Steve told them how the tower worked, and then they left. They all said so. One other simple point: Hanna testified, "I'm not sure where the water tower is. I still don't know where it is, but I'm guessing we were 10 or 15 minutes away from Alderson." If it had been so secluded, so way out in the boondocks, and took them ninety minutes to get there, as Rhonda claimed (it actually only took a few minutes), wouldn't Alderson have been much farther than 10 or 15 minutes away from it?

Fact: It was dark inside the truck, except when it wasn't. If they *had* been in a deserted area, with no street lights or other traffic, it actually might have been fairly dark. In the 22.8 miles between the rodeo and Rhonda's house, though, there were over 120 street lamps, light from businesses and homes, and probably some light from other cars on the road too. There were only two spots on the route where there were no street lamps, and they would have only been in those areas for a few minutes each.

Fact: Rhonda testified that she kept glancing over at Hanna and Steve, but didn't see anything sexual. Hanna testified that she kept glancing at Rhonda to see if she was noticing anything. Both Rhonda and Hanna described many things they saw in the truck as they watched each other, which proves there was plenty of light to see by, but Rhonda still didn't see anything happening.

Fact: Hanna said that Steve kept glancing at Rhonda, but he can't "glance" to his right. He has a glass right eye. To see Rhonda he would have to lean forward past Hanna, and turn his head and shoulders at least a quarter turn to the right (to see past his nose with his left eye), which would be a lot more obvious than an occasional "glance," not to mention difficult to do if you're driving, supposedly being masturbated, and trying not to call attention to yourself.

Fact: Rhonda and Hanna told different stories about arriving at Rhonda's house. Hanna said they just said normal goodbyes, but Rhonda said they both got out of the truck and she asked Hanna if she would be okay. She also gave two different versions of Hanna's response. In Trial #1, Hanna was silent. In Trial #2, she verbalized. Both can't be true.

Fact: Hanna said she directed Steve to a paved county road inside the city limits, and said that Steve pulled off the road into a deep ditch, which caused the truck to lean at "a really big angle," but there is no such road. I've searched all the roads that enter Alderson, especially those on the northern side of town. I only found shallow depressions, no ditches.

The Most Important Fact: Steve was recovering from hernia surgery, and ejaculation was a painful thing for him. The idea of him deliberately having Hanna masturbate him and give him oral sex (especially in a truck leaning at "a really big angle") is absolutely preposterous.

That's enough. Let's wrap this up.

The more I studied the trial documents, the more it seemed to me that many of Hanna's statements were designed to mislead and misdirect. By extension, the statements made by her mother, by Rhonda, and by anyone else who testified for her, were also misleading and often false (possibly because almost everything they said about the matter came from Hanna, who kept changing her versions of the story). Her statement, "He had come over to [*Rhonda's*] house, where I was spending most of my time, and picked us up to take us over to his house," is a perfect example. It seems simple and straightforward, but Rhonda was never at Steve's house. Did Hanna say that to convince the jury that Steve was always scheming to do bad things to young girls? Even if we agree that Hanna meant that Steve picked up her and her brother, Aaron, not her and Rhonda, it wouldn't have sounded that way to the jury, and Elmer Ross did nothing to correct her.

In my opinion, the reason that none of the so-called witnesses to any of Hanna's alleged incidents saw anything inappropriate was because nothing like that happened. Hanna was the generator of everyone's testimony because she was the one who told everyone around her what happened. All anyone could do was repeat what she had told them. This left her essentially free to say whatever she wanted as long as she cloaked it in reference to something verifiable that actually happened (like a ride home from a rodeo, or a ride to see a movie, or a night spent at a house after a birthday party).

Tom's interviews of Hanna, Josh, and Angie were never used in the trials. I wish they had been, because it seems obvious that the differences in Hanna's statements prove that she was lying to someone. Whether the lies were made to Tom or made in court is important in a legal sense (Hanna couldn't have been prosecuted for perjury for what she said to Tom because she didn't speak to him under oath); but an examination of the changes in her statements from her interview to the trials could have shown that she might have been attempting to deceive the defense, and possibly that she was lying in court. I think her pattern of layering what I believe were fantasies (like the masturbation and oral sex in the truck) onto a framework of truth (like the ride home from the rodeo) would have been noticeable to the jury if they had seen the frequent changes in her statements, but every jury heard her stories brand new. If they were, as I believe, invented scenarios that changed each time, the second jury had no way of knowing that the previous jury had been told something different, or that elements of what she said in court were different from the statements she made to Tom, or to Dixon.

I wasn't there the night of the rodeo, so I can't personally verify that nothing happened out on a county road that night; but no one else can prove that something did happen either. Steve said one thing, and Hanna said another. All I can do is show you that Hanna's and Rhonda's stories don't sync with each other; that no one thought this ride was significant until the summer of 2005 (over two years after the rodeo); that much of Hanna's story doesn't make sense, especially when compared with Rhonda's; that Steve couldn't physically have done what she said he did; and that she couldn't have done what she claimed without Rhonda catching her doing it.

As we saw in *The Night of Harry Potter*, just because Hanna dressed up her accusations with lots of little details doesn't mean they are true. You can dress a porcupine up in diamonds, Jimmy Choos, a Dior gown, and makeup, but it's still going to be dangerous to touch. This was just a stop at a water tower and a ride home, during and after which nothing happened.

Let's go to a birthday party.

The Night of Beau's 21st Birthday Party

"I don't think a whole lot happened that night. I don't believe it did. I do not think I stayed out there that night. I really don't remember."
Hanna Penderfield

"We came in at about 11:00, 11:30, and she sat there and talked to me until 2:30 in the morning."
Beau Sirois

[Subsections in this Chapter: The Questions // Final Thoughts About The Night of Beau's 21st Birthday Party]

This chapter covers what Hanna claimed were the last two incidents. She said they happened after a 21st birthday celebration for Beau, and they became the second and third counts against Steve. He was acquitted of both of them at his second trial (because of the deal I believe the jurors made), but even though they are both off the table because of double jeopardy, it is my goal to have you finish this book with no doubts about Steve's innocence. He can't be tried for these two counts again, but I think it's just as important to discredit them as any of Hanna's other accusations.

Beau was away at college when he turned 21, but they gave him a party the next time he came home. As the party wound down, some of the attendees left, but Hanna and Aaron stayed. At the time of the party, Darla Belisle was 47; Hanna was 14 (almost fifteen); Steve and Robin were both 43; Marri was 12; Aaron was 13; and Beau was, of course, 21. As with the previous chapters, I'll compare what Hanna said across all versions of her story to see the differences. Images mentioned in this chapter will be found on the blog at:

https://aggravatedbook.com/images-for-the-night-of-beaus-birthday-chapter/

The Questions

Here are the questions I hope to answer: "What kind of party was it?" "When and where did the party take place?" "What was the weather like?" "Who was there, and for how long?" Were Hanna and Steve ever alone at the party?" "Would Aaron have been alone at the fire?" "Who spent the night?" "When did everyone go to bed" "Where did everyone sleep that night?" "What did Hanna and Steve wear to bed?" "What happened at the house that night?" and "Did anyone see this happening?" Here's the first one.

What Kind of Party Was It?

Why is This Question Important? This is just to establish that it wasn't a traditional sort of birthday party (no clowns, balloons or party hats, etc.). It was just a get-together with some friends.

Hanna said, in her April 2004 affidavit, "I remember my mother, brother, and I had gone to Steve's home to have a BarBQ to celebrate his son's birthday."

[*A barbecue, food, and a birthday.*]

In the late-2004 brainstorming session, Steve said, "We were having a barbecue at my son's birthday party.

[*Another vote for a barbecue.*]

Tom interviewed Beau in 2005, and asked him what he remembered about it. Beau said, "Dad cooked, I think it was pork chops or something. I can't remember what it was. And we ate, and we had my little birthday party here in the kitchen, and we had a bonfire out back.

[*A little party, Steve cooked, and they had a bonfire.*]

In Trial #1, Hanna said (when asked about Steve's condition later that night), "Yes, he was stumbling around more than usual. And I know that everyone that night had quite a lot to drink. It was a birthday celebration, and 21st at that."

[*For the trials, Hanna (of course) suggested that it was a drunken party, which is something she hadn't previously mentioned, and is also something that no one else said about that night.*]

Analysis: Steve cooked, then they had a party for Beau to celebrate his 21st birthday. Everyone agreed with that. Also, yes, there was some drinking. Not for the kids, of course, but it wasn't as bad as Hanna tried to make the jury believe.

Conclusion: There was a party. It was for Beau's 21st birthday. They cooked, they ate, the adults drank, they partied.

So, where was it held?

When and Where Did the Party Take Place?

Why is This Question Important? Just to attempt to verify the location and date.

Hanna's affidavit said the party was on "February 14th of this year."

[*Her affidavit was created less than two months after February 14th.*]

Hanna also mentioned the birthday party to Ada Dixon. She said, "On February 13th or 14th, the night of his son's birthday party..."

[*Less specific than the affidavit, and still in the same ballpark, but she didn't give a year or say it was Beau's 21st birthday; or, if she did, Dixon didn't list that information.*]

In late-2004, Tom asked Steve if he remembered the date of the party. Steve said, "It wasn't actually on...February 10th [*Beau's birthdate*], but it was right in there, and we've had some discussions on that from my sister-in-law and my wife about whether we had it on Saturday or Friday night."

[*Beau was away at college on his birthday, but came home most weekends. The Friday after his birthday would have been the 13th.*]

When Tom interviewed Hanna, she said, "All I remember is it was close to Valentine's Day because I had a lot of those little Red Hot things. We called them Cupid Poops. It's a thing we did at school. I remember bringing a lot of those out there and giving them to Marri, and whoever else wanted them. Um, it was a celebration for Beau's 21st birthday."

[*Cupid Poops, close to Valentine's Day, Beau's 21st.*]

In Trial #1, Elmer Ross asked Hanna why she remembered it being near Valentine's Day. She said, "Because I had gotten candy and things like that from school that I brought over to share with Marri, and we were celebrating Beau's birthday." Ross asked her if it was held at the Sirois' house. Hanna said, "Yes, it was."

[*Around Valentine's Day, at the Sirois' house, but for the trial Hanna just called it candy, not "Cupid Poops."*]

Trial #2. Sanford asked Hanna if she recalled the party being held on February 14th, 2004. Hanna said, "Vaguely, yes." He asked if she remembered it because it was a barbecue for Beau. She said, "I don't recall it being a barbecue, but that -- I really don't know if it was or not. I really don't remember, sir. I'm sorry." He asked if it was a birthday party for Beau. She said, "Yes." He prompted, "His 21st, I believe you testified to?" She said, "Yes, sir."

[*When Sanford, the defense attorney, asked her about that night, she* "vaguely" *remembered it, even though she had already, in the same trial, told the prosecutor it was Beau's birthday, and had given him details about the Valentine's candy she brought Marri.*]

Sanford said to Robin, "I'm going to ask you about February 14th of 2004. Do you remember that date?" She said, "It was Valentine's." He asked if she remembered having a 21st birthday get-together for Beau. She said, "Yes, sir." He asked her if it was on February 14th, 2004. She said, "No, sir." He asked if it was in February 2004. She said, "Yes, sir. It was like the 20th."

[*February 20th was the next Friday after Valentine's Day. Is it possible that everyone else is wrong and Robin was right? Is that even important? It could be.*]

Analysis: The party was at the Sirois' home. There was no argument about that. There was some disagreement about the date of the party, though. Beau wasn't there on his birthday, so it was held the next time he came home. He didn't come home every weekend, but he did frequently. Almost everyone said the party was on the 13th or 14th, the first Friday or Saturday after the 10th. Hanna said that it was "either the day before or the day after Valentine's Day of 2004" (which would have been the 13th or the 15th), but Robin said "it was like the 20th," which would have been the next weekend.

Conclusion: In her affidavit, less than two months after the event took place, Hanna named February 14th as the date the party took place. During the brainstorming session, Steve mentioned a disagreement about which day it was, but, because of the affidavit, February 14th became the de facto date in most documents. In the trials, though, Robin said it was on the 20th. There is a good reason to believe Robin's date could be right, and that's covered in the next question. In the trials, the prosecution used the date of "on or about February 14th, 2004," regardless. Was this another example of data generated by Hanna becoming official just because she said it was?

Let's take a quick look at the weather now.

What Was the Weather Like?

Why is This Question Important? Yes, it's the weather question again. Oddly, no one said anything about the weather that night, not even Hanna, which is why a weather event might cast doubt on the date.

In his interview with Tom, Beau said that he left for a while to take his girlfriend to get her car, but returned about 10:00 pm. Then he added, "When I got here, our neighbor Matt was still here, and everybody was outside by the bonfire."

[*A bonfire makes a case for cool weather. Maybe the next item will make sense for the existence of a bonfire, or ruin it altogether.*]

From The National Weather Service archives, February 13 and 14, 2004.

> "A winter Storm swept across all of North Texas Friday night Feb 13 into Saturday afternoon Feb 14 as warm and moist air moved over a deep, cold Arctic air mass at the surface. As the low moved closer to North Texas Friday night, moisture was lifted into the atmosphere and snow, with a little sleet, began across much of the region.
>
> "The slow moving low and surface temperatures at or just below freezing set the stage for some of the heaviest snowfall totals seen in North Texas for over a decade! Some of the heaviest snow fell late Saturday morning across the Red River counties, as the slow moving system had moved far enough east to draw up even more moisture from the Gulf of Mexico.
>
> "The snow all but ended, even in the northeast, by late Saturday afternoon. Delays were reported at many airports and there were several traffic accidents, but much of the snow melted on many of the roadways. Icy bridges and overpasses seemed to be the major traffic problem areas with this snowfall event. In fact, as temperatures on Saturday rose into the mid and upper 30s, most of the snow had melted by Saturday evening. But not before many had enjoyed some of the most beautiful and heavy snowfall they had ever seen in North Texas. February 14, 2004 will be a Valentine's Day that many in North Texas will remember for many years."

An NWS map of the event is available on the blog. Deep Springs is on the southwest edge of the map, which put it in the mildest part of the storm, but National Weather Service data shows that a quarter-inch of freezing rain and/or melted snow fell in the Deep Springs area on Thursday, February 12th. There was none on the 13th, but 1.5 inches fell on February 14th. The temperature never got above 34° on the 13th, and was below freezing by 5:00 pm (meaning there would have been icy roads and bridges), and it got no higher than 46° by the afternoon of the 14th. It dropped to 23° by 5:25 am on the 13th, and dropped to 28° by 3:45 am on the 14th.

[*No one mentioned bitter cold or snow or freezing rain at the party, or when Beau drove his girlfriend to her car. Weather was a favorite subject of Hanna's, but there wasn't a single weather-related peep from her this time. Robin thought the party was on the 20th. Could she have been right while everyone else was wrong? The temperature on Friday, February 20th was 68° in the late afternoon, and dropped to 46° by 10:00 pm, but the visibility was clear that night, no sign of rain or snow clouds. Keep that chilly weather in mind (for both weekends) when you're reading Hanna's descriptions of how she and Steve were dressed after midnight that night.*]

Analysis: No one mentioned any rough weather on the night of Beau's birthday party, but the NWS recorded a severe winter storm in the region on February 12, 13 and 14, 2004. They said there were traffic accidents on icy bridges and overpasses, and snow and sleet, and a "beautiful and heavy snowfall." Admittedly, Deep Springs was on the far western edge of that region, but it did have temperatures in the 30's and mid-40's on the 13th and 14th, and received a quarter-inch of icy rain, sleet or snow on the 12th, and 1.5 inches on the 14th. It would have been cold enough to warrant a bonfire at the party, but how easy is it to keep a fire going in icy rain or sleet, and who wants to sit or stand outside and socialize in that kind of weather? On the 20th, the next weekend, there was no precipitation. The temperature rose to 68° late that afternoon, and dropped to 46° by 10:00 pm, certainly cold enough for a bonfire, but there was no icy rain or snow. A better forecast for a barbecue.

Conclusion: The weather on Valentine's Day weekend was very cold, likely sleeting or snowing. It was clear the next weekend, but cold enough for a bonfire. No one said anything about freezing rain or snow on the night of Beau's birthday party. The chances are good that Robin was right. It could have been the 20th. Did everyone else just accept Hanna's timeline on this because they didn't remember? The trial is full of examples of Hanna driving the narrative this way, but the revised date does generate an interesting thought. If the party was on the 20th, it would mean they had the celebration for Beau's birthday just a few days before Hanna's 15th birthday, and ten whole days after Beau's, but Hanna didn't get a party that night. Could that have pissed her off a little?

So, who came to the barbecue, and how long did they stay?

Who Was There, and For How Long?

Why is This Question Important? The obvious reason is because the more witnesses there were, the less chance there is of Hanna's story being true.

In her affidavit, Hanna said, "After several hours his wife Robin got drunk so she went to bed. I further remember my mother had left for awhile and so had Marri. I was in the house along with Steve while my brother, Aaron, was outside at the fire."

[*Hanna's first declaration under oath eliminated most of the witnesses by having her mother and Marri gone, Robin passed out, Aaron outside, and Beau and all the other guests just vanished.*]

In 2005, Tom asked Beau what he remembered about the party. Beau said, "I remember we had a bunch of people out here; my Aunt Nancy and Uncle Marvin, Matt and Vivian Percet, Les Etheridge from down the street. Let's see, Darla was out here. Hanna's brother, Aaron, was out here; Hanna was out here, and, of course I was here; and my ex-girlfriend, Jan, was here… And, well, I left and took my ex-girlfriend home." Tom asked him what time that was. Beau said, "I want to say I left about 9:00, and took her to Deep Springs to get her car, and she went on home, and I was back here by 10:00. But when I got back, I passed my aunt and uncle right up here on the road -- they were leaving -- and then when I got here our neighbor Matt was still here, and everybody was outside."

[*Beau left around 9:00. When he came back an hour later, his aunt and uncle were leaving and Darla was gone. Also, notice that he said nothing about ice or snow or bitterly cold weather.*]

When Tom interviewed Hanna, she was less than forthcoming about this night. She said it was the last time she was there at the Sirois' house. Tom asked her what she could remember about that night. She said, "You know, it's funny, but the last time is the hardest one to remember. One of the hardest ones." Then she added, "I don't think a whole lot happened that night. I don't believe it did. I do not think I stayed out there that night. I really don't remember."

[*What she told Tom and what she said in the trials were polar opposites. Was this another example of her trying to throw the defense off track?*]

In Trial #1, Ross asked her who was at the party. She said, "I didn't know some of the people real well. I don't remember their names. There was a lot of people. Some of Beau's friends were there. The main people I remember were Matt and Vivian Percet, my mom, Marri, Robin, of course, and Beau. I don't really remember. It was Beau's Aunt Nancy and a few of Beau's and Marri's cousins." Ross asked if her mother was still there. Hanna said, "She left. Beau had left. He had gone off with his friends to go do their own thing."

[*In the first trial, Hanna named a lot of people. A complete reversal from what she said in the affidavit and to Tom, but she made sure to mention that Beau and her mom weren't there.*]

In Trial #2, Hanna said, "And I brought over all sorts of candy, and was giving away red hots and all those little candy heart things to Marri." Hanna at first said that Marri was there, but later in the same trial Ross asked her, "Who else was present in the house on this last incident?" She said, "It was Sirois, of course, me, his wife, Robin, Beau, my little brother. And I don't believe Marri was there. I think she was staying the night over at a friend's house."

[*Early in the trial, Hanna said she brought Marri candy for Valentine's Day, but then she said that Marri wasn't there. Was she suggesting that Marri was only there during the party?*]

In Trial #2, Sanford asked Beau if, at any point during the night, he left the house. Beau said, "Yes, sir…I went to take my girlfriend back to her car." Sanford asked him if he went anywhere after that. Beau said, "Back to my parents' house."

[*Beau left, but he came back. He spent the night there at the house.*]

Their neighbor, Vivian Percet took the stand. Vivian had known Steve and Robin for over twenty years, and was frequently at their get-togethers. Sanford asked her if she remembered Beau's 21st birthday party. She said, "Yes, sir, I was there." He asked her if she was just there "for a few minutes or...?" She said, "No, I was there all night." To clarify, he said, "You didn't spend the night, did you?" She said, "No. I mean until the party was over. I was probably there till 11:00, 11:30, maybe 12:00." Sanford asked if she would agree that she didn't know what happened after she left. She naturally said "No." He asked, though, if she was there most of the evening. She said, "Yes."

When Elmer Ross cross-examined her, he asked, "You left the party in February of 2004 around 10:30 or 11:00?" She corrected him, "No, sir. 11:00, 11:30 or 12:00. I don't know the exact time." Ross asked if she knew what happened after she left. Vivian said, "No, but when I left, pretty much everybody was leaving. It was about time to go to bed."

[*Both Sanford and Ross established that Vivian didn't witness anything that might have happened after everyone went to bed at the Sirois' household that night. She said that the party was breaking up when she and her husband left, sometime between 11:00 pm and midnight.*]

I asked Steve about this in 2016. I said, "Nobody has ever established whether Marri was there or not, but I can't imagine she wouldn't have been there for his birthday party." Steve said, "Well, yeah." I asked, "And if she left, where would she go?" Steve said, "Nowhere. I mean, Marri didn't just run around everywhere. Marri stayed at the house."

[*Hanna said at various times that Beau was gone, her mom was gone, Marri was gone, and she usually only mentioned Aaron when she was asked. Why would Hanna need to make the jury believe that very few people spent the night after the party? Exactly, less witnesses.*]

I told Beau that Hanna made a comment in the trial about him leaving "with his friends to go do their thing." Beau said, "No, I left with my girlfriend to go take her home." I said, "You took Jan ...did you actually take her home, to Klemperer?" [*Klemperer, where Jan lived, was about 40 miles away, an 80 mile round trip.*] Beau said, "I took her back to town [*to Deep Springs*]. She met me in town." I asked, "To get her car so she could drive home?" Beau said, "Yes." I asked if any of his friends were there. "Beau said, "None of my friends were there for my birthday party, because the friends I had who would have been there were all in the military at the time."

[*Beau said that the only guest or friend of his at the party was his girlfriend, Jan, and he only left with her for about an hour to take her to her car. He did spend the night at the house, so did Marri, so did Aaron and Hanna, and so did Steve and Robin.*]

Analysis: Beau said that a number of people were there, and he left about 9:00 pm to take his girlfriend to her car, but returned about 10:00, passing his aunt and uncle as they were leaving. He said that "everyone was outside" when he returned except for Darla. She left just after Beau did. Five months after the affidavit, in August 2004, Hanna told Ada Dixon about being at the party, and said it was "on February 13th or 14th," but gave no information about who was there. In 2006, she told Tom that she and her family were there, but didn't say a word about any other guests, saying instead that nothing happened that night, and that she didn't think she even spent the night. In Trial #1, she said there were "a lot of people" there, and named some of them, but said that everyone was gone when the last incident happened, adding that Beau left "with his friends to go do their own thing." In Trial #2, she said, "It was Sirois, of course, me, his wife, Robin, Beau, my little brother. And I don't believe Marri was there. I think she was staying the night over at a friend's house." That's a switch from Trial #1, with Beau back in and Marri out. Beau and Steve both established (despite what Hanna said) that Marri and Beau both spent the night.

Conclusion: According to all accounts (except Hanna's first one, most of which was tossed aside soon after the affidavit was written) there were roughly a dozen people at Beau's party, which started breaking up around 9:00 pm, with the last guests leaving between 11:00 pm and midnight. Beau didn't leave permanently to go party with his friends, despite what Hanna said. Her attempts to remove people from the picture were, I believe, all done to convince everyone that there were fewer possible witnesses.

Hanna said that she and Steve spent a lot of time alone. Did that happen at the party?

Were Hanna and Steve Ever Alone at the Party?

Why is This Question Important? Hanna claimed that, over the space of two-and-a-half years, Steve molested her eighty to ninety times. If anyone saw them commit a single one of those acts, these would have been very different trials, but no one did. Not one person. Hanna claimed it happened that many times because they were either alone, or because everyone was oblivious, or were passed out, or asleep, or chose to ignore it. Other than Rhonda (who only claimed a possible touch on the knee or a hand on the back), everyone who was asked about it said they didn't see Steve and Hanna do any of the things she claimed, and that they never witnessed any kind of inappropriate behavior on Steve's part toward Hanna or anyone else. Read the following statements, and see if you can figure out when Hanna and Steve could have been alone. Some of the excerpts below are not about the party itself. Most of the witnesses were usually asked more general questions. Only a few were asked about anything related to the specific acts in the three counts.

In her 2004 affidavit, when asked about the night of the party, Hanna said, "Robin got drunk so she went to bed. I further remember my mother had left for awhile and so had Marri. I was in the house along with Steve while my brother, Aaron, was outside at the fire. I was helping Steve put up the food..."

[*She said that everyone else was gone, and Robin and Aaron were safely out of the way. What time of night was this supposed to be? Clearly, if Steve was putting up food, she was saying it was earlier in the evening.*]

This is a general comment from Tom's 2005 interview with Beau, not about the party specifically. He asked Beau if he remembered any time Hanna was alone with Steve. Beau said, "Well, there were times I wasn't there, but I don't think there was any time there wasn't anybody there. There was always my sister there, or my mom, or our neighbors, Matt and Vivian. They'd come over here. They'd be here, or there was always somebody here."

[*Even when Beau was away at college, somebody else was there.*]

Beau also told Tom that, when he returned around 10:00 pm that night after dropping his girlfriend off, "Everybody was outside by the bonfire. I was standing out there, talking to Aaron and Matt, and dad says, 'Well, I've got to go do the dishes,' and he walked in. I bet it wasn't two minutes, she walked in with him, but I walked in right behind them, and dad finished putting up stuff, and he came outside for a little while. And then he went in and went to bed." Tom asked him where Robin was. Beau said, "She was already asleep."

[*Hanna said everybody was gone, but Beau said people were still there when he returned. Steve and others were talking by the fire, and he followed Hanna and Steve when they went inside.*]

In Trial #1, Hanna undercut her own argument about the time she spent alone with Steve. Bevin Jenkins asked her "How often were you alone at the home with Steve?" She said, "Totally alone, no one outside or anything?" "Jenkins said, "Right." She said, "Extremely rare occasions. I don't even -- I can't even think of one that comes to my mind." He asked if it was fair to say that most of the incidents happened while family was there. She said, "Yes." He asked if other people were there too. She said, "Yes. I'm nearly positive there was one or two instances where we were totally by ourselves, but it was only for very few lengths of time. Maybe five minutes here, ten minutes there."

[*So, even Hanna said she couldn't think of a time when she and Steve were alone, and if it ever did happen, it was for brief periods. It would have been a miracle, with people constantly in and out, for any of those 80 or 90 incidents to happen without someone catching them. Naturally, Hanna didn't repeat that comment in Trial #2.*]

Trial #1. This next bit also wasn't about Beau's party. Bevin Jenkins asked Marri if Steve and Hanna ever spent any time alone. Marri said, "No." He asked her if she understood that the allegations in the case were that some of the "eighty to ninety" incidents happened at the house. Marri said, "Yes." He asked her if there was any way that could be true. Marri said, "No." He asked her why. She said, "Because she was never out there that much. She wasn't out there enough for it to happen that much." Jenkins asked her if Hanna could have been alone with Steve that much. Marri said, "No." He asked her how often they were alone. Marri said, "None that I know of." He also asked her if Steve and Hanna went off to other places by themselves. Marri said, "No."

[*Marri and others, including Hanna and her own mother, said that Steve was rarely alone; but also notice Marri's comment,* "she was never out there that much. She wasn't out there enough for it to happen that much." *Both Hanna and Darla (with some help from Elmer Ross) tried to make it seem like they were out there almost every weekend, but they weren't.*]

Analysis: Hanna's affidavit stated that her mother and Marri were both gone, and that she and Steve were inside while Aaron was outside and Robin was passed out drunk in her bed. There was no mention of Beau or any other guests. All of that was contrary to what she and everyone else said later. The affidavit's entire scenario (the time of night, who was present, the location inside the house, and the specifics of the incident) was replaced with an entirely different set of circumstances, and the original one was never mentioned again. I think the affidavit should have been considered invalid, as should the indictment that was based on it; but it wasn't.

About Steve and Hanna being completely alone: Even Hanna said they would be "totally alone" on "extremely rare occasions." She said, "I can't even think of one that comes to my mind." She also agreed that usually "there were other people there besides family." Marri, when asked if they spent time alone, flatly said, "No," adding that Hanna wasn't even at the house often enough for her accusations to be true (something I will thoroughly cover in the next chapter, *A Timeline as Final Proof*). Hanna's mother said the same thing in Trial #1 when asked about it. She said, "No. I mean, there was, I guess, times that he, not just her alone to my knowledge. There were times that he would take a few of them to the movies or, you know, here and there. But just one on one, no…I mean, he was rarely alone." That first jury was deadlocked, and their deliberations ended with a mistrial. Darla and Hanna didn't repeat their comments during the second trial about how rarely Steve was alone.

Conclusion: I hope it's clear that there wasn't an instance during the party when Hanna, Steve, Aaron, and Robin were the only people at the house. In other words, that part of Hanna's affidavit is a lie. Everyone else, including Hanna and her mother, said that Steve was rarely alone at any time. So, with that information in hand, is it feasible that Steve and Hanna could have found any time to be alone during the party, even for moments? No, it's highly unlikely.

Hanna said her brother was out at the bonfire by himself. Would he have been?

Would Aaron Have Been Alone by the Fire?

Why is This Question Important? In Hanna's deeply flawed affidavit, she claimed that while she was inside with Steve, Aaron (who was almost two years younger than her) was outside at the fire by himself. Would they have allowed him to do that? This will be very short.

In Hanna's affidavit. She said, "I was in the house along with Steve while my brother, Aaron, was outside at the fire."

[*She said that everyone else was gone or incapacitated except Aaron, and he was outside by the fire.*]

In his 2005 interview with Tom, Beau said, "Everybody was outside by the bonfire. I was standing out there, talking to Aaron and Matt.

[*Aaron was not alone, and people were still there after 10:00 at night, when Beau returned.*]

Steve told me in 2016, "Aaron is not going to be out there by himself. Not ever. I'm not putting a kid with a fire by himself. It's not happening. Marri got burned at the fire with five adults standing there, and three of us walked through coals to catch her on the way into the fire. And she really just got some superficial burns on her hand. I think they were maybe second degree." I asked him how it happened. He said they "were all sitting around it, and she had her little bicycle. She was little, but she just rode up and ...just fell over in it. Looked like the deal on *Laugh In*, like the guy on the tricycle. I mean, just literally fell over in it." He said that it "burnt the bottom of our feet. And that's with us all sitting there. That's how much we watched the fire. And it was quick. It happened really quick." I asked him if they were the same way about Aaron. Steve said, "I wouldn't have left him outside by himself. Well, that's Number One. Number Two, he wouldn't have *been* outside by himself... Aaron's not the type. Aaron wants to sit in front of the TV and play video games. We got him to do the fire…to get him to engage. But that was only when we're out there. I mean, we're calling him The Fireman. We're letting him poke the fire. We're damn sure not going to let him do that when we're not there. It's just not going to happen."

[*After the scare when Marri was younger, they were careful around the fire. A lot of people were there the night of Beau's party; so, no, Aaron wasn't alone by the fire. Why would Hanna say that under oath? Right. Fewer witnesses.*]

Analysis: Hanna said that in her affidavit, under oath. That statement allowed her to set up a situation where she and Steve were the only other conscious people inside the house. Beau, however, said that everyone was out by the bonfire late into the night, and that he talked to Steve, Aaron, Matt, and Hanna there. Their neighbor also testified that she and her husband were there at the house until at least 11:00 pm.

Steve said they would never have left Aaron alone at the fire by himself, citing the incident when Marri got burned in the fire when she was very young. They were super-vigilant after that.

Conclusion: It was obviously to Hanna's advantage to make everyone believe there weren't many people around, but it just wasn't so. The party wrapped up sometime between 11:00 and midnight, and while some people did go home earlier, there were still people there fairly late, several of them standing by the fire, talking. If Aaron was at the fire, he was with quite a few people. This was another statement that Hanna abandoned shortly after creating the affidavit. She never mentioned it again, but the inaccurate affidavit was still used to create an indictment against Steve.

After the party broke up that night, who stayed?

Who Spent the Night?

Why is This Question Important? It makes a huge difference whether one person spent the night or several did. The more people who are there to spot mischief, the less likely it is to happen. Conversely, the less witnesses there are, the easier it is for someone to convincingly peddle a story.

In her affidavit, Hanna said that she "was helping Steve put up the food," suggesting that the incident occurred right after they ate, but she didn't say that she or anyone in her family spent the night.

[*The affidavit, made less than two months after the party, was Hanna's first legal statement about the molestation. Why did she get it so wrong?*]

She soon added a new twist. In August 2004, she told Ada Dixon that there had been an attempt at intercourse that night, something not even mentioned in the affidavit. She said, "He entered me twice. I don't remember when he did it the first time. On February 13th or 14th, the night of his son's birthday party, when everyone went home and went to sleep…"

[*Within a few months Hanna had rewritten her story, telling Dixon that Steve attempted intercourse with her after everyone was gone, and indicating that she did spend the night after Beau's birthday party).*]

In 2006, Tom asked her what she remembered about the last time she was at the house. She said, "You know, it's funny, but the last time is the hardest one to remember. One of the hardest ones," and added, "I don't think a whole lot happened that night. I don't believe it did. I do not think I stayed out there that night. I really don't remember."

[*Hanna reverted back to the affidavit playbook. Was she attempting to deceive the defense by telling Tom that she didn't think she spent the night, and that she didn't think anything happened?*]

Just two months later, in Trial #1, Hanna told Ross that her mom went home, but she spent the night. He asked her where Marri slept, and Hanna said, "She was asleep in the twin bed that was <u>actually in</u> the living room.

[*Once the trial arrived, Hanna changed her story again, and said that her mom was gone, but she* did *spend the night. This time she said that Marri <u>was</u> there, but where were Beau and Aaron? And, if Marri was <u>actually</u> in the living room, was Hanna <u>not really</u> in the living room?*]

In Trial #2, Ross asked her who else was there. She said, "It was Sirois, of course, me, his wife, Robin, Beau, my little brother. And I don't believe Marri was there. I think she was staying the night over at a friend's house."

[*Less than a month later, Hanna contradicted herself again by testifying that Marri <u>wasn't</u> there, but Beau and Aaron were.*]

In that trial, Cleveland Sanford asked Hanna several questions about her testimony. He wanted to know if she had testified that she spent the night; and that Steve, Robin, Aaron, and Beau were there, but had said that Marri spent the night at a friend's house. She said, "Yes, sir," so he had her look at her testimony from Trial #1, pointing out that she had previously testified that Marri slept on a twin bed in the living room, but this time had said Marri was gone. She agreed that she had said that. Then he asked her if she also agreed "that Marri couldn't be at her friend's house and in her own house at the same time." Hanna, having been caught, agreed and said, "Yes, sir."

[*Marri was either there or she wasn't. She* was *there, but she would have been one less witness to consider if Hanna could have convinced the jury that she was gone. Fortunately, Sanford called her on it.*]

Analysis: In her 2004 affidavit, after disappearing a bunch of potential witnesses, Hanna claimed there was an incident earlier that night, when Steve was putting the food up, but she soon abandoned that, telling Ada Dixon that something happened later that night, after everyone else was asleep. Then, in 2006, she told Tom that she didn't think she even spent the night, and didn't "think a whole lot happened that night," but in both trials she reversed course and then reversed course again. In Trial #1, she didn't mention Aaron. She said that Marri was there, but both her mother and Beau were gone. In Trial #2, she said that Beau and Aaron were there, but Marri wasn't. Sanford challenged her on the differences between her testimony from one trial to the next (Beau gone in #1, but there in #2; and Marri there in #1, but gone in #2). Marri and Beau *were* both there that night. Does that mean that Hanna attempted to lie about who was there in both trials, or in just one?

Conclusion: Hanna said, at separate trials, that either Beau or Marri were gone. Which of those versions are we supposed to believe? Each jury only heard the story she was giving at that moment. Sanford did a good job of pointing out some of the differences between what she said in the two trials, but she told Tom she didn't think she even spent the night (should we consider that a lie?), and then told two very different accounts of who was there, one in each trial (were those lies too?). There are even more discrepancies tucked away in all of the minor changes to her story. No matter how Hanna might try to twist it, the occupants of the house that night were Steve, Robin, Beau, Marri, Hanna, and Aaron (plus Bob, the dog).

How late were they up?

When Did Everyone Go To Bed?

Why is This Question Important? Hanna made several claims about that night, but she not only disagreed with everyone else about when they all went to bed, she also disagreed with herself. She only claimed to have spent the night after Beau's birthday party in three of the documents I have (Ada Dixon's summary and the two trial transcripts), but for the trials she also changed what she said in her affidavit from a just-after-supper incident to a post-midnight one. She had already changed all of the affidavit's details for Count I, why would she add more contradictions by changing the time of night for Counts II and III too? Actually, she was just getting started.

Beau told Tom that Darla left the party around 9:00 pm. Tom asked him if she came back that night. Beau said, "No. She called and talked to Hanna, I think." Tom asked him what time that was. Beau said, "10:30 or 11:00? Somewhere around in there. It wasn't too long after I got back." Beau said that Darla offered to come back for the kids if they wanted her to, but Hanna and Aaron said they would stay.

[*Beau, Hanna, and Aaron were awake until sometime after 11:00. What was Darla doing that caused her to leave for the night? And why wouldn't she just return for the kids, instead of asking if they wanted her to come get them?*]

Early in 2005, before anyone knew what the prosecution's game plan was going to be,Tom asked Beau where Robin was that night. Beau said, "She was already asleep. And he [*Steve*] came in and went to bed. I want to say it wasn't long after that Matt [*Percet, their neighbor*] went home. And we all came in, me and Aaron and Hanna. I don't remember where Marri was at, but we all came in. When I come home on the weekends, I sleep on the couch because I like watching TV. And she [*Hanna*] sat down here and talked to me until 2:30 in the morning." Tom asked, "What time did y'all come in?" Beau said, "We came in at about 11:00, 11:30." Tom asked him what they talked about, and Beau said, "Just the same old stuff. About this guy that she liked that was supposedly going into the army, and about how she thought about some guy as a big brother, and he always took care of her, and stuff like that, and about how she didn't know if her mom liked him too much…I kept trying to go to sleep, and she just kept sitting there talking to me." Tom asked who the guy was, but Beau couldn't remember his name, and added that Hanna kept talking to him but he finally told her "'I've got to go to sleep. I'm tired,' and she's like, 'Okay.' And she went down there and went to sleep."

[*Beau said that Steve went to bed shortly before Matt and Vivian Percet went home around 11:00 to 11:30 pm, but said that Hanna talked to him until 2:30. If what she claimed was happening to her was true, would she have been talking to Beau about those typical teenage-type subjects? At first I thought the "big brother" could have been Josh, but in February 2004, he was already back in town, dating Steve's niece, Liz Brailford, and Hanna was aware of their relationship. This mystery guy, if he existed, had to be someone else. And remember, this was a recollection Beau' gave Tom a year-and-a-half before the first trial took place. That will be important later.*]

Tom wanted to know where Aaron slept. Beau said, pointing to a recliner to his left, "Right there. He always slept in that chair right there." He asked if Aaron was there while Beau and Hanna were talking. Beau said, "Yeah. He went to sleep. He didn't like what I was watching on TV, so he went to sleep." Tom asked what he was watching, and he said, "SportsCenter. That's like my favorite channel." He asked when Darla came back for the kids. Beau said, "The next day. I want to say it wasn't until about noon." Tom asked him what time he got up the next morning. Beau said it was "about 10:00, 10:30, something like that." He also asked when Hanna got up, and Beau said, "It was a little earlier than that, because she kept coming down here, sitting on my feet, trying to wake me up, giving me a hard time. And, so I would say 9:00 or so."

[*So, while Beau and Hanna talked on the couch, Aaron slept in the recliner. Darla came back about noon the next day to get her kids, but Hanna was up by around 9:00 am, acting playful.*]

In Trial #1, Hanna wasn't asked anything about when everyone went to bed; and Marri wasn't asked about that night in either trial, even though she could have had a lot to say. Steve wasn't asked about it either. In Trial #2, Ross asked Hanna what time she went to bed. She said, "My best guess is about 12:30, 1:00." In that trial, Sanford asked Beau if he spoke to Hanna that night. Beau said, "Yes, sir…Me and her sat there and talked till I'll bet 2:00 o'clock in the morning." Sanford asked him if he meant it was specifically 2:00 o'clock. Beau said, "No, sir." Sanford asked him if it was in that ballpark. Beau said, "yes, sir."

[*Beau told Tom he thought they talked* "until 2:30." *This time he said* "2:00," *but Hanna said she went to bed* "about 12:30, 1:00," *so even she was admitting that she and Beau talked for at least 60 to 90 minutes.*]

I asked Beau in 2016, "Hanna sat on the couch and talked to you until 2:00 in the morning?" Beau said, "Yeah. She talked to me for a long time when I got back."

[Beau said that Hanna didn't go to bed right away, they sat up and talked. He has been consistent about that since 2004.]

Analysis: In her affidavit, Hanna said she was assaulted just after Steve put up the food from the party, which would have been earlier in the evening. Then, contradicting the affidavit's account, she told Ada Dixon that a single incident happened after "everyone went home and went to sleep." The incident she relayed to Dixon was also completely different than the two items she claimed in the affidavit. We'll get to all of those details soon. Beau told Tom, "We came in at about 11:00, 11:30. And she sat there and talked to me until 2:30 in the morning." Two years later, though, Hanna told Tom that she didn't think she even spent the night, and that she didn't think "a whole lot happened that night." I believe she might have said that deliberately to confuse the defense, because in the trials, just a couple of months later, she reverted back to saying she did spend the night, estimating in Trial #2 that she went to bed "about 12:30, 1:00." In the trials, neither Robin nor Marri nor Steve were asked when they went to bed, but Beau was, and he testified that he and Hanna talked until around "2:00 o'clock in the morning."

Conclusion: The party broke up sometime around 11:00 or 11:30, and almost everyone was in bed shortly after that, but Hanna might have stayed awake to talk to Beau for a few hours. Very few of Hanna's statements on the time match up with any of her other statements, though, which will become even more apparent as we continue.

Was it still boys in the living room, girls in Beau's room? Let's see.

Where Did Everyone Sleep That Night?

Why is This Question Important? At first (in late-2001) the boys slept in the living room and the girls were in Beau's room. There was plenty of extra space in the living room, though, so eventually the boys and girls both slept there, each of them occupying one of the two twin beds, or the couch, or one of the two recliners. The beds had originally been moved in there when Robin and Steve were caring for their ailing parents, and were just never removed. The night of Beau's birthday the kids all slept there, but the question is: Where in the room were they located individually, and what could they see from their unique spots? You might want to view the floor plans on a monitor while reading this part. It will be easier to follow.

https://aggravatedbook.com/images-for-the-night-of-beaus-birthday-chapter/

Tom asked Beau where Hanna slept. Pointing to the far side of the room, Beau said she "went right down there [*past the TV cabinet*] and went to sleep." [*it's labeled* Hanna's Bed *on the floor plans*] Tom asked where Aaron slept. Beau, who was sitting on the couch, pointed at the recliner to his left [*labeled* Aaron's Recliner], and said, "He always slept in that chair right there."

[*Hanna slept on the bed behind the TV cabinet, Beau on the couch, Aaron in the recliner. Where was Marri?*]

Here's a description Hanna gave Tom of the living room. "I don't know how it's set up now," she said. "It's been years since I've been there, but in his living room, there should be an entertainment center…up against the wall, kind of pointed out [*i.e., perpendicular to the wall*]. Behind it there was a twin-sized bed [*labeled Hanna's Bed*]. I don't know if it's still there." Tom said it was. She said, "On that bed is where I was sleeping that night." Tom asked her where Beau was. She said, "When you first walk into that room, you're standing in the doorway. Right across from you should be that bed [*labeled Other Bed*]. That's where he was sleeping. My little brother was on the couch that would be to your left." Tom said, "I understand where that is." Hanna added, "He was either in that couch or on the recliner that was sitting beside the couch." Tom said, "Okay. So, y'all [*her and Steve*] were <u>behind</u> the entertainment center?" Hanna said, "Right."

[*I don't know how clear that is. The floor plan should help make sense of it. Beau said he usually slept on the couch, by the way, not the* "Other Bed." *Also, notice that Marri wasn't there in Hanna's description.*]

I need to pause to clarify something. They mentioned a piece of furniture called an entertainment center. If you're conjuring an image of something that will hold a modern 75-inch flat-screen TV, that's not what this was. See some pictures of it on the blog. What they called an entertainment center was really a fairly small cabinet (40 inches wide by 24 inches deep, and 60 inches tall). It's labeled a TV cabinet on the floor plan. I'll call it that from here on unless I'm quoting someone. The body of the cabinet, while only 40 inches wide, had a 48-inch wide flared base (four inches on each side). If the base had been pushed all the way up against the wall that night, someone facing it would have seen a four-inch gap along the right side of the wall. That meant that the left side of the cabinet would have been 44 inches from the wall. Hanna's bed was a standard twin (39 inches wide by 75 inches long). Anyone's head that was resting more than four feet from the right wall of the room would be to the left of the cabinet. The left side of the couch, the other twin bed, and Aaron's recliner would all qualify. Everyone could easily see part or all of the bed past the TV cabinet.

In Trial #1, Elmer Ross asked Hanna where she slept that night. She said, "There is a twin bed setting [*Texan for "sitting"*] behind their TV in their living room, and that is where I was to sleep." He asked her where Marri was, and Hanna said, "She was asleep in the twin bed that was actually in the living room." Ross asked her where those two beds were in relation to each other. She said, "If you're sitting on the edge of the bed I was to sleep on, her bed would be over caddy-cornered to the left, but you couldn't see it because of the entertainment center that the TV was setting on. So, it was blocked from view. You couldn't see anybody or anything."

[*Did Hanna imply, by referring to Marri's bed as "the twin bed that was actually in the living room," that her bed behind the TV cabinet wasn't even in the same room? Not true, of course, but I believe her big lie was saying that "you couldn't see anybody or anything" from Marri's bed. It's true that Beau, on the couch, probably couldn't see Hanna's head when she was lying down on her bed, especially if her head was near the TV cabinet, but Beau and everyone else could still see most or all of the bed itself from where they slept. In the trials, no one was asked whether they could see Hanna's bed (and whoever might have been on it) from the other locations in the room.*]

In Trial #1, Bevin Jenkins, referring to that night, asked Hanna if Beau was sleeping nearby, but she answered generically. "Some of the times, he was -- whenever I was in the twin bed that was behind the entertainment center, sometimes he was in the other twin bed that was out of sight from the one I was on, if that makes any sense." He asked her for a description of the area. She said, "It's one big room, but it's divided by kind of a small entertainment center." He asked her about the size of the room in comparison to the courtroom they were in. Was it "smaller than from me to you?" [*about fifteen feet*] "In width," she said, "but in length, it's about the length of the house." He asked her how close Beau was that night. She said, "The shortest distance would have been about five feet."

[*The living room was definitely smaller than the courtroom they were in, but it was still a big room, long and narrow. The interior dimensions were 33.5 feet by 13.5 feet. Jenkins did get her to establish that Beau was only about five feet away from her. That's not very far in a room that size, but even that might not be true because Beau was on the couch, not the other twin bed.*]

Ross asked Hanna where she was when that final incident happened. She said, "Behind the entertainment center there was another twin bed, still on the right side of the room. That's where I slept that night." Ross asked where Aaron was. Hanna said, "He was asleep in the recliner, in the living room. And Beau was asleep on the twin bed in the living room. Both were out of sight from the twin bed I was sleeping in."

[*Hanna said Aaron was in the recliner, and Beau was on the twin bed, but Beau usually slept on the couch so he could watch TV. Since he sat on the couch and talked to Hanna while watching SportsCenter, it makes no sense that he would have moved to the other bed when he went to sleep. Also, she disappeared Marri again. Was she still trying to push the idea that the small cabinet turned her bed into a completely separate room? If you haven't taken a look at the floor plan yet, you really should at this point.*]

In Trial #2. Sanford asked Beau if the entertainment center blocked one side of the room from the other. Beau said, "No, sir."

[*In addition to the cabinet being small, according to Steve, there was also a space of "about a foot, maybe 18 inches" between the head of the twin bed and the back of the TV cabinet to allow for wires and cables. They put the cabinet where it was so people could watch the TV or play video games while sitting on the couch, not to act as a divider.*]

Sanford, questioning Hanna about her testimony, asked if she had testified that Aaron was in the recliner. She said, "Yes, sir." He asked her where Beau was. She said, "I believe that he was on the twin bed that was in the living room." About her own location, she said, "There was another one that was kind of caddie-cornered to the right <u>behind</u> the entertainment center in the living room. That was where I was supposed to sleep. And <u>you cannot see anything from the head of the other twin bed that Beau was sleeping on</u>." He asked her if she had said that her bed "was secluded by this entertainment center." Hanna said, "Yes, sir." Sanford said, "So…it's perfectly possible, according to you, that you could have one person in the recliner and one person in the other bed and then you could have all this activity in the third bed…and they wouldn't know?" She said, "Yes, sir, it's perfectly possible." [*He showed her a photograph of the room, see it on the blog.*] He asked if she was saying that the room was secluded by that entertainment center in the picture. Hanna said, "Not the room. Just the bed." A long discussion followed that exchange, with Hanna insisting that the cabinet looked different, that it had been moved away from the wall. She also said, "I remember it being small, but I don't remember it being this small," but she did verify that it was the same piece of furniture.

["Next to" *the TV cabinet would be a more accurate way to describe her bed's position than* "hidden" *by it. The only way Hanna's bed would be hidden by the cabinet would be if there had been several of them completely surrounding the bed, walling it off. There was only one cabinet, placed near the head of her bed. The couch was two feet wider than the cabinet. Anyone lying down with their head on the left side of the couch could see a fair bit of the bed. The recliner was another foot or so to the left of the couch, angled toward the middle of the room. Anyone sleeping in it would be facing directly toward the twin bed and the TV cabinet. Hanna also wanted the jury to believe that anyone sleeping on the other twin bed couldn't see what was happening on her bed. Nonsense. The head of that Other Bed, placed along the left-side wall of the room, was about 10 feet from the front wall of the house, so the foot of it was about 16 feet from it. The head of Hanna's bed was about 18 feet along the right-side wall, with the foot of it resting at about 24 feet. Hanna's bed could obviously be seen from several spots in the room, but especially from the Other Bed and Aaron's recliner.*]

Neither Steve nor Marri were asked anything about what happened after Beau's party. Beau said that Hanna slept in the bed behind the cabinet, but he didn't say she was invisible because of it. Check out the sightlines on the floor plan. Also, on the blog, in the photograph of the room, can you see the rack filled with trucker caps? There were caps all over the house. Can you also see the fairly large opening in the back of the cabinet? Anyone on the couch could have seen movement on the bed through that opening as well.

Analysis: Beau and Hanna both told Tom that she slept in the small bed behind the entertainment cabinet. No one else was asked. Beau told Tom that he slept on the couch, that Marri was on the small bed on the left wall, and that Aaron was in the recliner. Hanna told Tom that Marri wasn't there that night [*but she was*], and said that Beau was asleep on the bed on the left wall [*he wasn't*], and that Aaron slept either in the recliner to the left of the couch [*he did*] or on the couch [*he didn't*]. In Trial #1, Hanna said that Marri was asleep on the bed on the left wall [*she was*], and that Beau was gone [*he wasn't*]. In Trial #2, Hanna said Aaron was asleep in the recliner [*he was*], that Beau was on the twin bed on the left side of the room [*but he wasn't*], and that Marri was gone [*but she wasn't*].

The cabinet was small. Anyone in the room could have seen movement on Hanna's bed from where they were sleeping, and could even see through the opening in the back of it. The best sightlines were from the recliner and the other bed, but some of the bed could be seen from the couch too. Her bed wasn't fully hidden from any vantage point in the room.

Conclusion: Hanna has changed her story so many times it's hard for me to give it any credence. Even her most favorable scenario for that night has at least one other person, either Beau or Marri, sleeping in the bed across the room from her, and that bed had the most complete viewing angle of any other location in the room. The primary thing to note is that the cabinet didn't visibly hide Hanna or the bed from everyone in the room, and probably not from anyone.

Now that we know where Hanna slept that night, and likely where everyone else was, what do you suppose they were wearing?

What Did Hanna and Steve Wear to Bed?

Why is This Question Important? In both trials, Hanna made specific comments about what she and Steve were wearing later that night. By comparing her testimony with what she said at other times, we can tell how radically her descriptions changed over time.

The only mention in the affidavit about Hanna's and Steve's clothing the night of Beau's party were, "He then <u>unzipped</u> his <u>pants</u>..." and "...he then pulled <u>the draw string</u> on my <u>pants</u>..."

[*Notice how specific Hanna was when saying that, stating that her pants had a drawstring tie. She never mentioned those pants again. If we assume that Hanna didn't bring any sleep clothes with her (which is logical), we could infer that she slept in some sort of pants, but her affidavit doesn't say she slept there that night. Also, when do most people wear drawstring pants? Yes, when it's warm. Was it warm in February 2004? Not a chance. Regardless of what she said in her 2004 affidavit, she had abandoned this scenario long before the trials.*]

In her 2006 interview with Tom, Hanna described an incident which she called "the second time" they unsuccessfully tried to have vaginal intercourse. She told him this didn't happen on the night of Beau's birthday, but she did describe some of the clothing she had on during that second attempt. Tom asked her if she remembered what she wore to bed that night, and she said, "Oh... ...no. I wouldn't ...well, hang on ...uh [*after a seven-second pause, with a smile in her voice, she said*] ...I *think* I remember …the pair of underwear I was wearing." Tom, keying off her tone, asked her what was special about them. She said, "They were different," and chuckled. Tom asked her what made them different. She said, "Um, they were kind of a …silky material." She paused, then said, "Um, they were a royal blue, and the seams were kind of bunched up a bit, had a little bitty bow at the top." Tom asked her what color the bow was. She said, "Same color as the rest of it." Tom asked, "Dark or light?" She said, "Dark." He asked her what made them special. She said, "They shone in the light." Tom asked her if she had intentionally worn them, thinking they were sexy. Hanna said, "Yes." He asked if she remembered what shirt she wore. She said, "No, I don't. I know that it was a big t-shirt, but I don't remember what color it was, or what was written on it or anything." He asked her what kind of pants or jeans she was wearing. She replied, "Well, I normally wore blue jeans. I hardly wore anything else. To this day I don't wear anything else. But, no, I don't."

[*Her drawstring pants are now jeans. Did Hanna seem a little too cheerful describing her dark blue silky panties with a bow on top that* "shone in the light?" *She told Tom that this was their second attempt at intercourse, but said it didn't happen the night of Beau's party. Two years earlier, however, she did tell Ada Dixon that the second time they attempted intercourse <u>was</u> on the night of Beau's birthday party, <u>after</u> everyone was asleep. Was this another stab at trying to confuse Tom about what her testimony would be at the trials?*]

Tom also asked her if she slept in her clothes on that not-Beau's-party night. She said, "I don't think so. I think I was just in a big t-shirt and a pair of underwear." Tom asked her if she was wearing a bra. She said, "I don't think so." He said, "Okay. I mean, being at that age..." She said, "It's really hard to remember." Tom also asked her if Steve slept in his clothes. She said, "Normally either in just a pair of underwear, or a pair of underwear and a pair of shorts."

[*Hanna said it was just a t-shirt, panties, and no bra; and said that Steve might have been wearing just underwear, or underwear and shorts. If he had been wearing a top hat and tails, we wouldn't know because he wasn't asked about it in the trials. He told me that he often wore swim trunks to bed in the summer and surgical scrubs when it was colder. It was cold that night. In all the documents I have, Hanna never mentioned Steve wearing scrubs.*]

In Trial #1, Hanna shifted course again, and said she did spend the night after Beau's birthday party. Ross asked her what Steve was "wearing when you aroused him from the bed?" She said, "Underwear." Ross asked, "Anything else?" Hanna said, "That was it." He asked what she was wearing. She said, "I was wearing a big t-shirt and a pair of panties." He asked if she had anything on under her shirt. She said, "A pair of panties and that was it." Trial #2 was a duplicate of Trial #1, about the clothes anyway, with Steve in underwear and Hanna in just a big t-shirt and a pair of panties.

[*Hanna told Tom that she intentionally wore the panties because she thought they were sexy. By the time of the first trial, though, they were just plain ordinary panties, not shiny blue ones with bows on them. And did you notice Ross saying* "when you aroused him from the bed." *Aroused? During a sex crimes trial? He couldn't have just said* "when you woke him up?"]

Was Hanna's description of her own clothing accurate? In 2016 I asked Beau about this. "She said your dad was just in his underwear, and she was just in underwear and a t-shirt. Do you...?" Beau interrupted, sounding shocked, "No!" I tried again. "Do you remember, when you guys were all sleeping in the living room there, did you ever get down to your underwear and...?" Beau interrupted again. "No!" He was surprised that I was even asking that. I asked him what he usually wore when they were all in the same room. He said, "Shorts and a t-shirt, stuff like that. It was never ...I mean, I might have slept in just my shorts, but never anything less than that." I told him that had felt peculiar to me too, and said, "If the boys and girls were in there together, you wouldn't have stripped to your undies, right?" Beau said, "Even when there was nobody there other than mom, dad and us, we still didn't do that." I asked, "So if just you and Marri were in there?" Beau said, "Yeah, I would have still had shorts on at least." I said, "That makes more sense to me than what Hanna was saying, because where would she get dressed and undressed?" Beau said, "Right. And that's just it." I said, "She could go off to the bathroom and change, but then she'd have to walk past your parents in her undies." Beau said, "Yeah, that's why that didn't happen."

[*For years I accepted that Hanna was in underwear and a t-shirt that night because she said so in her testimony, as if she and Steve were in another one of her bubbles. It wasn't until I realized that the rest of the kids were there that I began to view her comments in context. Context is everything.*]

Analysis: This is another instance where Hanna changed her story multiple times. In her affidavit, she didn't talk about spending the night, but instead said that Steve pulled her into his bedroom where Robin was drunk asleep, "unzipped his pants," and "pulled the draw string on my pants." A few months later, she dropped that in favor of telling Ada Dixon about attempted intercourse after Beau's birthday (a completely different situation than the affidavit), but she didn't mention clothing. Two years after that, she gave Tom a detailed description of the underwear she wore on some unspecified night, adding that Steve was wearing "just a pair of underwear." She followed that with a description of the exact incidents that she later testified happened on Beau's 21st birthday. In both trials, simply saying that Steve was wearing just underwear, and she "was wearing a big t-shirt" and "a pair of panties and that was it." Steve wasn't asked what he wore to bed that night.

In 2016, I had a conversation with Beau about whether any of the kids paraded around in their underwear. I didn't think they would have, because Beau, who was eighteen the first time Hanna spent the night, had been shy about even sleeping in the same room with her and Marri. Even though later they sometimes all slept in the living room, I couldn't believe they would strip down to their underwear to go to sleep. Beau said that never happened. In 2005, Beau told Tom that Hanna sat on the couch with him and talked to him while he tried to watch SportsCenter; but finally, around 2:00 or 2:30, he told her he had to get some sleep. He said "she went down to the twin bed past the entertainment center and went to sleep." He didn't say she went off somewhere to change and then came back to go to sleep, and I can't believe that she would sit there on the couch with Beau in just her underwear and a t-shirt, especially since no one else was undressed. The logical assumption is that she went to sleep with her clothes on, like every other time.

Conclusion: Hanna tried to paint a sexy picture to Tom of her silky underwear, but wandering around the house in just underwear on a night when the temperature was in the 30's or 40's, in a poorly insulated house, doesn't make any sense. And where would she have changed? This is just one more claim of hers that clearly didn't happen. She wasn't in underwear and a t-shirt, and neither were Marri, Beau, or Aaron. Or was Hanna claiming she was the only one in the room who stripped to her underwear in front of the others? I think not. More potential lies to add to the pile.

Let's see what everyone (mostly Hanna, of course) had to say about what happened that night.

What Happened at the House That Night?

Why is This Question Important? Steve was acquitted of Counts II and III, so why look at this at all? Because the jury acquitted him of those counts as part of the deal they allegedly made, not because all twelve of them accepted Steve's innocence regarding them. Some jurors did and some didn't. What I truly want is for you to finish this book with absolutely no doubts about what happened. Disproving both of those counts is just as important to me as disproving any of the rest of it. Hanna's story in the affidavit about this night was completely different from what she said in the trials, plus there are a sizable number of discrepancies between her later versions, so I need to refute all of them. Like much of what you've read so far, most of the quotes in this section are from Hanna because the storyline came entirely from her.

Let's start with her affidavit. Here's her original description of that night.

> "The last time I remember anything happening between Steve Sirois and me was February 14th of this year. I remember my mother, brother, and I had gone to Steve's home to have a BarBQ to celebrate his son's birthday. After several hours, his wife Robin got drunk so she went to bed. I further remember my mother had left for awhile and so had Marri. I was in the house

along with Steve while my brother was outside at the fire. I was helping Steve put up the food when he started trying to kiss me again. I told him this had to stop but he would not listen to me. He then grabbed my hand and led me into his bedroom where Robin was asleep. He then unzipped his pants and pulled out his dick. He then forced my head down and he stuck his dick in my mouth. He made me suck on his dick until stuff came out. After he let me up he then pulled the draw string on my pants and he stuck his hand inside them. He then stuck his finger inside my vagina. He did this for a few minutes and then he let me go. I then went into the bathroom."

[*The affidavit was created just seven weeks after the night that Hanna claimed this last incident happened. Since it was ostensibly the most recent incident, its description should also have been the most accurate, shouldn't it? It's worded in very specific, detailed language, as if it was a memory she was recalling. It also makes zero sense, and she ditched it almost immediately.*

In the affidavit, she tried to eliminate both Robin and Aaron as witnesses, and suggested that no one else was there right after supper, something several witnesses proved to be false. Unbelievably, Hanna also said that Steve took her to the room Robin was in to force his will on her (not to the living room, or the den, or Beau's room — all of which would have been empty in her scenario). After the affidavit was created she never made that claim again, even though Counts II and III against Steve were based on it. By the time of the trials, her narrative for Beau's birthday had been completely altered (different time of night, different room, different people present, and different actions). It clearly wasn't the same incident. I believe that Steve was indicted based on circumstances which were seemingly so false that Hanna herself rejected them.]

I need to pause here for a moment and explain something. I used the word "fingering" to describe an action that Hanna said Steve did to her. I could have called it masturbation or digital stimulation, but I didn't. That's a deliberate choice on my part because of the way Hanna referred to it. I don't know whether that decision was made by Deputy Knox because of the way Hanna described the alleged action to him, but it was also worded that way in the indictment. I used the same word here because she didn't indicate any motion of his digit after it was inserted, hence no masturbation. The first action described above (oral sex, fellatio) became Count II against Steve, and the second action (fingering her vagina) became Count III. Before we try to analyze both counts let's compare some other statements about that night.

By August 2004, Hanna was telling Ada Dixon, "He entered me twice. I don't remember when he did it the first time. On February 13th or 14th, the night of his son's birthday party, when everyone went home and went to sleep he said 'six more years and we can f***, then five years, four years, etc.'"

[*That's all Dixon listed in her summary about an attempt at intercourse that night, an act Hanna didn't claim in her affidavit (and apparently didn't mention to Dixon for over four months). Dixon's summary also didn't list the fellatio or the fingering, the only actions included in Hanna's affidavit about that night. I can't imagine Dixon would have left those out of her summary if Hanna had told her about them.*]

In 2006, Hanna shifted gears again when she told Tom, "I don't think a whole lot happened that night. I don't believe it did. I do not think I stayed out there that night. I really don't remember." A minute later Tom asked her, "Did he kiss you…or hold you, or grope you that night?" She said, "I believe so. I don't remember details exactly, but I ...believe so. I know it's kind of vague, but I really honestly don't remember that night, and I have no idea why."

[*Hanna told Tom that she didn't think much happened, that she didn't think she spent the night, and that she* "honestly" *didn't remember that night. The most logical assumption, in my opinion, was that this was another* "dishonest" *attempt to subvert the defense's case, since she clearly* "remembered" *the night two months later, in specific (but fluctuating) detail, once the trials were underway.*]

Tom asked Hanna to say more about this second intercourse attempt. She said, "Um ...I ...he told me to go wake him up, so I went in there to go wake him up after he had fallen asleep, and he came in there, and we were fooling around, <u>or whatever</u>. Then he got on top of me...and we started fooling around. He got on top of me, and he..." Tom asked if Steve undressed her. She said, "He undressed me." Tom asked her if she had been asleep. She paused, then said, "Mmmm. Yes. I was so asleep, and then I woke up, remembered I was supposed to go wake him up, and I did." Tom asked her what time that was. She said, "Uh, about 1:00 o'clock, maybe 12:25…I just remember because I looked at the time on the microwave on my way into his room." He asked her why Steve wanted her to wake him, and she said, "So he could come in there." Tom asked if he had pre-planned this with her. Hanna said, "Yes."

[*She said she woke Steve up, he came back with her, undressed her, and they* "started fooling around." *Did you spot the oddity about* "remembering" *the time? Also, what actions do the phrase* "or whatever" *describe?*]

Tom asked Hanna if Steve took his own clothes off, or if she did. She said, "He did it. He unzipped his own <u>pants</u>, unbuttoned them, and pushed them down." He asked her how far down. She paused, then said, "Um, let's see." Another pause. "I think he took the <u>shorts</u> off, but left his underwear on ...and just kind of kept them pushed down a little bit, not even to his knees." Tom asked her how she was positioned on the bed. Hanna said, "On my back." He asked her how she placed her legs, and what Steve did. She paused again, then said, "He, uh ...set them apart ...pushed my ...my knees apart, and ...got on top of me, and ...he put his penis inside me, and I felt the tightness, and I thought I was fixing to rip." Tom asked, "Did he continue to stroke you that way, or did he just pull out and stop at this point?" Hanna said, "He went in and out very slowly, but he didn't go in hardly at all." Tom began, "So, just enough to...?" She stopped him with, "So I could feel it. Yes." Tom asked how long that went on. She said, "It was very short. It was maybe like ...a minute." He asked if Steve ejaculated. Hanna said, "Not inside me, but yes." Tom asked her how that happened. After a brief pause she said, "He would make me do it with my hand or with my mouth. At that ...at that point in time, it was my hand."

[*Hanna said there was an attempt at missionary position sex, followed by her masturbating Steve, which caused him to ejaculate. Even though this description was ostensibly not about Beau's birthday, she did say it was the second time they tried to have intercourse, and she specifically told Dixon that the second time was on the night of Beau's birthday. Did she tell Tom this wasn't on Beau's birthday to confuse the defense team some more, or could she have been so disordered by her own lies that she was mixing versions up?*]

In Trial #1, Ross asked her if she knew what to expect that night. She said, "Sirois told me to come wake him up and take him into where I was sleeping whenever everyone else was asleep." He asked her what time that was. She said, "Whenever I looked at the clock on the microwave when I went in to go get him, it was about 1:45 in the morning…I went into his bedroom and to his side of the bed. And I had to shake him a couple of times to wake him up." Ross asked where Robin was. Hanna said, "Right beside him passed out." He asked her what happened next. She said, "He -- He followed me back into the living room. I don't even know if you would call it a living room. And by this time, I had been there so often I knew where all the squeaky places were in the floor, I could step right over them. I had good night vision, so, I was able to go through there with -- nearly without sound. And he bumped into something and he commented on how quiet I could be."

[*This time she said (after being asleep), that she went in at 1:45 to wake Steve up (not 12:25 or 1:00). She again said Robin was passed out drunk (a witness eliminated), and she pointed out how quiet and sneaky she was, but said that Steve was bumping into things. Notice that Hanna, who hadn't mentioned noisy floors during any of her previous interviews, was now admitting that they did squeak. Speaking of noise, where was Bob, the dog?*]

We're still in Trial #1. This is a long passage, so I'll use the compression style I used in the *Harry Potter, Part 2* chapter. Ross asked Hanna if Steve had been drinking that evening. Hanna said, "Yes sir." — Ross: Could you tell whether he was still feeling the effects of that? "Yes, he was still stumbling around more than usual. And I know that everyone that night had quite a lot to drink. It was a birthday celebration, and 21st at that. And also, but this time, I could tell if he had way too much to drink because his penis wouldn't get hard if he had a lot to drink." — Ross: Had that happened during previous encounters with him? "One other time that I recall, yes. And it disgusted me more than usual." — Ross: Where did you go when you left Steve's bedroom? "I tiptoed back to the bed I was sleeping in, and I laid down on my back." — Ross: What happened next? "He didn't sit down or anything. He just walked to where he was level with my bed and he pulled down the front of his underwear, took out his penis, and I didn't want to touch it, I had -- just hesitated." — Ross: Why did you do that? "Well, by this time, <u>we hadn't been out there as much</u>. My mom was beginning to argue with him more and more. I don't really know the details on that. I just know they weren't getting along as well as they had before. And so, we just went out there less frequently." — Ross: What did going out there less often have to do with your hesitation? "The best way I know how to put it is that I was beginning to come to terms, so to speak, with what was really going on, that it wasn't right, and I was beginning to feel I did have a right to say no. Because he had never physically done harm to me before other than leaving bite marks and bruises." — Ross: What happened next? "He grabbed the back of my head by my hair and yanked me toward his penis until I opened my jaws." — Ross: What happened after you opened your mouth? "He thrusted with his hips and it went into my mouth." — Ross: What did that feel like? "Like a slimy worm." — Ross: Was that different from previous times you had performed oral sex on him? "Yes." — Ross: How was it different? "It was just more revolting, just disgusting, like -- I don't really know of anything that would describe it." — Ross: Do you think the amount of alcohol he had drunk had an effect on him? "Yes." — Ross: What did you think about that? "It annoyed me a little. I kind of felt like I was being used because I wasn't getting any pleasure out of it. And it just -- It just disgusted me and annoyed me and I just wanted to leave." — Ross: Was he able to sustain his erection? "No." — Ross: How long did that continue? "Maybe one to two minutes. Not long at all." — Ross: Did anything come out of his sexual organ as a result of that taking place? "No."

Ross again asked, What happened next? Hanna said, "He bent down, and while he was kissing me on my mouth he lifted up my shirt and started fondling my breasts again. It was the same pattern, just moved down to my neck, to my chest." — Ross: Were you wearing anything under your shirt? "A pair of panties and that was it." — Ross: What happened next? "He pulled my panties down and kept them hung around one ankle, and he put his finger in my vagina. And then he climbed on top of me with my legs spread and he began -- with one hand rubbing his penis up and down on my vagina, then he put it in just so I could feel it. It wasn't all the way in. It didn't do any damage physically." — Ross: [*making sure he got it on the record, asked*] What do you mean by the word *it*? "His penis." — Ross: How long did that last? "Maybe a minute, minute-and-a-half." — Ross: When it stopped, what happened? "I started to get sore. It was hurting."

[*According to Hanna, this happened in the living room where Marri was sound asleep on the other twin bed, but she said nothing about Beau (on the couch) or about Aaron (in the recliner), and Ross didn't raise the issue. She said she went to get Steve at 1:45, so it was still before 2:00 am. It's generally agreed that everyone <u>except Beau and Hanna</u> went to bed around 11:30, so all of the others had been in bed for two-and-a-half hours before she claimed she brought Steve to the living room (I'll explain in the analysis why that amount of time is important). Think about something else for now, though. Hanna said that Steve wasn't on the bed for the first part of this. He would have had his naked rear exposed to the rest of the room, with his underwear down around his knees. How would he explain that if anyone had seen him (like Beau, who was still watching TV and talking to Hanna on the couch)?*]

Then Ross asked Hanna, Why wasn't his attempt at intercourse with you completely successful? "Well, his penis was in my vagina, but <u>it wasn't all the way in, as the medical report states</u>. It didn't go all the way in. I don't know how much. All I know is that I was sore for two or three days afterwards." — Ross: Was that <u>the same doctor's report that said there was a minimal amount of tearing noted in your hymen area</u>? "Yes, sir." — Ross began, "And the doctor indicated that was consistent with..." Bevin Jenkins objected, saying that Hanna repeating the doctor's words would be hearsay." Judge Hawes sustained the objection. Ross then made several further unsuccessful attempts to elicit the same information from Hanna before moving on to another topic.

[*Why didn't Jenkins object as soon as Hanna said,* "...as the medical report states?" *The medical report, which was part of the trial record, didn't mention a penis ever being in her vagina. The report, clinically stated that she had an* "...essentially virginal female introitus with the hymen mostly intact, with just a minimal amount of tear noted on the posterior aspect." *Jenkins' objection may have stopped Hanna from saying that the tearing could have been from penile penetration, but an earlier objection would have been able to point out that there was no cause indicated in the doctor's report. Ross did try to get Hanna to say that the doctor told her something along those lines, but that would have been a hearsay statement, and the doctor wasn't there to testify, so it couldn't be allowed; but I can't believe that Jenkins didn't also object to Hanna's mischaracterization of her exam results. Aside from penile penetration, there are many other possible reasons why a medical exam could show slight tearing. The exam, remember, was conducted ten weeks after the alleged incident, two weeks after she made the accusations, and also soon after she reportedly told her friends* "at a sleep-over that she had lost her virginity."]

Now we're up to Trial #2. This testimony is also all Hanna's. Did her story change by the second trial? Yes, some of the details did. Ross asked her what time she went to bed. She spilled everything out all at once. "My best guess is 12:30, 1:00. There was actually a birthday party for Beau. And it was his 21st birthday. And he had left for quite sometime, went and did his own thing after he did the family thing and he didn't come back until later that night. And I had waited till he got to sleep. Because I knew everyone else was. I was told beforehand by Sirois to come and wake him up, come get him and bring him back to where I was sleeping." — Ross: Why did he tell you to do that? "Oh, I knew why by this time." — Ross: Why? "It was going to be the same old thing, just wanting to mess with me." — Ross: Did you do what he wanted? "Yes, sir, I did." — Ross: What time was this? "When I looked at the microwave on my way in there, it was about 1:30 in the morning, I believe." — Ross: Where was Aaron? "He was asleep in the recliner, in the living room. And Beau was asleep on the twin bed in the living room. Both were out of sight from the twin bed I was sleeping in." — Ross: What did you do next? "I had gotten up out of bed and I had snook into Sirois and Robin's room. And I shook him awake and he followed me back into the bed I was sleeping in." — Ross: Are you talking about the bed that was secluded by the entertainment center? "Yes." — Ross: Where was Robin? "She was passed out drunk in the bed, in the master bedroom." — Ross: Did Robin wake up when you went in there? "She never woke up. Sometimes on some of the incidents, we would either be on the bed right beside her or on the floor on his side of the bed. She never woke up. She was always passed out, every night. She woke up with a beer in her hand, she went to bed with a beer in her hand." — Ross: What happened next? "He immediately -- all he was wearing was a pair of underwear. And he immediately pulled on the front of his underwear, took out his penis with his hand, and grabbed my head and pushed it toward his penis. And I didn't open my mouth. He had drank a lot. And I didn't know that this affected, at the time, but I know now just from taking health and classes like that, that alcohol does affect sexual performance of anybody. It is just -- it is more noticeable on a man. He didn't have a full erection, at all." — Ross: What happened when Steve tried to put his penis in your mouth? "I kept my mouth shut." — Ross: What happened next? "He kept taunting me. And I just -- I gave up. I had had it. I was tired. I wanted to go to sleep." — Ross: What do you mean by 'taunting' you? "He just kept saying things like, oh, come on, you always used to do it before. Why won't you do it now? Called me a chicken and a wimp, things like that. I performed oral sex on him." — Ross: Did anything come out of his sexual organ? "No, sir, it did not." — Ross: How long did this oral sex last? "Maybe a minute and a half, two minutes, tops." — Ross: What happened then? "I stopped." — Ross: Why? "I was disgusted." — Ross: Why were you disgusted? "Well, by this time, I -- I had gotten used to him having an erection and for him to not have one this time, I just -- I was disgusted. It was like a big worm, just kind of limp."

Ross asked her, What happened next? Hanna said, "I laid on my back and he started the same old routine. Kissing, the touching. Only this time, he went a step further." — Ross: What were you wearing? "A big t-shirt and a pair of panties." — Ross: Were you wearing a bra? "No, sir." — Ross: did something happen to your t-shirt? "He had pushed it up to my neck as usual." — Ross: Did something happen with your underwear? "Yes, he had it hooked around one ankle, as usual." — Ross: What did you mean when you said he went a step further? Hanna paused, then said, "<u>He had done this particular thing on several occasions</u>. He had gotten on top of me, I had my legs spread and he had taken his hand around his penis and had rubbed it against my vagina up and down. And this, I had almost gotten used to. It was kind of a new thing for me. And then, he <u>would</u> put it up against my vagina and I could feel it go in, not all the way, just a little bit. I don't know how much. All I know is it was incredibly tight and it hurt. I just could feel the stretching and I was -- I was just hoping I wasn't torn or anything." — Ross: How long did that last? "Maybe, I want to say, about five minutes. It wasn't long at all." — Ross: Did he ever put his penis fully inside you? "No, not fully." — Ross: Earlier you said that he wasn't able to maintain a full erection. Was that still the case then? "It was harder now, but not to its full extent." — Ross: Did he say anything to you while he was attempting to place -- or actually while he placed himself slightly inside you? "He just kept moaning, and saying, 'I want you so bad' and things like that." — Ross [*leading the witness again?*]: Did he say anything else to you about your age or anything like that at this point? "He said, I wish that -- he said <u>he wished I was 18</u>. And since this started, he kept saying, <u>just six more years, five more years, four more years</u>. He would countdown according to my birthdays.

[*There's a lot there to unpack. She described several sexual acts, which she said were complicated by Steve being so drunk that he couldn't keep an erection. Until we get to the analysis, here's something to think about. What time did Steve go to bed, and what time did Hanna say the incident occurred? Also, she kept insisting that her bed couldn't be seen from anywhere else in the room, but it was actually visible from nearly everywhere in it. And, considering that her 15th birthday was only a few days from then, did the countdown speech make any sense?*

One particular thing to notice, though, had to do with the phrase "He had done this particular thing on several occasions." *Before this trial, she referred to this final night's attempt at penetration sex as* "the second time." *Was she upping the number from* "two" *to* "several" *for the jury's benefit? Whatever her purpose, it's another change to her story.*]

Judge Hawes called a lunch break after that. When they returned, Elmer Ross had more work to do. Despite all of that testimony, he had only covered fellatio (Count II). He still had to establish that fingering (Count III) had occurred. After quickly reviewing the pre-lunch testimony, he brought that last element up, but Hanna didn't seem to be ready. He asked her, "Did anything else happen between you and the defendant on that date?" When she answered, "No, sir," Ross, probably shocked at that response, tried again. "Was there any type of penetration of any part of your body by anything other than his sexual organ?" That time she said, "Fingers and tongue."

Reading that in the transcript, it felt like she was suddenly blurting out a mantra she had been reciting all through lunch, "fingers and tongue, fingers and tongue, fingers and tongue," but had forgotten what she was supposed to say until Ross reminded her. It seemed to me that Ross had the same reaction. He started to ask, "And what did you mean by..." but paused before repeating "fingers and tongue" himself, and instead said, "I mean, tell us how that happened specifically with the fingers." Hanna said, "He would put his fingers in my vagina," then, seemingly unsure about what Ross wanted, quickly said, "…and his tongue in there also," then, almost as an afterthought, added, "And his tongue in my mouth." Ross asked her if he did all those things that night. She said, "Yes," but kept talking, trying to add more items. She said, "There was another occasion several months before this that I recall where he had done something totally different. This was the one time he did it, and it was bad." Ross didn't take the bait this time. Before she could add any more to the list, he asked her how many times, between September 2001 and February 2004, she and Steve did "something of a sexual nature." She said, "Eighty to ninety times." Then he moved on.

[*Did you notice that Hanna, by saying* "he would put his fingers in my vagina," *still didn't answer Ross' question, because that could simply mean that was something he did often, not necessarily something he did that night. Ross did cover for that, though, by asking her whether Steve did all those things to her that night. In what I believe was an additional attempt to game the system, just after she answered "Yes" to that question, she tried to squeeze in another incident that she said* "was bad." *She wasn't successful, but there were other times in both trials when no one stopped her. I believe that latitude allowed her to feed additional false information to the jury with impunity.*

It is worth noting, though, that when she told the same story to Tom, she also told him about the "bad thing" as soon as the above story was finished. It felt to me almost as if that was the order she had practiced them in.]

See the URL below for a blog post about the "bad" thing Hanna tried to introduce in the trial, but wasn't able to.

https://aggravated book.com/hannas-bad-thing/

Analysis: The question of what happened that night generated the longest set of excerpts in this chapter, but I'll try to keep this as brief as possible.

The first two statements Hanna made about what happened that night were in the affidavit and in Ada Dixon's summary, and those two documents completely contradict each other. Briefly, in the affidavit, she claimed that Steve had her give him oral sex on the night of Beau's birthday party until he ejaculated, and that he stuck his finger inside her vagina for a few minutes. Those supposedly happened earlier in the evening, within moments of each other, standing up in the master bedroom where Robin was passed out on the bed. Less than four months later, Hanna completely abandoned those accusations when she told Ada Dixon that the night of Beau's birthday party was the second time Steve attempted to have intercourse with her, but said nothing about any other sexual activity happening that night.

The next bit of information came when Tom interviewed Beau in 2005. Beau said that Hanna sat on the couch and talked until 2:30 in the morning (in the trials he said it was about 2:00). When sports are on, Beau is focused on them, especially if it's baseball; which means that Hanna probably did most of the talking while Beau was semi-listening to her and paying more attention to the TV. He said that Hanna was largely wrapped up in her problems, saying she liked a guy who was going into the military, and she didn't think her mom liked him. Finally, Beau said, "I've got to go to sleep." He said that she then walked over "to the twin bed past the entertainment center and went to sleep," but he said that she was awake by 9:00 the next morning, sitting on his feet, trying to wake him up. If Hanna had been awake until after 2:00 am, then waited until everyone was asleep before waking Steve, and after that endured an episode of groping and oral sex and fingering and masturbation and attempted penetration, would she have even tried to get up before anyone else, or try to bounce on Beau's feet to wake him up?

Hanna, though, said to different audiences that, after going to sleep herself, she woke up (at 12:25 or 1:00, or 1:30, or 1:45 am), and went to get Steve. Could Beau have been wrong about the time? Sure, but he has been consistent in saying they stopped talking about 2:00 or 2:30, and if he was watching familiar programs (like SportsCenter) he should have had a decent idea when he went to sleep. Hanna, on the other hand, gave all these different times for when she woke Steve up. She said she checked the time on the microwave, but still gave four separate times to describe one incident. My opinion is, of course, that she didn't look at the microwave, but instead slept through the night and didn't walk through the kitchen at all. Even so, all of her invented times were earlier than Beau's, and all were when he said they were both awake, talking on the couch.

Hanna told at least five different stories about that night. In her interview with Tom, she said that she didn't think she spent the night, and didn't think much happened. He asked her if Steve kissed her or groped her, and she said, maybe, but she really didn't remember. A few minutes later, though, she described an incident that was nearly identical to her trial descriptions of what she said happened after Beau's birthday party. Did she lie to Tom about remembering, or had she just not sorted out what to tell him? The version she relayed to him wasn't remotely close to the affidavit's version, but lined up perfectly with her trial testimony about that night, with a few exceptions. In Tom's non-birthday-night version, she said nothing about Steve being drunk, or the house making squeaky noises. In Trial #1, she didn't say whether she stayed awake or not, but did say she woke Steve up (at 1:45, not 12:25 or 1:00 like she told Tom). She said he followed her back, stumbling, still tipsy. Saying that he was drunk and had a limp, flaccid penis during the final incidents was brand new. She said nothing about it in the affidavit, or to Tom, and it isn't mentioned in Dixon's summary. Hanna said that disgusted her, and that he didn't ejaculate when she gave him oral sex (unlike in the affidavit, where she said he did). Then, she said, while fingering her, he rubbed his penis along the outside of her vagina before slipping it slightly inside (something she claimed they had done "several times" before, not just once before). In the same trial, though, she also said that that night was only the second time they had attempted penetration sex. In Trial #2, her version did have some other variations (1:30 instead of 1:45), but she still insisted that Steve was unable to get an erection. This time she referred to his penis as "a big worm" instead of a slimy one. And this time said he taunted her into giving him oral sex by calling her a "chicken and a wimp."

She also made other comments that don't make sense. To Tom and in Trial #1, she said she got on her back on the bed, and Steve stood next to it. In the trials, she said he grabbed her by the back of her hair and yanked her head toward his penis. Two things bother me about that. This is the only time she described Steve as having done something that aggressive, and she waited until the trials to use that description. Trial #1 also differs from Trial #2. In Trial #1, she got on her back right away. In Trial #2, the incident with the flaccid penis and the hair pulling happened first, then she got on her back. In Trial #1, she said his penis popped into her mouth after a hip thrust, in Trial #2, he sort of pushed her mouth onto it. Also, in Trial #1, she said that, after giving him oral sex <u>while</u> she was on her back, she said he fingered her while he was rubbing his penis on her vagina. In Trial #2, she said that, she got on her back after the oral sex, and then he rubbed his penis on her vagina, but never specified when he might have fingered her. Two different stories.

Her trial versions of everything are completely different from the affidavit and from the versions she gave Tom and Dixon, but they're also different from each other in various ways. Consider this too, according to Beau, at 1:45 am (Hanna's latest time for waking up to go get Steve), he and Hanna were still sitting on the couch, talking and watching TV. Beau's times have always been relatively consistent, but Hanna apparently didn't come up with her four very flexible times until 2006.

Drunken Performance: Hanna insisting that Steve was so drunk that he couldn't get an erection also made its first appearance during the trials. If we accept any of Hanna's times as correct, her comments about Steve's drunkenness could invalidate the rest of her story. To begin with, Steve and Robin didn't drink nearly as much as Hanna claimed, but even if he had been completely smashed when he went to bed, he would already have had a minimum of two hours to sleep it off and recover his functionality by the time she woke him up. If we use Beau's time as a measure, Steve would have had an extra hour beyond that. I won't speak for all men, but I think Hanna made a faulty assumption about the effects of alcohol on the average male. If a man is extremely drunk, yes, alcohol can have an effect on his libido, but that dissipates over time. Could she have added this to her story to spice it up because she was portraying Steve and Robin as alcoholics? Even if Steve had been drunk when he went to bed, though, a few hours later his "equipment" would likely have functioned better than she said it did.

In addition to that, her version in the affidavit destroys the description she came up with for the trials. In the trials, she portrayed Steve as so drunk he couldn't perform several hours later. In the affidavit, though, when the party was barely over, right after he would have finished drinking, she claimed he was more than capable of achieving an erection. If he had been so drunk that he couldn't perform an hour or two after midnight, he would have been much more likely to have been unable to perform earlier in the evening than later. She can't have it both ways. Her statements about this in the affidavit and in both trials just seem like invented hogwash to me, and all were told under oath.

Here's one more stray thought about Steve's inability to achieve an erection that night. In the trials she said this had only happened once before in all the time they had been doing this, and it disgusted her because he couldn't stay hard (like she said he <u>always</u> did). Was she suggesting that, in two-and-a-half years of fooling around, during her claimed 80 to 90 separate instances, she had never seen Steve's penis in a flaccid state, that it always popped out of his underwear completely ready for action? That undercuts her steady drumbeat of Steve and Robin being continually drunk. If Steve actually was drunk,"24/7," as she bluntly stated whenever she got the chance, shouldn't she have seen him unable to perform far more than just twice out of eighty or ninety times? Again, she can't have it both ways.

Taunting and Conversations: Scattered throughout Hanna's descriptions were conversations she claimed they had, and they didn't seem like whispered sweet nothings, some were more like near-arguments, rife with pleading and teasing ("you're a wimp," "a chicken," "you used to do this before"), or full of passion ("I want you so bad"), or instruction ("lift up so I can get your jeans off,"), and questions and answers back and forth. Wouldn't a lot of chatter like that wake up the room's other occupants? She testified that these discussions nearly always happened while other people were in the room with them or very close by (like Marri on the same bed with them the first night). Why, in all that time, didn't anyone hear any of these conversations? Or feel them moving around on the same bed with them? Or hear them sneaking around in their underwear on the squeaky linoleum floors, with Bob possibly trailing them, creating a racket with his toenails?

Bothersome Time Stamps: She told Tom she woke Steve up "about 1:00, maybe 12:25." Why would she use a number like 12:25, but still use the word "maybe" to soften the specificity? Why would she choose a number so oddly close to 12:30, but not just round it up like most people do? And she followed that statement, after giving those two different times, by saying that she remembered the time because she "looked at the time on the microwave." How did looking at the microwave clock help her "remember" both "1:00" and

"12:25" (two distinctly different times) as the single moment she looked at the clock? In both trials, Hanna again said she looked at the microwave on her way to get Steve, but in the first trial she said it was 1:45, and in the second she said it was 1:30. I know, that's not a huge difference, but it's another time change, which is a good indication that she was just making the numbers up. And all of them are shy of Beau's earliest bedtime of 2:00. Also, look at the floor plan on the blog. If she was coming from her bed in the living room, she would turn into the hallway before she could see the clock on the microwave.

In Trial #2, she said that Beau "didn't come back until later that night," and she waited until he was asleep before she woke Steve up. That's another change in her testimony, and a falsehood. If Beau didn't get back until everyone else was asleep, how did he manage to talk to Aaron and Steve and Hanna and the neighbors by the fire before they all went inside or went home? Several of the party guests said that Beau was back at the house from dropping his girlfriend off by around 10:00 pm. If everyone, Beau included, went in the house to get ready for bed by 11:00 or 11:30, doesn't that lend more credence to Beau's story that he and Hanna stayed up while he watched SportsCenter?

Conclusion: There's not much more to say here, except that almost nothing Hanna said about this night was consistent. She told different stories to different groups of people about who was there, when things happened, and what she and others wore. Importantly, nothing she claimed in her affidavit matches anything she claimed afterward, and the entire trial was designed by the prosecution (impossibly loosely, I believe) to fit the affidavit, even though it really didn't fit it at all. If she told the truth in her original accusation, why would she need to abandon all of it?

Exactly.

Let's look at another big question: Were there any witnesses?

Did Anyone See This Happening?

Why is This Question Important? Saying that potential witnesses happened to be nearby, but were handily unconscious or extremely unobservant, was one of Hanna's more frequent claims. Sometimes, though, she just didn't acknowledge their presence. In the affidavit she said that Aaron and Robin were the only two witnesses that night, but Aaron was outside and Robin was passed out drunk. Whose word do we have for this? Not Aaron's or Robin's. Aaron didn't testify, and Robin denied it. Plus, numerous people said they were at the party until late in the evening. Soon after she created the affidavit, though, Hanna changed that story completely. I often felt that pinning down the truth in her stories was something akin to shooting at a moving target with an empty water gun. Let's see whether any of the "witnesses" saw anything that night. Some of these quotes will be familiar by now.

In Trial #1, Elmer Ross asked Marri if Hanna ever spent the night at her house. Marri said, "Yes, sir." He asked if Hanna stayed by herself. Marri said, "She would do it with her brother sometimes. He would stay with us."

He asked if Hanna was usually alone or with her brother. Marri said, "With her brother." He then asked her if, during "all of that time from 2001 to 2004," she saw Hanna do anything inappropriate with Steve. Marri said, "No, sir."

[*According to Marri, when Hanna spent the night, Aaron was usually there too, but Marri never saw anything inappropriate happen between Hanna and Steve. I believe that Ross overstated the time again when he said,* "all of that time, from 2001 to 2004," *planting the idea that those* "80 to 90" *incidents could have taken place over three years instead of two years and a few months.*]

Bevin Jenkins had a number of questions for Marri. He asked her if she ever saw anything inappropriate happen between her dad and Hanna; or ever saw him touch Hanna on her bottom, or kiss her on the lips, or do anything she felt was inappropriate; or ever saw Hanna do anything inappropriate to Steve; or if Steve and Hanna ever spent time alone. Marri answered "No, sir" to all of those. He wanted to know if Marri was a heavy sleeper or a light sleeper. Marri said, "Light sleeper." He asked her what she meant by that. She said, "Like if someone walks into a room where I'm sleeping or something, I'd wake up." He asked if she would hear them walk into the room, and Marri said, "Yes, sir." He wondered what she would do if someone came to the front door. She said, "If I was close to the living room, I would be able to hear it." He also asked if she would wake up easily if there was movement in her bed, and if she and Hanna slept in the same bed sometimes, and if she would wake up if Hanna got up. Marri said, "Yes" to all of those too.

[*Marri didn't see anything inappropriate happening between Hanna and Steve, and didn't think they were ever alone. She also said she was a light sleeper. Did other people agree with that?*]

Judy Higham, Eddie Higham's niece, testified for the defense. Judy was a friend of Marri's, and became friends with Hanna in late-2001 when Hanna started coming to the get-togethers. She was sixteen at the time of the trials, about two years older than Marri and a year younger than Hanna. This is another long passage. Bevin Jenkins asked Judy how she knew Steve. Judy said, "Whenever I first moved out there at the lake, he was like the first people we met. Like me and his daughter are like really good friends." — Jenkins: So you live out there at the lake? "Yes, sir." — Jenkins: How long have you known the Sirois family? "Eleven years. Ten or eleven years." — Jenkins: How close are you to them? "Very close." — Jenkins: Are you friends with the kids? "Yes, sir." — Jenkins: Have you spent any time in the Sirois' home? "Yes, sir." — Jenkins: How often were you there? "Uh, a lot. I really can't give you a number." — Jenkins: Were you ever there when Hanna was there? "Yes, sir." — Jenkins: How many times were you there when Hanna was? "Almost every time she was there, I came over there because me and Hanna, we're really good friends."

Jenkins then asked her a series of questions. Did you ever see anything inappropriate going on between Mr. Sirois and Hanna Penderfield? "Did you ever see them going off by themselves at all? "Did you ever see anything inappropriate go on with any of the other young girls out there? *Any* of the other kids out there? And, finally… Has Mr. Sirois ever been inappropriate in any way with you?" She said, "No, sir" to all of that.

He asked her, What kind of relationship does Mr. Sirois have with his own kids? "Very loving father." — Jenkins: Are they close to him? "Yes, sir." To forestall a potential question from the prosecution, Jenkins asked her, Were you there 100% of the time Hanna was? "No, sir." — Jenkins: Were you there the majority of the time she was? "Yes, sir." — Jenkins: While you were both there, were you together 100% of the time? "Yes, sir." — Jenkins tested her, Did you even go to the bathroom with Hanna? Surprised, Judy said, "I -- Like I would walk with her, but I wouldn't actually go in there with her." — Jenkins: Okay. But an extremely large amount of the time, you were around her? "Yeah." — Jenkins wrapped up with, Did you ever see anything inappropriate happen between Steve and Hanna. "No." — He passed the witness.

Elmer Ross then asked her, Did you ever spend the night at the Sirois' house? "Yes, sir." — Ross: Have you spent the night when Hanna was there too? "Majority of the time." — Ross: Were there times Hanna spent the night at the house and you didn't? "Yes, sir." — Ross: Were there always a lot of people at the Sirois' house? "Not all the time." — Ross then threw three more questions at Judy. Were friends and family usually there? Including adults? and "Including a lot of kids? Judy said, "Yes, sir" to all of those.

[*Judy was there almost every time Hanna was, and spent the night many times, often when Hanna did. I would feel stupid if I didn't take this moment to mention that each time Hanna had one of her friends spend the night there with her, like Judy or Suzanna Bushnell, created another instance when more potential witnesses were present, making it more unlikely that any molestation occurred those nights.*

Judy had known the Sirois' most of her life, and said that she never saw Steve doing anything inappropriate with anyone. It's important to notice that Hanna didn't mention Judy spending the night in any of her stories, or even that they were friends. In fact, Hanna didn't mention her at all in either trial (or any other document or recording I have). Why wouldn't Hanna want the jurors to know that Judy was often there when she was? Exactly, because Judy was another witness who didn't see anything wrong, and also because of Judy's connection to Eddie Higham.

Also, I think Elmer Ross' final questions to Judy may have undercut his own argument by helping to establish that a lot of other people were frequently at the Sirois' house. More people means more potential witnesses, but none of them saw anything wrong either.]

Now we're up to Trial #2. Sanford asked Marri if she ever saw her father do anything inappropriate with Hanna. She said, "No, sir." He asked her if she was there most of the time Hanna was. Marri said, "Yes, sir." He asked her, "Do you think that you would have seen if there was something inappropriate going on?" Ross objected, "Calls for speculation." Hawes sustained it.

[*Sanford moved on to other questions. Variations on that same final question had been allowed previously, but it was disallowed this time because of the way Sanford worded it. He may have let it go at that point because he had made it clear that the prosecution didn't want Marri to answer the question, and that made his point anyway. Everyone else who was asked about it, though, said they had never seen Steve act inappropriately toward Hanna or any other child.*]

Sanford also had several questions for Beau. He asked if Beau would believe it if he was told that these incidents happened while he was in the same vehicle with Steve and Hanna; or while he was in the same house with them; or while he was in the same room with them. Beau said, "No, sir" to all of those. Sanford also asked him if, on the day of his 21st birthday party, he saw or heard anything inappropriate, and Beau said, "No, sir."

[*Hanna claimed that, during the vast majority of the times she was molested by Steve, someone else was in the room or the house or the vehicle while it was happening. The night of Beau's birthday party, three other people slept in the same room with her. Obviously, I don't know what Aaron might say, but Beau and Marri both said they didn't see or hear anything.*]

Here are more of Sanford's questions for Beau: At any time between September 1st of 2001 and February 14th of 2004, did you ever see your father do anything inappropriate relating to any kind of sexual activity in any form or fashion? Did you ever find any evidence that anything like that had ever happened? No stains? Never heard anything inappropriate? Beau answered "No, sir" to all of those. Sanford asked him what kind of sleeper he and Robin and Marri were. Beau said he was "a pretty light sleeper," and that both his mom and sister were too. Sanford asked him, if he would know what was happening on the other side of the entertainment center. Beau said, "Yes, sir." Sanford asked, "Pretty sure of that?" Beau said, "Yes, sir."

[*In Hanna's trial testimony, she claimed that Marri (Trial #1) and Beau (Trial #2) were sleeping in the other bed that night, and said that the other didn't spend the night. Marri slept in that bed and Beau slept on the couch. They were both there; and although she didn't mention him, Aaron was there too. Someone was always there. Hanna was rarely in any of these scenarios by herself. How likely is it that this kind of thing happened (especially eighty or ninety times) without someone noticing at least once?*]

A Related Side-Story: The mention of stains brings up another good point. Laundry. Hanna talked several times about Steve ejaculating. In Dixon's summary, Hanna is quoted as saying, "…he started ejaculating and he rubbed his penis on me from my neck to my bellybutton. His semen was all over me…I took the sheet and rubbed the semen off of me." In Trial #2, when she was asked if he had ever ejaculated onto the floor, she said, "Yes, sir, many times." In Trial #1, she was asked what happened to the semen after he ejaculated during another incident. She said, "It was on the floor. And he picked up a corner of a bedspread and wiped it off the end of his penis." Ross asked her if he tried to clean it off the floor, but she answered, "He just said, be careful, don't step there." She was asked if she knew what happened to the semen after that, and she said, "As far as I know, it just stayed there. They weren't the best housekeepers." In all of these accounts of ejaculation, she never indicated that the semen had been captured or wiped up with something like facial tissues, but, when asked, she said that the semen was wiped up with sheets or bedspreads or was left where it landed. According to Hanna, Steve often just stuffed his penis back in his underwear, where it would have left residue that would stain. In other words, Hanna was claiming that the linens and bedspreads in the house (especially those on the beds where she had slept) and Steve's underwear, would have ended up with semen stains on them.

During one of our weekly phone calls, I asked Steve, "Just out of curiosity, who did the laundry in your house?" He said, "Oh, that's a funny story. Robin did most of the laundry. Right after we got married, it probably hadn't been two weeks, I woke up one Saturday morning, and yawned and stretched and said, 'Breakfast would be nice.' She got out of bed and got everything out, a pan and eggs and bacon and bread, and said, 'Those make breakfast and I don't,' and went back to bed." He and I both laughed, and he continued, "So, about two weeks later she asked me to help her do some laundry, so I waited until I heard the pitter-patter of her feet coming around the corner and held the bleach over the washer like I was about to pour it on the blue jeans. She said, 'What are you doing?' I said, 'I put bleach in everything," and she said, 'Not in my laundry you don't.' So, for all of those years I stayed out of her laundry room and she stayed out of my kitchen, and we got along fine." He added that Robin *was* a good cook, but cooking was kind of his thing. It helped him wind down after a hard day's work. He said that Robin would help him wash dishes and he would help her fold clothes, but that was as close as they came to crossing over into the other's territory.

[*If all of that ejaculation had occurred, and semen had been left on various surfaces on a regular basis (but especially on underwear and sheets and bedcovers), it would have left noticeable stains. Since Robin did all of the laundry (something I confirmed with Marri and Beau as well), she would have noticed the stains showing up on the sheets and blankets that Hanna was using, and on Steve's underwear. That would definitely have raised a red flag for Robin. Since it didn't, I think we can assume that there weren't any semen stains where they shouldn't have been.*]

Another witness for Steve, his neighbor, Vivian Percet, said she had known Steve and Robin for over twenty years. Sanford asked her if she was ever at the Sirois' when Hanna was there. She said, "Several times." He asked if she had ever seen Steve doing anything inappropriate to Hanna. She said, "No." After a few other questions, he asked her once more, "You never saw anything inappropriate, did you?" Again, she said, "No, sir."

[*Hanna's witnesses (like Tiffany Sperger) were the only ones who claimed that Hanna visited the Sirois' very often (i.e., in the neighborhood of 80 or 90 times). Most of the others, like Vivian, said that Hanna visited "several times" or "often," but didn't attach a huge number to the visits.*]

In Trial #2, Sanford asked Judy Higham almost identical questions to those in Trial #1. About how often she had been at the house, she said, "Almost every time Hanna was." She also testified that she came over because Hanna called her, that she spent the night often, that she never saw Steve doing or saying anything inappropriate toward Hanna or her or anyone else, that Steve was just friendly and fatherly toward all of the other kids that were there, and that she had even spent the night there often, including between the two trials. Elmer Ross asked her similar questions, establishing that, although Judy was there often, she wasn't there every time Hanna was. Then Sanford asked her if she thought she had been around enough to have seen something inappropriate if it had happened. She said, "Yes, sir," and said she had never seen anything like that. He passed the witness back to Ross who took one more shot at it. He said, "Do you think sexual acts between an adult and a child would be done out in the open where people could see, or do you think that would be done in secret in a bedroom behind closed doors or at night when everyone else was asleep?" Sanford lodged an objection, "Calls for speculation." Judge Hawes sustained, and they excused Judy.

[*No, Judy wasn't at the house every single time Hanna was there, but she was there a great deal of the time, and had spent the night after Hanna filed the accusations, even staying once between the two trials. Ross did raise an interesting point in his last question to Judy, though. Hanna never claimed that the incidents had been done* "in secret in a bedroom behind closed doors." *She stuck to the ridiculous notion that most of them were done out in the open, usually with other people there.*]

Analysis: Did anyone see anything happening? The answer is, "No." In both trials, Marri was asked general questions about whether she had ever witnessed anything inappropriate happen between Hanna and Steve, and whether he did bad things to Hanna, or whether Hanna did inappropriate things to him. Marri answered, "No" to all of that, and said she was a light sleeper who would wake up easily if there had been anything happening nearby. One specific thing she wasn't asked, though, was whether she had seen anything improper happen on the night of Beau's birthday party.

Other people (Beau, Vivian Percet, and Judy Higham, among others) were asked similar questions, and they all said that they had never seen Steve do anything inappropriate to any child, and definitely not with Hanna. Judy said she had known Steve for about ten or eleven years, most of her life, and that she was at the Sirois' home almost every time Hanna was there. Judy spent the night often, but said (under extensive questioning) that she never saw or heard Steve do anything inappropriate to Hanna or to her or to anyone. She also added that she had spent the night at the Sirois' residence multiple times both before and after the charges were filed, a testament to her parents' common sense and confidence in Steve, but Hanna avoided even acknowledging Judy's existence, I believe because of her mother's relationship with Judy's uncle, Eddie.

Also, according to Hanna, while all these situations supposedly played out, Beau was either asleep on the couch or on the other bed, or Marri was, or they weren't there at all. Aaron usually was asleep in the recliner, but Hanna only mentioned him when she was asked where he was.

I believe that the problem most liars have is that their stories change because they can't remember all of the different nuances of the fiction they've just spouted for the tenth, or twelfth, or hundredth time, so they take a stab at it and say it with authority. Good liars say it as if it actually *is* a memory, when it's often just an image pulled out of the ether.

Conclusion: This is another instance where, despite Hanna's claims of multiple incidents occurring within earshot and eye range of several other people, no one saw or heard anything.

Are you ready to wrap this chapter up?

Final Thoughts About the Night of Beau's 21st Birthday Party

What follows is a summary of the reasons why I believe that none of Hanna's allegations about Steve that night are true. These are my own opinions, but are based on affidavits, trial transcripts, and statements made by Hanna and others.

First, a recap of the two opposing sides.

The prosecution claimed that "on or about" February 14, 2004, after a two-and-a-half year series of incidents, following a 21st birthday celebration for Beau Sirois, Hanna Penderfield was molested by Steve for the final time. According to the original affidavit, Steve pulled Hanna from the kitchen into the bedroom where Robin was drunk asleep. While standing up, Hanna gave Steve oral sex, and he fingered her briefly. Hanna claimed that her mother and Marri were gone and her brother was outside during this, but she didn't mention Beau or any of the party guests being there even though this supposedly happened just after dinner. That claim, made under oath, wasn't remotely similar to what she told Ada Dixon just a few months later. The affidavit's version was completely tossed aside and never revisited, but the indictment Steve was charged with was based solely on those statements in the affidavit.

By the time of the trials, over two years later, Hanna's completely revamped versions added a number of guests and heavy drinking. Hanna said that, after everyone was asleep, she went into Steve's bedroom, woke him up, and brought him back into the living room where her brother (who she only mentioned when asked) and either Marri or Beau were interchangeably sleeping, their presence varying from one trial to the next. Her story did include the two elements described in the counts (her performing oral sex on Steve, and Steve penetrating her vagina with his finger), although she appeared to not remember one of them in Trial #2 until she was prompted by Elmer Ross and suddenly spouted "fingers and tongue." She also, however, added actions for that night that weren't in any other versions, including a drunkenly failed attempt at penetration sex.

The defense had a much simpler story. The Sirois' had a party for Beau, several people attended and then left. Spending the night were Steve and Robin, Beau and Marri, and Hanna and her brother, Aaron. Steve slept in his bedroom with Robin. The kids all slept in the living room. Hanna didn't come into the bedroom to wake him up. He didn't follow her back to the living room. Nothing happened, including earlier in the evening.

It's important to be able to compare Hanna's various versions of her claims to determine whether she might have been lying during one or more of them. I hope I've been able to do that successfully. There are a few points in Hanna's story that everyone agrees with. The night in question was near the 14th of February, 2004 (but it might have been as late as February 20th).

Everyone also agrees that there was a 21st birthday party for Beau, that the adults did drink, and that it was held at the Sirois' home in Saddleview Cove. Let's look, though, at the areas where there are disagreements, and I'll make some judgment calls.

Clothing: Hanna often had problems giving logical descriptions of clothing. Shorts and t-shirts in cold weather. Double layers in scorching hot weather. Clothes changing form and style from one version to the next. What she said about this night was no exception. In the affidavit, she said she was wearing drawstring pants, and Steve was wearing pants with a zipper. In her interview with Tom, she said that Steve unbuttoned and unzipped his shorts (not pants) before pulling his underwear down, and that she was wearing shiny blue silky panties, a big t-shirt, and possibly jeans earlier in the evening (not drawstring pants). In the trials, though, she said she was wearing only panties and a large t-shirt, and Steve was just in his underwear. The weather for much of February 2004 ranged from cold to brutal, and the Sirois' house was poorly insulated. Would people have been wandering around the house in underwear and t-shirts when it was near freezing outside and not that much warmer inside, not to mention the modesty factor? No, of course they wouldn't.

The Verdict: I think she was just making the apparel up, and doing it badly.

Partygoers: There were some disagreements about who was there during the party and who wasn't. In the affidavit, Hanna tried to narrow it down to only her, Aaron, Steve, and Robin (with Aaron outside by the fire, and Robin unconscious in the bedroom), giving her and Steve the opportunity to fool around unnoticed. But if the rest of the house was empty, why would Steve pull Hanna into the bedroom where his wife was? In her interview with Tom, Hanna said very little about who was at the party, but in Trial #1, she reversed course and said there *were* lots of people: family, neighbors, relatives, and a bunch of Beau's friends. Beau said that his girlfriend was there, but none of his friends were because they were all in the military (Central Texas was sending a lot of young men to Iraq then). In Trial #2, Hanna just mentioned her family and Steve's, but said she didn't think Marri was there.

The Verdict: Hanna said something different each time she told the story. What she said didn't match up with anyone else's version, and, over time, it didn't even match up with her own.

Being Alone: As far as Steve and Hanna being alone long enough to do any of the vastly different things she claimed, they never were, not just in reality but also in Hanna's versions. The version in which they were the most alone was the affidavit's, and even that placed them in the room with Steve's wife. Hanna's idea that Robin was unconscious from drinking, and didn't know what was going on has been refuted by multiple people who have said they never saw her that incapacitated. When she did go to sleep after drinking, they said she was restless, often getting up and down several times a night. Also, put common sense into play, and realize that Robin (if she drank the way Hanna claimed she did) wouldn't have been able to maintain a 26-year exemplary record at her highly skilled, somewhat dangerous job as an engineering tech at a manufacturing plant. In addition, Hanna's very premise is faulty. If she wanted a scenario where they were truly alone, why not have her and Steve go to any one of the other rooms in the house that were away from Robin and Aaron. The reality, of course, was (if it happened after supper, as she claimed it did in the affidavit), the party was still going on and people were wandering in and out of the house until at least 11:00 pm.

The Verdict: No, they weren't alone at any point during the evening, and couldn't have been while the party was going on, which is why I believe she discarded the affidavit's version soon after creating it.

The Firepit and the Weather: No one but Hanna said that Aaron was by himself at the fire during the evening. Steve and the others said that someone was always there with him. They probably wouldn't have even had a fire in the pit on the 13th or 14th, because of all the snow and sleet. Under those weather conditions everyone would have been inside the whole time, and no one has said that they were. If the party did happen the next weekend (the 20th), as Robin suggested, the weather was clear and in the mid-40's. A fire then would make sense. Robin was the only one who thought it was the 20th instead of the 14th. Maybe she was more aware than all of them (which helps negate Hanna's theory that Robin was drunk "24/7").

The Verdict: Very little in Hanna's story has made any sense so far, and neither does this. If Aaron was by the fire, he wasn't alone.

The Timing of the Incident: As far as when the incident allegedly occurred, Hanna changed this part of her story completely by the trials, insisting that it happened after midnight (instead of after supper). Beau said that Hanna talked to him on the couch while he watched TV until 2:00 or 2:30 am. Think about that for a second. When Beau told Tom (in 2005) that he and Hanna sat up and talked on the couch until 2:30 am, nobody knew that Hanna was going to change her story's timeline (and the circumstances) from her version in the affidavit. That makes Beau's timeline even more believable. He was giving his own recollection of that night, based solely on his memory; and, unlike Hanna's story, whose final scenario I don't believe had been invented by 2005, his timeline didn't change four times like hers did. Which made me wonder how Hanna managed to lead Steve into the living room around 1:30 if Beau was still awake, watching TV, and talking to her on the couch. If she had known Beau's timeline, would she have changed hers again?

The Verdict: Unless she could harness quantum magic to bend time to her will, this didn't happen either.

Who Stayed Overnight: Hanna claimed that different people spent the night from one version to the next. Everyone else agreed that the overnighters were Steve, Robin, Beau, Aaron, Marri, and Hanna. In her affidavit, Hanna didn't say that she spent the night at all. She did say that her mother and Marri were both gone, but she didn't even mention Beau (at his own party). Shortly after that, she told Ada Dixon that she did spend the night, and mentioned herself and Steve but no one else. Two years later, she told Tom (supposedly referring to a different evening) that Beau slept on the other bed in the living room, that Aaron was on the couch, and Marri wasn't there. In the first trial, she said her mother and Beau were both gone, and Marri was in the other bed, but said nothing about Aaron. In Trial #2, she said that Beau didn't return until "later that night," that she waited on her bed for Beau to fall asleep, and said that Aaron slept in the recliner, but she didn't mention Marri at all.

The Verdict: She flip-flopped every time she told the story. Not credible.

What Time Was Bedtime? Some repeat information here. There are some disagreements about when everyone went to bed. Beau told Tom the party ended "about 11:00, 11:30," something that was corroborated by neighbors who left about that time, but he also said that he and Hanna then talked on the couch until 2:00 or 2:30 am. Hanna said, in Trial #2, that Beau "didn't come back until later that night," that she waited for him to go to sleep, and went to sleep herself "about 12:30, 1:00." Beau said, though (verified by several people), that he left about 9:00 to take his girlfriend to her car, but was back by around 10:00. Beau said that Robin was already in bed by around 11:00 (a little earlier than most of the crowd). Tom asked Hanna if she fell asleep before she woke Steve, and she said, "Yes. I was so asleep," and said that she woke him around "1:00, maybe 12:25." Beau's timetable plays havoc with all of Hanna's times, but even setting Beau's times aside, Hanna changed her story so much that her own times all contradict each other.

The Verdict: I call for a ruling of bullshit on this one. I think she was making it all up, and botching the job.

The View from the Rest of the Room: Hanna claimed she was completely hidden behind the entertainment cabinet. This is nonsense. Despite telling the jury, "you couldn't see anything or anybody," the TV cabinet did not separate her bed into its own little hidden room like something out of a fairy-tale. Everyone in the living room could have seen some or all of anything that happened (or didn't happen) on that twin bed.

The Verdict: Look at the floor plan. Insisting that the cabinet hid her from view was one of the least true statements Hanna made in either trial.

What Happened That Night? Hanna seemed to pull parts of each story from a Rolodex of endless possibilities. Affidavit: She said Steve molested her in the bedroom where Robin was passed out. To Ada Dixon: Steve attempted intercourse with her after everyone was asleep. To Tom: She didn't think she even spent the night, or believe that anything happened. In the Trials: She said she woke Steve up and brought him back to her bed in the living room, where there was not only attempted intercourse, but also oral sex, masturbation, and fingering. People who tell too many lies often can't keep their stories straight. Did Hanna lie to Willard Knox, or to Ada Dixon, or to Tom, or to both juries, or did she, as I believe, lie to everyone? The fact that she told five different stories to different people at different times suggests that she could have lied to at least four of those groups or individuals, which raises the possibility that she could also have lied to her mother, her doctor, the DA's office, and numerous friends.

The Verdict: Three of those disparate stories were told under oath. A simple comparison of Hanna's statements indicates that she had to have been lying at least part, if not all, of the time.

A Dumb Location: In her affidavit, Hanna said the last incident happened in the bedroom, with Robin present, but unconscious. In every other version, she said it happened on the twin bed in the living room, with Beau in the room (sometimes), or Marri (sometimes), or Aaron (almost always, though usually unmentioned). I assume that Hanna chose that room as the setting for this incident because that's where she actually did sleep that night, but it makes no sense as a location for people who were ostensibly trying to not get caught. Beau's bedroom was vacant that night, and was far more likely to conceal them than a 40-inch wide entertainment cabinet would. So, why did Hanna use the living room for her final story?

The Verdict: An incomprehensible choice, and another likely lie.

There Are More Differences: I could continue and spread this out over another few pages, but you've seen that Hanna rarely told the same story twice without changing something. She told several different versions of this night alone, changing the time, the clothes she and Steve were wearing, who was sleeping where, and (not counting her friends' sleepovers) gave five different accounts of her claims to five different audiences.

The Verdict: No verdict needed. The variability of her statements speaks for itself, but to sum things up:

a) Hanna made it all up, badly;
b) Her own stories didn't match her other own stories;
c) She and Steve couldn't have been alone during the party;
d) Aaron wasn't alone by the fire;
e) Hanna can't be in two places at once;
f) She flip-flopped several times about who slept where, or who was even there;
g) Her own times contradict her other own times;
h) Her bed in the living room wasn't magically hidden from everyone else;
i) Her own testimony proves she was untruthful to at least two people, and to the courts; and,
j) The multiple different stories to multiple people say it all.

Having read everything so far, I hope I've at least convinced you that Steve didn't molest Hanna. If I have, thank you for paying attention, but there's one more thing I would like you to see. In addition to the ridiculousness of Hanna's claims, what if I could prove to you that there simply wasn't enough time available for her claims to be true? I think I can do that.

Let's look at Steve's and Hanna's schedules during that time period.

A Timeline as Final Proof

"The truth will out."
William Shakespeare

"That which is obvious need not be proved."
Henry de Bracton

How often were Hanna and Steve actually together, alone and unseen? For the prosecution's argument to have any merit, a few things had to be true. First, for their grooming hypothesis to work, Steve would need a hefty amount of time, months and months of mental indoctrination, to prepare Hanna to accept the physical act when it finally arrived. During that protracted grooming period, they would both have to be in the same location multiple times for extended periods, with no one else around. And that would all have to be before the first incident of molestation. Then, after that, while they were allegedly committing those eighty to ninety acts, there would have to be enough separate occasions where they were alone, and under circumstances where they wouldn't be caught by witnesses; and, most of those occasions would also have to last long enough for extensive activity to occur, not just a couple of minutes here and there. Many of the actions Hanna described, according to her own testimony, required twenty minutes to an hour or more.

Proving that enough time and opportunity didn't exist for all of that to happen is what this brief chapter is about.

[Subsections in this Chapter: Misrepresentations of Time // The Timeline]

Misrepresentations of Time

First, we need to establish an accurate timeframe during which the incidents could have occurred. I've already mentioned that Elmer Ross and Hanna both seem to have made attempts to stretch the length of available time whenever they could. In his closing argument to the jury in Trial #2, Ross said, "Hanna was over at the Defendant's home so often that it was a goal mine for a perpetrator." He also repeated Blake Goudy's testimony, saying, "The one thing a perpetrator needs above anything else is access to the child," and added, "the testimony is uncontroverted that she was over there in the period from 2001 to 2004, at least every other weekend, if not more than that."

[*Let's start with access.* "The one thing a perpetrator needs above anything else is access to the child." *By Ross' own logic, and that of his expert witnesses, if there was little or no access, grooming couldn't occur. Without grooming, the chance of creating a climate for molestation to happen later would drop dramatically.*

You can chalk the court reporter's mis-transcription of "goal mine" *instead of* "gold mine" *either to Ross' Texas drawl, unless he actually said that (in which case, blame it on Texans' obsession with football), but his premise was still flawed. I believe that Ross (aware that grooming would require lengthy stretches of time) exaggerated the amount of time available to help the jury believe there was enough of it in advance to prepare Hanna to accept the first instance of molestation, and then enough additional time for the* "80 to 90" *incidents to happen. Hanna's own affidavit stated that the alleged molestation began in September 2001, not at the beginning of 2001, as I believe Ross tried to suggest by saying* "from 2001 to 2004."

I also believe that her September 2001 starting point was incorrect, but we'll cover that in the timeline. Hanna didn't say the molestation started near the beginning of 2001. She said the first time was in late-summer 2001. She also said that it ended in mid-February 2004, not the end of 2004. That's a little over two-and-a-half years, by her count, not the three-to-four years that "2001 to 2004" *might indicate. I also think that Ross oversold the dates at other times as well, like when he suggested that Hanna had been in counseling with Ada Dixon* "for three or four years." *She didn't start her sessions with Dixon until the end of April 2004, two years and four months before the start of the trials (not* "three or four years"*).*

Also, what was "uncontroverted" *about Ross' statement that Hanna's family visited the Sirois'* "<u>at least</u> every other weekend, <u>if not more than that</u>?" *Who proved that to be an absolute, undeniable fact? No one did. Even Hanna and her mother said they visited the Sirois' roughly every other weekend <u>on average</u>, not more often than that. Over time, there were actually fewer visits, not more, which is just one of the things I'll prove in this chapter.*]

Here's another statement from Ross. In his Trial #2 closing speech, he said, "...the consistency through which Hanna told this story is really quite amazing for a 17-year-old child, much less one that was 12 and 13 when many of these events took place."

[*Consistency? I have found very few instances where she told the same story the same way twice. Also, Hanna turned 13 in February 2002, so she was only 12 for a few months of the timeline, was 13 and 14 for the rest of it, and was just days away from turning 15 on the night of Beau's birthday (not* "12 and 13"*). Importantly, she* was *17 when she testified. Ross' statements often painted Hanna as younger than she actually was, sometimes stretching the truth in doing so. Was that to make her trauma appear worse to the jury?*]

I feel that one of the more egregious examples of time distortion came during Ross' opening statement to the jury in Trial #2. He said, "Hanna will tell you that she and her family met the Defendant sometime in the mid to late 1990's…around 1997, when Hanna was just seven or eight years old." He was wrong about two of those items. Hanna turned eight in February of 1997. Ross could have just said "when she was eight," but saying "<u>just</u> seven <u>or</u> eight" might have made her seem a year younger in the jury's eyes. It was also inaccurate to say it was in 1997. Hanna's mother testified that she didn't even come to the Sirois' house by herself until late-1998, and Hanna testified that she didn't meet Steve until 1998 when she was nine (which is neither seven nor eight, and wasn't 1997). By saying Hanna met Steve in 1997, the jury could have believed that Steve had two extra years to groom Hanna, even though that first meeting at her uncle's business may have only lasted minutes.

Then the time-twisting shifted into overdrive. Ross said, "And Hanna was often playing over at the Sirois' home, playing with Marri. And especially in the late 1990's when Hanna's father and mother separated and Hanna's father moved out of state, Hanna found herself spending more and more time over at the Sirois' house…and sometime around 2001, she began spending a great amount of time out at the Sirois' residence. Almost every weekend, she will tell you, that there were lots of parties there, lots of people over. The adults would eat and they would drink beer and alcohol and the kids would play." "He spent hours, Hanna will tell you, talking to her, leading up to September 2001. Spending time with her."

[*Did Ross list all those dates because those were dates Hanna gave him? Based on all the data I have, it just wasn't true. His statement made it sound like the two families were hanging out regularly from 1997 onward, but they weren't. Aside from a few visits by Darla alone (beginning late in 1998), and one visit with the kids in 1998 or 1999, Hanna and Aaron didn't attend any of the get-togethers with the Sirois' before September 2001. That could have been four years less than the impression the jury might have been given from Ross' opening statement.*]

I have no way of knowing whether Hanna misled Ross with distortions about when and how often she was at the Sirois' house; but Ross, whether intentionally or not, did describe a period of four years or more prior to the cross-country race, during which Steve and Hanna supposedly became acquainted with each other, and during which she was ostensibly "groomed" for molestation. I accepted those dates for a short period of time until I started comparing some of them to other dates. Darla and her husband got divorced in October 1996, and Darla started working for her brother's construction business in 1997. Steve had been working for Darla's brother since 1989, so it made sense that Hanna could have first met Steve one day at her mother's work, sometime in the late-1990's, but that doesn't mean that Hanna's family was frequently at Steve's house between 1997 and late-2001. Hanna told Tom that her mom "went out there the first couple of times by herself," specifically adding, "She did not bring me and my brother." Tom asked her how old she was the first time they visited. She said, "I was probably about ten…We did not go over there very often at first." She added, "…and, uh, nothing happened. Nothing happened for the longest time." Hanna turned ten in February 1999.

In Trial #1, Ross asked her if she visited Steve's family after she met him that first time. Hanna said, "Not for a long time…It was awhile before I was actually taken over to his house to meet his daughter." Ross asked if she remembered how old she was then. Hanna said, "No, I don't. I was probably about 9 years old." Hanna turned nine in February 1998, but notice that she reduced her age from the ten she told Tom to nine in the first trial. During the second trial, she dropped it again. She testified that they first came out to Steve's house as a family shortly after she first met him, and said, "I must have been about the same age, eight or nine. I don't really recall." Ross, though, despite Hanna's age-lowering testimony, still stated that Hanna was only seven or eight when she first visited the Sirois' home. If the jury accepted that she was twelve when she was first molested, but maybe seven when she first visited, they could have believed that there were as many as five years for Steve to work his evil ways on Hanna.

In Trial #2, though, when Ross asked Hanna how old she was when they started visiting more frequently, she said "I probably either just turned 12 or was fixing to." Ross asked if that would have been in January or February 2001. She said, "Yes, sir." Even though that statement negated Ross' previous statements about years of potential family visits, he continued to suggest otherwise, like he did in his closing statement when he said that the events of September 2001 followed "several years of socializing with the Defendant," and that it included "several months of the Defendant cultivating a relationship with her."

Hanna's Trial #2 statement about the family visits beginning seven or eight months before the affidavit's date of a September molestation may be seven or eight months too long, though. Neither Beau nor Marri remembered Hanna and Aaron spending the night before they went to see *Harry Potter* in November 2001; and neither of them remembered Hanna coming with her family and hanging out before the day of the cross-country meet on September 8th, 2001. Ross told the jury that Hanna visited the Sirois' home a great many times before then, and said that Steve had multiple lengthy conversations with her. He also said that there had been a "period of <u>several years</u> of social acquaintances and discussions with the Defendant that turned into this kissing and fondling of her," suggesting that Hanna's family had been visiting regularly for years. There weren't any extensive, lengthy talks between Hanna and Steve either before or after the cross-country meet, though, and her family only visited a few times between the meet and the movie. Even so, Ross still asked Hanna, in reference to the day of the cross-country race, "Did the <u>previous relationship</u> you had with him and his family <u>for several years</u> affect the way you responded that evening?" Hanna replied, "Well, by this time we had been talking for <u>several months</u>, like I said, for an hour or two hours, just talking." I don't believe either of those statements were true, not Ross' and not Hanna's.

Did Ross alter the amount of time himself, or was he just regurgitating statements Hanna had made to him during their attorney-client discussions before the trial began? I have no idea. There were other instances where it seemed like he misstated Hanna's comments, like when he asked Hanna, in Trial #2, how long she resisted Steve before letting him French kiss her. She said, "It seemed like I resisted it for a long time, but, in reality, it was only maybe <u>a month-and-a-half, two months</u>, " and Ross asked, "This was <u>two or three months</u> after the incidents began; is that right?" It seemed like he keyed off her maximum time of "two months," and added another month to it. She agreed with his assessment, though, when she answered, "Yes, sir."

[*Ross turned* "maybe a month-and-a-half, two months," *into* "two or three months." *I think that Ross' comments about* "several years" *worth of relationship and Hanna's about* "several months of talking" *are both untrue, though. The months of talking probably sounded more plausible to the jury than years of it, but neither one happened. The get-togethers with Hanna's whole family didn't begin until after the cross-country meet. Also, the very way the get-togethers were structured, with Steve doing the cooking, and the kids and adults being separated, prevented the creation of blocks of time when Steve could have spent hours talking with Hanna privately. That private time leading up to the night of the movie just wasn't there.*]

This is not to say that I think Ross was doing all the heavy lifting by himself. I believe Hanna's testimony was misleading too. In Trial #2, Ross asked her how often her family visited after the cross-county race. She said, "Anywhere from two or three times a month, sometimes more." Ross asked her if that was on "weekdays, weekends, or what?" She said, "A lot of the times, we would just go out there Fridays and Saturdays, very rarely on Sundays. And then, as time went on, my mom went by herself on Wednesdays." To verify, Ross asked her whether it was just Darla who visited on Wednesdays. Hanna said, "Yes."

[*More than three times a month would be every weekend, but Hanna's family didn't come over that often, and it was usually only Fridays (not "Fridays <u>and</u> Saturdays"). Even if we accepted her claim that they visited three out of four weekends per month, there were still only ten weekends between the cross-country race and seeing Harry Potter. Seven to eight weekends out of ten? Her own mother said it wasn't that often. Four to five weekends out of ten might be closer to the truth, but only at first. Visits tapered off after the first year or so, and quite a bit toward the end.*

That information about Hanna's mother visiting the Sirois' on Wednesdays has always intrigued me, though. Steve said that Darla didn't visit during the week, and they only had cookouts on the weekends. I can only speculate, but I do believe it's possible that Darla might have been using that time to get a weekly break from her kids. Maybe to see Eddie?]

Let's look at some actual numbers now, based on trial testimony and other data, about potential times when the incidents could have taken place.

The Timeline

When I first started gathering evidence for this book, I found so much contradictory information that I decided to construct a timeline of Hanna's and Steve's activities. I did it mostly so I could keep everything straight in my head. At first I thought it would be impossible to catalogue everything because there seemed to be so few actual dates to work with. Over time, though, as I studied trial testimony and statements from interviews, I began to notice how often dates and times had been misrepresented by stretching the amount of time available. I came to believe that it was being done to make it appear feasible for a jury to accept that so much molestation could have occurred. It's easier to sell snake oil to someone who's unaware of the true nature of your product than to someone who knows what it will do to their liver. In order for the jury to accept those few actions in the three counts, the prosecution also had to convince them that there was enough time and opportunity for Steve to have committed those 80 to 90 separate acts of molestation.

What if I could convince you that, in addition to all of the various misrepresentations you've seen so far, that there also wasn't enough time and opportunity to commit the acts Hanna claimed? When Bevin Jenkins asked Marri if Hanna's claims could possibly be true, she instantly said, "No, because she was never out there that much." Could Marri have been right?

The more I studied the trials, the more it became obvious to me, especially considering how many people were usually at the get-togethers and the constant foot traffic in and out of the house, that no one could have been molested that many times without being caught over and over again. How many times *were* they caught? Right, zero. What if there also was simply not enough time? At some point in my investigation I realized that no one had tried to track the dates and times when Steve and Hanna were both in the same location long enough for something to happen. To accomplish that, the first thing I would have to do would be to quantify how many times she spent the night, so let's start with that.

The information in Hanna's affidavit led to the indictment's range of dates (September 1, 2001 to February 14, 2004), so my search for the correct timeline obviously had to start and end with those dates. She characterized the first date hazily, as "late August or early September." The indictment basically split the difference to arrive at the date of September 1st, but at least that's a quantifiable item. Let's stick with it for just a moment, but it will be invalid within the next ten sentences. Here's where the math starts.

It's easy math, don't panic.

There were 897 days between September 1, 2001 and February 14, 2004 (and there were 128 weekends within those 897 days). That isn't an estimate, I counted them, days and weekends both. If you only considered the number 897, it would be easy to assume that someone could manage to find 80 to 90 opportunities. That's only about ten percent of the total number of days. It should have been simple for Steve, right? By 2006, though, Hanna had thrown away two-and-a-half months of that time. When she spoke with Tom, she was still maintaining (as she had in her affidavit) that the first time she spent the night was the first time she was sexually assaulted, but she admitted to Tom, and also testified in both trials, that she first spent the night after they went to see *Harry Potter*. So, September 1st isn't the correct starting point. We have to shift the timeline forward to late-November.

November 23, 2001, to February 14, 2004, is now the new timeline. That trims 76 days (or 12 weekends) off the total, leaving us with 821 days or 116 weekends. You can forget the total days, though, hold on to the number 116. Why, you ask? The weekends are the only important data point in this equation because Darla only brought Hanna and Aaron to visit on weekends. Summers are included in that because Darla, Steve, and Robin all worked year-round, so they still only had get-togethers on weekends. Has anyone noticed how remarkably close 116 is to 80 and 90? That's quite a drop from 897, isn't it? Once Hanna established the Night of Harry Potter as the new starting point, the maximum number of potential weekends during which Steve could carry out his degenerate activity was only 26 to 36 more than the number of deeds Hanna alleged.

Admittedly, there are two days every weekend, so you could argue that 116 x 2 = 232, doubling the possibilities, but that would only be a correct number if Hanna's family visited every weekend and spent the night both days each time. Darla and Hanna (along with all the Sirois' and their neighbors) have all said that they weren't there every weekend, and that they usually only visited one day each time (almost always on Fridays). That means, of course, that the number we're tracking (currently 116) doesn't refer to a weekend. It more accurately stands for single Fridays (or Saturdays). It was usually Fridays, but one or the other, not both.

I also mentioned another wrinkle above, though. Steve and Robin didn't have cookouts every weekend, and it was well-established in interviews and the trial record that Hanna and her family came, on average, *about* every other weekend. Even if we give them the benefit of the doubt and only cut the weekends by an exact half, dividing 116 by 2 drops the number to 58 days they visited. Just 58 days for Steve to potentially molest Hanna 80 to 90 times.

The formula for that is 128 - 12 = 116 ÷ 2 = 58

Even though it won't last long, forget 116 now, and remember 58.

A Different Calculation: Even though it's already that low, there is one bit of Darla's trial testimony that would drastically lower the number of dates even further. I'm not going to use it (even though it would definitely be to Steve's advantage), but I will tell you about it just so you're aware of it. Darla revealed something in her testimony which, if accepted at face value, would reduce the number of available days even more. It's very simple, and I believe it's the truth, the kids didn't spend the night every time they came to visit.

In Trial #1, Bevin Jenkins asked Darla where she usually was when the kids were at the Sirois' house. Darla said, "I was there, normally." He asked her if Hanna went home with her when she left. Darla said, "Most of the times. Sometimes she would stay the night, or her and her brother." Did she realize the importance of what she said? Despite Darla's testimony, Elmer Ross insisted repeatedly that Hanna spent so much time at the Sirois' house that there must have been huge swaths of time in which Steve could isolate Hanna and molest her. Darla testified, though, that Hanna came home with her most of the time, and that Hanna and Aaron only spent the night "sometimes." Since "most" clearly means more than half, and we already know they only visited every other weekend on average, the kids actually didn't spend the night there very often. In Trial #1, when Marri was asked if it was possible that Hanna could have been molested 80 to 90 times, she said, "No. Because she was never out there that much. She wasn't out there enough for it to happen that much." Could Marri have been right? If Darla's testimony was accurate, then the kids only spent the night on half or less of those 58 weekends. Even if we boosted that number in Hanna's favor a little, and said they stayed exactly half of the times they visited, the total number would drop to only 29 days.

58 days ÷ 2 would be 29 days (or less) that the kids spent the night.

Hanna's entire story relied on her and Steve having a huge number of opportunities to be alone long enough to remove clothes and participate in acts that required more than a few stolen moments. Given the nature of the get-togethers, though, with friends and neighbors and kids all around, that would be nearly impossible during the day and evening anyway; but Hanna's scenario would be even less likely if the kids had only stayed overnight fewer than 29 times in the space of two years and two months. I'm not going to use Darla's statement, though, even if it could potentially be accurate. Let's just stick with 58 weekends (for the next two paragraphs anyway). Darla, by the way, completely reversed her story by Trial #2, upping the numbers by saying things like, "We spent a lot of time out there," and "Maybe every weekend, every other weekend there for awhile." In that second trial she wasn't asked, and didn't offer, any specifics on how often the kids spent the night. Since her testimony altered substantially in her favor from one trial to the next, in which trial was she being truthful about how often they visited, and habout first trial or was it the second?ow often the kids stayed or went home with her? Was it the first trial. or was it the second? As you read earlier, I believe it may not have been the only lie she told. I think there might have been a few about Eddie.

Let's get back to the original timeline. What was the number you were supposed to remember? Right, 58. Good job. Here's another glitch in the timeline. From the 8th of November to the 23rd of December, 2002, Steve was in Massachusetts, taking his turn on Alzheimer's watch with our mother and doing some repairs on her house (that's 46 days, or 7 weekends when he wasn't even in Texas). In case you were wondering, I have documentation for that trip because I arranged his travel itinerary. Even if Hanna did spend the night at the house during that time period, Steve was on the other side of the country. We've already figured half of those dates in our first number reduction, so instead of 7 days, let's only remove another 3. That makes the new number 55 (58 minus 3 = 55).

[*Here's the new calculation, 128 - 12 = 116 ÷ 2 = 58 - 3 = 55.*] Remember 55 now.

Did Hanna give us any more clues? She told Tom, referring to the end of 2003, and leading up to Beau's birthday party, "I didn't see him for like two or three weeks at a time. We just didn't end up going out there that often." Tom seemed surprised, and said, "So, for about the last seven months, between say September and February, you didn't stay out there? Hanna said, "No." Tom asked, "From 2003 to 2004?" After a pause, Hanna said, "Not hardly at all." Tom gave her one more opportunity to say something different. He asked, "So, y'all had just stopped basically altogether staying out there?" Hanna said, "Yeah. I mean we traveled out there in the evenings, but my mom always made us go home. She didn't want to waste the gas to go out there because gas prices started going up." Gas prices could have been a factor, they were rising then, but there are a few other things to consider too. In September 2003, Steve's schedule changed when he started his new job at Lake Ashwell State Park. He wasn't on call like he had been with the city, but he did have to work two full weekends each month. The Sirois' had very few get-togethers that winter because of Steve's new schedule, and because they didn't have as many gatherings when the weather got colder anyway.

[*Darla apparently didn't mind going over there occasionally to "socialize" that fall and winter, but she apparently didn't want to have to make an extra 42-mile round trip in the morning to pick the kids up, so she brought them home each time. September through February is actually six months, not seven as Tom thought (which is 24 weekends, not 28, but we already counted half of those when I halved the original total number, so we'll only count 12 weekends now, not 24). I could probably also claim most of those days anyway because of the fewer cookouts in the winter, and Steve's weekend schedule, but let's just subtract the remaining half of those weekends on the basis of Hanna saying they didn't spend the night during that period at all.*]

128 - 12 = 116 ÷ 2 = 58 - 3 = 55 - 12 = 43, so the new number is 43.

Are we done? No, there's more.

None of what we've looked at so far includes times when Steve's family went to county and regional fairs for Marri and Beau to show their pigs, and it doesn't count the reduction in get-togethers during *all three* winters. It's not much fun to sit outside in the cold. We did count 2003 for that, but didn't deduct any extra winter days in 2001 or 2002. I realize that this argument becomes highly speculative at this point, and some of Steve's unavailable times are bound to overlap with some of the times when the Belisle/Penderfield family didn't visit, but we're already way below the 80 to 90 opportunities threshold. If we just stopped here, and didn't try to subtract another 12 to 15 days to account for the two winters and trips to out of town fairs (knocking the number down to 28 or 31), Steve would still have only had 43 opportunities to molest Hanna 80 to 90 times. He would have to have molested her an average of 1.86 to 2.09 times during each and every one of those 43 times, which would only likely happen under near-perfect circumstances. The equation still isn't complete, though.

We also haven't factored in the time it took Steve to recover from his hernia surgery. The injury was so painful that he couldn't have sex without extreme pain for six to eight months (that's 24 to 32 weekends if you're counting). In a 2016 phone conversation, he told me that the real pain started after the operation was over. I have copies of his medical records, and have read them thoroughly. In the surgery, as I understand it, the innards that had descended down into his scrotum were pushed back up into his abdomen, and a mesh was inserted to block the opening and repair the hernia. Steve said that, until sometime in the fall of 2003, any kind of sex was impossible for him; and let's not forget that the rodeo fell in the middle of that recovery period. Aside from what that does to Hanna's multiple masturbation and oral sex claims about the rodeo night, how many more weekends can be ruled out during those 24 to 32 weekends while he was recovering? We don't want to double-count some of the "every other weekend or so" cookouts, but just taking half of them (12 to 16) would drop our count of 43 to only 27 to 31 opportunities, about the same as if we had counted the extra winter dates and county fair weekends. If we only used one of those two scenarios (either winter get-togethers or the hernia recovery), using those figures, the average number of molestations would have to be somewhere between 2.58 and 3.33 times on each and every one of those nights when Hanna and Steve were both there and were both physically capable. Were Hanna and her family really only there a few dozen times in two years and two months? I don't know, but my best guess is that it was probably less than sixty visits during the entire time period, and likely much less than that. How many people drive 42 miles round trip to visit you 25 to 30 times a year? Even if Hanna's family *did* visit that often, Steve was gone part of that time, and physically incapacitated during a large part of it. So, accounting for Hanna and Aaron not spending the night every time they visited (and toward the end, apparently not at all), can I put a number to that? No, not easily, but we're still not done.

This isn't a late-night infomercial, but "Wait, there's more!"

There are also other possible complications for Hanna's claims, and they have to do with Hanna herself. Officials at Alderson ISD told me that she was very active in school. Beginning in the 7th grade, she participated in a variety of athletic and academic events, and some of those may have conflicted with weekends. An Alderson School official helped me look through Alderson's yearbooks from 2001 through 2004 to gather a list of her activities. During Hanna's 7th grade year, 2001-2002, she was on the cross-country team. In 2002-2003, her 8th grade year, she again ran cross-country, ran track, played basketball, was a cheerleader, and participated in UIL tournaments (which the school official said were probably speech and drama events). In 2003-2004, she played basketball and tennis, and was on the school's dance team. All those activities, except for the last part of the 2003-2004 school year, fell within the September 1, 2001 to February 14, 2004 time period. Possible conflict days are underlined below.

According to the school district's website, junior high and high school football games were played on Fridays and/or Saturdays (August-November). Cross-country meets (August-October) were on different days, but usually Monday through Wednesday, and an occasional Saturday. High school girls' basketball (November-February) was mostly Mondays or Tuesdays, with an occasional Saturday game. High school boys' basketball games (November-February) were mostly on Fridays, with an occasional Monday or Tuesday game. Track meets (February-April) were usually on Thursdays or Fridays.

Hanna's cross-country, track, and basketball teams would have had an occasional Friday or Saturday game or meet. As a cheerleader and dance team member, though, she would also have been at all football and basketball games, and the cheerleaders and the dance team probably attended some of the other sports events as well. Along with those Friday and Saturday commitments, she could possibly have had tennis matches on Fridays or Saturdays, and some of her UIL events might also have been on Fridays or Saturdays. In addition to that, we also have to consider all of the practices for those teams and events, and the rehearsals for her UIL events. If a team was playing another school on a Saturday, Hanna would probably have to board a bus at the school on Saturday morning, which would likely exclude a Friday stay-over at the Sirois' house. Obviously, I have no idea how many days we're talking about, but if you have kids of your own, ask yourself how much time a schedule like Hanna's would entail. Every Friday that she couldn't have been at the Sirois' home is another day we should eliminate.

The total number of days is unimportant. What's important is to determine on how many of those Fridays or Saturdays Steve and Hanna were both physically able and physically present at the same time. We have eliminated the weekends when Steve was gone to Massachusetts, and could eliminate some weekends when Hanna was involved in school activities. Without something like a full set of wall calendars or personal diaries from both families, I have no way of figuring out which of Steve's "away" days overlap with Hanna's unavailability, though; and—yes—some of Hanna's days will be the same as Steve's, but there must also have been some that weren't. However many that was, adding Hanna's school activity to the days we already have eliminated for Steve, and to things like trips to county and regional fairs, and Hanna's own sleepovers with her friends (some of which, according to her testimony, were on Fridays), I can't imagine there are too many days left. What's that number down to now? Practically nothing? Less than nothing?

Are we done? Are we done now? No. Here's one more item.

Hanna and Aaron visited their father in Michigan for a couple of weeks every summer. That's four more weekends, two in 2002 and two in 2003 (the summers of 2001 and 2004 were outside of the timeline, so they don't count). Hanna also said they visited him at Christmas every other year, so that's at least one more weekend that falls within the time period, possibly two. The 2001 and 2003 visits would have both been within the timeline, but if they visited in 2002 and 2004, the 2004 visit would have been after Hanna accused Steve. That's a minimum of five more weekends, though, maybe six.

Obviously, I can't prove which of Steve's and Hanna's days overlap and which of them don't, but it became very clear to me at some point that they weren't in the same place and time often enough, and the get-togethers weren't held under any sort of circumstance that would allow them to do the "80 to 90" things she claimed they did.

What if we had accepted Darla's Trial #1 testimony (under oath) about spending the night less than half of the time when they did visit, and had started our calculations with 29 days instead of 58? What number would we have ended up with?

Are we done now?

Yes.

After the Trials

Post-Conviction

"We who live in prison, and in whose lives there is no event but sorrow, have to measure time by throbs of pain, and the record of bitter moments. We have nothing else to think of."

Oscar Wilde

"Under a government which imprisons any unjustly, the true place for a just man is also a prison."

Henry David Thoreau

You knew the outcome from the start. Steve is in prison today because a jury rendered a verdict that none of them may have believed in. I came to that conclusion soon after I watched the court proceedings for Steve's motion for a new trial (October 26, 2006), which was the only part of the trials I witnessed firsthand. During that motion, Emma Barrens, one of the jurors, gave an affidavit, which was entered into the trial record. In her affidavit she said, "the jurors made a deal to find the Defendant guilty on count one and not guilty on the other two counts. If this deal had not occurred, a decision would not have been reached." All of the jurors agreed to vote to acquit Steve of Counts II and III, but also to vote to convict him on Count I. Ms. Barrens, in testimony at the motion, said that, when they started deliberating only one juror wanted to vote guilty on all of the charges against Steve. After several hours, it seemed as if the jury would be deadlocked like the first jury was. When asked about the deal they made, Ms. Barrens said that "one of the jurors suggested that he would vote on one guilty if they would vote not guilty on the two. And that's what we ended up doing." She was asked if she felt "that what happened in the jury room was that the jurors struck a deal," and she answered "Yes." She was also asked if she thought that "justice has been done in this case." She said, "No."

Some of the jury members believed Steve was guilty while others believed he was innocent, but they all agreed to swap votes. By doing that, I believe that each and every juror contravened the judge's orders. They voted against their conscience when they traded their votes for an outcome they didn't believe in, and Steve got screwed in the process. I say that none of them believed in it because those who wanted a guilty verdict won by voting to acquit on two charges (but that only gave them a conviction on one count instead of three), and those who wanted to acquit Steve voted against their conscience, and were duped into sending Steve to prison when they didn't believe he was guilty. I'm not going to spend much time on this section, or anything else about what it has been like for him in prison, or about his appeals after he was incarcerated. I have covered that on the blog a bit. This is just going to be an overview of what happened right after the trial.

[Subsections in this Chapter: The Night After the Verdict // The Next Morning]

The Night After the Verdict

Once the verdict was rendered, the jury was excused. It was already late in the evening, so Judge Hawes asked the attorneys when they could handle the punishment phase of the trial. Sanford asked for a two-week continuance so he could bring Dr. Stein in from Dallas to testify about Steve's PPG test. Ross wanted Hawes to revoke Steve's bail and take him into custody immediately. Hawes said there wasn't enough time for a continuance, so they would convene in the morning for sentencing, but he apparently thought Steve wouldn't be a flight risk because he said, "For tonight, you will remain on the same bond, Mr. Sirois. And I expect to see you up here in the morning at 10:30. It would only make matters worse if you are not."

Steve told me, "I spent most of that night sitting outside on my porch, staring at the free world for the last time. The three of us, Robin, me, and Marri, lay together just holding each other. I don't remember how long. The next day we were all in shock as we drove to the courthouse."

The Next Morning

Inside the courthouse, the first order of business was a pre-sentencing hearing, which Steve said, "is really just a joke." He added that an Officer Moffit took him into the empty jury room and asked him some questions about his criminal record. Steve said that, based on that five-minute conversation, Moffit "made a determination out of thin air to give the judge some sort of recommendation on the proper range" of sentencing.

Ross called Hanna and Darla to the stand. Each of their statements were brief. Hanna said, "I can't get my life back until I know that you can't do this to me or anyone else anymore." Darla said, "We have been through hell the last two-and-a-half years waiting for this to happen...This was a man I trusted, I trusted with my kids' lives, and he did unspeakable things to my child. And he needs to be put away." They both said they wanted the maximum sentence for Steve.

Sanford called Beau to testify for Steve. Beau said, "He has always been there for me and for our family and he has always been the person that holds everything together," and asked Hawes to consider giving him the lowest sentence. Steve told me, "Beau wanted to say what he did on my behalf. It tore me apart inside. I knew him well enough to know that if he didn't speak his mind and try to help me he would have harbored guilt for the rest of his life. He has always been the kind of person who does better if he gets things off his chest."

There wasn't enough time to get Dr. Stein to Deep Springs from Dallas, and there was no money left to pay him with anyway. Instead, Sanford introduced the results of the PPG test, hoping that Stein's assessment (that Steve "is not a psychopath," "is interested in adult females," and "showed no interest for underaged females") might help Steve get a lighter sentence.

Steve said, "The rest of the sentencing procedure was just a dog and pony show." Sanford asked for leniency, citing Steve's family ties and the PPG test, Ross demanded the maximum, citing the trauma caused to Hanna and her family. Judge Hawes announced that the range of punishment for aggravated sexual assault of a child was "a minimum of 5 years, a maximum of 99 years or life imprisonment with an optional fine of up to $10,000." He sentenced Steve to thirty-five years in prison, but didn't impose a fine. Steve said, "The judge was caught in the middle, because if he gave me too much he would look mean, and if he gave me too little he would look weak. Thirty-five years was apparently a safe number, but not a fair one. He did what any good politician would do."

I've often wondered how many years the jury, some of whom, like Emma Barrens, may have been feeling remorse for what they had done, would have given Steve if he had chosen to have them sentence him instead of the judge. It would certainly have placed them in the position of having to review the decision they made to trade votes. They wouldn't have been able to change the verdict once they had rendered it, but it may have compelled some of them to fight for a lesser sentence at least.

Once Hawes made his pronouncement, they handcuffed Steve, then allowed him to hug his family one last time before they led him back into the bowels of the courthouse and left him in a long narrow room. The room was split down the middle by a three-foot-high wall, which was topped with a Plexiglas panel that extended up to the ceiling. On the other side of the Plexiglas was an empty chair. A few minutes later, Sanford appeared there and sat down. Steve said it seemed odd that the man who had sat beside him throughout the trial, and had been to his home to discuss the trial less than a week before, now had to speak to him through a plastic shield. Steve said "Cleveland was as emotional as I was as he explained how he could not represent me just in case he had made a mistake. He promised to help my appeals attorney if he had," and slid an indigency form through a slot in the panel. Steve filled it out so Hawes could appoint an appeals attorney for him.

From there he was taken to the Ashwell County Jail, which would become his home for the next four months, and where he would get his first schooling about the realities of prison life. There are plenty of stories about his time there, and his time at the Stiles Unit in Beaumont since then, but I won't get into any of that here. I may post some of them on the blog, along with details of the appeals process, and why Steve was unsuccessful at winning a reversal in his case; but none of those are about why Steve was convicted in the first place. I believe that the real reason was a simple one, because Hanna lied to people and they took her at her word.

So, why did she say the things she did, and why should you believe Steve instead of her?

Logical Conclusions

"Facts are stubborn things; and whatever may be our wishes,
our inclinations, or the dictates of our passions,
they cannot alter the state of facts and evidence."
John Adams

"Three may keep a secret, if two of them are dead."
Benjamin Franklin

[Subsections in this Chapter: Why Hanna Accused Steve // Why You Should Believe That Steve is Innocent // A Final Word From Steve // My Two Cents Worth]

Why Hanna Accused Steve

The truth is that I don't know why Hanna named Steve as her abuser, and possibly never will, although I did find Karla Spivey's story about Hanna telling her that she was abused by her mother's boyfriend compelling. I wish Karla had been called to testify, but I believe that the prosecution and law enforcement accepted Hanna's word as fact without looking for other possibilities. My working theory is a simple one. Unfortunately, it's also largely based (by necessity) on statements Hanna made, so I can't be positive that I'm not basing part of the theory on falsehoods, but here it is.

Sometime in the spring of 2003, Hanna told Josh Chilmark she was being molested by an older man, so it stands to reason that she may have also said similar things to some of her friends. Did she tell them at several sleepovers in 2002 or 2003, as Angie claimed; or at a single sleepover in April 2004, as Rhonda testified? Was Rhonda not invited to the earlier sleepovers, and that's why she didn't hear about the abuse until after the charges were filed, or was the revelation at the 2004 sleepover actually the first one? Did Hanna, as she testified, tell her friends she was having sexual experiences with an older man or a football player or a student from another school or Beau? The trials were held at least two years after any of those sleepovers supposedly occurred, which would have given Hanna plenty of time to develop an accurate story, but instead she came up with several constantly shifting ones.

If the earlier sleepovers actually did take place, and these young girls were all trying to outdo each other in terms of experience with boys to gain popularity; <u>and</u> if, as Hanna said, she "always had the most experience," then she must have told increasingly racy stories over a period of time, maybe a year or two. As contests go, at each new brag session she would have needed to escalate the risque nature of her stories to stay ahead, adding new details to make her tales better than those told by the other girls.

In 2003, Hanna had "a huge crush" on Josh Chilmark. On the bus, after school one day, she sat beside him and saw an opportunity to get him to talk to her intimately by telling him some of the same stories she had been telling her friends. It worked, but only in the sense that he paid attention to her for the rest of the semester. She wanted to date him, but he kept saying *No, maybe when you're older, you're too young now.* She continued to communicate with him through the summer, but he left to join the Marines. She told Marri that Josh wrote her to say they would be together when she was old enough, and showed Marri a picture of him in uniform, but wouldn't let her read his letter.

In the fall of 2003, Hanna's family started visiting the Sirois' less and less. Darla said it was because gas prices were rising, which they were; but, based on her testimony that her relationship with Eddie Higham lasted 8 to 10 months, it's also possible that the relationship could have ended about then. If Darla was miserable about the breakup, Hanna could have blamed Steve because Steve had called Eddie's past to Darla's attention. This is all conjecture, of course, based on different versions of Hanna's story threading out in different directions.

When Hanna's family did visit, things didn't go well for her at the Sirois' either. She wanted to be included, but it didn't always work out to her advantage. One example: Marri was raising a hog to show at the Ashwell County Fair in January 2004. They had an extra hog, a feeder hog, whose primary purpose was to compete with Marri's for food. The rivalry for resources would encourage Marri's hog to eat more. Hanna helped with the hogs some (not much, because they weren't there that often), but she was told that, if the feeder hog qualified, she could enter it along with Marri's. Marri's ended up weighing enough, which qualified her hog to be shown at other fairs, but the feeder hog didn't qualify, so it became pork chops. Hanna wanted to go to the regional fair with them, but Steve told her she couldn't. He said the trip was just for family. That had to sting.

Marri's new braces also pulled some attention away from Hanna, and Beau's 21st birthday party might have too. Hanna turned fifteen just days later, but the party was only for Beau. I'm sure all of that made her angry (which Steve has said was a fairly normal setting on her attitude dial), but I think the biggest blow might have come from Josh. In January 2004, Hanna discovered he was back in town. His stay in the Marines ended up being a short one because, as he put it, "the small bones in one of my ears is messed up real bad, so I can't hear real good." Hanna also learned that Josh was dating a new girl, Steve's niece, Liz Brailford. She ran into Liz and Josh at the same Ashwell County Fair where she found out she wouldn't get to go to the regional competition with the Sirois family. A double whammy.

If that wasn't enough, Aaron had been lobbying since late in 2003 to go live with his father, which pulled even more of Darla's attention away from Hanna. I think all of those events shifted Hanna's anger toward the Sirois family, especially toward Steve. She wasn't able to date Josh, her mother was paying more attention to Aaron, she had been dismissed by Steve about going on the trip, and then also rejected by Josh when he (as she might have seen it) dumped her for Steve's relative. It was just too much. She might have been able to suppress that anger, and not do anything about it, but then Blake Goudy came to her school and talked about abuse, and about how to end it. Possibly for years she had been telling her friends that she was having sexual experiences with an older guy. She had even told Josh that the man was someone much older who had a couple of kids (maybe she was already basing the character of her molester on Steve). According to Angie, Hanna gave her and Suzanna enough information (in 2002 or 2003) for them to assume she was talking about Steve. In April 2004, as Blake Goudy spoke, Hanna probably felt the eyes of her friends on her, wondering what she was going to do.

She could have just ridden it out and then told them later that it was all over and done with and she didn't want to talk about it, but Karla Spivey forced her to go up and talk to Goudy. If Hanna actually did tell Karla that her molester was her mother's boyfriend (a logical choice, considering his past), she must have regretted it instantly, knowing how her mother would react. Needing another name, she may have switched from Eddie to Steve when she spoke to Goudy. Who better than Steve? She was pissed at him because of the hogs, Marri's braces, and Beau's birthday anyway; but especially because of Liz stealing her future boyfriend. Any one of those could have been a catalyst for Hanna striking out at somebody, but add them all together and it's easy to see why she might have zeroed in on Steve as her target. I know this theory seems like a house of cards. If one piece is removed, the whole thing could collapse, but most of those elements aren't crucial to the overall idea. Maybe it's more like a game of Jenga, several of the items could disappear and the structure would still stand. Of course, Hanna is the only one who really knows why she did what she did.

There are a couple of caveats to this theory, of course. Because some elements of Hanna's stories have been so changeable, pinning her motives to any one cause has been tough. Rhonda said she didn't find out about any of this until that April 2004 sleepover. It's even possible that Josh was the only person Hanna told about her abuse before Blake Goudy. If none of her friends found out about her story until after the accusations were made—and I am still calling it all a "story," a fiction, because I believe that it was something she invented—then several of her friends, by supporting her story, may have unwittingly told untruths themselves.

Is it conceivable that multiple individuals believed as early as 2002 or 2003 that Hanna was being abused but didn't tell anyone else for years? Yes, it's possible, but how likely is it? I don't know if you have ever lived in a small town, but the length of time that small-town secrets stay that way is usually measured in minutes or hours, not years. Alderson only had about 400 residents in the early 2000's. I find it difficult to accept that some of these girls knew about Hanna's predicament but didn't tell anyone else, not even a friend or a relative. People who grew up in the area told me that, in middle school, some of them would likely have told someone else "within three days or less." Wouldn't a few of the girls tell their parents? Angie Womack said she told her mother, but waited a year. If any of those parents heard that Hanna was being molested, wouldn't at least one of them report it to the authorities? No one did. Is it possible that none of the girls heard about it until after Hanna accused Steve? Maybe they didn't hear about it until later because Hanna didn't tell anyone except Josh? Maybe she was just using her story to get Josh to pay attention to her. Like everything else in her stories, it's hard to distinguish the truth from the fiction.

Why You Should Believe That Steve is Innocent

I could just refer you back to the *Proof of Innocence* section for this. The purpose of that section was to prove that Steve actually *is* innocent, and I hope I did that to your satisfaction. The reason why you *should* believe it, though, goes far beyond Steve. His case is representative of thousands of other cases of injustice in this country. Overzealous prosecutors, lazy or indifferent law enforcement, a corrupt judiciary, overworked public defenders, and a judicial system that is weighted heavily in favor of the rich and against the poor and the minority, combine to create a system that often fails to provide justice for the unfairly accused. Hopefully, if you can accept the simple premise that innocent people are convicted far too often, and have examined the data I provided you with, you will have come to the same conclusion I have, that Steve is innocent, and shouldn't be facing [*as of August 2020*] another 21 years in prison.

Steve's memory of everything is currently more akin to a reconstruction than an actual recall of specific events. He has been over the trial testimony in his head so often that it's all jumbled. He also hasn't had copies of the trial transcripts for several years now because the prison is far from watertight, and most of the copies he had were ruined in tropical storms. One thing he's said more often than anything else in response to my questions is, "Mike, I don't know. I don't remember. I just know I didn't do it."

In Season One of the wonderful podcast, *Serial*, Sarah Koenig, the podcast's producer and narrator, was interviewing Deirdre Enright, a University of Virginia Law School professor who runs UVA Law's Innocence Project clinic. They were talking about Adnan Syed, the principal character in the podcast. Adnan was accused of murdering his girlfriend, but had consistently maintained that he was innocent. Ms. Koenig was talking about how difficult it was to get to the truth of the matter, and that Adnan (who had nothing to lose and everything to gain by helping her), often wasn't able to provide any real information. Here's a bit of Koenig's and Enright's conversation.

> SARAH KOENIG: ...Adnan himself is not supplying anything super useful to say here's why I can prove I didn't do this. He has said out front, "I can't give you some clinching piece of information or evidence that's going to solve this, I wish I could, but I can't. I just don't have it. Like I don't know how to prove this."
>
> DEIRDRE ENRIGHT: That's kind of -- I love hearing that because somewhere along the line I've started realizing that when you have an innocent client, they are the least helpful people in the whole world, because they don't know. They don't -- they have no idea, like as soon as I realize I have an innocent client and that's the situation, I think like, "Okay, well, I'll talk to you again when I've solved it, because I'm not going to need you here."

It was the same with Steve. His position from the very first was that he didn't do it but had no way to prove it. How could anyone provide an alibi for some unspecified time period when the time and the narrative is allowed to shift and change at the whim of their accuser? Ms. Enright's position was that the truly innocent, the ones who had nothing to do with the crime, often can't say anything more than "I didn't do it." Steve would agree with that. He knows that Hanna's charges were false, and he doesn't know why she made those claims, but he does know that he didn't do what she accused him of.

He has now exhausted all of his appeals. From this point forward no courts will take his case unless he can provide new evidence, which might now be impossible for him, as it is for the vast majority of innocent inmates. The trial hinged on one basic premise: Hanna said that he did these things to her, but could provide no physical evidence of it, and he said that he didn't do them, but could provide no physical evidence that he hadn't. Unfortunately, Hanna was the one who created and modified the plot.

The prosecution's case consisted of Hanna telling her version (or versions) of the story, and providing a few witnesses who mostly had little to say. Rhonda Bresnick only said there might have been some hint of impropriety on Steve's part (a touch on Hanna's back or knee during a ride home in a small truck). Those had nothing to do with the charges against Steve, and weren't even what Hanna said happened during the ride. Tiffany Sperger said that Marri told her she had seen Steve and Hanna in an awkward position on a bathroom toilet. Marri denied seeing it or saying that to Tiffany, and even Hanna denied that it happened. That also had nothing to do with the three counts. Darla, Josh, Knox, Dixon, and Goudy all reinforced Hanna's story in various ways, but it was all largely by repeating what Hanna had told them. Dixon and Goudy were supposedly "experts," but they still could only echo what Hanna had said, and Deputy Knox could only say that he had spoken to a few people and had taken depositions. None of them had any personal knowledge. Hanna's other friends were also just as capable of repeating Hanna's words and offering opinions. Why weren't they called to testify? Hanna said she told a lot of them about the abuse. If all Blake Goudy did was talk to Hanna for a few minutes and advise her to tell her mother, why wasn't Karla Spivey, the girl who encouraged Hanna to talk to him, also subpoenaed? None of the witnesses actually witnessed anything, but Hanna said her brother, Aaron, did. Why wasn't he called? Why do we only have Hanna's word that Aaron saw a kiss in the truck? No one else saw it, and no one else heard Aaron ask about one.

Steve's witnesses (Marri, Robin, Beau, Del Weaver, Vivian Percet, Judy Higham, and a few others) didn't see anything either, but they had been present at many of the events. They were mostly there to testify to Steve's character. Del Weaver was a family friend and a former police officer who had often dealt with people under the influence. He testified that he had witnessed Steve and Robin at get-togethers, and that they did drink, but he had never seen either of them so drunk that they would pass out or be unaware of their surroundings, and that he had never seen Robin so drunk that she was "passing out on a regular basis," as Hanna frequently claimed.

Side Note: Weaver received a jury duty notice for Trial #1. Since he was on the witness list for the trial, he called the court, but they told him to show up for the first trial's voir dire anyway. He did, and was excused, as he knew he would be, because a witness can't serve on a jury and also be a witness. In Trial #2, Elmer Ross cross-examined Weaver for four pages of testimony. He spent three pages of that haranguing Weaver about showing up for the first trial's voir dire as if he had committed some sort of criminal offense. What was Ross trying to discredit him for? For being a responsible citizen? Completely irrelevant, and a rotten thing to do, in my opinion.

Vivian Percet, Steve's neighbor, testified that she had known Steve and Robin for many years, and had been to their house many times. She said she never saw anything inappropriate in all the years she had known them. She also verified that neither Steve nor Robin drank as much as Hanna said they did; and testified that Hanna "spent the night several times." Notice she didn't say hundreds, or even "80 to 90" times. Nancy Foxwell (Robin's sister) and Meredith Winstead (a friend of Marri's) also testified on Steve's behalf. Like his other witnesses, they both said they didn't think he was capable of this, and that they had never seen any inappropriate behavior on his part. We've already covered Judy Higham's testimony about Darla and her uncle, Eddie, but Judy and her sister, Jessica, had also known the Sirois' for most of their lives, and had spent the night many times. Judy, who was a friend of Hanna's, testified that she spent the night there nearly every time that Hanna did, and still never heard or saw anything inappropriate from Steve toward Hanna or anyone else, including her and Jessica. Hanna didn't mention Judy once; not in any of her testimony or during her interview with Tom, or even when she was asked about Judy's uncle, Eddie. Why wouldn't Hanna want to call attention to Judy? Maybe because she and Darla wanted Eddie and his background to remain hidden from the jury?

Betty Stavens and Rebecca Benway, who didn't testify, were interviewed by Tom. Both said they had known the Sirois' for years, and that Steve had never been anything but kind to them. That was also the pattern throughout all of the testimony and interviews. Even though Hanna said Steve was after her all the time, people who knew him said he might flirt with women his own age, but they had never seen him act improperly toward women or girls younger than he was. Hanna tried to convince Tom that Steve might have even molested Marri and Jenny Luborsky, and maybe some girls while he was in Florida. Those are, in my opinion, all blatantly false accusations, just rumors with no basis in reality; and I believe Hanna knew they were because she didn't mention any of them during either trial. I think she was attempting to mislead the defense when she told Tom those things. Would a person who had truth on their side try to rig the system with deceitful comments?

The more I look at Hanna's interview with Tom, in fact, the more it seems like an exercise in obfuscation. There weren't any teary instances where she had to break off for a moment to sob, as she did during the trials. Listening to the audio, she was occasionally angry, but often seemed cheerful and even playful. She did manage, though, for 2 hours and 28 minutes, to avoid telling Tom about any of the incidents charged in Counts I, II, or III; and also skipped telling him about the alleged incident in the ditch after they dropped Rhonda off at her house. Much of what she did tell him also differed from her trial testimony, plus she avoided giving him phone numbers of people who could have been key witnesses, like Karla Spivey. She did lead him to one witness, Angie. Did she think Angie would back her story?

As valuable as I found Hanna's interview for comparison purposes, I think it also served her as a preparation tool for the trials, as well as a way to confuse the defense.

Obviously, I can't tell you what to believe, but look at the lack of evidence. Look at Hanna's multiple stories (which I believe are largely falsehoods), ranging from insignificant things like her time and rank in a foot race to descriptions of unconcealed acts of molestation, supposedly conducted in front of multiple people, often under impossible physical circumstances. Acts which no one else saw. Look at the many changes she made to every element of her story, refining and altering it while she prepared it for presentation to a jury. Look at the misrepresentations from Elmer Ross, attempting to build extra non-existent months and years into the story to create "grooming" time. That inaccurate information wouldn't have been necessary if Hanna's story had been true and verifiable. In the timeline, look at the lack of potential days when this could have happened. Compare Hanna's sworn affidavit to her sworn trial testimony. They aren't remotely similar. Soon after affirming under oath that the affidavit was "true and correct to the best of my knowledge and memory," Hanna began changing each and every one of its elements (different dates and times, different circumstances, different clothing, different actions). The trial ended up ignoring nearly every detail in the affidavit, and tried Steve on things that Hanna claimed happened in completely different ways, often on different dates.

Ultimately, though, it was the decision of twelve jurors to trade votes that sealed Steve's fate. Some of them felt Steve was guilty, some felt he was innocent, and some of them might have been on the fence. Whatever each of them thought individually, I believe they were convinced by one or more of their fellow jurors to make a decision that would allow them to go home rather than voting on the evidence, or the lack thereof. Given the attitude and the rumors in Ashwell County, I don't believe Steve could ever have received a fair trial there, so the best outcome he could have hoped for in that second trial would have been another mistrial. The question then would have been how many times the DA would continue to try the case before giving up.

Years ago, I was briefly on a criminal jury, a statutory rape case. The accused male was nineteen and the girl was thirteen. After the basic accusation was read, but before the case could proceed any further, the judge read us the text of a letter from a psychiatrist who had examined the defendant. The letter stated that the defendant wasn't currently in a fit mental state to be tried. The judge instructed us to decide, based solely on that one piece of evidence, whether the trial should continue at that time. As soon as we entered the jury room, one of the jurors launched into a diatribe against the defendant, saying we needed to put this guy behind bars so the streets would be safe from scum like him. Several others echoed that same thought. It took a while before they would even accept that our instructions were specifically to examine the only evidence we had been given, the doctor's note. After about twenty minutes of spirited discussion, we all agreed to not let the trial go forward until the defendant had been cleared to do so.

I've often wondered if deliberations in Steve's trial started the same way, with suggestions that he be emasculated in a variety of inventive and painful ways. The problem with jury trials is that some jurors let their emotions cloud their sense of reason, and I think justice suffers when they do.

I've admitted to you up front that I have a bias in this case. I do believe that my brother is innocent, and nothing would make me happier than being able to prove that; but I have conducted every bit of my investigation and analysis seeking the absolute truth of the matter. If I had found proof that Steve had committed any of the things Hanna accused him of, I would have to change my position; but I haven't found anything to implicate Steve other than Hanna's word, and the only certainty I've been able to establish (over and over again) is that Hanna lied frequently.

A Final Word From Steve

In June 2015, I asked Steve a series of questions about what he wanted me to accomplish with this book, and what he thought an ideal outcome would be. Here's what he said:

> "Asking me what I want you to do or accomplish is the easy question for me. What you already do, and that is the undaunted and unconditional love that I don't think is achievable by any request (which is what makes it so special in the first place). That is already what benefits me the most. It's the only reason I'm able to hold on to a modicum of sanity.
>
> "The conclusion I came to is that there isn't an ideal outcome for me. Ideally, I want to hug my wife every night. I want to see my kids graduate — Beau's college graduation that I missed, and both college and high school for Marri. I want to be looking at my retirement and 401(k) from the State Park after I acquired the lead Ranger position. I want to struggle through Robin's disease and be there for her through that process so I can only blame myself for not helping her wake up in time.
>
> "I want to be able to say hi to someone, and not have to worry what they really think about me. I want to see Mom again before she dies. I want to see my brother-in-law Marvin before he dies. I want to see my friend and mentor Les Etheridge before he dies. I want to see my neighbor Ms. Bressler before she moves away because there was no neighbor around to help her. I want to tie all of our brothers and sisters together in one room until we can decide to be a closer family. You know, I could go on and on, but the point is I can't have any of this.
>
> "I want to eat when I'm hungry and not when I'm told. I want to take a crap or a shower without sixty or more people watching me. In fact, a bath would probably just complete my life at this point. I want BACON!!
>
> Other than that, my ultimate desires are to see my children get married [*Marri did in 2017*], be there for the birth (and spoilage) of their children, my grandchildren [*Marri gave birth to her first child in 2020*]. To build you and Minay whatever y'all want but can't afford (like new kitchens, or a back deck with a gazebo). Something I can leave behind that people will say I built. Something for everyone that they can be proud of and say, my brother built that.
>
> "I want to be awakened at two o'clock in the morning because someone in my family needs a tire changed or just needs some support. I want to be able to get in my vehicle and go help. I want to be able to knock on someone's door and say, Surprise!
>
> "But really more than anything, I want keys. Keys unlock doors. They give you access to known and unknown worlds alike."

My Two Cents Worth

I actually gathered much of the information for the book while Steve was preparing his own appeals. What I usually did for him was to find legal information that he couldn't get from inside prison [*his prison unit does have a law library, but the conditions are far from ideal or helpful*], and proofread his writs for grammar mistakes. As I did that, I started making brief notes of details in the trial transcripts that I found curious. Some of the "brief notes" grew to dozens of pages, and the idea for the book was born.

Steve began working on each new writ with a feeling of hope and optimism that "This will be the one." It didn't work out that way, of course. He also applied to various innocence projects, but they were all reluctant to take on a case like his. Most of the innocence projects have had a very good track record, but usually when there was some tangible evidence (especially DNA) that they could examine or have retested. Steve's case never had anything like that. It was entirely based on Hanna's word. That meant that none of Steve's writs were about his actual innocence. How could they be? They all had to be procedural writs, about some flaw in the trial process, or about some other element that made the trial unfair for Steve. There was plenty of that, but it was apparently never egregious enough to force a higher court to overturn a lower court's decision.

Having said that, it seems to me that a great deal of information that should have been available was missing (like Deputy Knox's notes from Hanna's and Steve's interviews, a written response to Ross' request for information about that nonexistent rape kit, Josh Chilmark's affidavit, any of Roland Mathis' or Bevin Jenkins' trial records, or any mention of Hanna's brother, Aaron, in the material I requested from the DA's office).

In order to catalogue what I had and what was missing, I started organizing my notes into lengthy digital files about particular aspects of the case (the different counts, the ride home from the rodeo, the jury, etc.). It was clear that the information I wanted to have was incomplete, but I thought the digital files I had created would be a way to preserve and sort details of the case for any lawyers who might believe in Steve and would be willing to take his appeals case pro bono (because I knew none of us would be able to afford to pay them). Once it was clear, though, that Steve's writs were going to fail, I realized that what I had gathered was much of the material I needed to write this book.

Hopefully someone with a better legal mind than either Steve or I possess, or someone who thinks further investigation would be worth doing, will see something in Steve's case that intrigues them. If you're that person, please contact me at michael@aggravatedbook.com. If not, I hope you got something useful from the book, and I would love to hear your opinion through email, or as a comment on the blog.

Michael Sirois

Endnotes

Source Materials

Over twenty hours of recorded interviews conducted by investigator, Tom Swearingen.

Hundreds of hours of interviews, conversations, and phone calls with a variety of individuals, but primarily with Steve.

Transcripts of testimony for eight witnesses from Steve's first trial (July 2006), plus the trial's motions in limine; and the entire transcript for Steve's second trial (August 2006), including all defense and prosecution exhibits, and motions in limine.

The transcript of Steve's motion for a new trial (September 2006), which includes Emma Barrens' affidavit.

Numerous records obtained through public information act requests from agencies and offices such as the Ashwell County District Attorney, District Clerk, and Sheriff's Office; plus Texas Parks and Wildlife, the Texas Department of Family and Protective Services (CPS), and the Deep Springs chapter of CASA, among others.

External Links

The Aggravated website
https://aggravatedbook.com/

The blog at the website
https://aggravatedbook.com/blog/

Truth Boots Publishing
https://truthbootspublishing.com/

Article: "Evaluating Truthfulness and Detecting Deception"
https://leb.fbi.gov/articles/featured-articles/evaluating-truthfulness-and-detecting-deception

Article: "Report of the APA Task Force on Appropriate Therapeutic Responses to Sexual Orientation"
https://www.apa.org/pi/lgbt/resources/sexual-orientation

Article: "Sensitivity and specificity of the phallometric test for pedophilia in non-admitting sex offenders," March 2002, Blanchard, Klassen, Dickey, Kuban, and Blak
https://www.researchgate.net/publication/12052561_Sensivity_and_specifity_of_the_phallometric_test_for_pedophilia_in_nonadmitting_sex_offenders

Article: "Ejaculatory Pain: A Specific Postherniotomy Pain Syndrome." Anesthesiology, August 2007, Aasvang, Møhl, Kehlet
https://anesthesiology.pubs.asahq.org/article.aspx?articleid=1931147

Serial Podcast: Season One
https://serialpodcast.org/season-one

People, Places, and Things

This is a complex book, with a large and varied cast of characters. Hopefully this list will help you keep everybody straight. The names below are arranged by category, not alphabetically, and they are all pseudonyms except for those in **bold**.

Defendant: (no pseudonyms)
Steven Barker Sirois (the accused)
Robin Henry Sirois (Steve's wife)
Marri and **Beau Sirois** (Robin's and Steve's daughter and son)
Michael, **Jamie**, **Cece**, **Maritia**, and **Phillip** (Steve's sibling's)
Joy Sirois Sen, **Stan Sirois** (Steve's parents)
Bill Sen (Joy's second husband)
Jeff and Iline Henry (Robin's parents)

Accuser:
Hanna Lee Penderfield (the accuser)
Darla Belisle, Hanna's mother
Aaron Penderfield, Hanna's brother
Nate Penderfield, Hanna's father

Law Enforcement:
Ashwell County Sheriff's Office (ACSO)
Deep Springs Police Department (DSPD)
Deputy Willard Knox (ACSO), created the affidavit
Deputy Craig Conner (ACSO), took over the case
Sgt. Lonnie Hartness (ACSO), took the original complaint
Officer Duke Chapman (ACSO)
Officer Theo Rossiter (DSPD), arresting officer

The Defense:
Roland Mathis, Steve's 1st attorney
Tom Swearingen (his real name), Steve's investigator
Warren Hathaway, briefly helped Tom with the investigation
Bevin Jenkins, Steve's 2nd attorney
Eugene Guthrie, Jenkins' associate
Charlotte Felton, therapist working with Jenkins
Cleveland Sanford, Steve's 3rd attorney

The Prosecution:
Elmer Ross, Assistant District Attorney (ADA)
Seymour Cooper, District Attorney (DA)

The Court:
555th District Court
District Judge Preston Hawes, the presiding judge
Associate Judge Jordan Decker
Mindy Camillo, court reporter
Officer Moffit, probation officer

Witnesses:
Rhonda Bresnick, possible friend of Hanna's, testified for the Prosecution
Tiffany Sperger, former friend of Marri's, testified for the Prosecution
Josh Chilmark, went to school with Hanna, testified for the Prosecution
Blake Goudy, expert witness for the Prosecution
Ada Dixon, expert witness for the Prosecution, Hanna's counselor
Judy Higham, friend of Marri's and Hanna's, testified for the Defense
Meredith Winstead, a friend of Marri's, testified for the Defense
Del Weaver, a friend of Steve's, testified for the Defense

Jurors: (and their voir dire numbers)
#2 Ronelle Wilcox
#5 Crystal Sue Benson
#20 Jerry Max Timmons
#23 Emma Pollard Barrens

The Billy Gasnick Story:
Billy Gasnick (rapist and murderer of Jenny Luborsky)
Martha Gasnick (Billy's mother)
Melanie Gasnick Gallison (one of Billy's sisters)
Erica Gasnick (one of Billy's sisters)
Karen Suhler (Jenny's mother, later married Andy Stavens)
Buddy Suhler (Karen's brother)
Jenny Luborsky (Karen's daughter, Billy's step-daughter)
Rebecca Luborsky Benway (Karen's daughter, Billy's step-daughter)
Deputy Otto Walton (one of the investigators, ACSO)
Arthur Seabury (former Ashwell County District Judge)
Roy Lane Dunnigan (Billy's court-appointed attorney)
Marcia Jagger (author of *A Gruesome End*)

Related to the Gasnick Story:
Andy Stavens (Karen Suhler's husband)
Wendy Stavens (Andy Stavens' former wife, Betty Stavens' mom)
Betty Stavens (Karen and Andy's daughter)
Greg Stavens (Andy Stavens' father)

Other Trials:
Gonzo v. Texas (2011 trial in which Dixon testified)
Texas v. Munsen (2013 trial in which Dixon testified)
Alan Munsen (defendant in the 2013 trial)

Social Media Contacts from the Deep Springs Area:

Burl Conley, Maggie Mae Joyner, and Nathan Brooks

Peripheral Observers, Other Misc. People

(Connected to Steve)

Clyde Sledge (editor of the Deep Springs Gazette)
Claude Tisbury (Deep Springs attorney)
Bernard Stein (a forensic and criminal psychologist)
Shawn Mansbach (Steve's high school friend)
Merle Pyburn (Steve's 7th Grade Science teacher)
Harry Newbold (partner in the Newbold Vanderhoop law firm)
Nancy and Marvin Foxwell (Steve's sister-in-law and brother-in-law)
Leo and Gail Foxwell (Nancy and Marvin's son and daughter)
Mrs. Bressler (a neighbor)
Bob and Linsey Laine, neighbors
Jan Sellers (Beau's girlfriend, 2002-2004)
Laura Hallmark, Beau's current girlfriend
Les Etheridge (Steve's friend and mentor)
Matt and Vivian Percet (neighbors)
Liz Brailford (Steve's niece)
Andrea Brailford (Steve's sister-in-law)
Peggy Higham and Fred Smith (friends of Steve's)
Jessica Higham (daughter of Peggy and Fred)
Patrick Houseman (Steve's boss at the State Park)
Yolanda Maldonado (co-worker of Steve's at the State Park)
Amy and Eldon Carragan (neighbors of Steve's)
Vince Amaral (a muscleman), and Edgar Madeiros (a gangster)

(Connected to Hanna)

Eddie Higham (Darla's boyfriend)
Eva Kern (Hanna's cousin)
Angie Womack (friend of Hanna's)
Leon and Rosie Belisle (Hanna's uncle and aunt)
Carl Belisle (Hanna's grand-uncle)
Karla Spivey (Hanna's classmate)
Margie Spivey (Karla's mother)
Suzanna Bushnell (friend of Hanna's)
Dan Dunbar (Suzanna Bushnell's husband)
Sean Luedeman (friend of Hanna's)
Gloria Moore (friend of Hanna's)
Cliff Polinger (friend of Josh Chilmark's)
Richard G. Wheeler (Hanna's 1st husband)
Shane Lancaster (Hanna's 2nd husband)
Jennilea Hubbard (placeholder name on ACSO's affidavits)
Hope Dawson (Hanna's 2001 cross-country coach)

(Connected to Both or to Neither)

Glenda and Gilbert Sperger (Tiffany Sperger's mother and father)
Patricia "Tricia" Lindeen (an attorney in Deep Springs)
Charlie Correll (former cross-country coach at Miler)
Curtis Hamner (current coach at Miler)
Barbara Osler (Executive Director of the Deep Springs CASA)
Toby Billings (an archaeologist, a justice warrior)
Zeke Yewdall, a Ford Courier collector

Places/Structures (All in Texas)

Ashwell County (where everything took place)
Deep Springs (county seat of Ashwell County)
Lake Ashwell (located north of Deep Springs)
Bloom (a city on the outskirts of Deep Springs)
Bloom Junction Mall (mall in Bloom)
Filmland Theaters (movie theater in Bloom Junction Mall)
Driskill (a town 10 miles from Deep Springs)
Alderson (where Hanna lived, 15 miles from Deep Springs)
Dwyer, Joubert Junction, Klemperer, Ritter, and Truesdale (other nearby towns)
Brewer, Cutter, Dutton, Keegan, and Seward (nearby counties)
Langford (city about 80 miles from Deep Springs)
Miler (town near Langford)
Locklin Memorial Hospital (regional hospital complex)
Deep Springs Gazette (local newspaper)
WTXD Radio (official weather reporting station for NOAA)
Ashwell County Rodeo (rodeo Hanna and Rhonda went to)
CASA of Deep Springs (child advocate organization)
Cradle's Rest (domestic violence shelter)
Bywater Baptist Church (Steve's church)
Deep Springs High School (DSHS)
Stockman University (local Baptist university)
Saddleview Cove (subdivision where Steve lived)
Galley Shores (another subdivision)
Orchid Beach (a third subdivision)
The Spinnaker (diner in Saddleview Cove)
Shaper Unit (state prison, just south of Deep Springs)
A-Plus Superior Roofing (Steve and Billy Gasnick both worked there)
Leon Belisle Builders (Steve worked there, owned by Hanna's uncle)
Magnolia St. Lift Station (a pumping station Steve monitored for Deep Springs)

Roads

In Deep Springs:

US 373 (runs NE to SW through the city)
US 179 (runs NW to SE, AKA as the Ritter Highway)
FM 29 (runs EW along the south side of Deep Springs, beginning at US 373)
FM 1517 (intersects with FM 29 on the SE side of Deep Springs, then heads NW)
Rock Squirrel Road (intersects with FM 1517, and heads NW into Deep Springs)

At Lake Ashwell:

Mustang Drive
Percheron Drive

In Alderson:

FM 3500 (Main Street inside town)
CO 982 (1st Street inside town)
Alderson has nine numbered E-W streets, 1 through 9, plus Main Street and six N-S streets with tree names (Elm, Alder, Pecan, Maple, Ash, and Pine)

Cities/Towns

These are mentioned in the book, but are far enough away from Deep Springs to retain their real names. **Arlington**, **Austin**, **Beaumont**, **Brady**, **Dallas**, **Keller**, **Houston**, **San Antonio**, and **Spring**.

About the Author

Michael Sirois was reading by the age of four, plowing through classics like *Treasure Island* before the first grade. In third grade he wrote a playground version of *Helen of Troy* (based on a *Classics Illustrated* comic book) so he could cast himself as Paris and Linda Leonard as Helen. She had great freckles. A poem about discovering lint in his navel and a story about fighting monsters on Mars soon followed, but in high school he fell in love with acting and added that to his repertoire.

After a few years as a radio DJ, along with an assortment of other jobs while working his way through college, he graduated in the late-1970's with degrees in Drama and English. For the next couple of decades he taught writing, drama, and technology in a Houston middle school, but continued to act and write. One of his stories, *Loony Louie*, placed in the top 100 of the 1989 Writer's Digest Short Story contest. The 1990's saw his one-act play, *Baum in Limbo*, produced in Houston. His screenplay, *An Ordinary Day*, survived the first round of cuts in the 2005 season of Project Greenlight, beating out over 5,000 other scripts. An excerpt from his first completed (but currently unpublished) novel, *If a Butterfly*, was featured in Rice University's 2006 Writer's Gallery, and a different excerpt from it won 2nd place in The Gutsy Great Novelist's Page One contest in 2020. Now that *Aggravated* is available, *If a Butterfly* will likely be published in 2021 in two volumes, *Chrysalis* and *Emergence*. The second novel he completed, *The Jagged Man*, was published in 2015. It's available as an e-book through Amazon and Barnes & Noble.

In 2009, Michael retired from his job as a program manager at Rice University, and lives with his wife, Minay, in Spring, Texas, a northern suburb of Houston, where he is now at work on a few more novels. One of the novels is a thriller, another is a mystery/thriller, and a third is a multi-volume *bildungsroman* which takes place in several alternate universes. References to them will pop up periodically on his social media pages.

https://www.facebook.com/michaelsirois.author/

https://twitter.com/michaelksirois

Made in the USA
Coppell, TX
17 December 2020